Reggae

THE ROUGH GUIDE

Other Rough Guide music reference titles

World Music • Jazz • Rock
Classical Music • Opera

Forthcoming

Music USA • Country Music

Credits

Commissioning editors: Jonathan Buckley and Mark Ellingham
Text editor: Jonathan Buckley
Picture research: Mark Ellingham
Typesetting: Judy Pang
Production: Susanne Hillen
Design: Henry Iles
Proofreading: Nikky Twyman

Publishing details

Published October 1997 by Rough Guides Ltd, 1 Mercer St, London WC2H 9QJ.
Distributed by the Penguin Group:
Penguin Books Ltd, 27 Wrights Lane, London W8 5TZ
Penguin Books USA Inc., Hudson Street, New York 10014, USA
Penguin Books Australia Ltd, 487 Maroondah Highway, PO Box 257, Ringwood, Victoria 3134, Australia
Penguin Books Canada Ltd, 10 Alcorn Avenue, Toronto, Ontario, Canada M4V 1E4
Penguin Books (NZ) Ltd, 182–190 Wairau Road, Auckland 10, New Zealand

Typeset in Bodoni and Gill Sans to an original design by Henry Iles.
Printed in the United States of America by R. R. Donnelley & Sons.

416pp.

A catalogue record for this book is available from the British Library.
ISBN 1-85828-247-0

Reggae

THE ROUGH GUIDE

Written by
Steve Barrow and Peter Dalton

Edited by
Jonathan Buckley

Photographs by
Adrian Boot, David Corio, Rick Elgood, Beth Lesser,
Everton Sharp, and others

THE ROUGH GUIDES

Acknowledgements

In putting together *The Rough Guide To Reggae*, we've had invaluable help from many people: artists, producers, record company personnel, fans and sound-system followers, journalists and photographers. Without their contributions our book would have been impossible to write.

In Jamaica we'd like to thank, in particular:

Monty Alexander, Doctor Alimantado, Prince Alla, Gladstone Anderson, Lynford 'Andy Capp' Anderson, Horace Andy, Peter Austin, Theo Beckford, Headley Bennett, Ken Boothe, Bertram Brown, Glen Brown, Hopeton 'Scientist' Brown, Hugh Brown, Prince Buster, Junior Cat, Johnnie Clarke, Carl Dawkins, Dillinger, Leonard Dillon, Dobby Dobson, Brent Dowe, Sly Dunbar, Vincent 'King' Edwards, Rupie Edwards, Alton Ellis, Jerry Haines, Niney Holness, I-Roy, Vivian Jackson, Lloyd 'King Jammy' James, Ranking Joe, Roydel Johnson, Pat Kelly, Ken & Gloria Khouri, Don Lee, Neville Lee, Hopeton Lewis, Little Roy, Winston 'Count' Machuki, Tony Mack, Don Mais, Larry Marshall, Derrick Morgan, Johnny 'Dizzy' Moore, Sylvan Morris, Blacka Morwell, Roy Palmer, Kentrick Patrick, Lee Perry, Sonia Pottinger, Ernest Ranglin, Cutty Ranks, Tony Rebel, Rudolph 'Ruddy' Redwood, Junior Reid, Lucille Reid, Glen Ricks, Max Romeo, Jah Screw, Edward Seaga, BB Seaton, Leroy Sibbles, Earl 'Chinna' Smith, Jah Stitch, King Stitt, Don Topping, Trinity, U-Roy, Winston Williams and Tappa Zukie.

All gave us the benefit of their experiences in Jamaican music in extensive interviews and conversations over the last few years. Sadly, four performers we interviewed have passed away: the foundation deejay Winston 'Count' Machuki, the young dancehall deejay Pan Head, vocalist Devon Russell, and the great singer Delroy Wilson. Each made significant contributions to our research as well as to Jamaican music: they are much missed.

Many of the interviews in this book were made as part of the Reggae Archive founded by Chris Blackwell. The Archive's video project aims to collect interviews with crucial figures involved in the creation of Jamaican music. To date there are 77 interviews, conducted during 1994 and 1995 by Steve Barrow and filmed by Don Letts and Rick Elgood. Carl Bradshaw was responsible for the logistics and production of the operation in Jamaica.

Also in Jamaica, Andrea Lewis was always willing to check facts and undertake additional research. And Steve Barrow would like to thank, especially, Dennis Alcapone and Bunny Lee, whose support opened many doors; they both went out of their way to help him in so many ways, in Jamaica and the UK, as did Clive Chin in New York.

In the UK, we would like to thank: Lol & Russ Bell-Brown for the understanding they gave us of the current UK roots/dub revival scene; Bob Brooks, whose Reggae Revive shop is the best in the world for vintage Jamaican music, for his always pertinent insights into the music; Roger Dalke for his painstaking discographical research; Duke Vin for giving us his time, opinions and knowledge; John McGillivray, Noel Hawkes and everyone at Dub Vendor for not only feeding our vinyl habit for 25 years but also for their always well-informed views; Dave Katz for allowing us to use his extensive interview material; Chris Lane for being the first person in the world to write intelligently about reggae; Reg Lowe for his reminiscences of 1950s' Kingston; Metro Downbeat for his hospitality, as well as knowledge of r&b and early sound systems in both Jamaica and the UK; Gaylene Martin of Coalition for years of information; and Rod Bloor, Florent Droguet, Grant Goddard, Matthew Harrison, Dave Home; Rangan Momen and Geoff Parker for lending us records missing from our collections, as well as crucial information.

Record companies have been generous with promotional copies and information. We would like to thank: Chris Cracknell, Chris Sedgewick, Chris O'Brien, Liz Greader, Ian Taylor and Brendan O'Leary at Greensleeves Records; Gary 'Dr Dread' Himmelfarb, Steve Cornwell and Teresa M Altoz at Ras Records; Neil Fraser at Ariwa Records; Adrian Sherwood and Pete Holdsworth at On-U/Pressure Sounds; Trevor Wyatt at Island Records; Martin Howell at Serengeti Records; Aad Van Der Hoek at Jamaica Gold Records; Ingmar van Wijnsberge at Munich Records; David Simmonds and Jeremy Collingwood at Anansi/Jad Records; and the press office of Jetstar Promotions.

Thanks also to the photographers featured in this book: Adrian Boot, David Corio, Rick Elgood, Beth Lesser and Everton Sharp, all of whom are responsible for some of the great images of Jamaican music.

Maximum respect to our editors, Jonathan Buckley and Mark Ellingham, whose patience we often tried, for their guidance and faith in the project, and to proofreader Nikky Twyman for her diligence in dealing with the chaos of Jamaican names and labels.

Finally, a special thanks to our partners Susan Green and Marian Whale, for their understanding of our obsession, their considerable patience and unfailing support.

Introduction

The Rough Guide to Reggae is a near-definitive guide to the music of Jamaica. The island has produced some 100,000 records over the last 45 years – an extraordinary output for a population of little more than two million. Although few of these recordings have crossed over to audiences beyond the Jamaican community, it's hard to think of any genre of popular music – other than the blues – that has had a greater influence in the past couple of decades. Mainstream rock stars from Clapton to the Stones, the Clash to the Fugees, have covered reggae hits, but more important has been Jamaican music's effect on the worldwide dance scene. Major features of Jamaican dancehall culture – the megawatt sound systems, the exclusive "one-off" recordings, the foregrounding of drum and bass, and the practice of rapping over rhythm tracks – have been appropriated by rave and dance culture. Other reggae innovations, like the dub remix, have been assimilated into wider popular music.

The Rough Guide maps a terrain that stretches from the music's folk origins to computerized ragga – via Jamaican r&b, ska, rocksteady, the varied strands that go under the name of 'reggae' itself, dub and dancehall. We've included interviews with crucial figures and have covered in depth the unique phenomenon of the sound systems, illuminating their pivotal role in the progress of the music, alongside the work of the legendary producers such as Coxsone Dodd, Duke Reid, Lee Perry, Bunny Lee and King Jammy. Giving an in-depth view of the whole history of reggae (including the off-shoots that have taken root in the UK, the US and Africa), we have covered the careers of such stars as John Holt, Dennis Brown, Gregory Isaacs, Freddie McGregor, Sugar Minott, Frankie Paul, and, most obviously, Bob Marley (the one truly global reggae superstar), in every phase of their development.

From the bewildering multiplicity of albums we have selected and reviewed the best, including plenty of singles compilations, as the humble 7" vinyl disc is still

A NOTE ON THE DISCOGRAPHIES

Discographies in this book are arranged chronologically with the exception of the discs we regard as essential to any decent reggae collection – these records, preceded by the symbol Ⓔ, are listed first, regardless of date. The symbol before the title indicates the format – ⦾ for CD, ● for vinyl, ◑ for records available in both. After the title we've indicated the country of release – the review makes it clear if the disc is currently available. As an example, here's a review of a record that should be the newcomer's first port of call.

VARIOUS ARTISTS

Tougher Than Tough: The Story Of Jamaican Music (Island, UK).

Ⓔ This 4-CD, 95-track set was compiled and annotated by one of the authors of this guide – and is a recorded counterpart to it. From late 1950s' r&b to ragga, the development of Jamaican music is charted through the island's major hits, with quite a few that scored internationally. Including a fully illustrated and annotated 64-page booklet, this is the fullest introduction to Jamaican music that has been released to date.

the main artery of Jamaican music. As much as possible we've concentrated on CDs and LPs that are currently available but there's also a number of vital albums that may require a hunt through the secondhand shelves. (And given the re-issue programmes from various UK, European and US record companies, it's likely they will eventually be re-released.) On the other hand, we hope we've done justice to the numerous performers who have yet to show strongly on solo discs – and wherever possible we've listed compilations on which they appear. A few worthwhile sets will no doubt have been omitted for reasons of ignorance, and we apologize to the artists concerned and their admirers. If you think we've neglected someone, let us know, and we'll put it right in future editions.

We have written this Rough Guide because we love this music, which has provided a major part of the soundtrack to our own lives. Our aim has been to share some of the excitement and pleasure we have found in this wonderful, multi-faceted music that goes under the name of reggae.

Steve Barrow/Peter Dalton July 1997

The beginnings: mento to ska

MELODISC RECORDS

1

1

previous page

Prince Buster (left, in cap) dancing in Orange Street, Kingston

The beginnings: mento to ska

August 1962, the month in which the largest of the UK's Caribbean islands was granted its independence, might seem the obvious date to begin any survey of Jamaican music. The new optimism and pride that took hold of the Jamaican people were clearly reflected in celebratory records like Lord Creator's "Independent Jamaica", Derrick Morgan's "Forward March" and Jimmy Cliff's "Miss Jamaica", but just as indicative of the national mood were the buoyant rhythms of the emergent style known as **ska**. While incorporating elements of American r&b and pan-Caribbean styles, ska was in effect the island's musical declaration of independence, and was the first music to be associated by the rest of the world exclusively with Jamaica. To many outsiders it appeared to have sprung from nowhere, and the notion of ska's spontaneous origin has its attractions for anyone wanting a neat beginning to the story of Jamaican music. It's a deeply misleading notion, however, for ska emerged from a musical culture of several diverse strands.

First amongst these was the **folk music** that had evolved to fulfil certain social functions, notably the music of the **Pocomania** church, the fife and drum music of the **Jonkanoo** masquerades, the adoption of the European **quadrille** and the long tradition of **work songs** derived directly from Jamaica's plantation system. The first recorded Jamaican music, **mento**, drew heavily on all of this folk music, both in its instrumentation and its repertoire. Although it has been commonly characterized as 'Jamaican calypso', mento was a distinct genre in itself, and like the island's folk forms it has continued to exert an influence on all the styles of Jamaican popular music that evolved after the introduction of local recording facilities during the winter of 1951–52.

As well as these local influences, Afro-Cuban forms like the rhumba, bolero and mambo all made an impact, as, crucially, did the music of black America – firstly big-band swing, then **r&b**. In the US after World War II, the smaller r&b bands proved both more economic and more in tune with popular taste than the big swing orchestras, which rapidly declined under the onslaught of r&b. This decline was repeated in Jamaica (where jazz had been strong since at least the 1930s), albeit with a significant difference. Whereas in the late 1940s 'orchestra dances' had packed out Kingston venues like Coney Island on East Queen Street, by the mid-1950s the phenomenon known as the **'sound system'** had largely replaced live musicians in any combination, large or small. Essentially mobile discotheques, the first sound systems were little more than record players with an extension speaker – liquor store owners especially favoured them because they drew crowds to their shops. Over the years they would evolve into huge systems, capable of playing bass frequencies at 30,000 watts or more, with a similar amount of wattage for the mid-range and high frequencies. These sound systems, and the fierce musical competition that they created, have been the main engine of development for all Jamaican popular music, spawning such practices as dub mixing and toasting (aka deejaying).

In the 1950s, the diet of the sound systems was US r&b. When r&b crossed over to white teenage audiences in the form of rock 'n' roll, it caused a problem for sound system owners in Jamaica, because they could no longer be guaranteed a continuing supply of their preferred music – the fast shuffle boogies and plaintive ballads of the (by now) outmoded US model. So they decided to record their own. For a couple of years the music they produced closely followed the US pattern, but then it began to sound more Jamaican – the rhythm guitar, strumming the offbeat, became more prominent, echoing the type of rhythm found in mento, where it was played on the banjo. The drums changed as well, with a bass-drum emphasis on the third beat that gave a real kick to the boogie-shuffle.

From there, the emphasis shifted to the afterbeat, the hallmark of later Jamaican music. Singer Derrick Morgan is probably right to claim that **Prince Buster** was the first to produce records that distinctly emphasized the afterbeat, as opposed to the offbeat of the Jamaican boogies. (Buster also dropped handclaps – derived from the 'claphand' songs of the Jamaican churches – into his rhythms, thus anticipating the 'one drop' rhythms of 1970s reggae.) By having guitarist Jah Jerry or harmonica player Charley Organaire play a chord on the afterbeat, beginning with a session that produced the huge hit "Humpty Dumpty" by Eric 'Monty' Morris and Buster's own "They Got To Go", Buster built into his productions the characteristic rhythm of classic ska. Another veteran vocalist, Alton Ellis, confirms this reliance on the afterbeat as the essential Jamaican syncopation: "I see the whole a dem as one sound, y'know – this is a lickle bit faster, this a lickle slower; this time the emphasis is on the drum, the nex' time the emphasis is on the bassline, but basically the nerve centre of Jamaican music is the afterbeat." This syncopation soon penetrated Jamaican r&b and turned it into ska, a transformation that was complete by late 1961, in plenty of time for the arrival of nationhood on August 5 the following year.

August 1962, Independence Day: dance poster

Jamaican folk traditions

Long before Jamaica had a recording industry, music played a vital role in the lives of its people – particularly the impoverished majority. Strong and varied traditions were maintained from one generation to the next, and there was no shortage of suitable musical accompaniments for funerals, religious occasions, work and social events of almost every kind. Unfortunately, as with most genuine folk musics, examples of these were only recorded after they had ceased, or were ceasing, to be central to most Jamaicans' way of life, even in rural areas. Nevertheless, musicologists have made a few albums of forms such as Revival Zion, the work songs known as ring play (or ring game), and Jonkanoo. From these it is clear how significantly these folk genres have fed into the mainstream of Jamaican music.

Most Jamaicans are at least in part descended from Central and West Coast Africans, forcibly brought by the English to work as slaves on the plantations that made the island such a valuable colony from the mid-seventeenth century to the abolition of slavery in 1838 – as countless reggae singers of the 1970s reminded the world. Not surprisingly, folk culture has directly reflected this heritage, not only in what it has retained from Africa – notably the central role of the drum – but also in elements from the culture that was imposed on them in Jamaica. To this cross-fertilization of African and European – especially British – elements were added those from the other races that made their presence felt on the island at various times, most notably the significant minority of East Indians descended from those brought to Jamaica as indentured servants and labourers after the end of the slave trade. The influences of the smaller ethnic groups on the island had a minimal role on the majority folk culture, though Chinese-Jamaicans and Syrian-Jamaicans were to play a considerable part in the development of Jamaican recorded music, especially in the areas of production and distribution.

Revival Zion and Pocomania

Two of the most influential Jamaican folk traditions date back to the upsurge in revivalist religious cults during the mid-nineteenth century, a period usually referred to as the Great Revival. Both **Revival Zion** and **Pocomania** combined African and Christian religious elements, and involved handclapping, foot-stamping and the use of the bass drum, side drum, cymbals and rattle.

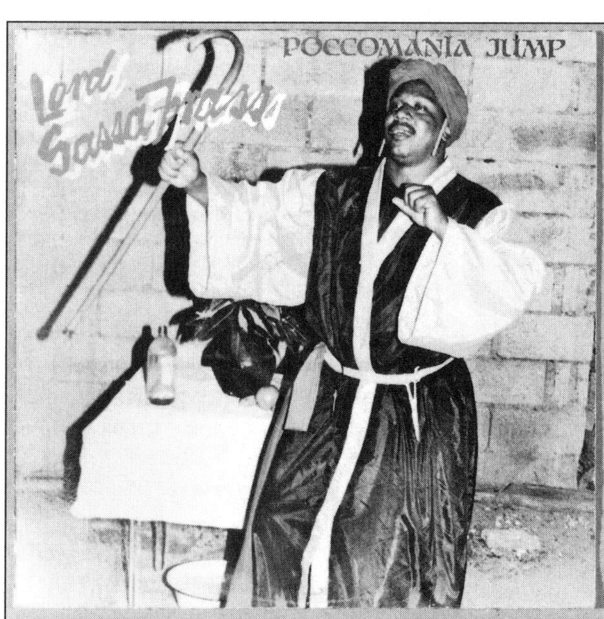

DJ Lord Sassafras in Pocomania shepherd garb

The influence of both is found, alongside that of American-style Baptist church services, in the early records of the most successful Jamaican vocal group of the 1960s, the Maytals (later the internationally successful Toots & the Maytals). The rhythms of Pocomania church services have also periodically been reborn in the dancehall – innovative producer Lee Perry, for example, is said to have been inspired to make his 1968 hit "People Funny Boy" (WIRL) by those rhythms, heard as he was passing a church on his way to a session. Nearly two decades later, the popular deejay Lord Sassafrass of Black Scorpio sound system was photographed in the vestments of a Pocomania 'shepherd' for the cover of his 1985 hit album *Poccomania Jump*. Still later, in 1990, a series of popular ragga productions from the drum and bass team of Wycliffe Johnson & Cleveland Browne (better known as Steely & Clevie) also adapted this aspect of the Jamaican tradition – beginning with the deejay Gregory Peck's massive local hit "Pocoman Jam" (see p.291).

Quadrille bands and Jonkanoo

There is another facet of Jamaican folk culture that might not, at first glance, seem to have exercised a direct influence on the island's musical future. This was the music of the **quadrille** bands, which provide early instances of the borrowing and adaptive practices used by later Jamaican musicians. Slaves were often taught to play European musical instruments, such as fiddles and fifes, so that they could entertain their owners and overseers at dances. In this way, the European eight-note diatonic scale was absorbed by the slaves and utilized alongside African retentions, notably the far more complex rhythms. A dance that was particularly popular with the slavocracy was the quadrille, and this was gradually adapted by the slaves for their own entertainment and as a subtle commentary on the manners and mores of the slave-owning class. The quadrille was just one of many dances invented in European ballrooms of the eighteenth and nineteenth centuries – others include the mazurka and the polka – that became subtly Africanized when played by the slave musicians and their descendants.

Quadrille bands were still active in rural areas in the immediate postwar years, also playing waltzes and reels. It is doubtful, however, if many of the hip Kingston dancehall kids who heard the **Wailers** sing "Ska quadrille, ska quadrille, ska quadrille" on their 1965 hit "Rude Boy" would have known the steps of this form of square dance. Nevertheless, as late as 1968–69 **Arkland 'Drumbago' Parks**, a master drummer of ska, but by then semi-invalid, was playing his fife on recordings for early reggae producer Clancy Eccles, and during the early 1970s the deejay Lizzy paid tribute to the quadrille dances on a Joe Gibbs 45 named, unsurprisingly, "Deejay Quadrille".

Fife and drum bands, which date back at least to the eighteenth century, also played their own variations of European dance music, including the quadrille, but they added military march tempos. While not restricted to any single style, they are best known for music played for a raunchy dance variously called 'John Canoe', 'John Connu' or 'Jonkanoo'. Revolving around a cast of colourfully costumed characters, **Jonkanoo** originated in a West African fertility ritual which was associated with the yam harvest, but then incorporated Christian elements such as the Devil into the overall presentation. It was further absorbed into Christmas carnival celebrations, and survives in this role today in various parts of the Caribbean. Some of the rhythms have even been incorporated into digital ragga recordings, particularly those introducing wild styles of dancing that resemble the Junkanoo dance itself. A less obvious heritage from Jonkanoo is audible in the press-rolls and percussive accents used by Jamaican drummers generally.

VARIOUS ARTISTS

● **From the Grass Roots Of Jamaica** (Dynamic, JA).

E Sleeve notes by Edward Seaga, when he was Minister of Finance and Planning, suggest this album was first released in the late 1960s. A folk research officer at the Jamaica School of Music, Olive Lewin, was responsible for the recordings, but none of the performers – all amateurs presumably – are credited. Nor are the different tracks identified according to the Jamaican folk styles they represent, which would have been useful for anyone not expert on the differences between Jonkanoo, kumina, mento, ring play et al. But quibbles like this do not prevent the music from being incredibly enjoyable – and for a far wider public than just serious musicologists. Re-released in 1995, this should still be available at specialist stores.

● **Jamaican Cult Music** (Folkways, US).

● **Bongo, Backra And Coolie: Jamaican Roots Volume 2** (Folkways, US).

Jamaican Cult Music is fairly esoteric stuff, covering various Revivalist religious ceremonies and celebrations, but of interest to anyone wanting to sample the roots of more familiar Jamaican musical forms. *Volume 2* is a wonderful chance to hear excellent examples of Zion Revival, set-up song, a quadrille band, and fife and drum music.

Mento and the birth of Jamaica's record industry

Well before the advent of recording in Jamaica, street singers would make up lyrics about the latest events and sell them in tract form for a penny a copy. Jamaican humorist Charles Hyatt cites **Slim and Sam** as the most popular of all the itinerant street singers of 1930s Kingston: "Ah suppose Slim an' Sam was the neares' thing to calypsonians we did have in Jamaica." In the next decade this role was taken over by **mento bands**. Contrasting with all later Jamaican musical styles, but in common with both its folk roots and the swing bands of the 1930s and 1940s, mento was principally a live music. Mento bands employed a very similar line-up to the quadrille bands, usually involving banjo, hand drums, guitar and the 'rhumba box', a large thumb piano which played the bass part. This basic line-up, frequently augmented by bamboo saxophone, penny whistle and the occasional steel pan, was used by the outfits who played during the interval of 'orchestra dances' as well as at weddings and parties. By the 1950s these mento bands were playing to the tourists in the large North Coast hotels, and even on the quayside at Montego Bay and Ocho Rios, where tourists would throw their loose change from the cruise liners to the serenading band.

Mento is often described as the Jamaican variant of **calypso**, and it's true that the more up-tempo mento tunes superficially resemble the Trinidadian form. Furthermore, its appearance on 78rpm singles in the early 1950s was in part due to the international vogue for calypso – in the UK, for example, the nightly BBC current affairs programme *Tonight* featured the Guyanan folk/calypso singer Cy Grant, who'd give a humorous rundown on the day's events. But in the final analysis, mento derives chiefly from Jamaican folk, and displays a wide range of tempos and song types.

Nevertheless, the terms 'mento' and 'calypso' were more or less interchangeable in Jamaica in the 1950s, when several top mento groups incorporated the latter term in their names – eg Lord Messam & the Calypsonians, Count Lasher's Calypso Quartet, Count Owen & His Calypsonians, Reynold's Calypso Clippers. Several of the mento discs included a reference to calypso in their titles or lyrics, including Lord Laro's "Jamaica Referendum Calypso" and Count Lasha's "Calypso Cha Cha", and one of the two most important labels on which the music appeared was named Kalypso – the name signifying similarity, the spelling, its difference.

Most mento songs were wryly humorous accounts of everyday life among the Jamaican poor, with plenty of references to the perennial topic of sex. Their tales of hardship and risqué descriptions of intimate acts can be seen as anticipating the preoccupations of reggae, though the social commentary of songs such as **George Moxey**'s "Monkey Talk" and **Boysie Grant**'s interpretation of the folk song "Linstead Market" were far removed from the 'protest' lyrics of reggae, particularly its Rastafarian strain. Instead, a certain level of material discomfort was taken as an inevitable aspect of existence, and acceptance of it was actually facilitated by the humour of mento. **Hubert Frier & George Moxey**'s "Dry Weather House" stands as a fairly typical example:

"Some of them rooms is so small
You can't turn around in them at all
When you want to turn around, you've got to go outside
Then you turn your back and go back inside
When the rainy weather was raising Cain
The house began to leak
And the whole foundation started to squeak
Some of the rooms the landlord rent
They're just like a scorpion tent."

The nearest to any active response to the situation comes in the following – decidedly distanced – comment:

"Tenants complaining why they shouldn't
Have to pay so much for the rent."

One mento record that was exceptional in its thematic content was **Lord Lebby**'s "Ethiopia", one of the first expressions of Rastafarian consciousness on record. Almost the same lyric and melody were used on Bunny Wailer's 1980s hit "Back In Jamaica". Nevertheless, the flip side, in more typically smutty mood, is titled "Dr Kinsey Report", a song all about the singer's "favourite indoor sport".

Stanley Motta and the first mento discs

With its roots in the hard rural life lived by the vast majority of Jamaicans during the immediate postwar period, mento was the folkiest of musical forms, yet it was also one that inspired hopes of commercial success and worldwide recognition for Jamaican music. The businessman who did most to bring that about was **Stanley Motta**, founder of a chain of electrical appliance stores on the island, and operator of one of the earliest sound systems. Because there were no mastering or pressing facilities in Jamaica, Motta used connections made through well-respected Jamaican jazz musician Bertie King, resident in London since 1935, to get his records manufactured. When King returned to Jamaica in late 1951 to lead a band at the Hotel Casablanca in Montego Bay, he recorded Harold Robinson and the Ticklers in Motta's small Hanover Street studio. The master tapes of "Don't Fence Her In"/"Glamour Girl" were then sent to London to be pressed by UK major Decca through the auspices of **Emil Shallit**'s London-based Melodisc company, which had previously issued Jamaican music recorded in London (eg Jamaican poet Louise Bennett's "Linstead Market" and "Bongo Man", made in 1951 with Leslie 'Jiver' Hutchinson).

Released in Jamaica in summer 1952, the Ticklers' record set the pattern for all the mento discs issued on the **MRS** (Motta's Recording Studio) label, with the fragile 10" 78s being pressed in London and then shipped back to Jamaica. Subsequently Shalit's own Kalypso label released almost fifty different titles on 45rpm singles (plus one EP) in the UK, suggesting that there was at least some following for the music among Jamaican émigrés. Kalypso issues of special interest include the first known recordings of future stars **Laurel Aitken** and **Lord Tanamo** (b. Joseph Gordon), who both recorded r&b as well as mento for the label, and the debut of future deejay and percussionist **Count Sticky**, with a couple of strongly Latin-influenced mento pieces.

Ken Khouri's Federal label also issued the mento recordings of people such as Count Owen on its Kalypso subsidiary in Jamaica. The other main producer of mento was **Baba Tuari**, an Indian who in the mid-1950s started the Caribou label for his mento (and Jamaican r&b) releases, recording such as Laurel Aitken; Tuari would go on to set up the Caribbean Distribution pressing plant by 1960.

The mento influence

Though many of the island's leading musicians of the 1960s served their apprenticeship in jazz or swing bands, the less sophisticated melodies and lyrics of mento come through more strongly in a lot of ska. "Hill & Gully Ride", the B-side of Justin Hinds & the Dominoes' first hit "Carry Go Bring Come" (Treasure Isle), was directly based on a traditional mento song recorded for Motta by **Lord Composer**. Two decades later, the song was to surface again as a 1980s hit for the consummate dancehall singer, Johnny Osbourne. In the same way, one of Eric Morris's best-remembered ska tunes, "Penny Reel" (also on Treasure Isle), shared lyrics with both **Lord Power**'s 1950s disc of the same name and **Monty Reynolds**' "Long Time Girl I Never See You". Similarly, the Maytals' "Little Flea" (Buster Wild Bells) can be traced back to "That Naughty Little Flea", which the trio from the market town of May Pen might have heard on a Stanley Motta 78 by **Count Boysie** – or simply heard being sung in their childhood homes by older family members.

The influence of mento spread even farther. **Phyllis Dillon**'s risqué "Don't Touch My Tomato" (Treasure Isle), an extremely popular rocksteady hit in the late 1960s, was an updating of a traditional mento number. Even Bob Marley drew from **Count Lasha**'s "Calypso Cha Cha" for his "Rocking Steady", while the great deejay originator of the early 1970s, U-Roy, was inspired by mento material on two occasions during his ground-breaking spell with Duke Reid: "Big Boy & Teacher" has lyrics based on a Kalypso 45 with the same title by **E. Bedasse**, while "Drive Her Home" drew from either a mento song, "Miss Goosie", or the glorious Jamaican r&b record it inspired – **Eric Morris**'s "No. 1" (Dutchess).

Traces of mento are to be found in the 'country' reggae style associated with groups like Stanley & the Turbines, the Starlights and the Maytones (and, to a lesser degree, the Ethiopians, the Gladiators, and even Peter Tosh). The Meditations, one of the leading 'roots' trios of the 1970s, also nodded to the mento tradition with the Winston Watson tracks "Do Mama Do" and "Woman Piabba" (both on the classic *Message From the Meditations* album – see p.193). And at the beginning of ragga in the mid-1980s, the leading producer King Jammy's two most popular deejays, Admiral Bailey and Lieutenant Stitchie, were among many who drew freely from mento imagery, for all the distance between their digital technology and the unamplified music that Stanley Motta recorded. In the same period, Jammy also had the singers King Kong and Echo Minott adapt

THE ALPHA SCHOOL

If you travel along South Camp Road to the east of Kingston's central district for about a mile, you will reach a building standing in a large dusty yard on the left-hand side of the road. This is the **Alpha Cottage School**, founded in 1880 as an institution for unmanageable or wayward boys. Run by Roman Catholic nuns, the school developed a formidable reputation for both the discipline it instilled into its charges and the first-class musical tuition it gave them. Since the 1890s Alpha has had its own band, and many of Jamaica's leading musicians have passed through it, including the majority of players in the dance bands of the 1940s and 1950s, who went on to create ska.

In 1938, for example, **Tommy McCook**'s mother entrusted him to the staff at the school; by 1942 he was playing saxophone in the prestigious orchestra run by Eric Deans, an instructor at the school who picked his most promising pupils for his band. The extraordinary trombonist **Don Drummond** was another pupil (he often returned to help with tuition), as were fellow Skatalites **Johnny 'Dizzy' Moore** and **Lester Sterling**. Alphonse 'Dizzy' Reece, Arthurlin 'Joe' Harriott, Harold McNair and Wilton 'Bogey' Gaynair, on the other hand, left Jamaica to pursue careers in jazz. Another Alpha old boy, trombonist **Rico Rodriguez**, sailed from Jamaica for the UK in 1962, returning periodically to record. Trumpeter **Eddie Thornton**, currently with the Jazz Jamaica band, followed Rico to London in 1964, playing in Georgie Fame's Blue Flames at the London Flamingo that year.

The tradition continues. Recent musicians like drummer **Leroy 'Horsemouth' Wallace** and vocalist **Leroy Smart** were both pupils at Alpha during the late 1960s and early 1970s, when the vibraphonist Lennie Hibbert was bandmaster. Today that post is held by Winston Sparrow Martin, a talented multi-instrumentalist who played with Carlos Malcolm in the 1960s and who ensures that pupils of today are well schooled on a wide range of instruments.

"Mandeville Road" (aka "Emmanuel Road"), a traditional children's game song which had been recorded thirty years previously by Lord Composer, again for Motta.

Mento now

Finding mento discs is a tricky task, as mento was recorded for a local market in the age of the 78, and was never well represented on vinyl. Several 10" albums were issued by **Stanley Motta** in Jamaica during the 1950s, and Decca in the UK also issued a 10" album entitled *Authentic Jamaica Calypsos*, featuring material from the same source. Sadly, both of these are nearly impossible to find. The same fate currently applies to a series of mento albums made by Count Owen for Federal subsidiary Kalypso from 1960, which culminated in *Mento Rock Steady* in 1968. Some examples of mento can be found on the folk music collections listed on p.6, as well as on albums which catered to the tourist market like *Yellow Bird* by **Jamaica Duke & the Mento Swingers** (Dynamic, early 1970s) and *Sunshine Is Golden* by the **Gaylads** (Coxsone, 1967), but there is an obvious need for at least one comprehensive CD of the best mento 78s from the 1950s.

Sugar Belly blowing a bamboo sax

Mento is still played in Jamaica today, both on the tourist circuit and less frequently for private functions such as weddings. Very occasionally new recordings surface: the legendary bamboo saxophonist **Sugar Belly** recorded for Clement Dodd in the mid-1970s, and again for Winston Riley over digital rhythms a decade later. In the late 1980s, coinciding with the 'world music' boom, both the UK Cooking Vinyl and the US Rykodisc labels issued CDs featuring the North Coast group the **Jolly Boys** playing mento and Jamaican folk songs. The group also toured to promote the CDs, appearing at the WOMAD festival, and proving that an audience and market, albeit specialist, still exists for this traditional form. At its best, like US country blues and string band music of the 1920s and 1930s, mento was a unique and exciting hybrid, poised at the cusp of folk and the commercial music that was to follow.

The birth of the sound system

Mento and Jamaican folk were largely the products of rural society. The people who flocked from the country to the rapidly growing Jamaican capital after World War II wanted a more assertive music, one that was more in tune with their new lives. The first to provide this was the hard-edged, boogie-based **American r&b** that was then reaching the island by various routes. It was brought in by returning seasonal migrant workers and by merchant sailors visiting Jamaica; for the minority of Jamaicans who had radios, it could be picked up from stations broadcasting from the southern USA, like WLAC in Nashville, WINZ in Miami and WNOE in New Orleans; most importantly, it was played by the **sound systems** that by the end of the 1940s were beginning to replace the dance bands who had been playing US swing or local mento.

As well as their selection of the latest and hottest r&b, there was another reason why the sound systems conquered the dancehalls – simple economics. As producer Bunny Lee tells it: "Y'see, after the orchestra play all an hour, dem stop fi a break, an' dem eat off all the curry goat, an' drink off all the liquor. So the promoter never mek no profit – dem did prove too expensive fi the dance promoter. Dem alone eat a pot of goat! So when sound come now, the sound no tek no break. When these few sound system come, it was something different…"

The very early sound systems were fairly basic, comprising one record deck, a valve amp and the largest commercially available loudspeakers. As the 1950s progressed, however, they became more powerful and technically sophisticated, to the extent that a sound system's theme tune was audible several streets away. By the second half of the decade, speaker cabinets known as 'House of Joy' – about the size of a wardrobe – were a common feature of the larger sets, and were serviced by specialists like Headley Jones, who could construct custom-built systems from scratch. The man who played and introduced the records became a crucial figure: the slang- and jive-talking Jamaican **deejay** – of whom **Count Machuki** (b. Winston Cooper) is remembered as the first – was master of ceremonies in every sense, as well as a precursor of today's rappers.

Then as now, the big dances drew crowds intent on having a good time and dressed to kill – during the 1950s women favoured petticoats (known as locally as 'crinoline') under their dresses, a look best appreciated in the energetic moves of the bop and jitterbug-style dancing then in favour. For men, dress was more simple, comprising trousers, shirt and the all-important handtowel for wiping off the sweat, although certain sounds, such as Doc's the Thunderstorm, would attract those who liked to pose in their best suits (this was known as the 'face man' sound). Top dancers like 'Pam Pam' Gifford, One-Eye Bostic, Pershom the Cat, and Bop (Mister Legs), already known as stylists from the orchestra dance days, worked out exciting and

Duke Reid's number one set, 1957

DUKE VIN ON EARLY SOUND SYSTEMS

It was Duke Vin who inspired Clement Dodd to build his Downbeat sound system in Jamaica, and was then the first man to run a sound system in the UK. Here he looks back on the days when American r&b ruled the dance, and explains what a Jamaican-style sound system meant to Caribbean émigrés living in Britain.

“I played with Tom the Great Sebastian in Jamaica. Tom was a lion in his day with sound system. I was a disc jockey that used to play records – not a deejay in the sense of someone who talks over tunes. Count Machuki was the first deejay to start chatting. That was when Coxsone came back from America, and say: ‘Machuki, I hear man on the radio in America who talk over the records. Boy, I want you to be like this.’ And Machuki started. He was the first man to talk over records in Jamaica. And then Stitt came in, and Whoopee. But I was the man who played records for Tom the Great Sebastian.

And then in 1954 I came to England, and I started my own sound system the next year. Other men follow about two or three years after that. There was guys, then – like Count Clarence. He used to pull a lot of crowd. That was before records started to be pressed in Jamaica. We used to have very good times. And all these people who used to follow the sound – if we went to Birmingham, they used to come from London. We used to play all over the country – Birmingham, Manchester, Reading, you name it. People were so glad to know there was a sound system here, because of what they were used to in Jamaica. We tried going to other people's places, but we didn't like the sort of music that we heard there. It was not our sort of music – the r&b that was the thing in Jamaica. I bring it here, and people were so appreciative, they would go anywhere to enjoy it.

The popular tunes of the time included “Page Boy Shuffle”, “Big Jay Shuffle”, “Coxsone Hop”, “Downbeat Shuffle”. Those records were tops, and if you didn't have them then people didn't come to your dances. Because people want to hear the sound that was number one at the time. I win two cups, one in 1956 and the other in 1957. I play with one sound named Boot, another called Rock & Roll, and Count Suckle. I beat them one night in Lambeth Town Hall, which was

complex steps. Gifford is still remembered for the dance he did to Joe Thomas's US r&b tune “Page Boy Shuffle”, and in 1992 he danced on stage with the Skatalites, during the celebrations for the thirtieth anniversary of independence at the National Arena, attended by Prime Minister P.J. Patterson (himself a former road manager for the band). The well-known Jamaican actor Carl Bradshaw remembers watching the best ‘legs men’ dancing with a beer bottle in one hand, flinging the bottle up in the air and then spinning through 360 degrees to catch the bottle before it could hit the floor, all in perfect time with the music.

The Kingston action was concentrated in the central area known as **‘Beat Street’**, which comprised top venues like Forresters' Hall on North Street and Love Lane, Chocomo Lawn on Wellington Street, and King's Lawn on North Street. However, there were numerous other dancehalls, many of them called ‘lawns’, usually referring to a plot of land owned by and adjoining a bar – hence the Bull Head Lawn in Central Road, Trench Town, and the Pioneer Lawn and the Barrel “O” Lawn, both in Jones Town. The sound would set up inside the fenced-in ‘lawn’ and begin to play, hoping to draw customers through the gate; inside, drinks and food – curry goat and the like – were sold by the promoter, who bought from the adjacent bar. Other dances took place in clubs (such as Club Monaco on the St Thomas Road), in various masonic lodges and Friendly Society halls, and in many locations outside Kingston – including Prison Oval in front of the Spanish Town jail, and Cane Hill, located in a quarry to the east of the capital. At times it must have seemed that the whole island was dancing.

Bunny Lee says of the early days of the sound systems: “The first sound was Goodie's, then

packed out. I remember playing "Big Jay Shuffle" by Big Jay McNeely, and "Dumpling" by Ernie Freeman, against Boot in 1957, and he get a beating then.

They started to press up 45s in Jamaica in 1958 or 1959. The first Jamaican-produced record I remember playing was "Boogie In My Bones" from Laurel Aitken. The other one was Owen Gray's "Please Let Me Go". And in 1962, Laurel Aitken had "Mary Lee", a bad, bad tune, for Mr Shallit's Melodisc label. I used to play for Mr Shallit at the Flamingo Club in Wardour Street, every Thursday, and then the original Marquee Club on Oxford Street, and after a couple of years, the new club in Wardour Street. We have a whole heap of fun there. By then ska had come in – about late 1963. The first ska music that I really love was Don Drummond's "Eastern Standard Time", on Treasure Isle. When I play that tune at the Flamingo, the people went mad. But I think the first man to produce ska was Coxsone. Then Duke Reid. The two of them make the most great ska in Jamaica; but one or two little men make better records some times. I have got some wicked music from the early sixties that small men do, and they only have the money to press about fifty or a hundred copies. And sometimes they tape something different over that tape, so you never hear the music again. That's what a poor man have to do.

No tune has been more associated with Duke Vin than "The Tickler". He explains how this early 1970s recording came to acquire such legendary status.

"The Tickler" was produced by Derrick Harriott. I was at home one day when the postman rang my doorbell. And when I opened the package there were two tunes, and one was "The Tickler". I didn't know about the recording, but when I played it, I thought this is a tune! And when my friends heard it, they said, 'You have to play it when you meet Coxsone.' And I did that at the Roaring Twenties that night. And from then, everyone talk about the tune. And then I get a letter from Derrick Harriott, and he said: 'Duke, I don't even have the tape any more for this record. You are the only man in the world who have this tune. The only way to get it back is to ask you to tape it and send it to me.' But he never did. That's why mine is the only copy in the world, now, and that's why I don't play it much. I just keep it for when a man want to play against me. And then I drop it! ”

Count Nick the Champ, then Count Jones. Nick the Champ now, his top tune was named "Hello Everybody", an' when Nick string up all a Maxfield Avenue, it's pure crowd." Most widely known of these pioneering sound systems was **Tom the Great Sebastian**, named after an act in the famous Barnum circus. With Count Machuki as MC and Duke Vin (who later set up the first UK sound system) as selector, Tom ruled Beat Street until the advent, in the mid-1950s, of the 'Big Three' who were to rule the dancehalls until the end of the decade. These were **Clement Seymour Dodd** (aka **Coxsone**), whose second and very successful system was called Sir Coxsone's Downbeat (eventually comprising four sets playing in different locations on the same day); **Arthur 'Duke' Reid**, whose Trojan sound was also a multi-set system; and **Vincent 'King' Edwards**, whose system gained the name Giant, and by 1959 was the most powerful on the island. The rivalry between the different sounds was fierce, and inspired loyalty akin to that of football supporters – it was virtually unheard of for someone to enjoy, for instance, Coxsone's Downbeat one week and Duke Reid's Trojan the next: you were either a Coxsone fan or a Reid fan.

Other notable sounds of the early and mid-1950s included Junior Sebastian and Son's Junior, both, like Tom the Great Sebastian, from the Charles Street and Luke Lane area of central Kingston. Playing just around the corner, in Orange Street, was a highly rated sound owned by a man named Jack Taylor, owner of a hardware shop. Roy White, a cabinet-maker based at Bridge View, played strictly blues and jazz. Yet more leading sounds during this time included V-Rocket from Manchester Square, whose speciality was playing back-to-back ballads from midnight, Doc's the Thunderstorm from Trench Town, who would only play opposite one of the Big Three, and Count Smith the Blues Blaster, one of the earliest from the Greenwich Town area.

The Big Three – and the arrival of Prince Buster

When Duke Reid and Coxsone arrived on the scene, Tom, described as a 'gentleman' by Count Machuki, moved his operations from downtown Kingston to the more select Silver Slipper club up at Crossroads. **Duke Reid** then became the new champion of Beat Street: he was crowned 'King of Sounds & Blues' for the years 1956–58 at the Success Club in Kingston's Wildman Street. Born in 1915, the colourful Reid had served in the police force, where he had been a champion marksman. After leaving the police he kept up his connections, ran a thriving liquor business with his wife, and continued to wear his guns at all times – pianist Theophilius Beckford remembers Duke with a .45 and a .22 tucked into his waistband and a rifle at his side, and Coxsone joked that he even kept them on in the bath. The armaments created a forceful impression that could often be intimidating, as singer Derrick Morgan recalled, talking about his 1959 audition: "I go down by Duke Reid, an' when I go down there I see this man in a him liquor store. I say: good mornin' mista Duke. 'Im say: What can I do for you now? I think he 'ave two gun a him side, an' him finger full a ring. I say: I hear that you havin' audition suh, an' I come fi sing too. 'Im say: you can sing? I say: yes, so 'im say: sing – in front of all who buyin'..."

The combination of powerful sound system and Duke's aggressive bearing also attracted the so-called 'bad men' of the day – men like Dapper Dan, Buggy an' Horse, Sam Jeggy and George Moore. They acted as 'enforcers' around the dance, and they or their friends would also sabotage dances held by other sounds, usually by lobbing stones over the fence or by starting fights. Occasionally there was even gunplay. In a clash with Reid, the promoter Count Buckram had a sound system that consisted of just a big American jukebox with an extension speaker, but had a selection of American r&b records which put Duke's to shame – until, that is, Duke decided he had taken enough punishment and ordered his followers to shoot up the offending juke.

Reid's main rival, **Coxsone**, was less flamboyant. He was younger (b. January 26, 1932), cooler and hipper, but equally capable of attracting followers by strength of personality. He had visited New York around 1954, checking stores like Rainbow Records in Harlem: "At that time we were in search of boogie woo-

Duke Reid crowned "King of Sounds and Blues", Success Club, Kingston, late 1950s

gie, good jazz, merengue and stuff like that. I was really lucky enough to find a lot of music also in Brooklyn, in different record outlets, and from there on I made regular visits to New York and Chicago and other [places].” An avid fan of US jazz stars like Charlie Parker, Coleman Hawkins, Dizzy Gillespie, Fats Navarro and Illinois Jacquet, Coxsone had excellent taste in music, an attribute which enabled his selectors to trounce the opposition in sound clashes. But Coxsone also had to show that he could take care of himself in other ways. “When I started, Duke had a batch of bad guys who come around and try to intimidate you. I remember this instance, I’m there playin’ my sound. Machuki’s operating, somebody call me because this guy was taking the player head off the record. I came up and show him it was the wrong thing to do. He did this again, and I knocked him out.” Nonetheless, in relation to Reid, he was still the underdog, as Lee ‘Scratch’ Perry notes: “I see Coxsone as a struggler, he was struggling under Duke Reid’s pressure. Duke Reid was well heavy, with bigger boys. If you have the most bad boys amongst you, then you’re stronger. It started from there, then me have to be compulsory on Coxsone’s side.” Perry was just one of several creative personalities – Prince Buster was another – who would be drawn into the orbit of Sir Coxsone’s Downbeat. As his success grew, Dodd would attract many more.

Coxsone had begun playing records on a thirty-watt Morphy Richards player for the customers of Dodd’s Liquor Store, which was owned by his parents and situated first on Laws Street, subsequently on Beeston Street. His father, a foreman on the docks, took r&b, swing and bebop records from the ships’ crews and passed them on to his son, who played tunes like Gene Ammons’ “Jug Head Ramble”/“Can Anyone Explain” outside the shop. From this Coxsone eventually progressed to his sound system, launching his legendary **Coxsone Downbeat** set in the mid-1950s, with **Count Machuki** introducing the sound’s choice of music to the dancers. Machuki had started making up spoken introductions for records, derived from the slang of US radio deejays and sustained by his reading of US publications like the Harlem-based magazine *Jive*, edited by Dan Burley, compiler of the well-known *Dictionary of Jive* in the 1940s. It was also Machuki who pioneered ‘peps’, the percussive effects produced by clicking with the mouth close to the mike.

At first Coxsone Downbeat played in venues like the Red Rooster on Tower Street, the Silver Dollar whorehouse on Hanover Street and the Bridge View lawn near Sutton Street in East Kingston, but it soon graduated to top venues such as Forresters’ Hall. By 1957 Coxsone had three sets, played by Machuki, Red Hopeton and **King Stitt** (aka Winston Sparkes), who got his break when Machuki, impressed by the young man’s spectacular dancing to Machuki’s

r&b selection, asked him to be his second, covering for him when he wanted a break. Forty years later, Stitt still works with Coxsone.

The third major sound system of the period was **King Edwards the Giant**, owned by Vincent ‘King’ Edwards. Like Dodd and Reid, he came to Kingston from the country, and he soon made a name for having an unparalleled selection of scarce US tunes. As he says: “I started to operate the sound in 1955, and after about four years I was made the number one sound in Kingston, taking over from Duke Reid and Coxsone.” With Red Hopeton as deejay, the sound enjoyed its most successful period in the late 1950s/early 1960s, and Edwards went on to produce records until 1964, releasing them on the King Edwards label. Subsequently, he entered politics and was elected as a member of parliament for the People’s National Party (PNP). He pursued a third successful career when he became a champion racehorse breeder, his eye for potential winners apparently as sharp as his ears were when searching for obscure r&b in the 1950s.

'KING' EDWARDS: HOW TO FLOP THE OPPOSITION

One of the top early sound system operators in Jamaica, King Edwards here gives an account of his search for obscure r&b records with which to 'flop' the competition, of the difficulty of introducing local records on the sound, and of his eventual withdrawal from the scene.

"The whole idea owning a sound came from my brother. In October 1954, I migrated to the United States, but I didn't like it. And while I was there, my brother wrote and told me if I didn't like it there and decide to come back home, then I should carry a sound system. And I accepted his advice, and bought an amplifier and many records. But when I came to Jamaica, I discovered that the typical sound system that they have in America was not suited to the type of dance they have here. People in Jamaica need to have a sound with a heavy bass. So I had to rebuild. I started off with a fifty-watt amplifier, made with seven or eight tubes. The first night I played at Galloway Road, I played against a sound called Cavalier, and I was flopped. So I had to regroup myself, build a bigger sound. And I was actually ruling in the West, around the Maxfield Avenue area, Greenwich Farm area. I couldn't play at Beat Street at that time, because you have to be on top [to play there]. But Duke Reid came one night to play and I flop him. The word 'flop' means that your dance fail. Thereafter, I was invited by the dance promoters to play on Beat Street, and when I get there I hold my own. I flop the other two competitors – Coxsone Downbeat and Duke Reid. And then I was number one in the area.

During that period, I have to do a lot of travelling to seek top-class records – rhythm and blues music – so as to stay on top. I realise that when you import records, you get more bad than good ones. So I decide that the best thing is to go and select them myself. From 1958, I started to ride the plane like a bus. And I find myself in most of the states south of Washington. In the West I went to California. I went to Chicago. Because of that effort, I was able to introduce top-class records that hadn't been available in Jamaica before.

We had a hard time introducing local records during the Fifties. We started to run out of foreign records, and we decided we had to introduce local records. We tried quite a few, but none made it until we had "Humpty Dumpty". That was the pioneer of local records. So everybody then switched to local records. At that time it was what we call free music. Most people don't write nothing. A guy just get an idea and sing a tune.

I didn't stay long in the local music business, because at that time – '61, '62 – the dancehall environment become very volatile. And of the seven sets of sound I had, I went down to about three sets. I went more into the recording business. But I couldn't take the studio because of the smoking. Each guy who sing, somewhere along the line feel that he have to get a good draw of smoke. Therefore, the artist be smoking, every guy in the band be smoking before he can take a solo – because in those days they were emulating the American music. Then you find the studio was totally full of pure smoke. You have to be a smoker to be in the studio. So I asked my brother to deal with that aspect. But he was too much of a businessman, so we didn't do much there. But Duke Reid and Coxsone did well."

As the 1950s drew to a close, the most serious threat to the triumvirate of Edwards, Reid and Dodd came from **Prince Buster**, born in 1938 as Cecil Bustamente Campbell. An assertive and quick-witted ex-boxer, Buster started out as a follower of Tom the Great in the late 1940s, and controlled a gang based around Luke Lane in central Kingston, a notoriously tough area. When Coxsone started his set in the mid-1950s, Buster and his followers ensured that Coxsone's patrons actually paid to come into the dance. What's more, his boxing skills proved useful in dealing with supporters of other sounds, in particular Duke Reid's bad-boy posse, from whom Buster once rescued Lee Perry. By 1959 he had set up properly on his own, starting the **Voice**

Of the People sound system, label and record shop at 36 Charles Street, premises that had been the site of the Prince Buster Record Shack outlet since 1957.

The sound systems and stateside r&b

The King, the Duke and the Sir spent a lot of their money on trips to the US, in search of r&b records that had yet to be heard on the island. The Southern states provided rich pickings, yielding plenty of discs that had been no more than local hits in the US. Thus Jamaican musicians and singers were influenced by a range of regional r&b styles, though Jamaican tastes very much veered towards one particular style. Despite the popularity in Jamaica of early rockers such as Ruth Brown, Fats Domino, Clyde McPhatter, Little Richard, Chuck Willis and Lavern Baker – several of whom performed in Kingston – the US r&b favoured by Jamaican audiences was usually quite different from the material that had enjoyed crossover success with the white American teenage rock 'n' roll audience. Rather, they tended to favour the more adult, harder-edged and 'blacker' style of jump blues.

All the sound systems needed exclusive recordings to attract followers and 'flop' the competition, which was the reason not only for the demand for the most obscure American 78rpm records, but also for the common practice of scratching out titles, names and even matrix numbers from the discs. In addition, a sound's top tunes would invariably be given new names. Thus, tenor saxophonist Willis Jackson's "Later For the Gator" became known as "Coxsone's Hop", and Harold Land's Savoy single "San Diego Bounce" was renamed "Coxsone Shuffle", while Eddie Chamblee's "Open Your Eyes And See" was identified simply as "Learn".

Typical of the sort of US jump blues that rocked the early Jamaican dancehalls was Wynonie 'Mr Blues' Harris's "Blood Shot Eyes", released on Cincinnati's King label in 1951, and an enormous Jamaican hit for a very long period. Other exponents of the genre, such as Lester Williams, Big Joe Turner, Amos Milburn, T-Bone Walker and Sherman Williams, were also popular in the dancehalls, while black American ballad singers like Johnny Ace, Charles Brown, Billy Eckstine, Nat 'King' Cole, Earl Connelly, Ivory Joe Hunter and Arthur Prysock enjoyed a large following, too. These ballad singers were to exert a lasting influence on singers like Wilfred 'Jackie' Edwards and Lascelles Perkins in the late 1950s, John Holt in the next decade and Gregory Isaacs in the 1970s.

Wynonie Harris's biggest Jamaican hit was one of several he recorded for King Records; other popular discs by this influential blues shouter of the late 1940s – such as "Good Rocking' Tonight" and "All She Wants To Do Is Rock" – had appeared on the Aladdin label of Los Angeles. Amos Milburn's "One Scotch, One Bourbon, One Beer", another American r&b hit that has proved something of a Jamaican standard, was also on Aladdin, which consistently provided the sort of records that appealed to Jamaican taste. But the American city that exercised the most obvious influence on Jamaica's musical development was **New Orleans**. This might simply have been a case of geographic proximity – Louisiana's largest city was, after all, near enough to Kingston for radio stations like WNOE to reach it. However, the rich cosmopolitan mix of musical traditions that went into New Orleans r&b might have had a particularly strong appeal to Jamaicans, whose national motto was to become "Out of many one people", and whose musicians have always proved adept at mixing and blending different styles. Jamaican musicians attempted to emulate both the shuffle boogies and the distinctive New Orleans syncopation of artists such as Professor Longhair – as on, for example, "Back To New Orleans" (Starline) by Laurel Aitken – and some commentators even claim that it was their failure to get those rhythms quite right that gave Jamaican r&b its unique character.

The beginnings of Jamaican r&b

Stanley Motta is best remembered for the mento he recorded in the early 1950s, but this pioneering figure also played a part in the development of the second – and more substantial – wave of the Jamaican recording industry. In 1954, before Ken Khouri launched Federal Records at 129 King Street (later relocating to Bell Road), Motta's small Kingston studio had been used by the very young vocal duo of **Lloyd 'Bunny' Robinson** and **Noel 'Skully' Simms**

COUNT MACHUKI: THE FIRST TALKER

Though only occasionally recorded, Count Machuki remains legendary as Jamaica's foundation deejay – the first man to speak over records at dances, initially for Tom the Great Sebastian and then for Sir Coxsone Downbeat.

"I got my professional break in the year 1950, with a sound, called Tom the Great Sebastian, in the Forresters' Hall. It was on Boxing Night, the 26th December. Previously I used to play every Friday night at the Jubilee Gardens, where I was able to create a selection of records that was entirely unknown to Tom the Great Sebastian. So on the 26th December, we had a shortage of liquors, and I got the opportunity there and then to open the Forresters' Hall. Because Tom went to get the liquors for the dance, and when he returned we were playing a lot of records that were strange to him. He said I shouldn't borrow any records to play on the set, and I smiled and said: 'No, Tom, I didn't borrow any records.' And when the record finish, I showed it to him. I did a good job, because I had the Forresters' Hall rammed to the seams by nine o'clock, and by ten-thirty Tom took over the controls and told me: 'Tell anyone, I, Thomas, want to say that Count Machuki is a great deejay.' From there on my professional career was launched.

On the 2nd January I promoted a dance at the Forresters' Hall, using two sounds – Tom the Great Sebastian and Nick the Champ. Nick, in those days, had a selection of records that was hard to beat, and he opened the dance and set the pace real hot for Tom. Nick was about to come off, when Tom said he was going to the toilet and would I mind putting on records until he returned. But

RICK ELGOOD

The original deejay

to cut a sentimental r&b ballad called "Till the End Of Time", probably the first post-mento Jamaican recording. At the time this was not commercially released as a single, but remained as an acetate (or 'dubplate') for sound system play, alongside US r&b records, on Beat Street. One of the first locally recorded r&b tunes that did gain commercial release (as a 78rpm on Federal) was "Silent Dreams" by the same Bunny & Skully.

Several of the sound system owners were prominent in the vanguard of post-mento record production. **Clement Dodd** released his r&b productions as 7" 45s on a host of labels, including All Stars (his first), Worldisc, Supreme, Cariboo (not to be confused with the earlier Caribou), Coxsone, Sensational and Muzik City, shortly followed by D. Darling, Rolando & Powie (owned in partnership with Roland Alphonso), Wincox, C&N and ND (the last two names a reference to his wife Norma). His famous Studio One imprint was introduced after he became owner of his own studio in late 1962. **Duke Reid** ran just three labels: Treasure Isle, Dutchess (in honour of his wife, Lucille) and Trojan, named after his sound system, which in turn was named after the trucks he used to haul the equipment around. (In addition to using their own sound systems to popularize the music they produced, both Dodd and Reid, like Tom the Great Sebastian before them, sponsored radio shows during the late 1950s – "Treasure Isle Time" was the Duke's slot, advertising the Duke's well-known rum bar/liquor store of the same name, situated first at Pink Lane and then 33 Bond Street.) **Prince Buster** at first concentrated on five main outlets – Prince Buster Voice Of the People (the same

Tom did not return until about six tunes after. Now, Nick had the habit of leaving the dancehall, and the people would always clamour: 'Bring back the Champ! Bring back the Champ!' They didn't have the opportunity that night. I took care of that properly, and from then on I was permanently with Tom, becoming his permanent selector. I spent a period of years with Tom. But when Duke Reid the Trojan came on the scene, Tom's policy was to put himself in safe enclaves where competition was hard to reach him. Then I joined a sound called Tokyo the Monarch, but this was not really my dream of a sound that would be number one, so that I could be the number one deejay of the day. So I step away, but fortunately I came into Clement Dodd, who was Sir Coxsone.

Duke Reid the Trojan had the sound of the day. He has the strength of money and equipment. But Coxsone had records and exclusive selecting. Not to be boasting, but being a man of the people, I was born of the people, and by the people and what the people wanted. Because what I set out to do was, at all times, to try to make other people happy. Well, there was a dance at Easter, where we were supposed to be playing, and I said to Mr Dodd: 'Give me the microphone.' And he handed me the mike, I started dropping my wisecracks, and Mr Dodd was all for it. And I started trying my phrases on Coxsone, and he gave me one or two wisecracks, too. I was repeating them all the night through that Saturday at Jubilee Tile Gardens. Everybody fell for it. I got more liquor than I could drink that night.

Well, I was not satisfied with that. So I said I had to get more things to say. Then I was passing Beverley's record shop, and I see a magazine called *Jive*. And I took up that magazine, and saw something that amused me, and paid for it. And from there on, I was able to create my own jives. The first I wrote for myself was: "If you dig my jive/you're cool and very much alive/Everybody all round town/Machuki's the reason why I shake it down/When it comes to jive/You can't whip him with no stick." That went down with the fans handsomely. And from there on I tried not to repeat myself, started creating. There would be times when the records playing would, in my estimation, sound weak, so I'd put in some peps: chick-a-took, chika-a-took, chicka-a-took. That created a sensation! So there were times when people went to the record shop and bought those records, took them home, and then bought them back, and say: 'I want to hear the sound I hear at the dancehall last night!' They didn't realize that was Machuki's injection in the dancehall! ❞

name as his own sound system), Buster Wild Bells, Buster Wild Flowers, Buster's Record Shack and Olive Blossom. In the 1960s Buster launched labels like Islam and Soulsville Centre, with re-presses appearing on the decidedly less colourful imprint simply called Prince Buster. King Edwards must be added to any roll call of important producers, as should Vincent 'Randy' Chin, Charlie Moos, Sir Dee's, Bells the President, and Wasp the Almighty.

Jamaica's r&b singers developed their skills in **talent contests** and **variety shows** on the theatre circuit, playing places like the Palace, the Carib, the Deluxe, the Gaiety, the Ward, the Majestic and the Ambassadors in Kingston, and many others elsewhere on the island. Dancers were especially popular in these variety shows – notable amongst these were Sparky & Pluggy, the brother and sister act Orville and Yvette Clark (known as the Little Twisters), and Errol Minto, who would bring the house down with his jitterbug dancing. The bills also featured novelty acts like fire-eaters, sword swallowers, the bicycle balancing act the Wisdom Brothers (who included future singer Audley Rollins) and the much-loved comedians Bim & Bam (Edward Lewis and Aston Wynter), who also put on shows such as *The Navy Goes A-Rocking And Healin' In the Balm Yard*, which were like farces with variety spots. Bim & Bam were in the audience at the Palace Theatre one night in 1956 when a 15-year-old **Derrick Morgan** (see p.31) beat Owen Gray, Wilfred 'Jackie' Edwards, Eric Morris and Hortense Ellis in the night's talent contest by imitating Little Richard. The following year, Bim & Bam took Derrick around the island touring as 'Little Richie', travelling in a canvas-covered truck

DAVID CORIO

Coxsone Dodd: Downbeat in his Brooklyn studio, late 1980s

supplied by the McCaulay liquor company. Bim & Bam usually worked with their own band – drummer Ian Pearson and saxophonist **Roland Alphonso** were members in 1958, the latter regularly bringing the house down with version of Louis Prima's "Robin Hood". In most stage shows the musical acts followed US models: another celebrated act on the circuit, the vocal group the Down Beats, who had Bob Weston, Winston Service and Count Prince Miller in their line-up, did cover versions of the Platters. Similarly, Derrick Morgan remembers Jackie Edwards as "a very good Nat Cole singer".

Right throughout the 1950s and well into the 1960s the talent shows flourished, staged by theatre owners like Victor Sampson or promoters like Horace Forbes. The most celebrated shows were run by **Vere Johns Junior**. Brent Dowe, who found fame as one of the lead singers in the **Melodians** vocal group in the 1960s, remembers him well: "Vere Johns was a man dedicated to music. He used to take the youth off the streets of the ghetto. Whether you a dancer, a comedian, a singer, he would accept you. Everyone was in the same category and could win through the crowd response. You used to have win twice before you reach the final. And on that night you have all people from the finals vying for the big prize." Some talent shows were also sponsored on radio by commercial concerns, like the *Lanneman's Children's Hour* which gave free sweets to the audience and promoted the confectionery company of that name. The first prize might be just a few pounds, with a chance to return as part of the variety show that took place before the talent show programme. Performers who achieved success on the talent shows were respected; ghetto youths would even fight each other for the privilege of carrying Jackie Edwards's stage suit into the dressing room. The singer **Hortense Ellis**, sister of Alton (then a dancer), used to walk from theatre to theatre dressed in her stage clothes late at night, and was never bothered.

Singers came to see these talent shows as a route into the recording studio, and by the late 1950s record producers had emerged from backgrounds other than the sound systems. Future prime minister Edward Seaga, for example, founded West Indies Records in 1958, after recognizing that the folk repertoire he had recorded during his university doctorate studies was not the music preferred by the urban ghetto dwellers. He recorded the duo of Higgs & Wilson, hitting immediately with the pounding "Manny Oh". **Chris Blackwell**, educated at Harrow, had been introduced to the dancehall scene through sessions at the Pinnis Club, where he met both **Owen Gray** and **Jackie Edwards**, whom he soon recorded. He also spent a lot of time in the Clocktower Music Record Shop at Half Way Tree in Central Kingston and started his own label, named R&B, in 1958. He began operating from premises in Odeon Avenue and scored soon after with **Laurel Aitken**'s "Boogie In My Bones", a record that used mostly white Canadian musicians and was clearly influenced by the Memphis bluesman Rosco Gordon. Seaga and Blackwell recorded at Federal Studios in 1958, the year before the sound system owners like Reid, Dodd and Buster entered commercial record production (as opposed to cutting acetates for their dances). Indeed, both "Manny Oh" and "Boogie In My Bones" were issued that same year in the UK on Starlite, a division of the British jazz label Esquire.

The r&b era was when **Clement Dodd**, **Duke Reid** and **Prince Buster** – the triumvirate who would dominate for the rest of the decade and into the next – established themselves as producers. They began recording in 1957, making acetate or 'soft wax' discs solely for play at their dances – a method still used by sound systems today. Clue J and his Blues Blasters' "Shuffling Jug", produced by Clement Dodd, began as one such exclusive acetate, and is often cited as the very first post-mento record, although it was not officially released on Worldisc until much later – it wasn't until 1959 that the producers began pressing 7" vinyl records for the public to buy. Acetates were an inexpensive way of assessing public demand, which could also be gauged by releasing blank-labelled 'pre-release' discs. If a tune failed to move the crowd at this stage, it had little chance of ever being released commercially with full printed label. By the time the UK pressings of successful Jamaican records were manufactured, some of the tunes had been circulating for anything up to two years after they had been recorded in Jamaica.

Singer **Alton Ellis** remembers participating with his then-partner Eddy in Coxsone's first commercially oriented session at Federal in 1959, cutting the moving prison ballad "Muriel" with Clue J's Blues Blasters backing them: "It was a one-track studio, an' when they count '1-2-3-4', everybody have to be there. Who is not there, the train is gone! One mike standin' in the middle of us, everything goin' through the same mike. The vocalist would go closest to the mike, an' everybody a lickle bit closer an' closer accordin' to the volume of what he's playin'. The engineer, he was mixin' at the time – we keep runnin' it down, an' 'im get a good balance. So when he say 'Go', what he took then – that's it. One take, no comin' back. That's it." Also present at this epochal session were singers **Basil Gabbidon** and **Lascelles Perkins**. Perkins, who became Coxsone's premier balladeer, remembers that the musicians were paid for each side they completed, which added a certain tension to the session: "When they were licking down, you had to be ready. They said: 'Come!', and when you missed one tune they became very upset, because they could have cut two songs in the time. The more records they cut, the more money they got."

The exact chronology of events is open to dispute, with Duke Reid's widow, Lucille, adamant that her late husband released records before Coxsone (his first release was the mento "Penny Reel" by Lord Power). What remains beyond doubt is that the three leading sound system owners at the end of the 1950s began making their music available to the public at about the same time, in 1959. Most important of all, the cultural network which would nourish and sustain Jamaican music was in place, with all its salient features – the dancehalls, the many specially designed sound systems, the deejays and selectors, the pool of musicians and singers, and the entrepreneurs who could record the material.

Jamaican r&b vocals: boogie

Boogie-style music dominated the first wave of Jamaican r&b vocal records. Along with Laurel Aitken, one of the most successful of these pioneering Jamaican singers was **Owen Gray**, whose "Jenny Lee" was a convincing Little Richard-style effort. Gritty or suave as required, and a very dynamic performer on stage, Gray was also the first Jamaican vocalist to sing the praises of a particular sound system on record, a sub-genre that continues to the present day. His song "On the Beach" (Cariboo, 1959), with the Coxonairs, celebrates Sir Coxsone Downbeat playing for Sunday picnic dancers at the Gold Coast, a popular beach spot east of Kingston. In the same year, pianist **Theophilius Beckford** dominated the sound systems with his boogie vocal "Easy Snappin'", from the Coxsone session mentioned above. Beckford had been playing piano since the middle of the 1950s, and had already taken part in mento sessions; he then became a leading session musician, his activity only curtailed by the arrival of the digital age in Jamaican studios in 1985.

Back in 1959, other singers were making their presence known in the studio, amongst them **Derrick Morgan**. Morgan's debut "Lover Boy" (Duke Reid) managed to add something new to the boogie formula and was particularly successful on sound system – when King Edwards the Giant played it at a dancehall off the Spanish Town Road, it became known as "S-Corner Rock" after the location, which was fairly typical of the way tunes would sometimes be remamed. **Eric 'Monty' Morris** was even more anxious to record after his friend's first success, so the pair went into Federal with tenor saxophonist Trenton Spence's six-piece combo, and cut "Now We Know" and "Nights Are Lonely" under Eric's name for the Hi-Lite label. The owner of this label, a shop owner called Mr Smith (who also produced Keith & Enid's monster hit "Worried Over You" with the same musicians), did not run a sound system, so his only outlet for the music was via commercial release, which was the very reason Derrick had approached him in the first place – Duke Reid favoured a period of exposure on his sound system before issuing records. At the same session, Derrick Morgan recorded his first sizeable hit "Fat Man" (Hi-Lite), a distinctly bolero-influenced effort that pushed the boogie in yet another direction. When Duke heard the song, he sent some bad men to bring Derrick to his store on Bond Street, where he warned the singer not to record for anyone else. Morgan then cut a duet with Patsy for Duke with the suitably penitent title "Love Not To Brag". Nonetheless, he showed little hesitation in cutting "Leave Earth" (All Stars) for Coxsone, a crunching boogie that Derrick recalls "mashin' down the place when Coxsone a throw it 'pon Duke an' get serious!" The dancehalls were getting pretty hot, but it was going to get hotter yet over the next couple of years.

RICK ELGOOD

Theophilius Beckford shows off one of his old pianos

Jamaican r&b: balladeers and duets

In contrast to the driving shuffle-boogies, there was a more romantic and tender sort of Jamaican r&b, which drew from both US blues balladeers and the more teenage oriented doo-wop groups. **Jackie Edwards**'s "Tell Me Darling" (R&B) was one of the early Jamaican solo ballads, soon followed by group and duo records like the **Jiving Juniors**' "Oh Pretty Girl" (Sensational), **Alton & Eddy**'s "Muriel" (Worldisc), the **Charmers**' "I'm Going Home" (All Stars) and the **Blues Busters**' "Donna" (Coxsone). As the 1960s dawned, **Lascelles Perkins**, who remains one of the most under-recognized of early Jamaican singers, scored strongly for Coxsone with the massive local hits "Lonely Moments" and "Together Forever" (both All Stars). But perhaps the most enduring of all the sentimental records of the time was made not by a Jamaican balladeer but by **Lord Creator**, who was born Kentrick Patrick in San Fernando, Trinidad. Creator's "Evening News" (Cooks International) was recorded in Trinidad with the Fitz Vaughan Bryan Orchestra around 1959, and was an important hit throughout the Caribbean, including Jamaica. Equally an early example of a 'reality' record, it told the story of a ragged boy who struggles to survive by selling newspapers on the street – a theme made more poignant by the contrasting buoyancy of the big-band arrangement. As a result of the record's success there, Creator took up residence in Jamaica from

Lord Creator (left) with calypso star Mighty Sparrow, around 1962

1962 and became a much-loved performer on the island. He twice remade the song in ska style for both Randy's and Studio One, around 1965, though the first cut remains the one to hear.

The popularity of r&b duos, some of whom made up for in enthusiasm what they lacked in finesse, was to continue into the ska years and beyond. Several of these early duos introduced singers who would later gain substantial solo reputations. Half of Alton & Eddy, for instance, was **Alton Ellis**, destined to be one of the major solo stars of rocksteady and early reggae; the Charmers were Roy Willis and Lloyd Tyrell – aka **Lloyd Charmers**, the reggae keyboard player, producer and singer; Chuck & Dobby featured **Dobby Dobson**, who was to have major hits for both Treasure Isle and Rupie Edwards.

Then there were (Joe) Higgs & (Roy) Wilson, who followed their debut disc and major hit, "Manny Oh" (WIRL), with further successes for Edward Seaga, including the sublime gospel of "The Robe" (WIRL) and the early ballistic lyric of "Gun Talk" (Luxor). **Higgs & Wilson** then went on to cut a series of popular records for Coxsone, Duke Reid and Prince Buster – most notably the life-affirming "There's A Reward" (Wincox), "Pain In My Heart" (Islam) and "If You Want Pardon" (Dutchess). These songs have lasted far better than the efforts of most of the duos of the time, not least thanks to the songwriting skills of Joe Higgs, later to be responsible for tutoring young vocal harmony groups like the original **Wailers** and the **Wailing Souls** in the kitchen of his home in Trench Town, and for a number of heartfelt records of his own, which have always fallen just outside the mainstream. Higgs himself was tutored by the classically trained singers Jimmy Tucker and Desmond Tucker, father of the popular Junior Tucker.

Gaynor & Errol, Winston (Stewart) & Robbie (Roy Robinson), Andy & Joey, Alvin & Cecil and Owen & Leon (Silvera) were among the other male duos who made worthwhile records, but the most consistently popular and vocally distinguished male duo of the time were the legendary **Blues Busters** (Lloyd Campbell and Philip James), whose refined harmonies – alongside those of Higgs & Wilson – set the benchmark for aspiring newcomers. The Blues Busters also took part in the informal Friday night cutting contests amongst the singers who gathered at Back-A-Wall, site of a shantytown which stood where Tivoli Gardens is now. Many future stars – among them **Keith 'Slim' Smith**, **Wilburn 'Stranger' Cole**, **Roy Shirley**, future Melodians **Brent Dowe** and **Tony Brevett** – hung out there. It was where **Ken Boothe**, then at elementary school, first saw these future stars: "I used to go to Back-A-Wall, where I can remember people like the Blues Busters and Higgs & Wilson. These guys were older than us. So when we sing, if we don't hear something from them, a compliment, then we don't feel like singing. Even Bob Marley, the first time I saw him was at Back-A-Wall. He just come from country. Everybody was just young. and pursuing the music."

Proto-roots and the rise of Ras Tafari

Another source of inspiration for young Jamaican performers, and one quite distinct from US r&b, was the gospel tradition of the various revivalist churches that commanded strong followings on the island, particularly in poorer rural areas, and among women. The lyrics of much of this church-grounded music were very close in their Old Testament orientation to the type of Rastafarian themes that were later to prove popular on record, and some members of the apocalyptic cult must have easily identified with the sentiments of, say, the Mellow Larks' "Time To Pray" (Worldisc), Winston Samuel's "Jericho Wall" (SEP), Busty & Cool's "What A World" (D. Darling), **Owen Gray**'s "Sinners Weep" (Coxsone) and Neville Esson's "Wicked & Dreadful" (Worldisc), all released in 1959–60. At about the same time, the singer and later successful producer **Clancy Eccles** recorded "River Jordan" (All Stars) and the truly moving "Freedom" (Coxsone), which boasts the earliest of his many directly political lyrics. In addition, the man who would later become a skinhead favourite in the UK, **Laurel Aitken**, was responsible not only for popular tunes about alcohol and women, but for such gospel-influenced items as "Zion", "Judgement Day" (both Duke Reid's), "What A Weeping" (Beverley's) and "Brother David" (Starline).

Arguably more original in their approach were the aptly named **Folkes Brothers**. The trio of John, Mico and Junior Folkes – all, incidentally, Christians – only made two sides, but their solitary single "Oh Carolina"/"I Met A Man" (Buster Wild Bells) was further distinguished by being the first Jamaican 45 to feature nyahbingi drumming from **Count Ossie** (Williams), a good example of just how innovative a producer Prince Buster could be. The Folkes Brothers had met Buster at Duke Reid's liquor store, where they had gone to audition; the fledgling producer was keen to make "Oh Carolina" and introduced them to Count Ossie, who was already rehearsing another act for Buster. As John Folkes recalls: "Bunny and Skitter were there too, practising "Chubby" up in the Wareika Hills where my brothers and I rehearsed "Oh Carolina" with Count Ossie. But of the songs with the drum sound released at that time from the Wareika Hills rehearsals with Ossie, "Oh Carolina" was the one that took off. It had the magic." Owen Gray, who just happened to be in the studio of radio station JBC (Jamaica Broadcasting Corporation) when the song was recorded, contributed the distinctive piano riff that set off the vocal perfectly.

Bunny & Skitter's "Chubby" (Buster Wild Bells) and "Lumumbo" (Worldisc), **Lascelles Perkins**' "Destiny" (Worldisc), Winston & Roy's "Babylon Gone" (Moodisc blank) and the Mellow Cats "Another Moses" (Sensational) and "Rock A Man Soul" (All Stars) followed the example of "Oh Carolina" by employing the nyahbingi drumming of Count Ossie and his five drummers, described variously as the Warrickas, his African Drums or his Afro-Combo. Where they differed from the Folkes Brothers' hit was in their 'conscious' thematic concerns. During the 1950s the **Ras Tafari** (see p.136) were gaining many converts. The Pinnacle community, controlled by Leonard Howell (aka 'Gangunguru' or 'Gong'), which was situated northeast of Spanish Town, was broken up by the Jamaican police in 1954. After this, many of the brethren relocated to the squatter camps of West Kingston, principally at Back-A-Wall and at the Dungle squatter camp by Trench Town. At Back-A-Wall, in particular, they came into contact with another group living on the margins of pre-independent Jamaican society, the 'burru' people. The music played by the burru people used African akete drums and sansa – similar to the rhumba box of mento – and its strong African feeling made a powerful impression on the Ras Tafari. Count Ossie was a regular visitor; eventually he was taught to play the funde drum and then the solo repeater by a burru man named Brother Joe.

By the close of the 1950s there were between ten and fifteen thousand Ras Tafari in Back-A-Wall, with an equal number of close sympathizers, and even more who might take their side given a suitable opportunity. As their militancy increased, provoked by the gap between the growth of the Jamaican economy and the conditions in the West Kingston ghettos, the Ras Tafari were penetrated both by leftist political activists and by criminal elements. In 1958, the police and some Ras Tafari brethren fought in Coronation Market in downtown Kingston; during the same year followers of the self-styled Reverend Claudius Henry took to the hills after their leader had been arrested, intending to launch a Cuban-style guerrilla campaign. The consequent deaths of two British soldiers and three Rasta men resulted in the demonization of Rastafarianism, but eventually a report was published that correctly characterized it as a peaceful movement. It was suggested that a branch of the Ethiopian Orthodox Coptic Church be established in West Kingston and that the Jamaican government should send a fact-finding mission, including representative Rastafarians, to Africa, in order to arrange for repatriation. In 1961 this mission was accomplished, a large public housing programme was initiated, and the tension dissipated. Independence was a year away and, though ska was to be the dominant musical form when independence arrived, Count Ossie's African-centred Rasta sound had a prominent place: an advertisement for Independence Night celebrations in the *Jamaican Times* of August 4, 1962, lists Count Ossie & his Afro Drums playing with both Jimmy Cliff and the most popular singer of the day, Derrick Morgan.

Jamaican r&b: the musicians

Throughout its subsequent development, the Kingston studio scene was to revolve around its **session bands**, among the earliest of which were **Herman Hersang's City Slickers**, **Ken Richards & the Comets**, **Aubrey Adams & the Dudroppers** and the **Drumbago All Stars**. Often, however, records were released bearing the names of such outfits as Smith's All Stars, Bell's Group or the Duke Reid Band, where the producer's name covered up the contributions of some of Jamaica's finest instrumentalists. The Duke Reid Band used musicians like trombonists Rico Rodriguez and Don Drummond, tenor saxophonist Roland Alphonso, trumpeters Oswald 'Baba' Brooks and Johnny 'Dizzy' Moore, and guitarist Ernest Ranglin. All of them except Rodriguez, who left for the UK in 1962, would feature prominently in the Skatalites a few years later.

These bands anticipated future Kingston recording habits by the way in which musicians would float from one fluid line-up to another. Thus one of the earliest discs released by Clement Dodd, a beaty Jamaican take on Bill Doggett by the City Slickers called "Oceans 11" (All Stars), magnificently displays the talents of both organist **Cecil Lloyd** and tenor sax man **Roland Alphonso**. Lloyd led his own modern jazz combo, which featured his own bop-derived piano; Alphonso, one of Coxsone's earliest session musicians, was a core member of the **Blues Blasters**, the most consistently distinguished and prolific of all the Jamaican shuffle-boogie groups of the 1958–61 period.

The Blasters were led by double bassist **Cluett Johnson** (aka Clue J) and recorded exclusively for **Coxsone Dodd**. Again, **Rico Rodriguez** was a frequent contributor to the band – his eloquent trombone is heard on many boogies from the time, including Clue J's reworking of Glenn Miller's "Little Brown Jug", the appositely named "Shufflin' Jug". **Ernest Ranglin** was another regular in the Blasters, as was the enormously influential **Aubrey Adams** (piano/organ). This line-up was often augmented by Ken Williams (drums), Herman Sang (piano), Keith Stoddart (guitar), Lloyd Mason (bass), **Theophilius Beckford** (piano), and the prodigously talented 14-year-old pianist **Monty Alexander**, who used to sneak out of school to hang out with the musicians at Federal studio: "I was welcome. They saw me and it was hey, man, this lickle guy play piano OK! I used to go and watch Ernie, and Aubrey Adams, who to this day is a number one hero of mine. Aubrey registered a real integrity in the midst of the roots things that was goin' on. Aubrey was a guy who was diggin' Errol Garner and Nat King

Cole (as a pianist), and Oscar Peterson. It was around Aubrey that I say, wow, what is this thing? He had a way of voicing chords on the piano, so he was my hero. He's dead and gone now. I don't know whether it was him, or Ernie [Ranglin], or somebody in that little group that said we're recordin' down at Federal, come on down there. I'd sneak out of school – we say t'ief out – I t'ief out a JC [Jamaica College] an' go there on the bus to the session. I guess the moment came when Aubrey couldn't play the piano on a session, and there I was. I just sat right down an' start lickin' the rhythm. From that day on they were askin' me to come down back an' play, because all I had to do was play that Louis Jordan kinda rhythm, y'know, ska."

ADRIAN BOOT

Guitar supremo Ernie Ranglin – better than ever in the 1990s

Ernest Ranglin also claims that the shuffle-boogies he made in company with many of the above musicians were the first ska recordings. This was after Coxsone called a meeting one Sunday morning with the musicians, and decided to change the beat from the dominant boogie style: "In those days we had the shuffle rhythm that organists use to play, Bill Doggett and people like those. So we getting into that shuffle rhythm, Louis Jordan and people. With the shuffle rhythm we could formulate a ska beat from it. That's where the ska beat came in. If you notice the second beat is much more emphasized. This is really from r&b that we formulate this rhythm of ska. The men who were instrumental to it was Coxsone, myself and Cluett Johnson." Although many of the Blues Blasters records have this different rhythmic emphasis, to the casual ear they still sound very close to their US models. Records made slightly later – such as **Roland Alphonso & the Alley Cats**' "Four Corners" (D. Darling) and **Don Drummond & the City Slickers**' "Don Cosmic" (Sensational) – were also essentially shuffle discs, but with a more pronounced mento feel in the guitar/piano rhythm, and thus more clearly pointing towards the coming eruption of ska.

The politicization of Rasta was reflected not only in the proto-roots vocals mentioned earlier, but also in instrumentals that employed the sort of minor chords that were to characterize much of the Seventies' 'roots' music of people such as Augustus Pablo, creator of the so-called 'far east' sound. Although it could be argued that this sound carries strong traces of Hollywood-tinged exoticism, a record like "El Bang Bang" (Muzik City) by the Carib Beats with Monty Alexander still has a power and moodiness that belies its inane title. Similarly evocative but more clearly Afrocentric is **Rico & his Blue Boys**' "Soul Of Africa" (Buster Wild Bells), one of the earliest titles to make direct reference to Africa as the blackman's spiritual home. As early as 1953 trombonist Rico Rodriguez had gone to live in the Rasta community of Count Ossie, based then at Renock Lodge in the Wareika Hills, and by the time of "Soul Of Africa" he was a committed Rastafarian.

'DIZZY' MOORE: GENESIS OF A SKATALITE

Trumpeter Johnny 'Dizzy' Moore is still best remembered as one of the original Skatalites, but his story goes back much further – to the renowned Alpha Boys School band.

"I was born in October 1938 and spent my learning days at Alpha Boys School. As far as I am concerned, my tenure there was fun. I anticipated that. I grew up in a home with music, but my family refused to impart it to me. At that stage, musicians were looked down upon. They were associated with bars and ting. They would be like heavy drinkers and not much money, and number one check for that. Well, a friend of mine was at Alpha, and he got holidays and started to play some heavy tunes. And I say: 'Hey, man, where'd you learn to do that.' And he said: 'At Alpha.' And I said, 'I've got to go there,' But he said, 'You have to be bad.' And I say: 'That's easy, man.' And that was it. After a couple of years my family figured: 'The kid is becoming unbearable, and we got do something, or we're going to lose him.' So one of my Mum's friends say you could take him to that place, and that was all I really wanted, you know. After that it was just me and music, so I can't complain.

RICK ELGOOD

Moore, in his Kingston backyard, 1995

They had one of the best boys' bands in the Caribbean, at that time. There was Don Drummond, Lester Sterling and Rico Rodriguez. I can't remember who else was involved in the music there. After Alpha I was called by the Jamaican Military Band. I got the job just like that: no test, no nothing. A few years after the military scene, most of us [the future Skatalites] were playing together in the studios. We were like a recording group in the studios. Well, what happened was that we had a band by the name of the Cavaliers, but things were never working out too right. So we decided to shelve that and go into a venture of our own. So from the Cavaliers we picked the ones that we figured would make the day right: that was myself, Jackie Mittoo, Lloyd Brevett and Lloyd Knibbs. And then we planned what the Skatalites would be like and call for different people that we want to work with.

The recording thing came about because of my mischievous nature, again. I got kicked out of the Military Band because of not being amenable to military discipline, though a good musician – that's what they say. After leaving the Military Band I joined Eric Dean's. At that time that was Jamaica's top dance band. Everything was all right – a nice family – but then this came along [indicates his long dreadlocks]. This was always there, but I just decided from this day onwards, no cutting. So I went up to the hills, chat with myself, and it came to me that day that I need some money. Things need to be done. So I went to Coxsone and said there's a possibility that we could produce a music here, and make a hell of a killing from it. Well, they laughed at me. Figured I was a nut, you know. That's where this 'Dizzy' ting came from. They say it's backward stuff, and America has beautiful music. But I say America is America – this is Jamaica. It took me a little while, maybe six months, to really convince them that we can make some money from it.

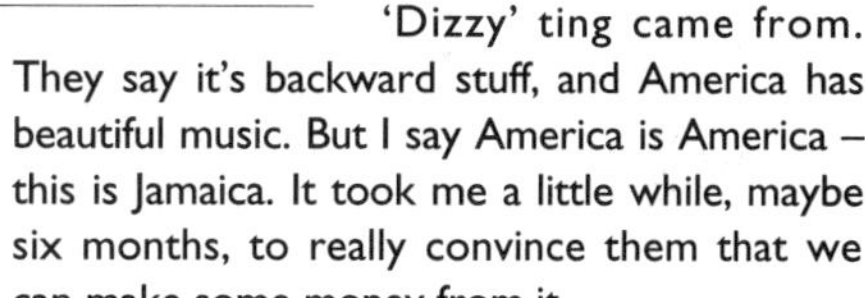

Most of the arrangements were more or less spontaneous. Like a melody would be submitted and everyone got to have their own line. Because no-one dictated anything to anyone. You've got to stand on you own two feet, spontaneous. So it was more or less spontaneous. But because of the love of the music and affection for each other, it was easy. We could feel one another. Most of the music that you hear today, that the younger ones are repeating over and over, that was where it came from. I think Top Deck got the best from the Skatalites, the best sessions. The music was clean. The choice of phrases was good. It was nice."

"Soul Of Africa" was just one of the many Prince Buster productions released on Emil Shallit's labels – Blue Beat, Dice, Fab and Melodisc – between 1960 and 1967 in the UK, which even then was beginning to shape up as the largest foreign market for Jamaican music. Other labels subsequently established in London in the early 1960s – such as Chris Blackwell's Island, Black Swan and Jump-Up, Rita and Benny King's R&B and Ska Beat, and smaller outfits like Planetone and Rio – further stimulated the record industry in Kingston. The music they issued was ska, the first Jamaican music to make a world impact: in 1964, an Ernest Ranglin-arranged cover of an obscure 1958 r&b tune by Barbie Gaye, "My Boy Lollipop", sung by 22-year-old **Millie Small**, sold millions and became a global pop-ska hit.

THE BLUES BUSTERS

The Blues Busters (Island, UK).

Unfortunately long deleted, but one to snap up should you come across a copy and have any interest in vocal harmony or the r&b/soul tradition in Jamaican music. Practically all the duo's most memorable hits of the late 1950s and early 1960s are here, including "Donna", their exquisite version of Jerry Jackson's "Wide Awake In A Dream", "How Sweet It Is" and "Wings Of A Dove".

JACKIE EDWARDS

The Most Of Jackie Edwards (Island, UK).

Some of Chris Blackwell's earliest productions were with the honey-voiced Wilfred 'Jackie' Edwards, and it is these late 1950s/early 1960s hits that are gathered here. "Tell Me Darling", "All My Days" and "One

METRO OF METRO DOWNBEAT

The man known to most people as Metro is a foundation figure in the UK's sound system scene. The popular Metro Downbeat sound, which he launched in 1959, was not the first in the country, but was the one that set new standards as far as the quality of equipment was concerned. In addition, the speakers he builds have made an incalculable contribution to the success of almost every other major UK sound, including the redoubtable Jah Shaka.

"In my early days in Jamaica, the first sound I heard was called Four Aces. That was a long time ago, before even Duke Reid and Coxsone. It was run by a Chiney bloke, and eventually it was very large. That was in about '51. And after a while I didn't hear anything more about that sound. And in that time you have V-Rocket, Sky-Rocket, all those, but the main sounds were Coxsone and Reid. A sound that a lot of people don't talk much about was Tom the Great Sebastian. All these sounds would have theme tunes. Tom would play "Blue Moon" by Lynn Hope; Duke Reid's main tune was "My Mother's Eyes", by Tab Smith. But a lot of people didn't know who the artists were, because in those days they didn't have the opportunity to buy records. They didn't even have anything to play them on.

Mostly we talk about the guys who were on top. But you have other sounds in the country, and quite a few of them that was very good. Where I grow up in St Mary's, my family run the Botanical Gardens; and most holidays, you have these sounds come to play, up to six sound systems at the same time. Even the first time I hear Laurel Aitken singing was at the same place. He was with a band led by the saxophonist Val Bennett. During that time these bands like Bennett's and Sonny Bradshaw's were the top-class type. They were playing like a Louis Jordan type of music – jump blues. But to me it didn't come up to the perfection of the American rhythm and blues. So whenever Coxsone or Reid, or whosoever, might get a good record, people didn't want to listen to the band any more.

I left Jamaica in 1958. Eventually, I came to England and got a job veneering furniture. But my intention from when I was in Jamaica was to build a sound. I had a friend in Dalston, with just a small amplifier and a speaker, who decide to throw a party. So I went to this place and was playing records like "This Is the Place", which was a bad tune that was in the ranking of "La La La Lady" with Eddie Chamblee. These were the type of records because they were the ones that were hits on sound systems in Jamaica. I remember Roy Milton's "I'm Going To Sit Right Down And

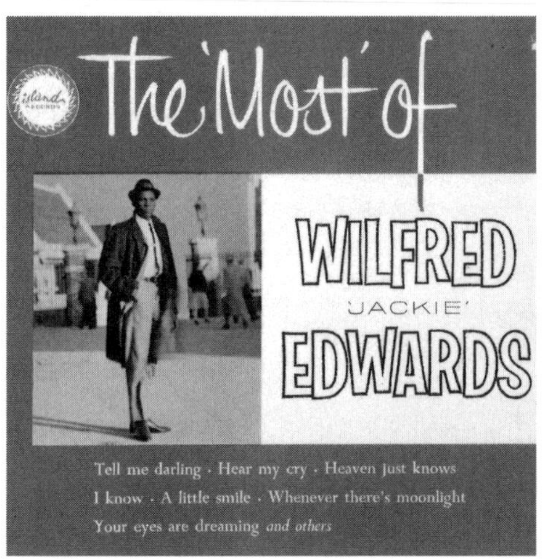

More Week" are superb examples of Jamaican music's sentimental side and the singer's already well-developed composing skills.

DERRICK HARRIOTT & THE JIVING JUNIORS

◑ **The Donkey Years** (Jamaican Gold, Holland).

The amazingly talented singer and producer Derrick Harriott's rocksteady and reggae material has been regularly recycled. This 1994 set from the aptly named Jamaican Gold label, however, was the first comprehensive selection of his pre-ska work with the Jiving Juniors. The group's name pretty much expresses the atmosphere of these doo-wop-influenced tracks, some of which were recorded in New York in 1960, and Harriott's own falsetto magic was already obvious. As usual with this label, the accompanying booklet is packed with informative notes and photos, and the entire package is an object lesson in how vintage material should be presented.

Cry Over You", which was a big tune there. Plus records like Louis Jordan's "Salt Pork, West Virginia" and "Texas & Pacific". Records like those were in a jump blues style, but jazzy. I started to play these records and people went wild. And eventually we made it a regular thing on a Saturday evening.

Then I got this job playing at Norfolk Road, in Stoke Newington. It was run by a lady called Miss Campbell. This was around Easter, in 1959. And when I finish, there was a lot of talk about the records I play. And Sunday, about four o'clock, Miss Campbell came down and ask me to play again in three weeks' time, but this would be at Down's Club in Mile End, and that was a big place. Now, during that time, I had started sending to Randy's in Tennessee for records.

Then I found an ad in *Billboard* magazine for this record shop called Ray Avery's, and he had a warehouse of the kind of tunes I wanted. My brother and I saved $100 for 100 records. But after sending the money we didn't hear anything for a whole year. Then one day I got home in the afternoon, and saw a slip saying the postman had been. I ran straight down the road to the sorting office, and just as I got there they closed. So I knocked and knocked. Then this bloke came out, and I explained about the parcel. And this guy went around and found the parcel! I came in and opened it. Then the first record I picked up just fell apart! and the second one, and the third! Over the year the package had run around, people had put things on it, and broken the top records. But I glued them together so that I could play them and know which ones I wanted to get back again. Among the rest I got about nineteen wicked tunes. Then I started getting more records from Ray Avery, and it was unbelievable. I got some tunes that even Coxsone and Reid didn't know about.

Over in Jamaica, Coxsone had been going to the States to buy records to sell. But always with the titles scratched out, so you didn't actually know what you were buying – only that they were good records because they were Coxsone's selection. Then there was this guy called King Edwards, who had his own sound system. And he went to the States and found a warehouse with all the top tunes that Coxsone and Reid were playing. He was the one that demolished the whole r&b scene in Jamaica. Because he brought records down to sell that the other sounds hadn't even heard. And this how the competition about reggae began. Before then you had bands, but they would never be let in the recording studio. Laurel Aitken had made a couple of records, but they were in a calypso sort of style – mento. Then there were a couple of guys called Bunny & Scully, and they made a record by the name of "Sweet Dreams", which came out on Federal, and that was the first Jamaican record that could be played on a sound system. ❞

KING STITT

● **Dance Hall '63** (Studio One, JA).

E A set from the legendary deejay, not recorded at the time he was shaking up Downbeat dances, but some thirty years later. Performing in the style of the late 1950s/early 1960s, when the man at the mike didn't totally dominate proceedings, Stitt simply adds to the excitement of tracks such as Owen Gray's "On the Beach", Theophilius Beckford's "Easy Snapping" and Billy Cooke's "Iron Bar" with his introductions and the odd jive-talk interjection. A large part of the set's appeal lies in hearing vintage vocals and instrumentals that are mostly otherwise unavailable on album. The 'Ugly One', as he was known, might not seem to be doing a great deal, but he adds an extra dimension to marvellous music, and the album gives some idea of what a Kingston dance of the time must have been like.

VARIOUS ARTISTS

◑ **Sir Coxsone & Duke Reid In Concert At Forresters' Hall** (Studio One, US).

E Not the historic live dancehall recording that the title promises (such a clash of the titans never took place), but a consummate selection of the type of r&b/early ska hits that would have been heard at such a dance in the late 1950s/early 1960s. Shuffle and boogie instrumentals are represented by tributes to key musical locations like Clue J & the Blues Busters' "Milk Lane Hop" and "Five Minutes On Beeston Street", as well as Duke's Group's "Pink Lane Hop"; important early vocals include Busty & Cool's "What A World" and Delroy Wilson's "Duke & the Sir" (aka "Spit In the Sky"). The emergence of the developed ska sound can be heard on Tommy McCook & the Supersonics' "Real Cool" and the Skatalites' "Twilight Zone".

⊙ **Jazz In Jamaica** (Treasure Isle, JA).

If you're curious about the links between jazz improvisation, Jamaican r&b and ska, look no further than this remarkable collection of Duke Reid-produced instrumentals from the 1960s. The Duke Reid Group represent the earliest efforts, and are joined by the Skatalites, the Baba Brooks Band and Tommy McCook & the Supersonics. Actually all these are variants of the same line-up, and display a facility for improvisation that has been consistently undervalued by the jazz world.

● **Jump Jamaica Way** (Coxsone, JA).

Originally released in 1963 on Coxsone's ND label, this is a mixture of the producer's late r&b and early ska work. The Maytals' revivalist-inspired "Four Seasons" and "6th & 7th Books" (aka "6 & 7 Books Of Moses") are among the most enduring of the vocal efforts, while the teen-oriented ballads have an amazingly innocent charm of their own. The instrumentals – variously credited to Don Drummond, Lester Sterling, Roland Alphonso and Tommy McCook – most clearly show how r&b evolved gradually into ska with no hard-and-fast dividing line between them. Historical interest aside, this is wondrous music.

● **History Of Ska Volume 1** (Studio One, JA).
● **History Of Ska Volume 2** (Studio One, JA).

Both these albums have a well-chosen mixture of shuffle tunes, ballads and fully developed ska, including several worthwhile items not otherwise available on album. The second volume is slightly stronger, featuring as it does the City Slickers' "Oceans Eleven", Delroy Wilson's "Spit In the Sky", Clancy Eccles' "Freedom", from the Coxsone selection, as well as the Folkes Brothers' "Oh Carolina", the Maytals' "Pain In My Belly" and trumpeter Raymond Harper's beautiful "African Blood", from Prince Buster at Orange Street.

● **Ska Boogie: Jamaican R&B, the Dawn Of Ska** (Sequel, UK).

Too many classics are missing for this to be the definitive compilation of Jamaican shuffle and boogie tunes, but it will do while we wait for one. Owen Gray's "On the Beach", the Folkes Brothers' "Oh Carolina" and Eric 'Monty' Morris's "Humpty Dumpty" are among the strongest (and best known) of the vocals, and there is scarcely a weak moment among the instrumentals, which include Rico Rodriguez's "Luke Lane Shuffle".

● **All Stars Top Hits [Jamaican Blues]** (Coxsone, JA; Blue Beat, UK).

This was Clement Dodd's first album and probably the rarest of the UK Blue Beat releases. The seven vocals and five instrumentals give some idea of the range of different styles that made up Jamaican r&b. The singers tend to display either doo-wop or gospel influences, while the instrumentals have dated far less – mainly because they more obviously presage ska. Aubrey Adams & Rico Rodriguez's "Stew Peas & Cornflakes" and Don Drummond's "Don Cosmic" particularly impress, though singers like Clancy Eccles, Alton & Eddy and the Jiving Juniors possess no shortage of charm.

Ska authentic

What set Jamaican r&b apart from its American models was in part its incorporation of elements from indigenous traditions – particularly mento – that had themselves merged African rhythms and song patterns with English, Scottish and Irish folk melodies. These ingredients were further cooked by musicians for the most part well schooled in US swing and bebop improvisation via the Jamaican jazz scene. These musicians were capable of spicing the mix further with Latin touches from elsewhere in the Caribbean – Ernest Ranglin, for instance, recalls bringing the merengue back to Jamaica from the Dominican Republic after the Eric Deans Band had toured there in 1953. Another crucial factor was the role of the bass-heavy sound systems for which the locally recorded discs were primarily intended, and which in turn determined their essential nature. Once vinyl 7" 45s started to be manufactured at the end of the 1950s, jukeboxes – not as powerful as a custom-built sound system, but also noted for heavy-duty bass – began to play a major part too, contributing markedly to local sales and disseminating the music beyond the dancehall. By late 1960 the distinctiveness of Jamaican r&b was no longer apparent only to connoisseurs – the unmistakably Jamaican rhythmic flavour of **ska** had now asserted itself.

VARIOUS ARTISTS – TOP DECK PRODUCTIONS

◑ **Ska Down Jamaica Way** (Top Deck, UK).

Ⓔ The first part of a project to make all of the inspired work on the Top Deck/Tuneico labels available again. The title track is the best from the Yap brothers' vocal mainstay, Ferdie Nelson, while the Deacons' "Hungry Man" and Bibby & the Astronauts' "Sweet Dreams" are the other vocal highlights. The labels' reputation, though, rests mainly on their instrumentals, represented here by alternate takes to the storming classics such as "VC10 (Shake A Lady)", "Red Is Danger" and "Shot In the Dark", as well as relative obscurities such as "Yogi Man" and "Tuff Talk".

VARIOUS ARTISTS – VARIOUS PRODUCERS

⦿ **Club Ska '67** (Mango, UK).

● **Club Ska '67 Volume 2** (WIRL, JA/UK).

Ⓔ Ska was already over in Jamaica when these were first released on WIRL, but nonetheless they were the most important ska compilations of their time, for they exposed the music to an audience far beyond Jamaica. Some tracks on the first volume – including those by Desmond Dekker, the Gaylads and Delroy Wilson – are in the rocksteady mode that had emerged in the previous year; about half are slightly older, and stand as classics of the ska style proper. Check Sir Lord Comic's "Ska-ing West", the Skatalites' "Guns Of Navarone" and the Maytals' "Broadway Jungle" for an indication of how varied and musically strong the form could be. There is a similar mix of styles on its companion, with Carlos Malcolm's "Bonanza Ska", Don Drummond's "Stampede" and Baba Brooks' "Independence Ska" among those fully living up to the ska title, and titles from the Ethiopians, the Clarendonians and Winston & George representing the shift to ska's cooler successor.

◑ **Intensified: Original Ska 1962–1966** (Island, UK; Mango, US).

◑ **More Intensified: Original Ska Volume 2 1963–1967** (Island, UK; Mango, US).

Two compilations drawing from a range of different producers, to bring together both classic vocals and instrumentals, including such as Justin Hinds' "Carry Go Bring Come", Stranger & Patsy's "Housewives Choice", and Desmond Dekker's "Mount Zion" among the former, and the Skatalites' "Dick Tracy", Baba Brooks' "Teenage Ska" and Don Drummond's "University Goes Ska" to represent the latter. There is even an early taste of deejay jive talk in the form of Sir Lord Comic's inspired "The Great Wuga Wuga".

◑ **Scandal Ska** (Island, UK).

An interesting selection of music used to accompany the film about the Profumo affair of 1962. That Don Drummond's "Scandal" and Roland Alphonso's "Christine Keeler" are here almost goes without saying. But it showed real imagination on the compiler's part also to include Bob Marley's "Judge Not", Ernest Ranglin's "Exodus", Jimmy Cliff's "Miss Jamaica", Roy (Panton) and Millie's "We'll Meet" and King Edwards' "Russian Roulette". The film is not bad, either.

Derrick Morgan and Prince Buster

Derrick Morgan, the first star of ska, was still with Duke Reid in the autumn of 1960, but Duke was not releasing his music to the public. Moreover, the producer and sound system man took a break from the music business around this time because of marital problems, and didn't return until he released Stranger Cole's "Rough & Tough" at the beginning of 1962. In late 1960, seeking a change, Derrick met up with a producer who was similarly inclined to change things: "One day now I goin' up Orange Street an' I met this guy call 'imself **Prince Buster**. [He asked] if me can come help 'im out an' do some tune fi 'im. So me go with Buster one day, an' me an' 'im siddung round by 'im house – 'im was livin' a Drummond Street, nex' door Patsy. Me write a song with 'im called "They Got To Go". His lyrics, but I help 'im set up the music. An' me tell 'im about Monty Morris." Buster lost no time in arranging a session, reputedly financed by Duke Reid, at which he recorded thirteen songs; every one was a hit. He had realized that the future lay in making the music more Jamaican. This partly came from necessity: he was not financially equipped to search the US for scarce r&b tunes, which were themselves getting harder to find. Even if he had the inclination to do so, at this stage he could never have matched the depth of Dodd, Edwards and Reid's US r&b selection.

ADRIAN BOOT

Lover Boy: Derrick Morgan

"They Got To Go" starts off with Buster singing "The rich man got money, the poor man got nothin'" – a clear reference not only to the economic situation in Jamaica, but also to his own position as a poor ghetto soundman, compared to the relative wealth of his rivals. The last verses of the song very clearly signalled Buster's intentions towards them:

"You've had your fun
Your time has come
You've played a game
That you're not worthy of
So make way, and take away
Since it's my sounds that goes around
They got to go, they got to go
They got to go, they got to go
They got to go, they got to go
They ALL got to go."

Even more crucially, the music backing these sentiments signalled a big change. Guitarist Jah Jerry strums a pattern of clipped chords throughout, but as the record fades saxophonists Stanley Ribbs and Lester Stirling join him, riffing emphatically with the guitarist on the afterbeat, and the characteristic trademark of ska is heard for the first time. Just over a year later the same rhythm, slightly faster and more emphatic, would propel the full-blown, classic ska "Madness Is Gladness" (Prince Buster Voice Of the People), and many more would follow. The biggest hit from this session, however, was **Eric Morris**'s "Humpty Dumpty" (Buster Wild Bells). Morris delivered a simple but insinuating nursery rhyme lyric, considerably enlivened by a definitively laid-back tenor sax solo that sounds like Stanley Ribbs played it from a spliffed-out horizontal position. The impact was immediate; soon Buster was selling dubplates of the song for the then astonishing sum of £50 each.

Between 1962 and 1967 Emil Shallit's Blue Beat label released around six hundred Prince Buster productions, the best of which matched anything by Duke or Coxsone. Stalwarts of his band included tenor saxophonist **Val Bennett** – who contributed the booting tenor sax to Buster's immortal UK chart hit "Al Capone" –

alongside another unsung saxophonist, **Dennis 'Ska' Campbell**, the man who played the single-note 'honks' heard on so many of Buster's ska classics (and was to join up with the Studio One group the Soul Brothers in 1968). Buster's ska was often noticeably percussive, with effects like handclaps and honks prominent in the mix. This percussion, together with Buster's laid-back vocalizing, distinguishes his work from that of his rivals, though the horn solos were often played by men who also recorded for Dodd and Reid. Ska instrumentals like the driving "Down Beat Burial", "Cincinnati Kid" and "Dallas Texas" (all Prince Buster Voice Of the People) also scored in the UK, where Buster toured for the first time in 1963 and cut his hit "Wash Wash" with Georgie Fame and saxophonist Red Price.

By the time the ska period ended, Buster had come to personify the 'one-man record company' that has become a particularly Jamaican mode of record production. He wrote, sang and produced much of the music on his label, and proved at the same time that he really was a "voice of the people". Although he ceased production in the early 1970s, he left behind some of the best Jamaican popular music ever made. But as the rude boy records began to slow the ska down from 1965, Buster still had much to say. He would go on to cut a series of records that are in turn swaggering and boastful, or evocative, almost elegiac.

PRINCE BUSTER & VARIOUS ARTISTS

I Feel the Spirit (Blue Beat/Fab, UK).

This long-unavailable album, first released in 1963, would form the basis of a wonderful CD compilation of the Prince's ska vocals. "Wash Your Troubles Away", "Madness" (aka "Madness Is Gladness") and "Blackhead Chinaman" are deservedly three of his best-remembered hits, and there are no throwaway tracks. Besides the hits featuring Buster's limited but effective vocals, there is Rico's inspired "Soul Of Africa", which brings home how badly a decent compilation of the producer's instrumentals is needed.

King Of Ska (Quattro, Japan).

Mostly instrumental – five vocals out of the sixteen tracks, including "Madness" and "God Son" – and compiled by Gaz Mayall, this is some of the best Prince Buster ever. A pity, then, that it is only available in Japan. Included are six previously unreleased instrumentals, the superbly moody "7 Wonders Of the World", and "Down Beat Burial", the mento-derived "Fire Stick", and Buster's tribute to Mohammad Ali, "Linger On", with deejay King Sporty supplying the peps. This latter track has been left in two-track form, with instrumental and deejay vocal on separate channels. Sound quality is first-class – everything was taken from the producer's original tapes. One to snap up if it ever gets issued in the rest of the world.

It's Burke's Law (Blue Beat, UK).

Pain In My Belly (Blue Beat, UK).

The merging of these two albums on one value-for-money CD would make a fine selection of the Prince's ska productions, with gems such as Don Drummond's "Ska Town", the Skatalites' "Supercharge" and Buster's All Stars' "Rhygin" (a tribute to "badman" Ivanhoe 'Rhygin' Martin), along with semi-instrumentals such as "Al Capone" and "It's Burke's Law", and the classic Maytals' vocals, "Pain In My Belly", "He Is Real" and "Treating Me Bad".

Ska-Lip-Soul (Blue Beat, UK).

A lesser-known and never reissued Prince Buster set that shows him in a distinctly local cultural context, in spite of the presence of the Beatles' "And I Love Her" and Steve Cropper and Otis Redding's "Respect". Otherwise, a folk medley featuring "Sammy Dead" and "Oil In My Lamp", tenor saxophonist Val Bennett's updated mentos "Cut Munno" and "Mek It Tan Deh Goosie" and Trinidadian calypsos like "Rum & Coca-Cola" and "Matilda" ensure a consistent Caribbean vibe. Even "Day-O" (aka "Banana Boat Song"), made famous by Harry Belafonte, gets Buster's unique ska treatment.

Fly Flying Ska (Blue Beat, UK).

A 1964 collection of Prince Buster productions that includes Owen Gray's "River Jordan", the Maytals' "Dog War", Don Drummond's "Down Beat Burial" and Roland Alphonso's "Roland Plays the Prince" among its highlights. Unfortunately, it has been passed over by the various reissue programmes of Buster's work in favour of far inferior sets.

JAH JERRY: THE SOUD OF SKA GUITAR

As much as anyone, the Skatalite guitarist Jerome 'Jah Jerry' Hinds can claim to having invented ska. Here he looks back to the late 1940s, when he was taught by the great Ernest Ranglin and 'boogie' reigned in the dancehalls.

"My father had a guitar and I play a little with it. Then I took it to Ernest Ranglin. That was in 1948 and part of 1949, and I asked him if he could help me out. He tell me yes and I went to 'im yard, and he learn me the tunes and beats I didn't know. He taught me all the great old tunes that he play, tunes that he used to play in the dance. The first one was "Sunny Side Of the Street", and "Swanee River". Then I started playing with the Val Bennett big band, at the Caribbean Hotel, in the middle 1950s. I play in a lot more bands 'til finally I reached Drumbago and go into the recording business.

HOWARD JOHNSON

Jah Jerry unplugged

Drumbago used to make recordings to play out in nightclubs all round town and country, and he say I the man for the job, and I go to make a special for Count Boysie's sound system, an instrumental called "Count Boysie Special". After Count Boysie I play for Prince Buster. I played on all the records that put Buster on top, like Derrick Morgan's first hit, "Shake A Leg". I play the introduction to that, all the great tunes that Derrick Morgan make. And I play for Beverley's, at the same time. Because in those days the money was small, you have to play for everybody: Buster, Beverley's and Duke Reid, and after a while Coxsone came in, and Randy's, Lyndon Pottinger, J.J. Johnson, King Edwards. In those days I play in all the All Stars. I used to play for all the promoters.

Then Skatalites came together. Only Roland Alphonso and Johnny Moore before me. And we play all around at live dances, and record in the studio at the same time. We play all the theatres on the island and 'nuff club. When we go into the studio, it was no good to play just one tune, 'cos you not make anything. Some days you have to play twenty tunes, some days ten tunes – it depends on what the man really want and what he can pay.

Ska was in a different style from the boogie. Most of the great ska tunes come off the boogie, through a change in the beat. It still have a boogie flavour, but the style change. Some things keep it up, like sometimes the bass man have the boogie thing going, but the piano and the guitar change it. That style of guitar, Prince Buster say, was the way gears change on a car, and I play the guitar like a man driving an automatic car. Like the way a man change gears on a car, I change chords on the guitar. All the other guitarists never play it like me, none. Through the jazz thing, I carry the jazz charts to the ska, because I don't play three chords, I play the six-string. So when you hear the guitar you hear the whole thing. That's why it take on with the people so. My style was the greatest style that come. If you listen to Irie FM playing oldies on Sundays, most of it them play are tunes I play on. I play with all the greatest artists – Millie Small, Jimmy Cliff, Bob Marley, Desmond Dekker. At least, I back them with the guitar, and send them out. I'm glad I know I did something with them. But when they had the vintage night at Sunsplash [1993], no one even call me to play one tune. And people say the ska don't sound so nice, because Jah Jerry don't play."

Leslie Kong starts up

Derrick Morgan had some hits with Buster in 1961, including "Shake A Leg" and "Lulu", written in the back of the Prince's shop at 36 Charles Street. But another producer was soon to enter his life – **Leslie Kong**. One day, late in 1961, a young boy named James Chambers came to visit Derrick in his tenement yard at Orange Lane. Recently arrived in Kingston, the boy soon to be better known as **Jimmy Cliff**, had already cut records for sound system operators Count Boysie and Sir Cavaliers. He had also written a song called "Dearest Beverley", and approached Leslie Kong and his brothers Fats and Cecil, because they owned a restaurant named Beverley's on Orange Street, and he hoped they would finance the recording of the title. Leslie Kong wanted to get into the record business anyway, and sent the boy to find Derrick. After a meeting, Kong set up a session, first getting Derrick to practise the songs with the great drummer Arkland 'Drumbago' Parks. "Drumbago did 'ave a rehearsal place in Greenwich Farm, right at West Avenue, Seaview Avenue corner. So me an' Jimmy go dung there the night fi rehearse with a piano. Same time me write dis tune "Be Still", an' "Sunday Monday", an' me write "Hurricane Hattie", that's 'im firs' tune, from me. We didn't do "Dearest Beverley" yet. The nex' day we go studio, an' we meet Owen Gray, an' rope 'im in. 'Im do "Darling Patricia", me do "Be Still" an' "Sunday Monday", an' Jimmy Cliff do "Hurricane Hattie". All a dem hit, an' deh so Beverley's start. He use to pay us better than all [the other producers], so I stick to 'im now, stick to the Chiney man." Naturally, the records were issued on the Beverley's label.

Derrick Morgan continued with a whole series of hits for Kong – at one time in 1962, he had seven records on Beverley's in the Jamaican radio Top Ten. Indeed, one song, titled "You Don't Know" when it was recorded, received so many requests from women listeners after it was played on acetate by JBC presenter Marie Garth that it was renamed and released as "Housewife's Choice". As the label's leading artist, Morgan also acted as its A&R man, auditioning performers and attending rehearsals. (He once turned down Frederick 'Toots' Hibbert, who auditioned as a solo singer in 1961, accompanying himself left-handed on the guitar.) He was in the position to give the go-ahead to record, and it was Morgan who judged when a singer was ready: "I 'ave **Desmond Dekker** in a Beverley's fi two years straight before 'im sing a tune. Me an' the man eat, we cook together, everyt'ing, but 'im never 'ave no tune." Dekker, born Desmond Dacres in 1942, finally had a disc released by Kong when "Honour Your Mother And Father" was issued in 1963. The young singer (a welder by trade) followed it up with a series of solid generic efforts for Kong, similarly cast in dutiful 'good boy' manner, but tracks such as "Parents" and "Labour For Learning" never really troubled the leading singers of the day. His reworking of the folk song "Soldering" (the basis of the Starlights' mid-1970s hit of the same title), the presumptuously titled "King Of Ska" and the proto-Rasta "Mount Zion" stand out from the period, though it would be very late in 1966 before he really came into his own with the classic 'bad boy' rocksteady of "007 (Shanty Town)". Another future star, a mellow-voiced 16-year-old named **John Holt** cut his debut ballads "Forever I'll Stay"/"I Cried A Tear" for Beverley's late in 1962. This former follower of the King Edwards sound recorded again for Randy's in 1964, before forming one of the greatest of the rocksteady vocal-harmony groups, the Paragons, early in 1965.

Most important of all, at least in retrospect, in February 1962 Derrick met a workmate of Dekker's named **Bob Marley**. The introduction was brought about by Derrick's girlfriend Pat Stewart, who knew Bob's aunt and heard him singing while visiting her. She told Derrick, who suggested that Bob come over to Beverley's restaurant, where there was a piano: "'im come up deh one day, an' I play the piano an' 'Im sing the tune "Judge Not", an' 'im sing another song. Me seh to Les: wha' you think about 'im? An' 'im seh: A'right, me could try 'im now." There is a general consensus that the young Marley at this stage was a better dancer than singer, but in March he cut three songs – "Terror", "Judge Not" and "One Cup Of Coffee". The last two were released, under the name Bobby Martell, but failed to make the slightest impression, an inauspicious beginning to a career that would bring Jamaican music to every corner of the planet. After a cutting a couple more tunes that were never released, Bob Marley left Beverley's, though he participated in Morgan's farewell shows, staged just before the older singer left for England in mid-1963. By Christmas that year, Marley would be back on the studio scene, this time as part of a new group, the **Wailers**.

BOY-GIRL DUOS

During the ska era a number of boy-girl duos became as popular as all-male duos had been since the beginnings of Jamaican r&b. Among the best-received boy-girl acts of the time – most of whom owed a debt to New Orleans' "Sweethearts of the Blues", Shirley & Lee, who were probably as popular in Jamaica as in the Crescent City itself – were Derrick & Patsy (Derrick Morgan & Millicent Todd), whose version of the New Orleans duo's "Feel So Good" was another of Duke Reid's comeback hits. They also cut some of their best duo recordings for Beverley's, including "Housewife's Choice", a track distinguished as much by Headley Bennett's splendid alto sax solo as by the duo's lively vocalizing. Derrick Morgan always had a liking for the duo format – after his success with Patsy, he went on to record with Naomi, Yvonne, Pat, Hortense and Paulette. After Derrick returned from the UK in the autumn of 1963, he found that Patsy had begun recording with Stranger Cole, a duo that enjoyed a big hit with "When You Call My Name" (Dutchess). So popular was this tune that Duke Reid had another hit when he remixed it a few years later. Almost as popular in this mould, if not as prolific, were Roy (Panton) & Millie (Small), Lascelles (Perkins) & Hortense (Ellis), Jackie (Opel) & Doreen (Schaefer), Shenley (Duffas) & Hyacinth, Roy & Paulette and (Lord) Creator & Norma (Fraser). Except among Jamaicans of a certain age, these duos await their long overdue recognition.

As independence came in August 1962, Derrick Morgan was scoring heavily with "Forward March", the lyrics celebrating Jamaica's new nationhood. According to Derrick, Prince Buster claimed that the alto sax solo in Derrick's song, played by Headley Bennett, copied Lester Stirling's solo on Buster's own "They Got To Come". Certainly Buster still insists that Derrick went to Kong with songs and ideas that had been worked out in the back of the Charles Street shop by Buster, Derrick and Eric Morris. All of this started a celebrated musical feud, though in private Buster and Derrick remained friends. Buster launched the first attack with "Black Head Chinaman", accusing his friend of taking his "belongings" and giving them to his "Chiney man" and warning Morgan that he will be discarded once he has served his purpose as the "first black head Chiney man". Derrick came back immediately with "Blazing Fire", complete with a genuine Chinese introduction by the singer which translates as "shut up you fool!" The feud continued with Buster's "No Raise, No Praise", and "Watch It Blackhead", reiterating the pertinent point about the singer getting the praise, Kong the raise – a notion hammered home with the horns playing a sarcastic musical quote from the show tune "We're In the Money".

DESMOND DEKKER

◑ **King Of Ska** (Trojan, UK).

The tracks that preceded his incredibly popular rocksteady/early reggae hits, made for the same producer, Leslie Kong. The title track is one of his most exciting ska tunes, and songs such as "Wise Man" and "Archawawa" deserve to be heard by a wider audience than they were at the time.

DERRICK MORGAN

● **Forward March** (Island, UK).

The title track of this 1960s album – only the third Island released – sums up the optimism of the immediate post-Independence period in Jamaica, as does Derrick Morgan's jaunty posture, complete with porkpie hat, on the front cover. Just as strong are "Housewife's Choice" (one of the most popular of his entire career) and "The Blazing Fire", his riposte to Prince Buster's scathing "Black Head Chinaman".

The Maytals: going to Broadway

Following his rejection by Derrick Morgan at the Kong audition, **Frederick 'Toots' Hibbert** made a dubplate for King Edwards, before linking up later in 1961 with **Nathaniel 'Jerry' Mathias** and **Henry 'Raleigh' Gordon**, as the **Maytals**. Born in May Pen, Clarendon, Toots sang regularly with his four brothers and three sisters in Baptist services, then in the late 1950s he came to town to work in a barber shop. He did more than just cut hair: "I used to sing all the time, and people would come around and listen, and say I was good and I should go and record my voice. That's when I met Raleigh and Jerry. They came around and said they liked my singing and wanted to form a group. We sang together, rehearsing and teaching each other. Then Raleigh came up with the name for the group – the Maytals."

After a number of auditions with other producers, the trio decided to record for Coxsone. From their debut "Hallelujah" (ND), they set a scorching pace, harnessing an "old time religion" feel to the powerful new ska beat laid down by Coxsone's crack sessioneers. The follow-up, "Fever" (ND), was a hot love song with a seamless call-and-response group vocal. **Lee Perry** was there too, producing their classic "6 & 7 Books Of Moses" (Rolando & Powie): featuring an astonishing vocal performance from Toots, it continued the religious theme and the barely controlled abandon of their first outing. Most of the two dozen titles they made for the producer would follow this model, Toots and his fellow Maytals digging deep into the hymnal and spiritual repertoire for tracks such as "He Will Provide" and "Shining Light" (both Coxsone), "Study War No More" (Muzik City) and "I'll Never Grow Old" (Rolando & Powie).

Eventually dissatisfied with Dodd, who was paying them as little as £3 a side, the Maytals left him and made a handful of fine tracks for Randy's, Kentone and Beverley's, including the devastating "Neither Silver Or Gold" for the latter label. In 1964 came equally successful records in a similar vein for Prince Buster, such as "Light Of the World" (Islam), "Judgement Day" and "He Is Real" (both Buster Wild Bells). By now they were receiving the sincerest form of flattery from such imitations as Priest (Bongo) Herman Davis's first cut of "We Are Praying" (Prince Buster Voice Of the People), and the Pioneers' superb double-sider "River Bed"/"Golden Opportunity" (Wincox). Other highlights of the Buster sessions included "Pain In My Belly" and "Broadway Jungle", also known as "Dog War", presumably because the song incorporated snatches of an old mento tune, "Dog War A Matches Lane", with barking and yelping noises contributed by one of the group. Identifying with the imagery that the

THE GLEANER

Drifters had projected on their US hit "On Broadway" the previous year, Toots could hardly contain the excitement in his voice as he sung a farewell to Coxsone: "We're out of the jungle, we're going to Broadway."

THE MAYTALS

- **Prince Buster Record Shack Presents The Original Golden Oldies Vol. 3** (Prince Buster, JA, UK & US).

E A twelve-track compilation of the Maytals' singles on Prince Buster's Wild Bells and Islam labels. If anything the trio's work for Buster has endured marginally better than their output for Studio One, mainly because with the switch of producers they largely abandoned ballads for what they did best – revivalist jump-ups. Begins with the incredible frenzied "Dog War" (aka "Broadway Jungle"), and keeps the pace throughout. This is the group's best album, but it would be good to have a CD reissue with "Looking Down the Street" and "Lovely Walk".

- **Never Grow Old** (Coxsone, JA; R&B, UK; Studio One, US).
- **Life Could Be A Dream** (Coxsone, US).

The first of these sets was originally released in the 1960s, the second in 1992; together they collect most of the Maytals' singles for Clement Dodd ("6 & 7 Books Of Moses" and "Marching On" are the most surprising omissions). The more gospel-drenched tracks have perhaps best weathered the passing years, but Toots Hibbert's hoarse voice is wonderfully effective throughout, and the musicians who became the Skatalites are flawless.

⦿ **Sensational Ska Explosion** (Jamaican Gold, Holland).

A re-release of their previously rare and much sought-after *Sensational Maytals* album for Byron Lee, which appeared after their stays with Dodd and Buster, and before Toots' incarceration and the trio's subsequent move to Beverley's. A strong mixture of late ska/revivalist stompers and soulful ballads, plus eight alternate takes for the more scholarly of mind.

Coxsone's ska – the birth of Studio One

At the time Prince Buster was striking gold with Derrick Morgan, **Clement 'Coxsone' Dodd** was in the US, trying to find out how to record blues. When he returned, he found "Humpty Dumpty" had become the biggest hit of the year in Jamaica, and that his former gateman had changed the music into something much more the island's own. By late 1962 Coxsone had **Lee Perry** hard at work in the studio for him, producing, among others, a young teenager called **Delroy Wilson**, thereby initiating a trend for juvenile performers that would become a perennial feature of Jamaican dancehall culture. Delroy's first hits, all issued on various Coxsone labels, included the proto-Rasta "Lion Of Judah", the spiritual-cum-dance hall boast of "I Shall Not Remove" and several barbed attacks on Buster, including "Prince Pharoah". Coxsone was obviously stung by Buster's success – "Prince Pharoah" is the only record in which his speaking voice can be heard, likening Buster to the Egyptian oppressor. These tunes were used in what the late Delroy referred to as 'sound war': "In days like that you have a sound war. It was like Prince Buster against Coxsone against Duke Reid against King Edwards . . . I came along, and it seems was like I was the missile that could get rid of Prince Buster. I made a whole heap of records with lyrics aimed at Prince Buster: "Spit In the Sky", "Joe Liges". But Buster was like a super power: he stood his ground."

In 1963 Coxsone opened the Jamaica Recording and Publishing Studio at 13 Brentford Road (previously home to a club called The End) and launched a new imprint appropriately called **Studio One**, which was to be the label most associated with his name. Dodd had bought the Federal studio one-track mixing-board when they upgraded to two tracks, and his cousin Sid Bucknor installed it in the new studio, which was constructed by the sound-system builder Headley Jones. In 1965 he would replace this with the Federal two-track when they further upgraded to eight tracks.

As was obvious from the name he had chosen for his label, Dodd had serious ambitions for his studio: he was confident that he could occupy the same trendsetting position in the recording world as he had in the fiercely competitive dancehall scene. Prince Buster and Duke Reid might have made the initial impact with a musical style that was already known as 'ska', but neither of them had his own studio when Dodd moved into Brentford Road, nor were their productions to be as prolific over the next four years. Duke did not build his studio until 1965, when he installed facilities over his liquor store; Buster never controlled his own studio, preferring to invest his money in lucrative jukebox distribution.

No doubt inspired by the initial success of Prince Buster's new beat, and further encouraged by his own successes with the Maytals and Delroy Wilson, he began assembling a team of musicians. He had already employed many of the players who would soon come together as the legendary **Skatalites** – the tenor saxophonist **Roland Alphonso**, for example, had been arranging for Coxsone throughout the r&b days. Coxsone was also interested in another tenor man, **Tommy McCook**, whom he had been asking to lead a band ever since McCook had come back from a long-term engagement in Nassau in 1962 – and, indeed, since his return McCook had already cut impressive early ska sides like "Ska Ba", "Adams Apple" and "Below Zero" for Dodd, as well as titles for Reid. With the establishment of Dodd's own studio, the time seemed right.

McCook had been working with pianist **Aubrey Adams** in a group at the Courtleigh Manor Hotel; apparently he had taken some convincing that ska was as serious as his first musical love, jazz, despite having cut some ska sessions for the money. **Lloyd Knibbs**, the drummer whose innovative use of bass-drum 'kick' and snare rimshots had added significantly to the development of ska, was particularly keen to be in a band led by McCook – in fact it was he who suggested that the saxophonist organize the top players into a group. Other leading and seasoned musicians who were already thinking along similar lines included three fellow members of the never-recorded Cavaliers band: the bop-loving trumpeter **Johnny 'Dizzy' Moore**, the teenage keyboards player **Jackie Mittoo** and the important double bassist **Lloyd Brevett**. During 1963 different permutations of these musicians held jam sessions in a club above the Regal Theatre on Sunday afternoons; soon they would begin touring as the Skatalites (see p.43).

Late 1963 was an exceptional time for Coxsone: not only did he release the Wailers' first hit in December, but he also began work with another future star, **Ken Boothe**, in the same period. When Coxsone recorded the duo **Stranger & Ken**, they had already recorded for Treasure Isle and Sir Mike The Dragon, while Ken's partner and mentor **Wilburn 'Stranger' Cole** was already a solo hitmaker for Duke Reid. As Ken recalls: "The first recording we do was for Duke Reid. The song was in some Chinee language, and was called "Mow Sen Wa". We don't know what it meant, but Stranger made a song from the words, and we both sing it!" The duo's partnership with Coxsone began with "At the World's Fair" ("We didn't even travel at that time, but we make a song about the World's Fair!" commented Ken), then cut the storming "Artibella", a record on which Ken literally cannot stop singing – even during the solos from Johnny Moore and Roland Alphonso, he can be heard soulfully wailing and moaning in the background. This must have made an impression on the astute Dodd, who called the younger member of the duo into his office to tell him that he would have to go solo. After this would come the first records credited to Boothe himself, beginning with "You're No Good".

Ska child star Delroy Wilson

With two extremely gifted youth singers – Ken and Delroy Wilson – Coxsone showed he was ready to develop serious new talent, a direction confirmed by his signing of the **Wailers** to an exclusive contract just before Christmas. What the youthful Wailers had in their favour was rude-boy attitude and the best band on the island, the Skatalites, behind them, and this was all they needed to challenge – though not topple – the two greatest ska vocal groups, the Maytals and Justin Hinds & the Dominoes. Indeed, their mentor, **Joe Higgs**, remembers them as being pretty raw: "The Wailers weren't singers until I taught them. It took me years to teach Bob Marley what sound consciousness was about, it took me years to teach the Wailers. For example, they will be going to make a record and I would go with them, and there is somebody making constant mistakes. I would just have to take his part in order to get the record finished in time."

Bob Marley began singing in informal sessions at Joe Higgs' yard on Trench Town's Third Street in 1960. The Wailers first got together there in 1961, initially calling themselves the Teenagers (no doubt after the successful Frankie Lymon group).

Alongside Bob was **Bunny Livingston** (b. Neville O'Riley Livingston, 1947), **Peter Tosh** (b. Winston Hubert McIntosh, 1944; d.1987) and **Junior Braithwaite**, plus two backing singers, Beverley Kelso and Cherry Smith. After intensive practice, Higgs decided the group was ready. His friend **Alvin 'Seeco' Patterson**, a professional hand-drummer who eventually became the Wailers percussionist, knew of Coxsone's auditions at Brentford Road, and one morning in mid-1963 the Wailers turned up at one.

ADRIAN BOOT ARCHIVE

The Wailin' Wailers, around 1964: from left, Bunny, Bob and Peter

Though their talent was still unrefined, the Wailers did enough to convince the producer they were worth recording. Two titles were cut, "It Hurts To Be Alone" and "I'm Still Waiting", with Braithwaite singing lead on the former and Bob on the latter. Dodd pressed up pre-release copies and circulated the tunes on the sound systems. The response was positive and he quickly called the group back in the studio to cut "Simmer Down", with **Don Drummond** in the band. It was the first song to acknowledge and address the rude boy constituency in a direct manner, and the message got through – "Simmer Down" stayed at the top of the Jamaican charts for two months following its release in late 1963.

The Wailers recorded several more titles on the rudie theme, which, as well as giving a fresh impetus to singers from the same West Kingston background, were important in slowing down the pace of ska (as was the Clarendonians' hit, "Rudie Bam Bam"). Tracks such as "Rude Boy" and "Jailhouse" (which are discussed more fully in the next chapter – see p.54) rank alongside such classics as the first cut of the anthemic "One Love" and the defiant "Put It On" as highlights of this phase of the group's career. Not all their Studio One material was of such a high standard, however: the Wailers also tried their hand, with varying degress of success, at doo-wop ballads, raucous ska, spirituals, dance-craze celebrations, and covers of the likes of Bob Dylan and the Beatles. Even the theme from the film *What's New Pussycat?* was given a going-over.

When Bob left Jamaica to live in Wilmington, Delaware in February 1966, both Peter and Bunny continued recording at Studio One. They sang backing harmonies for Ethiopians lead singer Leonard Dillon, on a couple of excellent titles he made under the name Jack Sparrow; they can also be heard on the beautiful Bob Andy song "I've Got To Go Back Home" – which Andy thought was by the Wailers when he heard it for the first time on dubplate at a Coxsone dance. Peter and Bunny also cut solo titles in this period that were the equal of anything the group had done together. Tosh made the swaggering "I'm the Toughest" and "Rasta Shook Them Up", the latter a celebration of Haile Selassie's visit to Jamaica in April that year; Bunny cut "Who Feels It Knows It", "Sunday Morning" – a masterpiece of fragile soul – and the equally fine "Dancing Shoes". When Bob returned in October the music was on the point of changing again – to rocksteady proper.

BOB MARLEY & THE WAILERS

⦿ **One Love At Studio One** (Heartbeat, US).

A well-presented package that covers every facet of the original Wailers' work at Studio One. Musical directions were still being sought by the rude boys' favourite group, and the forty tracks, selected from the hundred-plus the group recorded at the studio, are stylistically wide-ranging. A fair portion of obscurities and alternate takes, as well as all the important hits, make this a worthwhile overview.

LEE PERRY

◑ **Chicken Scratch** (Heartbeat, US).

Clement Dodd never got around to releasing an album by the young Lee Perry, and his 45s from the ska and early rocksteady eras had to wait almost three decades to be collected. It is true that if the future Upsetter had retired from music after these records, he would be considered a footnote to the story of Jamaican music, rather than a major figure. But there is no denying that he used his limited vocal range effectively and that what he was doing was different from everyone else. Anyone waiting to be convinced about Perry's ska work should hear the joyous "Feel Like Jumping" on this compilation, though tough reality songs like "Help the Weak", "Wishes Of the Wicked" and "Give Me Justice" are missing. The musical accompaniments from the Skatalites and Soul Brothers are, of course, perfect.

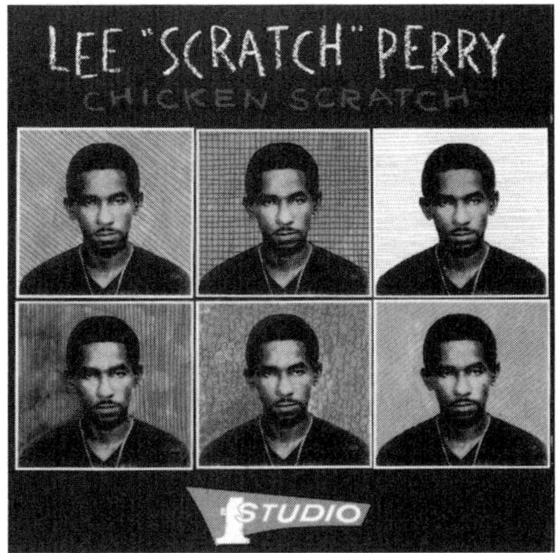

DELROY WILSON

● **I Shall Not Remove** (Studio One, JA; R&B, UK).

◑ **Dancing Mood** (Studio One, JA).

The late Delroy Wilson was a great singer, even when he was just a kid. The vintage *I Shall Not Remove* collects the tunes cut in his early teens, and includes "Joe Liges", "Lion Of Judah" and "I Shall Not Remove". Everything is distinguished by the adolescent star's sheer energy and self-assurance, and by the exemplary

musicianship behind him. *Dancing Mood* features the sublime title track and "Won't You Come Home", both of which helped mark the emergence of rocksteady, but otherwise – except for one ballad – concentrates on glorious r&b and ska.

VARIOUS ARTISTS – CLEMENT DODD PRODUCTIONS

⦿ **Ska Bonanza: The Studio One Ska Years** (Heartbeat, US).

E An extremely well-packaged two-disc set that brings together all the tracks from the *All Star Top Hits* LP (which are actually r&b rather than ska) and all except one from *This Is Jamaica Ska*, and adds such as the Skatalites' "Nimble Foot Ska" and "Spread Satin", Ken Boothe & Stranger Cole's "Artibella", Owen Gray's "Jezebel" and the Maytals' "Shining Light". Digital clarity makes this unmissable even if you have almost half of the selection on the original albums. The stunning music is complemented by a booklet containing two excellent essays by Jamaican journalist Julian Jingles and series compiler Chris Wilson, plus a selection of atmospheric photographs from the period.

● **This Is Jamaica Ska** (Studio One, JA).

For anyone who wants a taste of r&b/ska vocals, as well as the better known instrumentals, this includes the Wailers' "Simmer Down", and the far more obscure "Go Jimmy Go" and "How Many Times", as well as Jackie Opel's excellent double-entendre "Push Wood". "Heaven & Earth" from Don Drummond & Roland Alphonso, along with "Sucu Sucu" and "20-75", credited to Alphonso alone, are the instrumental highlights.

● **Ska Strictly For You** (Studio One, JA).

Alongside Skatalites classics such as "Guns Of Navarone", "Ball Of Fire" and "Man In the Street", this includes the Wailers' beautiful "Love & Affection" and Delroy Wilson's "I Want Justice". Great cover shot of Clement Dodd and Roland Alphonso, as well.

Original Club Ska (Heartbeat, US).
A worthwhile compilation of Studio One material that mixes undisputed classics of the genre – Roland Alphonso and the Skatalites' "From Russia With Love", "Guns Of Navarone", "Phoenix City" and "Ball Of Fire" – with more obscure items that should attract those who already have a few ska/Skatalites compilations – "Timothy", for instance, has not appeared on album before, but is as hot a ska instrumental as any. To give variety, a couple of tracks – like the Gaylads' "Stop Making Love" and Delroy Wilson's "Dancing Mood" – are from the end of the ska era and look forward to rocksteady. Sound quality and presentation are of Heartbeat's usual exemplary standards.

Duke Reid's ska

Stranger Cole was the biggest hitmaker to emerge from under **Duke Reid**'s wing in the early days of ska. Backed by a band led by trumpeter **Baba Brooks**, Cole had enjoyed substantial hits with such early 1960s sound war titles as "Rough & Tough" and "Nothing Tried" (both Dutchess). "Out Of Many One" celebrated the arrival of independence, with the newly returned **Tommy McCook**. Cole also made a series of duets with Patsy for the producer, their liaison lasting until 1966, by which time they were recording for Sonia Pottinger. A gifted songwriter, his lyrics were quite often moralistic, as on "Things Come To Those That Wait", "Love Your Neighbour", "Look Before You Leap" and "We Are Rolling (Under the Tree Of Life)" (all Treasure Isle or Dutchess). These songs were not imbued with quite the same degree of 'jump-up' revivalist feel as the Maytals, but their messages were just as serious. Unfortunately, these Duke Reid productions have never been reissued as a coherent set, remaining scattered instead on various compilations and hard-to-find 45s.

Reid also had hits with Eric Morris, including "Drop Your Sword", and "Penny Reel", a ska updating of the old song about a well-known Kingston prostitute. More importantly, in early 1963 Duke discovered a singer who would prove the equal of the Maytals. Right from his first record, "Carry Go Bring Come", **Justin Hinds** (b. 1942, Steertown, St Anns) proved himself a master of the rich Jamaican tradition of proverb and biblical parable. With that mainstay of the ska period, **Don Drummond**, in the band, and drummer Drumbago Parks pushing everyone along on a fast ska rhythm very similar to "Simmer Down", Hinds' startlingly pure tenor easily rises above the unison vocal of the **Dominoes**. The lyric starts out apparently accusing a woman of rumourmongering (the

RICK ELGOOD

Duke Reid hitmaker Stranger Cole in Duhaney Park, Kingston, 1994

KIM GOTTLIEB/MANGO

Justin Hinds (front) and the Dominoes

"carry go bring come" of the title), but by the end he is singing about something else entirely:

"This carry go bring come my dear, bring misery
This carry go bring come, bring misery
You're going from home to home, causing disturbances
It's time you stopped doing those things, you old Jezebel
The meek shall inherit this earth, you old Jezebel
It needs no light to see you are making disturbances
It's better to seek our home in Mount Zion-I
Instead of heaping oppression upon an innocent man
Time will tell on you, you old Jezebel
How long shall the wicked reign over my people?"

One of the first records to articulate a Rasta point of view, it was a huge hit – its impact can be gauged by the fact that the song was quoted in a poster campaign run by the JLP in the 1967 election, almost four years after its initial success. Hinds followed his powerful debut with more of similar quality – some, like "Botheration", expressed the sufferings of ghetto people in like manner, while others, such as "Corner Stone", "King Samuel" and "The Ark", drew more directly on the Old Testament as a source of parable.

JUSTIN HINDS & THE DOMINOES

● **From Jamaica With Reggae** (High Note, JA).
Justin Hinds & the Dominoes deserve a multi-CD box set, but in the absence of such a survey this album and the one below will serve as collections of representative material from the Treasure Isle vaults. The title for this LP is a little misleading as it begins with "Carry Go Bring Come", which is pure ska, progresses through rocksteady, and only includes a couple of examples of true reggae. But no complaints about the selection, which includes gems such as "Drink Milk", "The Little You Have" and "Here I Stand".

◑ **Early Recordings** (Esoldun, France).
This fourteen-track set has two more items than the High Note album, though with so much Justin Hinds material still to appear on album it is a pity that four of the tracks should be duplications. Includes the rare and fine "Corner Stone" and "Over the River".

The Skatalites

No group of musicians were more central to the ska age than the **Skatalites**. They backed most of the top singing stars of the day, including the Maytals, Stranger Cole, Lord Creator, Jackie Opel, the Wailers and Delroy Wilson. Under their own name they made great instrumental music that stands unparalleled in any popular music form worldwide. The Skatalites were responsible for hundreds of 45s released under the band name or that of individual members. In view of this, the brevity of the band's career is astounding. The Skatalites were officially formed in June 1964, at a meeting in the Odeon Theatre: inspired by the early space shots, drummer Lloyd Knibbs suggested the name 'Satellites', to which Tommy McCook is said to have replied: "No, we play ska – the Skatalites." Shortly after that, the band played their first official gig at the Hi-Hat club in Rae Town. During their all-too-brief life as a band they played regular dates at locations like the Orange Bowl, the Bournemouth Beach Club, the Blinking Beacon and La Parisienne. Shortly after the Independence Day celebrations in August 1965, during which they played on a parade float sponsored by the Cable & Wireless Company, they held their farewell show at a police ball held at the Runaway Bay Hotel.

The drums of **Lloyd Knibbs** and the bass of **Lloyd Brevett** were the high-powered engine of the group. Guitarists **Ernest Ranglin**, **Jerome 'Jah Jerry' Hinds** and **Harold McKenzie**, together with pianist **Jackie Mittoo**, built on this foundation, supporting the driving force of saxophonists **Tommy McCook**, **Roland Alphonso** and **Lester Sterling**, along with trumpeter **Johnny 'Dizzy' Moore** and

Skatalites at Studio One: Knibbs on drums, Mittoo on piano, McCook standing with sax, and Don Drummond (inset)

trombonist **Don Drummond**. Other talented individuals who travelled with the core band included the trumpeters **Reverend Billy Cooke** and **Percival Dillon**. The band always featured top-quality singers like **Lord Tanamo**, **Doreen Schaeffer**, **Jackie Opel** and **Tony Gregory**.

Maybe there were too many drivers – it has been suggested that rivalry between Tommy McCook and Roland Alphonso contributed to the break-up. What seems more likely is that the band suffered a blow to their collective spirit when Don Drummond was incarcerated for the murder of his girlfriend, the dancer Margarita Mahfood. He was subsequently confined to the Belle Vue Mental Hospital, where he died in 1969. Drummond was a superb musician, whose abilities were recognized by leading international jazz figures such as George Shearing, J.J. Johnson and Sarah Vaughan. With his taste for minor chords and his Rastafarian faith, he anticipated later developments in Jamaican music, including the 'Far East' sound of Augustus Pablo. Though seriously troubled by mental instability, he was responsible for some of the most innovative work of the ska era, and his trial was a harbinger of the demise of ska.

The standard of the Skatalites' records was phenomenally high, and their best discs are small miracles of invention under pressure: With the singer on one track and all the musicians on the other, there was no room for mistakes, creating a tension that was often inspirational. Their most widely known sides were made for Clement Dodd, Duke Reid and the still undervalued Justin and Duke Yap, but band members made equally distinguished work as sidemen for other producers. Often these records were simply credited to the session leader. Thus Baba Brooks made records for King Edwards and Duke Reid in which he played trumpet in place of the equally talented Johnny Moore, but still with the rest of the Skatalites present. Likewise, Brooks recorded "Cork Foot", an updating of the mento "Cork Foot Simpson" for Lindon O. Pottinger, on which he and Drumbago replaced Moore and Knibbs from the band. Similar aggregations made records for Prince Buster, Randy's and Leslie Kong, as well as countless smaller producers who paid them for just a session or two, sometimes pressing the 45s in quantities of one hundred copies or less.

The two producers who released the greatest number of 45s by the Skatalites were, not suprisingly, **Clement Dodd** and **Duke Reid**. Among the instrumental classics the band recorded at Dodd's Brentford Road studio were furious up-tempo workouts such as "Timothy", "Crime Wave" and "Tear Up", and more reflective jazz-oriented pieces in the mould of "Schooling the Duke", "Looking Through the Window" and "Scandal". Additionally, there were moodier minor-key pieces including such enduring favourites as "Cleopatra", "Beardman Ska", "Sudden Destruction" and "Addis Ababa". Similar examples could be given of their equally fine work for Reid, beginning with the record that some sound-system owners remember as one of the first and most striking indications of the shift to ska: Don Drummond's beautiful "Eastern Standard Time". Other records the band made with Duke, such as "One Eyed Giant" and "Alcatraz", have a different atmosphere, with early deejays adding extra excitement via shouted catchphrases and lots of percussive vocal effects. Tunes like these were major hits on the UK club and sound-system scene as well.

Arguably, the cream of the Skatalites' work was for **Justin and Duke Yap**, not least because the Chinese-Jamaican producers were willing to spend more time and money on their sessions. The Yaps had recorded the singers Larry Marshall, Ephraim 'Joe' Henry and Ferdie Nelson at Federal in 1962–63, and these first sessions also resulted in a minor instrumental hit in the form of trumpeter Baba Brooks' "Distant Drums". By 1964 Justin had linked up with Allan 'Bim Bim' Scott, a friend of Coxsone. Scott introduced Justin, just twenty years old, to the Skatalites: "He (Scott) started to say, well you could get the Skatalites band, which was on fire at the time. Then he got me introduced to Roland, Johnny Moore, the basic band at the time, Knibbs and everybody. And then we hook up with Don Drummond too. Bim drove me downtown, [and] went in and talked to him first. I remember he [Don] just took off! When he came back, he came with his answer...it's OK! I admired Don Drummond. I call him a maestro – he takes over, he's in charge, he knows what he's doin'. He's very professional. And when you hear my recordings with Drummond, you know that he took charge." Sessions followed at Studio One in November 1964 and the radio station JBC the following year.

Justin's first session at Studio One was an all-night marathon. He and his brother laid on food, drink, herb and money for the musicians, and were not afraid to try for retakes, always a fairly rare practice in cost-conscious Jamaican disc production. What they got in return was a batch of the best ska instrumentals ever made – "Confucius", "Chinatown", "Marcus Junior", "Ringo", "Smiling" and "The Reburial", as well as Roland Aphonso's "Ghost Town". These tunes put the Yaps' Top Deck, Tuneico and Top Sound labels on the map; the following year they held further sessions at Studio One, recording the similarly excellent "Red For Danger" and "Yogi Man", featuring trumpeter Johnny Moore. A session later that year at JBC produced two more classics with Roland Alphonso: a superbly relaxed cut of jazz pianist Ray Bryant's "Shake A Lady" (aka "VC-10") and, even better, an hypnotic version of the Henry Mancini theme from the Peter Sellers movie *A Shot In the Dark*. Both Roland Alphonso and the very gifted Bajan singer **Jackie Opel** were credited with many of the arrangements, all of a consistently high standard.

Ska demonstrated the typical Jamaican gift of being able to make effective use of pieces drawn from a variety of often unlikely sources: almost every ska outfit, the Skatalites included, recorded instrumentals based on film themes or pop hits from anywhere in the world. The Skatalites also supported the Wailers on a couple of interesting vocal interpretations of movie material: Burt Bacharach's "What's New Pussycat?", already a gigantic international hit for Tom Jones, and Irving Berlin's vintage "White Christmas" – even if the group's interpretation owed more to the Drifters' 1950s cut than the Bing Crosby original. Moving away from the small and large screens, but staying with foreign sources of inspiration, Roland Alphonso recorded a creditable instrumental version of the Claude King county/pop hit "Wolverton Mountain", retitled "Twin Double" (C&N), while Lord Tanamo, who regularly sang with the Skatalites, was responsible for changing "I'm In the Mood For Love" – made particularly popular in Jamaica by Fats Domino's cut – into "I'm In the Mood For Ska" (C&N). It was the first of several outstanding Jamaican interpretations of this standard: the Techniques were to cut the consummate rocksteady version, then the Heptones did the reggae one. Perez Prado and Mongo Santamaria were regularly covered – the latter's *Watermelon Man* album providing several tracks that were to be given ska treatments; from instrumental soul, Roland Alphonso copped Alvin Cash And the Crawlers' "Twine Time" and renamed it "Dr. Ring Ding" (Coxsone).

As committed **Rastafarians**, the Skatalites backed a few vocalists who were not professional singers but Ras Tafari brethren who were able to deliver a song. Particularly noteworthy among these was "Far I Come"/ "Babylon" (Coxsone) by Vernon Allen, perhaps the earliest song to express clear Rasta sentiments. Then there was a little-recorded singer known as Bongo Man (Byfield), who anticipated the Rastafarian boom by cutting a handful of artless but sincere expressions of faith: "Where Is Garvey?" (Muzik City), "Jack Ruby Is Bound To Die" (Rolando & Powie) and "Bongo Man" (Treasure Isle). The first of these was on the flip of the best-selling ska record of all time, "Guns Of Navarone", and so is not hard to find (particularly on the UK Island pressing, where it was simply credited to the Skatalites), but his other two discs remain among the scarcest of the period.

For all the brevity of the period in which they were officially together as a band, the Skatalites' contribution to Jamaican music was incalculable. After they split, nearly all the musicians involved were to continue playing important roles in studio bands, occasionally reforming for tours and to record albums such as *Return of the Big Guns*, which Island released in 1984.

DON DRUMMOND

◑ **The Best Of Don Drummond** (Studio One, JA).

Ⓔ This really does live up to its title, mixing Studio One material with very welcome tracks from both Treasure Isle and Top Deck. An indispensable album.

● **In Memory Of** (Studio One, JA).

● **100 Years After** (Studio One, JA).

Buy these two in addition to the above set and you'll have most of his best work for Studio One. *100 Years After* contains the superb "Freedom Sounds" and "Last Call", which are truly essential Drummond.

JACKIE OPEL

● **The Best Of Jackie Opel** (Studio One, JA).

● **Cry Me A River** (Studio One, JA).

The quality of Jackie Opel's voice puts him among the all-time Jamaican greats, in spite of his Trinidadian nationality. Yet he has been consistently undervalued by the crossover audience. This can only be explained by his tendency to sing in an American r&b/soul style, rather than sounding particularly Jamaican. Any CD release of either of these soulful sets should add the incredible "I Am What I Am", a ska scorcher of the first order.

THE SKATALITES

◑ **Ska Authentic** (ND/Studio One, JA).

● **Ska Authentic Volume 2** (ND/Studio One, JA).

Ⓔ When originally released in 1964, both volumes of *Ska Authentic* featured a mixture of instrumentals and vocals. The first title then reappeared a couple of years later in a UK pressing as an instrumental set, with only a couple of tracks in common with the original. To confuse things even further, a Studio One CD appeared in 1994 called *Ska Authentic Volume I* that had the second selection of tracks, minus three, but with the addition of seven extra ones (including a couple of vocals from the 1964 set). The very rare coloured vinyl original now fetches three-figure sums, but fortunately the all-instrumental set, which is seldom unavailable, is stronger, both in its vinyl and its CD form. *Volume 2* has remained unaltered, and is only marginally less impressive than the second variation of its predecessor; it includes only a couple of tracks that have ever appeared on other albums.

● **Ska Boo-Da-Ba** (WIRL, JA; Doctor Bird, UK).

E The 1966 press of this – on Top Deck in Jamaica, Doctor Bird in the UK – remains the definitive ska album: twelve scorching instrumentals, with Don Drummond well to the fore (five of the composing credits are his, including "Confucius", "Chinatown" and "Marcus Junior"). Producer Phillip Yap paid the participating musicians twice the normal rate; in return the musicians rehearsed the music fully, and it shows. For some reason, the reissue on WIRL, which receives periodic represses, replaced two of the original gems with a couple of relatively weak Studio One vocals from the Wailers. Even in this truncated form, however, there is still no ska album to touch it.

● **Best Of the Skatalites** (Studio One, JA).

● **Celebration Time** (Studio One, JA).

Two more high-grade compilations of the Skatalites' Brentford Road output. The former includes the UK club hit "Phoenix City", and the great "Beardman Ska"; the second, compiled by Coxsone in the mid-Eighties, has the 'Far East' sound of "Cleopatra Rock", as well as the Skatalite reading of the classic "Peanut Vendor", with blistering trumpet from Frankie Anderson. The most recent vinyl pressings carry two extra vocal tracks as bonus.

● **Scattered Lights** (Top Deck, JA).

Released in the 1980s, this repeats five of the tracks from *Ska Boo-Da-Ba*, but is essential for gems like "Determination", "Ska Ta Shot" and "Shot In the Dark".

◑ **Ska – Tribute To the Skatalites** (Essoldun, France).

◑ **Music Is My Occupation: Ska Instrumentals 1962–1965** (Trojan, UK).

● **The Skatalites** (Treasure Isle, JA).

The Skatalites' work for Duke Reid was easily the equal of that for Clement Dodd, as shown in all three of these well-selected collections. There are enough differences between each to make it worthwhile buying all three.

THE SKATALITES AND FRIENDS

◑ **Hog In A Cocoa** (Essoldun, France).

The Skatalites in the role of backing band for various vocalists at Treasure Isle. Quite a few acknowledged classics – Justin Hinds' "The Higher the Monkey Climbs", Stranger Cole's "Run Joe", Derrick & Patsy's "Housewife's Choice", Eric Morris's "Penny Reel" – plus enough worthwhile obscurities to interest those who already have the well-known tracks.

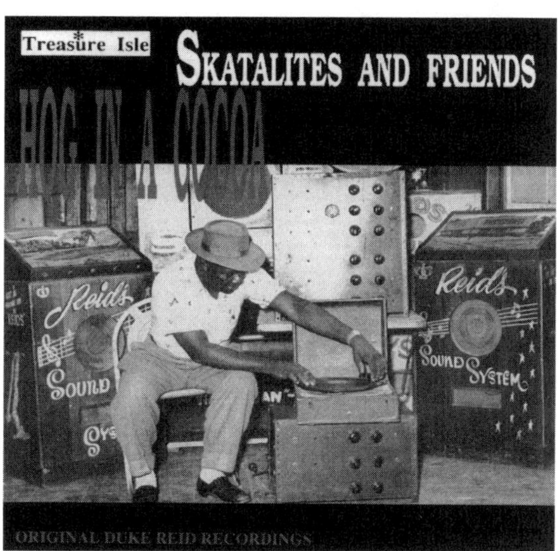

Other ska producers

Among the outstanding instrumental 45s made outside of the Coxsone/Reid/Buster axis were Baba Brooks' "Shank I Shek" for **King Edwards**, who finally retired from music production at the end of 1964. He, more than the other producers, had concentrated on cutting music primarily for his sound system; although he made vocals with such as Eric Morris, Lord Tanamo, Bobby Aitken and Shenley Duffus, his instrumentals were exceptional. **Leslie Kong** continued to enjoy vocal hits with Jimmy Cliff – including the spirited "King Of Kings" – and Derrick Morgan, and also made top-notch instrumentals like "Dreadnought" and "Sly Mongoose" (all Beverley's). **Lindon Pottinger**'s big vocal star was Winston Samuels, a fine singer who has been unjustly overlooked. Pottinger also scored a huge hit with Jimmy James, later to find fame in the UK as a soul man. Instrumentally, "King Size" and "Faberge" (Gaydisc) did the business for him. The Chin family, headed by **Vincent 'Randy' Chin** soon established themselves as leading retailers; the shop known as Randy's at 16/17 North Parade became a Kingston music business landmark by the early 1960s. The biggest success for Vincent Chin was the balladeer **Lord Creator**, but Chin also produced vocals by the soul-styled Jackie Opel, John Holt and Alton Ellis. Randy's instrumentals include a now much-sought-after Don Drummond EP, as well as the Skatalites' "Siberia" and "Sam the Fisherman". Just before trombonist Rico Rodriguez left for the UK he made "Rico's Farewell" and "Cuban Blockade", the latter featuring Johnny Moore, Tommy McCook and Lester Sterling. The Chin family moved to the USA in the mid-1970s and now runs the famous VP Distribution Company from Queens, New York.

The trombonist and percussionist **Carlos Malcolm** produced his own band – which included Karl Bryan (saxophone), Kart McDolald (conga), Boris Gardner and Lascelles Perkins (vocals) and Winston 'Sparrow' Martin (drums). The band's best-remembered hit was a version of the TV Western theme "Bonanza", though they were responsible for several more fine instrumentals. With a repertoire drawing equally from hard bop – Horace Silver's "Filthy McNasty" and Neal Hefti's "Splanky" – and traditional sources like the mentos "Sly Mongoose", "Cut Munoo" and "Rukumbine", their three albums on the Upbeat and Top labels show a satisfying mento/jazz/ska hybrid just outside of the ska mainstream. (Incidentally, Malcolm also arranged all the local music featured in the James Bond movie *Dr No*.)

LORD CREATOR

◉ **Don't Stay Out Late** (VP/Randy's, US).

Ⓔ Lord Creator was always in a class of his own when it came to handling smooth ballads, and no slouch when it came to either calypso or vocalizing over steaming ska tracks. Everything of worth that he recorded for Vincent 'Randy' Chin in the 1960s is gathered for the CD version of this stunning collection (the vinyl version misses out ultra-rare cuts of "Evening News" and "Such Is Life"). These and well-known hits like "Independent Jamaica", "Man To Man" and "Don't Stay Out Late" are among the most moving sides ever to emerge from a Kingston studio, and quite unlike what everyone else was doing then – or has done since. When UB40 honoured the quality of his "Kingston Town" and included it on their *Labour Of Love* cover version album, Creator was able to buy a house in Jamaica from the royalties.

CARLOS MALCOLM & HIS AFRO-JAMAICAN RHYTHM

● **Skamania** (Up-Beat Records, JA).

The only album from this exciting band features a spirited mento medley in the six-minute title track, as well as a version of the South African hit "Skoian" and several Malcolm originals. The band is tight and punchy, and showcases some good soloing. Overall perhaps not as funky as the Skatalites, but nonetheless well worth seeking out.

VARIOUS ARTISTS – KING EDWARDS PRODUCTIONS

◑ **Man About Ska Town** (King Edwards, UK).

◑ **King Edwards Presents Ska-Volution** (King Edwards, UK).

◑ **Ska-Ba-Dip – The Essential King Edwards** (King Edwards, UK).

◑ **Ska-Lutations From King Edwards** (King Edwards, UK).

As a producer, Vincent 'King' Edwards remains best remembered for trumpeter Baba Brooks' version of "Shank I Shek" (ie Chiang Ki Chek, the Chinese Nationalist leader), one of the hottest of ska instrumentals with the haunting minor-key 'Far East' sound. These four collections constitute his swansong and demonstrate that his eponymous label was responsible for a great deal of top-drawer ska, even if the producer's first love was r&b. Instrumentals like Lester Sterling's "Man About Town", Baba Brooks' "Bus Strike" and the Upcoming Willows' "Red China" are in the same class as the much-versioned "Shank I Shek". The vocals tend to be more variable, excellent titles by Lord Tanamo and Eric Morris notwithstanding.

Rude boys and rocksteady

2

2

Rude boys and rocksteady

As **rocksteady** emerged during 1966 it developed characteristics that identified it as almost the opposite of its predecessor, ska. In a nutshell, rocksteady was slower, more refined and, most of all, cooler. Firstly, the regularly paced 'walking' basslines that ska inherited from r&b became much more broken-up – in rocksteady the bass didn't play on every beat with equal emphasis, but rather played a repeated pattern that syncopated the rhythm. In turn, the bass and drums became much more prominent, with the horns taking on a supportive rather than lead role. For further emphasis, **Lynn Taitt**, the most significant musician of rocksteady, would play a line on the bass strings of his guitar in unison with the bassist. Taitt was the arranger for all the records generally cited as the first examples of rocksteady, and his guitar sound was a trademark of the genre. The impact of various soul styles on Jamaican music was also apparent in the more refined style of rocksteady vocalists, which meshed perfectly with the slower tempo. Several already-established singers, such as **Alton Ellis**, **Ken Boothe** and **Delroy Wilson**, would go on to reach even greater heights in this period, which also saw the emergence of a new generation of talented youngsters, often singing in trios.

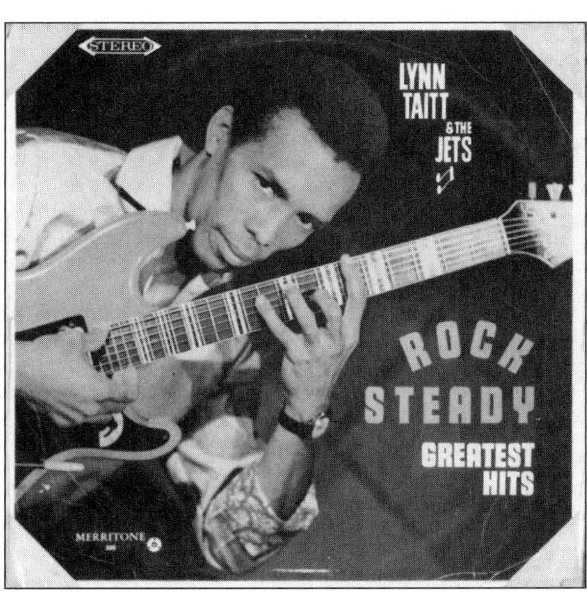

The brief flowering of rocksteady – between the autumn of 1966 and the summer of 1968 – was the most important episode in Jamaican musical history, exerting an influence on almost every subsequent development. The shift of rhythmic focus onto the bass and drums has remained a feature of all later stages of Jamaican music. This emphasis on the bass in particular followed on from the first instrumental remixes of **Treasure Isle** songs made by sound-system owner **'Ruddy' Redwood** in 1967, a development which would lead directly to the dub of the 1970s. When the deejay **U-Roy** first made an impact with his dancehall lyrics on record in 1969, it was the classic rocksteady rhythms that he used to showcase his new style, in which he interacted with snatches of the original vocals by bands such as the **Melodians**, **Silvertones** and **Paragons**. The rhythms from **Roland Alphonso**'s **Soul Vendors** at Brentford Road and **Tommy McCook**'s **Supersonics** at Bond Street would also be adapted later on, notably for the 'flying cymbals' and 'rockers' styles of the mid-1970s, early 1980s dancehall, and computerized ragga. And crucially, the practice of 'versioning' – whether in the form of dub or deejaying – had its genesis in this period. From now on the focus of production

The Melodians

would shift away from the big sound-system owners and studio bosses, and onto a new generation of freelance entrepreneurs.

During its relatively short period of dominance, rocksteady was the music of choice in the ever-important dancehall. Before the first records were made in the new style, however, there was a transitional period in which the fast tempos of ska slowed down and the rhythms became more emphatic. So any survey of rocksteady has to look first at the period of **rude-boy** music, and at the musical and social trends that prepared the ground.

VARIOUS ARTISTS

Catch This Beat (Island, UK).

E The packaging was obviously designed to cash in on the 1980s' Two Tone craze, but the selection is pure rocksteady, and far too refined for the boys from Coventry to have tried emulating. One advantage this compilation has over most others is that it draws from a number of producers and labels to give a comprehensive overview of the music, with tracks ranging from Slim Smith's "The New Boss" and Jackie Mittoo's "Got My Bugaloo" for Studio One, through the Melodians' "Train To Expo '67" and Alton Ellis's "Shake It" for Treasure Isle, to Derrick Harriott's self-produced "Do I Worry" and the Defenders' "Set Them Free" for WIRL.

Put It On – It's Rock-Steady (Island, UK).
Released in 1968, this is one to search for in the secondhand bins. Besides the title track from the Wailers, there is Justin Hinds' "Save A Bread", the Clarendonians' "Rude Boy Gone A Jail", Delroy Wilson's "Dancing Mood", Ken Boothe's "Feel Good" and another nine hits that trace the shift from rude-boy music to rocksteady. Despite the cover and label credits, "Won't You Come Home Baby" is not by the Gaylads, but Ken Boothe) and Delroy Wilson, while the Tree Tops are actually the Three Tops, and Bob & Andy's real identity is revealed when you drop the ampersand.

Feel like Jumping (Receiver Records, UK).
Another sterling collection that draws from several sources, including Studio One, Derrick Harriott, Joe Gibbs, the obscure Leeward Robinson, and J.J. Johnson. Historically the most significant track must be Roy Shirley's "Hold Them", Joe Gibbs' debut as a producer. But the album is clearly not meant to be a dry history lesson, and important rocksteady hits like the Federals' "Penny For Your Song", the Kingstonians' "Winey Winey", the Gladiators' "Train Is Coming Back" and the Pioneers' "Long Shot" equally make the title of Marcia Griffiths' classic appropriate for the entire set.

Rude-boy music

From early 1965, when the Kingston studios were still turning out ska instrumentals in quantity, to 1967, the year of rocksteady's domination, the youths of West Kingston listened and danced to a different style of music, one that was to act as a bridge between two more fully developed forms. It was a style that was characterized by two factors above all else: musically it carried a far more dynamic **bassline** (the electric bass had only recently replaced the stand-up variety); and lyrically its performers addressed their target audience – the **ghetto youth** – as their own kind. For the latter reason, the label '**rude-boy music**' is as good as any.

There had always been something essentially adult about ska, with its swing- and bop-influenced horn solos; these new records spoke to a younger audience. Looking forward to rocksteady and later reggae, the horns tended to stay in the background, while the slower pace allowed the vocals to gain a fresh prominence. The status of the vocals was in itself a factor in the music's ability to communicate with the ghetto kids, who could have their collective identity confirmed by the lyrics of singers of their own age and – for the most part – from the same West Kingston background. Although the full flowering of Jamaican vocal styles was going to need the further slowing down of the rhythms and the greater incorporation of American soul influences, the starring role was moving from the musicians – such as Roland Alphonso, Tommy McCook and Jackie Mitto – to the new wave of vocalists and harmony groups, like the **Gaylads**, the **Clarendonians**, the **Ethiopians**, **Desmond Dekker & the Aces**, the **Silvertones**, the **Tennors**, **Alton Ellis & the Flames**, the **Melodians**, the **Techniques**, the **Wailers** and many, many more.

Because of the sheer productivity of the highly competitive Jamaican music business, and the speed with which new ideas are seized upon with an almost total indifference to notions of individual originality or copyright, major stylistic shifts occur every few years. That said, the developments that took place in this period can be related to additional specific factors, both within the tightly knit community of professional musicians and the larger social sphere.

VARIOUS ARTISTS

● **Dance Crasher: Ska – Rocksteady** (Trojan, UK).

Covering the change from ska to rocksteady, though going back as far as 1962 for Stranger Cole's prescient "Rough & Tough", as well as the late ska instrumentals "Bonanza Ska" and "Let George Do It". Keeping up the musical standards are ground-breaking proto-rocksteady classics like Alton Ellis's title track, Lee Perry's lewd "Doctor Dick", the Ethiopians' familiar complaint about "Owe Me No Pay Me" and the Rulers' "Don't Be A Rude Boy".

⦿ **Rudies All Round: Rude Boy Records 1966/7** (Trojan, UK).

A collection of twenty singles from various producers, but with a common thematic concern, variously condemning, glorifying or simply noting the phenomenon of the rude boys. Most of the tracks are acknowledged classics, with the others not falling far short. Particularly welcome are gems by artists not often anthologized, including the Rulers, the Spanishtonians, Joe White, the Rio Grandes, the Overtakers and the Valentines. Historically important records by Prince Buster and the Wailers are missing, but this is almost the complete story of the rudies on record. A pity that most tracks are dubbed from disc and not from producers' original tapes.

"Rudies all around"

The buoyancy of ska – despite the melancholy sometimes found in the horn solos – had expressed the optimism that accompanied the achievement of independence. But by the mid-1960s it was becoming increasingly clear that Jamaica had exchanged the political rule of Britain for the economic domination of the United States. As far as the sufferers of the ghettos were concerned, there had been no great qualitative change in daily life, and the mounting resentment felt in Trench Town and the other ghettos of West Kingston frequently found expression in outbursts of violence – often employing German-made knives known as ratchets and sometimes guns. Not that the **rude-boy** phenomenon was new to the island – in 1948 Ivanhoe 'Rhygin' Martin, the model for the Jimmy Cliff part in the film *The Harder They Come*, had become the archetypal rudie with a series of gun fights with the police. However, the years following independence brought a marked rise in the crime rate.

A major reason for the growth in lawlessness was the sheer number of young men attracted to the city from the country. A high percentage of these migrants from the rural areas found themselves without hope of employment in the overcrowded shanty towns, and unable to fulfil the dreams that had prompted their move. By 1967, it was possible for Garth White, writing in the *Caribbean Quarterly*, to claim that "Rudie culture has so developed as to command adherents among the majority of lower class youth." The spaghetti westerns of directors like Sergio Leone, and Sergio Corbucci, along with James Bond's celluloid adventures, also made their own contribution to rudie culture, providing rough and tough heroes to be emulated. Many of Kingston's young criminals named themselves after the characters and actors they saw on the screen, as did later streetwise deejays, from Dennis Alcapone, through Trinity, Clint Eastwood and Dillinger, to Josey Wales.

Back in 1962, **Duke Reid**, an ex-policeman with credible claims to toughness himself, had released **Stranger Cole's** "Rough And Tough", a fast early ska number that was one of the first instances of a musician giving warnings to the unruly youth. The following year record producers discovered the large audience for moralistic messages that also managed to glamorise the rudies. Duke Reid produced an instrumental called "Rude Boy" in 1963, but the **Wailers**' early single "Simmer Down" was the hit that sent a warning to the disaffected youth in their own language:

"Chicken merry
Hawk deh near
And when 'im deh near
You must beware, so
Simmer down
Ooh, control your temper
Simmer down,
Cause the battle will be hotter
Simmer down
And you won't get no supper
Simmer down
And you know you're bound to suffer."

The teenage Wailers followed their initial rude-boy hit with two others on the topic. "Rude Boy" (Coxsone) borrowed the chorus from the Impressions' US hit "Keep On Moving" to convey the plight of the rude boy on the run. But it was to be with the group's third single about the rudies that was to have the greatest significance in purely musical terms, for the 1966 hit "Jailhouse" (Studio One) helped to crystallize the sound of the rude-boy era, with both its slower pace and buoyant pumping piano (the latter reminiscent of New Orleans r&b, but perfectly expressing the rude-boy swagger).

Before the Wailers left Coxsone, and while Bob Marley was earning money in a Delaware car factory, **Bunny Livingston** and **Peter Tosh** recorded another couple of 45s on the rude-boy theme, one ambivalent in its position, the other a great deal less so. In its chorus at least, Tosh's "I'm the Toughest" (Studio One) seemed to give expression to the rudies' challenge to their neo-colonial and class oppressors; yet other lines warned the youth to change their ways, and the title's boast could be read as directed to, rather than from, the rude boys. Far less open to more than one interpretation was Bunny Livingston's equally strong "Let Him Go" (Studio One). No doubt a response to the theme of the Clarendonians' "Rudie Gone A Jail" hit, it was essentially a reminder to the authorities that the rudie languishing in jail was smart and strong, and would live long – that the rudie, in fact, represented the future.

Joe White's "Rudies All Around" (WIRL) presented the rude boy as an island-wide phenomenon: "From Kingston to Montego Bay, from Negril to Port Royal, rudies everywhere", coolly adding that "Cop shoot rudie, rudie shoot cop". **Keith McCarthy**'s one major hit, "Everybody Rude Now" (Studio One), advises at its close "don't just be a rudie", but for most of the side McCarthy merely notes – in slightly alarmed tones, admittedly – that it will be "gun against gun/ratchet against ratchet/tough against tough." The other rude-boy classic by the **Clarendonians** (Peter Austin and Fitzroy 'Ernest' Wilson), "Rudie Bam Bam", a sequel to their earlier hit, also cuts both ways to some extent. It begins with the singers, who were clearly the same age as the rudies, exuberantly singing: "I hear say that Rudie got out of jail/I hear say Rudie got bail". The lyrics then tell of how the archetypal Rudie soon cuts a man with a ratchet, and ends up back in jail, concluding that: "This looks like the end of Mr Rude boy/Because the judge gave him life sentence, friend." But what could be a morality tale is undercut by both a relentless pumping piano that might be celebratory of the bad boy's misdeeds, and the chorus of "What a bam bam, yeah/What a bam bam/What a bam bam", which seems regretful about his undoing.

Sentiments not far removed to the Wailers' declaration that the youth were going to one day rule the land, but without the overtly rudie imagery, were voiced by **King Rocky** (aka future Leroy Sibbles and Little Roy associate Anthony 'Rocky' Ellis), with "I'm the Ruler" (Studio One), as well as the **Ethiopians**' first 45 for Coxsone, "I'm Gonna Take Over Now", the latter disc proclaiming: "For I know that our time has come/We must wear the crown". The **Clarendonians**, too, referred to being king on "You Can't Keep A Good Man Down" (Coxsone), though their throne in mind might well have been a musical one. Even former Techniques member and future leader of the Uniques, **Slim Smith**, best remembered for his tormented love songs, recorded "The New Boss" (Studio One), which contrasted the past and present tribulations of the black diaspora with their promised destiny:

"Someone just tell them for me
They just can't see
Someone like me was born to be
The boss and king of everything."

All of these records shared their musical style with those that directly addressed the rudies, as did the winner of the 1966 Festival Song Competition, the **Maytals**' "Bam Bam" (BMN). Recorded for Byron Lee (a bandleader whose music was usually aimed at the middle class and tourists), this advanced production did not make any direct reference to racial pride, but was nonetheless a statement about personal dignity, with Toots declaring: "But if you trouble this man/it will bring bam bam, what a bam bam".

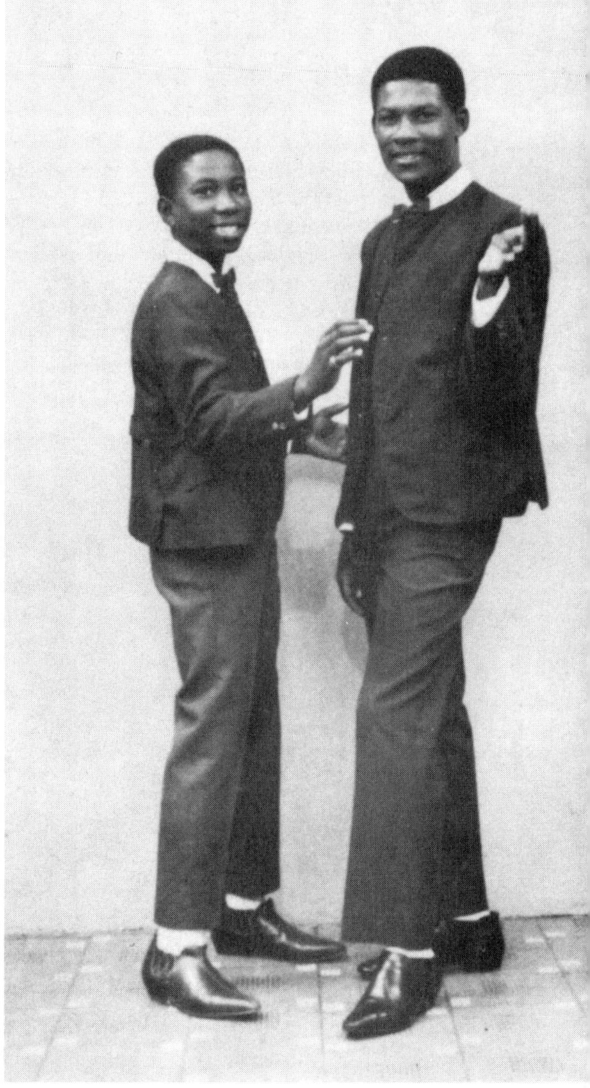

The Clarendonians: Ernest Wilson (left) and Peter Austin

THE CLARENDONIANS

The Best of the Clarendonians (Coxsone, JA).

Recorded in the hiatus between ska and rocksteady, though what tips the balance to the latter category are the relatively sophisticated musical arrangements for the beautiful "Ten Guitars" and their first recording of "Darling Forever", as well as the presence of the two seminal rude-boy hits, "Rudie Gone A Jail" and the more developed "Rudie Bam Bam".

PETER TOSH

The Toughest (Heartbeat, CD).

E "Rasta Shook Them Up" and "I'm the Toughest" are just the two most stunning tracks of the thirteen from Studio One collected here (the singer's complete work for Dodd but for two tracks), and presented free of crackle and hiss. The other six items are from Scratch, and include the ground-breaking early reggae tracks "Earth's Rightful Ruler", "Downpresser" and "Brand New Secondhand". This is the only truly essential Peter Tosh set ever released, though enough worthwhile Joe Gibbs and self-produced singles exist for another.

Prince Buster and the Judge

The best-known condemnation of the rudies was the facetious one that came from **Prince Buster**. His "Judge Dread" (Prince Buster), from early 1967, might not have prompted many of the ratchet and gun users to hang up their weapons, but it did initiate some sort of debate. On Buster's original hit, four rude boys appear in court, charged with a variety of crimes, including "robbing school children", "killing black people" and "burning homes." The draconian judge, who announces that he is from Ethiopia, sentences them to a total of several hundred years, with any pleas for mercy treated as contempt of court and deserving another century behind bars.

The case for Two Gun Tex, Adolphous James, Emanuel Zachariah Zakipon and George Grab-and-Flee was subsequently presented on other records, some using the same melody. Buster himself contributed two more instalments of the saga, remaining firm with "The Barrister" (when the appealing barrister is also sentenced to jail), but showing a change of heart (or perhaps awareness of record buyers' sympathies) with "Judge Dread Dances the Pardon", the new leniency being celebrated with an excellent trombone solo by the great Rico Rodriguez. Among the best of the further variations on the theme were **Honeyboy Martin**'s "Dreader Than Dread" (Caltone), and **Lee Perry & the Defenders**' "Set them Free"/"Don't Blame the Youth" (WIRL). Like most of the pro-rudie answer records, the Martin record was content to confirm the young delinquents' unbowed bravado, while the future Upsetter based his appeal against the sentences on the grounds of black history and related contemporary social conditions:

"But as you can see, they're from a poor generation
Having no education, no qualification
So they're driven to desperation
Can't get no job so they're forced to rob
I'm not saying they should, but as you know
A hungry man is an angry man
So think it over before you bind them over
Please give them a break to mend their mistakes
As you already know, robbery was from creation
For robbery befell the black nation
Our ancestors once ruled the world and all its gold
But now we're poor."

Again, it was probably Prince Buster who most eloquently invoked the social context, with his January 1967 disc "Shanty Town". The squatter camp known as Back-A-Wall had recently been razed to the ground and the inhabitants, including many Ras Tafari brethren, dispersed. The JLP government was getting tough on an area that had long been a haunt of the rude boys and had attracted considerable comment from politicians. Over a great slowed-down ska rhythm, without any of the bombast (or humour) of his Judge Dread persona, Buster sings from the heart:

"Too late, shanty town get scanty
Too late, shanty town get scanty
Too late, there is no more place to capture

Too late, the people can't do no better
Too late, the rude boys gon' to jail
Too late, dem can't get no bail
Too late, seven years in dem tail
Too late, the minister put on the pressure

A woman with a baby, cryin'
The same time all dem big bulldozer come in
The cops was standin' by
Dem baton sticks was long
An' all the people could do
Is tan up an' watch dem mash dem belongs

I saw a woman with a baby, cryin
She says: I got no place to sleep
I got no place to eat
What is now am I to treat?
The cops was standin' by (Lord Lord Lord)
Baton sticks was long
An' all the rudies could do
Is stay in jail an' sing a song
Too late, dem a go put on the pressure
Too late, the people can't do no better
Too late, shanty town get scanty
Too late, the squatters start to scatter
Oh God I am sorry fi dem."

Buster remained a force in the rocksteady era, even if he might have presented a greater challenge to Reid and Dodd had he worked with more of the emergent youth talent. Instead, he mostly concentrated on his own vocals, which, admittedly, included the wonderful two-part saga of "Johnny Cool", the equally inspired "Shepherd Beng Beng" and his evocative tribute to the sound men of his youth, "Ghost Dance".

PRINCE BUSTER

◉ **Fabulous Greatest Hits** (Sequel, UK).
While Buster is more often associated with ska, some of his most exciting records were in the rocksteady mode, and it is these that are best represented here. Built around the famous 1967 Fab LP of the same title, but with twice as many tracks, this still falls short of the compilation the Prince deserves. To begin with, a couple of tracks from the original set were always less than top-drawer, while the choice of extra ones is – to put it kindly – curious. Recommended, though, for including his best-known ska classics, "Al Capone" and "Ten Commandments", as well as some of the finest rocksteady outside the Treasure Isle/Studio One axis, including "Freezing Up Orange Street", "Judge Dread" and "Ghost Dance", the last his atmospheric tribute to the characters from the dancehall scene of his youth.

Derrick Morgan and Desmond Dekker

More typical of the manner in which the majority of rude-boy records simply glamorized the violent bad boys was the series of hits on the topic cut by both **Derrick Morgan** and **Desmond Dekker** on Leslie Kong's Beverley's label. Morgan cut a trilogy of singles on the theme beginning with his huge hit "Tougher Than Tough", recorded in January 1967. Like "Judge Dread", this was set in a court room, and has the unbowed defendants answering the judge:

"Your honour, rudies don't fear
Rougher than rough, tougher than tough
Strong like lion, We are iron
Rudies don't fear."

Derrick followed this with "Retrial Of Rudie" in March and "Judge Dread In Court" was cut in May of the same year. The origins of these records, which were grounded in the reality of West Kingston's rude boy culture, can be traced to late 1966, when a well-known rude boy by the name of Busby asked the singer to make a

TROJAN RECORDS

Rudie Got Soul (and shirt): Desmond Dekker

CURTIS MAYFIELD AND THE SOUL CONNECTION

The Sensations' "A Thing Called Soul" was just one of many Jamaican celebrations of the US counterpart to rocksteady, and Jamaican artists have continued to cover or transform contemporary American soul hits down to the present day. The full flowering of Jamaican vocal styles came about through the incorporation of influences from harmony groups like the Miracles and the Temptations, and solo stars such as Sam Cooke, Ben E. King, Jerry Butler, Marvin Gaye and Chuck Jackson. Nobody was more important to this process than **Curtis Mayfield**, whom the British radio deejay David Rodigan rightly identified as the "godfather of reggae".

Even a cursory survey of rocksteady hits reveals several versions of songs written by Mayfield and originally recorded by either his group of the 1960s, the Impressions, or by artists he produced in the same period, such as Major Lance and Gene Chandler. Among these rocksteady gems are the likes of the Techniques' beautiful "Queen Majesty" (modelled on the Impressions' "Minstrel & Queen") and "You Don't Care" (based on "You'll Want Me Back", a US hit for Major Lance), as well as outstanding versions of Mayfield songs by the Wailers, the Minstrels, Pat Kelly and Ken Parker.

The Impressions, the most gospel-influenced of all the major soul vocal groups of the time, originally featured the baritone of Jerry Butler on lead. But in 1961 Butler left later to embark upon a successful solo career, and Mayfield reorganized the group around his own fragile but effective lead voice, and the harmonies of Fred Cash, Sam Gooden and the Brooks brothers, Arthur and Richard. The exquisite "Gypsy Woman", recorded for ABC-Paramount in 1961, was the one major hit associated with this second line-up of the Impressions, and it was successfully covered in Jamaica by the Uniques (with Slim Smith on lead vocal), and later by Marcia Griffiths, Milton Henry and the Mighty Diamonds.

In 1963 the Brook brothers departed, and over next three years the Impressions made a consistent run of US hits that were fundamental to the development of rocksteady, for both Mayfield's romanticism and his Civil Rights consciousness struck a cord with Jamaicans, while the Impressions' records provided young Jamaican performers with material that could not have been better suited to cool rocksteady rhythms. Even when Jamaican performers were not dipping into the Curtis Mayfield songbook, they were drawing from the vocal arrangements of the Impressions, and Mayfield's high-tenor lead was to be a model for, among others, Slim Smith (who sounded like a much edgier Mayfield), Ken Parker, Pat Kelly and Cornell Campbell. Even Bunny Wailer could – once upon a time, at least – project a convincing Mayfield-type falsetto. What made these covers and adaptations uniquely Jamaican were the 'rhythms' built for them, and these instrumental backing tracks have proved to be at least as great a legacy for successive generations of Jamaican musicians as Mayfield's well-crafted and soulful songs. They were continually updated in the Channel One and Joe Gibbs studios in the mid- and late 1970s, and then again – by practically every producer – in the dancehall period of the early 1980s. When reggae went digital, rhythms such as "Queen Majesty" were once again given new treatment, bringing the influence of Curtis Mayfield into the ragga era.

record about him. Derrick responded by cutting "Cool Off Rudies" for Coxsone, but the sentiments of the song were not to the real-life rude boy's liking – he insisted that he was far too tough to cool off. Derrick then cut "Tougher Than Tough" and handed the dubplate to the rude boy, who played it at a dance in Greenwich Town that night. The tune was a success and Busby duly celebrated by shaking up some beer and spraying it over some girls who happened to be followers of a gang of rude boys called the Vikings. Soaked and humiliated, the girls left the dance. The next day Busby paid the price for his misbehaviour. While on his way to another dance to hear "his" tune again, the rude boy was shot dead.

Producer Kong had further successes with the rude-boy style, most famously with "007

(Shanty Town)" by **Desmond Dekker**. Dekker had sung the backing vocals on Morgan's series with his brother George, but "007", the most enduring and archetypal of all rude-boy records, took the rudies to an international audience, charting in the UK and, even more surprisingly, the USA in the summer of 1967. Dekker's song borrowed lyrics from previous local hits on the topic but, in keeping with the rudies' love of lawless imagery from the movies, added memorable references to both James Bond and *Ocean's Eleven*, a caper film staring Frank Sinatra and friends. One of the most infectious rhythms ever to come from the Beverley's studio band further ensured the record's phenomenal success. Desmond Dekker & the Aces (Wilson James, Easton Barrington Howard) followed it with the almost as striking "Rudie Got Soul" and "Rude Boy Train".

DESMOND DEKKER & THE ACES

⦾ **Action!** (Esoldun, France).

E Before the international success of Marley, Desmond Dekker was the pop face of reggae, with early hits in both the UK and US (the latter particularly extraordinary for the time). Not that many outside of the music's target audience understood the lyrics of "007" (rude boys) or "Israelites" (repatriation) – they were just good to move to. A couple of decades later, the welcome CD release of *Action!*, a scarce late-1960s Beverley's album (with a handful of sought-after 45s added), shows just how under-appreciated both Dekker (his singing here much improved from the ska days) and producer Leslie Kong have been.

● **This Is Desmond Dekker** (Trojan, UK).

Several different packages have collected Dekker's greatest hits over the years, but none of the later compilations supersede either *Action!* or this 1969 Trojan release. Four of the tracks are found on both albums – "007" (a classic that stands any number of plays), "Sabotage", "Unity" and "Mother Young Girl". No less worthy of attention are Jamaican hits like "Hey Grandma", "Rudy Got Soul", "Wise Man" and "Beautiful & Dangerous". The Beverley's All Stars must remain one of the most undervalued session bands in the history of Jamaican music.

DERRICK MORGAN

● **Best of Derrick Morgan** (Beverley's, JA).

One of the first Jamaican recording stars, Derrick Morgan remained popular into the rocksteady era and beyond. He enjoyed particular success with 1967's "Greedy Girl" and a series of rude-boy records for Leslie Kong. His range might have been limited compared to the more expressively soulful vocalists who arrived with rocksteady, but given the right lyric Morgan could use it to telling effect. This is superbly demonstrated on an album that actually lives up to its title. It's a real rarity now, but it's well worth seeking out, while keeping your fingers crossed that it will be re-released in digital clarity.

Alton Ellis

One of the few popular Jamaican singers to take an unequivocal and consistent anti-rudie stand on record was **Alton Ellis** (b. 1944, Kingston), arguably the consummate vocalist of the rocksteady era. With his group, the Flames, he recorded five classic anti-rude-boy singles for Duke Reid. The first, "Don't

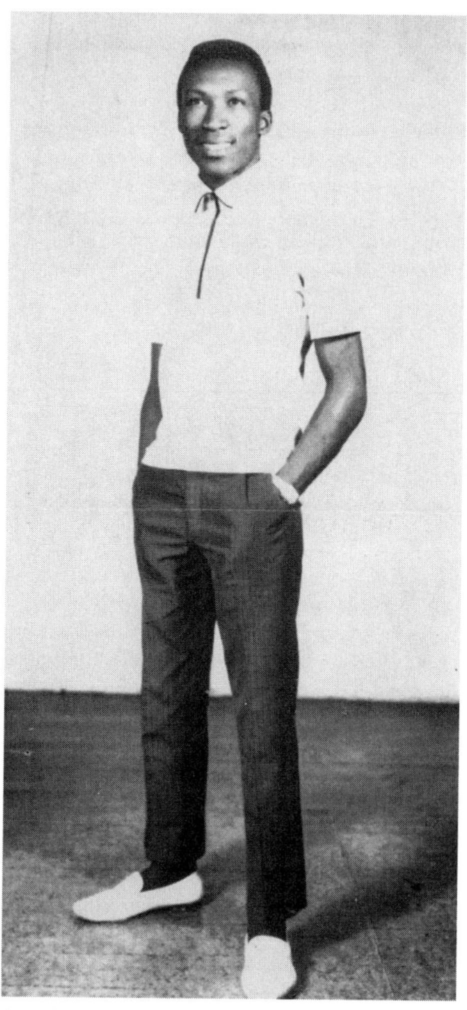

Alton Ellis, the godfather of rocksteady

Trouble People", was a relatively muted plea to "have your fun while you're young", but still to live according to the title. Two of the subsequent harder-edged tunes were again about the rude boy Busby. "Dance Crasher" was concerned with the trouble caused at dances by bottle-crashing bullies like him. Ellis advised rude boys to direct their aggression and need for status towards activities like boxing; as the song ends, he is singing: "You could be a champion, just like Mr Bunny Grant" (a reference to the successful Jamaican boxer). On "Cry Tough", which Ellis sings with a deep-voiced Lloyd Charmers, he informed the youth in no uncertain terms that time will catch up on them. Charmers could be heard intoning the foreboding chorus: "How can a man be tough, tougher than the world." "Blessings Of Love" simply warned the disaffected youth to throw away their ratchets and stop the killing; "The Preacher", the final record in the series, confirmed the message already given and stated that there were better things to be than a rudie.

Many singers cut both pro- and anti-rude-boy records, changing their angle to fit the producer or shifting public taste; but Ellis, who has blamed Marley for glorifying the rudies, remained constant in his attitude, before deciding it was safer to concentrate on more romantic concerns, including many of the most masterful interpretations of US soul material to emerge from Jamaica. He was, however, to return to warning the rude boys some five years later, with the exceptional "Big Bad Boy" for the innovative youth producer Keith Hudson's Mafia label.

ALTON ELLIS

⦿ **Cry Tough** (Heartbeat, US).

E The CD release of the classic ***Mr Soul Of Jamaica*** with the addition of another eight tracks. The original collected together most of his greatest rocksteady hits for Treasure Isle, and was always his strongest album – despite the overdubbing of "modern" drumming (circa mid-1970s). The track listing is flawless, with titles like "I Can't Stop Now", "All My Tears Come Rolling", "Remember That Sunday" and "Chatty Chatty" standing as part of the bedrock of Jamaican music, always suitable for updating. The original songs are marvellous, and Ellis's interpretations of US soul hits are no less so, with his distinctive vocal approach – along with the Supersonics' rhythms – giving "Ain't That Loving You", "Willow Tree" and "Ooh We Baby" a fresh identity. Despite a few errors in the sleeve notes, this is a first-class presentation from Heartbeat, all in crisp remastered sound.

Get ready, it's rocksteady – Duke Reid and Coxsone

When, in late 1966, the young singer **Hopeton Lewis** recorded "Take It Easy" at Federal Studios for club owner Winston Blake's Merritone label, he asked the band led by Lynn Taitt to play the rhythm slower, because he was having difficulty fitting the lyrics over the ska-style rhythm. When the take was finished, pianist Gladstone 'Gladdy' Anderson remarked on the 'rock steady' nature of the slowed-down rhythm. The new name stuck. Hopeton's advice to "Take your time/There's no need to hurry" could be taken as either directed at the rude boys, or simply to dancehall patrons adapting to the new musical pace. Further tracks recorded at the same sessions, and rush-released for the popular Hopeton's first album, included the sound-boy boasts of "Sounds & Pressure" and "A Deh Pon Dem"; the first 'herb' song ever recorded in Jamaica, "Cool Collie"; a couple of nods to US soul in "Music Got Soul" and the ballad "Why Must I Cry"; and the anthemic "Rock Steady", which celebrated the arrival of the new dance in a direct way:

"People are you ready
This is rocksteady
Shoulder jerk, heads a movin'
Feel the beat now
Move your feet now
Then go steady
If you're ready
People are you ready
This is rock steady."

The advent of rocksteady allowed many fresh young producers an entry into the business, but the best rocksteady of all was made by the long-established Duke Reid, who now entered a period in which he seemed unassailable.

HOPETON LEWIS

● Take It Easy (Merritone, JA; Island, UK).

An unjustly ignored figure, Hopeton Lewis won the 1970 Festival Song Competition with "Boom Shacka Lacka" for Treasure Isle, but this Merritone production from three years earlier remains his most worthwhile album. Three rocksteady anthems are included – "Sounds & Pressure" (the infectious rhythm of which was revived for Sugar Minott's "Hard Time Pressure"), "Take It Easy" (the template for Johnny Osbourne's big dancehall hit, "Water Pumping") and "Rock Steady", alongside his interpretation of Billy Bland's US hit, "Let the Little Girl Dance". This album has been long deleted, but hopefully a record company with taste will reissue it – alongside a Merritone "various artists" compilation.

Gems from Treasure Isle

The producer whose work best exemplified the cool and elegant feel of rocksteady was **Duke Reid**, who since the end of the previous decade had issued countless first-order boogie and ska records on the Treasure Isle, Trojan, Duke Reid and Dutchess labels, without ever quite dethroning Clement Dodd at Studio One. The colourful Reid recorded proto-rocksteady in 1966, using the rhythms that had developed during the rude-boy phase to propel big hits such as Alton Ellis's "Shake It Girl (For Me)" and "Girl I've Got A Date" as well as little-known nuggets like the Silvertones' "It's Real". Even nearer to the full-blown romanticism of the following year's outpouring of rocksteady hits were other Reid productions of 1966, like Slim Smith & the Techniques' "Telling Lies", the Silvertones' "True Confession" and the Paragons' "On The Beach".

In 1967 came a major, if temporary, shift in the two rivals' respective positions. While great records continued to pour from Dodd's studio at Brentford Road, it tended to be the Latin-American tinged sound of **Tommy McCook**'s **Supersonics** at Bond Street that best summed up the refined, romantic appeal of rocksteady in its maturity. The session band employed by Reid was one of the greatest ever assembled, with virtuoso guitarists **Ernest Ranglin** and **Lynn Taitt** both playing key roles, as did saxophonists Tommy McCook and **Herman Marquis.** Extra sweetening in the recipe was supplied by McCook's deft flute voicings. Occasionally, as on Alton Ellis's "Cry Tough" and the Paragon's "Tide Is High" classic, an effective violin, played by a character known as **'White Rum' Raymond**, can be heard. Reid also drew on the distinctive talents of organists **Neville Hinds** and **Winston Wright,** as well as pianist **Gladstone Anderson**, a nephew of the great Aubrey Adams. In the drum chair it was either **Arkland 'Drumbago' Parks** or **Hugh Malcolm**, the latter a man further renowned for his tendency to swear profusely at the smallest provocation.

The Treasure Isle studio was made entirely of wood and situated over the top of Reid's liquor store. The timber construction made for a warm environment and a responsive acoustic, which proved ideal for expressive vocalists. The great **Alton Ellis** recollects spending hours in the studio at this time: "The bright light was jus' the music an' the studio, bright in a mi mind all the while, so me nah bother the big riches y'know, me jus' gone singin'.... I use to go in a Duke studio an' siddung [sit down]. Me alone, the studio empty. Me jus' go in there, play 'pon piano, 'til me jus' drop asleep. Duke forget an' lock me up in there. Me never did get that high 'pon Downbeat [ie Studio One] studio, but I really did get a high 'pon Duke's studio. Me jus' feel at home there so."

The studio also attracted most of the leading harmony trios (and occasionally quartets) who had largely taken over from the earlier, more r&b oriented duos. A roll call of vocal groups from the top drawer who recorded for Treasure Isle during the rocksteady period includes the **Techniques**, the **Jamaicans**, the **Three Tops**, the **Sensations**, the **Silvertones**, **Justin Hinds & the Dominoes**, the **Melodians**, the **Conquerors** and, arguably the most exceptional of them all, the **Paragons**. An indication of the quality of this vocal talent is given by a tally of the group members who went on to solo success: both John Holt and Garth 'Tyrone' Evans from the Paragons (Bob Andy was a founder member, but had left by the time they joined Treasure Isle); Jimmy Riley from the Sensations; Slim Smith, Pat Kelly, Bruce Ruffin, Jackie Paris and Lloyd Parks from the amazing Techniques; and both Brent Dowe and Tony Brevett from the Melodians. The Jamaicans' Tommy Cowan might not have gone

DOBBY DOBSON: THE LOVING PAUPER

Dobby Dobson was a perfectly controlled, soulful singer who really hit in the rocksteady era, having originally made a name for himself in the boogie years as half of Chuck & Dobby. His "Loving Pauper" remains his most enduring disc: the perfect expression of the poor man who has nothing to offer a woman but his loving.

"I was attending primary school in Jamaica, and they had the usual end of term concert, and I was chosen to play the part of Ali Baba. A portion of the play required me to sing a song called "Do You Think That It's Easy To Be Poor", and I sung it pretty good. And I say, 'Hey, I can sing'. After leaving primary school and going on to secondary, Kingston College, I tried out for the Vere Johns Opportunity Hour, and I won a couple of the contests, beating out some very well-known names. I was competing with people like Count Miller & the Downbeats, Derrick Harriott & the Jiving Juniors, Lascelles Perkins: sometimes they would beat me and sometimes I would beat them. I was singing solo then, but my first recording was done while I was at Kingston College with a group called the Deltas, who were my classmates, and our first song "Cry the Cry" went to number one on the RJR chart, and stayed there for about six weeks. So you can image me as a young boy in short pants with a number one record and a head as big as a balloon. I also sang a duet with a friend called Chuck, as Chuck & Dobby. We had a song called "Sweeter Than Honey" that we recorded for Edward Seaga, who later became prime minister. That was another big hit in Jamaica. But most of the time I've sung solo.

Those talent shows had finally brought me to the attention of Lindon Pottinger, who at the time owned Tip Top Records, along with his wife Sonia Pottinger. It was for them that we did "Cry the Cry". At the same time, both Coxsone and Duke Reid had heard of me, and I did "Loving Pauper" and "Cool School" for Reid, and "Seem To Me I'm Losing You" for Coxsone. These were at first what you would refer to today as 'specials'. They were exclusive to a particular sound system; they were what they used to compete with each other. If Coxsone was playing at one 'lawn', on one side of the street, and Duke Reid was on the other, both would be playing sounds that the other couldn't get. Coxsone would be playing "Seems That I'm Losing You", and Reid would be playing "Loving Pauper". They wouldn't be commer-

on to make such a significant impact as a solo singer, but instead became a proficient and popular producer in the mid-1970s (the Sweet City, Talent, Arab and Top Ranking labels) and then a very successful Sunsplash MC. Similarly, the founder of the Techniques, Winston Riley, named his very successful record label after the group and helped define the shift to reggae itself, before going on to become a hitmaking producer right up to the present day.

There were also equally gifted solo singers being recorded at Bond Street, including the sometimes underrated **Dobby Dobson** (whose "Loving Pauper" is another record that is endlessly reinterpreted), Ken Parker, **Phyllis Dillon**, **Freddy McKay** (with his first hit, the beautiful "Love Is A Treasure"), Vic Taylor, Joya Landis and, having parted from his Flames, the astonishingly soulful Alton Ellis. Duke also attracted **Hopeton Lewis** to the studio while he was still under contract to Federal; uncredited, Hopeton contributed many arrangements and backing vocals for other artists at the studio. When he became free to record for Treasure Isle, he soon scored, winning the Song Festival in 1970 with "Boom Shacka Lacka", easily the equal of his pioneering rocksteady hits.

PHYLLIS DILLON

⊙ **Love Is All I Had** (Rhino, UK).

⊙ **One Life To Live** (Treasure Isle/Studio One, JA).

Until these two collections appeared almost simultaneously in 1995, Phyllis Dillon was not well represented on LP or CD, despite having been Treasure Isle's most successful female singer. Unfortunately, there's a lot of duplication between them – even if different

cially available until they had run their times with the sound systems. We were recording in a little box, two-track studio at Federal, with all the musicians and the singers recording at the same time. Therefore, you had to make sure you were doing the right thing, because you could get right down to the end of the song, and mess it up and have to do it again. So it required you to be perfect.

Duke Reid was quite a character. He was a big fat man, with a big belly, who had a very pleasant personality, but at times he could also be tyrannical. People still talk about the time when the studio session wasn't going well, and he drew his gun and fired shots in the ceiling. To dispense with the evil spirits, was his idea. But he was quite an amiable person – very nice in terms of his dealings with the artists. But I must say that when it came to payments he was a bit on the stingy side. He could have afforded more, but it was what was being paid in those days – the £5 and £10 flat payment. But what people don't realize about those times was that, though the singers didn't know anything about publishing and royalties, they never gave Duke Reid the complete rights of the song. It was just the performance they gave him. So they still retained – though they didn't know about it – the publishing rights.

At the time, I wrote "Loving Pauper", I was singing with a band called Charles & the Teddy Boys, and their bass player, Steve Bachelor, was living a little above me on Arnold Road, and I went to his house one morning and to talk about the song. I knew the words would be popular; because who in Jamaica at that time had money to be a sugar daddy? What you had to offer a woman was love. I was a schoolboy, so I didn't know anything about supporting a woman. He sat down and listened, and said it was a great song. So I went to Duke Reid with it, and he liked it instantly. I think it was the Techniques that did the backing vocals.

Coxsone was the Berry Gordy of Jamaican music. He had a bunch of singers around him, and he helped them to a degree – in terms of working out lyrics and that sort of stuff. But he was less of a producer than producers nowadays, in my estimation. Because he didn't know a lot about music, but he just had the right singers, and the studio, and he picked the right songs for them. Most of his recording sessions were incident-free. He would listen to the song you have and tell you to come and record it. But there was one thing he did that I was kind of miffed at. When we recorded "Cool School" for Duke Reid, he called in Bunny & Skitter, and had them re-record the identical words, but with "Cherry" instead of "Baby". And to this day, I resent that. ❞

rarities on each CD will compel the true fanatic to fork out for both. Though tracks like "Right Track",

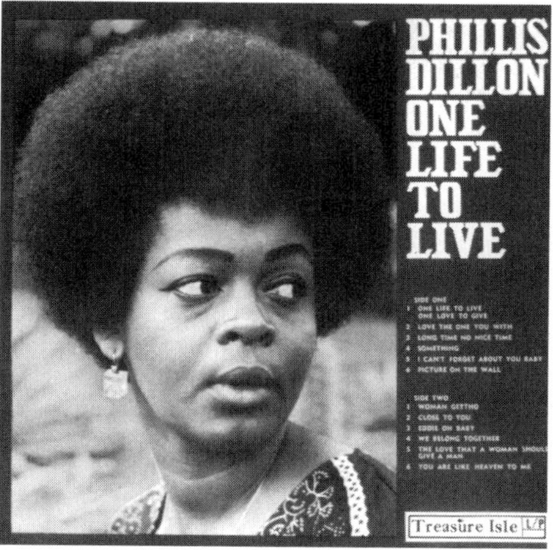

"Don't Stay Away" and her definitive interpretation of Glenn Miller/Dorothy Claire's "Perfidia" have the most familiar rhythms, the moving "One Life To Live" arguably remains her single most impressive effort.

TOMMY McCOOK & THE SUPERSONICS

⦿ **Down On Bond Street** (Trojan, UK).

Proof, if any was needed, that the Treasure Isle instrumentals, while not 'versioned' as often, were the equal of those from Studio One, and as worthy of consideration as the glorious harmony groups most associated with the studio. Ignore the subtitle ("20 Great Ska Hits"): this brings together twenty superb examples of the understated, Latin-influenced sound of the coolest rocksteady session band of them all.

⦿ **Run Rhythm Run** (Heartbeat, US).

Another superb instrumental set, featuring the Supersonics, and wonderful soloists such as Tommy McCook, Winston Wright and Sugar Belly. The only really well-known track is "Our Man Flint", but obscure and previously unreleased versions of celebrated Treasure Isle vocals – including Alton Ellis's "Girl I've Got A Date", the Techniques' "Love Is A Gamble" and the Melodians' "Everybody Bawling" – are just as revelatory of the strength of the studio's rhythms.

THE MELODIANS

⊙ **Swing & Dine** (Heartbeat, US).

E The Melodians rank alongside the Paragons, the Techniques and the Heptones in the upper echelon of rocksteady groups. They had the advantage of possessing two exceptional lead voices in Tony Brevett's warm baritone and Brent Dowe's anguished tenor, plus an excellent harmonies singer in Trevor McNaughton, and a fourth member in a purely songwriting capacity, Ranford Cogle. They were later to have perfectly good records on Beverley's, Jam-Can, Mellos and Lee Perry's Wizzdom label, but their most consistent body of work belongs to the 1960s, when they recorded for both Duke Reid and Sonia Pottinger. This is the body of work represented here, with ten tracks from the former, and six from the latter: sixteen classics, with only "Passion Love" missing (though some would argue this was their finest ever).

THE PARAGONS

◑ **Golden Hits (The Great Treasure Isle Collection Volume 2)** (Treasure Isle, France).

E This French collection duplicates nine of the tracks from the group's classic *On the Beach* set, but presents them in digital clarity, and adds "The Same Song", "My Best Girl" (possible their finest record) and four more of a similar standard. The best of John Holt's hits after leaving the group might have equalled his wonderfully assured and smooth performances here, but none quite surpassed them. This pretty much sums up what rocksteady was all about.

● **On the Beach** (Treasure Isle, JA).

Their classic Treasure Isle album has been regularly re-released, and is still available in the specialist retailers at the time of writing. Besides the title track, highlights include the original cut of "The Tide Is High" (covered by the rock group Blondie), "Only A Smile", "Happy Go Lucky Girl" and "Village Girl".

THE TECHNIQUES

⊙ **Rock Steady Classics** (Rhino, UK).

E The title is spot-on for a set including two takes of both "You Don't Care" and "Travelling Man", and most of the rest of their best rocksteady material for Treasure Isle, including their two most 'versioned' tracks, "Queen Majesty" and "Love Is Not A Gamble". Exquisitely refined but infectious rocksteady rhythms plus sweet vocal harmonies – it doesn't come much better than this.

● **Little Did You Know** (Treasure Isle, JA).

This is the Techniques' debut album, named after one of their biggest hits, re-released with its original cover. At the time Duke Reid obviously lacked enough titles by the group, so he made up the shortfall with five strong tracks by the Baba Brooks Band. The Techniques' tracks are divided between the earliest for the label, with Slim Smith as lead, and those with the less frenzied Pat Kelly. Most of the group's offerings here are available elsewhere, but not all the instrumentals – or the back cover photographs from the period.

VARIOUS ARTISTS

⊙ **Duke Reid's Treasure Chest** (Heartbeat, US).

E With some five companies re-releasing Treasure Isle material, there is not surprisingly a problem with duplication of material, so non-fanatics are well advised to compare like with like before making their choice. Having given due warning, there really is not a better start to any Treasure Isle rocksteady selection than the 41 examples of Duke Reid's elegant magic collected on this double CD set. Besides the most comprehensive selection of the best-known classics from Alton Ellis, the Techniques, the Jamaicans, the Paragons, the Melodians, the Silvertones, etc, there are also more obscure gems – as well as previously unreleased alternate takes, for the sake of those collectors suffering under the illusion that they heard it all years ago.

◑ **Hottest Hits Volume 1** (Treasure Isle/Studio One, JA).

The vinyl original of this album was one of the most important rocksteady compilations, containing as much of the best of the Treasure Isle catalogue as it was possible to fit onto a single LP. Premier vocal groups the Sensations, Alton Ellis & the Flames, the Melodians, the Silvertones, the Techniques, the Jamaicans, the Paragons and the Three Tops, along with the solo singers Dobby Dobson, Vic Taylor and Phyllis Dillon, are represented not only by major Jamaican hits, but in most cases their best records. The CD offers digital clarity, plus bonus tracks of a comparable quality. Only the Heartbeat set, which remains the best value-for-money Treasure Isle package, surpasses this.

Hottest Hits Volume 2 (Treasure Isle, JA).
The next volume in the series kept up the standard of the above, with another twelve rocksteady classics, including Freddy McKay's first hit, "Love Is A Treasure" and the record for which Joya Landis is still best remembered, "Moonlight Lover".

Hottest Hits Volume 3 (Treasure Isle, JA).
The least satisfying of the three volumes, because it's not quite as focused. Tracks from the early 1970s – John Holt's "Ali Baba" and Hopeton Lewis's "Boom Shacka Lacka" – are superb, but they don't fit with the classic rocksteady of the Paragons and the Techniques.

More Hottest Hits (Heartbeat, US)
A satisfying blend of rocksteady classics – the Paragons' "On the Beach", the Conquerors' "Lonely Street" and the Jamaicans' "Dedicated To You" – with later reggae from such as Dave Barker, Leroy Sibbles and Tyrone Evans. The compilation also contains fascinating and previously unreleased material including a studio conversation between the Duke and U-Roy, followed immediately by a further unreleased cut of the deejay's "Rock Away". Superb sound quality – taken from original tapes, Heartbeat's Treasure Isle reissues are by far the best on this score.

Rock Steady Beat: Treasure Isle's Greatest Hits (Treasure Isle, JA).
A wonderful collection that was first released in the rocksteady era, but appeared again in the early 1990s, and should not be too hard to find now. Most of the tracks are available elsewhere, but it's worth finding for the original cover, with its photograph of the Treasure Isle studio.

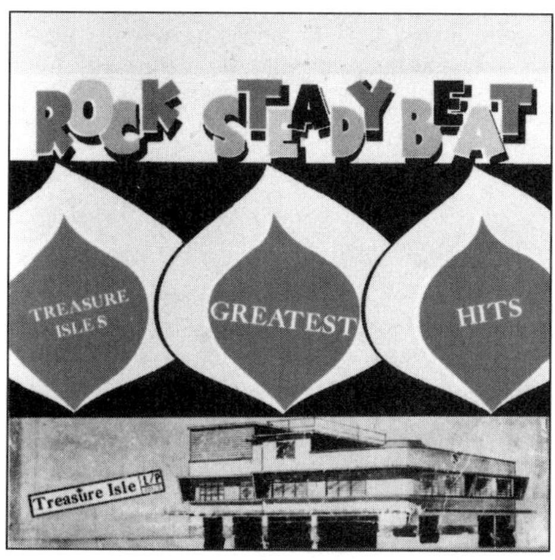

Greatest Jamaican Beat (Treasure Isle, JA).
Another Treasure Isle album originally compiled without the advantage of hindsight, and which has been re-released several times since. The only problem is that most of the best-known tracks have appeared elsewhere, but it does play very well as a set, with only Tommy McCook's version of Jimmy Castor's Latin-soul hit, "Hey Leroy", slightly out of mood.

Baba Boom: Classic Rocksteady And Reggae 1967–72 (Trojan, UK).
Covering more than pure rocksteady, but all from Treasure Isle and totally in the harmonious spirit of that too-brief era. The Tennors' "Hopeful Village" and "Weather Report" are the group's all-time strongest, and "Passion Love" and "Only A Smile" have arguably the same place in, respectively, the Melodians' and Paragons' oeuvres. The main strength of the set is its avoidance of the obvious: John Holt & Joya Landis' "I'll Be Lonely" and the Three Tops' "Do It Right" are seriously under-rated records, and what appears to be the best-known track, Justin Hinds & the Dominoes' "Carry Go Bring Come", turns out to be the rare second cut, which is at least the equal of the better-known ska original.

It's Rocking Time: Duke Reid's Rocksteady 1967–1968 (Trojan, UK).
A Treasure Isle rocksteady collection made up of seldom-anthologized items. The Conquerors' wonderful "Lonely Street"/"I Fall In Love" 45 has almost legendary status, and the inclusion of both sides is reason enough to buy this album, while the obscurity of the other tracks says something about the sheer amount of worthwhile music produced in the era. The three instrumentals from the Supersonics – "Train To Skathedral", "Indian Love Call" and "Spanish Eyes" – show how much could be made of unpromising material, though the Three Tops' "Sound Of Music" has nothing to do with Julie Andrews.

Studio One rocksteady

Though **Clement Dodd**'s records never epitomized rocksteady in the way Reid's did, many first-class recordings continued to emerge from Brentford Road throughout the period, largely under the supervision of organist/pianist **Jackie Mittoo** (b. 1948, Kingston). It was under the tutelage of the prodigiously gifted Mittoo that the Heptones' lead singer **Leroy Sibbles** (b. 1949) learned bass, which he first played in a jazz trio led by Mittoo during early 1967. When the gigs came to an end, Sibbles was ready, and he began to create some of Jamaican music's most insinuating basslines for the studio. Interestingly enough, while Duke Reid productions favoured cool and sweet vocals over decidedly tough rhythms, Dodd's studio still turned out the most enduring instrumentals of the period. The Brentford Road session band,

BRENT DOWE: SINGING KING ALPHA'S SONG

The singer of "Rivers Of Babylon" and numerous other Melodians hits of the late 1960s and early 1970s looks back to early days at Back-A-Wall, and subsequent recording sessions for Clement Dodd, Duke Reid, Sonia Pottinger and Leslie Kong.

"I'm the leader of the Melodians. We've been in the business since 1964, when we first recorded for the Studio One label. We met in '62 in a competition for Vere Johns. He used to keep Opportunity Hour at the Ambassador Theatre in Spanish Town Road. That was where John Holt, Alton Ellis, Lascelles Perkins, everybody, made their bid. Vere Johns was a man dedicated to music. He used to take the youth off the streets of the ghetto. Whether you a dancer, a comedian, a singer, he would accept you.

The Melodians started rehearsing at a place called Back-A-Wall. That is where Tivoli Gardens is now. Slim Smith, Ken Boothe, Roy Shirley, all of us, would meet there. It was a wide space, and then people started living there, and they called it Back-A-Wall – because it was behind a wall. It was the roots of the music. All of us would gather some times, especially Friday night. I remember Slim Smith used to call it his domain. We were the main singers. There was the Wailers and Alton at Trench Town, the Gaylads from the East, the Blues Busters from Montego Bay. So at that time, singers centred around one place. That's Trench Town to Greenwich Farm and Back-A-Wall. On Friday night at Back-A-Wall, I remember everyone up to daylight, because everywhere you go a sound system playing.

I remember going down to Coxsone for the first time in 1965, on a Sunday morning. His yard was full of artists, trying to make a rise for themselves. At that time, B.B. Seaton was in charge of audition. And when we went there and sang the first couple of lines, he told us to stop. We thought that he was going to push us out. But he didn't want to hear anymore because he wanted us to record that day! We watched other guys come in and some were told they should never come back! In those days, it was rough. You had so many singers in Jamaica, you had to be good. You had the Zodiacs, the Gaylads, the Clarendonians. Bob Marley was there, the Techniques. It was pure group. Jackie Opel was the only one man singer. There was Ken Boothe, but he came with Stranger Cole as a group. They were a group but Coxsone saw the potential of the lead singer and took him away.

Coxsone is a creator – the creator of all of us. But when you do music at those times, you have to sign a paper. He pay you £10. Every time we sign a paper for Dodd, we thought it was payment for that song; we didn't know it was for publishing. Coxsone was a very smart man. Now, if you went to him and ask for money he give it to you. The only problem was that we didn't know what we were signing. We did four tracks for him in two sessions. The first time we record a song called "Lay It On". Coxsone accepted it

the **Soul Vendors**, cut instrumental hits under their own name, or sometimes that of Jackie Mittoo, that have struck an even deeper chord with successive generations than those of Treasure Isle's Supersonics. The rhythms for such infectious and well-crafted gems as "Real Rock", "Drum Song", "Swing Easy" and "Psychedelic Rock", most of which were driven by Sibbles' basslines, have been copied ever since. Thus, rhythms devised to rock dancehall patrons in 1967 have endlessly been recycled, whether supporting the singing sensation of the moment, or any number of hot new deejays. Soon, in 1968, Leroy's bass, combined with the guitar of **Eric Frater**, would propel Studio One into the age of reggae.

Of the solo singers to cut exemplary records at Dodd's studio during the period, the very soul-influenced **Ken Boothe** (b. 1948, Kingston) was the most successful. Stranger Cole's former partner was responsible for many massive hits of the time, most of which have been collected on albums; especially notable are the relentlessly rocking "The Train Is Coming" from 1966, and the following year's "Feel Good" (a version of Roy Shirley's "Hold

immediately, and he put it out the same day. That's what used to happen. If they hear you in the morning and you sound good, you know by the evening the record will be out. They don't let you walk away with that song. We record just four songs for Coxsone. Then we hear of this Treasure Isle label.

So the next week we decide to go to Duke Reid. You have to pass through Gladdy Anderson first, him and a man called Cuttins. And immediately we go down there, the whole place was full. I remember a door opening and a guy go in, and I hear him start to sing. Then someone say 'Shut up,' and I see him come out. Then the next guy go in and sing, and he says, 'Oh come on! Get out!' So when we went into the rehearsal, we were scared. We start to sing the song "I'll Get Along Without You". And he say, 'Stop singing. Go upstairs.' We were so pleased that we pass the test. And when we went upstairs we see Alton Ellis. He come to Duke with a song called "Dance Crasher". He record it the same day as we did "I'll Get Along Without You". And then we did a song, "You Don't Need Me". We did two songs the same day. Duke gave us £30. When we was with Coxsone, he give us £10 for the three of us. So £10 each was a big thing.

Then when we were at Duke Reid's, we hear that another producer was paying bigger money. So we check it out, and it was Mrs Pottinger. So I went over there to see her, and she say she do business with us. And then I went to call Ken Boothe and the Gaylads and Delroy Wilson, and they come over, and that same night we record "Little Nut Tree", "Swing & Dine"; the Gaylads did "Hard To Confess"; Ken Boothe did "Lady With the Starlight" and "Say You"; Delano Stewart did "That's Life". So, Mrs Pottinger had six hit songs in one session. Then word spread around that there's money down here; and everybody started going down to Tip Top, leaving Coxsone. Coxsone must have heard about that, because he started to raise his money.

I went to Beverley in 1969. The first international producer we had was Leslie Kong. Because Coxsone and Duke Reid wouldn't travel. When we went there, he was the first one to give us the money for our publishing. So everybody start going to Leslie Kong. He was the most honest producer of those times. When we went down there with the words of "Rivers Of Babylon", we tell him it's a Christian song, that we want to sing to reggae. He say it can't work; but we say listen to it. He call Warrick Lynn, his main man at the time. When we started "Rivers Of Babylon", he say 'I'm going to put it to music.' When Leslie Kong put "Rivers Of Babylon" out, they ban it from the radio, because I sing "Oh Fari". And Leslie Kong protest, and it did some good. Because the song started playing again and in two weeks it get to number one. He was very good. He saw things before they happen. So that was really the first song that was recorded in a Christian sort of way over a reggae rhythm. Because after that Maxie Romeo record "Let the Power Fall For I". And people started to record God words on top of reggae. ”

Them", retitled by Coxsone) and "Home Home Home", a bravura performance of superbly controlled emotional power. Boothe also gave a definitive reading to Bob Andy's composition "I Don't Want To See You Cry". He left Studio One, along with the **Gaylads**, in the spring of 1968, and continued to be a major figure in the music throughout the first half of the 1970s, even notching up a number one hit in the UK pop charts of 1974 with the Bread song "Everything I Own".

Coxsone also recorded the most gifted woman singer in Jamaica, **Marcia Griffiths** (b. 1954, Kingston), who enjoyed success with further Bob Andy compositions like "Mark My Words", "Tell Me Now" and "Melody Life". (She also cut the joyous "Feel Like Jumping", driven by a monumental rhythm that would resurface the next year recut by Leslie Kong under the Maytals' smash "54-46 (That's My Number)" and has been successfully versioned not a few times since.) Coxsone's other important solo hitmaker was the 19-year-old **Delroy Wilson**, who recut the Tams US soul tune "Dancing Mood" and made it his own, aided by a sympathetic arrangement from

Jackie Mittoo. The good-looking Wilson was by now something of a heartthrob, but his appeal was far greater than that of the mere pin-up. In the words of Ken Boothe: "When I see him on the street, I see a lot of people gather around him. He was Jamaica's first baby star. He inspire Bob Marley; he inspire me; he inspire a lot of us. He was the first one to put his voice on records that start to establish Jamaica's name, all over the world."

Marcia Griffiths with writer-singer and then-partner, Bob Andy

Wilson's other popular sides during the rocksteady era included the emotive love songs "I'm Not A King", "Riding For A Fall", "I Shall Not Remove" and "Run Run". All of these featured spirited, soulful vocal performances over some of the Soul Vendors' most infectious rhythms – updated versions of which became staples of the dancehall era almost two decades later.

Then there was **Dawn Penn**, who covered a Memphis blues tune called "You Don't Love Me", retitling it "No No No" and enjoyed a sizeable hit in the process. Twenty-seven years later, leading ragga producers Steelie & Clevie recut the tune with Dawn, in a virtual note-for-note copy of the original, as part of a project designed as a tribute to the enduring appeal of their favourite label. It became a huge international hit, reaching the #1 slot in several national pop charts and was even featured on the soundtrack of a Nissan car ad in the UK and Europe. The later hit offered a striking illustration of the power of Coxsone's music, which was still commercially potent nearly three decades after it was first recorded.

Not unexpectedly, Dodd also showed an interest in the best of the harmony groups not recording exclusively for Duke Reid. His mainstay for the period were the **Heptones** – Leroy Sibbles plus **Barry Llewellyn** (b. 1947) and **Earl Morgan** (b. 1945). Just as successful as the most popular of the Treasure Isle trios, the Heptones contributed little but classic recordings to the studio's catalogue, during both the rocksteady and the early reggae years. Bittersweet tracks like "Tripe Girl" and "I Hold the Handle" express fairly negative attitudes towards women of Leroy Sibbles' acquaintance, but are delivered in the most seductive manner possible. "I've Got A Feeling", "Why Must I", "Baby" and many further local hits demonstrate how satisfying the conventional love song can be when both writing and performance are informed by a genuine sensitivity.

Sweet harmony singing was one of rocksteady's outstanding features, and no survey of the subject could omit the limited but extraordinary output of **Carlton & his Shoes**. **Carlton Manning**, composer of several of the greatest love songs in the history of Jamaican music, handled the exquisitely tender lead vocals, while his brothers, Donald and Lynford, were responsible for the crystalline

The Heptones, from left: Earl Morgan, Leroy Sibbles and Barry Llewellyn

harmonies that have only been matched by their own work in the roots trio, the Abyssinians. After an unsuccessful debut for Sonia Pottinger, Carlton & his Shoes relased their initial single for Dodd, "Love Me Forever"/"Happy Land", in early 1968 on the Supreme imprint, and both songs eventually gained classic status. The unashamedly romantic sentiments of "Love Me Forever", which has been re-released regularly on both single and album, were supported by what has become one of the most versioned rhythms of the period; the cultural and just as absorbing "Happy Land", on the other hand, has been more talked about than actually heard – mainly on the grounds that it is known as the template for the Abyssinians' "Satta Massa Gana" roots classic. After the rocksteady era, Carlton & his Shoes maintained the sublime standard of their Studio One work with occasional recordings for Dennis Brown, the UK's Fashion label and themselves. Yet, even counting the later work on which Carlton Manning maintained the group name and harmonized with himself to comparable effect, Carlton & his Shoes remain that rare phenomenon in Jamaican music – an act that has tasted acclaim, but remain under-recorded.

In Coxsone's camp as well were the golden-voiced **Gaylads – Harris 'BB' Seaton** (b. 1944), **Winston Delano Stewart** (b. 1947) and **Maurice Roberts** (b. 1945). The trio's illustrious recording career began with ska, but blossomed in the rocksteady era with hit after hit – including "Lady With the Red Dress On", "Love Me With All Your Heart", "You'll Never Leave Him", "You Should Never Do That" and "Red Rose". Subsequent rocksteady tunes for both WIRL and Sonia Pottinger maintained the quality of their Studio One output, and both Seaton and Stewart went on to achieve degrees of popularity as solo performers, without ever quite scaling the same heights that they did with the trio.

The quality of the Brentford Road recordings of the **Sharks** was never consistent enough to take them into the premier league, but they made one beautiful late rocksteady classic, "How Could I Live", on which evocative Spanish guitar and heartfelt voices interplay to truly spine-tingling effect. Among the other harmony outfits who at least made the occasional record of note during this period at Dodd's studio were the **Viceroys**, showing a promise that would only be truly fulfilled over the next couple of decades; the **Bassies**, who impressed with both the cautionary (if vague) "Beware" and the truly sublime "River Jordan"; and the **Termites**, a duo who consistently made strong records but are best remembered for launching the career of bass player, solo singer and record producer **Lloyd Parks**.

BOB ANDY

◑ **Song Book** (Coxsone, JA).

Ⓔ His first and best collection, with thoughtful 'reality' and love lyrics, as well as beautiful bittersweet melodies that are not easily forgotten. The title – chosen by Mr Dodd apparently – is only too fitting, and it is surprising that more non-reggae singers have not covered the material collected here: titles like "My Time", "Unchained" and "Feeling Soul", however rooted in the particular, have a universal application. But the album makes clear that Andy's might well be the definitive versions. One of the half-dozen or so Jamaican albums that belong in the collection of anyone interested in the art of either the singer or songwriter, whatever the genre.

KEN BOOTHE

● **A Man & his Hits** (Studio One, JA).

Ⓔ The gritty tones of Ken Boothe, one of the most distinctive voices in Jamaican music, were first heard in the ska era, with the underrated Stranger Cole, and it's a pity that most of the hits credited to Stranger & Ken still wait to be collected in album form. The earliest track on *A Man & his Hits* is "Train Is Coming", one of the best rocksteady tunes to use the popular gospel motif. Other notable inclusions are "Moving Away", "When I Fall In Love", "Crying Over You" and his powerful version of Garnett Mimms' "Thinking". Even "Puppet On A String" seems acceptable.

● **Mr. Rocksteady** (Studio One, JA).

This set repeats "Puppet On A String", but stands as just as important a collection, with hits like "I Don't Want To See You Cry", "My Heart Is Gone" (successfully recorded twice by John Holt), "The Girl I Left Behind", "Home, Home, Home", "Feel Good" and his delicious duet with Norma Fraser, "Give Me the Right". Ken Boothe was sometimes billed as Jamaica's Wilson Pickett, and it is not surprising that he also does justice to Sir Mack Rice's "Mustang Sally", previously a US hit for the US soul star.

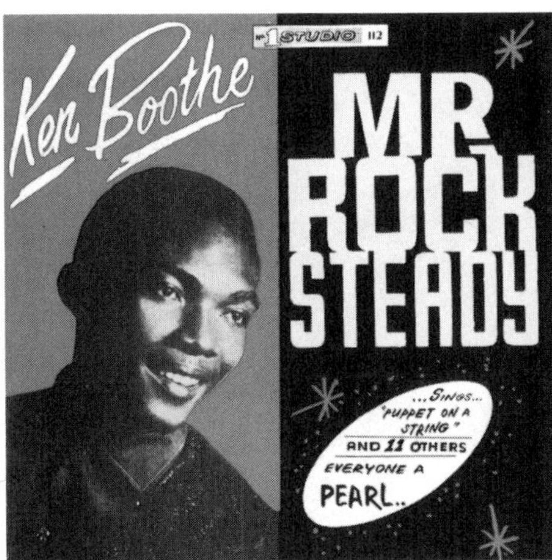

CARLTON & HIS SHOES

● **Love Me Forever** (Studio One, UK).

Covering not just rocksteady but the first years of reggae, this remains the ultimate album for both sweet harmonies and original Jamaican love songs. To complete the story of Carlton Manning at Studio One, any future re-release of the album should add both "Happy Land" and "Let Me Love You", his last glorious record for Coxsone (and one for which he supplied all the voices).

ALTON ELLIS

● **Sings Rock & Soul** (Coxsone, JA).

Not the perfect Ellis album, because of "Whiter Shade Of Pale" and "Massachusetts", two tracks obviously designed to broaden his appeal and justify the first part of the title. But there is no argument about the quality of the local tunes, which include "I'm Still In

Love With You" (the original to Althea & Donna's "Uptown Top Ranking"), "Mad, Mad, Mad", "I'm Just A Guy" (versioned countless times, but most successfully with Michigan & Smiley's "Rub A Dub Style") and "Never Love Again".

THE GAYLADS

◑ **Soul Beat** (Studio One, JA).

This late 1960s album was always the trio's best – featuring "Love Me With All Your Heart", "I Am Free" and "Red Rose" among the timeless hits. The CD adds extra instrumentation, without detracting from the feel of the original set, plus some extra tracks. Purists might want to stick with the vinyl original (which is still available), but for anyone else the CD is the better buy. Coxsone has also released a *Best Of* set that would be essential if only it had been remastered properly; as it is, a selection that could hardly be bettered has been rendered virtually unlistenable.

MARCIA GRIFFITHS

● **The Original (At Studio One) Marcia Griffiths** (Studio One, JA).

Jamaica's premier female vocalist, classic Studio One rhythms from the Soul Brothers/Vendors, and several songs written by the wonderful Bob Andy (with whom Griffiths had a long-term involvement). Reggae snobs argue that Dodd should never tamper with the original 45 mixes of Studio One classics, but these remixes don't detract from the exuberance of her debut hit, "Feel Like Jumping", or the beauty and power of love ballads like "Truly", "Melody Life", "Mark My Word" and "Tell Me Now". It is a cliché to say that some Jamaican singers would have sold millions if only they had been born in the USA, but it's undeniably so in the case of Marcia Griffiths, who no doubt earned more money as one of Marley's I Threes than for all the gems gathered here.

THE HEPTONES

◑ **On Top** (Studio One, JA).

E The trio's second album, covering the period when rocksteady was transmuting into reggae, was an even greater triumph than the debut, and the CD release offers not just digital clarity but three bonus tracks of the same calibre: "A Change Is Gonna Come" (not the Sam Cooke song), "When You Are Down" and "Oil In My Lamp". The voices are sublime and the songs – covering both love and 'reality' themes – are even more accomplished than before. It is impossible to imagine the course of reggae without the basslines for tracks like "Heptones Gonna Fight", "I Hold the Handle" and "Pretty Looks Isn't All", or for that matter their horn parts, usually devised by saxophonist 'Deadly' Headley Bennett.

◑ **Fattie Fattie [The Heptones]** (Studio One, JA).

The vinyl original of the Heptones' debut album was always a classic, and the retitled CD substitutes a previously unreleased cut of "Mama" for "Land Of Love", and adds the perennially popular "Why Did You Leave" (with extra harmonies) and "Get In the Groove". The fact that Leroy Sibbles was responsible for basslines and songs that are still being versioned today, as well as most of the emotive lead vocals, demonstrates the breadth of his seminal talent. It can only seem a bonus that both Barry Llewellyn and Earl Morgan also came up with the occasional song and lead vocal, without any discernible drop in quality.

JACKIE MITTOO

◑ **Evening Time** (Studio One, JA).

Jamaica's top Hammond man in a rocksteady mood. This was always a worthwhile item if only for "One Step Beyond" (the original cut to Freddie McGregor's "Bobby Babylon") and "Drum Song" (reworked for countless titles, including Dillinger's "Dub Organiser" and Burning Spear's "Joe Frazier"). The CD adds Mittoo's excellent interpretations of Dawn Penn's "You Don't Love Me" and Delroy Wilson's "Dancing Mood" (both over the original rhythms), making it even more desirable than the vinyl original.

THE TERMITES

◑ **Do the Rock Steady** (Studio One, JA; Heartbeat, US).

The Termites were one of the few successful duos of the rocksteady era. None of the records collected here launched a rhythm that was massively popular later, but their only album demonstrates the appeal of their charming, innocent-sounding rocksteady. The title track, "Corporal Jones" and "Beach Boy" are among the highlights.

DELROY WILSON

● **Original Twelve – The Best Of Delroy Wilson** (Coxsone, JA; Heartbeat, US).

E Essentially, the best of his rocksteady material for Coxsone not included on the above. Every track is a classic, though deserving a special mention are "Run Run", "Riding For A Fall", "Conquer Me" (successfully revived by, among others, the deejay Dr Alimantado) and "True Believer".

● **Good All Over** (Coxsone, JA).

Only in his late teens – but already a musical veteran – by the time rocksteady developed, Delroy Wilson really hit his stride with a glorious series of hits for Coxsone that captured the buoyancy and relative sophistication of the new style. As a soul stylist, he was clearly the equal of either Alton Ellis or Ken Boothe, and here he particularly shines on "Run For Your Life", "Rain From the Skies" and "I'm Not A King".

VARIOUS ARTISTS

◉ **Mojo Rocksteady** (Heartbeat, US).

E Just to completely confuse everyone, three sets bear this title, with some variation in the track listings. The Heartbeat CD beats the original Jamaican vinyl press for sound quality and has two more tracks than the American vinyl one. A couple of the tracks are not rocksteady at all, but the musical quality couldn't be more consistent. Just the inclusion of "Whipping the Prince", the very first cut of the perennial "Arena" rhythm, would justify the price; but the general quality – including the balance between instrumentals and vocals – lifts this far above the usual hit-and-miss Studio One compilations.

Ride Me Donkey (Coxsone, JA).
Another vintage collection that is still available (well, most of the time). The tracks cover both rocksteady proper – the Heptones' "Pretty Looks Isn't All", for example – and examples of the form transmuting into early reggae – Marcia Griffiths' anthemic "Feel Like Jumping" and the Cables' "Baby Why". Other highlights include a beautiful Soul Vendors cut of Bacharach & David's "A House Is Not A Home" (always a favourite for Jamaicans to cover), Ken Boothe's "Tomorrow" and the Westmorlites' "Miss Hiti-Tite".

Rocksteady Coxsone Style (Studio One, JA & US).
Not one of the best rocksteady compilations, but it's of interest on historical grounds at least. Besides three tracks by a young Winston Holness (aka the producer Niney), two of them as half of a duo known as Winston & Robin, there is Bumps Oakley's obscure "A Get A Lick", the rhythm of which became far better known when revamped in the 1980s for Shinehead's "Billy Jean" dancehall smash. There are also very listenable contributions from Carl Bryan & the Soul Vendors, the Termites and an extremely young Jacob Miller, whose voice had yet to break when he sang "Love Is A Message".

Blue Beat Special (Coxsone, JA).
The title is misleading, as the tracks have nothing to do with the UK label of that name – or ska, for which the term served as a synonym. Instead, there is a mixture of strong rocksteady instrumentals and vocals, all emanating from Brentford Road. Particularly outstanding among the former are the Soul Vendors' hit "Something Special" and their version of the Ethiopians' "The Whip", while from the latter there is both Alton Ellis's interpretation of "Let Him Try" and Dudley Sibley's most memorable record, "Run Boy Run".

12 Carat Gold (Studio One, JA; Melodisc, UK).
A mixture of rocksteady and compatible early reggae of the first order. Highlights include Cornell Campbell's beautiful tenor on the Eternals' "Stars", both the Heptones' soulful "Why Did You Leave" and first cut of "Love Won't Come Easy" (later re-recorded with Augustus Pablo), Bop & the Beltones' innocent-sounding "Dancing Time", and two masterful versions of foreign hits: Ken Parker's cover of Joe Simon's southern soul classic, "Choking Kind", and Norma Fraser's take on P.P. Arnold's "The First Cut Is the Deepest", written by Cat Stevens.

Get Ready Rock Steady (Coxsone, JA).
Appearing initially in 1968, this is one of the best original compilations and is still regularly re-pressed. No throwaway tracks at all, and several out-and-out classics of the genre, including Alton Ellis's "Never Love Again", the Bassies' otherwise impossible to find "Big Mistake", Ken Boothe & Delroy Wilson's cut of "Won't You Come Home Now", and the Soul Vendors/Jackie Mittoo serious instrumental "Darker Shade Of Black".

Catch this beat: the new producers

While Duke Reid and Clement Dodd were the dominant producers in the flowering of rocksteady, this was a period in which the number of producers grew – whether of the "hands-on" variety, meaning those who made considerable creative contributions to the sessions, or those who simply financed them, leaving the musicians to produce themselves. In this respect, as in so many others, rocksteady was a harbinger of a significant future development: the constant influx of fresh producers who have helped keep the established names on their toes.

Joe Gibbs

Joe Gibbs (b. Joel Gibson, 1945, Montego Bay) represented a new generation of enterepreneurial producer. His first contact with the music business came through selling records in his TV repair shop on Beeston Street, then in January 1967 he financed recording sessions with Lynn Taitt's band, hiring **Lee Perry** to supervise them, and releasing the music on his Amalgamated label. Perry, who had just left Coxsone, scored immediately. The first releases on the new imprint – "Please Stop Your Lying" by the teenage **Errol Dunkley** (b. 1951, Kingston) and Perry's own barbed message to his former employer, "I Am the Upsetter" – were important hits. Gibbs had shown that you did not have to own either a sound system or a studio to produce records. Further best-selling tunes followed, such as "Hold Them" from **Roy Shirley** (b. 1948, Kingston), probably this distinctive singer's most satisfying record, the **Pioneers**' first account of the legendary Jamaican racehorse "Long Shot", and the heartfelt "Seeing Is Knowing" and "Just Like A River" from **Stranger & Gladdy**, the partnership of the already-established Stranger Cole and the keyboards player and sometime vocalist Gladstone Anderson.

VARIOUS ARTISTS – JOE GIBBS PRODUCTIONS

⊙ **Joe Gibbs: Amalgamated Label: Explosive Rocksteady 1967–1973** (Heartbeat, US).

E The continuity of this set is disrupted by a couple of Nicky Thomas tracks from the mid-1970s, but otherwise this album is faultless, with superb presentation and sound, as well as a selection of the some of best rocksteady ever made. Lee Perry was the actual producer of the gems on display here, and his own "I Am the Upsetter" was to set the pattern for many future "grudge" records of his. Tracks like the teenage Errol Dunkley's heartfelt "Please Stop Your Lying", the Pioneers' true tale of the racetrack, "Long Shot", and Roy Shirley's ground-breaking "Hold Them" are anthems of the genre.

Bunny Lee and Winston Lowe

Other new producers soon followed, like **Bunny Lee** (b. Edward O'Sullivan Lee, 1941), a former record plugger for both Reid and Kong, who had started working with former Skatalites road manager B.J. Kalnek (aka Ken Lack) for his Caltone label in 1966. Lee, in turn, introduced his friend **Winston Lowe** to the music business soon after; Lowe was a gambler from Greenwich Town, who started a label called Tramp and produced several hits by the **Uniques**, featuring one of the most expressive vocalists in Jamaican music, **Keith 'Slim' Smith** (b. 1948), on lead vocal, and Lloyd Charmers and Jimmy Riley providing harmonies. Bunny himself was responsible for further classic recordings from Smith, continuing until the mentally unstable singer entered the Belle Vue mental hospital in 1972. (The following year Smith died when he thrust his

Bunny Lee (right) with his brother Don (centre) and uncle

arm through a window of his parents' house and bled to death on the pavement.) The first of the impressive series of records that Slim and the Uniques made for Bunny was the timely "People Rock Steady"; more hits followed, the most devastating in its impact being the massive "My Conversation"/"The Beatitude" (Lee's). The first side has provided subsequent generations with a particularly distinctive and popular rhythm to 'version'; the second, also known as "Blessed Are the Meek", remains one of Smith's most accomplished and moving

REALITY AND RAS TAFARI

Although rude-boy records led the way, the increase in the number of songs voicing disquiet about Jamaican social conditions in the rocksteady era can also be related to trends in Anglo-American popular music, which was then finding 'protest' lyrics commercially viable.

Many local hits presaged the 'reality' lyrics associated with the next decade. The **Heptones**' "Equal Rights", "Soul Power" and "Fight It To the Top" (all for Coxsone), for instance, looked forward to the early reggae work of the trio, when they would be among those very obviously influenced by US expressions of black consciousness. The **Slickers**, in their turn, contrasted humanity's technological and social progress on one of the most original lyrics of the era with "Man Is Going To Leave Earth" (Dutchess), while the **Gaylads** made an exquisite plea for repatriation with "Africa" (Studio One), the advanced arrangement of which was hardly altered when revived by Dennis Brown ten years later. **Joe Higgs**'s first cut of the reflective "I Am the Song" (Studio One), and almost the complete output of the **Ethiopians, Justin Hinds & the Dominoes** and **Bob Andy**, were further examples of the move towards greater social/spiritual consciousness that was eventually to be tagged 'cultural' or 'roots' music, and find a worldwide audience through the work of such as Bob Marley, Burning Spear and Black Uhuru.

Bob Andy (b. Keith Anderson, 1944) is a particularly interesting case. He might be best known to the outside world for his strings-sweetened duets of 1969 with Marcia Griffiths, "Young, Gifted and Black" and "Pied Piper", but he created far more substantial work both before and after this brief period of international pop success. Although Andy was to write strong love songs (several made famous by Griffiths, with whom he was having a relationship), his greatest moments on record were mostly well-crafted expressions of the sufferers' tribulations. In contrast to many of the later roots singers, the founder member of the Paragons never simply relied on heavy rhythms and chant structures to carry his incisive lyrics. Instead he wrote memorable melodies that could equally have suited the most romantic love songs. The music he made at Brentford Road in the mid–late 1960s had the added advantage of some first-class arrangements, most of them by the keyboards player Jackie Mittoo, a musician rated by Andy himself as one of the most important figures in the evolution of reggae.

Andy's first single for Clement Dodd after leaving the Paragons in 1966, "Crime Don't Pay" had much the same message as Alton Ellis's "Cry Tough", warning the rudies to think about their futures. Further recordings at Studio One that ensured his reputation included "Let Them Say", "Feeling Soul" and the very dignified and moving "My Time". There was also "I've Got To Go Back Home", with harmonies by Bunny Livingston and Peter Tosh, a call for repatriation which could equally be heard as the cry of a home-sick country boy in the less than hospitable city. Each was a 'real' song, and all the more effective for the avoidance of cliché. Jamaican music has never produced quality songwriters in the anything like the same numbers as singers, but Andy's writing skills place him in the select company of Joe Higgs, Larry Marshall, Leroy Sibbles and Bob Marley (all graduates of the Brentford Road Academy). It can seem a bonus that he is one of the most soulful vocal stylists the island has ever produced.

An event of long-term significance for Jamaican culture was Haile Selassie's state visit in April 1966. News film of the welcome given to the Emperor of Ethiopia at Kingston airport (by newly married Rita Marley among others) leaves no doubt there was a growing interest among the city's dispossessed in Rastafarianism (see p.136). For the biblical imagery of this uniquely Jamaican religion, along with the imported (and more politicized) Black Power ideas then in circulation, helped give expression to the discontent of the poor, as well as producing a more positive self-image than given them by their daily experiences. In 1964, the body of Marcus Garvey, the Jamaican who in the 1920s had advocated the return of all black people to Africa, had been shipped from England back to Jamaica – an occasion celebrated by at least one great ska instrumental, Don Drummond's "The Reburial" (Coxsone). But Haile Selassie was a living, and thus more potent, icon.

Rastafarianism was to become the dominant ideology of Jamaican music in the mid-1970s, and no singers of that period were to be more widely associated with Rastafarianism than the **Wailers**. The group first expressed their faith during the rocksteady period, a few years before it became fashionable or commercial to do so. Always in contact with the latest feelings of the shantytown inhabitants, they recorded several of the few overtly Rasta songs of the period. Musically, **Peter Tosh**'s celebration of Haile Selassie's visit to Kingston, "Rasta Shook Them Up" (Coxsone) – cut without Marley but with Norma Fraser, as well as Rita Marley and her cousin Constantine 'Dream' Walker – was a cross between a typical rude-boy record, complete with pumping piano, and a traditional Rasta chant. It neatly combined the contrasting expressions of social unrest, and prefigured how the best-known spokesmen for the rudies would later become world ambassadors for Ras Tafari. Two more singles with the same line-up were among the most mature they cut for Dodd. The powerful "He Who Feels It Know It" also had the distinction of being one of the first tunes by anyone to employ the Rasta phase "I & I" (expressing unity between man and God, as well as man and man); "I Stand Predominate" still stands as one of the most accomplished statements of Rasta-inspired racial pride ever made by any variations of the group.

These were also two of the last records that the Wailers made for Dodd, and the next stage in their career was very significant in the present context. For the output on their own **Wail 'N' Soul 'M** label, set up in 1967 in a record shack owned by Bob at 18a Greenwich Park Road, was almost entirely made up of 'conscious' material informed by their recently found Rastafarian faith. Combining the name of the Wailers with Rita's group the Soulettes, the label repeatedly released what would one day be considered some of the greatest back-to-back classics ever to appear in Jamaica, including "Hypocrites"/"Nice Time", "Stir It Up"/"This Train" and "Pound Get A Blow"/"Burial". Nearly all were in. A CD set of the complete Wail 'N' Soul 'M catalogue of some thirty titles – including Rita Marley's most sought-after record, "Play Play" – is long overdue.

A project that was even more extraordinary for the time was the recording of the undiluted Rastafarian music of **Ras Michael & the Sons Of Negus**. This appeared in very small presses on the outfit's own Zion Disc label, and included "Ethiopian National Anthem", which was to be used three years later to introduce one of the deejay **U-Roy**'s first records – "Earth's Rightful Ruler".

If expressions of Rastafarianism were to surface only occasionally in the rude-boy and rocksteady periods, other strains of black consciousness were very much in the air. Jamaicans, like black people throughout the world, were very conscious of the emergence of independent black states in Africa, and were also paying attention to much closer struggles taking place in the United States. In the summer of 1965 Jamaicans gave an enthusiastic reception to Martin Luther King, but far more disturbing to the emergent middle class on the island were the Black Power teachings of Walter Rodney at the University of the West Indies in Kingston. Their unease must have seemed even more justified when the refusal to let the Guyanese lecturer back into Jamaica after a trip abroad prompted student demonstrations and rioting among Kingston's poor. The latter disturbance was put down by the Jamaican Defence Force, which intensified many ghetto dwellers' hostility towards the right-wing JLP (Jamaican Labour Party) government. Prince Buster might have been named after the JLP's founder, Alexander Bustamante, but he still paid tribute to the man the party saw as a disrupting influence, with the great "Dr Rodney Black Power" (Prince Buster). Throughout its rich history, Jamaican music has always been the voice of the dispossessed, though it would not be until the 1970s that this became overwhelmingly obvious to the outside world.

ADRIAN BOOT

Watch This Sound: Slim Smith

vocal performances. Bunny Lee was almost as successful in this period with another former lead singer from the Techniques, Pat Kelly (b. 1948, Kingston), the Caribbeans, Ken Parker, the vintage saxman Val Bennett and Glen Adams. The last of these is probably best remembered as the organist in the Hippy Boys/the Upsetters, one of the best session bands of Jamaican music's next phase; in the rocksteady era, he was primarily known as another convincing singer in the Curtis Mayfield mould.

SLIM SMITH

Early Days (Total Sounds, JA).

E Slim Smith was the greatest vocalist to emerge in the rocksteady era. Whether heard as part of a group (the Techniques, and then the Uniques) or solo, his emotion-racked high tenor was always in a class of its own. This collection should perhaps be credited to "Slim Smith And the Uniques", as the harmonies of Jimmy Riley and Lloyd Charmers are also in evidence throughout. No argument, however, about the near-definitive selection that includes "Give Me Some More", "Let Me Go Girl", "Out Of Love "Love & Affection", "Version Of Love" and "Watch This Sound" – all of them exquisitely soulful.

VARIOUS ARTISTS – BUNNY LEE PRODUCTIONS

Jumping With Mr Lee 1967–68 (Trojan, UK).

Not to be confused with the 1968 Island compilation *Leaping With Mr Lee*, with which it has only one track in common. This is a far stronger collection of Lee-produced rocksteady and early reggae, mostly compiled from the producer's original tapes, and features his star vocalists of the time – Pat Kelly, Slim Smith & the Uniques, Ken Parker, the Sensations and Derrick Morgan – as well as instrumentals of the first order from Val Bennett, Lester Sterling and Vin Gordon, all of whom were members of the Bunny Lee All Stars. If standout tracks have to be picked from out of a superbly consistent set, check Slim Smith's "My Conversation" and "The Beatitude", as well as the very different "Bangarang" from Lester Sterling & Stranger Cole, adapted from a UK jazz original by Kenny Graham's Afro-Cubists.

Ken Lack, Sonia Pottinger, J.J. Johnson and Lloyd Daley

Among those new to production, the most unjustly ignored has been **Ken Lack**, who released a stunning series of 45s on his Caltone label, nearly all of them featuring artists of the first order. The **Heptones**, for instance, cut their first two 45s for Lack, one of which was the extraordinary "Gunmen Coming To Town", which was a rude boy record with a difference – it took its melody from Rossini's "William Tell Overture". Comparably fine harmony-group efforts came from the **Clarendonians**, fresh from their sojourn at Studio One, the **Tartans** (featuring Prince Lincoln Thompson, Lindbergh 'Preps' Lewis, Cedric Myton and Devon Russell), the **Pioneers**, who were soon to be international stars, the **Emotions** (fronted by **Max Romeo**, but also including future Hippy Boy Leroy Brown) and the **Diplomats**. **Alva Lewis**, better known as the excellent session guitarist Reggie Lewis, showed he could also sing – with the effective Lynn Taitt-arranged "Return Home". Perhaps the most enduring of all the Caltone tunes, though, were a handful of fine understated instrumentals, which were credited to bands led by either **Tommy McCook** or **Lynn Taitt**, and featuring gifted soloists such as Johnny 'Dizzy' Moore and Vin Gordon. The infrequency with which original Jamaican copies of Lack's productions turn up suggests that limited pressings were given to some of the most accomplished rocksteady ever recorded – a major reissue programme on CD is needed.

The most successful woman producer in Jamaican music, **Sonia Pottinger**, formerly married to producer Lindon O. Pottinger, was owner of the Tip Top record store on Orange Street, and from 1966 released excellent sides on her Gay Feet, Tip Top and Rainbow labels (with High Note following). Important hits recorded by Sonia Pottinger at the Treasure Isle studio included the likes of the **Gaylads**' "It's Hard To Confess", covered by the Heptones at Studio One and arguably the Gaylads' finest record, Ken Boothe's "Say You", the **Melodians**' incredibly popular "Swing & Dine" and "Little Nut Tree", **Delano Stewart**'s "That's Life", the **Conquerors**' "Won't You Come Home", which received the honour of being covered by Delroy (Wilson) & Slim (Smith) at Studio One, and the **Ethiopians**' much-versioned "The Whip". All were distinguished by clean and vibrant-sounding rhythms from **Lynn Taitt & the Jets**, as well as some of the most beautiful vocal performances of the era. Perhaps a more prolific output would have ensured that Sonia Pottinger was mentioned as often as Reid and Dodd.

Successful jukebox distributor **J.J. Johnson** recorded classic sides by the **Kingstonians**, the **Ethiopians**, **Carl Dawkins** and the **Rulers** on his Sir JJ label (at first, simply JJ), beginning a run of hits that would continue into the next decade and the shift to reggae. **Lloyd Daley**, who had previously cut some boogie and ska tunes for play on his Lloyd the Matador sound system, and was to make his presence really felt at the close of the decade, initiated the label named after his sound with a couple of worthwhile rocksteady singles by the **Overtakers**, with all four sides recorded at Studio One. The still underrated Daley also produced a beautiful late rocksteady/early reggae record by the Hamlins called "I Don't Care At All", perhaps better known in its instrumental incarnation as "Love Kiss Blue" by trumpeter Johnny 'Dizzy' Moore and altoist Carl Bryan. And the more obscure Leeward Robinson produced at least one classic, with the **Gladiators**' "Train Is Coming Back", one of the first records from a group who were to be a major force in the roots music of the next decade.

RICK ELGOOD

First Lady of Reggae, Mrs Sonia Pottinger at her Kingston home, 1994

AN AUDIENCE WITH MRS P

Jamaica's only woman producer of note entered the music business at the same time as rocksteady was born, and found her own take on rocksteady while using Duke Reid's studio. She now has interests outside music, but her memories are still vivid of the days when her productions rivalled those of any of her male peers.

"I needed to work and not work for someone, and so I invested in the music industry. My first release was "Every Night" by Joe White & Chuck, and I got an award for this, and went from strength to strength from there. That first session, I had Baba Brooks, and I put him in charge of it, and he did a splendid job. When they made the cut of "Every Night", it was just one cut, and I said: 'Please don't do it over.' Because I just felt it was right, and it was a great success. Even today, I feel very proud when I speak of it. In those times, we explored. We tried something. We'd maybe use one roll of tape, and just do jam sessions. Out of that, sometimes you'd find something meaningful. That's why I came up with so many instrumentals. I was one for drums. It was a dream of mine that when I go to Africa I would tape drums and more drums, and come back and work with it. Unfortunately when I went, I never had the chance to. But I used what I could fine – like Count Ossie, and some men from Portland, and some of those have never been released. I have a beautiful drum sound on tape that I made, and I used Aubrey Adams and Ernest Ranglin to play jazz on top of it. And it is wonderful!

The Melodians, I think, were dissatisfied with where they were, I don't know for what reason, but it was nearing Christmas, and they come wanting me to record them. I realized they need some money for the holiday, and I did two tunes, but they were not of the standard to go out on the street. However, I gave them some money, and they came back after Christmas, and we had a wonderful session. When we did "Little Nut Tree", we did it in the middle of the night at the Dynamic's, and Tony Brevett became very ill and was taken to the hospital from the studio. And while he was in there, he wrote a tune for me. The only thing I can say about the artists of yesteryear is that they were poor but they were lovely people. They had love, and they shared. If you showed them kindness, they would give it back to you in return. I can't say too much about today's artists, because I'm not working with them. But in those times, they really were wonderful people to work with. And they would listen. They wanted to be upgraded. You could easily talk to an artist and say when you're going on stage you should do so and so, groom your hair, and they would listen. Because they realized it was a growing process for them, too.

Marcia Griffiths is like my relation. We do have a very good rapport with each other. I remember when I was in New York, and so was she, and she called and said: 'Mrs P why don't you record me.' And I said to her: 'The first thing we will record will be a lot of your hits that you've done as a duo [Bob & Marcia], we'll do them singly, and make a good album.' And so we came up with *Naturally*, which is a classic. And then we went on to release "Dreamland", first, from that album, and that was a very successful single. Quite recently, I heard Marcia on an interview, and she said she was from my stable, and coming from my stable she had to be disciplined, because that what I stand for. And I felt very tall about that."

VARIOUS ARTISTS – SONIA POTTINGER PRODUCTIONS

⊙ **Put On Your Best Dress (Sonia Pottinger's Rocksteady 1967–1968)** (Attack, UK).

Sonia Pottinger launched her Hi Note label in the year ska metamorphosed into rocksteady, and this superb collection, all dubbed from 45 rpm discs, takes up the story the year after – when she and the music's new phase were really firing. The Gaylads' "Hard To Confess", from the end of the rocksteady era, is among the best records from one of the most talented Jamaican harmony groups, and as good an example of the fully developed rocksteady sound as any. The Conquerors' "Won't You Come Home" and "Blam Blam Fever" from the Valentines (aka the Silvertones), on the other hand, are superb earlier examples of the genre, while the Melodians' "Swing &

Dine" and "Little Nut Tree", Ken Boothe's original mix of "Say You" and Monty Morris's title track are further undisputed classics.

⊙ **Musical Feast: Mrs Pottinger's High Note and Gayfeet Label** (Heartbeat, US).

This duplicates several tracks on the Trojan collection above, but has far better sound from the producer's original tapes. It also has a good selection of tracks not otherwise easily available, like the deejay version to the Conquerors' "Won't You Come Home" and the instrumental version of the Melodians' "Swing & Dine". One negative point: Ken Boothe's "Say You" is an inferior version with 1970s organ overdub, but overall this compilation is classy stuff, further enhanced by Mrs Pottinger's own reminiscences in the CD booklet.

WIRL

West Indies Records Limited (WIRL) was founded by future prime minister Edward Seaga then taken over by businessman Ronnie Nasrullah, who constructed a new WIRL studio in the mid-1960s. Graeme Goodall, an Australian resident in Jamaica, was the first engineer; he was joined by **Lynford Anderson**, who learned how to use the two-track Ampex board there and subsequently became one of the most creative engineers on the scene (see p.87). As the music changed from rocksteady to reggae, the studio became a mecca for the freelance producers who couldn't get in the door at Federal, Studio One or Treasure Isle – including such as Bunny Lee, J.J. Johnson, Lee Perry and Clancy Eccles. Notable among the rocksteady discs that appeared on the WIRL imprint were early discs by the **Gladiators** and, more importantly, the **Ethiopians**, fresh from their successful run of local hits at Studio One (see p.55). Scoring principally with "Train To Skaville" and "Engine 54", they remained essentially a group with roots in the music of the Jamaican countryside. Often reliant on folk sayings for inspiration, their leader Leonard Dillon never wrote typically romantic rocksteady songs, instead

ROCKSTEADY SESSION BANDS

Though the prolific Soul Vendors and Supersonics were the top session bands of the period, there were several proficient rival outfits. **Lynn Taitt**, as well as playing with the latter outfit, also led the Jets, the other band to lay down tough, infectious rhythms for Treasure Isle, as well as Ken Lack, WIRL, Bunny Lee, Derrick Harriott, Leslie Kong, Derrick Morgan, Sonia Pottinger and Joe Gibbs. Another exemplary collection of musicians led by a guitarist was **Bobby Aitken**'s Carib Beats, who recorded for J.J. Johnson, Bunny Lee, Joe Gibbs, Ewan McDermott and Clancy Eccles. The **Fugitives**, fronted by Jo Jo Bennett, deserve a mention, as well, if only for two wonderful and much 'versioned' sides (released on the trumpeter/cornetist's own Fugitive label), "The Lecture"/ "Cantelope Rock", as well as the glorious rhythm they supplied for the **Conquerors**' original cut of "Won't You Come Home" on Sonia Pottinger's Gay Feet imprint (a tune successfully covered by Delroy Wilson for Studio One).

BOBBY AITKEN

⊙ **Presents Rock Steady Original & Red Hot 1966–67** (Next Step, UK).

The guitarist Bobby Aitken, brother of Laurel Aitken, was one of the top session musicians of the rocksteady era, and deserves far greater acclaim than he's so far received. The appearance of thirteen previously unreleased productions by him is a move in the right direction, though it has to be said that it is obvious why most of the vocals have not appeared before. The instrumentals are another matter, though, particularly when Val Bonnet's tenor sax is to the fore. One for the rocksteady specialists, rather than those with a more casual interest.

LYNN TAITT & THE JETS

● **Sounds . . . Rock Steady** (Merritone, JA).

● **Rock Steady Greatest Hits** (Merritone, JA).

Nothing to choose between these two instrumental sets, which are full of subtle musicianship from the leader himself, and others of the calibre of saxman Roland Alphonso and organist Aubrey Adams, all underpinned by the innovative drum and bass of Joe Isaacs and Bryan Atkinson. The repertoire is exclusively cover versions, but it doesn't matter at all – lovers of rocksteady will want both albums.

pursuing his own distinctive style, but for a while doing so over some great rocksteady rhythms from Tommy McCook's Supersonics.

THE ETHIOPIANS

● **Let's Ska & Rocksteady [Engine 54]** (WIRL, JA).

The Ethiopians never made typical rocksteady – instead, like the Maytals, and Justin Hinds & the Dominoes, they went their own way through most of the different phases of Jamaican music, with just the supporting rhythms changing. Trains were obviously on Dillon's mind at the time, as, besides "Engine 54", there are the equally anthemic "Train To Skaville" (almost an instrumental) and "Train To Glory".

VARIOUS ARTISTS – WIRL PRODUCTIONS

● **Rock Steady – Intensified (Jamaica's New Dance Craze)** (WIRL, JA).

The subtitle tells you how long ago this was originally released. If you have a taste for rocksteady at all, you can not afford to miss tracks such as the Tennors' "Ride Yu Donkey", Monty Morris's "Say What You're Saying", David Isaacs's version of "Place In the Sun", the Gaylads' "Joy In the Morning" and Lee Perry's biting "People Funny Boy".

Singer-producers

In addition, several singers also set themselves up as producers, a trend that has continued ever since. The foundation vocalist **Derrick Morgan**, for instance, took the duo **Lloyd & Devon** (Lloyd Robinson & Devon Russell) into the studio, having a huge hit on his own Hop label with their infectious "Red Bum Ball", as he did with his own "Conquering Ruler". (A few years later, on the same label, he was to release Max Romeo's PNP anthem, "Let the Power Fall For I".) **Derrick Harriott**, a former member of the early group the Jiving Juniors, but a solo singer and producer since 1962, was responsible for a considerable body of classic work on his Crystal, Derrick's and Move & Grove labels, not only from himself, but the likes of **Keith & Tex** (Keith Rowe & Texas Dixon), **Rudy Mills**, the **Kingstonians** and **Noel 'Bunny' Brown**, as well as instrumentals featuring the trumpeter, **Bobby Ellis**. Having initial success with the singer **Monty Morris**, former Studio One hitmaker **Clancy Eccles** secured his reputation as a producer, and established his New Beat and Clandisc imprints, which were to play an important role in the next phase of the music.

DERRICK HARRIOTT

⊙ **The Sensational Derrick Harriott Sings Jamaican Rocksteady-Reggae** (Jamaican Gold, Holland).

If Harriott had written more of his own material he might be better known today. As it is, he usually turned his marvellous tenor voice to US hits from such as the Tams and various Motown acts. When he did sing one of his own compositions – "Tang Tang Festival Song", say – the results were just as worthwhile.

KEITH & TEX

● **Stop That Train** (Crystal, JA).

Derrick Harriott remains an underrated producer, though he was responsible for some of the best rhythms of the rocksteady era and always brought out the best in the artists with whom he worked. Keith & Tex are a case in point. Thanks to the film *The Harder They Come*, they are best known to the general public for "Stop That Train", the vocal toasted by Scotty; but as their only album amply demonstrates, they were far from being one-hit wonders. "Tonight" is the other track familiar to most rocksteady lovers, but the remaining originals and their versions of US soul hits are of a similar calibre. Because Derrick Harriott only possessed eight tracks by the duo, these are complemented with four pieces from Noel 'Bunny' Brown, the wonderful high tenor singer from the Chosen Few.

VARIOUS ARTISTS – DERRICK HARRIOTT PRODUCTIONS

⊙ **From Chariot's Vaults Volume 1: 16 Rocksteady Hits** (Jamaican Gold, Holland).

Superb collection of Harriott productions, including – as is usually the case with this reissue label – obscure gems as well as the major hits. An informative booklet, complete with ultra-scarce photographs, completes the package.

Early reggae

ADRIAN BOOT

3

3

previous page

Kingston rum bar, early 70s

Early reggae

There's no question which record was the first to use the term **'reggae'** in any of its various spellings – it was the **Maytals'** "Do the Reggay", released by Leslie Kong on his Beverley's label in 1968. However, it remains debatable which was the first to signal the shift from rocksteady in early 1968. **Larry & Alvin**'s much-versioned "Nanny Goat" (for Studio One) and the **Beltones**' "No More Heartaches" (for Harry Johnson) are the records most frequently cited, but something fundamental was happening before these, with **Lynford Anderson**'s "Pop A Top", produced and engineered by Anderson for his own Upset label right at the start of the year. "Pop A Top" was based on a style of rhythm that was noticeably faster than rocksteady, a development taken further in mid-1968 when Anderson collaborated with Lee Perry on "People Funny Boy". This huge hit was firmly in the 'musical war' tradition (Joe Gibbs was the target), but the rhythm over which Scratch voiced his invective was a lot faster than rocksteady, with an insistent guitar motif that seemed to quicken the pace further. The integration of a baby's cries in the mix not only enhanced the atmosphere – it also anticipated the greater role of the recording engineer and experiments with different mixes.

Yet it's too simple to say that reggae was all about quick tempo, for alongside the faster rhythms most associated with early reggae were a few records that were slower paced than rocksteady. In fact, Jamaican music now took on a greater diversity than it had ever displayed before. What tied it all together was a new rough quality to the tunes, and the assigning of an even more pivotal role to the electric bass. Reggae in all its variations signalled a break from the smoothness of rocksteady and the aspirations of producers like Duke Reid and Clement Dodd to replicate the refinement of Detroit and Chicago soul. The music was now more extrovert, and nearer in spirit to James Brown than to the Impressions.

It's fitting that the word 'reggae' has endured as the favoured label for all Jamaican popular music, because reggae began in a period of extraordinary experiment, in which almost all later styles were prefigured and all previous styles absorbed. The music of 1968–74 ranged from the fast, jerky instrumentals of session bands such as **Lee Perry**'s Upsetters, **Clancy Eccles**' Dynamites and **Derrick Harriott**'s Crystalites, through the work of vocal harmony groups like the **Heptones**, **Carlton & his Shoes**, the **Cables** and the **Beltones**, to the minor-chord sounds and Rasta imagery of tracks that anticipated the roots revolution of the mid-1970s. It was in the early reggae era that it became common for sound-system deejays to chat on record, and the origins of dub techniques lie here as well (see pp.197–228). Central in the development of these multifarious strands was the emergence of younger producers, as men such as Anderson, Lee Perry, **Bunny Lee**, Clancy Eccles and **Winston Riley** all invented new types of rhythm to challenge the dominance of Dodd and Reid, generally using musicians who were not yet established sessioneers. To borrow the prescient imagery of Bob Marley (then recording for another former Coxsone employee, Lee 'Scratch' Perry), there were an increasing number of small axes to whittle away at the big trees.

THE UPSETTERS

◑ **Return of Django** (Trojan, UK).

As reggae LPs tended to be in 1969, this is essentially a collection of singles, including the wonderful "Night Doctor", "Man From MI5" and "Live Injection" (the latter one of the best examples on record of Glen Adams's keyboard skills). A long way from the Black Art sound of a half a decade later, but one of the best of the cheesy organ-dominated instrumental albums synonymous with the time.

VARIOUS ARTISTS

◑ **Monkey Business** (Trojan, UK).

Ⓔ Pretty near to a definitive compilation of up-tempo reggae of the early 1970s. Everything here has stood the test of time: from Desmond Dekker's rocksteady classic "007", through the more characteristic instrumentals of a couple of years later, such as the Harry J All Stars' "Liquidator", the Upsetters' "Return Of Django" and Dave & Ansell Collins's "Double Barrel", to wonderfully vibrant vocals like the Pioneers' "Long Shot (Kick De Bucket)", and Eric Donaldson's 1971 Festival Song winner, "Cherry Oh Baby".

Jimmy Cliff in "The Harder They Come"

The Harder They Come (Island, UK).

E The soundtrack to the most popular film ever made in Jamaica, and the album that – along with the Wailers' *Catch A Fire* – turned white middle-class kids on to reggae. Jimmy Cliff was the star of Perry Henzell's movie, and is well represented with the title track, "You Can Get It If You Really Want", "Sitting In Limbo" and the sublime "Many Rivers To Cross". Just as much of a revelation to an audience previously hostile to the music were the Melodians' haunting "Rivers Of Babylon", the Maytals' gospel-hot "Pressure Drop" and "Sweet & Dandy", and the deejay Scotty's "Draw Your Brakes".

Tighten Up (Volumes 1 & 2) (Trojan, UK).

Tighten Up (Volumes 3 & 4) (Trojan, UK).

Tighten Up (Volumes 5 & 6) (Trojan, UK).

A now legendary series that began as a budget line in early 1969 and introduced many white kids to reggae. It is a pity that the standards of the earlier volumes were not maintained for the entire series, but there is no denying the imagination and sheer charm that went into practically everything collected on these sets: from the Perry-produced track that gave the series its title, through soulful vocals like Ken Boothe's "Freedom Street", to harmony-group outings such as the Kingstonians' "Sufferer" and early examples of the deejay's art, in particular King Stitt's "Fire Corner". Not a great deal here that doesn't appear on other readily available sets, but it's still a treat to have them together.

The Magnificent Fourteen (Trojan, UK).

Successors to the Hollywood themes popular in ska, these fourteen examples of mainly instrumental reggae celebrate celluloid Westerns in spirited fashion, often employing gunshots and/or quotes from the films in question. The Upsetters' "Return Of Django" might seem a little too familiar, but it fits well alongside less common examples of the genre, such as the Crystalites' "A Fistful Of Dollars", Richard Ace's "Hang 'em High", King Stitt's "Lee Van Cleef" (aka "The Ugly One"), the Rupie Edwards All Stars' "Magnificent Seven" and Sir Lord Comic's "Django Shoots First". A pity about the minimal information on the sleeve, though.

Crab Greatest Hits (Pama, UK).

Crab was one of the UK record company Pama's many subsidiary labels, and released countless sterling records in the late 1960s/early 1970s from producers such as Lloyd 'Matador' Daley, Harry Mudie, Derrick Morgan and Lee Perry. This collection of hits from 1969 is dominated by vocal groups, and particularly outstanding are the Ethiopians' "Reggae Hit the Town", the Viceroys' "Work It" and the Versatiles' "Children Get Ready". Well worth a scour of the secondhand bins.

Gas Greatest Hits (Pama, UK).

Drawing hits from another Pama subsidiary, and a similar sort of collection as the above. Exceptional tracks include Roland Alphonso's "1,000 Tons Of Megaton" (an instrumental cut of Slim Smith's "Everybody Needs Somebody To Love"), Slim himself on the Uniques' version of the Temptations' "Ain't Too Proud To Beg" and Pat Kelly's moving "How Long Will It Take".

Reggae Hits '69 Volumes 1 & 2 (Pama, UK).

These repeat some of the best tracks from the Crab and Gas collections, but also have Stranger Cole & Lester Sterling's "Bangarang", Derrick Morgan's treatment of the traditional "River To the Bank" and the Techniques "Who You Gonna Run To". In your search for all these Pama LPs, be prepared for serious competition from middle-aged skinheads.

The Big Three in the reggae era

The three dominant forces of the previous era – **Prince Buster**, **Clement Dodd** and **Duke Reid** – were never again to lead the pack in quite the way they had up to 1968, neither in the studio nor as sound-system operators. Nevertheless, Dodd remained a prolific producer, and the one most obviously in touch with new trends – as shown by important hits with Larry Marshall, the Bassies, the Heptones and Freddy McKay at the beginning of the new phase. Shortly afterwards, Dodd was to anticipate the roots era by releasing goundbreaking tunes from the likes of the Abyssinians, Burning Spear and Horace Andy. Both Buster and Reid displayed a more cautious attitude, though each produced fine records from singers informed by the melodic values of rocksteady and the expressiveness of current US soul. In addition, Reid was responsible for ushering in one genuinely new and important trend: the practice of 'toasting' (rapping or talking) over recent hits, already established in the dancehall but new on record.

Brentford Road reggae

The founder of the most influential studio of all, **Clement Dodd** gathered around him musicians who very quickly adapted to the changes in the air and managed at least to follow the trends set by the new producers who were beginning to arrive. Records of a very high quality continued to appear on the Studio One and Coxsone imprints, as well as a myriad of smaller labels, including Supreme, Winro, Bongo Man, Money Disc and Iron Side.

Coxsone's session bands were usually led by **Jackie Mittoo**, and included musicians like **Leroy Sibbles** on bass, **Eric Frater** on guitar, **Bunny Williams** on drums, **Roland Alphonso**, **Headley Bennett** and **Cedric Brooks** on saxophones. Jamaica's most renowned guitarist, **Ernest Ranglin**, would often take time off from jazz gigging to sit in on sessions (one of which resulted in the marvellous "Surfing"), as would Alpha bandmaster **Lennie Hibbert**. They usually recorded under the name **Sound Dimension**, named after an echo unit favoured by Frater. During the period from late 1967 until Mittoo's departure for Canada in 1968, they made a series of rhythms that have been continually recut ever since. Confident, dynamic instrumentals like the propulsive "Full Up" and the brassy "Mojo Rocksteady" (despite its name) represented the next step on from Coxsone's take on rocksteady, which had always been tougher than the polished Reid style.

The Studio One **singers** of the period included some who had recorded with Coxsone through the rocksteady era, plus a few new names who were to display the same sort of enduring qualities. Prominent in the first category were the **Heptones**, who continued with much the same approach as previously, but supported by rougher rhythms in the new style, and with even more of their lyrics addressing the subject of Black self-determination. Of particular note were their covers of the Motown hit, "Message From A Black Man", Curtis Mayfield's "Choice Of Colours" and Bob Dylan's "I Shall Be Released", as well as Sibbles' own "Be A Man", "Freedom Line" and "Time Will Tell".

Alton Ellis, too, continued to provide both Reid and Dodd with important hits – some in the gloriously romantic strain with which he had been successful before, but also proving just as comfortable with the type of socially conscious material that was to become increasingly popular in the 1970s. Most notable among these were such as "African Descendants", "Set A Better Example" and the incisive "Blackish White", all recorded at Brentford Road. **John Holt**, similarly flitting between Studio One and Treasure Isle, did excellent work at the studio, most notably the huge hits "Stranger In Love" and "A Love I Can Feel". The latter effectively versioned the Motown original by the Temptations, reflecting the still-pervasive influence of US soul. This influence was also felt in the music of **Carlton & his Shoes**, who continued cutting infrequent but brilliant records, nearly all in a lushly romantic vein. Lead singer Carlton Manning was also an important session musician for the label, playing guitar and occasional bass.

The **Cables** – Keeble Drummond, Elbert Stewart, Vince Stoddart – did not begin recording their marvellous harmonies for Dodd until 1969 (they had previously cut the very rare "Good Luck To You" for Sonia Pottinger). Though never prolific, the quality of their output for Dodd was impeccable, and a handful of fine records subsequently appeared on the Sir JJ, Harry J and Electro labels.

ADRIAN BOOT

John Holt, post-Paragons, at Studio One

Of the other artists to distinguish themselves at Brentford Road, **Larry Marshall** was outstanding. In addition to making classic records such as the epochal "Nanny Goat", "Mean Girl", "Throw Me Corn" and "Thelma", Marshall also worked as an assistant to recording engineer Sylvan Morris, searched out dubs for sound system use, and wrote and arranged for other artists. These included former Treasure Isle hitmaker **Freddy McKay** (b. 1947, St Catherine) who enjoyed a massive hit with "Picture On the Wall", and cut several similarly memorable tunes in his grittily soulful style, all employing the Soul Defenders band. Marshall also had considerable input in the early work of **Horace Andy** (b. Horace Hinds, 1951, Kingston), whose strikingly effective falsetto spawned a whole new school of Jamaican male singers.

Larry was further involved in the creation of some of the most startlingly different records cut at Brentford Road in the immediate post-rocksteady years. These sessions were with a singer from St. Ann's Bay who had been christened Winston Rodney in 1948, but styled himself after the name taken by Jomo Kenyatta, the leader of the struggle for Kenyan independence – **Burning Spear**. Nothing could have been more uncommercial in 1969 than his debut single on Dodd's Supreme label. "Door Peeper" was a reflective chant delivered in a way that was frighteningly serious, and much the same can be said about all the two albums' worth of material he recorded over the next five years. But if Burning Spear's chosen themes – the oppression of the black race, Marcus Garvey and repatriation to Africa – prefigured the dominant roots style of the later 1970s, his individual style was largely to defy imitation and leave him always outside the music's mainstream.

ROLAND ALPHONSO

◑ **Best Of Roland Alphonso** (Studio One, JA).

● **King Sax [King Of Sax]** (Winro/Studio One, JA).

Tenorman Roland Alphonso is one of Jamaica's most important musicians, with a career dating back to the beginnings of the island's recorded music. Both these sets were released in the 1970s, employing rhythms already considered classics – including

LYNFORD ANDERSON: 100 SONGS A DAY

Lynford Anderson, born 1941 in the parish of Clarendon, was among the most gifted recording engineers ever to work in Jamaica. Employed at the radio station RJR from 1959, he recorded "Thirty Pieces Of Silver" for Prince Buster there. In the mid-1960s he moved to WIRL where, taught by the Australian Graeme Goodall, he refined his engineering skills on the studio's Ampex two-track machine. He recorded most of Leslie Kong's hits, and his own productions like "Pop A Top" were significant moments in the transition to early reggae. In this interview by reggae historian David Katz, Anderson talks about the birth of talkover and the workload of a 60s Jamaican studio engineer.

Can you remember the first session you recorded?

"I did quite a few Leslie Kong productions. I did all of his stuff. I cut everything for Kong; name a tune and I probably cut it. I started a label, I did "Pop A Top", the first talking record in Jamaica. I was the one who put King Stitt, if you listen to King Stitt, I have the record here right now, "Herbman Shuffle", I'm talking on there. You can hear my voice along with King Stitt. He talks and I'm [makes puffing sound] "Hot it from the top..." I did the first talking song ever, "Pop A Top". Yeah, that was when the talking really started, it's the first talking record.

"Pop A Top" was inspired by a Canada Dry advert?

I heard the commercial, the guy said "Pop A Top". Then I had this rhythm. [It] was "South Parkway Mambo". All I know, it was an instrumental kind of song but it didn't work, the instrumental type of song I was trying to create. I had it sitting down for about seven years. We didn't touch that tape for years. One day I got it out, Lloyd Charmers started playing "pop pop pop, pop pop", I said, "Oh, Pop A Top!" That's how that song came about. Then we realized the same [chord] changes become "Fat Man", it's the same rhythm, Derrick Morgan did it. Later on we did some versions with some guys going "chick chick chick", we had about thirteen versions of it. Derrick Morgan came down and was listening to it, and realized that it's the same song that he did years ago.

You also did "The Law". Who played on that?

I think it was the same set of guys, Gladdy's All Stars. Gladdy is on all of my songs, Hux Brown, Lynn Taitt, I think. I mixed it, I mixed everything.

What inspired you to put so much delay and non-standard sounds on "Pop A Top" and "The Law"?

I know that the playback of the machine, if you do it at low speed you get a lot of delay, I don't remember why but..."Pop A Top", I just keep doubling up, I don't remember exactly but I know you can hear the delay on that song. I use to try to mix different, I never want to do the same thing twice.

What do you recall recording with Byron Lee?

I do a lot of stuff. I do the stuff with Roberta Flack, "Killing Me Softly", I made the rhythm track for that at Dynamics Sound. Yeah! Drum and bass. The bass you hear, it's from Jamaica, it was done in Jamaica [by] Jackie Jackson. I only did the bass and drums. I used to record and I used to master, almost a hundred songs a day, for foreign and local. I used to have to work right through the night, after working in the studio, then go down and cut again until three, four in the morning. I was involved with almost everything in that period! Every song, I had something to do with it – either I record it, I mix it, I voice it, or I cut the master; I have to be involved with it in some way."

the Heptones' "Why Did You Leave", the Sound Dimension's "Full Up", the Eternals' "Queen Of the Minstrels" and the Victors' "Things Come Up To Bump" – plus a smattering of equally well-crafted originals. There is really very little to choose between the two: *Best Of* has the most outstanding original in "Jah Shakey", which itself has been versioned countless times, but both sets are of an

IT'S THE DRUM AND BASS: LARRY MARSHALL

Widely known as one of Jamaica's most talented singers and songwriters, Larry Marshall (b. Lawrence Park, 1945, St Ann's) also played a considerable role at Clement Dodd's Brentford Road studio as an engineer and arranger.

"I leave country in 1957 and come to Kingston. I went to a lot of dances in ska days, and enjoy myself with ska music. But my project was something more soft and easy. In 1960 I met some musicians. They know the music, the chords. But they were ska-ing. I tell them I don't want any ska. Play what I'm singing, go with my mood. Then I join together with Joe Henry and Ferdie Nelson. They two cousins, you know. When it take a start it with the Top Deck label. There was a Chinee fellow by the name of Philip Yap, and he was familiar with the Skatalites. They would do his backings for his records. Joe and Ferdie had the first recording session with him, but it wasn't that effective. Then he called me because he heard that I had some nice songs, and he want to do some recordings with me.

The first tune I then really do was "Too Young To Love". But in those ska days it seem that every foreign number one tune get on the Jamaican chart. Ben E. King, Solomon Burke, Brook Benton, Sam Cooke and all those foreign men. So I look into this to see how there could be a Jamaican tune on the chart for every foreign one. And I say it's the drum and bass, man! Because I remember when they play the calypso and rumba sort of thing, it have that basic sound. It was the bass!

After my first record, I did "Promise Is A Comfort To A Fool" for Philip Yap. Then he went to foreign, and bought back a song called "Snake In the Grass". He ask me to do a cover version, and it got to number one. From there I go to Coxsone. Clement Dodd said 'Come on and do some recording for me,' and I do "Nanny Goat". He had this rhythm with a guy singing some lovers thing, and he get me, Alvin and Ernest Wilson to sing over that song. Then we record "Throw Me Corn", "Your Love", "Can't You Understand" and "Thelma". But no money. When you need some money, you have to go beg a bus fare and so forth. They don't want to pay. I get paid £29 for "Nanny Goat". £29! I was at home, listening to the radio when "Nanny Goat" started. A brother called King Victor had a little sound in Spanish Park, used to play in Papine's Square. For six months, every sound that play in Papine's Square get flopped. Every man go to Coxsone and ask for that song. They don't know the name of the song. They just know it's Larry Marshall. But even Coxsone's sound get flopped when it play Papine's. Because Coxsone did not approve of "Nanny Goat". So I had to take it as a dub and promote it myself.

People talk about where reggae come from. But let me tell you. When I am a little youth, my mother sent me down the road to

almost flawless standard. The only qualifications to that last statement are that the Studio One press of *King Of Sax* adds a final track that you are unlikely to play more than once, and the others have been subjected to a remix – but only to seriously deleterious effect on "Theme From the Baba".

HORACE ANDY

Skylarking (Studio One, JA).

The best of Horace Andy's material at Brentford Road is collected here. He has recorded several of the songs more than once – including "Every Tongue Shall Tell", "Just Say Who", "See A Man's Face", "Something's On My Mind" and "I'll Be Gone" – and it is a tribute to his interpretative powers that in most cases all the versions are essential. Few Jamaican singers have possessed such an original style, or been as influential, and though he might have matched the music here with later recordings, he never superseded its heartfelt qualities.

CEDRIC BROOKS

Im Flash Forward (Studio One, JA).

E This was not released until 1977, but the rhythms suggest it was cut at the beginning of the decade. Whether blowing his tenor saxophone (or flute) over an original rhythm or an established classic, Brooks brought a serious, reflective feel to bear that was completely his own. Early roots classics, such as the Abyssinians' "Declaration Of Rights" or Keith Wilson's "God I God I Say", might seem the most appropriate to this approach, but versions of Freddy McKay's "Picture On the Wall" and Horace Andy's "Skylarking" are as every bit as suc-

the grocery store to buy things, and my girlfriends see me in my raggy pants. So I ashamed and go back to the house ask my mother if I can wear some other pants. But she says 'No – go on to the shop!' I don't like them to see me in my tear back pants. I afraid they break off with me, and I don't like that. Anyhow, it goes on and on, and I have to live with it. You see, there's where the raggedness comes in. When we say 'reggae', 'ragged way of life', it down to earth. No one listen to the poor man. If you want to talk to the boss, most times you have to ask five or six person, first. Tell them you need some money to buy some pants.

Well, in the Studio One days I was so busy, round Coxsone, selling dub and helping promote the music. Because Dodd didn't know what he had. When Sylvan Morris was there, he was chief engineer, and he and I good friends. He the one to tape "Nanny Goat". And I become his assistant, learning. Dennis Brown came in and sang "Love Grows", and I sit in and tape his second recording, "No Man Is An Island". Alton Ellis was there, as well, and I tape him. Horace Andy came in, and I tape "Skylarking". Freddy McKay came in and I tape "Picture On the Wall". Burning Spear came in. I tape a lot of Burning Spear, Dennis Brown, Horace Andy.

But I first met Burning Spear when I went to St Ann's Bay with Jackie Mittoo, for a show in Sommerville. I went around to the beach to find a smoke. Because I smoked then. And I see a lot of smoke, and Burning Spear came up to me, and say 'Mr Marshall, I would like to do some recording, but don't know how to go about it.' So, I said 'Find your way to Studio One, and I'll set you up.' Then he goes to Jack Ruby, and there he rehearses and rehearses with this band. And he bring them to record with Coxsone – the Soul Defenders. I was the one to help him, show him how to sing and portray this African sound. All those [Burning Spear] songs I know because I help arrange them. A whole lots of artists, I sit down, and I put my vibe into them. When Sylvan Morris left, Coxsone wanted me to stay and be the engineer. But I wasn't getting any money.

When I leave Coxsone, I meet a youth called Carlton Patterson, who had a label called Black & White. He came to my house, with a song, "Not Responsible". Carlton used to practise with me, and I learn him the way of things. I even help him arrange things, and help him deal with it. Then he said 'Come and do some recordings, and we split 50-50.' Then we went into Randy's studio, and record "I Admire You". And then we leave and go to King Tubby's, and he mix the song, and a new version called "Watergate Rock". That the dub that made King Tubby's name. Him tell me! King Tubby tape a couple of my songs. I have Tubby on my tapes, right now: 'Roll them, Larry!', 'Larry, ready.' I would like to produce an album. Put out them songs with Tubby. He was a great man. Help many youth have bread. ❞

cessful. Will Mr Dodd ever draw together the Cedric Brooks 45s not included here – his versions of "Java" ("Ethiopia"), say, or "Satta Massa Gana" ("Sata") – for a second essential album?

BURNING SPEAR

Presenting (Studio One, JA).

Rocking Time (Studio One, JA).

E The incomparable Winston Rodney's earliest material, with all the distinguishing characteristics of his music well in evidence. Whatever people might say about Clement Dodd's treatment of his artists, there were not many producers who would have spent time and money on such seemingly uncommercial material as this. The Spear was to re-interpret several of the tracks later, and it says something about his artistry that it is impossible to choose between the raw originals on these two sets and the more 'produced' later versions.

THE CABLES

What Kind Of World (Studio One, JA).

The Cables are one of the few talented Jamaican acts that have been under-recorded, and their best is collected on this one – not particularly long – album. Presumably the surfeit of talent at Brentford Road in the late 1960s was the only reason Dodd did not record them more. The hits "Baby Why" and the title track are classics that have been versioned again and again, but gems like "Love Is A Pleasure", "My Broken Heart" (the original flip side of "What Kind Of World") and especially "Be A Man" (the flip of "Baby Why") are easily their equal.

ALTON ELLIS

Sunday Coming (Studio One, JA).

E This remains his finest album. The title track places romance in a realistic social context, and is the more powerful for it, while the intense "Hurting Me" is the other exceptional original. Ellis's own view that his talent lies primarily as an interpreter seems credible when you hear his readings of Jerry Jackson's "Wide Awake In A Dream", the Royalettes' "(It's) Gonna Take A Miracle", the Guess Who's "These Eyes", Brenda Holloway's "You Make Me So Very Happy" and Harvey Fuqua & Johnny Bristol's "What Does It Take To Win Your Love" (a US hit for Junior Walker). The only point at which Ellis sounds less than totally convincing is with the too-funky "Alton's Groove".

The Best Of Alton Ellis (Studio One, JA).

The CD release of the *Best Of* collection of Studio One classics presents them in digital clarity and with the addition of some strong Treasure Isle tracks. As usual with Jamaica's premier vocal stylist, there is little to choose between the self-penned material and his reworkings of US hits (only Eddie Floyd's "Knock On Wood" doesn't quite come off). Tracks like "Still Trying" and "Breaking Up Is Hard" have been versioned countless times, but even Coxsone has yet to put out a next cut to "Set A Better Example", which deserves similar status.

THE HEPTONES

Freedom Line (Studio One, JA).

Released in 1971, this shows the trio's harmonies honed to even greater perfection than during the rocksteady era, but over rhythms that were unmistakably in the rougher – more funk-influenced – reggae style. The influence of socially conscious themes in US soul is discernible on the title track, "Show Us the Way" and even Paul McCartney's "Let It Be", while elsewhere Leroy Sibbles sounds even more agonized in his affairs of the heart. Includes a version of Elvis Presley's hit "Suspicious Minds" that vies with the Dee Dee Warwick interpretation as the definitive one.

LENNIE HIBBERT

Creation (Studio One, JA).

If the vibraphone is not an instrument you associate with reggae, you can't have yet heard Lennie Hibbert. In contrast with most Studio One instrumental sets, this features a high percentage of original rhythms, though Mr Hibbert sounds just at home on the Heptones' "Pretty Looks" and the Studio One version of Keith & Tex's "Tonight". Any doubters should listen to "Village Soul", simply one of the most beautiful instrumentals ever to emerge from Brentford Road.

JOHN HOLT

A Love I Can Feel (Studio One, JA; Bamboo/Attack, UK).

Another standard-setting Studio One album. The ultra-smooth Holt had not long left the Paragons when these were recorded and was obviously pulling out all the stops to establish his solo career. The title track has one of the most popular rhythms in reggae

RICK ELGOOD

Larry Marshall, one of the claimants to the title Originator of Reggae

(Holt himself was to cut an excellent dancehall version for Junjo Lawes), and the other massive hit singles are "Stranger In Love" and "My Heart Is Gone" (which he also successfully recorded for Phil Pratt). Every track a blues party gem (with several extra on the tastefully remixed CD version).

LARRY MARSHALL

◑ **Presenting Larry Marshall** (Studio One, JA; Heartbeat, US).

E Larry Marshall never failed to deliver his best at Studio One, and it can only be regretted that Dodd released just one album by him. However often his rhythms are recycled by others, there is no substitute for hearing the writer of some of the most heatfelt records ever to emerge from Jamaica, including "Nanny Goat", "Thelma", "Mean Girl" and "How Can I Go On" (aka "Can't You Understand"). Most of his best-known tunes are on the *Presenting* album, though it is a pity that the CD could not have added "Press Along Nyah", "Run Babylon" or "Lonely Room".

◉ **I Admire You** (Java, UK; Heartbeat, US).

I Admire You, which originally appeared on Carlton Patterson's Black & White label, is the most distinguished record Marshall made after leaving Brentford Road, and almost achieves the impossible task of matching the Studio One set.

FREDDY McKAY

● **Picture On the Wall** (Studio One, JA; Attack, UK).

The late Freddy McKay never achieved the degree of consistent success his talent deserved – or left an album that quite did it justice. Instead, his best work was scattered over obscure 45s on many different labels, with his debut album for Studio One remaining his most consistent. Whatever the lyric or rhythm, his voice had a catch in it that always expressed heartache, as witnessed by the title track, the cultural "Father Will Cut You Down", or even the lightweight lyric of "High School Dance".

JACKIE MITTOO

◉ **Tribute To Jackie Mittoo** (Heartbeat US).

E Superb 31-track compilation that collects various singles and unreleased performances and presents them in a satisfying overview of Mittoo's talents: the organist excels, whether vamping over an already familiar Brentford Road rhythm like "Nanny Goat" or "Fattie Fattie", or delivering Memphis/New Orleans-influenced funk workouts such as "Hot Tamale" or "Memphis Groove". The crack session bands involved range from the Soul Brothers through the Soul Vendors to the Sound Dimension.

● **Macka Fat** (Studio One, JA).

Jackie Mittoo's importance to Jamaican music cannot be overstated – both as a virtuoso keyboards player and the arranger on countless sessions. Of all the Mittoo albums issued at the time, this is the most consistent, employing the same formula found on equally successful sets by hornsmen Roland Alphonso and Cedric Brooks: a selection of classic Studio One rhythms (plus a couple of originals), over which the featured musician makes his statements. Some of Dodd's strongest early reggae tracks are featured – including several from the Heptones, Burning Spear's "This Population", Alton Ellis's "Live & Learn" and Dawn Penn's "You Don't Love Me" – and Mittoo's playing is inspired throughout.

ERNEST RANGLIN

◉ **Sounds & Power** (Studio One, US).

Though not released until the 1990s, this contains recordings of uncertain date and consists entirely of vintage-style performances from the master guitarist over the most enduring Studio One rhythms from the late 1960s and early 1970s. Besides more expected rhythms such as "Stars", "Love Me Forever" and "Swing Easy", another highlight is a previously unreleased Coxsone cut of "Pop A Top".

THE WAILING SOULS

● **The Wailing Souls** (Studio One, JA).

E The Wailing Souls' lead singer, Winston 'Pipe' Matthews, has been compared with Marley (a fellow pupil of Joe Higgs), but he is no copyist and his songwriting skills are certainly his own, while belonging to the same 'country' school as Justin Hinds and the Gladiators' Albert Griffiths. To complete the package, the group's harmonies have always been immaculate, and among the most heartfelt in reggae. The eponymous first album shows them at their best.

● **Soul & Power** (Studio One, US).

The second album – released some eight years later – is much more than a collection of rejects. Particularly interesting are the original cuts of three songs that the group also recorded elsewhere – "You Should Have Known" ("Back Biter"), the title track ("Feel the Spirit") and "Rock But Don't Fall" ("Walk the Chalk Line").

VARIOUS ARTISTS

Money Maker (Coxsone, JA).

One of the best Studio One album jackets, and one of the few compilations from that quarter that has been put together with some consistency of mood in mind. The emphasis is on serious instrumentals, with five from Im & David (Cedric Brooks and David Madden), three from Jackie Mittoo and one rather mysteriously credited to the Boss (maybe the gentleman who introduces it), plus a soul-inflected vocal to the rhythm used for the Wailing Souls' "Back Out With It" from the obscure Lloyd Williams. File next to Cedric Brooks' *Flash Forward*.

SKINHEAD REGGAE

Up-tempo reggae was the chosen soundtrack for Britain's **skinhead** cult – another of the recurring examples of white youth being comfortable with a more hectic, less sensual style of Jamaican rhythm. The term 'skinhead reggae' might be something of a misnomer, in that Britain's native rude boys didn't actually create any reggae, but there is no denying that skinheads were an important record-buying market, with a consuming power that was a good deal greater than that of the young inhabitants of the Kingston ghettos. Jamaican musicians and producers domiciled in Britain – particularly Dandy Livingstone, Joe Mansano and the great Laurel Aitken – were the most adept at catering directly for their needs, but there was also an awareness of this audience in Kingston itself. The forward-looking Bunny Lee, for instance, named one of his record labels Agro Sound, and his session band the Aggrovators, after skinhead argot for "trouble".

It was thanks to the skinhead audience that reggae 45s made a concentrated impact in the British pop charts. Jamaican records had occasionally enjoyed crossover success in the UK before, however. **Millie**'s 1964 version of Barbie Gaye's r&b hit, "My Boy Lollipop", had been a favourite of London's sharply dressed mods, and subsequently an international pop hit. Three years then went by before **Prince Buster**'s "Al Capone" and then the **Skatalites**' "Guns Of Navarone", which came out a few months before the biggest hit of all in this period – **Desmond Dekker**'s "007 (Shanty Town)", which eventually hit the #14 slot during the summer of 1967.

These early reggae hits were seen as isolated novelty items, but between 1968 and 1971 more than twenty reggae singles reached the UK pop charts, with many narrowly failing to do so. Among the most successful – and enduring – of these hits were two instrumentals that reached the Top Ten in the same month: the **Upsetters**' "Return Of Django", featuring the tenorman Val Bennett (#5 in October 1969), and the **Harry J All Stars'** "Liquidator", with the distinctive Hammond organ of **Winston Wright** (#9).

Another instrumental hit that registered with UK pop fans was **Boris Gardiner**'s "Elizabethan Reggae" (#14 in 1970), while **Dave** (Barker) **& Ansell Collins** combined the sort of organ sound already familiar to many white listeners with an early taste of Jamaican deejaying, and were spectacularly successful with, first, "Double Barrel" (#1 in 1970) and then the "heavy monster sound" of its follow-up, "Monkey Spanner" (#7 in 1971). Vocal records over similarly fast rhythms – sometimes with strings added in London – made the UK charts, as well: Desmond Dekker's "Israelites" (#1 in 1969) and "It Mek" (#7 in 1969); **Max Romeo**'s rude "Wet Dream" (#10 in 1969); **Jimmy Cliff**'s "Wonderful World, Wonderful People" (#6 in 1969), "Vietnam" (#46 in 1970) and "Wide World" (#8 in 1970); the **Pioneers**' continuation of the Jamaican racehorse saga, "Long Shot (Kick De Bucket)" (#21 in 1969); **Bob & Marcia**'s version of Nina Simone's "Young, Gifted and Black" (#5 in 1970) and "Pied Piper" (#11 in 1971); the **Melodians**' "Sweet Sensation" (#41 in January 1970); and **Nicky Thomas**'s "Love Of the Common People" (#9 in July 1970).

The decline in skinhead interest in new reggae came at the start of the new decade, when Rastafarianism became the dominant force in Jamaican music. As the "heavy monster sound" gave way to what seemed like hippy attributes – long hair, dope, calls for "peace and love" – the skinheads stopped buying, and the chart entries dried up.

⊙ **Clement 'Coxsone' Dodd: Musical Fever 1967–1968** (Trojan, UK).

The line of continuity between rocksteady and early reggae is made obvious in this double CD set. Brought together are the *Rocksteady Coxsone Style* album (see p.72) and a collection of sixteen singles. The only real hits are Jackie Mittoo's "Ram Jam" (a version of the Heptones' "Fattie Fattie") and Slim Smith's beautiful interpretation of Larry Williams & Johnny 'Guitar' Watson's "Mercy, Mercy, Mercy"; but there are several effective cuts of familiar rhythms, among them Ed Nagle's "Good Girl" variation of "The Lecture", Jackie Mittoo's treatment of the Jamaicans' "Ba Ba Boom", and Bob Andy & Tyrone Evans' original cut of "I Don't Mind" (more familiar through the Bassies' version).

● **Tribute To Peckings** (Studio One, UK).

The late Leroy George Price (aka Peckings) was Coxsone's main representative in the UK, and someone who contributed enormously to the reggae scene – many London followers of Studio One used to visit his Askew Road shop to hear his lessons in musical history. He died in 1994, and this is his sons' memorial to him. Every track will delight any Studio One fan, but of particular note are the first cut of the Heptones' "Ting A Ling" (over a different rhythm from the more familiar one), Freddie McGregor's "Wise Words" (adapted from Cat Stevens' "Wide World") and a serious instrumental apiece from Cedric Brooks, Reuben Alexander, Roland Alphonso and Don D. Junior. Timeless music that transcends fashion or categorization.

● **Tuffest!** (Studio One, UK).

An appropriate title for a wonderful selection of rare instrumentals that have never appeared on album before. The tracks, mostly from the early 1970s, are some of the most serious that Dodd ever recorded and, for the most part, very much ahead of their time – collectors have long sought gems like Big Willie's "College Rock", Bobby Kalphat's "Ans-A-Wa-Wa" and Karl Bryan & Count Ossie's "Black Up".

⊙ **Soul Defenders At Studio One** (Heartbeat, US).

Though not the most celebrated of the Studio One session bands, the Soul Defenders possessed a distinctive and effective sound, as demonstrated by this superb collection. The two best-known hits with which their punchy and very tight approach is associated must be Freddie McKay's "Picture On the Wall" and "High School Dance", though the Selected Few's "Selection Train" and several scorching instrumentals delight just as much. An object lesson on how to present historically important records, bringing together both acknowledged classics and more obscure gems, with a profusely illustrated booklet. (How many reggae fans will have seen a photo of the singer Clifton Gibbs before?)

Meanwhile, back at Bond Street...

While Dodd, with the help of some of the best session musicians in Jamaica, seemed to shift to the new style of rhythm with a minimum of difficulty, his old rival **Duke Reid** – whose productions had epitomized rocksteady in a way no other producers did – found it less easy to come to terms with the changes. Using a line-up generally led by pianist **Gladstone 'Gladdy' Anderson** and often known as Gladdy's All Stars (this band also worked with Leslie Kong and Harry Mudie), Duke produced discs characterized by a sound that was more refined than the hard-edged Studio One style of the day. But, though the hits on Treasure Isle or Dutchess were less frequent in the new decade, several of them maintained his standards of old – **Joya Landis**'s "Moonlight Lover", anything by former Paragon **John Holt** (in particular the much-versioned "Ali Baba"), a couple of tunes by the **Ethiopians**, **Cynthia Richards**' best-selling disc, "Aily I", and **Hopeton Lewis**'s 1970 Festival Song winner, "Boom Shacka Lacka". Lewis performed a role similar to that of Larry Marshall up at Studio One: he coached singers, contributed vocal arrangements and sang backing vocals on many Treasure Isle recordings in rocksteady and early reggae styles. As he was under contract to Federal he did this work uncredited until "Boom Shacka Lacka" returned him to the limelight.

ADRIAN BOOT

Hopeton Lewis: Taking It Easy

But it was significant that the Trojan's real resurgence only came in 1970, when he initiated the deejay craze with, first, **U-Roy** 'toasting' Treasure Isle's vintage rocksteady hits, and then his fellow chatters **Dennis Alcapone** and **Lizzy** (for more on deejays, see p.113). It would be late 1973 before Duke hit again – with B.B. Seaton in charge of the studio, Reid then scored with **Claudette Miller**'s plangent "Tonight Is the Night", **Justin Hinds**' extraordinarily beautiful

"Sinners Where You Gonna Hide", and **Pat Kelly**'s successful version of MOR king John Denver's "Sunshine". This handful of inspired records was to be the Duke's parting shot: he died from cancer in 1974.

JOHN HOLT

● Like A Bolt (Treasure Isle, JA).

A collection of the solo material that Holt recorded at Treasure Isle immediately after splitting from the Paragons. The lyrically playful "Ali Baba" has the strongest rhythm cut at Bond Street in the post rocksteady years, and it is little wonder that it has been a favourite for other producers to revive – Doctor Alimantado's "I Shot the Barber" being the most famous 'version'. The rest of the material is more romantically conventional, but confirmed that Holt's assured tenor could easily stand on its own. The sound quality isn't great, but if you're used to Jamaican vinyl the music will nevertheless triumph.

VARIOUS ARTISTS

● Greater Jamaica – Moon Walk Reggae (Treasure Isle, JA).

There might be a glut of Treasure Isle rocksteady reissues around at present, but that label's contribution to early reggae remains seriously under-represented. The re-release of this collection of hits and near misses would go some way to rectifying that. The one track that makes this reasonably scarce album worth hunting for is the very original "Lock Jaw" (actually a Lee Perry production). Not as eccentric, perhaps, but nonetheless worth hearing are keyboard variations on the Techniques' "My Girl", Joya Landis's "Moonlight Lover" and the Paragons' "Only A Smile" (the first from Glen Adams, the others from Winston Wright), as well as outstanding vocals from John Holt, Justin Hinds and the Gladiators.

...and on Orange Street

Prince Buster continued producing records as well, if not in quite as prolific a manner as before. His belief in Islam might have made him – like Duke Reid – unsympathetic to the Rastafarianism of many of the up-and-coming performers, or perhaps one of Jamaican music's great innovators simply become bored with making new music. When he did apply himself to the task, however, the results were the equal of most of the competition or, for that matter, his own illustrious past. Though Buster's name is synonymous with the 1960s, no-one interested in Jamaican music of the next decade should ignore minor classics like **John Holt**'s "Rain From the Skies", "For Your Love" and "Get Ready", **Dennis Brown**'s "One Day Soon" and "If I Had the World", the **Heptones**' "Our Day Will Come" and "God Bless the Children", or **Alton Ellis**'s "Since I Fell For You".

And, as if to show he was not simply a traditionalist, Buster was also successful with the newly fashionable deejay version – recording half a dozen of the most inspired performances from **Dennis Alcapone**, including "Dub Machine" ("For Your Love"), "Giant" (over an original rhythm), "Kings & Castles" (John Holt's "I'm Not A King"), "Let It Roll" (Max Romeo's "Words, Sound & Power") and "Sons Of Zion" (Buster's own "My Happiness"). When the deejay style changed, he produced **Big Youth**'s "Chi Chi Run" (a cut of "Rain From the Skies") and "Leave Your Skeng" ("Get Ready"). Other records that confirm he could have played a much greater part in the dread half of the 1970s had he been more inclined to do so include a version of Augustus Pablo's "Java" (credited to a "Senor Pablo", who was in fact **Pablove Black**) and his own "Police Trim Rasta Hair", as well as one of the superior dub albums of the period.

BIG YOUTH/VARIOUS ARTISTS

● Chi Chi Run (Fab, UK).

Manley Augustus Buchanan's first album – or, rather, third of an album, as eight tracks are credited to others. Greater things were to come, but he had the right delivery and could clearly ride a rhythm (some of Buster's best of the period, as it happens). The shortfall in Big Youth tracks is made up with excellent vocals from Dennis Brown, Alton Ellis and John Holt, one track from a disciple, Little Youth, and instrumentals from Buster's All Stars.

VARIOUS ARTISTS

● Jamaica's Greatest (Melodisc, UK).

Prince Buster is so associated with ska – and, to a lesser extent, rocksteady – that his productions from the early 1970s have been ridiculously underrated by most writers on reggae. It was not his most prolific period, but – as this collection makes clear – he was still responsible for some outstanding records. The accent is on well-crafted love ballads over crisp rhythms, performed by some of the music's all-time great singers: Dennis Brown, the Heptones, John Holt and Alton Ellis. Try Alton Ellis's "Good, Good Loving", which matches any of the singer's Treasure Isle or Studio One classics, or the Heptones' sublime version of Ruby & the Romantics' "Our Day Will Come".

Promotions to the premier league

In the years of early reggae the new producers who made the strongest and most consistent impact in Jamaica – as well as among the island's increasingly important diaspora – included several who had already started to establish themselves. **Lee Perry**, for example, had already produced records for Coxsone and Joe Gibbs (see pp.72–73); **Bunny Lee** had learned his trade as a plugger for Duke Reid and Leslie Kong before working with Ken Lack's Caltone label and setting up his own label (see p.73); **Clancy Eccles** had been a singer, recording for Coxsone, Lindon Pottinger and the little-known Mike Shadadd; and **Derrick Harriott** had enjoyed a singing career that went back to the late 1950s, and had run his own Crystal label from 1962. To this tally of reggae's new big hitters should be added **Lloyd Daley**, who had launched his Matador imprint in the rocksteady era, and **Joe Gibbs, J.J. Johnson** and **Sonia Pottinger**, all of whom had made some fine rocksteady discs. Both **Leslie Kong** and **Harry Mudie** had produced records back in the days of Jamaican r&b; though the latter's career had been put on hold for a decade, the early reggae era saw both of them scale new heights of commercial and artistic success.

Joe Gibbs

Joe Gibbs (or Joel Gibson, as he was known then) could not play an instrument but he knew what he was about. He picked only the best musicians to work in his studio in the newly built Kingston suburb of Duhaney Park, and selected some very talented men to engineer the recordings he financed and distributed from his shop at 32 Beeston Street. The musicians included **Carl Bryan** (alto saxophone), **Tommy McCook** (tenor saxophone), **Jackie Jackson** (bass) and **Lynn Taitt** (guitar), while for production duties he continued to employ **Lee 'Scratch' Perry** at first, and then, from mid-1968, the equally mould-breaking **Winston 'Niney' Holness** (see p.120). The studio engineer **Errol Thompson**, who contributed to the success of recordings made at Randy's Studio 17, stepped in after Niney's departure, and was eventually to become half of the Mighty Two to whom all productions on the Joe Gibbs group of labels came to be credited – as well as having the Errol T imprint named after him in the mid-1970s. But before the phenomenal success enjoyed by Gibbs and Thompson in the last half of the decade, the creative input of both Scratch and Niney was well in evidence on numerous tough and progressive records that appeared on the Jogib, Amalgamated, Pressure Beat and Shock labels.

These included adventurous instrumentals like "Hi Jacked", "Mad Rooster" and – inspired by the star of Sergio Corbucci's Django Westerns – "Franco Nero", featuring the legendary Count Machuki. But there were also excellent vocals by harmony groups such as the **Immortals**, the **Versatiles** (fronted by the phenomenal **Junior Byles**), the **Slickers**, the **Young Souls**, the **Overtakers** and, most consistently, the very popular **Pioneers** (including the first of their two hits about the fabled Jamaican racehorse, Long Shot). After they left Studio One in 1971, the **Heptones** freelanced in the usual Jamaican manner, and made some of their best records for Joe Gibbs, most notably the melodic but pungent "Hypocrites". Gibbs at this stage had a particular talent for vocal groups, but also worked successfully with established and new solo stars, including **Delroy Wilson**, **Nicky Thomas** (who gave Gibbs his first UK pop hit with "Love Of the Common People"), **Judy Mowatt**, **Ken Parker** and the feistiest of the Wailers, **Peter Tosh**, catching him on some of his first and hardest-hitting solo discs. The vocalist who was to be his major star for most of the decade, however, was the still very youthful **Dennis Brown**, who scored a massive local hit for him in 1972 with the original version of "Money In My Pocket" (he was to re-record it for Gibbs seven years later and have an international smash). The deejay versions he released should not be forgotten, either, and included gems from Dennis Alcapone, (Sir) Lord Comic, Winston Scotland, Prince Williams, Caly Gibbs, Count Sticky, King Smiley, Lizzy, Little Johnny Jones and Cat Campbell.

DENNIS BROWN

The Best Of Dennis Brown (Joe Gibbs, JA).

E Not a collection of hits as might be expected, but simply his fourth album, and first for Joe Gibbs, with whom he was to have a very long and rewarding relationship. A non-original – Al Wilson's soul hit, "Poor Side Of Town" – stands out, and the influence of US producer Willie Mitchell is all over the rhythm employed for the Niney-produced "Westbound Train". Arguably still his most accomplished set – and one to be checked by all fans of the first African dub album, several of the rhythm tracks of which originally appeared here.

THE HEPTONES & VARIOUS ARTISTS

The Heptones & Their Friends Volumes 1 & 2 (Trojan, UK).

By adding hits from other artists, Joe Gibbs was able to stretch the Heptones' output for him to two LPs, and now Trojan have placed them together on one CD. In case anyone feels that presence of the 'friends' is a bit of a cheat, it should be enough to say that they include Judy Mowatt (under the nom de disque of Julianne), Nicky Thomas and Peter Tosh. Indeed, there is a strong argument for Mowatt's "The Gardener" being the most exceptional track here – though the

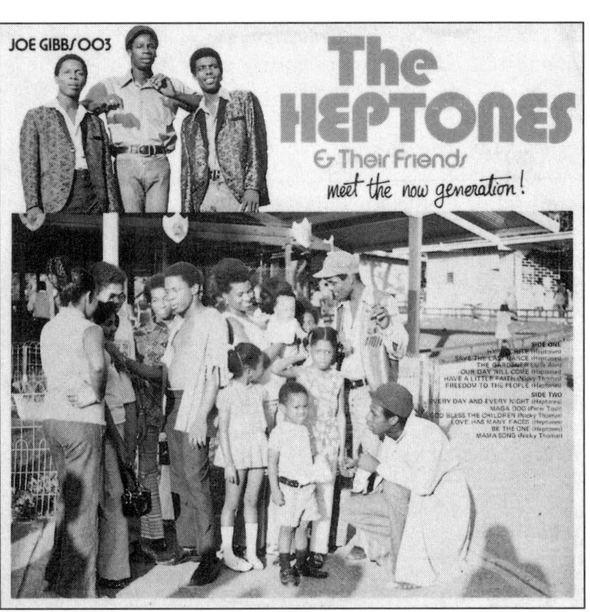

Heptones' own "Hypocrite" (once covered by UK pub-rock band, Brinsley Schwartz), Tosh's "Maga Dog" and "Them A Fe Get Beaten", and Thomas's "Have A Little Faith" are all serious contenders.

THE PIONEERS

Greetings From the Pioneers (Amalgamated, UK).

Because they enjoyed considerable UK pop success (and their later releases were admittedly lightweight), the Pioneers tend to be unfairly overlooked these days. Nevertheless, at their peak they were an excellent vocal harmony trio, and both their Joe Gibbs and Beverley's material is well worth investigating. This set from the former producer includes their first major local hit, "Give Me A Little Loving", as well as one of their superb tales of the track, "Jackpot". Like all their decent sets, this was deleted aeons ago.

VARIOUS ARTISTS – JOE GIBBS PRODUCTIONS

Rocksteadyin' To Reggae – Early Years Volumes 1, 2 & 3 (Rocky One, JA).

For those wanting to dig deep into the seminal music that appeared on Joe Gibbs' labels in the late 1960s/early 1970s, the man's son has put together three CDs' worth. With sixteen tracks on each, there are plenty of gems – and not just the obvious ones. For instance, Dennis Brown's original cut of "Money In

My Pocket" is followed with Big Youth's commentary, "Ah So We Stay". And then there are killers of the order of the Versatiles' "Wareika Hill", Stranger & Gladdy's "Seeing Is Knowing" and "Just Like A River", and Hugh Malcolm's "Good Time Rock". The only grouse is the lack of informative sleeve notes.

◑ **The Reggae Train 1968–1971** (Trojan, UK).
An eighteen-track compilation that provides a strong case for Joe Gibbs's most inventive period being the immediate post-rocksteady years (even if all the tracks were produced by either Scratch or Niney). Perry's own "The Upsetter" remains the best of his many revenge tunes; more obscure but just as worth hearing is Gibbs himself having a go at Scratch with "People Grudgeful". Away from ex-colleagues' reproaches to each other, further highlights include glorious vocal harmonies from the Versatiles, the Slickers, the Young Souls and the Reggae Boys (who were probably the Pioneers) – as well as Peter Tosh showing his militancy with "Arise Blackman".

Derrick Harriott

At the begining of the reggae phase, **Derrick Harriott**, a former member of the Jiving Juniors, was recording his superb session band, the **Dynamites**, on a series of tough instrumentals, many featuring the ubiquitous Hammond organ of Winston Wright, and some the percussionists Bongo Herman and Bongo Les. Harriott also had the same set of musicians provide the backing for vocals from artists such as the **Kingstonians**, **Dennis Brown**, the **Ethiopians**, **Junior Murvin** (or Junior Soul as he was then known), the **Chosen Few** and **Rudy Mills**. In addition, the former lead singer with the Federals, David Scott, was – as **Scotty** – cutting wonderfully original deejay cuts to many of the vocal hits that had appeared on Harriott's Crystal, Move & Groove and Derrick's labels, including Keith & Tex's revival of the Spanishtonians ska hit "Stop That Train" and Harriott's own anthemic "Solomon". Harriott's own performances were saturated with US soul influnces, a direction he had taken since establishing himself as one of the first singers to control his own productions and career. His beautiful falsetto, similar to that of Temptation Eddie Kendricks, was strong and pure, and ideally suited to covering soft soul hits from Detroit, Chicago or Philadelphia. This lack of original songs has led to his being underrated in certain circles, although it was precisely through his use of such material that Harriott anticipated the lovers rock form that successfully developed in the UK from 1974 onwards.

DENNIS BROWN

● **Super Reggae & Soul Hits** (Crystal, JA; Trojan, UK).
Derrick Harriott produced Dennis Brown's third album a couple of years after the young singer's Studio One debut and captured the same freshness – and wonderful interpretative powers. It includes more fine originals from the teenage singer – "Concentration", "He Can't Spell" and "Changing Times" are outstanding – but his versions of foreign hits – the Rays' "Silhouettes" and, perhaps more surprisingly, Glen Campbell's "Wichita Lineman" – are at least as successful.

Teen sensation Dennis Brown

DERRICK HARRIOTT & THE CRYSTALITES

⊙ **For A Fistful Of Dollars** (Jamaican Gold, Holland).
The Crystalites' classic 1970 *Undertaker* album, with the addition of another four tracks. Several tracks employ rhythms from well-known Harriott-produced vocal hits, including his own "Solomon" ("The Undertaker"), and even a fast reggae version of the Beatles' "Lady Madonna" fits in. With both Winston Wright and Ike Bennett featured extensively, no Hammond fan can afford to miss this.

THE KINGSTONIANS

◑ **Sufferer** (Attack, UK).

Jackie Bernard's group remain under-represented on CD, and there is a particular need for their Sir JJ singles to be collected and packaged in the way they deserve. Until that time, this Harriott-produced set from 1970 is still available, and at least includes their two major hits for that producer – the title track and "Singer Man" – as well as the lesser-known but marvellous "Hold Down".

VARIOUS ARTISTS – DERRICK HARRIOTT PRODUCTIONS

⦾ **From Chariot's Vault Volume 2: 16 Reggae Hits** (Jamaican Gold, Holland).

Sixteen crisp Derrick Harriott productions, covering the period 1969–73, with the emphasis on quality vocals. The best-known tracks are Glen Brown's chant-like "Love I", Augustus Pablo's "Bells Of Death" and "Bedroom Mazurka", and I-Roy's seriously sought-after "Melinda". But the set's main strength lies in its avoidance of the obvious to confirm that many excellent reggae 45s are not even local hits. Among the wonderful obscurities are a young Junior Murvin (as Junior Soul) with "The Hustler", Noel Brown's "Phoenix" (yes, the Jimmy Webb tearjerker), the Kingstonians' "Right From Wrong", Bongo Herman & Bingy Bunny's instrumental cut of Rudy Mills's "Long Story", and Denzil Laing's "Medicine Stick".

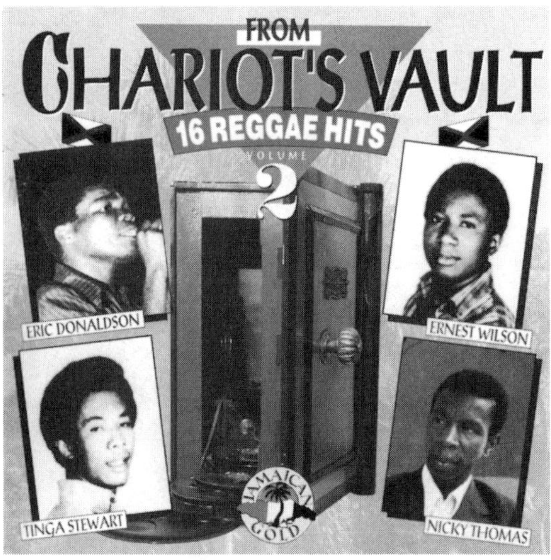

● **Blockbuster Reggae Instrumentals** (Crystal, JA).

This repeats a couple of tracks from the *Fistful Of Dollars* album, but adds plenty of further instrumentals of note, such as "Bells Of Death" from Augustus Pablo, the much-sought-after melodica versions of Harriott's "The Loser".

Bunny Lee

Meanwhile the unstoppable **Bunny 'Striker' Lee** continued to produce **Slim Smith** until the troubled singer's untimely demise in 1973, and also had major local hits throughout the period with **Pat Kelly, John Holt, Delroy Wilson, Eric Donaldson, Cornell Campbell** and **Derrick Morgan**. His first big reggae hit, however, was **Lester Sterling & Stranger Cole**'s unforgettable and much-versioned "Bangarang", an adaptation of a UK jazz tune named "Bongo Chant" by Kenny Graham's Afro-Cubists. Lee played a crucial role in establishing major UK outlets for reggae: his productions formed the backbone of the labels run by the Palmer brothers as well as a significant part of the early Trojan catalogue, both created to take over the market position previously occupied by Island Records in the years immediately prior to 1968. He first visited the UK with his brother Don 'Tony' Lee in 1967, staying in the East End of London and making many contacts who would prove useful in later years.

Lee's business sense, as well as his musical acuity, ensured he was to remain a major player throughout the decade. He produced so vast an amount of music between 1969 and 1975, particularly from 1973 onwards, that he has been often taken for granted and hence undervalued. But the ground-breaking hits from 1969 to 1973 speak for themselves: in 1969, Slim Smith's "Everybody Needs Love"; in 1970 Pat Kelly's "How Long"; in 1971 Eric Donaldson's Festival winner "Cherry Oh Baby" and Delroy Wilson's election-winning "Better Must Come". With "Better Must Come", Lee changed the sound again, and in early 1972 John Holt's cover of Shep & the Limelites "Stick By Me" – which also rode the slow, tough rhythm called the 'John Crow' – proved perfect for the 'skank' moves then in favour in the dancehalls. Although it carried love lyrics, "Better Must Come", heralded a new era of 'dread', tension-filled rhythms that would underpin the more militant stance of mid-Seventies 'roots' music; the bass and drum team of Aston 'Family Man' Barrett and his brother Carlton, who played the dynamic, stop-and-go rhythms on these two records, would also propel this music onto the world stage with Bob Marley and the Wailers.

CORNELL CAMPBELL

● **Cornell Campbell** (Trojan, UK).

The former Eternal was to reach the peak of his solo popularity with the 'flying cymbals' sound of the mid-1970s, and his variations on the Gorgon and Greenwich Farm themes. It is necessary, however, to turn to 1973 for his best album. Produced by Bunny Lee, it was only ever released in the UK, and with the naffest sleeve design imaginable. But nothing can detract from the magic of hits like "My Confession" and "Didn't I" (here titled "Don't I Always"), or his solo cut of "Queen Of the Minstrels", and a remarkable version of Gregory Isaacs' "My Only Lover".

ERIC DONALDSON

⊙ **Love Of the Common People** (Jamaican Gold, Holland).

A definitive collection of his work for Dynamic and Bunny Lee, complete with the type of informative booklet that is expected from Jamaican Gold. Though Donaldson was the most consistent winner of the Jamaican Festival Song Competition, the local popularity of his distinctive falsetto never extended to the crossover audience that reggae found in the 1970s – he was obviously not considered 'rootsy' enough. This set, including virtually all of his major Jamaican hits (including the title track, the much-revived/covered "Cherry Oh Baby" and "Blue Boots"), deserves to rectify that.

DERRICK MORGAN

● **Seven Letters** (Trojan, UK).

A 1969 album that draws from Bunny Lee, Lynford Anderson and Leslie Kong productions. The title track is a fast reggae version of Ben E. King's soul hit, which, because of the tempo, sounds less than soulful; but other tracks – "Hold You Jack" (the original of Max Romeo's "Wet Dream" rhythm), his second cut of "Fat Man", "Blazing Fire", "Conquering Ruler" (the original of Cornell Campbell's "Gorgon") – are bona fide classics. The dated cover's forlorn but sexy-looking postwoman makes this an easy one to spot in the secondhand racks.

Sonia Pottinger

Sonia Pottinger, Jamaica's only female record producer until the 1980s, benefitted from the dissatisfaction that various singers felt with the established producers: the **Melodians** came to her after their sojourn with Duke Reid; similarly, **Ken Boothe**, the **Heptones**, **Errol Dunkley** and **Delroy Wilson** all recorded for her after their days at Studio One. Bunny Lee also released music through her auspices, including songs such as "The Time Has Come" by **Slim Smith**. Like most producers of the time, Mrs Pottinger also released successful instrumentals, hers being often credited to the **Hippy Boys**, who typified the new breed of session musicians playing in a deadlier style that anticipated roots reggae. Based in Greenwich Farm, they came into the business via their lead singer, a young **Max Romeo**. "So I formed a band called the Hippy Boys," Romeo later recalled. "That was the great Family Man and his brother Carlton Barrett – I brought them into the business – and Alva Lewis and Glen Adams. We did our first record, "Dr No Go", but after a while went our separate ways. It was hard to keep people together then, because there was no money in the business." Not unsurprisingly, Mrs Pottinger enjoyed a special relationship with female singers, dating from her rocksteady hits with **Millicent 'Patsy' Todd**, continuing into the 1970s with singers such as **Judy Mowatt**, **Marcia Griffiths** and **Carlene Davis**.

ERROL DUNKLEY

◑ **Presenting Errol Dunkley [Darling Ooh!]** (Gay Feet, JA; Attack, UK).

The 1972 debut album of another unsung Jamaican vocal hero, and still his most consistent. Includes the original recording of "A Little Way Different", which he successfully recut at the end of the decade and which remains the most memorable of his own compositions. Other highlights are interpretations of "Created By the Father" and "Baby I Love You", both of which bear comparison with anyone's. One of the most expressive voices in Jamaican music, here given musical settings that could not be more fitting – which was not always the case in his long career.

Leslie Kong

Active since the early 1960s, **Leslie Kong** reached his peak with early reggae. He was one of several Chinese Jamaicans to make a serious contribution to the music's development, and one of the first producers to make inroads into the international pop market. Operating from an ice-cream parlour/restaurant and record shop that he and his brothers owned at 135a Orange Street, Kong was always the consummate professional in his approach to recording, insisting on a 'clean' sound and bouncy commercial rhythms – which is perhaps why he has tended to be underrated by self-conscious 'roots' fans, who too often confuse shoddy production values with authenticity.

His most consistent hitmakers in Jamaica were the **Maytals**. The exuberant trio missed the rocksteady era because of a two-year jail sentence for ganja possession given to their leader, **Toots Hibbert**, but they made a triumphant return with their debut for Kong. "54-46 That's My Number" (the title referred to Toots's prison number) was one of the biggest hits of their career, and they went on to cut an epoch-defining run of records for Kong's Beverley's label. Their "Monkey Man" even reached the lower regions of the UK pop charts, as did other Kong-produced discs by Jimmy Cliff, the **Melodians**, the **Pioneers** and **Desmond Dekker**. Indeed, Dekker reached the #9 position in the US with "Israelites", and was the first Jamaican-recorded song to break into the US chart. The **Melodians**' "Sweet Sensation" charted in the UK in January 1970; the same trio's classic anthem "Rivers Of Babylon", with a beautifully understated accompaniment featuring guitarist **Ernest Ranglin** and percussionist **Larry McDonald**, narrowly failed to repeat the feat, but was a massive underground hit. Curiously, the album's worth of material Kong recorded in 1969 with the Wailers did not sell spectacularly at the time and is disappointing, especially when compared with the material the group had released on their own Wail 'N' Soul M imprint immediately before. Kong's premature death from a heart attack in 1971, when only in his late thirties, was a serious blow to reggae's trajectory towards international recognition in the period before the Wailers signed to Island.

THE MAYTALS

◉ **Bla Bla Bla** (Esoldun, France).

This set covers the same period, but has better sound quality and manages to include worth-

DELROY WILSON: THE COOL OPERATOR

An acclaimed star since his teenage years, the soulful Delroy Wilson reached even greater heights of popularity in the reggae era, beginning with massive hits such as "Better Must Come", which became an electoral anthem for the PNP in 1972. Numerous sides for Bunny Lee followed, mostly of a very high quality, including "Cool Operator", "Here Comes the Heartaches", "Mash Up Illiteracy" and "Trying To Wreck My Life". Just as impressive were outstanding recordings from the first half of the decade for, among others, Joe Gibbs, Keith Hudson, Gussie Clarke, A. Folder, Harry J. and Niney. Possibly the high point of his career, commercially and artistically, came in 1976 with his masterful interpretation of Bob Marley's "I'm Still Waiting" for Lloyd Charmers.

Wilson promo shot for "I'm Still Waiting"

"I used to sing in concerts at Boys Town School. I used to be the number one singer in my class. I used to listen to some foreign singers and sing their songs. I used to listen to, like, Marvin Gaye and Lou Rawls, and the Temptations and other Motown singers. My recording I started when I about twelve. We went to Coxsone, me and another singer. He came to my mum and asked if he could take me to Coxsone, and we went down and started singing. But Coxsone didn't like his singing. Coxsone took me to one side and gave me five shilling, and say I must come back another day.

while tracks not in the Attack collection, such as "Pressure Drop", "Bla Bla Bla" and the skinhead favourite, "Monkey Man".

◑ **Do the Reggae: 1966–1970** (Attack, UK).

This album begins with "Bam Bam" (for Byron Lee, and the trio's last record before their leader's incarceration), and then jumps to some of their best Kong-produced material, including "54-46 That's My Number", "Struggle" (another scorcher expressing Toot's unbowed defiance), "Do the Reggay" and "Night & Day". Sound quality is not all it could be on some tracks (the whole album was dubbed from 45s), but the music – unrestrained, soulful Baptist vocals over Stax-tight, chugging rhythms – is beyond criticism.

THE PIONEERS

● **Long Shot** (Trojan, UK).

One of the best fast reggae albums, with its fair share of hits, plus some album tracks of a similar standard. This was recorded for Leslie Kong before Rastafarianism became fashionable, but the trio's concerns with everyday Jamaican life made their records just as much 'reality' ones. The title track is, in fact, "Long Shot (Kick De Bucket)", not the Joe Gibbs hit named after the legendary racehorse, and "Poor Ramases" is another tale of an unfortunate nag, while the massive Jamaican hit "Samfi Man" is about a confidence trickster. "Trouble Dey A Bush", which employs one of Leslie Kong's most memorable rhythms, deserves to be as famous as their UK hit.

VARIOUS ARTISTS – LESLIE KONG PRODUCTIONS

● **The King Kong Compilation** (Island, UK).

● **The Best of Beverley's** (Trojan, UK).

Leslie Kong's contribution to ska, rocksteady and reggae from 1968 to his death in 1971 is incalculable, and a multi-CD set of his most important recordings

So Coxsone say I must come to Federal. But I was little so they put me on a Red Stripe beer box, and I sing my first song. And after that another song, and then it became a hit – "Spit In the Sky". In days like that you have a sound war. It was like Prince Buster against Coxsone against Duke Reid against King Edwards. So both of them wanted to get rid of Prince Buster. So I came along, and it seems was like I was the missile that could get rid of Prince Buster. I made a whole heap of records with lyrics aimed at Prince Buster: "Spit In the Sky", "Joe Liges". But Buster was like a superpower: he stood his ground.

I had hit after hit. They used to call me "The Boy Wonder". In those days it was ska, but then we cross over to a thing called rocksteady. Then I came with other songs – like "Dancing Mood" now becomes one of my biggest hits. And I've got other songs like "Ungrateful Baby", "Good All Over", "How Can I Love Someone". But I feel I wasn't getting enough, so eventually I leave Coxsone. And me and another singer called Stranger Cole start out own thing, our own label [W&C]. We go into the studio and make a song called "Once Upon A Time", and the other side was "I Want To Love You". Then we form another group, me, Ken Boothe, the Gaylads and the Melodians, named the Links, and we put out some records, but some of the guys get a little too crazy, so the Links get broke up. We then went to Beverley's, and then we split up again, and some of us went to Sonia Pottinger, and others stayed with Beverley's. I went to Mrs Pottinger, and had two hits – "I'm the One Who Loves You" and "Put Yourself In My Place".

Then we switch now to the rhythm reggae beat, and Bunny Lee enter the business and he really get himself in a way so you have to sing for him. I started singing for him. Everybody started to sing for him. I was there singing for him a long time, in and out. I went to London with him, and did some shows, with a sound called Coxsone, Lloydie Coxsone. He first let me know London. Then I went back to Jamaica and sang again for Bunny Lee. I made songs like "Better Must Come" for the politicians and the youth, and the PNP used it to help win the election. I wrote that song, "Better Must Come", when things were going on that were a little hard for me. And I get the idea, and so write the song. The election time was coming on, and Mr Manley and his party decide to use it. Then we, the singers, get together, like me, Ken Boothe, Clancy Eccles and other singers, to state that Mr Michael Manley should win this election. And we go with him all over Jamaica. And after that I made a song named "Cool Operator". I made enough hits for Bunny Lee. ”

is needed. These 1981 compilations, both of which concentrate on the early reggae years (though their selections are totally different), will do in the meantime. Contributions from the Melodians, the Wailers, Desmond Dekker, the Maytals and the Pioneers will be familiar to anyone with even a casual interest in Jamaican music, but just as worthwhile are gems from the Gaylads, Delroy Wilson, Tyrone Evans, the criminally underrated Bruce Ruffin, Ken Boothe and the organist Ansell Collins.

Lloyd 'Matador' Daley

Another producer who built upon his earlier achievements was former sound-system man, and noted builder of 'sound boxes', **Lloyd 'Matador' Daley**, who was responsible for distinguished records by such as the plaintive **Little Roy**, nearly all of whose records, beginning with "Bongo Nyah" in 1969, had Rastafarian/cultural themes. Just as impressive were acts who recorded far less frequently for the producer, including the **Uniques** (not the Slim Smith group), **Dennis Brown**, the **Wailing Souls**, the **Paragons**, **Audley Rollins** (both solo and with his group, the **Emotions**), the Gladiators, Alton Ellis, the Hamlins, John Holt and the Caribbeans. Daley also released top-quality instrumentals featuring such as organist **Neville Hinds** and trumpeter **Johnnie Moore**, and there were sterling deejay versions of his vocal hits from **Big Joe**, both **U-Roy** and his disciple **U-Roy Jnr** (aka Froggy), **Sir Lord Comic**, **Winston Blake** and **I-Roy**.

FEEL THE RHYTHM: CLANCY ECCLES

Clancy Eccles started as one of Clement Dodd's first singing stars, beginning with the beautiful "Freedom", a major Jamaican hit in 1961. By the late 1960s, however, he had set up his own Clandisc label, and was soon successfully producing not just himself, but such varied talents as Eric 'Monty' Morris, Cynthia Richards, Lord Creator and the early deejay sensation, King Stitt.

"I was born in 1940 in the parish of St Mary. By attending church, as a kid, music was always part of me. One of my uncles was a spiritual revivalist, who always did this heavy type of spiritual singing, and I got to love that. Earlier, in Ochos Rios, I met the Blues Busters, Higgs & Wilson, Buster Brown. At night we all used to jam. And by jamming, and listening to the r&b music from America, we started to develop our own thing. We used to copy and we used to create.

So, later on, I came back to Kingston and there was a talent show at the Royal Theatre. I entered the show, which I didn't win. Tony Gregory won that night. But it did a lot for me – because I was offered a recording contract by Coxsone. I hit the first time with him when I did "Freedom". The session was at Ken Khouri's studio, and it was November 1959. The musicians for the session was Aubrey Adams on piano, Ernest Ranglin on guitar, Cluett Johnson on bass, Roland Alphonso on tenor sax and Drumbago on drums, and Coxsone played percussion with his hands. Coxsone really didn't like that side. He wanted the B-side to be the hit, "I Live And I Love". But the crowd didn't want that side. They wanted "Freedom". And Count Machuki, as the dean of the dancehall then, fell in love with it. It was a year in which we was then thinking about repatriation to Africa. We wasn't thinking yet about independent Jamaica. The song took over. At first Machuki put that record on the sound. He started playing it at around 8.30, just the introduction, and he say: "Later will be greater when I turn you on." And around 12, he said to the crowd: "When I want it, I want it bad/If I don't get it, it makes me sad/When I do get it, it makes me frisky/Don't get me wrong, Daddy, I'm talking about my freedom." And he played that song about 21 times that night. The crowd came, roadblock and everything. And from there on, the Coxsone sound went very big.

I spent some time with Coxsone. But then no reward, and I had to move on. But

VARIOUS ARTISTS – LLOYD 'MATADOR' DALEY PRODUCTIONS

◉ **Lloyd Daley's Matador Productions, 1968–1972** (Heartbeat, US).

◉ **From Matador's Arena: Vol. One (1968–1969); Vol. Two (1969–1970); Vol. Three (1971–1979)** (Jamaican Gold, Holland).

Lloyd 'Matador' Daley was ignored by European and US record companies for a couple of decades, but in the 1990s Heartbeat and Jamaican Gold have released well-packaged and well-annotated sets, with the former concentrating on the Matador's biggest hits, and the latter a larger cross-section of his work. Those with a more casual interest in Daley should go for the Heartbeat set, but they'll be missing what is arguably the Matador's greatest production of them all – the Uniques' "Secretly" (on Volume One). Curiously, none of the four sets includes "Righteous Man", Little Roy's most sought-after tune (recorded with the Heptones and released under his real name, Earl Lowe). That grouse aside, all four CDs belong on any serious reggae collection, and superbly demonstrate how Jamaica's musical heritage should be presented.

Clancy Eccles

Singer-producer **Clancy Eccles**, who has been credited with deriving the name 'reggae' from 'streggae' (Kingston street slang for a kind of good-time girl), gained his biggest successes during the transition from rocksteady to reggae. His own vocal on the risqué "Fatty Fatty" was a skinhead favourite in the UK, as were the deejay tunes he produced by the distinctive **King Stitt**, and a whole series of atmospheric, organ-dominated instrumentals by his session band, the **Dynamites** (who became the Crystalites for

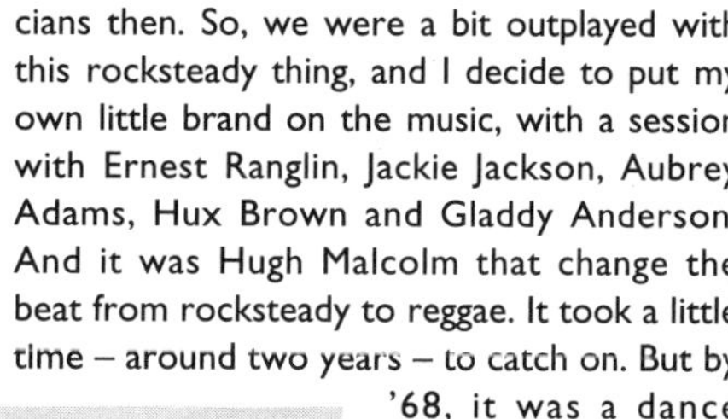

two years later, I went back to Coxsone and did "River Jordan". And I did a song with Jimmy James. People say who the first deejay, but Jimmy James – who was in England with the Vagabonds – was Jamaica's first rap artist.

After Coxsone, I went into oblivion for a while. But then I came back in 1967. I set up a production house, and did "Say What You're Saying" with Monty Morris, and I also did a song for Larry Marshall. I tried to move away from what was happening, because rocksteady was the major thing. Duke Reid gave me some free time in his studio. He say: 'Clancy, I know you got some sounds in your head. Go get it done.' And I went around there and I did songs like "Say What You're Saying". We try to change it from rocksteady, because that was here for quite a while. Remember, we came in pre-rocksteady, pre-ska, with Ken Richards and those musicians then. So, we were a bit outplayed with this rocksteady thing, and I decide to put my own little brand on the music, with a session with Ernest Ranglin, Jackie Jackson, Aubrey Adams, Hux Brown and Gladdy Anderson. And it was Hugh Malcolm that change the beat from rocksteady to reggae. It took a little time – around two years – to catch on. But by '68, it was a dance that eventually got a name, and that name was reggae. The Larry Marshall tune, "Natty Goat", came in, and I followed right after with "Feel the Rhythm". That was the beginning of reggae from that session. Thanks again to Ernest Ranglin, because he played a very important part in that session. It was a free session really, with brethren and brethren jamming, and Ernest came down and said: 'Aubrey, Clancy don't want no rocksteady thing. He want something new.' So Aubrey said: 'You count it.' And Ernest did. And it started there. ❞

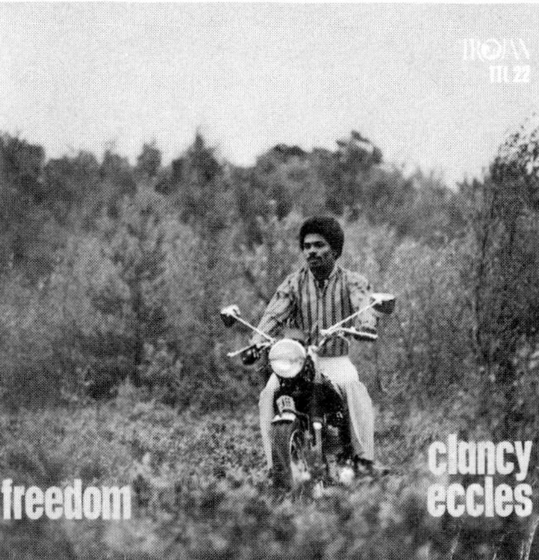

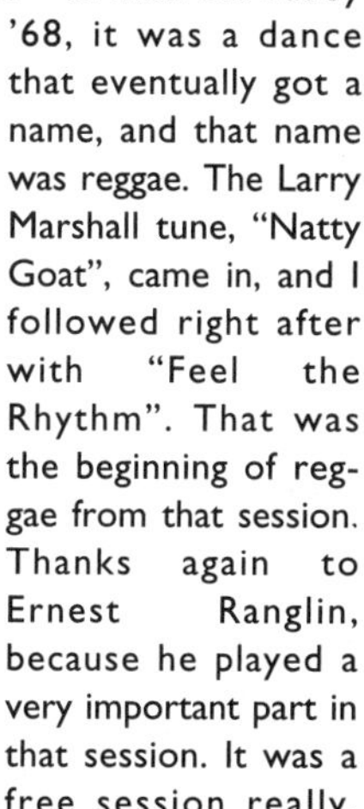

Derrick Harriott, and also played for Leslie Kong). Eccles' New Beat and Clandisc labels also issued classic records by **Alton Ellis, Lord Creator** (the wonderful "Kingston Town"), **Cynthia Richards, Monty Morris, Higgs & Wilson** and **Busty Brown**. Moreover, Clancy helped both **Lee Perry** and **Winston 'Niney' Holness** set up as producers – in late 1971, he lent Niney the money to press "Blood & Fire", the first hit on the Observer label, and a harbinger of the sort of socially conscious religious anger that was to dominate the second half of the decade. A lifelong socialist, Eccles became closely involved with the election campaign of PNP candidate Michael Manley, and although he made records into the Eighties, his concentration on politics eventually pushed music into the background.

THE DYNAMITES

⦿ **The Wild Bunch Are the Dynamites** (Jamaican Gold, Holland).

A retrospective compilation of the Dynamites' instrumentals for Clancy Eccles, including the best from *Fire Corner*. A set compiled with considerable taste and with the sort of packaging that gives the music the respect that it has always deserved.

● **Fire Corner** (Clandisc, JA; Trojan, UK).

Possibly the most interesting of the organ-dominated instrumental albums that appeared at the turn of the decade. Winston Wright, the man at the Hammond, particularly impresses on three tracks in the middle of the first side – "I Did It", "This Is the Night" and "One Way Ticket" – while horns are also employed effectively on "Eternally", "Sam-Fie" and "Skokiaan (Mr Midnight)". To further help maintain interest, there are two hits from the foundation deejay, King Stitt – "Vigorton 2" and "Fire Corner", as well as his even more wonderful "Soul Language", which was perhaps just too strange to be released as a single.

CLANCY ECCLES

⦿ **Joshua's Rod Of Correction** (Jamaican Gold, Holland).

Gathers tracks from the singer-producer on which he voices his support for Michael Manley's PNP in no uncertain terms. Includes both cuts of "Power For the People", "Rod Of Correction" and another thirteen expressions of the "democratic socialist" vision that so frightened the CIA, the IMF and international corporations wanting cheap bauxite.

VARIOUS ARTISTS – CLANCY ECCLES PRODUCTIONS

⦿ **Clancy Eccles Presents his Reggae Revue** (Heartbeat, US).

E At first glance this might seem to duplicate a couple of tracks from the selection below, but these are alternate takes of Larry Marshall's "Please Stay" and Eric Morris's "My Lonely Days". Then there are killers like Alton Ellis's "Feeling Inside" (aka "True Loving"), arguably the best record with which Eccles was ever associated, and more obscure tracks that deserve to be far better known, such as a previously unreleased 'sound clash' stormer from Eccles himself, "Don't Brag, Don't Boast". Add to those an early taste (circa 1972) of Beres Hammond's phenomenal talent. Wonderful stuff.

● **Fatty Fatty (1967–1970)** (Trojan, UK).

Clancy Eccles has yet to receive the credit that is his due. As demonstrated by this sixteen-track compilation, his productions were the equal of anyone's. Besides the title track from the man himself, there is his very first production (and hit), Monty Morris's "Say What You're Saying", its inventive deejay version, "CN Express", the glorious instrumental "Mr Midnight", one of Cynthia Richards' best vocals in "Foolish Fool", King Stitt with an early anthem to Jamaica's most popular natural resource, "Herbsman Shuffle", and the groundbreaking proto-dub version of it – the Dynamites' "Phantom".

J.J. Johnson

Yet another consistently successful producer of the time who deserves to be celebrated more widely is **J.J. Johnson**, one of the main jukebox suppliers on the island, who is best remembered for work with the **Ethiopians** (including the anthemic "Everything Crash"), **Carl Dawkins**, the **West Indians** and the **Kingstonians. Lloyd Young**'s "Soup" (Sir JJ) – an inspired early deejay version of the Jamaicans' rocksteady hit, "Things You Say You Love", also stands as among his most exciting records. More of a businessman than a music person, J.J. generally left the mechanics of production to his musicians, but he displayed a sure touch in deciding what to release. The series of performances recorded for him by the Ethiopians remain a high point in the history of Jamaican vocal groups.

THE ETHIOPIANS

◑ **The Original Reggae Hit Sound** (Trojan, UK).

E As near to a definitive Ethiopians compilation as it's possible to have on a single disc. The album begins with examples of their best-known ska and rocksteady hits, before moving into the early reggae era, which was palpably their most consistent period. Their work with J.J. Johnson is particularly well represented, with a dozen of their best tracks for this often overlooked producer, and then there are the duo's two biggest hits for Derrick Harriott, and a great late Treasure Isle production. Leonard Dillon, who was in effect the Ethiopians, remains one of the unsung heroes of Jamaican music, and this collection should have brought him to a far wider audience.

Harry A. Mudie

Undoubtedly the most refined early reggae productions came from the under-celebrated **Harry A. Mudie** (b. 1940, Spanish Town). He had recorded a handful of sides, including "Babylon Gone"/"First Gone" with the master Rasta drummer **Count Ossie** in the early 1960s, but only began producing on a regular basis almost a decade later, when two UK record companies – first Trojan, then R&B – began regularly releasing his records on labels they set up for that purpose. His rhythms – often recorded on the 'open' Sundays at Studio One – were distinguished for being as heavy as any, but also very melodic and well crafted. The most daring of his innovations was to add strings (recorded in London) to some records, an odd combination that he made work – the best examples being **John Holt**'s version of

JOSHUA AND HIS ROD OF CORRECTION

Most Jamaican singers and musicians avoid publicizing their political sympathies, which is understandable in view of the violence often accompanying general elections on the island. The major exception to this rule occurred in the early 1970s, when Michael Manley addressed his promise of justice and equality directly to the ghetto 'sufferers', with singer and producer Clancy Eccles organizing some of the best youth singers to show their support for the opposition party's version of 'democratic socialism'.

During the 1972 Jamaican general election, the charismatic PNP leader took on the persona of the biblical "Joshua" – complete with "rod of correction", the walking stick given to Manley by Haile Selassie during the former's visit to Ethiopia in 1970 – while his JLP opponent Hugh Shearer was identified with the Pharaoh. The nickname of 'Joshua' had been coined some eight years earlier when, as a trade unionist leading a demonstration of striking workers outside the Jamaican Broadcasting Company building, he had declared: "There are the walls of Jericho." For the 1972 election this image fitted easily into a PNP campaign that borrowed freely from the ghetto dwellers' way of seeing the world, catching the desire for radical social change already voiced in the 'rebel' lyrics of Junior Byles, Max Romeo, Niney and the Wailers.

Among the outstanding singles associated with Manley's victorious campaign were Delroy Wilson's "Better Must Come", the title of which became a PNP slogan, Junior Byles's "Joshua Desire" and "Pharaoh Hiding", Niney's "Hiding By the Riverside" and Max Romeo's "Let the Power Fall For I", another inspirational PNP slogan. In "Rod Of Correction" Clancy Eccles converted a song about the 1920s preacher Bedward ("Dip them Bedward dip them, dip them in the healing stream") into a celebration of the stick that became the dominant symbol of the campaign – "Lick dem, Joshua, lick dem, lick dem with the rod of correction". Clancy even placed a Manley campaign speech over the rhythm of his own "Power For the People", releasing it as a two-part 45 with the same title.

To many it must have seemed an almost revolutionary moment in modern Jamaican history, even if the social democratic PNP's slogan of "Power For the People" was somewhat less radical than "Power To the People". Whether the Manley governments of 1972–76 and 1976–80 were too ambitious or not radical enough remains a moot point. What is undeniable is that a widespread disillusionment set in among many of his ghetto supporters before his first term had run its course, and this too was reflected in the lyrics of some of the singers who had been associated with the 1972 campaign, including Junior Byles and Max Romeo. One little-known singer, Bill Gentles, even recorded "Take the Rod From Off Our Back" (Attack) over the rhythm for "Let the Power Fall For I", to suggest that Joshua had become the new Pharaoh.

American blues balladeer Ivory Joe Hunter's "It May Sound Silly", and the same singer's classic *Time Is the Master* album. As part of his concern with quality control, Mudie worked with only the most professional of vocalists, who, besides Holt, included **Dennis Walks**, the **Heptones**, **Winston Shand**, **Lloyd Jones**, the **Eternals** (with Cornell Campbell), **Joe White** and the **Ebony Sisters**. He also released successful instrumental versions of his major hits, variously featuring the cornet player **Jo Jo Bennett**, the vibist **Lennie Hibbert**, the pianist **Gladstone Anderson** (the leader of his excellent studio band) or percussionist **Bongo Herman**, as well as deejay cuts by **I-Roy** (including his debut disc, "Musical Pleasure"), **Big Joe** and **Count Sticky**.

GLADSTONE ANDERSON

It May Sound Silly (Moodisc, JA).

The combination of Gladdy Anderson's piano and strings may never have sounded 'ethnic' enough for the crossover audience that reggae attracted in the mid–late 1970s, but the formula repeatedly worked for Jamaicans, both on the island and abroad. This beautiful album was a reggae best seller in 1972, and has remained in demand ever since. Several of Harry Mudie's heaviest rhythms – Lloyd Jones's "Rome" among them – are the third part of the equation.

JO JO BENNETT

Groovy Joe (Moodisc, JA).

Harry Mudie's regular hornsman revives his own rocksteady hit, "The Lecture", to good effect (as "Lecture Me"), and does what is expected of him over some of the producer's best-known hits. Includes his popular 45, "Leaving Rome", which features some of the best use of strings on a reggae record, and a stunning cut of the Ebony Sisters' "Let Me Tell You Boy" (without strings).

JOHN HOLT

Time Is the Master (Moodisc, US).

A 1974 *tour de force* originally released in the UK by Creole. If any Jamaican voice was suited to string

accompaniments, it was John Holt's mellifluous tenor. The rhythms are crisp on this series of exceptional songs, including the title track (an enormous Jamaican hit), "It May Sound Silly" and Brook Benton's "Looking Back". Lovers rock before the term was coined.

VARIOUS ARTISTS – HARRY MUDIE PRODUCTIONS

Let Me Tell You Boy (Trojan, UK).

E Any single-disc compilation for a producer of Harry Mudie's stature will inevitably omit some favourite tracks; but there can be little complaint about the selection of vocals and instrumentals collected here. John Holt's "It May Sound Silly" should help broaden the mind of anyone who thinks that strings and reggae are incompatible, and major hits like Slim Smith's "Give Me Some More Loving", Winston Shands' "Time Is the Master" and Dennis Walk's much-versioned "Drifter" similarly combine outstanding material, strong rhythms and flawless performances. Some of the most unformulaic reggae ever.

Mudie's Mood (Moodisc, US).

A best-selling 1970 compilation that has been made available again. Most of the tracks overlap with the above set, but there is also Lloyd Jones's wonderfully understated "Rome" (the original of Jo Jo Bennett's "Leaving Rome"), plus the original cover for period charm.

New producers enter the arena

A substantial contribution to the restless innovation of early reggae was made by the large number of entirely new producers who arrived on the scene, eager to make their mark with a sound of their own. They came from a variety of backgrounds – some had been singers, while others had been involved in business activities outside music. Indeed, about all they had in common when they embarked on record production was a feeling that they had something fresh to offer. All those who found favour with Jamaican record buyers did so by forging a unique and easily identifiable sound of their own. These ranged from the solid, obviously commercial stylings of **Harry Johnson**, through the smooth romantic offerings of **Rupie Edwards** or **Lloyd Charmers**, to the minor-key experiments of **Herman Chin Loy** or **Clive Chin**. Similarly **Glen Brown**, **Keith Hudson**, **Alvin Ranglin**, **Winston Riley**, **Prince Tony Robinson** and **Phil Pratt** all forged individual styles in a period when it seemed that practically anything was possible in the studio.

Harry Johnson

Early in 1968, a former insurance salesman named **Harry Johnson** hired time at Clement Dodd's studio in Brentford Road to produce a group called the **Beltones** (formerly Bob & the Beltones, who had recorded "Dancing Time" and "Smile Like An Angel" for Dodd). The result was the group's biggest hit, "No More Heartaches", which Johnson used to launch his own successful Harry J label and which, with its fast and assertive rhythm, arguably launched the new phase of Jamaican music. More local hits followed, including **Lloyd Robinson**'s "Cuss Cuss" (also recorded at Studio One, and possessing Harry J's most enduring rhythm), and then came the producer's taste of international pop success with the instrumental, "Liquidator", credited to the **Harry J All Stars**, and **Bob & Marcia**'s "Young, Gifted and Black" and "Pied Piper".

VARIOUS ARTISTS – HARRY JOHNSON PRODUCTIONS

◑ **The Return Of the Liquidator: 30 Skinhead Classics 1968–1970** (Trojan, UK).

A double CD set that brings together the original *Liquidator* album of instrumentals and another eighteen Harry J-produced 45s from the same era, including two more cuts of his international hit, Tony Scott's vocal "What Am I To Do", and Val Bennett's tenor sax version, "Tons Of Gold" (aka "Return Of the Liquidator"). Other rhythms from the 1970 set that reappear on the second disc: "The Big Three" ("Marcia Griffiths' "Put A Little Love In Your Heart"), "Jay Moon Walk" (Dave Barker & Glen Brown's "Festive Spirit") and "Reach For the Sky " and "Elcong" (Bob Andy's "Peace Of Mind" and "Weep"). Karl Bryan's alto sax cut of Lloyd Robinson's "Cuss Cuss" is a further highlight, and then there are the Cables' "Equal Rights" and its deejay version, "Cambodia" by the Blake Boy (aka Winston Blake).

Herman Chin Loy, Clive Chin and Augustus Pablo's Far East sound

Harry Johnson was just one of many new producers establishing individual styles and making their presence felt locally and among Jamaican communities abroad. **Herman Chin Loy**, a cousin of Leslie Kong, was specializing in quirky, innovative instrumentals on his Aquarius and Scorpio imprints, including "Reggae In the Fields", "Invasion" and Inner Space". Several of these left-field productions, usually involving the Hippy Boys session band, were released in the UK on Junior Lincoln's progressive Ackee label, but not the record that was the most important of all, judged from any historical perspective. This was "Iggy Iggy", the 1969 debut of one Horace Swaby, who took on the house name that the producer used for many of his discs featuring a keyboards player – **Augustus Pablo**.

The young Mr Swaby's follow-up was another instrumental, and it was to gain a far greater reputation than its initial sales suggested – the first cut of "East Of the River Nile". It was a masterpiece of understatement, with Pablo alternating rudimentary but spooky solos on melodica and organ over a jagged rhythm reminiscent of the Temptations "Papa Was A Rolling Stone". The first example of what would soon come to be known as Pablo's "Far East sound", it was typified by the employment of minor chords which imparted a supposedly oriental feel to the music, and it soon spawned imitators such as Bobby Kalphat, Joe White, Glen Brown and the similarly named Pablo Black. This Eastern feel was often further emphasized by the titles, as in the case of the first record by Pablo which really struck a chord with Jamaican record buyers – "Java", produced by another Chinese-Jamaican, **Clive Chin**, a friend since schooldays. Working at the family-owned Randy's studio, Chin not only produced further exceptional instrumentals from the frail-looking melodica/clavinet player, but also recorded a fine series of vocals with such as Dennis Brown, Junior Byles, Hubert Lee, Jimmy London, Carl Malcolm and the Lyrics, who included future roots hero Fred Locks in their line-up.

Alvin Ranglin

Alvin Ranglin, employing the organist **Winston Wright** as part of his session band, had important local hits on his GG's, Hit and Typhoon labels. These included **Billy Dyce**'s "Take Warning", **U-Roy**'s version of the Dyce record, "Way Down South", **Max Romeo & Glen Adams**' "River Jordan", and several early hits by **Gregory Isaacs** which contributed greatly to establishing him as a major vocal stylist. Like all the other producers of the time, Ranglin was also responsible for a series of instrumentals, including the popular "Man From Carolina" (loosely based on the Folks Brothers' "Oh Carolina"), "Flight 404" and "Ganja Plane". He established his position with a keen awareness of one sector of the market ignored by the other early reggae producers – from 1969 he produced religious music, selling huge quantities of records by singers like **Claudette Clark**. However, he remains best remembered for his pivotal role in establishing the mento-influenced 'rural' style of reggae that was to command a large local following in Jamaica for the next decade (particularly with hits from the **Maytones**, with whom Ranglin originally sang, and the **Starlights**).

THE MAYTONES

⦿ **Brown Girl In the Ring** (Trojan, UK).

The vocal duo of Vernon Buckley and Gladstone Grant have been the leading exponents of the rural style of reggae – a simple approach that has always enjoyed a much greater following in Jamaica itself than among the island's sophisticated expatriates. This collection, a generous 28 tracks, misses their one best-selling record in the UK, "Madness", but includes practically everything else they recorded of interest. "Loving Reggae", one of their first successes, is infectious fast reggae of the first order; slower tracks – such as "Serious Love", "Hands & Feet" and "All Over the World" – are more representative of their mature style, and allow greater scope for some delightful vocals.

Lloyd Charmers and Rupie Edwards

Lloyd Charmers, formerly a member of the Uniques and a gifted keyboards player, launched his Splash label in the early 1970s, and was noted for his sophisticated arrangements, which tended to incorporate strong elements from current Philadelphia soul styles. What is most important about Charmers, whose work also appeared on the Soul Beat and Wild Flower labels, is that he invariably brought out the best in the performers with whom he worked, including guitarist **Mikey Chung** and his crack **Now Generation** session band, **Ken Boothe**, **Harris 'B.B.' Seaton** (both solo and with the **Gaylads**) and **Lloyd Parks**. Excellent vocal and instrumental records also appeared under the name of the **Conscious Minds** – which involved variations of Boothe, Seaton and Charmers himself. Another outstanding guitarist who worked on sessions for Charmers was former Sonny Bradshaw sideman **Willie Lindo**, whose marvellous instrumentals included the evocative "Breezing" and "Samba Pati". Charmers himself displayed a quirkier side of his production style in tunes like the witty "Aily Sound" and the proto-dub of tracks like "Touching the President".

Charmers scaled the heights of commercial success with Ken Boothe: local hits like "Have I Sinned" ensured Boothe a massive female following, and his Trojan album *Black, Gold & Green* was a massive UK seller. Boothe consolidated his position with the UK chart-topping cover of Bread's "Everything I Own" (and the album of the same name); typically the song had been a sound-system favourite for a year before its eventual release outside of Jamaica. Although producer and singer followed up this success with the similarly well-crafted and soulful *Let's Get It On* set, further gain was thwarted by the collapse of the UK licensor, Trojan Records.

Another fine singer also responsible for attention-grabbing records was **Rupie Edwards**, who recorded local hits for his Success and Opportunity labels by Joe Higgs, Bob Andy, Dobby Dobson, the Ethiopians, Gregory Isaacs, Max Romeo, Time Unlimited (featuring a young Junior Delgado) and Johnnie Clarke, as well as plenty of superb instrumental and deejay versions. Edwards scored a monster hit in the UK in 1974 with "Ire Feeling", a dub-influenced instrumental with a nagging "skenga, skenga" vocal refrain, which spent several months in the charts that summer. He moved his operations to London the same year, but was never able to repeat that success, or the musical quality of earlier records.

KEN BOOTHE

◑ **Everything I Own** (Trojan, UK).

A superb set that captures one of the quintessential Jamaican soul voices at its peak, making even unlikely material – "Impossible Dream" from the musical *Man Of La Mancha*, "Speak Softly Love" from the movie *The Godfather* – seem totally natural. As well as the celebrated UK #1, there are Jamaican hits like the Charmers' composition "Crying Over You", alongside Boothe's own moving "You Will Reach Your Goal" and a pair of songs contributed by the Cimarons, the UK-based reggae band who also play on the album.

KEN BOOTHE, B.B. SEATON & THE GAYLADS

● **The Great Ken Boothe Meets B.B. Seaton & the Gaylads** (Jaguar, JA).

Not actually a Charmers production, but a fine showcase for some of his finest artists. Seaton and the Gaylads get a side apiece and both begin with medleys of their Studio One hits, before moving onto new material. "Black, Gold & Green" must have been one of the first overtly Rasta-influenced sides cut by Boothe, and the Gaylads' "My Jamaican Girl" similarly displays the sort of racial/national consciousness that was playing an increasingly important role in the music. The voices are, of course, sublime.

WILLIE LINDO

● **Far & Distant** (Wild Flower, JA).

An 'easy listening' album that sheds all the negative connotations of that phrase. Lloyd Parks (the best bass player in Jamaica in 1974) and drummer Paul Williams provide the solid foundation, Lloyd Charmers vamps away on piano and organ, and the guitarist Willie Lindo obviously enjoys himself extemporizing on their themes. The format could not have been simpler or worked to more beautiful effect.

VARIOUS ARTISTS – RUPIE EDWARDS PRODUCTIONS

● **Pure Gold** (Success, UK).

E A marvellous collection of instrumentals from the Rupie Edwards All Stars, who included – at one time or another – Tommy McCook, Winston Wright, Ansell Collins and Vin Gordon. Tracks such as "West Of Parade", "Bubbling Horn", "East Of Africa" and "Magnificent Seven" have an incredibly bright, clean sound that never slips into blandness. One of the most delightful instrumental reggae sets ever to surface.

● **Rupie's Gems** (Cactus, UK).

A collection of hits produced by Rupie Edwards, with some complemented by their dub cuts. There is no arguing with the term "gems" to describe tracks like Dobby Dobson's "Endlessly", the Heptones' "That Loving Feeling" (a cut of the Righteous Brothers' hit), the Ethiopians' "Pray Mama Pray" or Errol Dunkley's delicious "Darling Ooh". Curious, though, that Johnnie Clarke's "Everyday Wandering" is not followed by Rupie's own dubonic hit version, "Ire Feeling".

◑ **Ire Feelings: Chapter & Version** (Trojan, UK).

Both "Everyday Wandering" and "Ire Feeling" are included here, alongside another twenty cuts of the rhythm. The Heaven Singers' "Rasta Dreadlocks" will be of interest to some because of the group featuring a young Junior Delgado. But, as was so often the case with Edwards's music, the most exciting tracks are the instrumentals – including Rupie's own amateur-hour melodica version.

Prince Tony Robinson and Winston Riley

With the rapid enlargement of the UK market from 1968 onwards, UK licensor companies like Trojan and Pama needed a steady supply of new product. The ranks of freelance producers based in Jamaica were accordingly swelled by men who, like Bunny Lee, never owned their own studios but hired the facilities of others to make their discs. Like Lee, these producers had usually been involved in some aspect of the music business before venturing into full-time production. **Prince Tony Robinson**, for example, sold records from his shop on the Slipe Road before founding his High School label. Robinson was unusual in that he made a speciality of deejay records, finding particular success with **Dennis Alcapone**, **Winston Scotland** and **Lloyd Young** (and so prefiguring the wide appeal of his later production work with Big Youth and U-Roy). He was also among the first producers to realize the potential in updating rhythm tracks from the recent past. He produced the Chosen Few vocal trio on an excellent version of the Techniques' Treasure Isle classic "You Don't Care", which in turn provided further chapters of commentary from his deejays.

TROJAN RECORDS

Ansell Collins (left) and The Magnificent Dave Barker

Winston Riley, who had been in the business since founding the **Techniques**, used the group's name for the label he started in 1968, and recorded several more Techniques tracks that were fully the equal of their Treasure Isle rocksteady classics, namely "Man Of My Word", "One Day" and "Go Find Yourself A Fool". The **Sensations**, who in this period featured **Johnny Osbourne** (whom Riley also released as a soloist), impressed just as much with the enduring "Warrior", which more than two decades later would be 'versioned' by both Bunny Wailer and Marcia Griffiths. Commercially, Riley's most successful record was **Dave Barker and Ansell Collins**' funky, piano-led "Double Barrel" (featuring Barker's deejaying), which reached the UK pop charts in 1970, but Riley's greatest legacy to Jamaican music was "Stalag 17", an instrumental by the **Soul Syndicate** band and featuring the organ of Ansell Collins. The "Stalag 17" rhythm was to provide hits over the next two decades for, among others, Big Youth, Horace Andy, Augustus Pablo, Frankie Paul, General Echo and Tenor Saw.

DAVE & ANSELL COLLINS

◑ **Double Barrel** (RAS, US).

Both the title track and their other international pop hit, "Monkey Spanner", are classics; the other tracks are made up of straight instrumentals from Ansell Collins that are of the same standard, and the chronically underrated Dave Barker demonstrating that he could sing as well as deejay (he was a member of the Techniques vocal group, after all). An album that was originally rushed out after the hit singles, but has stood the test of time remarkably well.

JOHNNY OSBOURNE

● **Ready Or Not** (Big Shot, UK).

First put out when he was largely unknown, this includes some amazingly mature performances, not least the original – and best – cut to "Purify Your Heart" (Riley perversely released an inferior second cut as a single). The title track, "Nyah Man" and "My Name Is Man" are other strong tracks that anticipate future greatness, and weight is made up with a couple of mildly interesting instrumental versions, and two (more interesting) deejay ones – one of which is Prince Far I's first recording of his "Deck Of Cards" lyric.

Phil Pratt

Phil Pratt is another figure who deserves to be better remembered. He first ventured into production with a very young Horace Andy around 1966, but only established a distinctive sound for himself in 1972–74 with soulful vocals over raw, hard-driving rhythm tracks. His touch was best demonstrated by **John Holt**'s second version of "My Heart Is Gone" (Sunshot), which stands as a rare example of a recut record that betters the Studio One original. Pratt enjoyed further success with the same singer's "Strange Things", **Dennis Brown**'s inspired interpretation of Peter Green's "Black Magic Woman", **Ken Boothe**'s "I'm Not For Sale" and, as the era moved towards the roots phase, two exceptional discs from former Techniques member, **Pat Kelly** – "Soulful Love" and "They Talk About Love". Deejay cuts of his most popular rhythms from such rising names as Big Youth, Dennis Alcapone and Dillinger further added to his reputation at the time. Pratt's undervalued output from this period has yet to find its way onto CD; the producer has run a Caribbean café in north-west London for many years.

Keith Hudson

A sometime ghetto dentist (no anaesthetic!), **Keith Hudson** (b. 1946, Kingston; d. 1984, New York) possessed a pretty dismal voice himself, but clearly knew how to get the best out of others in the studio. His first hit was one of **Ken Boothe**'s most memorable records, "Old Fashioned Way" (Inbidimts); besides the singer's forceful performance, this was further distinguished by an early example of a typically rough and rugged Hudson rhythm. Not surprisingly, given its popularity, this was followed by excellent deejay interpretations by both **U-Roy** and **Dennis Alcapone**, which set the pattern by which Hudson-produced vocal hits were soon followed by outstanding deejay or instrumental cuts.

Hooking up with the young band from Greenwich Farm called **Soul Syndicate**, with George 'Fully' Fullwood and Carlton 'Santa' Davis providing the propulsive bass and drums, Hudson produced a series of perfectly realized records in the first half of the decade. Noteworthy among these were trumpeter **Johnny 'Dizzy' Moore**'s "Riot", an inspired reworking of a Hugh Masakela tune. Other gritty instrumentals included trombonist Don D. Junior's "Evil Spirit", melodica wizard Augustus Pablo's "Fat Baby" and "The Killer", and the haunting "Satan Side", credited to Chuckles. The young producer coaxed superb vocals from stars like **Horace Andy** ("Don't Think About Me"), **Alton Ellis** ("Big Bad Boy"), **John Holt** ("Hurt My Baby") and **Delroy Wilson**, whose version of "Run Run" was stronger than the original he cut for Studio One.

Hudson's deejay records were no less notable. After producing U-Roy, Alcapone and I-Roy, he turned his hand to the new toasting sensation **Big Youth**, providing him with his first major hit, "S.90 Skank" (printed "Ace 90" on the label), a tribute to the Honda motorcycle. Hudson actually brought a motorbike into the studio, revving up the engine to provide a suitable atmosphere for the record's intro. The popularity of the record easily exceeded Hudson's own vocal version on the rhythm, "True True To My Heart". Hudson even persuaded fellow youth producer Clive Chin to record a creditable deejay record under the name Little Clive, "African Bread".

Eventually Hudson put his own unorthodox voice to highly effective use on 1973's totally original *Flesh Of My Skin, Blood Of My Blood* – reggae's first true concept album, with all tracks relating to Black history and consciousness.

KEITH HUDSON

● **Flesh Of My Skin, Blood Of My Blood** (Mamba, UK).

E Keith Hudson's enigmatic masterpiece opens with one haunting instrumental, "Hunting", featuring the drums of Count Ossie, and closes with another, "Stabiliser". In between the man himself is totally convincing as he intones in mournful but dignified style on the subject of the Black race's history and destiny (with a couple of the vocals followed by their even moodier dubs). The only track that was not self-penned – Bob Dylan's "I Shall Be Released" – fits the serious mood surprisingly well. A seriously different album that was a long way from anything that preceded it or has followed since.

VARIOUS ARTISTS – KEITH HUDSON PRODUCTIONS

● **Studio Kinda Cloudy** (Trojan, UK).

E The definitive collection of Hudson singles, omitting only the most obscure. Ken Boothe's "Old Fashioned Way" must have been one of the most advanced records of 1968 when it launched his Inbidimts label and topped the Jamaican charts. Here it is joined by the equally exciting Dennis Alcapone and U-Roy versions (the latter with a different bassline and extra sax). Among the other gems are the instrumental "Riot", Alton Ellis's "Big Bad Boy" (as well as the trombone version, "Evil Spirit"), and Horace Andy's "Don't Think About Me" (with deejay versions from both Dino Perkins and Jah Woosh). Anyone not convinced of the late Mr Hudson's genius should start here.

Glen Brown: God Son in Caledonia Place

If Keith Hudson was idiosyncratic in bringing motorbikes into the studio and insisting on singing despite his limited vocal prowess, **Glen Brown** was even more left-field. He began his career in the 1960s as vocalist with Sonny Bradshaw's jazz group, singing standards on the North Coast hotel circuit. Subsequently he recorded duets with Hopeton Lewis, Lloyd Robinson and Dave Barker. In the new decade he produced and released records on the Shalimar imprint in partnership with businessman M.G. Mahtani, who had premises in the Kingston Arcade downtown. Then in 1972 he set up his own Pantomine [sic] and Dwyer imprints, operating from various premises – some records bear the legend "Blake's Autos, New & Used Cars, Caledonia Place", while others were available from "Radio & Television Sale & Service, 10 Old Hope Road, below Regal Theatre".

Record production was largely a hand-to-mouth affair for Glen Brown, whose tunes were often pressed in tiny quantities with labels re-used from previous releases, or occasionally on blank labels. But drop the needle into the groove and Brown's ability as rhythm master is immediately evident. Though some strong vocals appeared on Brown's labels – **Gregory Isaacs**' "One-One Cocoa Fill Basket", **Roman Stewart**'s "Never Too Young", **Lloyd Parkes**' "Slaving", **Little Roy**'s "Father's Call" and **Richie MacDonald**'s "Boat To Progress" to name some of the most outstanding – the self-styled God Son is mainly associated with the top-quality instrumental and deejay versions of his highly original rhythms. Supremely tough backing tracks, underpinned by sinuous, muscular basslines and laced with emphatic, crackling percussion were regularly coaxed by the producer from studio bands like the In Crowd or Soul Syndicate.

Though never a virtuoso on the melodica, he nevertheless seldom failed to sound interesting on the records he personally fronted. "Merry Up", a melodica duet with Joe White, was his first major local hit, boasting a distinctive, choppy rhythm, one to which he was to return again and again for fresh chapter and version. His records were punctuated with false starts and unsettling breaks, as on "Dance Good", another version of "Merry Up", in which a studio visitor interrupts the record after thirty seconds or so, declaring forcefully that "Man can dance more better than that". Glen replies that he is enjoying himself, restarts the rhythm and begins playing his simple melodica melodies again. His own vocals are heard to best advantage on a duet with Richie MacDonald, "Realise", which employed the same backing track as "Dirty Harry", the masterful horns workout from saxophonists Tommy McCook and Richard Hall that gave the latter musician his nickname.

Like Hudson, Brown also developed a fruitful rapport with deejays, resulting in outstanding versions of the "Dirty Harry" rhythm by **I-Roy and Prince Jazzbo**, as well as **Big Youth**'s "Opportunity Rock", **Dean Beckford**'s "Father's Call", **Berry Simpson**'s "2 Wedden Skank" and **U-Roy**'s "Number One In the World". Almost all of these records featured exceptional dubs by **King Tubby** (see pp.204–205), including some of the very first the master engineer mixed for commercial release. Glen was accustomed to leave his rhythms with Tubby, asking the dubmaster to mix "five or six styles" of each; not unexpectedly, Brown was also the first to actually credit Tubby on a record, with "Tubby's At the Control", yet another cut of "Merry Up" from 1972.

Glen had barely a handful of hits in Jamaica – he rarely had enough money to press large runs – but the scarcity of his discs ensured that he became a cult figure.

VARIOUS ARTISTS – GLEN BROWN PRODUCTIONS

● **Double Attack: The Original Pantomine DJ Collection 1972–74** (Greensleeves, UK).

● **Boat To Progress: The Original Pantomine Vocal Collection 1970–74** (Greensleeves, UK).

● **Check the Winner: The Original Pantomine Instrumental Collection 1970–74** (Greensleeves, UK).

These superb compilations of mostly rare 45s appeared in 1989 and were deleted a few years later. Luckily, they still crop up in secondhand record shops often enough to be worth seeking out. Those unfamiliar with Glen Brown's skills as a producer might try U-Roy's "Number One In the World" or Prince Jazzbo's "Mr. Harry Skank" from the deejay material, Roman Stewart's "Never Too Young" or Gregory Isaacs' "One-One Cocoa Fill Basket" among the vocals, or virtually anything on the instrumental set, including both horns and melodica workouts. Once the man's distinctive touch is appreciated, every track suddenly becomes essential listening.

Wake the town: how the deejays came to rule the nation

The early 1970s marked the beginning of the ascent of the deejay, a trend that continued during the roots era, and went on to become dominant throughout the dancehall and ragga phases. The story of the Jamaican deejay record can be traced back to the ska era, when the men who took the mike at the dances could occasionally be heard on vinyl, shouting an introduction and/or interjecting their catch phrases. The voice of the fabled **Winston 'Count' Machuki**, for instance, can be heard on the Baba Brooks Band's steaming "Alcatraz", while **Sir Lord Comic** made an impact with two massive hits that were actually credited to his name – "Ska-ing West" and "The Great Wuga Wuga". The role of the deejay at this point, however, was still largely confined to the dancehalls of the day, encouraging the dancers, and promoting the sound systems on which they were appearing. The first deejay to be recorded on more than an occasional basis was **King Stitt**, longtime MC for the Sir Coxsone Downbeat sound system.

VARIOUS ARTISTS

◑ **Keep On Coming Through the Door (Jamaican DJ Music '69–'73)** (Trojan, UK).

Deejay music is still underrated by many, but at its best it's just as creative as any of reggae's other forms. Proof lies in any one of the eighteen tracks gathered here – with the exception of "Deck Of Cards", where the superb Prince Far I toast has been accidentally replaced with its dub version. This collection draws from a variety of top producers – including Joe Gibbs, Glen Brown, Harry Mudie and Lee Perry – as well as several very different and distinct deejay approaches. A collection to be checked by anyone curious as to where the styles of Buju Banton or Shabba Ranks – or US rap, for that matter – began.

● **U-Roy & Friends – With A Flick Of My Musical Wrist** (Trojan, UK).

A worthy companion to the above set, with a similar variety of producers and men at the mike. Besides the Originator himself on top form, there are impressive pieces by I-Roy, Big Youth (including his toast to the Wailers' "Keep On Moving"), the seriously eccentric Ramon (aka Amblique, dancehall singer of the 1990s), and three regal gentlemen, King Tony, King Sporty and the always compelling Prince Jazzbo.

King Stitt

Winston Spark, aka **King Stitt**, was born with features not designed to win hearts, or even basic social acceptance, but he used these to his advantage, taking a cue from the 1966 Sergio Leone movie *The Good, the Bad & the Ugly* to promote himself proudly as 'the Ugly One'. Clement Dodd, on whose sound he appeared, went on to record him later, but Stitt's most successful records were with Clancy Eccles, for whom he cut a startling series of discs at the close of the 1960s. Eccles placed him over rhythms in the tough new reggae mode, built by his brilliant session outfit, the

RICK ELGOOD

'The Ugly One': King Stitt in the Studio One printery, 1994

Dynamites. Local hits – including "Fire Corner", "Lee Van Cleef", "Vigorton 2" and "Herbman" (aka "Herbman Shuffle") – also sold well to the skinhead audience in the UK, and played their part in establishing reggae as the favoured music for the stomping of Dr. Martens. But for all the success of these records, King Stitt belongs to the prehistory of the deejay's art. For, like Machuki and Sir Lord Comic, he excelled with a style that was taken largely from the jive talk of the American radio deejays heard on broadcasts from Miami and New Orleans. Stitt would introduce Coxsone's latest recordings at the dance in ceremonial fashion – "And now let the musical spotlight fall on the man called...Delroy Wilson" – before playing the record and interjecting the odd shouted phrase. Another deejay, Scotty, remembers Stitt "didn't have a magnetism, he recorded mainly because he was ugly – yunno, it was 'I am the ugly one' – an' people would go an' see if he was really ugly – it was like a laughin' ting." Stitt raised the profile of the deejay, but the men at the mike were yet to take centre stage. That came about in the first months of 1970 when Duke Reid recorded one Ewart Beckford (b. 1942, Kingston), better known as the incomparable U-Roy.

KING STITT

⊙ **Reggae Fire Beat** (Jamaican Gold, Holland).
In his own unique way King Stitt was the equal of any deejay who followed. He might not have had quite as much to say as his successors, but what mattered was how he delivered lines like "This is the days of wrath, Eastwood/I am the Ugly One/If you want me/Meet me at the big gun down/Die! Die! Die!/I am Van Cleef" – and, of course, the stunning Dynamites rhythms he was given. This well-presented compilation tells the whole story of his time with Clancy Eccles: sixteen amazing tracks, including his much-sought-after commentary on early dancehalls, "Dance Beat", and the even more original "Soul Language".

U-Roy

Though not the first deejay to make records, **U-Roy** is often referred to as the 'Originator' because of the unprecedented popularity of his early records and the influence of his style. His recordings for Duke Reid dominated the Jamaican radio charts during 1970 and had an enormous influence on every deejay who followed him into the studio. U-Roy's style of talking over the rhythm was radically different from that of people like his early inspiration, Count Machuki

KING STITT, YOUR BOSS DEEJAY

While U-Roy is referred to as the Originator because of the manner in which he established deejaying on record as a popular form, King Stitt (b. Winston Spark) was the first to have hits. The main difference between them was that most of Stitt's discs were almost instrumentals, but livened up considerably with his distinctive introductions and interjections. Facially disfigured from birth, Stitt was also a wonderful and characteristically Jamaican example of the man who turns misfortune to his advantage, styling himself the Ugly One.

"I started my musical career in the year 1957, when I came to the attention of Sir Coxsone's Downbeat sound. I started on a Friday evening at a barbecue lawn on Fleet Street, and Count Machuki took on to me because he found I was really interested in dancing, and I could dance to his opening selection, because in those days you had some hard up-tempo r&b. And he found I could dance to all of them. He said, 'If you can dance to all these records that I'm playing, you'd make a good deejay.' Well, I started and for about three months was the second deejay on that set, with Count Machuki.

I started playing on my own at dances at places like Carnival Lawn and Chockomo Lawn, and I find that I start to draw a certain amount of followers. It so happened that when Count Machuki retired from the sound, I took up the baton. Well, the Duke was still in his glory, and the deejay he had was Cuttins. But most of the time Sir Coxsone was the victor, because we had the better records, and a more intelligent set of followers. They know when a tune was good, so it create a storm.

The series of records that I made with Clancy Eccles started with "Fire Corner". Now he made a tune on that rhythm called "Shoobeedoo", but it didn't sell that much. I was in Ocho Rios, because in those times, '68 and '69, was when violence took the city by storm, and Mr Dodd had to pack up his sound, because he wouldn't play in that sort of environment. Well, I was in Ocho Rios with Jack Ruby, and I was at a dance one night when Clancy Eccles came by with the rhythm and said he wanted me to do something on it for him. 'All right,' I said. So he gave me the rhythm on a dub, and I played it a couple of times. Well, it so happened that I wrote all the top part of "Fire Corner": "No matter what the people say/These sounds leads the way/It's the order of the day/From your boss deejay, I, King Stitt/Haul it from the top to the very last drop." We recorded that at Dynamic studio, now. In the studio, the rhythm started, and I heard them play the punch line, and that was how "Fire Corner" was made. "Van Cleef", now, came from seeing films like *Day Of Anger*, *The Good, the Bad & the Ugly* and *For A Few Dollars More*. Clancy, again, said he wanted to do a tune by the name of "Lee Van Cleef". And we went into the studio, and the punch line now was: "These are the days of wrath, I am the Ugly One." For in the show, *The Good, the Bad & the Ugly*, Van Cleef was the ugly one. That was how "Van Cleef" was made.

"Herbman Shuffle" – down at the studio, Dynamic, they was playing, redoing, "Beardman Ska", and at that time you had an engineer by the name of Lynford Anderson – they call him Andy Capp. The tune was playing, now, and one of my friends in the studio made a big spliff. And I took the spliff from him. and light it, and I just say, 'Smoking is a habit.' And Andy Capp say 'Drag it! Crab it!' That was how "Herbman Shuffle" was born. "Vigorton 2", again, I was down at Dynamic one day, and Clancy was having a session, and playing the rhythm, and said do something over this. And I said: "Look how you sad and blue/I, King Stitt, has got a new discovery for you/The bad, bad Vigorton 2". And "I For I", again the same thing. Clancy had a track by Monty Morris called "Say What You're Saying", and he say he want me to do something on it. So I write the punch line: "I for I, a tooth for a tooth/I am the one you've got to salute." "King Of Kings" – when U-Roy did "Rule the Nation", I answer him back on another Monty Morris tune ["Tears In Your Eyes"], and say "You say you rule nation with version/Well, I'm the King of Kings, I rule Kingdoms!""

– his rich-toned voice proclaimed sizzling, jive-saturated lyrics rather than simply inserting a few phrases. Moreover, he rode the pared-down instrumental track all the way through, rather than interjecting at crucial points. As Scotty com-

U-Roy rules the nation on the cover of Swing, 1970

ments : "U-Roy come across as an individual who was a serious music person."

When U-Roy joined up with sound-system owner Osbourne '**King Tubby**' Ruddock in 1969 as deejay, he soon took the sound to the top. Such was U-Roy's power that he could hold a crowd with his voice alone. The deejay Trinity remembers an early 1970s dance with Tubby's Hi-Fi when the electricity was turned off because it was raining; the crowd remained standing in the downpour, listening to U-Roy's lyrics. In 1969 he made his first discs for Lee Perry, Bunny Lee and Keith Hudson. He recorded for Duke Reid the following year. and the initial effort, "Wake the Town", did just that, soaring to #1. It was followed by "Rule the Nation" and "Wear You To the Ball", and U-Roy soon had the top three records on the chart. All the Reid records rode rocksteady hits of recent memory, the staple diet in the dancehalls of the time. Soon deejay records were selling more than even the most popular singers: the deejay as recording phenomenon had arrived.

U-Roy went on to make records with Glen Brown, Joe Gibbs, Alvin Ranglin, Niney Holness and Lloyd Charmers, and by 1972 he had set up his own labels, Mego-Ann and Del-Ma. His classic toasting style has proved durable. He enjoyed a revival courtesy of producer Prince Tony Robinson in the mid-1970s (see p.110), going on to score further successes with Tappa Zukie in the late 1980s, and UK's Mad Professor in the 1990s. He still tours and records in the classic style he created.

U-ROY

◑ **Super Boss** (Esoldun, France).

E Comprising all of the Originator's known work for Treasure Isle, including both the *Version Galore* and *U-Roy* (aka *Words Of Wisdom*) LPs, plus the 45s that never made it onto album – such as the much-sought-after "Merry Go Round" (a cut of Errol Dunkley's "Where Must I Go"). His debut album has always been considered a bench mark, and 25 years later still sounds remarkably fresh – not least because of the rocksteady classics U-Roy was given to work with, as well as his own deftness of touch. No deejay before had 'ridden' a rhythm in quite the way Mr Beckford did – or so totally dominated proceedings. The eponymous second album was its equal in terms of the rhythms and U-Roy's inspired jive talk, but was slightly let down by the remixes given to the original singles.

Dennis Alcapone

Reid, who always knew a good thing when he saw it, soon found another distinguished deejay to repeat the success of U-Roy – **Dennis Alcapone** (b. Dennis Smith, 1947, Clerendon), from the El Paso Hi-Fi. Soon practically every other producer on the island followed suit, but there is no doubt that Dennis Alcapone was U-Roy's main rival. A deejay of comparable talent, he was even more prolific than U-Roy during this period – between 1970 and 1973, when he was at the peak of his popularity and powers, he cut more than 130 tracks, mostly for Reid, Dodd, Bunny Lee and Keith Hudson, but also for Lee Perry, Joe Gibbs, Prince Buster, Alvin Ranglin, Prince Tony Robinson, J.J. Johnson and Phil Pratt.

Fed some of the best rhythms of the day, Alcapone was a highly original stylist – whereas U-Roy rapped in an excitable jive talk, Alcapone delivered his lyrics in a half-sung,

U-ROY: THE ORIGINATOR

The initial impact and continuing influence of U-Roy on Jamaican music cannot be overstated. Almost single-handedly he showed that the deejay's jive talk, long popular in the dancehalls, could be successfully transferred to vinyl, and that producers could have more than one hit on a popular rhythm track. He was not the first man to chat on record, but he was the best for a very long time.

"First, I used to love this deejay by the name of Count Machuki. He used to play a sound named Sir Coxsone's. I like his style, because this man is a man who you can understand what he talking about. He don't talk no stupidness. He don't clash with no vocals, and stuff like that. I used to love that. That's really the man who inspire me to do certain things. But my style is kinda different from Machuki or other people's style. Because I just do things the way I feel.

My very first sound was Doctor Dickie's Dynamic. I was going to school at the age of 14 or so, and I had to ask my grandmother, who I was growing up with, if I can go to dance. Sometimes, she say yes, and sometimes she say read a book or something. But dance was just something I have such love for that I would sneak out and go anyway. No matter if she lock me out, and I have to sleep outside, I would reach dance somehow. That was my sort of fun. When I small my greatest pleasure was to hear a sound system play. Dickie's was a Chinese guy. He have a business and this sound system, so I used to go with them, when ever I could go. But I didn't start holding mike until a couple of years after that, because I was kinda shy. Then I start taking the mike and introducing the singers, and giving an invitation for the dance next week. Then I leave Dickie's and start playing Sir George. That was in about 1968, and at that time it was rocksteady. When I was playing Dickie it was mostly American music – like Louis Jordan and Ruth Brown, and stuff like those. And then I leave and start play Sir Coxsone's for a little while. I play his number two set, because King Stitt was playing the number one. King Stitt was the big deejay then, but I used to have my own crowd, because my style different from Stitt. I leave Coxsone's and go back to Sir George. Then I start playing King Tubby's, and I become a lot more versatile, and a lot more people start follow my sound. It change a lot of things.

Tubby's used to play a lot of Duke Reid and Coxsone music. John Holt came to a dance one night and hear me deejaying on one of his records, and went back to Duke Reid and tell him about this. So Duke Reid tell Tubby's that he want to talk to me. To tell the truth, I didn't really want to talk to him. I know this man have a whole heap of gun round him. When I see him, I think he try to intimidate people, and I never like that. But then I go to him, and we talk, and I do the first two tune for him – "Wake the Town" and "Rule the Nation". Believe you me, when I do the two tunes, I never had the slightest idea that it was going to be the way it was. Because we never thought people would ever make money out of this deejay business, talking over records. But the tunes release, got played on the radio, and people started to check me different from now. The two tunes come out and play on the radio a lot, until they reach number one and two. That was a big surprise. I was never checking for that. Even when I start deejay sound system, if somebody ever tell me a time would come when I'd buy a $100 shirt, I'd laugh. I did it for fun. Then a few weeks after the first two tunes, I did "Wear You To the Ball", and that chase the other tunes up the chart. So I have numbers one, two and three for six weeks on the two stations."

rhyming style that was peppered with sudden high-pitched whoops and imitations of crowing cockerels. He started out on a sound system known as El Paso Hi-Fi, which enjoyed the patronage of well-known ghetto enforcers like Jack Massop. Alcapone, named after the infamous gangster, was the first deejay to introduce gun lyrics with his enormous hit, "Guns Don't

Argue", and his Studio One album jacket even shows him astride a cannon. At his best, Alcapone also proved capable of sly humour – his "Teach the Children", a witty Jamaican #1 hit in 1972, is still used on literacy programmes on Jamaican radio today.

He had his share of followers, too. Among these was **Scotty** (previously the singer David Scott from the Federals and the Chosen Few), who went on to record as deejay for Derrick Harriott, Harry Johnson, Sonia Pottinger and Lloyd Charmers. Working on the El Paso sound with Alcapone was **Lizzy**, who cut a handful of great sides for Duke Reid, Bunny Lee, Joe Gibbs and Byron Smith. The deejay **Dillinger** was another follower of the sound as a youth; he initially styled himself Young Alcapone before taking the name of another American gangster at the suggestion of Lee Perry. Alcapone's influence can also be heard, alongside that of U-Roy, in the early Harry Mudie-produced records of the great I-Roy, later the pre-eminent lyricist of deejay music.

DENNIS ALCAPONE

My Voice Is Insured For Half A Million Dollars (Trojan, UK).

E A retrospective collection that appeared as part of Trojan's major reissue programme in the late 1980s. It's probably the best place for the newcomer to Alcapone's work to start, simply because it draws from a number of different producers. "Rocking To Ethiopia" (his cut of the Ethiopians' "Selah" classic) is worth the price of the album, and the same can be said about "Mava" (Augustus Pablo's "Java"), "Jungle Of Crime" (Alton Ellis's "Big Bad Boy"), the title track (the Techniques' "Queen Majesty"), or practically any of the other nine tracks from the deejay's peak in the early 1970s.

Forever Version (Studio One, JA; Heartbeat, US).

Clement Dodd's answer to U-Roy's classic *Version Galore* set on Treasure Isle, and very much its equal. The title track is a classic deejay version of a classic vocal, Carlton & his Shoes' "Love Me Forever", but no less compelling are the treatments given other timeless Studio One hits, such as Larry & Alvin's "Nanny Goat", Delroy Wilson's "Run Run", John Holt's "A Love I Can Feel", the Heptones' "Baby", the Cables' "Baby Why" and Alton Ellis's "Sunday Coming". As was the fashion then, snatches from all the original vocals are included, with the Alcapone interacting to add his comments. The only reservation about its CD

reissue is that none of the eleven Alcapone singles for Coxsone that failed to find their way onto the original 1971 album have been added.

Soul To Soul – DJ's Choice (Trojan, UK).

The best of several Treasure Isle deejay albums released by Trojan in the wake of U-Roy's phenomenal success. Dennis Alcapone has the majority of tracks – including the marvellous "DJ's Choice" and "Wake Up Jamaica" – but there are also compelling contributions from Lizzy, Little Youth and even the Originator, U-Roy. If you possess the original vinyl pressing, the CD is still worth considering for the eight extra tracks.

Guns Don't Argue (Jamaican Gold, Holland).

Musical Liquidator (Jamaican Gold, Holland).

The two LPs that Bunny Lee released in the 1970s, with some extra tracks for value. His first album for Bunny was not surprisingly named after the hit with which his name is still most associated – "Guns Don't Argue" (his version of Eric Donaldson's "Love Of the Common People") – and the rest of the album followed the same formula, with the producer's best rhythms inspiring the deejay's totally confident jive talk. The second CD is based on the album named after another massive hit, "King Of the Track" – a version of John Holt's "Stick By Me". Again, he was given only the hottest rhythms, including hits from Cornell Campbell, Slim Smith and Delroy Wilson. To the original album are added four tracks recorded when Dennis was living in the UK by Bunny Lee associate, Count Shelly.

SCOTTY

● Unbelievable Sounds (Trojan, UK).

Scotty prefigured the 'singjay' style of a decade later, and this is essentially his great 1972 *Schooldays* album for Derrick Harriott, with a few extra tracks thrown in. Top rhythms employed include the producer's own "Solomon" and "The Loser", as well as Keith & Tex's biggest hits, "Tonight" and "Stop That Train" (the latter for "Draw Your Brakes" – by far Scotty's most famous record).

Deejays galore

The success of U-Roy and Alcapone spurred a stampede of deejays on record. Of these the most consistently interesting included the plummy-voiced **Winston Scotland**, who recorded largely for deejay specialist Prince Tony Robinson; **Big Joe**, who made his best records for Studio One, Lloyd Daley, Leonard 'Santic' Chin and Harry Mudie; and **Charlie Ace**, who produced himself but also cut wonderful records for Studio One, Sonia Pottinger, Clive Chin, Bunny Lee and Lee Perry. Ace also sold his records himself, operating a converted van with the legend "Swing A Ling Record Shack" emblazoned on the side. Others who had at least the odd moment of glory on disc included Shorty the President, King Sporty, U-Roy Junior (aka Froggy), Sir Harry, Prince Francis, Carey Johnson and Lloyd Young (the latter two sometimes joining forces as Carey & Lloyd). The fine singer Dave Barker also made deejay records – most notable are the international hits "Double Barrel" and "Monkey Spanner". Conventional radio deejays also made talkover records – the producer Bunny Lee scored local hits with American-style raps from both Jeff Barnes and the alliteratively inventive Winston Williams. Even the famed Studio One drummer **Leroy 'Horsemouth' Wallace** had his turn, calling himself Mad Roy for "Universal Love", an accomplished enough deejay version of John Holt's "A Love I Can Feel"; while Holt himself toasted his own "Linger A While" for Lloyd Daley, and **Winston Blake**, owner of the uptown sound system, Merritone, cut several 'toasting' records in the clearest of dictions.

In the same period, several of the deejays who were to reach their widest audience in the subsequent roots era also made their recording debuts, including **Prince Jazzbo**, **Trinity** (as Prince Glen) and **Jah Lloyd**. From the Lord Tippertone Hi-Fi sound system, run by Jah Wise and Clive, came **Jah Stitch** and **Doctor Alimantado**, who made his earliest sides under the names Winston Cool, Winston Prince and Youth Winston. Tippertone also brought to prominence the deejay who was to be the most innovative and influential stylist since U-Roy, the dreadlocked **Big Youth**. But, whereas the Youth was not to make his presence felt on vinyl until 1972, the music's premier lyricist, **I-Roy**, arrived two years earlier with "Musical Pleasure" and "Drifter" for Harry Mudie, both of which registered strongly with record buyers in Jamaica and the UK. I-Roy had deejayed most of the important Spanish Town sound systems, including Son's Junior, Stereo, and Ruddy's Supreme; he went on to V-Rocket and then to King Tubby's Hi-Fi. Always the most erudite deejay, he peppered his records of this period with references to such diverse cultural icons as Mickey Spillane, Alfred Hitchcock, Stokely Carmichael, Florence Nightingale and Cleopatra. All these deejays had distinct microphone styles, and opened the way for the multitude of roots deejays who were to follow them.

BIG YOUTH

◑ Screaming Target (Gussie, JA; Trojan, UK).

E The first set that Big Youth had to himself had the advantage of being produced by a fellow youthman also out to prove himself – Gussie Clarke, who was then barely 20. Almost anything would sound acceptable over rhythms such as Leroy Smart's "Pride & Ambition", Gregory Isaacs' "One One Cocoa Fill Basket", K.C. White's "No, No, No" and Lloyd Parks's "Slaving", but Mr Buchanan was breaking new ground with a chant-like style that would set the pace

for almost the next decade of toasting. The most important deejay set after U-Roy's debut, and one that few have matched since.

PRINCE JAZZBO

● **Choice Of Version** (Studio One, JA).
It was Prince Jazzbo more than anyone who established the 'rockstone' tradition of gruff deejay delivery – of voices sounding as it their owners had seen it all and only just lived to tell the tale. This should have been his stunning early 1970s debut set, but Dodd kept it back for nearly a quarter of a century. It was worth the wait, with the best-known hits like "Imperial I", "School" and "Fool For Love" complemented by hitherto unreleased versions of rhythms just as classic – including the Wailing Souls' "Mr Fire Coal Man", the New Establishment's "Rockfort Rock" and the Ethiopians' "I'm Gonna Take Over Now".

I-ROY

● **Presenting** (Gussie, JA; Trojan, UK).

● **Hell & Sorrow** (Trojan, UK).
The deejay's first two albums: one for Gussie Clarke, the other a self-production. The debut set from Gussie appeared the same year as Big Youth's, and is comparable in terms of its mould-shattering quality. There are occasional touches of both U-Roy and Dennis Alcapone in I-Roy's approach, but also an intimate tone and literate storytelling ability that was very much his own. "Blackman Time", over the "Slaving" rhythm, was the enormous hit, but every track displayed a major and very inventive chatting talent. It set a daunting standard to follow, but *Hell & Sorrow* hardly fell short, with important hits like "Monkey Fashion" and "Buck & the Preacher", alongside new tracks of the same calibre, such as "Dr Phibes" (another cut of the legendary "Sidewalk Killer").

Rebel music and Rasta chants

By 1975 a seismic shift had occurred in the mainstream of reggae, with the eruption of Rastafarian-dominated 'roots' records. This development was clearly anticipated by the so-called **'rebel music'** of the first half of the decade, a term used to refer both to the influx of younger producers at that time and to the social discontent often expressed in the music of their artists – many of whom were committed Rastafarians. The **Wailers** exemplified the changes in youth music, having evolved from representatives of West Kingston's rude boys into more conscious 'soul rebels' (even if such distinctions were often more blurred on the street). In this period the Wailers benefited from the distinctive and radical production ideas of **Lee 'Scratch' Perry**, whose vocal phrasing was also greatly influential on Bob Marley's new style of singing. As well as the Wailers, solo singers such as **Junior Byles** and **Max Romeo** gave expression to their Rastafarian beliefs over slower, 'dreader' rhythms that producers like Perry and **Winston 'Niney' Holness** were getting their musicians to play. Furthermore, traditional Rastafarian chants, which had occasionally surfaced on record before, were now increasingly being recorded – sometimes given a more commercial gloss by non-Rastafarian producers such as Derrick Harriott, Lloyd 'Matador' Daley and Leslie Kong.

VARIOUS ARTISTS – ASSORTED PRODUCERS

◑ **Rebel Music** (Trojan, UK).
E This double album remains the most comprehensive compilation of singles exemplifying the 'rebel music' phase. Don't be put off by the truly naff cover: this is music that is innovative, daring, quirky, heartfelt and committed to expressing both the tribulations and dignity of the Jamaican majority. Includes seminal works by Gregory Isaacs, Horace Andy, Big Youth, Dennis Brown and I-Roy.

◑ **Sufferer's Choice** (Attack, UK).
A selection similar to the one above in the period covered, as well as producers, artists and topics. Just

the titles of the two tracks that open the album – the Kingstonians' "Sufferer" and the Ethiopians "Condition Bad A Yard" – sum up the concerns expressed throughout, and it closes with Bob Marley's "Nice Time" ("Long long time, we have no..."). The Abyssinians, Alton Ellis, the Versatiles and Dennis Brown are among those offering further highlights.

Scratch and Niney

Significantly, in the period immediately subsequent to their departure from Joe Gibbs, the equally progressive **Lee 'Scratch' Perry** and **Winston 'Niney' Holness** often co-operated on productions – the composition of **Max Romeo**'s "Rasta Bandwagon" (which surfaced on Niney's Observers label) and of his "Babylon's Burning" (which was on Scratch's Upsetter) is credited to Maxie, Perry & Niney, while Scratch's voice can be heard on the brilliant 'version' side of the former. Another Max Romeo hit of the time, "The Coming Of Jah", appeared on Niney's Observers label, but those boring enough to check these things will find an LP (Lee Perry) matrix number on the Jamaican disc. Besides regularly recording the often inspired Max Romeo in this period, the two producers also shared a taste for distinctive, unorthodox rhythms, and their roles in the development of 'rebel music' cannot be overstated.

Scratch's session players, appositely called the **Upsetters**, were in fact Max Romeo's old band the Hippy Boys, featuring the drum and bass partnership of Carlton 'Carly' Barrett and Aston 'Family Man', along with the distinctive organ of Glen Adams. They had already recorded for producers like Bunny Lee, Sonia Pottinger and Lloyd Daley, but Scratch brought out something in them that was even more in tune with the 'dread' mood of the time – slow and edgy, with an implied threat of physical violence. Their rhythms couldn't have been more suited to the Rasta/rebel vocal styles of Scratch's two major acts of the time, **Junior Byles** and the **Wailers**.

Niney achieved a similar mood at his sessions, and before recording some of Max Romeo's greatest sides performed one of the seminal 'rebel music' sides himself – "Blood & Fire" (Observer). Appearing at the close of 1970, this raw masterpiece remains one of the most uncompromising reggae records ever – not only musically, but lyrically:

"There is no more water to put out the fire
Let it burn, let it burn, let it burn
Blood and fire
Judgement has come, and mercy has gone
All weakheart shall lick out and spit up
All righteous shall stand."

The fact it was a massive Jamaican hit suggests that many of the island's inhabitants could relate to its vengeful message, and Niney pursued a similar apocalyptic tack with further records by himself ("Brimstone & Fire", "Message To the Ungodly", "In the Gutter") and a series of equally impressive 45s by the very gospel-influenced Max Romeo.

THE UPSETTERS

Kung Fu Meets the Dragon (Justice League, UK).

In 1974 Perry had just set up his Black Ark studio at Washington Gardens, and was beginning to develop the sound with which he's most associated by the crossover audience that belatedly discovered his music. Kung Fu movies were influencing a number of producers then, though perhaps none took them to heart in quite the way Scratch did. Any excuse for weird sounds and a touch of mysticism was enough for Jamaica's most adventurous producer.

VARIOUS ARTISTS – WINSTON 'NINEY' HOLNESS PRODUCTIONS

Blood & Fire (Trojan, UK).

E A fitting title for a collection of the Jamaican hits that established Mr Holness's labels in the early 1970s, pretty much defining the 'rebel music' phase. The title track is still arguably his supreme statement on record, and it is understandable why some Jamaicans felt uneasy about the new developments in the music. Besides three further chapters to "Blood & Fire", there are further voicings from Niney himself, Max Romeo, and even the well-established Delroy Wilson, all giving appropriate expression to a dread time.

VARIOUS ARTISTS – LEE PERRY PRODUCTIONS

The Upsetter Collection (Trojan, UK).

E As definitive a collection of Upsetter hits as possible on a single album – the first side covers the early instrumentals, the second has the slower records that followed. The Gatherers' "Words Of My Mouth" is to many fans Scratch's greatest achievement ever, but also brilliantly ahead of their time were such as "Cow Thief Skank" by Scratch and deejay Charlie Ace, "Better Days" by the Carltons (aka Carton & his Shoes), and the Upsetters' "Black Ipa".

Give Me Power (Trojan, UK).

The title track is from the Stingers, and they were lucky enough to be given one of Lee Perry's most compelling rhythms of the early 1970s – further borne out by the deejay cut from one King Iwah. Other legendary Scratch productions from the same period include Junior Byles' "Rasta No Pickpocket", Max Romeo's "Public Enemy No One", Dillinger's "Mid-East Rock" and the mysterious Prince Django's "Hot Tip", a version of the Gatherers' "Word Of My Mouth".

Shocks Of Mighty (Attack, UK).

A next collection of Scratch's productions from the first half of the decade that is not quite as consistent as the above, but worth picking up for gems such as the title track from Dave Barker, the Classics' rootsy "Civilisation" and the Upsetters' "Tackro" (the next chapter to the better-known "Clint Eastwood"). Three hitherto obscure vocals to tracks from the Revolution Dub album are interesting, but slightly out of place.

Version Like Rain (Trojan, UK).

Versions of three magnificent Upsetter rhythms from the early 1970s. The most haunting is the one employed for Junior Byles's reading of Little Willie John's r&b classic, "Fever", the five cuts including "This World" from King Medious (aka Milton Henry) and "Hot & Cold" from Augustus Pablo. Leo Graham's "Want A Wine" is followed by just two further versions – its original dub side and U-Roy's marvellous "Stick Together". Then the entire second side is devoted to Junior Byles' "Beat Down Babylon", including Max Romeo's just as dread "Babylon's Burning".

The Upsetter Box Set (Trojan, UK).

This double CD, triple vinyl set brings together *Africa's Blood*, the legendary *Rhythm Shower* and *Double Seven*, seminal Scratch work that provides a link with the producer's fast reggae of the early 1970s and the Black Ark sound of the decade's second half. Mastered from original tapes, each mixes quirky instrumentals, inchoate dubs and pioneering deejay versions. Together the albums chart the development of reggae's greatest innovator in what was the most experimental period of the music's history. Consistently interesting as the first two albums (both from 1972/3) certainly are, the most fully satisfying has to be the following year's *Double Seven*, featuring not only classic instrumentals, but soul-tinged vocals from Dave Barker, and deejay gems from both U-Roy and I-Roy, plus Scratch's own meditation on Colonel Sanders, "Kentucky Skank".

Junior Byles

The most inspired – and anguished – of all the 'rebel music' singers was **Junior Byles** (b. Kerrie Byles Junior, 1948, Kingston). Coming from a devout family, he had his first chance to sing in church, and the intense spirituality that infuses his best records can no doubt be traced to these early years. His entry into the record business came in 1967 when he formed the **Versatiles** with Louie Davis and Dudley Earl. The group's first recording was for Joe Gibbs' recently launched Amalgamated label, and the man supervising the session was Lee Perry, who was soon to strike out on his own. The session that resulted in "The Time Has Come" for Gibbs was a more than promising start to a professional relationship that would last for the next seven years, yielding some of the most impressive tunes of the careers of both Perry and Byles. A year or so after Perry split from Joe Gibbs, the Versatiles followed suit and went to their first producer to record again. Perry quickly produced several titles with them, which then surfaced on Deltone, a label owned by a Mrs Dorothy Barrett.

In 1970, Junior Byles embarked on his solo career (though his fellow Versatiles would sometimes contribute harmonies), beginning with the Perry-produced "What's the World Coming To", released under the name of King Chubby. Two years later came the Jamaican Festival Song competition entry "Da Da", and another major local hit that was as much a cry of pain and anger as any of Niney's – the phenomenal "Beat Down Babylon". Most of his other records for Perry in this period – as well as the self-produced "Black Crisis (Love Power)" – were just as highly charged, and nearly all had social/spiritual themes. "A Place Called Africa", for instance, is possibly the most moving repatriation plea ever recorded.

Few singers could touch Junior Byles at his peak, for either the intensity of his vocals or his sheer commitment to a vision. The voice, in particular, was unique – expressing a potent mixture of militancy, vulnerability and spiritual faith. A singer who anticipated the 'roots' phase of the music, he went on to cut a handful of the greatest records of that period as well, and only severe mental problems – he attempted suicide after hearing about the death of Haile Selassie – curtailed his career during the latter half of the 1970s.

JUNIOR BYLES

Curly Locks: Best Of Junior Byles & the Upsetters 1970–1976 (Heartbeat, US).

E Misses "Beat Down Babylon", as well as "Pharaoh Hiding", "King Of Babylon", "Auntie Lu-lu", and "Rasta No Pickpocket", but otherwise this handsomely packaged set lives up to its title. Anyone at all familiar with the singer's work will salivate at the thought of three cuts of the title track (two previously unreleased), "Cutting Razor" with the Versatiles, "A Place Called Africa", and another seventeen prime tracks produced by Scratch.

Beat Down Babylon: The Upsetter Years (Trojan, UK).

Byles's classic first album, plus some extra tracks from the same inspired period (including the wonderful "King Of Babylon"). Perry obviously knew he was dealing with someone as special as the Wailers, and never gave him rhythms of less than equal worth.

The Wailers meet the Upsetters downtown

After the failure of their own Wail 'N' Soul 'M' enterprise, the **Wailers** joined those working with Scratch. Recording the trio whom he had originally met at Studio One, the diminutive but charismatic Perry played a key part in giving Marley a new voice – the tone and phrasing from this period onwards having clear echoes of the producer's own. The Wailers' "Duppy Conqueror" (Upsetter), only the second track the group cut with Scratch at Randy's studio, arguably became the inspiration for Niney's "Blood & Fire" – certainly it caused an acrimonious dispute between them. The Wailers then maintained the pressure with the most striking and original series of records either they or their producer had yet cut. "Mr Brown" continued the 'duppy' (or ghost) theme, while equally explosive tracks on the Upsetter or Justice League labels included "Kaya", "My Cup", the anthemic "Small Axe" (and its next cut, "More Axe"), "Man To Man" and the definitive version of Richie Havens's "African

Herbsman". There was also the incredible two-sider, "Sun Is Shining"/"Run For Cover", which Perry produced, though it was to be the initial single on the trio's own Tuff Gong label (see p.132).

All these confirmed not only the full fruition of the Wailers' songwriting and interpretative powers, but also a new stance in Jamaican music: unmistakably tougher, yet simultaneously more spiritual. The rhythms from the Upsetters were in an appropriate slower, 'dread' mood, and black self-determination was the central theme. What is still open to speculation is how many of the songwriting credits for the tracks collected on the *Soul Rebels* and *Soul Revolution* albums that Perry put out in Jamaica can be given to either Marley or Perry alone, and how many were in fact co-written. What is unarguable is that all three members of the original trio were now very near to their creative peaks, with Marley as the dominant figure, but the less prolific **Peter Tosh** and **Bunny Wailer** also displaying their own very distinctive perspectives – with the former's militant "400 Years" and the latter's beautifully moving and dignified "Dreamland" defining the contrasting but complementary strains that were to dominate Jamaican music's next phase.

BOB MARLEY & THE WAILERS

◑ **African Herbsman** (Trojan, UK).

Ⓔ The Wailers' work with Scratch represents a summit that even the best of Marley's subsequent recordings failed to scale. Certainly, the two LPs' worth of Upsetter-produced material (plus a smattering of 45s that did not make it onto album) was seminal music that remains without parallel. Every track collected here is a classic, and the cornerstone for the music's subsequent development.

◑ **All the Hits** (Rohit, US).

◑ **The Upsetter Record Shop Vols 1 & 2** (Esoldun, France).

Three albums that provide the most economical way of adding particularly scarce – and musically important – Wailers items to the collection. The Rohit set looks much like any number of cheapo Wailers compilations currently available, but rather than simply repackaging what every Wailers fan already has, it brings together four tracks from the trio's own Wail 'N' Soul 'M' label, two from their early Tuff Gong period, one from Bunny Lee and three from Scratch. Half of these vocals are otherwise unavailable on album, and each is followed by its instrumental version. The second of the Esoldun albums provides a package of even scarcer recordings – largely self-produced, despite the title – also complete with their instrumental cuts. Most of the titles will be familiar – but these are alternate takes that are different enough to be of real interest to a wider public than those who strain their eyes reading matrix numbers. The vocal tracks on the first volume have all been available on album before, but are presented with instrumental versions (which haven't).

Rasta chants, nyahbingi drumming and dread rhythms

In parallel to the aggressive 'rebel music' discs, there were some more reflective 45s that tended to be even more directly informed by Rastafarianism and were not associated with any particular producers. Instead, they often appeared – almost out of the blue – on a number of different imprints, including those of the very established Clement Dodd.

Among the most advanced in this context was "Happy Land", the flip of **Carlton & his Shoes'** gloriously romantic "Love Me Forever", released on Dodd's Supreme label in early 1968. "Happy Land" was to act as a template for the **Abyssinians'** 'cultural' anthem, "Satta Massa Ganna", recorded the following year at the same studio, though not released until two years later and on the trio's own Clinch label. Both records shared the same concern, the Rastafarian dream of repatriation to an Arcadian paradise in Africa, and also employed similar minor-chord melodies and dread-slow rhythms. The Abyssinians – Bernard Collins plus two members of Carlton & the Shoes, Lynford and Donald Manning – recorded two more classic sides at Brentford Road in the same period. "Jerusalem" appeared as the flip of the first (very limited) pressing of "Satta Massa Ganna", while "Declaration Of Rights" was released on Dodd's Coxsone label. Both were serious cultural records that employed minor chords, while the latter was over a rhythm that has been 'versioned' almost as often as "Satta".

His Imperial Majesty

But the Abyssinians' records were not the only pioneering 'cultural' sides to be cut at Brentford Road before the end of the decade. The **Royals**' first recording of "Pick Up the Pieces" was recorded in 1967, and would have been far ahead of its time had it only been released sooner. As it was, Dodd held back this understated and very dignified cultural classic until after the group had tasted some success with several tunes in a more typical early reggae mode for Joe Gibbs, Byron Smith and Lloyd Daley, and had released – almost six years after the original – a self-produced second cut of the tune.

Another stunning record that was released on Supreme nearer the time that it was recorded – and must have seemed all the more radical in 1969 – was **Burning Spear**'s amazing debut, "Door Peeper". Rasta lyrics and musical motifs had been adapted for commercial release before, but none sounded quite like the disc that announced the arrival of Burning Spear (b. Winston Rodney, 1948, St. Ann's Bay). Before the heavyweight rhythm emerges, a solitary voice in the gravest of tones announces:

"I and I, the son of the Most High
Jah Rastafari
Whose heart shall correspond
And beat in harmony
Sounds from the Burning Spear."

What follows is not a conventional song but a chant structure, delivered in a manner that owed little to any previous Jamaican styles. The calls to "Chant Down Babylon" are repeated and repeated, interspersed with advice to "Give thanks and praise to the only man of creation". In glaring contrast to the fast instrumental reggae records that were striking a chord with white teenagers in the UK, this was starkly uncompromising music that demanded to be taken on its own terms or not at all.

Just as lacking in any obvious commercial appeal was **Vivian Jackson & the Ralph Brothers**' "Conquering Lion" (Now), a self-production released in 1972, though conceived a couple of years earlier. The nearest the record has to a conventional 'hook' was the chorus of "Yabby you, Yabby, yabby, yabby you/you yabby, yabby you/La la la lala la la la". This is repeated for almost the entire length of the side, with Jackson coming in at a couple of points to sing:

"Everyone come to see Jah
72 different nations bow
Before Jah glory.
Because he's the King of Kings
The Lord of Lords
The Conquering Lion of Judah."

The idea might seem fairly minimal, but the effect – over one of the great minor-chord rhythms of the period – was phenomenal.

In the same period of 1969–74, more commercial takes on Rastafarian chants were forthcoming from producers like Leslie Kong (the **Melodians**' "Rivers Of Babylon"), Lloyd 'Matador' Daley (**Alton Ellis**'s "Deliver Us" and "Back To Africa"), Derrick Harriott (**Bongo Herman & Bingy Bunny**'s "We Are Praying" and "Know For I"), and **Lloyd Charmers** ("Rasta Never Fails", by himself and **Ken Boothe**, and "Africa Is Paradise", on which he was joined by former Gaylad **B.B. Seaton**). Several of these records adapted the lyrics and/or the melodies of Rastafarian chants, and incorporated variants of nyahbingi drumming. In this way they looked forward to developments that were to take place later in the decade, while harking back to the dawn of the post-mento recording business in Jamaica – when the master Rasta drummer **Count Ossie** had contributed to several pre-ska hits. By the early 1970s, even relatively pure Rasta music, untempered by commercial considerations, was finding its way onto disc quite often, with several excellent examples from Count Ossie and the tenor saxophonist **Cedric 'Im' Brooks** appearing in 1970/71 on various Studio One labels, including "Black Is Black", "Black Up" and the archetypal "So Long Rastafari Calling".

Though records such as those discussed in this section were a minority of the total released at the time, the scene was set for the roots explosion that was to take place in 1975. Then what had seemed rather daring issues to put on record became *de rigueur* – and arguably lost some of their freshness.

Roots reggae

ADRIAN BOOT

4

4

previous page

Bob Marley, late 1970s

Roots reggae

The term **'roots reggae'** means different things to different people, but to most Jamaicans a roots record is simply one that concerns itself with the life of the ghetto sufferer – with 'reality'. Though often informed by the millennial cult of Rastafarianism, it takes in a range of music, from the ska of Justin Hinds & the Dominoes to a modern record like "Untold Stories" by the ragga deejay Buju Banton. The term 'roots' was first widely used in the mid-1970s to describe the work of artists such as the **Wailers**, **Burning Spear**, the **Abyssinians**, **Junior Byles**, the **Royals**, the **Wailing Souls**, **Big Youth** and **Vivian Jackson**. The music that they (and countless others) made was largely concerned with 'truth and rights' and the legacies of colonialism. Occasionally, though, the same people cut love songs, such as the Abyssinians' haunting "Love Comes And Goes", over the same sort of rhythms that underpinned their cultural material. These rhythms shared certain musical motifs, such as nyahbingi drumming and/or minor-key horn chords, and were played in the 'rockers' and 'steppers' styles that are still indelibly associated with the roots genre. Demonstrating the underlying continuity of Jamaican music, 'rockers' was essentially a militant update of classic rocksteady rhythms, while 'steppers' was an even more assertive take on that, tailored for a high-stepping, march-like dance move.

If the term is taken to encompass its broadest definition, 'roots' artists are to be found in every chapter of this book. Here we've narrowed the focus to concentrate on music produced in Jamaica during the period when roots reggae was the clearly dominant style – roughly 1975–80. As well as dealing with the most popular producers of the period, including **Bunny Lee**, **Joseph 'Joe Joe' Hookim** and **Joe Gibbs**, this chapter covers influential innovators who operated slightly outside the mainstream, such as **Lee 'Scratch' Perry**, **Winston 'Niney' Holness**, **Augustus Pablo**, **Yabby You**, **Keith Hudson** and **Glen Brown**, plus a wide range of smaller producers, some of whom would indicate future directions for reggae. Some records that fall outside of this era, but are inseparable from it through a particular performer's consistency of style – those produced by Augustus Pablo, Bunny Wailer and Israel Vibration after the 1970s are just three obvious examples – are also included here, as is the work of the most popular singers in the dancehalls and blues dances during the 'roots' period – men like the astonishingly successful and talented **Dennis Brown** and **Gregory Isaacs**, who mixed both cultural themes and the most romantic of lovers' laments.

Records with 'roots' themes – the ghetto people's suffering, repatriation to Africa, Haile Selassie as a living deity, slavery in Babylon – had been released during and since the days of ska. The majority of discs by two talented vocal groups, Justin Hinds & the Dominoes and the **Ethiopians** (note the name), fell into this category, and those of many others more occasionally did so – the Gaylads' repatriation call, "Africa", for one marvellous instance. In addition, what can be spoken of as 'pure' Rasta music, in the form of the nyahbingi drumming and chant-like vocals, can be traced back to the pre-ska era and master drummer **Count Ossie**'s (see p.24) contributions to recordings for Prince Buster Harry Mudie and Clement Dodd. Rocksteady, which drew much of its inspiration from American soul harmonies, tended to concentrate on affairs of the heart, but even in this most romantic phase of Jamaican music the Wailers were drawing on the inspiration of Rastafarianism for records like "Selassie In the Chapel" (even if this particular example was based on the US doo-wop disc, "Crying In the Chapel"). The early reggae years then saw a significant increase in the number of records with Rasta/cultural themes, and by the middle of the decade these had achieved a position of dominance. This was particularly obvious in 1974–75, when Rasta-oriented roots records became such a craze that Max Romeo was provoked into releasing a caustic 45 called "Rasta Bandwagon".

There were a couple of likely reasons for this popularity. Disillusionment with Michael Manley's initially well-received PNP government played a part in turning the ghetto youth towards Rastafarianism, with its message of spiritual and social salvation. The Black Power movement in the United States had also made an impact by then, though the message of American militants such as Eldridge Cleaver and Angela Davis found more of an audience with the young intellectuals at the University of the West Indies than with the ghetto dwellers. By the mid-1970s even the intelligentsia were switching to Rastafarianism. The other important – and perhaps clinching – factor in Rastafarianism's wide acceptance was that the cult was embraced by all three of the Wailers, the first reggae act to have an album financed by a foreign record company. By mid-decade all three were wearing their hair in dreadlocks – as celebrated by the title of what was in effect Bob Marley's first solo album, *Natty Dread*.

VARIOUS ARTISTS

◑ **Classic Reggae (Definitive Revival Reggae Mastercuts Volume One)** (Mastercuts, UK).

A dozen very popular classics, drawn by deejay David Rodigan from a range of producers/labels: Channel One, for instance, for the Wailing Souls' steppers classic "Very Well", Lee Perry for the Jolly Brothers' "Conscious Man", Augustus Pablo for Jacob Miller's "Keep On Knocking", Jack Ruby for Fabian Miranda's "Prophecy". The best of UK roots productions are also represented, with anthems such as Aswad's militant instrumental "Warrior Charge" and Pablo Gad's account of "Hard Times". Beginners' stuff, maybe, but what a beginning!

◑ **Rockers** (Mango, JA/US).

The soundtrack to the Theodoros Bagfaloukas movie, and an album that can be recommended to newcomers and aficionados. To the former, the selection is a wonderful introduction to the music, bringing together classics such as Junior Byles's "Fade Away", Junior Murvin's "Police & Thieves" and Gregory Isaacs' "Slave Master"; to the latter it offers the only way to get hold of a totally a cappella version of Burning Spear's "Jah No Dead", on which he is backed only by the surf on the beach.

◑ **Knotty Vision** (Nighthawk, US).

One of the finest-ever roots collections, compiled with real vision. The emphasis is firmly on the most serious but understated examples of the genre, with all the artists – Bunny Wailer, Big Youth, Gregory Isaacs, the Wailing Souls, Sylford Walker, the Itals and Little Roy – on their most heartfelt form. A pity that this did not begin a series of similar sets.

Bob Marley & the Wailers

The main stimulus for the rock world's belated interest in reggae in the mid-1970s was Island Records' adroit promotion of **Bob Marley & the Wailers** as a rock act, even if initial record sales were modest by then-current international standards. The Wailers – the vocal trio of Bob Marley, Bunny Wailer and Peter Tosh – signed to the UK's top independent record label in 1972, following the group's first visit to London in order to promote the debut CBS single, "Reggae On Broadway" (a track credited to Bob Marley alone). The single didn't sell, and Marley wisely – or perhaps desperately – turned up at Island Records' studio to make contact with the label's owner Chris Blackwell.

Presumably, Bob remembered Island as the UK company that had released some of the Wailers' ska output in the UK. He might also have been aware that, after concentrating on more lucrative rock acts like Traffic, Jethro Tull and Free, Chris Blackwell had returned to the Jamaican music with which he had established his company, releasing the soundtrack to *The Harder They Come*, starring Jimmy Cliff as an archetypal rude boy. Following the success of the album, which sold to hippy types who hadn't previously bought a reggae record, Cliff left Island, wanting to sign with the sort of larger company he felt could give him greater promotion on the world stage. When Marley met Island's boss he must have seemed the obvious replacement for Cliff: not a Jamaican singer who could convincingly play the role of a West Kingston rude boy, but the real thing. Nevertheless, a couple of changes would have to take place before the Wailers could be sold to a wider album-oriented audience. To begin with, black harmony groups were almost entirely associated in the rock world with soul – which by this time couldn't have been more unfashionable. What's more, there was a perception, fostered by rock critics, that any music deserving to be taken seriously was made by self-contained bands featuring a lead guitarist and 'meaningful' lyrics. And progressive music appeared on albums, not 45s.

Fortunately for Island's strategy, the Wailers were already accustomed to playing with the former Hippie Boys/Upsetters bass and drum team: Aston 'Family Man' Barrett and his brother Carlton. Thus the basic Wailers line-up – Bob (vocals, acoustic guitar), Bunny (vocals, percussion) and Peter (vocals, guitar, keyboards), supported by the Barrett brothers and Earl 'Wire' Lindo (organ) – was formed as an outfit that could tour in the manner of a regular rock band. This was the group that made the historic *Catch A Fire* at the Harry J, Dynamic and Randy's studios in Kingston. Overdubs by such rock luminaries as Stevie Winwood (organ), Wayne Perkins (guitar) and Chris Karen (tabla) were added in London, and the finished item was packaged in an eye-catching cover in the shape of a Zippo lighter. The first reggae album made with a rock audience specifically in mind, *Catch A Fire* was released in the UK in December 1972, and in spring of the next year the Wailers returned to tour the country, attracting not only long-time fans from the Jamaican communities but also the hipper representatives of the rock press. Though the performances were low-key compared to the shows Marley was to put on later, the gigs at venues like London's fashionable Speakeasy and the more down-to-earth Greyhound pub were stunning, and left no doubts that this was an outfit to be taken very seriously indeed. This was confirmed when the Wailers appeared with Marvin Gaye at the Carib Theatre and the National Arena in Kingston; later that year they toured the USA with Sly & the Family Stone, upstaging them regularly.

The first cracks in the band soon began to show. Bunny became unwilling to leave Jamaica, so Joe Higgs, the group's original Trench Town mentor, took his place for an American tour. Peter, too, was starting to feel restricted in his role in the band, though his anthemic "Get Up Stand Up" appeared on their second album for Island, *Burnin'*. This 1973 triumph also included a new Marley song "I Shot the Sheriff", which became a sizeable hit for Eric Clapton the following year – bringing welcome royalty payments and a further broadening of the Wailers' audience. Towards the close of 1974, after eleven years of recording together, the strain within the trio became too much, and Peter and Bunny left, both feeling that too much attention was given to Bob. Earl Lindo also left, taking up an offer from US roots musician Taj Mahal, who had recorded part of his album *Mo' Roots* in Jamaica that year. This may well have been a relief to Island, as it was fairly obvious by then that Marley, always

ADRIAN BOOT

Catch A Fire: Bob and herb

the keenest worker of the original trio, was also the easiest Wailer to promote as a rock star. In the last instance, both Bunny and Peter proved, in their different ways, too difficult to integrate into the marketing process that is necessary for crossover success. In any case, both had already launched their own Jamaican labels, and they soon became separately contracted to Virgin and Island, which made the promotion of the charismatic Marley even easier.

Another smart move in the packaging of Marley for international consumption was made after Peter and Bunny had departed to pursue their solo careers. Instead of attempting to replace their cool and characteristically Jamaican male harmonies, the more gospel-inflected backup vocals of the I-Threes were brought in, to supply a sound much more familiar to rock audiences of the time. As the three women involved had already established careers as singers in their own right, there was never any doubting the individual talents of **Rita Marley** (b. Alvarita Anderson, Kingston), **Marcia Griffiths** (b. 1954, Kingston) and **Judy Mowatt** (b. 1952, Kingston), but their voices also blended seamlessly together and they helped give a more striking visual image to the stage shows – which would eventually reach a global audience.

The Tuff Gong: Bob Marley

Though his move to Island was a giant step forward, **Bob Marley**'s colossal successful success owed much to past achievements – ones that had been largely ignored by the world outside of Jamaica and that island's communities in the UK. While not afraid to incorporate elements from outside reggae for the sake of wider acceptability (most obviously the rock/blues guitar of Junior Marvin and the harmonies of the I-Threes), Marley also looked back to the Wailers' music of the turn of the decade. Essentially, Marley and his band spruced up variants of the skank-type rhythms developed with, first, **Lee Perry**, and then on the early releases on the group's own **Tuff Gong** label. This was despite the fact that, by the middle of the 1970s, the style of rhythm originally forged with the Barrett brothers under Scratch's supervision had become passé in the dancehalls of Kingston. It was Marley's genius to adapt his music for international appeal, while never forgetting where he came from.

The self-produced material released on Tuff Gong had been firmly based on what the Wailers had learned in their couple of extremely prolific years with Scratch (late 1969–71). Early but totally confident Tuff Gong singles, such as "Craven Choke Puppy", "Screw Face", "Lively Up Yourself" and the anthemic "Trench Town Rock" were, like the Upsetter hits before them, distinguished by tough sinuous rhythms and the strength of Marley's songwriting. (Several of his triumphs from this period, like those cut previously with Scratch, were to be re-recorded on Island/Tuff Gong albums.) Peter Tosh and Bunny Wailer were just as distinctive in their visions of the world – Peter was the outspoken 'rebel', the more soulful Bunny was the spiritual Rasta man – but on the Tuff Gong releases their main contribution was as superb harmonizers.

In 1975, Island/Tuff Gong released what can be termed the first Bob Marley solo album. The **I-Threes** took the place of Bunny and Peter's harmonies on *Nattty Dread*, a title obviously designed to catch the mood of the moment in Kingston – and to captivate young rock fans in Europe and the USA with its rebel image. To promote the album they performed two concerts at London's Lyceum Ballroom, and from these acclaimed shows came the live album that further broadened Marley's appeal. It was in the following year, however, that Marley for the first time entered the American album charts. Again, it was with a title that served to emphasize an exotic and now very marketable image. *Rastaman Vibration* was weaker than any of the preceding Island albums, but this didn't stop American music journalists proclaiming it as the "Jamaican rock & roll". Prepared by a busy touring schedule, the time was at last right for Marley's breakthrough in Jamaica's powerful neighbour.

Unfortunately, 1976 was also the year when the Jamaican reality of outlaws and firearms intruded into the carefully managed image. On the eve of a concert to be held at Kingston's National Heroes Park on December 4, gunmen broke into Marley's home and made an attempt on his life. Though wounded, Marley performed at the concert, and later celebrated his survival with the single "Ambush", a record whose power lay in the way Marley drew more general principles from his personal drama:

"See them fighting for power, but they know not the hour
So they bribe dem with their guns, cars and money
Trying to belittle our integrity
They say what we know is just what they teach us
We're so ignorant 'cos every time they can reach us
Through political strategy, they keep us hungry
Every time you gotta get food
Your brother is your enemy."

The reasons put forward for the shooting have ranged from Marley's supposed sympathies for Michael Manley's PNP to the involvement of some of his considerable entourage in a horse-racing scam. But whatever the reason, from this point onwards Jamaica's only true international superstar was to spend far less time on the island. At the beginning of the next year he left Jamaica for eighteen months, going on to further enormous successes in the international market – the album

Exodus spent 56 weeks in the UK album chart during 1977–78, and his live performances were extraordinarily popular. A 1980 show in Milan attracted 100,000 fans, the Wailers' largest ever audience, and a performance the same year in the the new nation of Zimbabwe reputedly inspired many African musicians to play reggae. Towards the close of that year, Marley fell ill in New York, and was diagnosed as suffering from cancer, probably caused by a football injury. In April 1981, he received the Jamaican Order of Merit for his services to his country's culture. On May 11, Bob Marley, the greatest Jamaican artist ever, died in a Miami hospital. His funeral in Jamaica drew unparalleled crowds and was attended by both political leaders.

Taken together Bob Marley's Island/Tuff Gong albums represent a phenomenal achievement, one unequalled by any other Jamaican performer. The music found on them is, for the most part, far removed from the mainstream of what was being recorded in the Kingston studios in the period 1973–80, but only a reggae snob would find fault in this. It remains a tribute to the integrity of the Third World's only global superstar that none of the moves towards an 'international reggae' style detracted from the message or the quality of the music. This is the essential nature of Marley's talent: he expanded reggae's musical and commercial perimeters while remaining true to where he started.

The Stepping Razor: Peter Tosh

Even before the original three Wailers split up to pursue solo careers, **Peter Tosh** had released the first singles on a label of his own, Intel Diplo H.I.M. (Intelligent Diplomat for His Imperial Majesty). The move to launch his own label, financed by payments for Wailers material from Island, was not that surprising. From the late ska days of "Rasta Shook Then Up" and "I'm the Toughest" for Coxsone, the oldest Wailer had carved out an identity for himself that was distinct from the group one: that of the angry rebel who was increasingly conscious of black history. He was also the Wailer who provided the early group with much of its 'bite', as he proclaimed on "I'm the Toughest":

"Anything you can do, I can do better
I'm the toughest, I'm the toughest
I can do what you can do
You never try to do what I do."

Solo records then appeared in the early 1970s on Joe Gibbs' labels (credited to Peter Tosh/Peter Touch), as well as a couple on Lee Perry's imprint – "Second Hand" and the typically angry "Downpresser". On Intel Diplo, Tosh made a

DAVID CORIO

Peter Tosh, the Toughest, takes the spotlight

vibrant series of singles between 1973 and the end of the decade that showed a more fully developed musical and social vision. These 45s – committed, militant and focused – impressed far more than the higher-profile but patchier albums he made for the Rolling Stones label and EMI. The most striking singles were imbued with a sense of outrage against past and present injustices dealt the black nation, and included the apocalyptic "Babylon Queendom" and "Mark Of the Beast", as well as "Legalise It", a defence of the herb that was to become the anthem of the 1975 Notting Hill Carnival in London and remains the tune most associated with his name.

Tosh's life was eventful, even by the standards of the Jamaican music world. He survived a serious car crash on Spanish Town Road in 1973, which left his girlfriend dead, and there were numerous run-ins with the law. These ranged from his arrest on an anti-apartheid demonstration in the late 1960s to being taken in several times for possession of the herb he so forthrightly defended. Finally, on September 11, 1987, armed men entered his Plymouth Avenue house, in St Andrew. Despite the trial and conviction of one of these, Dennis 'Leppo' Dixon, the motives for what followed remain unclear. The intruders shot all seven of the people present: Tosh's common-law wife Marlene Brown, the drummer Carlton 'Santa' Davis, Yvonne Dixon and Michael Robinson survived; Tosh, the broadcaster/ singer Jeff 'Free I' Dixon and Wilton Brown were killed. The incident might simply have been a robbery carried out with maximum violence, but the attempt by gunmen a month later to murder Marlene Brown could be taken to support her view that murder had been the whole purpose of the raid. Whatever the full facts of Tosh's murder, the reggae world had lost an artist whose work expressed both a clear-sighted political consciousness and a blazingly righteous anger. These qualities have only recently resurfaced in the work of the more conscious dancehall performers, such as Anthony B, whose 1996 "Fire 'Pon Rome" could have been written by Tosh.

The Blackheart Man: Bunny Wailer

Though not as prolific as either Bob or Tosh during the Wailers' times with Coxsone or Scratch, **Bunny Wailer** matured the quickest as both singer and songwriter. His vocal style, initially a less fragile version of Curtis Mayfield's tenor, was ideally suited to the romanticism of much of his early material – the best example of which was the sublime "Sunday Morning". Nevertheless, he was

ADRIAN BOOT

Wailers football action: Bunny waits for Bob to pass

capable of applying himself to other topics – the rude-boy anthem "Let Him Go" was one of the finest of the genre, and 'cultural' statements such as "I Stand Predominate" and "He Who Feels It Knows It" anticipated the future. During the Upsetter years, his output shrank to just a couple of tunes, though one of these was the beautiful repatriation plea "Dreamland", quite possibly his most enduring composition. From then on, his romanticism would be transposed into something more reflective and spiritual.

His 1971 cut of "Dreamland" demonstrated Bunny's increasing commitment to the Rastafarian faith, and this found its fullest expression after the Wailers had signed to Island and he was able to launch his own imprint, **Solomonic**, beginning with his best love song of all, "Looking For Love". Interestingly enough, the strongest of the records released on Solomonic tended to be those released shortly before and just after he had parted from the Wailers – including such sublime shots as "Trod On", "Life Line" (both these credited to the group), the exquisite "Bide Up" and "Arab's Oil Weapon", and then 1975's "Battering Down Sentence" and "Rasta Man", which were to be two of the highlights of his classic first album. As the decade drew to a close, his self-produced 45s became less consistent, though there is no denying the power of, say, 1979's "Bright Soul" and "Free Jah Children", 1980's "Gamblings", or 1981's exceptionally militant "Rise & Shine". Curiously, a new burst of sustained creativity for the man who had always seemed the most spiritual of the Wailers was to come in the early 1980s, when Jamaican music shifted from roots to the more hedonistic concerns of dancehall.

BOB MARLEY & THE WAILERS

◑ **Legend** (Tuff Gong, JA; Island, UK/US).

◑ **Natural Mystic** (Tuff Gong, JA; Island, UK/US).

E The two best-selling Bob Marley albums (*Legend* has sold an incredible twelve million copies worldwide), and deservedly so. Every set he recorded had its share of classics, but these two collections of his most popular records comprise nothing but tracks of that order.

◑ **Songs Of Freedom** (Tuff Gong, JA; Island, UK/US).

E A four-CD/eight-LP set, complete with lavishly illustrated booklet, that is unlikely ever to be superseded by any single reggae artist. Much more than 'greatest hits' compilations, it covers every period from raw ska, through beautiful rocksteady (that was never quite typical of the genre), to the reggae classics that brought him to the world's attention. The set includes much that has not appeared on album before, as well as previously unreleased material; highlight of the latter must be the revelatory acoustic medley recorded in a Stockholm hotel room that sheds new light on Bob's creative processes. The most essential of all essential reggae sets.

◑ **Catch A Fire** (Tuff Gong, JA; Island, UK/US).

◑ **Burnin'** (Tuff Gong, JA; Island, UK/US).

Both the Wailers' first two albums for Island included contributions from Peter Tosh and Bunny Wailer, though Marley is very much the dominant figure. The debut makes concessions to the rock market in the mix and extra instrumentation, which is entirely dropped for the second album, one of the most uncompromised reggae sets ever to appear on a major label.

◑ **Natty Dread** (Tuff Gong, JA; Island, UK/US).

The first album on which the I-Threes take the place of Peter and Bunny. The Jamaican hits included were the title track, "Talkin' Blues", "Belly Full" and "Rebel Music". There was also the first cut to one of Bob's best-known songs, "No Woman No Cry".

◑ **Live!** (Tuff Gong, JA; Island, UK/US).

Recorded in front of a multiracial audience in London, this was an unalloyed triumph that consolidated Marley's achievements and considerably broadened his audience. One of the most exciting live albums ever.

◑ **Rastaman Vibration** (Tuff Gong, JA; Island, UK/US).

Though it rightly never received the rapturous praise garnered by its immediate predecessor or successor,

RASTAFARIANISM

Most of the world only became aware of **Rastafarianism** through the elevation of Bob Marley & the Wailers to international superstar status, but the cult first emerged in Jamaica during the late 1930s. In 1930 the Prince Regent of Abyssinia, **Ras Tafari Makonnen** had been crowned King Negus Negusta, and on November 2 had assumed the official title of **Emperor Haile Selassie I**, an event that made a huge impact on black people round the world. Media coverage showed a powerful African king, receiving the tributes of leaders of the developed world, an event which had been forecast by **Marcus Mosiah Garvey**, the other main philosophical influence on Rastafarianism. Garvey, born in the Jamaican parish of St Ann in 1887, came to prominence after moving to New York in March 1916. There he set about fundraising for the Universal Negro Improvement Association, which he had founded in Jamaica after he returned from England in 1914. By the 1920s the UNIA had five million members, and under Garvey's leadership the organization published the Negro World newspaper and established the Black Star Line, a shipping company intended to transport black people to a new independent state in Africa.

Black nationalists in Harlem, in particular the organization known as the Abyssinians, gained impetus from the coronation of Haile Selassie I; they advised their fellow black people to burn the American flag and sold certificates of Abyssinian citizenship. These incidents found an echo in Jamaica, where **Leonard Percival Howell**, a Jamaican who had returned to the island in December 1932, began preaching that the poor should pay allegiance to the Emperor of Ethiopia and not to the British crown. Howell sold pictures of Haile Selassie I to his followers, a seditious act that earned him two years' hard labour in 1933. But his message had not fallen on deaf ears, and in the 1940s Howell established the Pinnacle community (see p.24), which would become a focus for Rastafarianism. In the meantime the Ethiopian World Federation had been founded in 1937 in New York by Haile Selassie I's cousin, Dr Malaku Bayen, to organize support for Ethiopia, then being invaded by fascist Italy. By 1938 a Jamaican branch was in existence. Many tenets of the Rastafarian philosophy, in particular the culture of the Ethiopian Orthodox church with its emphasis on Selassie as the Elect of God, were derived from this organization's newspaper *The Voice*

Marley's 1976 album includes three out-and-out classics – "War", "Rat Race" and "Crazy Baldhead".

◑ **Exodus** (Tuff Gong, JA; Island, UK/US).
An album divided into supposedly "heavier" cultural and "lighter" romantic sides, the two elements coming together in the final track, "One Love". "Natural Mystic", "The Heathen", "Exodus" and "Waiting In Vain" match anything Marley had previously done; even more important is the totally self-assured manner in which the album stands as a complete work.

◑ **Kaya** (Tuff Gong, JA; Island, UK/US).
Another set that only seemed disappointing when measured against the classic that preceded it. "Running Away" and "Is This Love" were the best of the new material, while reworkings of "Sun Is Shining", "Kaya" and "Satisfy My Soul" were different from (rather than superior or inferior to) the originals.

◑ **Survival** (Tuff Gong, JA; Island, UK/US).
Marley's response to the attempt on his life at the end of 1976, "Ambush In the Night", towers over everything here, though "So Much Trouble In the World" and "One Drop" seem stronger as time goes by.

◑ **Uprising** (Tuff Gong, JA; Island, UK/US).
The strongest collection of new Marley songs since *Exodus*. "Coming In From the Cold", "Bad Card", "Forever Loving Jah" and "Could You Be Loved" are outstanding by any standards, while the reflective "Redemption Song" must be the strongest track he ever recorded after meeting Chris Blackwell.

◑ **Confrontation** (Tuff Gong, JA; Island, UK/US).
Standards were maintained here, on an album that boasts at least four classics – "Buffalo Soldiers", "Chant Down Babylon" "Blackman Redemption" and "Rastaman Live Up".

Of Ethiopia. Poor Jamaicans were primed for the message of Rastafarianism, having long sought solace in the Bible – the Book of Revelations ("Weep not, behold the Lion that is of the tribe of Judah", etc), along with the Apocrypha, provided many texts that yielded to reinterpretation by Kingston's 'sufferers'.

Following the granting of independence in 1962, and the failure of the main political parties to offer hopes of a better life for the majority of Jamaicans, Rastafarianism rapidly spread. It was of course fuelled by the Black consciousness movements in the US, but gained an extra dynamic from conditions that were unique to Jamaica, an underdeveloped Caribbean island situated close to the world's wealthiest and most powerful nation. The desire of struggling singers to jump on a bandwagon was undoubtedly an element in the explosion of Rastafarianism in the 1970s, and the seeming omnipresence of dreadlocks and Rasta-speak among the ghetto youth. But it would be a mistake to question the sincerity with which many grasped a faith that offered a positive alternative to a life of crime or the despair of the ghetto.

Although some Rastas attempted to establish a coherent system of beliefs along the lines indicated by Ethiopian Orthodoxy, Rastafarianism is not a church with a hierarchy and official doctrine. Rather, ever since the name first came into use in the late 1940s, it has always consisted of a core of spiritual, historical and social tenets open to a range of interpretations, as espoused in more recent times by such Rastafarian associations as the United Ethiopian Body, the Ethiopian Youth Cosmic Faith, the Ethiopian Coptic League and the **Twelve Tribes of Israel**, a group formed in the early 1970s and which attracted a number of high-profile adherents, notably Bob Marley. Even the stereotyped image of the Rasta, with dreadlocks and spliff, doesn't hold for all Rastafarians: some neither combing nor cutting their hair, whereas others have it cut conventionally; some view ganja as a religious sacrament, but others do not smoke at all. What all Rastafarians share is the belief that Africa is the Black race's spiritual home, to which they are destined one day to return. The West, where their ancestors were taken in chains, is vilified as 'Babylon', after the place where the Israelites were enslaved. Most Rastafarians recognize a divine line of royal sucession descended from King David, with Haile Selassie I as the 225th in that line. Even his death after the communist coup on September 12, 1974, failed to shake this belief, presumably since God is ever-living.

⊙ **The Complete Wailers 1967-1972 Part I (JAD/EMI, France)**

This superb three-disc set is the first part of an ambitious nine-disc series covering the Wailers output during the transition years between Coxsone and Island. The first CD consists of the sessions previously issued on Chances Are album, here presented in original-mix form. The songs are done US soul style, and show Marley already reaching tentatively for an international audience. The second CD has the rarities, including the transcendent "Selassie Is The Chapel", while the third collects material from Leslie Kong and Bunny Lee.

PETER TOSH

◑ **Legalise It** (Intel Diplo, JA; Virgin, UK).

The most outspoken of the original Wailers never quite maintained the standards of his best singles over the length of an album. The first LP under his own name comprises recuts and remixes of his most successful local hits, compiled with one eye on Bob's crossover market. It remains the nearest he came to a completely satisfactory set.

BUNNY WAILER

◑ **Blackheart Man** (Solomonic, JA; Island, UK).

E The international labels that became involved with reggae during the 1970s made plenty of mistakes, but were also responsible for a handful of classics that otherwise would probably not have taken quite the form they did. Bunny Wailer's debut set, originally issued in the UK and Jamaica with a gatefold sleeve, is a case in point. This was a reggae album on which considerable time and thought had obviously been spent, and was aimed far beyond the dancehall. The effort was more than justified by the strongest songs Bunny ever wrote – including "Fighting Against Conviction" (aka "Battering Down Sentence"), "Bide Up" and "Dreamland" – and the most considered treatments imaginable. Sublime music.

In I Father's House (Solomonic, JA).
A 1980 set that represented something of a return to roots form after the disappointing *Protest*. Highlights include a majestic "Love Fire", and a version of his own "Let Him Go", originally recorded by the Wailers in the 1960s. The trite "Wirly Girly" brings the standard down a little, but otherwise everything is typical Bunny Wailer prior to his dancehall phase.

Sings the Wailers (Solomonic, JA).
Bunny has often returned to the Wailers catalogue over the years; easily the most successful is this set, recorded with Sly & Robbie in 1980. The ten songs covered – four written by Bob, three by Bunny, two by Peter, plus Curtis Mayfield's "Keep On Moving"– serve as a pretty accurate indicator of the contributions made by each member of the trio, and are sung by Bunny with powerful sincerity.

Tribute (Solomonic, JA).
Issued shortly after Bob died, this includes further covers cut at the *Sings the Wailers* sessions. Both of these sets put to shame the rather perfunctory workouts on the overblown 52-track *Hall Of Fame* set, which won a Grammy in early 1997.

The UK connection

The attempt by certain UK labels to bring Jamaican reggae to a rock-oriented audience was fraught with problems. To begin with, even after the international success of Bob Marley & the Wailers, self-contained bands were a rarity in Jamaica. With the exception of the North Coast hotel circuit, the emphasis on the island was on sound systems rather than live groups of any description, and the usual method of recording was for singers to voice-over pre-recorded rhythm tracks built every day by studio musicians. But whereas Jamaican artists were accustomed to release singles almost on a weekly basis, recorded for a wide variety of producers, both Island and Virgin were used to dealing with artists and/or management who targeted the very different album market.

Bearing these cultural differences in mind, it's remarkable that the investment in Jamaican music by two of the UK's leading progressive rock record companies, Chris Blackwell's **Island** and Richard Branson's **Virgin**, worked as well as it did. They provided finance for a number of fine reggae albums by artists as diverse as the **Mighty Diamonds** and **Burning Spear**, as well as enabling various performers to start their own Jamaican labels. Island concentrated on Marley and a couple of other self-contained bands, but also did deals with the producers Lee Perry, Jack Ruby and Harry J that brought some excellent music to a wide audience. Virgin also started strongly, licensing material from 'Joe Joe' Hookim, Bunny Lee and Prince Tony Robinson, while Virgin Front Line albums by the Mighty Diamonds, Johnnie Clarke, Peter Tosh, U-Roy and the **Gladiators** all sold exceptionally well.

But an even more important factor than the rock audience's appetite for roots reggae was the development of an audience among the offspring of Jamaican immigrants to the UK. In the immigrant areas of Britain's cities, sound systems like Battersea's Sir Coxsone Outernational and the Mighty Moa Ambessa, Lewisham's Jah Shaka, Brixton's Sofrano B and D'Nunes, and Birmingham's Quaker City were the equivalent of an underground radio network. Though the well-distributed and well-packaged albums turned out by Island and Virgin were bought by black youth in the UK, they were far better served by the dozens of small and struggling independent labels that sprung up in the wake of Trojan's demise in 1974. Labels such as Dip, Third World, Black Wax, Grounation, Ethnic Fight and Burning Sounds all drew on the work of a wide range of Jamaican producers, a policy in contrast to Island's or Virgin's rush to sign performers who might follow the Marley route. These small companies knew far more about what was being played in 'blues parties' or sound-system clashes than any major label ever could, and the fact that only Hawkeye and Grove Music have survived demonstrates the difficulties of running an independent record company with very limited financial backing, rather than reflecting errors in musical judgement. The foreign market that exercised the main influence on studios in Kingston was the one for which these companies catered, and not the white crossover audience that often seemed receptive only to large advertising budgets and the related articles in the pop weeklies.

The Man In the Hills: Burning Spear

After the Wailers, the reggae act that had the greatest international impact was another vocal trio signed by Island – **Burning Spear**. However, there were crucial differences between the two acts. For one thing, Burning Spear had too uncompromising a sound ever to achieve quite the same kind of stardom as Marley; for another, whereas the original Wailers trio comprised three strong personalities, each with his own musical approach, Burning Spear (aka **Winston Rodney**) was a powerful solo performer, who simply employed two harmony singers to help flesh out his unique vocal style – one that seemed to owe a great deal more to traditional Rastafarian chanting and jazz-like improvisation than to mainstream reggae.

Born in the same St Ann's Bay area as Marcus Garvey and Bob Marley, Winston Rodney made two albums' worth of exemplary tracks for Studio One, nearly all of them informed by his Garveyite believes and faith in Rastafari. He then became one of the handful of artists to have begun by making ground-breaking records at Brentford Road, and then gone on to surpass them with even more dynamic and commercially successful recordings. Upon leaving Clement Dodd, Burning Spear brought in the harmonies of **Rupert Wellington** and **Delroy Hines**, and moved to North Coast sound-system operator and record producer, **Jack Ruby** (b. Lawrence Lindo), for a far fuller, 'dreader' production style, driven by the horns of Richard 'Dirty Harry' Hall, Herman Marquis, Vin Gordon and Bobby Ellis.

The epochal singles "Marcus Garvey" and "Slavery Days" were sizeable Jamaican hits in 1975, but it was the album named after the former hit, released the same year, that really established Burning Spear as the leading force in the new generation of 'cultural' singers concerned almost exclusively with black history, its relation to contemporary ghetto conditions, and the salvation promised by Rastafari. After *Man In the Hills*, another Ruby production featuring Burning Spear as a trio, Rodney returned to his original solo status, and to self-production. "Travelling", "Free Black People", "Spear Burning" and "Throw Down Your Arms" were among the exceptional 45s then released, the first on Total Sounds, and the others on his own Spear and Burning Spear imprints, though – unusually for a Jamaican artist – it was to be albums on which his reputation was largely to rest. Indeed, with the possible exception of Marley, no other Jamaican performer has been better suited to the album format – lacking immediate hooks, his music has relied on the general smoky ambience of the studio recordings and an astonishingly intense vocal style that is best appreciated over an entire set. His message has not changed over the years, and he remains the most compelling live performer in reggae, who at his best almost hypnotizes his audience. The albums reviewed below are the strongest crystallizations of his musical and social vision.

ADRIAN BOOT

Winston Rodney: Behold the Spear Burning

BURNING SPEAR

◑ **Marcus Garvey** (Fox, JA; Island, UK).

E Winston Rodney's first set for Ruby was also one of the first reggae albums after Bob

Marley's *Catch A Fire* and *Burnin'* to work as a unified creation, and it made an impression on trend-conscious rock fans beginning to suspect that there was more to reggae than the charismatic Marley. Even in the remixed form of its UK release by Island, it was an amazing document, both musically and in the vision expressed.

◑ **Social Living [Marcus's Children]** (Burning Spear, JA; Blood & Fire, UK).

E First released in 1978, this remains the most fully accomplished Spear set after *Marcus Garvey*. From the pain-racked opening, "Marcus Children Suffer", through similarly dread-serious tracks such as "Marcus Say Jah No Dead" and "Institution", there is no doubting the total integrity.

◑ **Man In the Hills** (Wolf, JA; Island, UK).
The next LP under the guidance of Ruby, which appeared the following year, expressing to a greater degree the rural lifestyle that Rodney had chosen, and only just falling short of the standard already set.

◑ **Dry & Heavy** (Spear, JA; Island, UK; Mango, US).
The first self-produced solo album, from 1977, made obvious his fully developed musical vision, as well as the social, historic and religious world-view that had always informed his work. The dense sound that now engulfed his material perfectly complemented the unique vocal approach that sometimes touched an almost jazz-like abstraction. Includes the marvellous "Throw Down Your Arms".

◑ **Hail H.I.M.** (Burning Spear, JA).
The final classic Burning Spear album, released in 1980. The power of tracks like "Cry Blood Africans" and "Columbus" belie any notions about the redundancy of an orthodox roots approach by that date.

VARIOUS ARTISTS

◑ **Black Slavery Days** (Clappers, US).
Recorded in 1975, this collection of horn-soaked roots productions from St Ann's displays much the same feel as the Jack Ruby-produced work of Burning Spear. The title track from the Skulls, led by Tony Thomas (one of Justin Hinds' original Dominoes) attracted some attention as a 45 (then called "Bondage"), and remains the set's highlight. But almost matching it are the group's other contributions, as well as those from two more fairly obscure groups, Arrows and the Original Survivors, each of which features one of Burning Spear's original harmony singers. Worthwhile dubs to some tracks, as well.

Third World, Black Uhuru and Justin Hinds & the Dominoes

Third World – initially, Stephen 'Cat' Coore, Michael 'Ibo' Cooper, Richard

ADRIAN BOOT

Roots with quality: Third World

Daley, Willie 'Roots' Stewart, Irving 'Carrot' Stewart, Milton 'Prilly' Hamilton – were the best of the self-contained Jamaican reggae bands after the Wailers and, as such, no doubt made much more sense to Island than outstanding vocal harmony trios like the Abyssinians, the Royals and the African Brothers (or, for that matter, the Wailing Souls or the veteran **Heptones**, whom they did sign, but failed to promote sufficiently). Reggae snobs have dismissed these sons of the Jamaican middle class – guitarist/cello player Stephen 'Cat' Coore is the son of former Deputy Prime Minster David Coore – as a slick crossover act, ignoring the quality of first Milton 'Prilly' Hamilton's vocals and then William 'Bunny Rugs' Clarke's, as well as the entire band's high level of musicianship. They have also always been capable of making records as 'rootsy' as they want – witness tracks such as the 1981 gem "Roots With Quality", the title of which pretty much sums up their broad appeal.

The third, visually more striking, line-up of **Black Uhuru** (**Michael Rose**, **Derrick 'Ducky' Simpson** and **Puma Jones**) also appealed to Island, at least once they had joined forces with the drum and bass partnership of **Sly Dunbar** and **Robbie Shakespeare**, to become a band in the accepted rock sense. It is unlikely that either of the previous all-male vocal line-ups of the group that Simpson founded – originally with **Rudolph 'Garth' Dennis** (later of the Wailing Souls) and future solo star **Don (Mc)Carlos**, then with **Errol Nelson** and Michael Rose – would have been deemed to possess quite the same crossover appeal. Indeed, the very strong 1978 album made by the second incarnation of the group for engineer-turned-producer Prince Jammy had failed to make the breakthrough to a wider audience. An excellent interpretation of Bob Marley's "Sun Is Shining" then appeared on the Channel One label Hitbound, but their real impact in the reggae world took place when they were produced by Sly & Robbie on tracks like "Plastic Smile" (Gorgon), "Abortion" and "General Penitentiary" (both Taxi). In this initial period with Sly & Robbie, the group also took time off to cut a couple of equally strong 45s for Dennis Brown's DEB imprint – "Wood For My Fire" and "Rent Man". Unfortunately, the most dynamic and progressive reggae act of the late 1970s/early 1980s were simply too militant in their poses and music to quite fill the international reggae superstar slot left vacant by the death of Bob Marley – despite having three excellent albums given international distribution by Island/Mango, as well as a compilation of their first hits with Sly & Robbie released by Virgin (and then the US Heartbeat label). Over the course of their first five albums, they pursued a course of uncompromising roots music that also transcended most of the genre's limitations.

ADRIAN BOOT

Black Uhuru, from left: Ducky Simpson, Puma Jones and Michael Rose

Another Island vocal group was one of the first obviously Rasta-inspired trios, **Justin Hinds & the Dominoes**, who dated back to the ska years. They had never possessed the rude-boy panache of the teenage Wailers – their heartfelt and deeply cultural music instead gained its impact from the superior songs of their leader and his distinctive lead vocals. Island matched Justin Hinds' distinctive rural feel to the horns-dominated production style that had already broadened the audience for Burning Spear, and the result was the great *Jezebel* album – amazingly, only the second album since the 1960s from what was one of Jamaica's premier vocal and writing talents. It demonstrated that his abilities were in no way diminished since the initial Jamaican hits for Duke Reid, which were released in the UK on Blackwell's old red-and-white Island label.

BLACK UHURU

Showcase (Taxi, JA; Heartbeat, US).

E Their promotion to the premier league came when the group replaced Errol Nelson with the visually arresting, American-born Puma Jones, and started to record and tour with Sly & Robbie. This 1979 'showcase' album (vocals followed by dubs) brought together five of their initial hit 45s – including the mighty "General Penitentiary" – and added a couple of fresh tracks calculated to have a similar impact.

Black Sounds of Freedom [Love Crisis] (Jammy's, JA; Greensleeves, UK).

Black Uhuru's debut album for Prince Jammy appeared, seemingly out of nowhere, in 1978. Tracks like "I Love King Selassie" and a stunning version of Marley's "Natural Mystic" announced the arrival of a serious new force in Jah's music. Perhaps because there were too many hard roots albums at the time, it initially met with limited success, but the Greensleeves edition both remixed and retitled the album four years later to far wider acclaim.

Sinsemilla (Taxi, JA; Island, UK).

Showcase sold well, but the next Taxi album, *Sinsemilla* (1980), created even more excitement. The themes were familiar, but no one before had created roots music that sounded quite like the title track, "World Is Africa" or "Endurance".

Red (Island, JA & UK).

Appearing the following year, *Red* built on the style already established, without taking any great steps forward. The most powerful track, "Guns Of Eglington", proved popular enough for Island to release a dub cut as a single.

Chill Out (Taxi, JA; Island, UK).

This 1982 release was the last Uhuru album of any real interest, even if the weaker *Anthem* was the one to win a Grammy. The chemistry was still working to good effect, particularly on "Darkness", "Chill Out" and "Mondays".

THE HEPTONES

Night Food (Island, UK; Mango, US).

One of the two albums that the legendary trio cut for Harry Johnson in the 1970s. Several of the tracks are reworkings – complete with string arrangements – of classics they had originally recorded for Studio One, but there is also original and quite stunning material that had appeared as Harry J and Jaywax 45s in Jamaica, including the popular "Book Of Rules", "Country Boy" and "Mama Say".

JUSTIN HINDS & THE DOMINOES

Jezebel (Island, UK).

While Justin Hinds' greatest achievements belong to ska and rocksteady, he was still making convincing records a decade later, first for Jack Ruby, then for Sonia Pottinger. His rural-style voice and proverb-based lyrics were never as fashionable in the dread 1970s as they should have been, though "Fire Is A Desire" and "Prophecy A Fulfil" were popular enough 45s in Jamaica, and the update of his first hit, "Carry Go Bring Come", was a reasonable seller in the UK reggae market.

THIRD WORLD

96 Degrees In the Shade (Island, UK).

Their second very accomplished album that left no doubts about the band's cohesive musical vision. "Third World Man" might be a little overproduced, but check the title track or the stunning "Human Market Place". A set they have yet to eclipse.

Reggae Ambassadors (Mango, US).

A two-CD compilation that covers their career from the eponymous debut album to a Mikey Bennett-produced 'combination' effort with ragga deejay Terror Fabulous, taking in a couple of minor masterpieces on the way that were previously available only as scarce 45s: "Railroad Track" and the Niney-produced "Roots With Quality", arguably their greatest track to date. Their version of the O'Jays' "Now That We've Found Love" remains the definitive one. Curiously, "Human Market Place" is missing, but it is hard to pick fault with any of the 31 tracks that are collected.

Rico Rodriguez and Ijahman Levi

Island also financed highly successful, if untypical, reggae albums from the contrasting figures of **Rico Rodriguez** and **Ijahman Levi** (b. Trevor Sutherland, 1946, Manchester, Jamaica). The former was a trombonist who had recorded prolifically in Jamaica in the years immediately preceding ska, and whom many saw as at least Don Drummond's equal. He had been living in England since 1961, where he had maintained both his Rastafarian beliefs and his capacity for inspired improvisation. When Island paid for him to return to Kingston for sessions with the city's leading contemporary studio musicians, including the ubiquitous Sly Dunbar and Robbie Shakespeare, the master musician effortlessly adapted to modern studio techniques, applying his jazz-influenced playing to a meditational roots context.

Ijahman Levi, on the other hand, was a much younger Jamaican-born singer and songwriter then living in north London, who came to Chris Blackwell's attention through three locally recorded singles. His "Chariot Of Love", "I'm A Levi" and "Jah Heavy Load" for Dip label-owner Dennis Harris remain among the strongest UK-produced roots reggae singles ever released; but Blackwell's attempt to steer this very distinctive performer towards appealing to the far larger audience who had bought Van Morrison's *Astral Weeks* disappointed many who had enthused over the 45s – especially as two of the songs were treated to extended (some thought pretentious) versions on the debut album, *Hail I Hymn*. Only in retrospect has this adventurous set gained near-classic status.

IJAHMAN LEVI

◑ **Hail I Hymn** (Island, UK; Mango, US).

Released in 1978, this was a reggae album of a type that had never been made before, nor has been since. Only four extended tracks, and drawing on the talents of not just the best Kingston session players, but rock star Steve Winwood and Del Richardson from Afro-rock band Osibisa. The set sounds far better now than it did at the time; it might not have represented the future of reggae – or even Ijahman Levi – but it stands as a more than interesting divergence from the mainstream.

RICO RODRIGUEZ

● **Man From Wareika** (Top Ranking, JA; Island, UK; Blue Note, US).

⊙ **Roots To the Bone** (Mango, UK).

Though Rico Rodriguez is one of Jamaican music's founding fathers, *Man From Wareika* was suitably licenced to the Blue Note jazz label in the US when first issued in 1978 on vinyl. It is a superbly accomplished Jamaican jazz set, most of which has been reissued on the CD *Roots To the Bone*, with a couple of tracks missing from the original. Additional tracks – Paul Desmond's "Take 5" and Chuck Mangione's "Children Of Sanchez" – more than compensate. Most importantly, Rico's beautiful, reflective compositions – "Free Ganja", "Lumumba" – have never been heard to better effect.

ADRIAN BOOT

I'm A Levi: Ijahman

Virgin groups – the Gladiators and the Mighty Diamonds

It was to Virgin's credit that, amid a throng of mostly mediocre deejay albums, they released excellent debut sets from two of Jamaica's finest vocal harmony groups, the **Gladiators** (Albert Griffiths, Clinton Fearon, Dallimore Sutherland) and the **Mighty Diamonds** (Donald 'Tabby' Shaw, Fitzroy 'Bunny' Shaw and Lloyd 'Judge' Ferguson) – even if they were also responsible for the latter's not very well-received collaboration with noted New Orleans r&b producer Allen Toussaint, *Ice On Fire*. Together, the first Mighty Diamonds and Gladiators sets demonstrated how the modern 'rockers' sound – largely brighter, brasher and more militant updates of rocksteady rhythms from the late 1960s – could support a range of vocal styles, ranging from the modern Philly/Chicago soul-influenced approach of the former group to the more traditional Jamaican rural tones of the latter.

THE GLADIATORS

Trenchtown Mix-Up (Virgin, UK).

It's impossible to recommend too highly the Prince Tony Robinson production that was the Gladiators' debut album (though recorded after most of their Studio One set). The local hits "Know Yourself Mankind" and "Eli Eli" are the equal of anything that had preceded them, and the mixture of originals and new interpretations of their old material (as well as a couple of Marley hits) updated their rural style to marvellous advantage.

Presenting the Gladiators (Studio One, JA).
This one tardily released album from Mr Dodd tells only half the story of their career with Studio One. It is worth picking up, however, for tracks like "Hello Carol", "Jah Jah Go Before Us" and "On the Other Side", even if it misses at least as many great numbers, including the essential "Roots Natty" and "Mr Baldwin".

The producer as auteur

Developments in Jamaica were stimulated by interest from abroad, particularly the UK, but the music would not have grown in quite the same way without the fierce competition between producers and their ability to respond to the demands of a new generation of West Kingston ghetto dwellers. As in previous periods, some of these producers owned their own studios while others had to use facilities owned by others. Among both groups there were two broad types of producer: highly creative figures who actively fed ideas into their sessions; and those who developed the sounds associated with their labels through employing particular musicians and/or engineers who would, in effect, supervise the sessions. By their skilful manipulation of various resources (singers, musicians, studio technicians) all the major producers developed easily identifiable styles of their own – in effect, they were like film directors controlling the crucial aspects of production to impose their vision. **Bunny Lee**, **Joseph Hookim**, **Joe Gibbs** and **Winston 'Niney' Holness** were the most consistently popular and widely imitated, and they dominated the dancehall scene of the day, using many of the same musicians on their sessions and releasing huge numbers of records. A handful of producers were more idiosyncratic, but markedly less successful in Jamaican terms. Prominent in this contingent was **Lee 'Scratch' Perry**, who – along with **Augustus Pablo** and to a lesser extent **Yabby You**, **Keith Hudson** and **Glen Brown** – has found the greatest acclaim outside Jamaica, usually in non-reggae circles. Perry, for all the brilliant work he did at his Black Ark studio, only scored a few isolated hits in Jamaica, but luckily his productions were released on Island albums for the international market.

Bunny 'Striker' Lee and the flying cymbals sound

The man who more than any other first showed how old rhythms could be updated and freshened for the youth audience of the mid-1970s was the ever-resourceful **Bunny Lee**. Precisely because he did not have his own studio but had to buy time from producers like Clive Chin at Randy's or Joseph and Ernest Hookim at Channel One, it was a matter of economic necessity to keep studio time to a minimum. One way of doing this was to use each rhythm more than once; another was to spend less precious studio time in the first place by having the musicians 'do-over' classic rhythms with which they were already familiar.

In making the updating of Studio One or Treasure Isle tracks a common practice, Bunny Lee anticipated not only the approaches of Channel One and Joe Gibbs, but the dancehall revolution of the next decade. His most successful vocalist, **Johnnie Clarke** (b. 1955, Kingston), could be called the first dancehall singer in the modern sense. Clarke spent so much time hanging around the studios he became known as the 'studio idler', but it paid off for the singer who became capable of fitting his distinctive tones and fresh lyrics onto the new versions of classic rocksteady rhythms Striker was building with his session musicians. During 1974 Striker had led the way with the 'flying cymbals' sound he had his drummer **Carlton 'Santa' Davis** develop, as a response to the then-popular 'Philly bump' style of US soul; it also became known as 'flyers', after the dance moves it engendered, which involved a kind of flying motion with the arms, done in time to the pronounced beat on the hi-hat cymbal.

Striker's session musicians, a fluid line-up known as the **Aggrovators**, also usually included Bobby Ellis on trumpet, Bernard 'Touter' Harvey, Winston Wright or Ansel Collins on organ, Ossie Hibbert, Keith Sterling or Errol 'Tarzan' Nelson on piano, Tony Chin or Winston 'Bo Beep' Bowen on rhythm guitar, Earl 'Chinna' Smith on lead guitar, Tommy McCook on tenor sax, Lennox Brown on alto sax, Robbie Shakespeare, Aston Barrett or Lloyd Parks on bass, Vin Gordon on trombone, and Barnabus or Noel 'Scully' Simms on percussion. Sometimes Sly Dunbar or Carlton Barrett (in between sessions with the Wailers band) would replace Santa at the drum kit, and Bunny's favourite singer, Johnnie Clarke, might sit at the piano. Cornell Campbell also played rhythm guitar from time to time.

While Bob Marley was broadening reggae's audience, Striker's productions dominated the Jamaican dancehalls – at least until the Channel One variation of the 'rockers' rhythm took over. Beginning with "Move Out Of Babylon Rastaman" (Justice) in 1974 (over an updated cut of John Holt's "Sad News" rhythm, a Studio One hit from four years earlier), Johnnie Clarke, who had already had a couple of local hits for Rupie Edwards, rapidly became one of the hottest young singers in Jamaica. This was with both his own (mostly 'cultural') lyrics and equally successful revivals of old romantic favourites, such as John Holt's "Stranger In Love" and "Fancy Make Up", and always employing familiar rhythms given a new lick of paint by Striker's studio band. The producer's other major singing star of the mid-1970s was **Cornell Campbell**. The possessor of a highly distinctive falsetto, Campbell had started back in the early 1960s making records in the ska vein for Clement Dodd. His Curtis Mayfield-tinged vocals, however, were even more suited to the romantic rocksteady era, when he was a member of the Uniques and the Eternals. Professional contact with Bunny dated from then. In the early 1970s, the Eternals split up and Campbell began recording as a solo performer for Bunny, cutting a distinguished debut album for release in the UK only. But it was in 1975 that he made his greatest impact on the Jamaican dancehalls, promoting himself on the "Gorgon" series of records (the initial hit based on Derrick Morgan's popular 1968 tune "Conquering Ruler"), and adapting to fashionable 'dread' lyrics with discs such as "Dread In A Greenwich Town" (Justice) and "Dance In A Greenwich Farm" (Attack).

The rhythms that supported Campbell on his mid-1970s hits were all in the same 'flying cymbals' style as the Johnnie Clarke hits, and other Brentford Road alumni to benefit from Striker's formula included **Horace Andy**, **Delroy Wilson** and **John Holt**, plus two vocalists with even longer recording histories – **Owen Gray** and **Jackie Edwards**. When the dominance of Channel One from the close of 1975 prompted another shift in the rhythm ruling the dancehalls, the Aggrovators adapted accordingly, and Bunny's combative attitude was expressed in wild 'version' sides like "Channel One Under Heavy Manners", "Channel Is A Joker" and "Channel Get A Knockout". Over the next couple of years, the producer who often used the Channel One studio for building rhythms notched up a further string of hits from Johnnie Clarke (including "Blood Dunza", "Don't Trouble Trouble" and "Peace And Love In the Ghetto"), as well as scoring with such triumphs as Cornell Campbell's "The Investigator" (which sounded like an Impressions song from the 1960s) and the gravel-voiced **Leroy Smart**'s biting "Wreck Up My Life". There was also a new generation of young contenders to prevent the established singers from resting on their past achievements, and the most notable of those recorded by Bunny were **Linval Thompson**, who scored his first big hits like "Cool Down Your Temper" and "Ride On" with Striker, and **Barry Brown**, whose rough-and-ready style anticipated the dancehall explosion. When with Bunny, he was heard near his best on the angry "Politician" (Jackpot), which recycled Horace Andy's fearsome "Money Money" rhythm.

Because Striker was among the first producers to realize the potential of using the same rhythm tracks time and time again ('version to version, chapter to chapter', in 1970s dancehall parlance), it was no surprise that he produced numerous deejay cuts of the most popular Aggrovators rhythms. There were perhaps too many, recorded too quickly, but genuinely interesting ones included at least some by **I-Roy**, **Prince Jazzbo**, **Big Joe**, **Little Joe**, **Tappa Zukie**, **Doctor Alimantado**, **U-Brown**, **Jah Stitch** and the Originator himself, **U-Roy**. Indeed, in the case of the man who had preceded Big Youth as the top 'toaster' on the Lord Tippertone sound system, Jah Stitch, some of the most pungent sides of his career were the result of his sessions with Bunny. Only his first hit, "Danger Zone" for Errol 'Flabba' Holt, along with a couple of sides for Yabby You, ever sounded quite as focused as rough culturally oriented tunes like "Give Jah the Glory", "African People" and "Watch Your Step Youthman" for Bunny Lee. Not long after Stitch left Tippertone to form his own Black Harmony sound, he also earned the distinction of being one of the few men in the world to survive being shot straight through the head, supposedly the result of the intermingling of sound-system and political rivalries.

None of Striker's numerous deejay hits created more excitement than the series of feuding 45s released in 1975 from the already well-established I-Roy and Prince Jazzbo. This variation of the 'sound wars' of the past began with the former's "Straight To Jazzbo's Head", and the latter's answer, "Straight To I-Roy's Head", continuing over "Jazzbo Have Fe Run", "Gal Boy I Roy" and, for Channel One, I-Roy's "Pad Lock", which opens with one of the funniest and most protracted spoken introductions to any Jamaican record. The two rivals apparently remained friends away from the mike, though this can seem hard to believe when hearing them trade insults that extended to casting aspersions on the other's masculinity – the "Pad Lock" intro involved trying to wake up "Princess Jazzbo".

The Aggrovators' rhythm tracks were inevitably further recycled on sundry instrumental albums and 45s, which were credited either to the Aggrovators or featured soloists such as **Tommy McCook**, **Bobby Ellis**, **Bernard 'Touter' Harvey**, **Earl 'Chinna' Smith**, **Winston Wright** or **Augustus Pablo**. At times, it seemed as if the sheer amount of vinyl bearing production credits to Bunny Lee caused his work to be taken for granted, but Striker is a pivotal figure, for he showed the way for innumerable hustling ghetto producers. His practice of versioning old rhythms and reusing those he had already made clearly demonstrated how to maximize limited resources; this, and his willingness to travel far from the ghetto in order to sell his product, makes him the archetypal Jamaican producer.

HORACE ANDY

● **Sings For You & I** (Striker Lee, JA; Clocktower, US).

Twenty tracks that bring together all of Horace Andy's major hits for Bunny Lee, with the exception of "A Serious Thing", alongside versions of Studio One classics like the singer's own "Skylarking", Dennis Brown's "No Man Is An Island" and Delroy Wilson's "Riding For A Fall". The 'do-overs' slot in surprisingly well with hits like "Money Is the Root Of All Evil" (aka "Money Money"), Zion Gate" and "You Are My Angel", and serve to further demonstrate what a truly astonishing vocal technique Andy has always possessed.

BARRY BROWN & JOHNNIE CLARKE

◉ **Sing Roots & Culture** (Fatman, UK).

Some of Bunny Lee's roughest rhythms and both singers on blistering form. Barry Brown's "Politician" and Johnnie Clarke's "Peace In the Ghetto" are just two highlights on a very consistent set. Anyone who already possesses much of the Striker-produced material by these singers, however, should be aware that several of the tracks are retitled – Clarke's "Fight For Money", for instance, is better known as "Blood Dunza", while Barry Brown's "International Step" turns out to be "Step It Up Youthman".

CORNELL CAMPBELL

◉ **Natty Dread Ina Greenwich Farm** (Striker Lee, JA).

The ultra-cool tones of Cornell Campbell and Santa's 'flying cymbals' when both were at their peak of popularity. The title track is a classic of the period, and was among the first to celebrate that musically rich area of Kingston. Other highlights include "Natural Facts", "Girl Of My Dreams" and his beautiful interpretation of Gene Chandler's "Duke Of Earl".

JOHNNIE CLARKE

◑ **Don't Trouble Trouble** (Attack, UK).

Ⓔ Johnnie Clarke cut virtually all his most interesting music for Bunny Lee, so there's no shortage of tracks from that quarter, many of which are still available on LP or CD. This set was compiled retrospectively, and so has certain advantages over those from the time. "Cold I Up" (aka its Jamaican title, "The Ruler") and the title track both exemplify what most roots fans appreciate about his records: a militant rhythm, and Mr Clarke intoning upon a suitably righteous theme.

● **Movin' Out** (Total Sounds, JA).

● **None Shall Escape** (Total Sounds, JA).

● **Enter Into his Gates With Praise** (Trojan, UK).

Between them these three albums contain most of Johnnie Clarke's early hits for Lee. The Trojan issue is the most easily available, and contains seven of the twelve tracks on *None Shall Escape*, plus another seven including the title song, a big Jamaican hit in 1975. The two Jamaican issues display a similar mix of Studio One covers – usually John Holt or Delroy Wilson songs – and original roots material. *Movin' Out* has the hit that established him, "Move Out Of Babylon", as well as "I Don't Want To Be A Rude Boy", one of his toughest-ever tunes.

● **Authorised Version** (Virgin, UK).

● **Rockers Time Now** (Virgin, UK).

A couple of solid Striker/Johnnie Clarke sets from 1976. Clarke maintains his propensity for covering the material of others with Marley's "Crazy Baldhead", Roy Richards'/Little Richard's "Freedom Blues" and Culture's "See Them A Come" on the appropriately titled *Authorised Version*, and the Abyssinians' "Satta Massa Gana" and "Declaration Of Rights", as well as the Mighty Diamonds' "They Never Love Poor Marcus", on *Rockers Time Now*. Originals like "Roots Natty Congo", "Stop the Tribal War" and "African Roots" impress as well. Unfortunately, the singer lacked an image that made sense in rock terms, and Virgin lost interest after these two fine albums.

◑ **Originally Mr Clarke** (Clocktower, US).

The 'steppers'-style rhythm that developed in the late 1970s was even more militant than the Channel One 'rockers' sound, and ideally suited to Clarke's railings against the iniquities of Babylon. This US collection of Bunny Lee-produced sides includes two of the singer's best records from the era, "Blood Dunza" and "Every Knee Shall Bow", but unfortunately omits the U-Roy toast that made the 12" release of the latter such an essential purchase.

JAH STITCH

◑ **Original Ragga Muffin (1975–77)** (Blood & Fire, UK).

The deejay known as Jah Stitch never entirely escaped from the shadow of Big Youth, though he began his career on the Lord Tippertone sound system before the man who established cultural toasting on record. At his best, Stitch approached Mr Buchanan's level of penetrating ghetto talk, and consistently cut fine records. The most exciting were for Bunny Lee and Vivian Jackson, and it is these that are collected here (a dozen from the former producer, and a couple of the latter's). A bonus on this superior deejay set is Horace Andy's classic vocal, "Zion Gate", which precedes Stitch's equally compelling "Every Wicked Have To Crawl" commentary.

TOMMY McCOOK & THE AGGROVATORS

● **Brass Rockers** (Total Sounds, JA).

Along with the glut of dub albums rushed out in the mid-1970s, most of Jamaica's leading producers released at least one straight instrumental set, and this is among the best. King Tubby was responsible for the mixing, but, rather than deconstructing the Aggrovators' rhythms to just raw drum and bass, the serious qualities of tenorman Tommy McCook, altoist Lennox Brown, trombonist Vin Gordon and trumpeter Bobby Ellis are allowed to come to the fore – along with the ubiquitous 'flying cymbals' of Carlton 'Santa' Davis. Popular tracks like "Dance Ina Greenwich Farm", "A Love I Can Feel" and "Duke Of Earl" in a different – and very musical – style.

AUGUSTUS PABLO AND VARIOUS ARTISTS

◉ **Pablo & Friends** (RAS, US).

Nine Striker-produced vocal or deejay tunes, and their melodica versions from Mr Swaby. The quality ranges from the sublime to a couple of tracks you will want for reference only. I-Roy's "Cow Town Skank"/Pablo's "Cow Town Skank" fully justifies purchase.

LEROY SMART

● **Superstar** (Attack, JA; Third World, UK).

This is a collection of the singer's strongest records for Striker, including a more than worthwhile second cut of the most outstanding song he ever wrote, "Pride & Ambition" (originally recorded for the Wailers' Tuff Gong label). The nearest to a "best of" Leroy Smart package currently available.

U-ROY

⦿ **Rock With I** (RAS, US).

The original foundation deejay's work of the mid-1970s has been largely overlooked in favour of his more ground-breaking records of the beginning of the decade. A pity, as his tunes for Bunny Lee showed no loss of verve or panache, and he sounded just as happy interacting with the voices of Johnnie Clarke, Cornell Campbell, Jackie Edwards and Linval Thompson as Alton Ellis or the Paragons.

VARIOUS ARTISTS – BUNNY LEE PRODUCTIONS

◑ **If Deejay Was Your Trade** (Blood & Fire, UK).

E Not all the deejay versions of Bunny Lee's rhythms were of the very highest standard – an inevitable result of Striker's rush-them-out policy – but this sixteen-track compilation collects the best. I-Roy's "War & Friction", a version of Vivian Jackson's "Death Trap" instrumental, was the track most sought-after by collectors, though Dillinger, Prince Jazzbo, the underrated Jah Stitch, both Big Joe and Little Joe, Dr Alimantado, Tappa Zukie and Prince Far I are all represented by fine efforts.

Channel One

One studio that Bunny Lee used took note of his activities and soon developed its own variations of rocksteady rhythms – the Hookim brothers' **Channel One**, located north of Spanish Town Road on Maxfield Avenue. The studio and label, operational from 1973, followed the sound system of the same name, launched in the early 1970s by **Ernest** and producer **Joseph 'Joe Joe' Hookim**, who had entered the music business through operating jukeboxes (as well as one-armed bandits).

Despite some strong initial 45s – Stranger & Gladdy's "Don't Give Up the Fight", Alton Ellis's version of Lorraine Ellison and Jerry Butler's "I Dig You, Baby", Junior Byles' roots masterpiece, "Fade Away", and Leroy Smart's "Blackman" – the truly distinctive Channel One sound was not to emerge until mid-1975. **I-Roy**'s lewd toast "Welding" was one of the first records with the distinct 'clap' sound on the drum that became synonymous with the studio, and was an important hit for the outfit that summer, even gaining release by UK major Philips. Both deejay I-Roy and keyboards player **Ossie Hibbert** also had a considerable input on the Channel One sound in their alternative roles as in-house producers, but the two musicians mainly responsible for the new style of rhythm that was soon to dominate the Kingston dancehalls, and be copied in every other recording studio on the island, were the astonishingly prolific and inventive drum and bass partnership of **Lowell 'Sly' Dunbar** and **Robbie Shakespeare**, who began playing together regularly in 1975.

The Channel One house band, the **Revolutionaries**, were built around Sly and Robbie, plus keyboard players Ossie Hibbert, Ansel Collins and Errol 'Tarzan' Nelson, all of whom also played with Bunny Lee's Aggrovators. Other regular Revolutionaries included guitarist Radcliffe 'Dougie' Bryan, keyboards player Robbie Lynn, percussionist Uziah 'Sticky' Thompson and horn players Tommy McCook, Vin Gordon and Herman Marquis. Bertram 'Ranchie' McClean sometimes took Robbie Shakespeare's place and contributed equally strong basslines.

What became known as their 'rockers' rhythms were mostly based on Studio One classics from the previous decade, made totally modern by the many drumming styles created by Sly (formerly a member of the Upsetters and Lloyd Parkes' Skin, Flesh & Bones band), and Robbie's complementary basslines. Rhythms originally built for the romantic themes of rocksteady suddenly sounded militant enough to mirror the upheaval and conflict that was shaking Jamaica in the mid-1970s. It is not stretching a point to suggest that Sly Dunbar's drumming, whether rockers or steppers, 'double-drumming' or subtle 'one-drop', was the musical counterpart of the rapid fire of the gunmen's M.16s and Bushmasters.

The most successful of the performers to record over the Revolutionaries' rhythms were the **Mighty Diamonds**, a vocal trio (Donald 'Tabby' Shaw, Fitzroy 'Bunny' Shaw and Lloyd 'Judge' Ferguson) who sang Garveyite lyrics like those of Burning Spear with the type of harmonies associated with Philly and Chicago soft-soul groups such as the Stylistics and the Chi-Lites. Their early discs for Channel One included the former's "Country Living", and the latter's "Stoned Out Of My Mind", but then came the militant "Back Weh A Mafia" and

"Right Time" in 1975; the following year there was the equally hard-hitting and successful "Have Mercy", "I Need A Roof" and "Africa", as well as the release by Virgin in the UK of their first album – which brought together most of the hit 45s, and came complete with gatefold sleeve to hook the white rock audience. The Mighty Diamonds went on to be one of the most enduring harmony groups in reggae, with further local hits for a number of leading producers – including Joe Gibbs, Tappa Zukie and Gussie Clarke – but their Channel One work remains the benchmark.

The other first-rank vocal harmony groups at Maxfield Avenue at this time were the **Wailing Souls**, who managed to keep up the incredibly high standard they had set with Clement Dodd at Brentford Road. Even when reworking their earlier classics – "Back Out", "Fire Coal Man" and "Backbiter" – the results were made fresh by the Revolutionaries' rhythms. Even better was the quality of their new material, with "Very Well" ranking as perhaps their greatest single achievement.

Vocalists to have one of two fine records in this period on Channel One – or its sister labels Steady, Hitbound, Disco Mix and Well Charge – included Horace Andy, former Clarendonian **Ernest Wilson**, **Gregory Isaacs**, the **Enforcers**, **Creole** (who disappeared after just a couple of 45s) and **Freddy McKay**. More prolific on the Hookim brothers' labels were two well-established singers, **Leroy Smart** and **John Holt**. Both showed themselves in tune with current concerns by cutting singles that addressed the political strife that divided Kingston along party lines into mutually antagonistic and heavily armed camps. Smart, who himself carried something of a bad-boy reputation, compared the current state of affairs with a more peaceful past on "Ballistic Affair", written by Greenwich Farm-based singer Frankie Jones, which employed a ferocious updating of the "College Rock" rhythm:

"Ballistic affair, ballistic affair
We used to lick chalice, cook ital stew together
Play football and cricket as one brother
Now thru' you rest a Jungle,
Or you might block a Rema
You a go fight 'gainst your brother
That no right, my sister
Let us all live as one, yeah
Throw away your gun
Throw away your knife
Let us all unite
Everyone is living in fear
Just thru' dis ballistic affair."

Holt took one of the most memorable updates produced at Channel One – Sly's "Up Park Camp", a powerhouse take on the Heptones' "Get In the Groove" – to warn the youth of the possible fate in one of the government's notorious detention centres:

DAVID CORIO

Posing outside Channel One

"When I used to go to school
You know they taught me the golden rule
They say, 'Son you better know yourself
Because in time to come, it's going to be dread'
An' now me gone a Up Park Camp
Me never want to go a Up Park Camp

Why didn't I take their advice
If I did, I would be living in style
God knows I wasn't born to grow wild."

Several Channel One 45s from the duo **Earth & Stone** (Albert Bailey & Clifton McWell), including the haunting "In Time To Come", also made an impression, though little is known about them other than that similarly worthwhile records credited to them subsequently appeared on High Note, Joe Gibbs and Roots From the Yard. Even the Michael Rose-led **Black Uhuru** made one stunning single at Maxfield Avenue – a version of Bob Marley's "Sun Is Shining" – before finding a larger audience with records on, first, Dennis Brown's DEB label, and then, taking them into the truly international arena, Sly & Robbie's progressive Taxi outlet (see pp.260–261). **Barry Brown** also cut definitive youth music for the Hookim brothers at the end of the decade. "Far East", his most enduring Channel One record, employed a plea for peace in the ghetto over a blinding reinterpretation of the Roland Alphonso instrumental classic, "Jah Shakey", to become as common a title for the much-used rhythm as the original.

Not surprisingly, there were versions of all Channel One's most popular rhythms from the top young deejays of the period, including Trinity, his younger brother Clint Eastwood, the popular U-Roy disciple Ranking Trevor and Jah Thomas. The often highly original Doctor Alimantado recorded an atypical singing track there, "Born For A Purpose", which was not only his one sizeable Jamaican hit but also registered with punk rockers in the UK. The most consistently popular of all the Channel's chatters, however, was **Dillinger** (b. Lester Bullocks, 1953, Kingston), who rode the rhythms from the brightest and brashest Mighty Diamonds hits as confidently as he did his famed CB 200 motorbike around the Kingston streets (the bike was the topic of one of his best-received 45s and the title of his debut Channel One album). The Hookims got yet more mileage from the rhythm tracks that were ruling the dancehalls in London as well as Kingston, with a very successful series of instrumental cuts credited to the Revolutionaries, most of which sported timely militant/revolutionary titles like "MPLA", "Angola" and "Leftist".

No other Jamaican studio was to have quite the same impact in 1975–76, or exert as much influence on the direction of the music. Soon every producer on the island was trying to lure Sly Dunbar and Robbie Shakespeare' into his studio, or instructing other musicians to imitate their style. Channel One's undisputed reign only ended in 1977, when the mantle passed to two men who had obviously paid careful attention to the Maxfield Avenue approach– the Mighty Two.

BARRY BROWN

● Far East (Channel One, US).
Besides the title track, which remains one of the singer's most enduring moments, this set has several tough, late 1970s roots songs running it pretty close – most notably "So Jah Jah Sey".

DILLINGER

◑ CB 200 (Black Swan, UK; Mango, US).
Dillinger, a deejay in the Big Youth mould, made some strong records before he arrived at Channel One, but it was when he was put over that studio's hits – especially Gregory Isaacs' "Sun Shines For Me" for the title track – that he jumped into the premier league. On "Crank Face" he's joined by the slightly younger Trinity for the first of several successful 'combination' discs that the deejay pair cut. The rest of the time, though, his own no-nonsense, very dread approach is enough. Some of his later 45s are worth checking, but he was never again to be quite as impressive over an entire album.

EARTH & STONE

◑ Kool Roots (Pressure Sounds, UK).
Originally a double LP, released in 1978, and featuring one disc of vocals and another of concomitant dubs. The duo's all-time classic, "In Time To Come", is included, and tracks such as "Three Wise Men" and "False Ruler" come very close.

JOHN HOLT

● Up Park Camp (Channel One, JA).
John Holt was seeking to relocate himself in the Jamaican dancehall after his UK chart successes during 1973–74; he achieved his aim with ease on this totally accomplished set, which perfectly combined old Studio One classics with new items such as the powerful title track. The singer was to prove capable of reinventing himself at all stages of development in modern Jamaican music.

THE MIGHTY DIAMONDS

◑ When the Right Time Come/I Need A Roof (Well Charge, JA; Virgin, UK; Channel One, US).
E The breakthrough for Channel One came with a staggering series of 45s from the Mighty Diamonds. The trio's debut album then more than lived up to expectations, with the previ-

MY NAME IS DILLINGER

A highly successful run of singles and two albums for Channel One remain Dillinger's best-remembered work, though he also recorded striking 45s for, among others, Studio One, Lee Perry, Yabby You, Augustus Pablo, Bunny Lee, Winston Riley, Niney, Ossie Hibbert and Joe Gibbs. Originally influenced by pioneer deejays such as Dennis Alcapone, his career really took off when he incorporated elements of Big Youth's cultural chanting into his increasingly distinctive style. "Cocaine In My Brain" was not the best track on the *CB 200* album, but it brought him to the attention of new audiences in both Europe and the US.

"My name is Dillinger, otherwise known as Ragnam Pizza, the Dub Organizer, the Dub Supervisor, come into make you wiser, so you got to realizer all reggae music and deejay business get started in Jamaica. I come into reggae music as a youth. I heard about U-Roy, Dennis Alcapone, King Stitt, Sir Lord Comic, Muchuki, and all them great guys there, who make some nice music. I wanted to be like one of them man there, 'cos I hear music alone shall live and never shall die. I loved music as a youth that me started following sound system. I like Sir Coxsone Downbeat, who play then time at 28 Waltham Park Road, and Lloyd the Matador and all them sounds. I came on as a deejay and ting, and look upon man named Scratch at Dynamic's studio. Perry my first producer. He asked me my name and I said: 'Dennis Alcapone Junior'. And he said: 'No, man, you're different from Alcapone. You're Dillinger.' My first session for Scratch was a very long one, and me do like "Dub Organiser", and many other tunes. Before then I follow Dennis Alcapone's El Passo sound. Me a youth but they sometimes pass the mike to me, and I just go on and keep on. Me help to lift the soundboxes onto the truck. But me don't mind that, because me love the music.

RICK ELGOOD

A beer in the yard with Dillinger, 1994

Enough man come into the music to get rich quick and make a lot of money. But it's more than money. Because when the money spent out, the music still liveth to showeth the corruption and foolishness. So you have to love the music and love the people. The music is a big message carrier. The music is the biggest informer that tell you what is happening in the world. I give people wrong information if I say "shock him, stab him, kill him, put him in a coffin." But I deal with joy, one love, one heart, get up and stand up for your rights.

After being inspired by Dennis Alcapone, U-Roy, and them original deejays before my time, I start to break the eggshell, and show my true potential by doing my own thing. This is at Channel One, now, with tune like "Plantation Heights" and "CB 200". Joe Joe had a sound called Channel One, and it play out. And he had some specials and asked me if I would deejay pon dem. Then the Mighty Diamonds come across, and, and I deejay pon dem rhythms for the *CB 200* LP. That go all over. Even "Cocaine In My Brain" was from that LP. Most artists, I tell you, grateful for an LP, 'cos a 45 like a little slug from a gun, but the LP like a rocket launched, long-distance missile that shoot far."

ously unreleased tracks matching successful 45s like "Right Time", "Have Mercy" and "Africa". The combination of the Revolutionaries' updates of classic Studio One rhythms and the trio's immaculate harmonies more or less defined the 'rockers' phase that ruled the music for the next couple of years.

● **Stand Up To Your Judgment** (Channel One, JA).

The second Channel One set from the trio collects a couple of marvellous early singles omitted from its predecessor, "Back Weh" and "Country Living"; their best subsequent one for the label, "Stand Up To Your Judgment"; and adds some new material very near the same calibre.

THE WAILING SOULS

● **The Best Of the Wailing Souls** (Channel One, US).

Not to be confused with Greensleeves' *Very Best Of* compilation, which draws from the group's work with several different producers. This is restricted to their 1970s recordings at Channel One, which means some of the greatest of their long career. Classics like "Very Well", "Things & Time" and "War" are part of a flawless selection – though it is a pity that "Lawless Society", which appeared as a Hitbound 45 some time after the event, is not included.

VARIOUS ARTISTS – JOSEPH 'JOE JOE' HOOKIM PRODUCTIONS

⊙ **Hitbound! The Revolutionaries Sound Of Channel One** (Heartbeat, US).

This falls just short of the definitive collection it should have been (the Mighty Diamonds are represented with a lesser effort, and John Holt's "Up Park Camp" is omitted), but is still well worth a place in the collection for undisputed classics like Junior Byles' "Fade Away", the Meditations' "Woman Is Like A Shadow", Horace Andy's "Girl A Love You" and Black Uhuru's "Sun Is Shining".

The Mighty Two – Joe Gibbs and Errol Thompson

The first records on the **Joe Gibbs** group of labels to bear credits to the **Mighty Two** (Gibbs plus **Errol Thompson**) appeared in 1975, though Thompson – previously the chief engineer at Randy's studio on North Parade – had played a role at Gibbs' controls since the late 1960s, when Gibbs opened his studio in Duhaney Park. Thompson became a pioneer of dub techniques – witness the ground-breaking *Java, Java, Java, Java* LP of 1973 – and it was on the version sides, and then on entire dub albums released by Gibbs, that his input was most obvious. Even if the ubiquitous **Ossie Hibbert, Ruddy Thomas** and **Blacka Morwell** assisted in running and arranging sessions, Thompson was the dominant presence after Gibbs opened his new sixteen-track studio on Retirement Crescent in 1975, a situation acknowledged by his being given equal production credits as half of the Mighty Two. Thompson also continued releasing sides on his own Errol T label.

Several strong roots records appeared on various Gibbs labels in 1975 – **Sylford Walker**'s searing "Burn Babylon", **Jacob Miller**'s update of Marley's "Soul Rebel", retitled "I Am A Natty", and the obscure **Snuffy & Wally**'s deejay version of Lloyd Parks's "Mafia" smash, "Dreader Mafia", to name just three. But the floodgate was opened in 1976–77, when a new youth audience in the UK and Kingston lapped up rejuvenated Studio One and Treasure Isle rhythms, as well as exciting new cuts of Bob Marley & the Wailers' biggest rocksteady hit, "Hypocrites".

Dennis Brown (b. 1957, Kingston), whose first cut of "Money In My Pocket" had appeared on Gibbs' Record Globe label in 1972, was the most consistently successful solo performer to record for the Mighty Two. Besides a string of hit 7" and 12" 45s that covered both roots and lovers concerns (the militant "Cup Of Tea" and "Slave Driver", plus updates of the Sharks' "How Can I

Leave" and Alton Ellis's "Ain't That Loving You"), he also recorded three of the outstanding vocal albums of the period in the best-selling *Visions*, *Words Of Wisdom* and *Joseph's Coat Of Many Colours.*

Almost as successful in the international marketplace was **Culture** (Joseph Hill, Albert 'Randolph' Walker, Kenneth Paley), a vocal trio with an approach based on that of Burning Spear when he was recording with the supporting harmonies of Rupert Wellington and Delroy Hines for Jack Ruby. Culture's front man, Joseph Hill, never quite touched the heights of his model, either as a vocalist or lyricist, yet for a while he reached a broader audience, including many white punk rockers. Subsequent work for Sonia Pottinger showed that the charismatic Hill was not entirely dependent on the Mighty Two's rhythms either, and had developed a style of his own, for all his debt to Winston Rodney.

Other impressive roots singles on the Joe Gibbs, Belmont, Town & Country, Crazy Joe or Errol T labels in this period included gems from **Gregory Isaacs**, **Junior Delgado**, the **Mighty Diamonds**, **Junior Byles**, **Dolphin Morris**, **Cornell Campbell**, **Earl Sixteen** and one of the few female singers to cut convincing militant roots records, **Dhaima**.

At the same time as catering to the demand for 'dread' deliberations on the coming apocalypse, gun courts and the waving of dreadlocks, the Mighty Two did not forget the blues-dances market for more romantic records. This audience was kept happy with well-crafted offerings like **Marcia Aitken**'s "I'm Still In Love With You Boy" (based on one of Alton Ellis's Studio One hits), **Wayne Wade**'s "After You", **Ruddy Thomas**'s "Let's Make A Baby" and his revival of Dobby Dobson's "Loving Pauper", and hit after hit from Dennis Brown, including his even more popular second cut of "Money In My Pocket". The Mighty Two even scored a gigantic crossover success in the UK with **Althea and Donna**'s "Uptown Top Ranking", utilizing the same rhythm track as Trinity's "Three Piece Suit".

Following the Channel One model, there was also a deluge of deejay versions from talents such as **Trinity**, **Little/Ranking Joe**, **Jah Thomas**, **Nigger Kojak** (totally bald, of course), **Bo Jangles** and future crossover star **Clint Eastwood**, as well as those with claims to veteran status like I-Roy and Dillinger. The most interesting and popular of the Mighty Two's talkers after Trinity and Dillinger, both of whom had already established their reputations at Channel One, was the gruff-voiced **Prince Far I** (b. Michael James Williams, 1944, Spanish Town). His major hit for Gibbs, titled "Under Heavy Manners" after the get-tough measures initiated by Michael Manley's PNP government towards violent crime, was a brutal

ADRIAN BOOT

Culture, with Joseph Hill (centre)

critique of that policy, delivered in the most sombre of tones:

"Manners is like unto to a dog
Discipline is wha the world needs today, baby
Heavy, heavy discipline, yu know
Nuh true
Well, watch ya, man
War in the East, war in the West.
War in the North, war in the South
Crazy Joe get dem out
What a terrible bout
I tell yu what a terrible bout
Crazy Joe get dem out
Well, watch yu, man
Natty dread don't borrow
Cos he remembers tomorrow."

The record prompted an answer from the other side: Bunny Lee and Clive Chin produced Jah Stitch on a record called "Crazy Joe", in which the deejay warned "we're gonna chase Crazy Joe an' his baldhead followers out a town". Clive Chin used to play the record continually from his base in Randy's shop at 17 North Parade, just a few feet away from Joe Gibbs' shop. The rivalry thus encompassed politics, music and business.

Of course Gibbs also put out his own instrumental cuts, credited to **Joe Gibbs & the Professionals**, though never in the same quantities as the Revolutionaries on the various Channel One labels. In accord with Gibbs' conservative JLP sympathies, titles such as "State Of Emergency" and "No Bones For the Dog" reflected the social crisis being experienced under Michael Manley's PNP government, rather than expressing identification with leftist revolutions abroad as favoured at Channel One; note, too, the contrast in the house bands' names, even if they did feature mostly the same musicians.

What, in the end, made Joe Gibbs records the ones for the youth to check in the final half of the 1970s were Errol Thompson's dubs, which, complete with the attention-grabbing sounds of dogs barking, car horns hooting and toilets flushing, reached a far wider audience than his more subtle – and now perhaps less dated – efforts at Randy's.

DENNIS BROWN

◑ **Visions** (Joe Gibbs Record Globe, JA).

Ⓔ One of the Crown Prince of Reggae's most compelling albums, and the one that helped establish his and producer Joe Gibbs' dominant position in late 1970s reggae. The voice of the still very youthful veteran was amazingly assured, his performances achingly felt. Add a thoughtful selection of material, Jamaica's leading session musicians on top form and the prowess of Errol Thompson at the controls, and the result was a hit album in a field that was (and still is) run by the humbler 45. Sales were further helped by the fact that some of the best tracks – "Malcolm X", "Deliverance Will Come", "Concrete Castle King" – were never released as singles, though they were played by sound systems as if they were. "Stay At Home", incidentally, is better known as "Ghetto Girl", an incredibly popular 45 that's been a 'revive' favourite ever since.

● **Words Of Wisdom** (Rocky One, JA; Laser, UK).

● **Joseph's Coat Of Many Colours** (DEB, JA; Laser, UK).

These two 1979 Dennis Brown sets from Joe Gibbs further refined the approach found on the above album, with the singer equally at ease with both lovers and cultural concerns. The former includes the second cut of "Money In My Pocket", which deservedly made the UK pop charts, and "Ain't That Loving You", which was also a gigantic hit in the reggae world; among the latter are wonderful versions of Marley's "Slave Driver" and John Holt's "Man Next Door", as well as the popular self-written 45s, "Three Meals A Day" and "A Cup Of Tea".

CULTURE

◑ **Two Sevens Clash** (Joe Gibbs Record Globe, JA; Lightning, UK).

Ⓔ The time for Culture would have come anyway – it was always unfair to dismiss Joseph Hill as a mere Burning Spear copyist – but the Mighty Two's production style hurried it on, and ensured the trio was heard by a far wider audience. Hit singles like the title track, the even stronger "I Am Not Ashamed" and "See Them A Come" are included, and the rest of the selection easily competes for attention.

◑ **Baldhead Bridge** (Joe Gibbs Record Globe, JA; Shanachie, US).

The album that followed from Joe Gibbs was released after Culture had moved to rival producer Sonia Pottinger's camp, and collected tracks recorded at the same sessions as the debut set. Not all the material is quite as strong, but it has its moments – most notably "Love Shines Brighter".

JOE GIBBS & THE PROFESSIONALS

● **State Of Emergency** (Joe Gibbs Record Globe/Rocky One, JA).

Whether or not Mr Gibbs was in the studio when these sessions took place remains a moot point. Keyboard player Ossie Hibbert was certainly heavily involved – he produced the similar *Earthquake Dub* around this time. Nevertheless, these are the rhythms that supported several of the most popular records of the time, here given straight instrumental treatments. The title track, for example, is familiar as Culture's "See Them A Come" (originally the Sound

Dimension's "Heavy Rock"), and the entire set confirms the strength of the Professionals' updatings of rocksteady/early reggae rhythms.

PRINCE FAR I

◑ **Under Heavy Manners** (Joe Gibbs Record Globe/Rocky One, JA).

Prince Far I never sounded like a youthman, but rather a gnarled prophet who had just descended from the mountain top. Accordingly, he stated a preference for being called a chanter rather than a deejay, and you can hear what he meant. The title track was his most successful record in Jamaica, and impresses with its sheer seriousness. Similarly, "Deck Of Cards" adapts the lyric of the country song of faith, and places it over a very appropriate rhythm – the Mighty Two's version of "Satta Massa Gana". Against the odds, his righteous doom and gloom maintains interest throughout.

TRINITY

◉ **Three Piece Suit** (Joe Gibbs Record Globe/Rocky One, JA).

It is easy to forget just how popular Trinity was in the late 1970s. Singles on Well Charge and Prophets had established him as one of the best of the generation of cultural deejays emerging in the wake of Big Youth, but prepared hardly anyone for the popularity of the "Three Piece Suit" single for Joe Gibbs. With its use of an updated cut of Alton Ellis's "I'm Still In Love With You" and lyrics about the deejay's dapper attire, it anticipated the dancehall era that was to come. More conventional cultural lyrics dominate the rest of the album, and everything is over *African Dub*-style rhythms – that is, the best of their era.

VARIOUS ARTISTS – JOE GIBBS PRODUCTIONS

◉ **Joe Gibbs Revive 45s Volumes 1 & 2** (Rocky One, JA).

Pretty near to definitive collections of the major vocal hits of the mid–late 1970s from the Mighty Two. Only Delroy Wilson's "Oh Pretty Girl", from earlier in the decade, seems out of place (fine record though it is). Standout tracks include those from Junior Byles, Prince Allah, Dhaima, Sylford Walker, Naggo 'Dolphin' Morris and Gregory Isaacs. Presumably Culture and Dennis Brown were felt to be adequately represented on their own albums, as theirs are virtually the only significant names missing.

Yabby You: the Jesus Dread

The career of **Yabby You** (b. Vivian Jackson, c. 1950, Kingston) began in the first half of the decade, when he cut two superb records, "Conquering Lion" (Now) and "Love Thy Neighbours" (Defenders), the former credited to Vivian Jackson & the Ralph Brothers, and the latter to Vivian Jackson & the Deffenders [sic]. Though pressed initially in small quantities (one hundred in the case of "Conquering Lion"), they made the enigmatic Jackson enough money to launch his **Prophets** label in 1974. Most of the initial releases on Prophets are now considered roots classics, including "Jah Vengeance", "Chant Jah Victory", "Warn the Nation" and "Valley Of Jehosophat", all credit-

DAVID KATZ

Another Channel One patron: Yabby You

YABBY YOU ON RASTA CULTURE

Deeply committed to Rastafarianism of a highly individualized kind, Yabby You forged a style based on traditional Rastafarian chants, and the best of his work formed one of the plateaus of 1970s roots music. Not surprisingly for a man who has always placed his faith at the centre of his music, here he begins by talking of some of the different strains of religious belief in East Kingston.

“My first involvement with the music was once in the late ’60s, early ’70s. You have the Rasta culture, and you have the Bobo culture, and you have the Ites culture. I’ve always carried a special type of life, of living – where you don’t eat things that grow under the Earth, or things where you have any form of killing. And what we used to do, we don’t eat salt or any of those sort of things. Like you have the Rastaman, now, who call himself the wholesome Rastaman, them worship Emperor Haile Selassie, Rastafari. My first home was with Ites. We used to have a belief the Almighty is the power for Creation, and live within man. Meanwhile the Rastaman used to have a belief that Haile Selassie was the returned Messiah.

So you always have a conflict between reasonings. On this day in particular – it was sometime in about 1969 – I was reasoning, and I was saying that I don’t see Rastafari is the Supreme – because, I say, the Supreme live in we, as the higher Ites, the highest Ites in Creation. And it cause a big dispute with the whole of them Rastaman. Me hold on to my opinion, and they hold on to them opinion, and it become boring. And then all of a sudden the rain start up, and them go asleep, and when them asleep it’s like I hear a sound – a strange thing – I hear a sound within my thoughts – like an angel sing. And when the thunder roll, it become like music to me, and I hear these sounds, you know: “King of Kings, Lord of Lords, Conquering Lion of the Tribe of Judah.” So what I try to do now is sing along with the song I hear in my thoughts. And eventually them wake up and listen to me and say things like it is a new kind of sound to put on record. I penetrate that and decide I should go into recording.

From that moment, I have to understand what studio is like, what musicians is like. And I find out about money to book studio, to book the musicians. What I do now is look for this brother called Leroy Wallace – him called Horsemouth – and sing the song to him, and tell him the idea. And he say “Yeah, it sound like a new kind of sound

ed to either **Vivian Jackson & the Prophets**, or individuals from the fluid membership of the group, such as Errol ‘Dada’ Smith, Alric Forbes (who had been one of the Ralph Brothers) and various Gladiators. Jackson also produced the teenage **Wayne Wade**’s sublime “Black Is Our Colour”, a perfect blending of ‘lovers’ and ‘roots’ that has remained popular ever since.

Jackson’s first album, essentially a collection of the early 45s, was followed by further Prophets discs over the next couple of years, most notably “Run Come Rally”, “Judgement On the Land”, “Judgement Time”, “Undivided World” (the latter credited to Vivian Jackson & Horace Andy) and one of the first and most popular reggae 12" 45 releases, 1977’s “Babylon Kingdom Fall”/“King Pharaoh Plague On the Land”. Just as perfectly realized expressions of his world-view were found on further records from the sweet-voiced Wayne Wade, as well as the singers **Patrick Andy** (a Horace Andy soundalike who specialized in adapting his model’s songs), **Tony Tuff**, **Charlie Morrison**, **Willie Williams** and **Junior Brown**.

The most consistently successful of all his discoveries after Wayne Wade, however, was a conscious youth singer called **Michael Prophet** (b. Michael George Haynes, 1957, Kingston). The possessor of a distinctive swooping tenor, Prophet first made an impression on roots followers with 45s like “Praise You Jah Jah” and a version of the Heptones’ Studio One classic “Fight It To the Top” for Yabby, as well as a brace of 45s for proto-dancehall producer Don Mais. But it was his debut album, *Serious Reasoning*, released in the UK by Island, that established his reputation outside of Jamaica. After that, Prophet adapted just as successfully to the raw dancehall productions of Junjo Lawes and, eventually, to lively ‘combination’ efforts

come to music." And he say him bring bass man and guitarist, from a band called Generation Gap, and what he do is go and bring these instruments to Gully Bank. Well, Gully Bank is in Waterhouse, the most remote place, and him bring Chinna and bring Family Man, and when they hear it and play the chords to the music and ting, they say, 'Yes, it can go far as a record.'

What it need is money. Well, I have this trust fund from hospital because of this complaint. We eat Ital and didn't sleep inside house. I eventually reach hospital. Them say I have malnutrition, ulcerated stomach, diarrhoea, pneumonia. Them say I have brain fever. Say I eat too much of one thing, less of a certain thing, and they have to operate on me stomach. So when I come out of hospital, I couldn't work, and to find the money was very difficult. The only money I could find was to book this studio – Dynamic – and the only tape I could afford was a two-inch tape. Well they [the musicians] so believe in the song that they say, bwoy, them play for free. Because they feel there's a message in this that deserve to reach the Earth.

Then I carry the tape now over to King Tubby's, it just the rhythm, and he play the tape. And him get fascinated over it. And then I sing the song to convince him it mine, he agree to voice it because a song like this deserve to reach the Earth. When I voice it, take me another two year to save to build a stamper. Then it take me another six month before I can press a hundred of the record. I never record before – and I no want anyone to know it was we. So if it flop we won't get the blame. Well, eventually I play it to people, to soundman, and to record shop, and everyone I play it to like it and patronize it. And after the hundred sell I go back and press another two hundred, and when that sell I press five hundred and that sell, and then it get popular. People, now, start to want to know who sing it. I no tell them that it me. I just say it was Tubbs.

Me go back after that and sing one "Love Thy Neighbour" and the same thing start to happen. Another one was called "Jah Vengeance". That was the time, now, then that Tubbs started to make them know that it was me. When people used to ask for the song – me call the song "Conquering Lion" – but when people ask for the song after what the beginning say: "Yabby You, Yabby, Yabby You." And they always ask for the song as "Yabby You". When they realize it was me singing now, they start to call me 'Yabby You', and that's how me get the name, and the name stick on. ”

with an upfront ragga deejay over digital rhythms made in London.

In keeping with the trend of the time, Yabby You also issued compelling deejay versions of his most enduring rhythms. The most popular included "Yabby Youth", a cut of "Conquering Lion" from the great **Big Youth**. Unfortunately, this was the only record that the deejay – who was then rivalling even Marley in terms of local popularity – ever made for Yabby. Among the other fine 'toasting' tunes from those working under the Youth's shadow were "Words Of the Prophet" and "Consumption Tax" from the up-and-coming **Trinity** (b. Wayne Brammer, 1954, Kingston), who would go on to enjoy a truly massive hit with Joe Gibbs, while his already more established friend **Dillinger** (b. Lester Bullocks, 1953, Kingston) offered advice on dietary matters from a strictly Rastafarian perspective on "Freshly". Dillinger's record employed the devotional "Jah Vengeance" rhythm, which also supported "Natty Dread On the Mountain Top", one of the better tunes from **Tappa Zukie** (b. David Sinclair, 1955, Kingston). "Judgement", arguably the greatest record from **Jah Stitch** (b. Melbourne James, 1949, Kingston), revitalized the Prophets' "Judgement On the Land" hit, and Yabby You's "Prince Pharaoh Plague" was reworked on a stunning disc from Trinity (with Dillinger on the intro) titled, appositely for its producer, "Jesus Dread", a version of its producer's "Prince Pharaoh Plague". High-quality instrumental cuts of the same rhythms also appeared, featuring (variously) Augustus Pablo, saxman Tommy McCook and trombonist Don Drummond Junior (aka Vin Gordon), but there were not nearly enough of them, making the now-deleted album credited to **Tommy McCook** and trumpeter **Bobby Ellis** all the more precious.

An intensely spiritual but unorthodox Rastafarian, Vivian Jackson was undoubtedly able to release more records thanks to UK sales, but this hardly seemed to make a difference to the vision he was intent on expressing. Clothed in the imagery of orthodox Rastafarianism, but with Jesus Christ rather than Haile Selassie as the central figure, the vision was his before he set foot in a recording studio and never wavered. Yabby You, the self-styled Jesus Dread, was no 'waggonist'.

YABBY YOU

Conquering Lion (Vivian Jackson, JA).

E Essentially the Jamaican press of the UK debut set, *Ram A Dam*, but with "Defend Thy Enemies" taking the place of the much weaker "Beyond the Hills". If the Old Testament themes of tracks like "Conquering Lion", "Run Come Rally" and "Jah Vengeance" were soon to sound tired in lesser hands, both the musical freshness and Jackson's own palpable sincerity make them still sound some of the most inspired and inspiring cultural tunes. An album that helped define roots music, with every track a classic of the genre.

King Tubby Meets Vivian Jackson (Prophet, UK).

Originally pressed in Jamaica without a cover, under the title *Walls Of Jerusalem*, and in the UK (with a cover) as *Chant Down Babylon*. The first side has another half-dozen prime Vivian Jackson & the Prophets vocals, most of which had already been released as 45s, while the second delivers their dub counterparts. Tracks like "Walls Of Jerusalem" and "Chant Down Babylon" are flawless, while the dubs are fully the equal of those on the classic *Prophecy Of Dub* set from Tubby.

Deliver Me From My Enemies (Vivian Jackson, JA).

The quality slips a little with the third album, though four tracks – "Deliver Me From My Enemies", "Judgement Time", "Blood Ago Run Down King Street" and "Zion Gate" – are vintage Yabby You, and the remainder stands as strong roots material by the standards of most singers/producers.

TOMMY McCOOK & BOBBY ELLIS

Blazing Horns (Grove Music, UK).

A solid instrumental set that showcases the enduring partnership of tenorman Tommy McCook and trumpeter Bobby Ellis over strong Yabby You rhythms. Released in the same year as *Beware Dub*, but with the emphasis on the sheer untampered-with musicianship of the rhythm tracks.

MICHAEL PROPHET

Serious Reasoning (Island, UK).

Something of a swansong for Vivian Jackson. He established new youth wailer Michael Prophet by producing this assured debut album, which appeared in 1980 and more than fulfilled the promise of the LP's worth of dub versions that had preceded it. "Peace & Love" (aka "Mash Down Rome") is the equal of anything with which Yabby You had been associated previously, and none of the other tracks are far behind it.

TRINITY

Shanty Town Determination (TR Groovemaster, JA).

The debut album from the best of the graduates from the Big Youth toasting academy. Trinity's style was to develop more individuality later on, but there is no denying the effectiveness of these strictly cultural tirades, including the singles "Consumption Tax" and "Words Of the Prophet" (the latter retitled "Hold Dem Jah Jah").

WAYNE WADE

Black Is Our Colour (Vivian Jackson, JA).

The title track successfully combined black consciousness sentiments with the type of sweet voice and rhythm usually employed for more romantic efforts, and as a 45 (minus the horns on the version here) it reached most parts of the reggae audience. The album's other rhythms are mostly in the more rootsy style associated with Vivian Jackson's productions, and include cuts of "Conquering Lion", "Run Come Rally" and "Fire Round Town". Wade has been undervalued by some because of his penchant for lyrics and themes already familiar through Yabby You's own records, but a voice that could not be more different ensures the individuality of his own cuts.

Rockers Time – Augustus Pablo

Vivian Jackson has become a cult figure among non-Jamaicans with a retrospective interest in Jamaican roots music. Another hero to this new audience is the slight, somewhat frail-looking Rastaman known as **Augustus Pablo** (whose arrival on the Kingston recording scene is covered on p.107). After his spell with Aquarius he made an amazing contribution to roots reggae, both as a melodica/keyboards player and as a producer with an immediately recognizable style. His Hot Stuff and Rockers labels (the latter named after his brother Garth's sound system) were launched in 1972, and soon established him as a stupendous session musician. Releases under Pablo's own name also made clear his principal influence, as they were mostly fresh-sounding interpretations, on melodica or clavinet, of Studio One instrumentals from keyboard virtuoso Jackie Mittoo and/or the Soul Vendors. In several cases, this was made obvious

Dub instrumentalist Augustus Pablo

CORIO

by the new titles – "Skanking Easy" was an update of the rocksteady classic "Swing Easy", "Frozen Dub" of "Frozen Soul", "Rockers Rock" of what was to become the most versioned of Studio One instrumentals, "Real Rock". Precedents for his so-called 'Far East' sound, with its heavy reliance on minor chords, could also be found in the moody ska records of key musicians like the trombonist Don Drummond, and the trumpeters Johnny 'Dizzy' Moore and Baba Brooks.

In common with Vivian Jackson, Lee Perry, Bunny Lee, Glen Brown and several others, he employed King Tubby to mix the 'version' sides of these singles, and this eventually led, in 1977, to the release of his *King Tubby Meets the Rockers Uptown*, the album that both confirmed and spread both men's reputations (see p.208). Besides dub versions of Pablo's instrumental hits, this groundbreaking set also included Tubby's treatments of several of the recordings he had made earlier in the decade with other artists, including Paul Whiteman/Blackman's "Say So", legendary as the first vocal record that Pablo produced.

Three vocals from **Jacob Miller** were versioned on the King Tubby album, including "False Rasta" and "Who Say Jah No Dread", both featuring the type of 'dread' lyrics that were to become increasingly popular. However, the singers with whom Pablo was to have the most fruitful associations were **Junior Delgado** (b. Oscar Hibbert, 1958, Kingston) and **Hugh Mundell** (b. 1962, Kingston; d. 1983). A gritty, seemingly always pain-racked vocalist in the tradition of the great Ken Boothe, Junior Delgado had already recorded for Rupie Edwards, Scratch, Niney and Dennis Brown before cutting "Blackman's Heart Cries Out", a classic cut of Pablo's instrumental "Zion High", itself a version of the Paragons' Treasure Isle tune, "Riding On A Windy Day". This was followed by "Away With You Fussing And Fighting", which if anything made an even greater impact on roots listeners when it appeared on a Rockers 12" single with Hugh Mundell adopting the name 'Jah Levi' to take care of the 'toasting' part. The mutually rewarding relationship between producer/musician and singer was renewed in the late 1980s, when Pablo adapted digital technology for his own rootsy needs, and was particularly successful with a series of hard-edged tunes from a revitalized Delgado.

Mundell was extremely young when he recorded his initial hit for Pablo, being barely in his teens when he became one of the first Jamaican vocalists to voice the soon to be popular sentiment that "Africa Must Be Free By 1983". He went on to make other distinguished records for Pablo and maintained the association with his mentor on his own Muni Music label; then, as a new decade opened, he went on to record for the dancehall king Junjo Lawes and the partnership of Prince Jammy and the leading UK sound operator, Fat Man. But less than ten years after his recording debut he was dead – shot in a dispute over the ownership of a fridge.

Mundell had also produced "Speak the Truth", the debut single of **Junior Reid** (b. Delroy Reid, 1965, Kingston), released on Pablo's Rockers International imprint in 1979. A spirited cultural lament inspired by his grandmother's store of proverbs and songs, the record did well enough as an import single in the UK to give Reid a name and alert roots fans to any further records from the youthman, despite the limitations of his unbroken voice. (As Reid recalled – "Augustus Pablo an' the man dem, they was sayin' that I sound flat. But at the time, I didn't know what flat mean, or nothin' at all.") Indeed, Reid was set to become one of the major vocalists of the 1980s and beyond.

Though Pablo's most consistent and creative period was over by the end of the 1970s, strong records have still continued to appear on Rockers and the newer Message label. The roughhouse spirit of the last two decades might not seem conducive to Pablo's laid-back approach, but he's issued good music by Junior Delgado, as well as Bunny Brissett, Yami Bolo, Spliffy Dan, Johnny Osbourne and the young cultural chatter, Blacka T. On his recent albums Pablo has not always been able to keep up the standard of his best singles, though there has been one classic instrumental set in *Blowing With the Wind*, and an interesting enough dub excursion in *One Step Dub*.

Because of the amount of interest in recent years in Pablo, largely from outside Jamaica, most of his back catalogue has been re-released. What remains to be made generally available are the numerous 45s for other producers, which helped finance his own labels. Contemporaneous with the first discs on his own labels were sessions with most of the more progressive producers, including Keith Hudson, Clive Chin (with whom he had attended school), Joe Gibbs, Lee Perry, Bunny Lee and Derrick Harriott. Then there were occasional recording dates for the partnership of Leroy Hollett and Dudley Swaby (whose Ja Man imprint was one of the more dependable smaller operations of the time), Vivian Jackson, pioneer deejay Dennis Alcapone, Ken Boothe's brother Douglas Boothe, Roydale Anderson and Winston Riley. As if this were not enough, the prolific Pablo was also closely involved with the work of the young **Leonard Chin**, who persuaded Pablo to record the first single on his Santic label, "Pablo In Dub", which was a major local hit. Pablo then played a significant part in the subsequent Santic sessions, including those that yielded striking records by Paul Whiteman, Horace Andy, Roman Stewart and Gregory Isaacs. Most of the Santic sessions are on CD, but anyone willing to endure the headache of negotiating with all the producers Pablo worked for could assemble one of the most important multi-CD sets in the history of Jamaican music.

AUGUSTUS PABLO

◑ **Original Rockers** (Rockers International, JA; Greensleeves, UK).

Ⓔ A superb selection of most of the best early self-produced instrumentals from Pablo. The deejay Dillinger crops up on one track – the brilliant "Brace A Boy" – but other than that, it is the young Mr Swaby following in the footsteps of Jackie Mittoo, drawing a little from Don Drummond and coming up with something that was very much his own. Some of the tracks employ Studio One rhythms ("Real Rock" for the opening track, "Rockers Dub", for instance), others are originals, and Pablo's musical vision unites everything. Anyone who has yet to join the initiated should check this immaculate album.

◑ **This Is** (Kaya, JA; Above Rock Records, US).

One of the most impressive and original debut albums in reggae's history, yet the approach could not have been simpler: over a dozen popular Randy's rhythms, Pablo improvised on what had previously been simply a child's plaything, the melodica (as well as clavinet, and the more conventional piano and organ). The choice of rhythms from Clive Chin was immaculate – among them, Alton Ellis's sublime "It's Too Late", a cut of Burning Spear's "Joe Frazier" and two of Horace Andy's major hits, "Children Of Israel" and "Problems". The effect was almost that of 'easy listening', but with a certain edge. After this album, practically every producer with a few rhythm tracks in stock was pursuing the magic that Pablo could add. The CD adds his first hit, "Java", and the equally compelling "Guiding Red" (a version of the Heptones' "Guiding Star").

◑ **East Of the River Nile** (Message, JA; Greensleeves, UK; RAS, US).

His first self-produced instrumental (as opposed to dub) set, this appeared in 1978, four years after *This Is*, and three after the most recent of the singles included on the above album. The sound is mellower – more 'meditational' – and just as ground-breaking. He was never again to release instrumental 45s that had quite the impact of his work of the first half of the 1970s, but on its own terms the album could not have been more successful.

◑ **King David's Melody** (Message, JA; Greensleeves, UK).

Something of a hotchpotch, drawing from tracks recorded between 1977 and the early 1980s. This is not usually seen as Pablo's golden period, though much of this material does sound better in retrospect, and "King David's Melody", the version to

Junior Delgado's "Away With You Fussing And Fighting", always seemed one of Pablo's better pieces of the time.

● Rockers Comes East (Rockers International, JA).

Perhaps the most underrated Pablo album, as traditionalists in 1988 found it difficult to accept their hero employing digital rhythms, or quite such a low-key approach. But given time, the set gradually reveals subtle qualities. Includes cuts to his two finest rhythms of the digital age – Junior Delgado's "Raggamuffin Year" and Delroy Williams's "This Love".

◑ Blowing With the Wind (Message, JA; Greensleeves, UK).

Just when the reggae cognoscenti were writing Pablo off, his reputation was restored by this truly amazing return to form in 1990. The new element that made a difference was nyahbingi drumming, half a decade before it returned to fashion with employment on Cobra and Buju Banton records. True, it is only featured on two tracks – "Blowing With the Wind", itself, and "Drums To the King" – but these are the longest on the album, and the non-nyahbingi workouts still have Pablo sounding far more focused than on most of his modern material. The trumpet of Johnnie 'Dizzy' Moore, one of the original Skatalites, is a further link with tradition, and another delight.

● Golden Melodies (Rockers International, JA).

This compilation, which appeared in 1992, includes several tracks of uncertain vintage. Of immediate interest are previously unreleased versions of Lloyd Parks's "Slaving" and the Gatherers' "Words Of My Mouth" (both on the original rhythms from Parks/Glen Brown and Lee Perry). There's also a cut of "Satta Massa Gana" that is different from either side of the "Pablo Satta"/"Silent Satta" single, as well as the very rare version of Vivian Jackson's "Conquering Lion", and the almost as rare "Islington Rock", "Eastman Sound" and "House Is Not A Home". An exceptional set, with a wicked cover photograph of the young Pablo.

JUNIOR DELGADO

● Raggamuffin Year (Mango, US).

The definitive Junior Delgado album with Augustus Pablo would draw from the best of this and *One Step More*, plus a handful of earlier and subsequent 45s. *Raggamuffin Year* includes their strongest single work together in the title track, an impressive duet with Johnny Osbourne, and the momentous "King Of Kings", but is otherwise slightly disappointing.

● One Step More (Message, JA; Mango, US).

Their second set together is a good deal more consistent, with the 45s, "Hanging Tree", "Riot In A Juvenile Prison" and "Forward Revolution", joined by the equally impressive "What Am I Doing Here", "One Day" and "King James" (the latter employing a new cut of the "East Of the River Nile" rhythm). Even "Hey Good Looking", which seemed disconcertingly lightweight when it appeared on the back of "Hanging Tree", fits in surprisingly well.

JACOB MILLER

◑ Who Say Jah No Dread (Greensleeves, UK).

E The late Jacob Miller flirted with international crossover success fronting the instrumental/vocal group Inner Circle, but few would deny that his most compelling work was under the guidance of Pablo. "Baby I Love You So" became better known through its version side, "King Tubby Meets the Rockers Uptown", and it makes perfect sense for all six vocals (his complete oeuvre for Mr Swaby) to be followed by their King Tubby mixed versions. At the heart of the set are "False Rasta" (with Tubby himself introducing the dub), "Who Say Jah No Dread" and "Each One Teach One", three of the most convincing expressions of the Rasta doctrine ever released by anyone.

HUGH MUNDELL

● Time & Place (Muni Music, JA).

A co-production from Pablo and Mundell, this second album was a natural progression from its predecessor, and showed a new maturity in the singer's voice (he was all of 19 when it appeared). Several tracks had already been released as singles – "Great Tribulation", "Short Man" and "(Rastafari Says the) Time Has Come" on Pablo's Rockers or Message labels, and "Rastafari's Call" on Mundell's own Muni Music. Two years after this album he was a victim of the gun culture he warned against.

HUGH MUNDELL/AUGUSTUS PABLO

◑ Africa Must Be Free By 1983/Africa Must Be Free By 1983 Dub (Greensleeves, UK; RAS, US).

A classic roots set, accompanied by its dub counterpart. The original vocal album said much about the

NYAHBINGI MUSIC

Nyahbingi (sometimes spelt 'nyabhingi' or 'nyabinghi') music in its purest form is the music played at Rastafarian meetings or 'grounations', and is based around a style of relentless drumming and chanting. Sometimes a guitar or horns are used (ska musicians such Johnnie 'Dizzy' Moore and Don Drummond developed their approaches at such gatherings), but no amplification at all is employed.

The drumming, which usually involves three hand drums of different sizes (the bass, the funde and the repeater), exercised an influence on early recorded Jamaican music – the Folks Brothers' 1960 hit, "Oh Carolina", for instance. However, though the drumming style – and even the master Rasta drummer Count Ossie – appeared on major hits in the 1960s, nyahbingi music was heard too sporadically to be considered a commercial trend until the computerized 1990s, when hardcore ragga deejays like Capleton, Shabba Ranks and Buju Banton chose to mouth 'cultural' concerns over rhythms that included traditional Rastafarian percussion. The one period in which Rastafarian ensembles regularly made records that were untampered by commercial considerations was the roots era of the 1970s.

HIGH TIMES RECORDS

Ras Michael: bongo man a-come

Though serious musicologists had made occasional field recordings of nyahbingi sessions, the first album to give the music the studio time it deserved, while remaining as true to its original forms as possible, was the triple LP set *Grounation*, from **Count Ossie & the Mystic Revelation of Rastafari**. The MRR was an aggregation of accomplished musicians which brought together both Count Ossie's African-style hand drummers and the horns and bass of tenor-sax man Cedric Brooks's Mystics band. This historic set has never been superseded, but the establishment of Rastafari as the dominant reggae ideology in the mid-1970s, plus the emergence of an audience for reggae albums that were more than collections of hit singles, created a climate in which more sets of nyahbingi-based music could be produced.

The most noteworthy of these were by **Ras Michael & the Sons of Negus** and the **Light of Saba**. The latter group was led by Cedric Brooks, who had played tenor sax, clarinet and flute on *Grounation*, as well as being its musical arranger. Ras Michael (b. Michael George Henry) was a drummer and singer who had been leading groups of Rastafarian musicians since at least the mid-1960s, and had spasmodically released music on his own Zion Disc label. The albums from both ensembles of percussionists, horn players, chanters and guitarists brought the music of Rastafarian meetings closer to the commercial reggae mainstream, initiating new musical hybrids that foreshadowed the concept of 'world music'. In reverse of the usual Jamaican practice, little music from either group appeared only on 45, but each produced at least one outstanding single. The Light of Saba's atmospheric instrumental "Lambs Bread Collie", featuring the trombone of Ronald 'Nambo' Robinson (also associated with the MRR), appeared in 1978 on their own label, and has become their most sought-after single track. Ras Michael's "Good People", a Studio One release from the same period, sounds as if the regular Brentford Road session musicians of the time were employed, but is no less inspired than previous work with the Mystic Revelation.

COUNT OSSIE & THE MYSTIC REVELATION OF RASTAFARI

◑ **Grounation** (MRR, JA; Ashanti, UK).

E The first triple-LP (now a double-CD) set to be cut in Jamaica, and a project that must have seemed very uncommercial at the time. Presumably it only happened because of the higher profile given Rastafarianism after Island's signing of the Wailers. The orations from Brother Samuel Clayton might wear a bit thin after a couple of plays, but do place the music in its context: the Rasta chants, drumming, a couple of songs that sound akin to British folk airs, and the jazz-based instrumental workouts bear any number of hearings. Music marked with integrity that should be heard by anyone interested in Jamaican culture, percussion or the roots of roots music.

◑ **Tales Of Mozambique** (Dynamic, JA/UK).

Released a couple of years after the ground-breaking *Grounation*, and along similar musical lines – a mixture of Rasta chants, nyahbingi drumming and jazz-based horns work.

THE LIGHT OF SABA

● **The Light Of Saba** (Total Sounds, JA).

● **The Light Of Saba In Reggae** (Total Sounds, JA).

The eponymous first album for a commercial record company included one of their most impressive 45 releases, the plaintive "Words Of Wisdom", a version of Horace Silver's US jazz hit "Song For My Father", and much that was an extension of Brooks's work with the MRR. As the title implies, the second album fitted even more into a conventional reggae mould – though few reggae outfits as such would have dared to base a piece on an Ethiopian marching song. Their treatment of dub poet Mutabaruka's "Outcry" most immediately stands out, and was released as a single.

RAS MICHAEL & THE SONS OF NEGUS

● **Dadawah Peace & Love** (Wild Flower, JA; Trojan, UK).

In 1975, Ras Michael's group were joined by some of Kingston's top studio musicians for this riveting album, produced by Lloyd Charmers. Unique in its synthesis of musical forms and the length of its tracks (there were only four), it uses traditional Rasta chant as its basic material, but subjects it to elements from the reggae mainstream, US funk and even rock.

◑ **Rastafari** (Rastafari, JA; Greensleeves, UK).

The album that followed the Tommy Cowan-produced hit single, "None A Jah Jah Children No Cry", and featuring the same line-up as the above, with the addition of Peter Tosh and Earl 'Chinna' Smith on guitars, Robbie Shakespeare on bass and Robbie Lynn on keyboards. Released in 1975, this was the nearest that the Sons had come to a conventional reggae album, and it worked wonderfully.

◑ **Kibir-Am-Lak** (Top Ranking, JA; Greensleeves, UK).

This is very close in mood and instrumentation to *Rastafari*, simply adding Geoffrey Chung on keyboards and Tommy McCook on flute. The results are almost as satisfying, with the first two tracks, "New Name" and "Wicked Men", approaching the anthemic nature of "None A Jah Jah Children".

● **Movements** (Ras Michael & the Sons Of Negus, JA).

Another strong album that mixes nyahbingi drumming with more commercial elements. "Numbered Days" borrows a motif from Marley's "Slave Driver" but adds enough to stand as a contender for Ras Michael's single most outstanding track.

● **Love Thy Neighbour** (Jah Life, US).

Lee Perry receives a credit on the last Ras Michael album of interest, and it does have the characteristic Black Ark sound about it (though it was apparently recorded at Dynamic). This makes it Ras Michael's most accessible album to those not 100 percent sure about nyahbingi music.

VARIOUS ARTISTS

● **Churchical Chants Of the Nyahbingi** (Heartbeat, US).

◑ **Rastafari Elders** (RAS, US).

These two sets – the former a field recording of a seven-day Rasta meeting in the Upper Trelawney hills, the latter a Washington studio session with Rasta elders visiting the United States – represent nyahbingi music in its purest form, and have yet to appear on a Jamaican label.

commitment that Pablo, as a producer, could inspire in even the most youthful of singers. Other successful singles included are "Let's All Unite", "Book Of Life" and "My Mind", while at least two of the tracks that only appear on the album are at least their equal: "Why Do Blackman Fuss & Fight" and the even harder "Run Revolution Come" (the first cut of the rhythm used for Junior Delgado's "Away With You Fussing And Fighting"). The dub set that makes up the rest of the Greensleeves CD (separate discs on RAS) deconstructs six of the tracks (plus another two by the young singer).

NORRIS REID

● **Give Jah the Praises** (Rockers International, JA).

A decade and a half after the earliest tracks first appeared as 45s, Pablo collected them together for the second and better of Norris Reid's two albums for him. There are only six vocals, but each is followed by its corresponding dub/instrumental version, with the most exceptional over three of Pablo's best-known rhythms: "Black Forces" ("King Tubby Meets the Rockers Uptown"), "Give Jah the Praises" ("Pablo Satta") and "Entrance Of Jah World" ("East Of the River Nile").

TETRACK/ROCKERS INTERNATIONAL BAND

◑ **Let's Get Started/Eastman Dub** (Greensleeves, UK).

Another classic vocal album produced by Pablo, doubled up with its Sylvan Morris-mixed dub counterpart (the latter never released in Jamaica). The title track remains the trio's best-known record, but interest is maintained throughout, not only by Pablo's rhythms, but all three members taking equally effective lead vocals, and Carlton Hines's songwriting skills. The other singles included are "Only Jah Jah Know", "Let's Get Together" (a surprisingly successful version of Dino Valenti's hippy protest-rock song recorded by the Youngbloods) and their ultimate work, "Isn't It Time".

VARIOUS ARTISTS – AUGUSTUS PABLO PRODUCTIONS

⦿ **Classic Rockers 2** (Mango Reggae Refreshers, UK).

E A set that fully lives up to its title, with many of the man's most popular productions, including the Heptones' "Love Won't Come Easy", the Immortals "Can't Keep A Good Man Down", Horace Andy's "Rock To Sleep" and Paul Whiteman's legendary "Say So".

◑ **Rockers International** (Rockers International, JA; Greensleeves, UK).

◑ **Rockers International 2** (Rockers International, JA; Greensleeves, UK).

Two Pablo-produced collections that deserve a place alongside the *Original Rockers* compilation. Certainly, the second volume is just as potent – with its fifteen tracks based on five different rhythms, and the strength of each confirmed by these variations. Its only slightly less impressive predecessor took a slightly different approach, with four cuts of "El Rockers"/"Real Rock" that had appeared as 45s, plus previously unreleased tracks that are almost as strong.

⦿ **Augustus Pablo Presents Rockers Story** (RAS, US).

⦿ **Augusts Pablo Presents Cultural Showcase** (RAS, US).

These two compilations are both mixed bags, drawing from classic and lesser-known (but interesting) items. *Rockers Story* is worth picking up for an obscure Dillinger cut to "Love Won't Come Easy"/"Frozen Dub", while *Cultural Showcase* demonstrates how the best of his 1980s work sits comfortably alongside more vintage material.

VARIOUS ARTISTS – LEONARD CHIN PRODUCTIONS

◑ **Santic & Friends – An Even Harder Shade Of Black** (Pressure Sounds, UK).

A reissue of a classic compilation from the mid-1970s, to which Augustus Pablo made significant contributions, with the addition of half a dozen extra tracks. Leonard 'Santic' Chin was one of the period's most original producers, as demonstrated not only by his two major hits, Horace Andy's "Problems" and "Children Of Israel", but also by their instrumental counterparts from Pablo, and further gems such as Gregory Isaacs' "I'll Be Around", Pablo's appropriately named "Harder Shade Of Dub" and contributions from the deejays I-Roy, Big Joe and Jah Woosh. The omission of Paul Whiteman's "I Don't Want To Lose You", the equal of his legendary "Say So", is made the more glaring by the presence of Tubby's magnificent dub cut.

The Black Ark man: Lee Perry builds his own studio

The diminutive **Lee Perry** (b. Rainford Hugh Perry, 1936, Hanover) made his initial impact performing at Studio One in the ska era. He had then been instrumental in Joe Gibbs' early success, and went on to produce for himself, making radical impressions with the most innovative work of the Wailers' entire career, as well as a further string of classic vocal discs from the likes of Junior Byes and one of the most impressive early dub albums, *Blackboard Jungle*. In the mid–late 1970s, Scratch, with Augustus Pablo, Vivian Jackson and Glen Brown, was one of the quartet of innovative Jamaican producers destined to find a larger audience after the event – particularly among those coming to reggae from the outside. The main reason for this was the studio sound he developed at the **Black Ark** in Washington Gardens from the middle of the decade. Ears attuned to the more experimental areas of rock or ambient music, or simply interested in the use of the studio itself as a musical instrument, delighted in the dense, 'underwater' ambience of Black Ark productions.

ADRIAN BOOT

Scratch on fire, 1976

Like so much cutting-edge reggae, the Black Ark sound exemplified the Jamaican approach of making maximum demands of minimal resources. Sound textures that were unique anyway were developed further through working with four-track equipment, and the necessity of dumping completed tracks onto one track so as to free them for further overdubbing. This meant a loss of what would normally be thought of as 'sound quality' every time it occurred, but contributed to the incomparable feel of the Black Ark sound. Perry's fascination with new technology (drum machines, an Echoplex reverb unit, a Mutron phaser) and his propensity for imaginative risk-taking were the other essential components in the process.

Sometimes the result disguised what were really rather weak rhythms and/or inferior performances, but many recordings cut at the Black Ark have stood the test of time. Among those that immediately spring to mind are several from **Max Romeo**, an often underrated singer who had previously cut cultural tirades like "Babylon Burning", "Public Enemy Number 1" and "Ginal Ship" for Perry. In the mid-1970s their association produced an even more impressive series of records, beginning in 1975 with a major local hit, "Three Blind Mice", which adapted the nursery rhyme to tell the story of a police raid on a party. This was followed by the records that brought Max to the attention of an international rock press that had previously dismissed him as simply the smutty singer of "Wet Dream" fame. "Sipple Out Deh", released in Jamaica in 1975, then issued by Island in a remixed version titled "War Ina Babylon", was one of those tunes which seems to sum up perfectly the mood of the time. Bob Marley heard the song before it was recorded and said he'd like to voice it himself, but Scratch said Max should be given the break – a smart move, it

ADRIAN BOOT

The legendary Black Ark studio

turned out, as the Island LP built around the hit remains Maxi's best-selling album. (A couple of years later Marley was to adapt the rhythm for his popular album track, "Three Little Birds".) The follow-up single, "One Step Forward" was just as serious, featuring another mesmerizing rhythm, unmistakably recorded at the Black Ark, and lyrics that similarly addressed the climate of social crisis in Kingston.

Romeo, who enjoyed a long professional relationship with Perry, offers witness to the unique Black Ark atmosphere. "Black Ark is a studio that if you walk in it was like someone's study. It doesn't look nothing like a studio until you hear it. No one knows what technique Perry used. Because he used those small track tape, and he seemed to get sixteen tracks stuffed into that four-track. It was a marvel – until today, no one knows how he did it. The vibe of the Black Ark studio was like all these people gather around. It start like ten o'clock in the morning. Guys start gathering. There's a kerosene pan on the fire bubbling some dumpling, some jelly roll, some ackee and ting. Everyone throw in something to buy what we need. There might be a guy outside with his guitar, chantin', and Scratch's inside with a spliff, tunin' in to the guy, who doesn't even know Scratch is tunin' to him. Then Scratch jus' go out and say 'Let's go inside here,' and find him a riddim. He say: 'I hear that, and on this riddim'." This was the process out of which Scratch's most successful recording of the period came about. Max, again: "That's how we did "Police & Thieves". Junior Murvin was just playing and Scratch come out and immediately say 'Here's the rhythm, let's do it.'" The result was out on the streets in just a couple of days, which was fairly typical of Scratch's production mode.

Just as notable an Upsetter release from 1977 was one of the first 12" singles to appear in Jamaica. The top side, **Carlton Jackson**'s "History", perfectly fused one of Scratch's most serious rhythms with a lyric that exemplified the word 'conscious'. Beginning with an account of how he was sold as a slave in Africa to a European and taken in chains to the Caribbean, the singer tackles the different versions of history to which he has been exposed:

"Then I really get to realise
A Rastaman first bring civilisation on yah
Rasta civilise yah
Israel, your history say from 1695
We have been working on the same plantation
Chanting the same recitation
Say Jah Jah is loving and a who don't love him never
know Jah
Oh no, a could never know Jah, oh no
Robbing, cheating, hatred and scorn
That is the culture the Babylon taught
Saying they teach us of so-called civilisation
Babylon, you are a sly old fox
Lock you ina box and throw away the key
For all those tricks you played when I was me
Jah, Jah, Jah, Jah, Jah, Jah, Jah got the master key."

A similar theme of tradition and cultural identity was continued on the other side of the single, with "Sons Of Slaves", arguably the strongest record by Junior Delgado.

Other exemplary Black Ark productions in a strictly 'conscious' mood from the mid–late 1970s included **George Faith**'s "Guide Line", **Jimmy Riley**'s "Sons Of Negus", the **Heptones**' "Mystery Babylon" and former Melodian **Brent Dowe**'s Twelve Tribes favourite "Down Here In Babylon". To show that the Black Ark sound could fit love songs as well as dread 'cultural' expressions, **Keith Rowe**, formerly half of the Keith & Tex duo, offered a soulful version of Gene Chandler's soul hit, "That Girl (Groovy Situation)"; **Junior Byles**' "Curly Locks" similarly transcended divisions between 'cultural' and 'lovers' tunes. And though the albums Perry produced tended to be inconsistent, the **Congos**' *Heart Of* set was the most consistently brilliant album of Scratch's entire career. Deejays were represented by records from **Prince Jazzbo**, **Lord Sassafrass**, **James Brown** and **Jah Lion**, as well as Perry's own semi-sung/spoken commentaries, most notably the 1977 revenge classic "White Belly Rat", which was supposedly aimed straight at former associate Max Romeo.

Curiously, the stream of quirkily brilliant instrumental 45s credited to Perry's session band, the **Upsetters** (who, after the departure of brothers Aston and Carlton Barrett to join the Wailers, usually included Boris Gardiner on bass and Michael Richards on drums, alongside hornsmen Bobby Ellis, Richard 'Dirty Harry' Hall, Herman Marquis and Vin Gordon), ran dry

ADRIAN BOOT

The Congos at Black Ark, 1977; from left, Roy Johnson, Cedric Myton and Watty Burnett

by the middle of the 1970s, with the last great flurry ("Cane River Rock", "Enter the Dragon", "Bury the Razor") appearing in 1974–75. To some degree this can be explained by the fact that the dub techniques that Perry had encouraged **King Tubby** to develop proved more interesting to dancehall audiences than the straight organ- or horns-dominated instrumentals with which most producers had scored previously.

THE CONGOS

◑ **Heart Of the Congos** (Blood & Fire, UK).

Ⓔ The most completely successful of all the albums recorded at the Black Ark, and not simply because Perry had perfected his use of the studio he was soon to destroy. The sound is breathtaking, but of equal importance are the vocal talents with whom he was working. The interplay between Cedric Myton's falsetto and Roydel Johnson's tenor would have been enough under most circumstances, but Scratch also chose to utilize comparable talents for the backing vocals – Barry Llewellyn and Barry Morgan from the Heptones, Watty Burnett, Gregory Isaacs and the Meditations. This is thus one of the prime examples of Jamaican vocal technique, and the CD is even more essential for including another disc's worth of dub and 12" versions.

THE HEPTONES

● **Party Time** (Island, UK).

The variable quality of the rhythms prevents this from being the *tour de force* that might have been expected. Worth picking up, however, for "Sufferers Time" (which deserved to be the title track), "Mr President" and the trio's second cut of "Crying Over You".

JAH LION

◑ **Columbia Colly** (Island, UK; Mango, US).

When recording for Scratch, the deejay Jah Lloyd became the more dread-sounding Jah Lion. His approach remained the same as usual, though, and his one Perry-produced album has him chanting in fairly typical style – with debts to both Big Youth and Prince Jazzbo. Favourite Upsetter rhythms employed include the marvellous "Fever" and "Dub Organiser".

JUNIOR MURVIN

◑ **Police & Thieves** (Island, UK).

The title track is so perfect that everything Junior Murvin later recorded remained in its shadow. However, tracks like "Tedious", "Roots Train" and "False Teaching" all deserved a wider audience than they received.

PRINCE JAZZBO

◑ **Ital Corner [Natty Passing Thru]** (Black Wax, UK; Clocktower, US).

This was originally released in the UK by Black Wax under the title of *Natty Passing Thru* at about the same time as the Jah Lion set on Island, and it drips with the same steamy tropical jungle atmosphere. Those interested primarily in Jazzbo should perhaps check his self-productions and Studio One work first, but Black Ark fans cannot afford to be without it.

MAX ROMEO

◑ **War Ina Babylon** (Island, UK).

The title track is a remix of "Sipple Out Deh", which was Perry's biggest Jamaican hit of 1975, and at least three other tracks – "Norman", "One Step Forward" and "Chase the Devil" – are of a similar standard. Romeo's gospel-inflected voice never sounded more poignant, and Scratch wisely resisted the urge to dominate totally. Unfortunately, producer and singer went their separate ways after this, to nobody's benefit.

VARIOUS ARTISTS – LEE PERRY PRODUCTIONS

◑ **Open the Gate** (Trojan, UK).

Ⓔ The second in Trojan's series of two-CD Perry sets bring together singles that were mostly under-appreciated when they first appeared in the late 1970s. A few years later, collectors were willing to bankrupt themselves for rare copies of tracks such as Devon Irons' "Vampire", Carlton Jackson's "History" and Watty Burnett's "Open the Gate", all included on *Open the Gate*.

◑ **Build the Ark** (Trojan, UK).

Ⓔ The third instalment in the Trojan series is a similar collection of fairly obscure but striking Black Ark productions, including Perry's own "White Belly Rat" (aimed at Max Romeo, apparently), the Sons of Light's "Land Of Love", Junior Dread's seriously off-the-wall "A Wah Dat" and Danny Hensworth's "Mr Money Man". Scratch did make his share of weak records in this period, but this selection goes for the heady peaks.

◑ **Heart Of the Ark** (Seven Leaves, UK).

Concentrating on Scratch's late 1970s work at the Black Ark, and including one bona fide classic in Leroy Sibbles's "Rasta Fari" (only previously available on a scarce 12"), as well as obscurities like his own "Nuh Run It Down" and Prodigal's "4 & 20 Dreadlocks". It will delight Scratch's followers, but is unlikely to win new ones.

⊙ **Arkology** (Island UK/US).

A three-CD set that covers the Black Ark period handsomely and with few overlaps with other Island/Perry sets. Among the 52 tracks – all mastered from first-generation producer tapes – are unissued dubs, songs from the Heptones and Congo Cedric Myton, more than a dozen variant mixes which have never been released in this form, and tracks which only appeared on hard-to-find Jamaican singles. Hits like Max Romeo's "War Ina Babylon" and Junior Murvin's "Police & Thieves" (and four more versions) are scattered throughout the programme, which covers all the major artists Scratch worked with during the period, except Bob Marley. The fifty-page accompanying booklet features previously unseen photos and interview material with many of them. Suitable for newcomer and hardcore fan alike, the set supplies convincing evidence to support the 'Scratch as creative genius' argument.

⊙ **Excaliburman** (Seven Leaves, UK).
A superb collection, including Scratch's own "Free Up the Prisoners", Debra Keese's "Travelling" and Jackie Bernard's "Economic Crisis" from the late 1970s, and also Dillinger's inspired "Dub Organiser" and Jah T's "Lick the Pipe" from earlier in the decade. The tunes from disparate periods blend surprisingly well, and belie the bargain-basement packaging.

Niney: flat foot hustling

While his friend Scratch was building his Black Ark studio, **Niney** was continuing on his way as a less adventurous but nonetheless distinctive producer, a role he would maintain into the 1980s and beyond with Channel One, Tuff Gong and Sonic Sounds. He had begun with Joe Gibbs, and by 1970 was supervising sessions for both Lee Perry and Bunny Lee. The 1970 hit "Blood And Fire" got his Observer label off the ground in a big way; for the next six years he produced a steady stream of high-quality roots music, injecting his own authorial voice into the work of such vocal stylists as Dennis Brown, Gregory Isaacs, Freddie McGregor, Michael Rose, Junior Byles, Delroy Wilson, Jacob Miller, Junior Delgado and Tyrone Taylor, all of whom were inspired to cut some of their best music with the producer. Other Niney productions were more experimental, like the monologues he recorded with engineeer **Errol 'ET' Thompson**: "Ital Correction" was exactly that, a Rasta correction to the "names white men have given" to various foods, while "False Ship" utilized the same rhythm to underpin an incomprehensible diatribe against false Rastas. His dubs were also innovative, being among the first to feature sound effects and disruptive false starts and breaks.

Although Niney is not generally celebrated for his deejay records, they were rarely less than top quality. Outstanding was Big Youth's "6 Dead 19 Gone To Jail", which extended its eloquent outrage at Kingston violence to the whole world. I-Roy proved his versatility again with the sly slackness of "Sister Maggie Breast" and the contrasting hard-reality message of "Point Blank". But perhaps the highlight remains the exceptional "Flat Foot Hustling", on which Dillinger, fresh from his Channel One hits, rapped over a ferocious dub of Dennis Brown's "Have No Fear", seamlessly incorporating snatches of the mento "Linstead Market" into his compulsive narrative of ghetto survival.

DAVID CORIO

Niney observes the scene

VARIOUS ARTISTS – WINSTON 'NINEY' HOLNESS PRODUCTIONS

⊙ **Observation Station** (Heartbeat, US).
E Covering a five-year span in the producer's career, this set demonstrates how Niney was able consistently to develop his hard-edged approach into a fully developed roots mode. The music here is all from the producer's original tapes, and exceptional tracks like Junior Byles' "Weeping", the monumental disco-mix cut of Tyrone Taylor's "Sufferation", and Michael Rose's first cut of "Guess Who's Coming To

Dinner" have never sounded better. Also present are premier-league singers like Delroy Wilson, Slim Smith, Ken Boothe and Gregory Isaacs, as well as the relatively little-known Glassford 'Porti' Manning – lead singer of the similarly obscure harmony trio the Jewels – whose "Prophecy Call" has become something of a cult in the UK.

Ital Observer Style (Jah Live, France).
This album received limited distribution when issued in France in 1983, but is well worth searching for in secondhand racks. As well as Niney vocals to Max Romeo tunes, there are excellent deejay cuts from Dillinger, Big Youth, I-Roy and the little-recorded Jah Bop, alongside oddities like "The Harp Sound", an unlikely but riveting meeting between ET's dub technique and Chinna's Swiss music-box effects on guitar.

Truths & Rights Observer Style (Heartbeat, US).
A further selection from Niney's tapes, similarly featuring two cuts of "Blood And Fire". Rarities uncovered include Michael Rose's alternative vocal on the "Guess Who..." rhythm, titled here "Clap the Barber", Johnnie Clarke riding the well-known Augustus Pablo rhtyhm "555 Crown Street" on the extended mix of "Warrior", Junior Delgado's "Long Way" (originally titled "Every Natty Want To Go Home"), and the double drum steppers underneath the producer's own vocal backed by the Morwells on "Mutiny".

Bring the Couchie 1974–1976 (Trojan, UK).
Dubbed from clean Jamaican 45s, this collection is roots and dub all the way. Three cuts of Dennis Brown's "Wolf & Leopard", two lesser-known Horace Andy tunes and their dubs, plus both sides of the rare title track. Max Romeo, Michael Rose and Niney himself are the other featured vocalists.

Glen Brown

Another great left-field producer of the early 1970s, **Glen Brown**, was not as prolific as before, presumably because of financial constraints, but in retrospect it can be seen that his rhythms of the roots period were at least the equal of their predecessors. He deftly adapted to the sort of 'steppers'-style rhythms dominant in the closing years of the decade, but left his individual stamp upon them – perhaps a mark too individual for wide acceptance.

For a couple of years after 1975, when he launched the South East Music imprint, there were no new Glen Brown productions on vinyl, except for a few on the enterprising UK label Grove Music, the strongest of which was **Richard MacDonald**'s apocalyptic "Wicked Can't Run Away". Then came a couple of 45s on Tappa Zukie's Stars label, and a few more on his own South East Music. But rather than the instrumentals or deejay outings that proved his most compelling records in the early 1970s, Brown now concentrated on rootsy vocals, mainly by MacDonald, **Sylford Walker** and **Wayne Jarrett**. The youthful Walker was the most prolific of these: an archetypal roots singer in the Burning Spear mould, he cut a couple of worthwhile 45s for Joe Gibbs, but his cult reputation otherwise rests on the album's worth of sides he recorded for Glen Brown in the mid–late 1970s. They all feature truly heavyweight rhythms, with "Lamb's Bread" and "Eternal Day", respectively a tribute to the herb and a warning to the wicked, being particularly notable.

Glen Brown, the God son

Brown's few forays during this period into the instrumental territory for which he had been previously noted were also noteworthy – a Tommy McCook version of Sylford Walker's "Chant Down Babylon"/Lloyd Parks' "Slaving", entitled "Music From South Side", and a superb album of the tenorman's versions of Brown's best-known rhythms that received only a very limited and unofficial release in the UK. Perhaps he had gone off deejays, as well; except for a version of "Wicked Can't Run Away" by **Tappa Zukie**, the only talker with whom he worked in this period was the Lone Ranger's former spar, the undervalued

Welton Irie, who impressed with "Lamb's Bread International", his variation of the Sylford Walker theme.

WELTON IRIE

Ghettoman Corner (Pantomine, US).
Eight of Glen Brown's heaviest rhythms, over which the seminal dancehall deejay adds his commentaries to good effect. The much sought-after "Blackman Stand Up Pon Foot" is included, and the entire set bears comparison with the producer's earlier deejay classics.

SYLFORD WALKER

Lamb's Bread (Greensleeves, UK).
E The only album by Sylford Walker that has ever been available, and one released about a decade after the event. "Lamb's Bread" itself was one of the last of the producer's 45s to make any sort of impact, and all the tracks depend on the more apocalyptic style of rhythm he favoured in the mid–late 1970s. None was a major hit, but each is a minor masterpiece – and three come complete with their Tubby-mixed dub versions.

VARIOUS ARTISTS – GLEN BROWN PRODUCTIONS

Green Bay Killing (Pantomine, US).
Best known as Wayne Jarrett's "Youthman" or Glenroy Richards "Wicked Can't Run Away", the most enduring Glen Brown rhythm ever is given the full version-album treatment (ten cuts in all). The absence of a proper sleeve rather undersells the marvellous contents.

Keith Hudson

Keith Hudson, another maverick producer/performer of the first half of the decade, moved in the late 1970s to New York, where he became more even more eccentric in what he produced, perhaps because he was removed from Kingston's latest trends in the dancehalls.

Following the impact of his classic *Flesh Of My Skin* and *Pick A Dub* sets, Hudson was signed to Virgin as part of the rock label's venture into the newly fashionable area of roots reggae; the resulting album, *Too Expensive*, was a disastrous attempt to broaden his audience that only too fittingly bore out the warning of its title. Only when he started a new label of his own did the enigmatic Hudson regain his old form with, first, a dub album that stood comparison with his former work, and then a vocal set on the same rhythms that only just fell short of *Flesh Of My Skin*. Unfortunately, he was to show little interest in this later period either in singers other than himself, or even in deejays, with whom he had previously been particularly successful. This hugely talented figure died prematurely in 1984 from lung cancer, leaving a considerable legacy of recorded work that was of inconsistent quality, (but always at least interesting), and unmistakably his own.

KEITH HUDSON

Rasta Communication (Greensleeves, UK; Joint International, US).
The first of three vocal albums made after relocating to New York has the vocal cuts to the rhythms on the esteemed *Brand* dub set (see pp.205–206), with the expected tortured vocals from the idiosyncratic Mr Hudson, over spare, jagged rhythms (just drums, bass, guitar and keyboards) that remain among the most serious associated with his name.

From One Extreme To Another (Joint International, US).

Playing It Cool & Playing It Right (Joint International, US).
These are even more eccentric sets. Hudson's voice is not to everybody's taste but on these albums he employed it to quite incredible effect. The title track on *Playing It Cool* is yet another excellent cut of the great "Melody Maker"/"Don't Think About Me" rhythm. Everything on all three Joint albums is in the same slightly unnerving mood, and quite removed from the reggae (or any) mainstream.

The small axes

Every era in Jamaican music has been dominated by two or three producers, who have reaped most of the rewards and set the major trends. In the ska era it was Clement Dodd and Duke Reid; during the roots period the nearest equivalents were Joseph 'Joe Joe' Hookim, Joe Gibbs and Bunny Lee. Nevertheless, the number of '**small axes**' attempting to cut down the 'big trees' increased greatly in the early 1970s, and it was these small operators who were largely responsible for bringing about a major shift in the direction of Jamaican music – one that made it less dependent on US influences, and more in tune with the ghetto youth. This process accelerated even more in the second half of the decade.

Some of the new labels were founded by performers who, dissatisfied with their share of the rewards from hits made for established producers, decided to take greater control over their recordings and finances (as the Wailers had done when they launched their Wail 'N' Soul 'M label way back in 1967); others were launched by sound-system operators following directly in the tradition of Dodd, Reid and Prince Buster, or by individuals with an interest in music and sufficient entrepreneurial spirit and skills. Many did not last very long – sometimes just a single or two. But sheer number of fiercely competing producers meant that ever more youthmen were given the chance to move from the dancehall audience to the studio. Moreover, whereas self-production in most areas of popular music leads to self-indulgence and pretentiousness, in Jamaican music these vices are rare, for the very different market for reggae has always put a block an albums about the performer's 'personal growth'.

The Abyssinians

The **Abyssinians** – Bernard Collins plus Lynford and Donald Manning – were the vocal trio who defined the roots variation of close-harmony singing by moving away from its US soul origins and imbuing it with a sombre spiritual feel. Their Clinch label, launched in 1971 (see p.124), never released a record that was not either by the group, or Bernard Collins on his own, or a version of one of his rhythms.

ADRIAN BOOT

The Abyssinians: Bernard Collins (left) with the Manning brothers

But the consistent brilliance of these 45s fully justified the policy. The initial single on the label was the legendary "Satta Massa Gana", which had been recorded at Studio One in 1969, but whose left-field nature (for the time) ensured it was never released by Clement Dodd. When it appeared a couple of years later on Clinch the record eventually earned classic status and prompted further cuts of the rhythm – built by a stellar band that included Leroy Sibbles (bass), Richard Ace (piano), Vin Gordon (trombone), Carlton Manning (guitar) and Bongo Herman and Bongo Les (percussion) – such as Big Youth's "I Pray Thee", Dillinger's "I Saw E Saw", Richard Ace's "Charming Version" and the Abyssinians' own inspired talking cut, "Mabrak", on which all three members recite biblical phrases in the Ethiopian language, Amharic. When the trio's debut album, *Forward On To Zion*, appeared in 1976, it not surprisingly included a recut of their first hit, along with new versions of "Declaration of Rights", which they had originally cut for Coxsone, and "Yim Mas Gan", their only record for Lloyd 'Matador' Daley.

Subsequent 45s on Clinch by Bernard Collins and the Abyssinians were few in number by Jamaican standards but all were of an extremely high standard – from "Poor Jason White", which related the true story of a fisherman's son who floated seventeen days at sea before being picked up by a German ship, to equally reflective songs of history, culture and faith, such as "Let My Days Be Long", "Leggo Beast", "Forward Jah" and "Prophecy". *Forward On To Zion* brought them to the attention of a wider audience than their singles, especially after being released in the UK; a second LP, courtesy of Virgin, then disappointed some of their followers, and they had to wait until the beginning of the next decade before a third album appeared (and that was largely a compilation of singles). After a quiet period in the 1970s and 1980s, Bernard Collins relaunched the label with new material that was almost of vintage standard, and even released a couple of previously unheard cuts of "Satta Massa Gana" – a vintage performance from the late Prince Far I and a presumably more recent vocal version by the Abyssinians themselves declaring (quite correctly, of course) that "Satta rules the dance". Another album of fresh material is probably too much to hope for, especially since at the time of writing there are two versions of the group in existence – one led by Bernard Collins, the other by the Manning brothers.

THE ABYSSINIANS

◉ **Satta Massa Gana** (Heartbeat, US).

E This release presents their stunning debut album in digital clarity, and adds another four tracks that equal the original ten in quality. Even the reworkings of the roots anthems "Satta Massa Gana", "Declaration Of Rights" and "Yim Mas Gan" are worthwhile, and fit in perfectly with marvellous fresh material like "Good Lord", "I & I" and "African Race".

◑ **Arise** (Tuff Gong/Clinch, JA; Virgin, UK).

Their second album, initially released by Virgin in the UK, was generally found disappointing at the time, though in hindsight this could only have been because of the phenomenal impact of the first set. The best tracks – such as "This Land Is For Everyone", "Let My Days Be Long" and "Wicked Men" – now stand comparison with any vocal-group records of the period.

◑ **Forward** (Clinch, JA; Alligator, US).

The final album repeats two of the additional tracks on the Heartbeat set, and slots them alongside other rarities of the same calibre, including the beautiful "Jerusalem" (originally the flip of the very limited first press of "Satta"), "Prophecy" and Bernard Collins's solo "Forward Jah Jah".

The Royals

The genesis of **Roy Cousins**' Wambesi/Tamoki labels was similar to that of Bernard Collins's Clinch. Just as Dodd had kept "Satta Massa Gana" in the vaults, so he also sat upon the original cut of the song most associated with Cousins' name, "Pick Up the Pieces", as recorded by his group, the **Royals** (Cousins plus Bertram Johnson, Keith Smith and Errol Wilson), in the late 1960s. Coxsone at last released the record under the group name of the Tempests in 1973, when Cousins himself released a self-produced cut as only the second disc on Wambesi/Tamoki; three years later Coxsone re-released the original with a more modern drum track. All versions went on to gain classic status. Before this the Royals had enjoyed minor success (in terms of sales, if not financial reward) with recordings for Joe Gibbs, Byron Smith and Lloyd Daley. Supporting himself with a post office job, Cousins had launched the Wambesi/Tamoki labels in 1973 with the Royals' "Down Comes the Rain", backed by "Heart In Pain", credited to a Vinnie O'Bryan. The new version of "Pick Up the Pieces" followed in the same year, complete with a more contemporary-sounding rhythm than the Brentford Road original and a splendid early King Tubby's dub side, titled "Llongo".

A perhaps more important parallel with the Abyssinians lies in the reflective nature of several of their songs on Wambesi, as well as the obvious care they took over their limited number of releases. Just the titles of 45s like "Ghetto Man", "Sufferer Of the Ghetto", "Blacker Black" and "Promised Land" give a fair idea of Cousins' concentration on concerns more enduring than fashion. Eventually most of these early self-productions were collected on an album that was released in a limited press in Jamaica, before being picked up by the Ballistic label in the UK. This international exposure gave Cousins the freedom to leave the post office and devote himself full time to music, though only occasionally did subsequent releases quite match the sublime standards of the material collected on the Royals' debut album.

At the same time as the Royals' classic work was appearing, Cousins sometimes recorded other artists, imparting a very Royals-like feel to tracks such as "Way Of Life", one of the greatest tunes ever from **Gregory Isaacs**, "Genuine Way" from **Lloyd Ruddock** (King Tubby's brother) and, on the eve of the next decade, **Naggo 'Dolphin' Morris**'s "Down In the Ghetto". Though Cousins at this stage avoided the relatively easy option of producing numerous deejays over his classic rhythms, there was I-Roy's "Monkey Fashion"/"Fashion Monkey", a pair of splendid toasts from one of the most intelligent of the chatters over what else but the "Pick Up the Pieces" rhythm.

THE ROYALS

◑ **Pick Up the Pieces** (Wambesi, JA; Magnum, UK).

E The Royals' debut set collected 45s recorded over a four-year period, when Roy Cousins' job at the post office was paying for the studio time. Perhaps the easing of the usual financial pressures allowed by his regular employment was a major factor in the carefully crafted nature of the material. The title track is arguably stronger than the Studio One original (a more modern rhythm was used), and gems like "Ghetto Man", "Sufferer Of the Ghetto" and "When You Are Wrong" are equally dignified and moving.

◑ **Ten Years After** (Wambesi, UK).

The more hurriedly recorded second album is not quite in the same class as its predecessor, but does includes one of the last classics cut by the group, "Make Believe" (featuring Errol Davis on lead vocal rather than Roy Cousins), along with the earlier "Down Comes the Rain" and tracks that only just fall short of the skyscraping standards of its predecessor.

The Wailing Souls

Managing to keep up a standard similar to the Abyssinians and the Royals, while being a great deal more prolific, were the **Wailing Souls**, who even turned out a worthwhile album in the 1990s. Their incredible body of work for producers ranging from Dodd to Linval Thompson has appeared over the course of three decades, but its consistency has largely

ADRIAN BOOT

The striped-hatted Winston Matthews with fellow Wailing Souls

been down to **Winston Matthews**' aching voice and his superb songwriting talent – though fellow members Lloyd 'Bread' McDonald, Rudolph 'Garth' Dennis and George 'Buddy' Hayes have also provided strong songs, and both Dennis and Hayes have sung the occasional lead. The group launched their Massive label in 1976, recording at the Channel One studio, and scored almost immediately with two superb 45s: "Bredda Gravalicious" and "Feel the Spirit". Their output on their own label was never prolific – little more than the material that appeared on their *Wild Suspense* album – but a substandard record has yet to appear on it. Their work for top 1980s producers like Sly & Robbie, Henry 'Junjo' Lawes and Linval Thompson was to show no drop in standards, but that part of their story belongs to the dancehall chapter (see p.251).

THE WAILING SOULS

◑ **Wild Suspense** (Massive, JA; Mango Reggae Refreshers, UK).

E The self-produced second album from the Wailing Souls was not released until seven years after their Studio One debut, some eleven since their first 45. But *Wild Suspense* was a triumph that easily equalled standards previously set. In fact, both their harmonies and songs sounded unaltered – the difference came from hearing them over what were then state-of-the-art rhythms from the Revolutionaries. Three tracks – "Bredda Gravalicious", "Feel the Spirit" and "Very Well" – had already appeared as 45s (the last on Channel One, where all the recordings took place) and defined the tone of a set that can be compared with the Royals' *Pick Up the Pieces*, the Abyssinians' *Forward On To Zion* and the Mighty Diamonds' *Right Time*. Roots harmonies *par excellence*, and the CD adds dubs to seven tracks.

⦿ **The Very Best Of the Wailing Souls** (Greensleeves, UK).

"Bredda Gravalicious" also appears on this collection, alongside other self-produced gems, and those from Taxi, Henry 'Junjo' Lawes and Linval Thompson. "War Deh Round A John Shop", a big seller on UK single release, reaffirms its exalted status.

Prince Lincoln

Just as selective in its releases was the God Sent imprint of **Prince Lincoln Thompson**. Entering the music business in the late 1960s as part of the rocksteady group called the Tartans, this very original singer and songwriter has never quite fulfilled the promise of his solo work in the first half of the 1970s (three consummate 45s for Studio One) or the singles that he recorded with various harmony singers (including Cedric Myton of the Congos) as the **Royal Rasses** towards the close of the decade.

The first two releases employing the group name appeared on God Sent in 1976, and arguably Prince Lincoln has yet to match either the "Kingston 11" or "Love the Way It Should Be", two of the finest expressions of Rastafarian consciousness ever released. Unfortunately, a record contract with the UK's Ballistic outfit failed to bring the desired crossover success, despite musically adventurous albums with UK rock singer Joe Jackson, and much of Lincoln's original roots audience was lost in the process.

THE ROYAL RASSES

◑ **Humanity** (God Sent, JA; Ballistic, UK).

The Royal Rasses once seemed on the verge of crossover stardom with their very progressive variation of international reggae. Prince Lincoln Thompson wrote memorable melodies, as well as incisive lyrics, and was open to far wider influences than most of his roots compatriots. For some obscure reason, the initial promise of both the 45s under his own name (for Studio One) and with additional singers as the Royal Rasses (for his own God Sent label) were not fulfilled, and this remains the only first-rate album with which he has been associated. Includes the wonderful hits "Love the Way It Should Be", "Kingston 11", "Old Time Friends", "Unconventional People" and "San Salvador".

Natty Dread Ina Greenwich Farm

The Greenwich Town/Farm area of West Kingston, which was celebrated on record in 1975 by Cornell Campbell, continued to thrive musically throughout the rest of the decade and into the next. Max Romeo, who lived in the district for several years during the 1970s, has spoken of how young songers and musicians from the country would be attracted to the area, where they could sell farm produce and perhaps be discovered by a man successful in the music like Bunny Lee. The two producers most associated with the district were Bertram Brown and Errol 'Don' Mais, owners respectively of the Freedom Sounds/Redemption Sounds and Roots Tradition labels.

It was at at 14 East Avenue that **Bertram Brown** (b. 1950) ran the Freedom Sounds setup. Though he used Channel One studio at Maxfield Avenue and Randy's on North Parade for his recording sessions, and had them mixed by King Tubby at Dromilly Avenue in Waterhouse, the artists he produced were mostly resident in his own area. They included roots wailers such as the sometimes brilliant **Earl Zero** (b. Earl Anthony Jackson), who is perhaps best remembered as the writer of "None Shall Escape the Judgement", one of the Bunny Lee-produced hits that took Johnnie Clarke into the premier league in 1974. The 20-year-old Zero had already recorded his song for Bunny, but the astute producer thought it had a better chance sung in the more obviously commercial tones of Clarke. The Greenwich Farm resident and devout young Rastaman then wrote and recorded several tracks that brimmed with the same dread conviction and force, most notably "Please Officer" and "City Of the Weakheart" (both for Tommy Cowan's Arab label), and "Righteous Works" (for the singer Al Campbell's Addis Ababa), before "Shackles & Chains" for Brown's Freedom Sounds.

Then there was **Michael Prophet**, who made his greatest impression in the late 1970s with work for Yabby You, but still had reason to be proud of the searing "Poverty", which appeared in 1979 on Freedom Sounds. Perhaps no one typified the culturally conscious youthman singer of the second half of the decade as much as **Rod Taylor**, who cut two of his most important hits for Brown, "Ethiopian Kings" and "In the Right Way", both of which were helped by the rugged Soul Syndicate rhythms employed, as well as their deadly dub sides. In the same period Taylor also recorded for the deejay Prince Hammer, Ossie Hibbert, and a former radio deejay-turned-producer who for a short while created an extraordinary impact – Michael Campbell, aka Mikey Dread. Yet another stalwart of the Greenwich Farm music scene, **Philip Frazer**, followed the formula of the popular "Ethiopian Kings" for "Come Ethiopians", which made a considerable impact in dancehall in London as well as Kingston, for all its lack of originality.

The most consistently successful artist recording for Freedom Sounds was **Prince Alla** (b. Keith Blake, 1950, Kingston). He had recorded in the rocksteady period as a member of the vocal group the Leaders; more importantly, from the late 1960s he had lived in the Rasta camp of Prince Emmanuel Edwards at Bull Bay. After six years he came back to Greenwich Farm where Brown, who had grown up with Alla from boyhood days, persuaded him to begin serious recording. Alla then recorded with Soul Syndicate a series of utterly convincing sufferer's laments such as "Stone" and "Bucket Bottom". Old Testament themes, as on "Lot's Wife", for example, were sung with an urgency that made them sound as if snatched from the newspaper headlines. Alla also recorded top-quality material for Tappa Zukie (see pp.181–182) in this period; he has made infrequent visits to the studio since, resulting in only two more albums (in 1983 and 1996) and a few singles. He still lives in Greenwich Farm, where he works cleaning fish; he is, however, planning to return to live performance sometime soon.

Errol 'Don' Mais (b. 1950) also specialized in artists from Greenwich for his Roots Tradition label. His way of 'versioning' old – especially Studio One – rhythms, as played by either the Soul Syndicate or the musicians who were to become the Roots Radics, played a key role in the development of 'dancehall'. Further details of this transition will be given in the next chapter (see p.223) – here it suffices to say that the label was launched in 1976 with Earl Zero's "Home Sweet Home", and had further successes in a roots vein from Michael Prophet, Philip Frazer and Sammy Dread.

PHILIP FRAZER

● **Come Ethiopians** (Redemption Sounds, JA).

Never as popular as stablemate Prince Alla, Philip Frazer nevertheless wailed over some strong roots rhythms in the late 1970s. The title track is a near relation to Rod Taylor's "Ethiopian Kings", and "Righteous Works" is (not unexpectedly) the next cut to the Earl Zero classic. Generic roots, maybe, but worth acquiring after the Alla set from the same producer.

PRINCE ALLA

◑ **Only Love Can Conquer 1976–79** (Blood & Fire, UK).

A compilation of Prince Alla's work for Freedom Sounds , plus a couple of offerings produced by Tony Mack, and "Dread Locks Nazarene" and "Their Reward", both produced by the singer himself. The momentous opening track, "Stone", stands as perhaps the most powerful of the singer's career, a definitive fire and brimstone statement of the mid-1970s, though further sound-system favourites like "Only Love Can Conquer", "Lot's Wife" and "Bucket Bottom" run it very close. Of Alla's significant work for Freedom Sounds, only "Children Of God" is missing.

ROD TAYLOR

● **If Jah Should Come Now** (Belva, JA; Little Luke, UK).

A consistently popular youthman singer in the late 1970s, Rod Taylor still needs a compilation that draws together his best work from several sources. In the meantime, this deleted album from deejay-turned-producer Prince Hammer is well worth seeking out. The title track is the strongest here, but everything else stands as representative of the tough singer's work and the time.

Cultural toasters

Several of the most talented deejays who came to notice in the early 1970s – notably **Big Youth** (see p.119), **Dillinger** (see p.111), **I-Roy** (see pp.119–120) and **Prince Jazzbo** (see p.119) – continued to make fine records in the roots era, some for their own labels. They and their numerous rivals from the next generation no longer simply added to the excitement of the dance with hip catch-phrases: the deejay now offered commentaries on the ghetto sufferers' tribulations, history lessons from a black perspective, and the chanting of psalms. By the mid-1970s times were truly dread, with Marcus Garvey and Haile Selassie as likely to be praised as the sound on which the deejay was employed.

ADRIAN BOOT

Big Youth, 70s style

Big Youth

The most influential talker by this time was the dreadlocked man known as **Big Youth**, the Lord Tippertone sound's top deejay, and it's instructive to compare the type of lyric he was employing on his records of 1972 with those he was at home with just a year later. On the Augustus Clarke production "Tippertone Rocking", released in mid-1972, he had little more to say – in a rather mumbled and indistinct manner – than most deejays of the time:

"When I tell yu about the sound that lead the way
The sound called Tippertone rocking
Tipper mek you rock so
Tipper mek you born so
Let me tell, yu born so
Come on, come on, mek yu rock so."

By the summer of the following year, his diction had become much clearer, symptomatic perhaps of a greater confidence, but also as if to emphasize the gravity of his new messages. His "I Pray Thee", over the Abyssinians' "Satta Massa Gana", drew directly from the Bible, not jive talking in the U-Roy/Dennis Alcapone manner, but chanting phrases about the heathen raging and false kings "setting themselves up 'pon the earth as the anointed". On "All Nations Bow", a stunning version of the Winston Riley-produced instrumental "Stalag 17", he proclaimed:

"All nations got to bow
When the fourth and fifth generation stand
The wicked got to fall
And only the fittest of the fittest of the fittest
Of the fittest of the fittest shall stand."

Other versions of classic cultural records made by Big Youth during the period 1973–75 included "Craven Version" (Tuff Gong), over Bob Marley's "Craven Choke Puppy", "Bide"/ "Black On Black" (Solomonic), both sides of which were inspired cuts of Bunny Wailer's "Bide Up", "Yabby Youth" (Micron) and "Mosiah Garvey" (Fox), which had Jamaica's hottest deejay adding his commentary to Burning Spear's ground-breaking Jamaican hit, "Marcus Garvey". By the summer of 1973 he had also set up his own imprint, Negusa Negast, which was followed by Agustus Buchanan, and it was on these (plus a couple more that arrived later) that his most consistent work for the next three years appeared, usually featuring Earl 'Chinna' Smith's excellent Soul Syndicate band, and nearly all of it of a cultural nature.

The later releases on Big Youth's own imprints showed a decline in quality, but this was after four prolific years of exceptional self-produced music that defined cultural toasting and gave a lead to such deejays as Dillinger, Jah Stitch, Trinity and Clint Eastwood. The dominance of the Jah Youth style was to continue until the likes of Ranking Joe, U-Brown, General Echo and Lone Ranger reinstated the U-Roy style and initiated the next wave in the dancehall. Popular records like "Streets In Africa", "African Daughter", "Wolf In Sheep's Clothing" and "Ten Against One" – as well as a wonderful duet with U-Roy, aptly titled "Battle Of the Giants" – were nothing if not extremely serious, and obviously informed by what the deejay/toaster/chanter had seen and experienced in the tough, sometimes brutal world of the West Kingston ghettos.

BIG YOUTH

- **Dread Locks Dread** (TR Groovemaster, JA; Front Line Classics, UK).

In developing a highly original chanting style to comment on the lot of Kingston's ghetto dwellers and express his Rastafarian faith, Big Youth took the art of the deejay a major step forward. The eye-catching packaging undoubtedly contributed to the crossover success of this set, and though not representing the deejay at his very best, it has stood the test of time well.

- **Natty Cultural Dread** (Trojan, UK).
- **Hit the Road Jack** (Agustus Buchanan, JA; Trojan, UK).

These self-produced albums, despite including examples of his forays into singing (which remain contentious to say the least), represented the Youth in complete control, and demonstrated how a deejay's records could be much more than adjuncts to popular vocals. Among the important hits on the former are "Wolf In Sheep's Clothing", "Natty Cultural Dread" and Jim Squashey", while the latter has his witty and confident re-reading of the Ray Charles title number and "Ten Against One" (a superbly 'dread' reworking of the Mad Lads' "Ten To One").

- **Everyday Skank: The Best Of Big Youth** (Trojan, UK).

E Mixing self-produced hits with some of his best for other producers, *Everyday Skank* stands as a brilliantly compiled collection. The variety of prediction styles covered makes it the place for the newcomer to start.

U-Roy and his disciples

Big Youth was sold to the rock audience with the strikingly packaged *Dread Locks Dread* album for Prince Tony Robinson, and Virgin tried a similar tactic with **U-Roy**. Though the pioneering deejay had previously avoided using his Rastafarian beliefs for self-promotion, he was pictured on the cover of his initial Prince Tony/ Virgin set with dreadlocks and enveloped in clouds of smoke from a 'chalice'. On the record, he chatted commercial dread lyrics over updates of rocksteady classics. In both Big Youth's and U-Roy's work for Prince Tony, the sheer number of references to "natty dread" can be wearisome, though the albums seem more acceptable in retrospect, and tracks from U-Roy like "Run Away Girl" and the cheeky "Chalice In the Palace" (over a recut "Queen Majesty") showed he had retained a fair degree of wit and panache.

In this period of international exposure, U-Roy also played an important role in the Kingston dancehalls through his Stur-Gav Hi-Fi sound system – in effect the deejay academy, with Daddy Roy as the founder of the school. The first graduate, **Ranking Joe** – newly promoted from Little Joe – deejayed the set during 1977–78 before going on with selector Jah Screw to the champion set of the late 1970s, the reborn Ray Symbolic. A live sound-system deejay *par excellence*, Joe enjoyed several big hits: his version of Gregory Isaacs' "Soon Forward" ("Stop Your Coming And Come") was the first deejay success for the Taxi label; "Weak Heart Fade Away" successfully rode the Junior Byles hit; and his toast on Bobby Ellis and the Revolutionaries' recut of the dancehall staple "Shank I Shek" ("Shine Eye Gal") for Sonia Pottinger was similarly massive, and very influential.

Joe was followed on Stur-Gav by **Charlie Chaplin**, **Josey Wales** and **Brigadier Jerry**, all of whom would play influential roles in establishing the dancehall styles of future years. **U-Brown** was the most notable disciple of U-Roy not to come through the Originator's sound system: he followed the master onto King

Tubby's Hi-Fi before deejaying for sets such as King Attorney, Socialist Roots – alongside another dynamic U-Roy disciple **Ranking Trevor** – and the Ocho Rios-based set of Jack Ruby. After his debut recordings for Winston Edwards, U-Brown recorded extensively during the latter half of the decade for various producers. His output included several albums for Bunny Lee and hit singles for Gussie Clarke, Jack Ruby, Ossie Hibbert, Carlton Patterson and his own label, Hit Sound. His personal variant on his model's style – at times he sounded like a newly energized U-Roy – suited perfectly the more dynamic 'rockers' updates of vintage rhythms then ruling the dancehalls.

RANKING JOE

● **The Best Of Ranking Joe** (State Line, JA).
Ranking Joe, so close to U-Roy that the dancehall crowd often never knew when they swapped the mike on Daddy Roy's Stur-Gav set, hit the spot on a number of occasions. This Prince Tony Robinson production has the young deejay sounding like U-Roy's younger brother with traces of Big Youth, and riding the rhythms employed on both their LPs for the producer.

U-BROWN

● **Weather Balloon** (Gorgon, JA).
Another of the leading U-Roy disciples, U-Brown successfully produced himself on this selection of Studio One and Treasure Isle rhythms updated for the late 1970s at Channel One. The nearest the deejay got to capturing the excitement he created on King Tubby's sound system.

U-ROY

● **Dread Ina Babylon** (TR Groovemaster, JA; Virgin, UK).
Some of his old followers looked down their noses at U-Roy toasting Prince Tony Robinson-produced recuts of Treasure Isle and Studio One rhythms in 1975. In retrospect the deejay was still turning in lively enough performances, and the Soul Syndicate and Skin, Flesh & Bones bands used for the rhythms were also pretty nifty. Buy after the early 1970s material.

Prince Jazzbo

Prince Jazzbo was another deejay who at least equalled the records that established his name at the beginning of the decade, and did so largely with self-productions on his own labels, Count 123, Brisco and Mr Funny. In common with Big Youth's output of the mid-1970s there was an air of unmistakable authority about them, of his having lived the life of which he spoke. Jazzbo had begun his career on a "lickle three-box sound" named the Whip, in Spanish Town, where he had troubled the well-established sets like Ruddy's and Stereo – in the deejay's own words he "ran them out of town". Subsequently he came to the attention of Coxsone, who recorded him during 1972–73 on the tracks that were to eventually find release in 1990 as the *Choice Of Version* album. He recorded a handful of tracks for Glen Brown and Bunny Lee before starting his own labels and forming an association with producer Lee Perry with the successful 45 "Penny Reel", a prelude to the excellent *Ital Corner/Natty Passing Thru* album (see p.168). One of the singles on his own label, "Concubine Donkey", drew a response from the Big Youth, the positive and non-misogynist "African Daughters". This sound war turned physical when Jah Youth's associate Trevor 'Leggo' Douglas chased Jazzbo under a bus, prompting a memorable commentary from deejay I-Roy on "Jazzbo A Fe Run":

"This incident happen on North Parade
'Im run past Kincaid
'Im couldn't get no first aid.
Jazzbo, wha' mek you do that?
A serious ting."

If Jazzbo came off the worse in the exchanges with I-Roy, then he triumphed on self-produced hits such as "Wise Shepherd", "Every Nigga Is A Winner" and "Step Forward Youth", all of which were brooding and impeccably dread. He continued production up to the present, his Ujama label offering an outlet to vintage deejays and quirky new talents like Zebra and Manchez. His successes have been limited, though he has produced good albums from longtime friend Frankie Paul and roots singer Horace Ferguson.

Other deejay-producers: Doctor Alimantado, Jah Lloyd and Prince Far I

Another deejay who shone when producing was **Doctor Alimantado**, with his Ital Sounds and Vital Food labels. The doctor's self-productions employed rhythms from a number of different sources, and showed how off-centre a deejay he was. In spite of working with Perry and Randy's, his unique talent only flowered when he had complete control over the sessions. **Jah Lloyd** – real name Pat Francis – was another who benefited from self-production, issuing a series of interesting and often powerful sides on his Teem label between 1974 and 1977. With limited resources – certain rhythms, like "Ain't No Sunshine", "Have Some Mercy" and the Mighty Diamonds' "Shame & Pride", were employed again and again – he achieved a distinctive style that was typified by his commentary on the 'poison flour' scare of early 1976, "Killer Flour", dropped nicely onto a dub cut of the Diamonds' tune. The most popular of his singles (eg "Soldier Round the Corner" "Channel One" and "Green Bay Incident") mark him out as an under-celebrated deejay of the period.

The Best Dressed Chicken in Town: the good Dr Alimantado

Prince Far I had begun his recording career with Bunny Lee in 1969, cutting a version of alto saxophonist Lester Sterling's "Spring Fever" called "The Great Wooga Booga". In his early career he used the name King Cry Cry; by the time he made the version of Larry Marshall's "Mean Girl" titled "Natty Farmyard" for Coxsone Dodd, he had begun calling himself Prince Far I, at the instigation of singer Enos McLeod, for whom he also recorded. Under this new name he scored hits for Joe Gibbs which financed the setting-up of his own label, Cry Tuff. On this label his style – gruff chants delivered over tough rhythms from an early incarnation of the Roots Radics – never varied a great deal but was always effective. The label also made an impression with fine vocals from Errol Holt, Rod Taylor, 'Reggae' George Daley, Bobby Melody, and Carol Kalphat, many of which were released on Hit Run Records in the UK, run by Adrian Sherwood. Far I was able to tour Britain and Europe, forging an alliance with the young English producer that continued until the peace-loving deejay's brutal murder in 1983.

The vast majority of toasters continued to record for a variety of producers with the rhythms and money to entice them into their studios. Popular talkers like **I-Roy**, **Dillinger**, **Jah Stitch**, **Trinity** and **Jah Woosh** would occasionally release music on labels of their own, but still found it more profitable or convenient to record for others.

DILLINGER

Ready Natty Dreadie (Winro/Studio One, JA).
Lester Bullocks' impressive second LP over classic Brentford Road rhythms, including the Mad Lads' "Ten To One" (imaginatively retitled "Natty Ten To One"), the Soul Vendors' "Real Rock", Horace Andy's "Fever" and Alton Ellis's "Breaking Up". Unless you are fortunate enough to find a copy of the first press, however, you will search in vain for the title track, a version of Burning Spear's "Creation Rebel": all the subsequent presses replace it with "Natty Kung Fu" (over Roy Richards' "Freedom Blues").

DOCTOR ALIMANTADO

Best Dressed Chicken In Town (Greensleeves, UK; RAS, US).

Doctor Alimantado sold to UK punks after being lauded by the likes of Johnny Rotten, and failed to deliver much after that. But, for the preceding three-year period (1973–76), the 'Ital Doctor' could do no wrong. His even earlier 45s had hardly prepared anyone for self-produced classics like "Poison Flour", the completely over-the-top "Best Dressed Chicken In Town" (engineered by Scratch), or the dread defiance of "I Killed the Barber". Sporting a strikingly dread cover photograph taken in downtown Kingston by Dave Hendley, this compilation collects the best examples of this work, and still stands as one of the most original deejay albums ever.

◑ **Born For A Purpose** (Greensleeves, UK).
The second album from Greensleeves brings together what was omitted from its predecessor, including the Bunny Lee-produced "Chant To Jah" and another strong version of the "Best Dressed Chicken"/"Ain't No Sunshine" rhythm, "Oil Crisis", and adds his only subsequent records of note: the title track (with dub) and its next cut, "Still Alive".

I-ROY

◑ **Don't Check Me With No Lightweight Stuff 1972–75** (Blood & Fire, UK).
E As near as it is possible to get to a definitive collection of the prolific I-Roy's mid-1970s work on a single CD. From the opening version of Tommy McCook's "Sidewalk Killer", produced by legendary sound man Ruddy Redwood, this is deejaying of the roots era at its most varied, pertinent and pithy. For prime examples of his sly humour and powers of observation, check Mr Reid's tribute to the movie "Buck & the Preacher" and his thoughts on "Sound Education", or what he has to add to classics like Augustus Pablo's "Java", Marley's "Talking Blues" or Desmond Young's "Warning".

● **Truth & Rights** (Micron, JA; Grounation, UK).
A compilation of some of I-Roy's most popular records from 1975. It includes two tracks from the above, but is worth seeking out for further gems like "Every Mouth Must Be Fed", "Teapot" and the Perry-produced "Dread In the West". As the man says, "It's easier for a camel to go through a needle's eye/than a version to die, believe me."

JAH LLOYD

◑ **Soldier Around the Corner** (Teem, UK).
Practically everything of worth that appeared on the deejay's own Teem label, including the classic title track and "Ganja Crop" (both over the "To Be A Lover"/"Have Some Mercy" rhythm), "Zion Dub", and "Sunshine Girl" and "No More Tribal War" (both over "Ain't No Sunshine"). As a showcase for Mr Francis's deejaying skills it is arguably a stronger album than the Perry-produced *Columbia Colly*.

JAH WOOSH

● **Jah Woosh** (Cactus, UK).

◑ **Chalice Blaze** (Student/Original Music, UK).

● **Psalms Of Wisdom** (Jah Man, JA; Black Wax, UK).

Jah Woosh was unusual among deejays in that he established his reputation in the UK market with these three albums, rather than a couple of dozen 45s. Produced by, respectively, Rupie Edwards, Leonard Chin and the partnership of Leroy Hollett & Dudley Swaby, the LPs are generic roots toasting of the time (1974–76), with strong stylistic elements derived from Big Youth, Prince Jazzbo and practically everyone else who was successful at the mike. An uncompromising approach on all three, with the Jah Man set having the slightly stronger rhythms.

Tappa Zukie, Junior Ross & the Spear, and Knowledge

There was one popular deejay who turned out to be arguably a more gifted producer than performer. On his first visit to the UK in 1973, the young **Tappa Zukie** had recorded the cult favourite *Man A Warrior* album for UK producer Clement Bushay. On his return to Jamaica in 1975, Tappa acted as bodyguard for Bunny Lee, occasionally venturing into Tubby's studio to voice, but the producer still was not convinced about the youth's abilities. After an argument with Bunny the young deejay launched his own Stars label, largely with Bunny's rhythms. Tappa now seemed to find himself musically, and besides his own efforts (of which "She Want A Phensic" and "Oh Lord" were the most successful in Jamaica) he was responsible for several strong records by vocalists, most of whom were based in Greenwich Farm.

Patti Smith's mate, Tappa Zukie

Among these were two rootical groups, the most popular of whom was **Junior Ross & the Spear**, who also recorded for Bertram Brown, and as the **Palmer Brothers** had one classic 45 – "Stepping Out Of Babylon", produced by Brent Dowe on Tommy Cowan's Sweet City imprint. Stylistically, their approach showed the salutary influences of Vivian Jackson and, hardly surprisingly, Burning Spear. Tappa met his other vocal group, **Knowledge**, when he was involved in setting up a youth centre in Trench Town. They managed to get their debut album released on the international A&M label, who unsuccessfully marketed it to the new white audience for reggae, though the set was an above-average roots album of the time, and at least one of their 45s, "Sentry", has endured as a minor classic.

Just as suited to Tappa's manner of producing were the relative veterans **Errol Dunkley**, **Horace Andy** and the former member of the Leaders vocal group, **Prince Alla** (b. Keith Blake, 1950, Kingston). Alla was from the same Greenwich Farm scene as Junior Ross & the Spear, who also sang backing vocals for him: his powerful songs "Bosrah", "Daniel" and "Funeral" are filled with Old Testament dread, as is the distinguished album made with Tappa, *Heaven Is My Roof.*

JUNIOR ROSS & THE SPEAR

Babylon Fall (New Star, JA).

As the group's name suggests, Junior Ross & the Spear were influenced by Winston Rodney, and they cut some solid roots records in a decidedly apocalyptic mood. Though variations of the group also recorded as the Palmer Brothers (for Brent Dowe and Ossie Hibbert) and Soft & the Nazarines (for Freedom Sounds), this remains their only album release to date. Typically strong Tappa Zukie production from the mid-1970s, with the title track a masterpiece of the Jah-judgement school, and only the great "Liberty" missing.

KNOWLEDGE

Word, Sound & Power (Stars, JA).

Originally released by A&M at the close of the 1970s, this has sensibly been re-released by Tappa Zukie on his own label. "Centry" remains the group's most convincing pronouncement in the dread mode of the time; but nothing here should disappoint lovers of the producer's heavyweight, always rootsy approach.

PRINCE ALLA

Heaven Is My Roof (Tappa, JA).

E This collects all Prince Alla's most significant work for Tappa Zukie, including the glorious title track, "Bosrah", "Funeral" and "Daniel". "Gold Diver" was amazingly never released as a single, though fully the equal of those that were.

TAPPA ZUKIE

MPLA (Klik, UK).

Thanks largely to the patronage of Patti Smith, Tappa Zukie's reputation as a deejay was overinflated in the late 1970s. But he did, as shown here, have his moments at the mike. It helped to be working with only the hottest rhythms from Bunny Lee and Yabby You, but there is no denying the excitement and energy he brought to them. Strange, though, that a sometime activist of the conservative JLP in Jamaica should have chanted the praises of Angola's Marxist MPLA.

From the Archives (RAS, US).

A retrospective collection that repeats eight of the tracks from *MPLA*, and adds his biggest Jamaican hit, "Oh Lord", and three more. A pity that "She Want A Phensic" is not included, but perhaps a second volume is planned.

The mainstream

In the last half of the 1970s, reggae was dominated by Rastafarian-influenced 'cultural' lyrics to such an extent that practically every singer or deejay thought it appropriate to appear on his album sleeve sporting locks, and have at least some of his lyrics in Rasta-speak. Yet the most popular singers never concentrated entirely on 'dread' messages. Instead, singers like **Dennis Brown**, **Gregory Isaacs** and **Freddie McGregor** mixed expressions of their Rastafarian faith with the most romantic love songs. This versatility made good economic sense: because the reggae market is relatively small, it is necessary for a singer wanting a reasonable living to cover as wide a base as possible. Burning Spear, of course, never wavered from his Rastafarian convictions, but the commercial reality that allowed him to make so many albums in a 'conscious' mode was a new crossover audience – as was the case with Marley. Brown and Isaacs, on the other hand, only made slight inroads into this global audience. Rather, they rose to the very top in the Jamaican reggae market by reaching all parts of it. It's a gauge of what was happening in the dancehalls and blues parties of Jamaica and the island's diaspora that Delroy Wilson's marvellous updating of Marley's ballad "I'm Still Waiting" was possibly the biggest reggae hit of 1976, and certainly of the singer's career.

Dennis Brown

Not unexpectedly, Dennis Brown and Gregory Isaacs, by far the two most popular singers in the reggae world of the second half of the 1970s, both ran labels of their own – DEB and African Museum respectively. But the fact that they partly financed these endeavours by recording prolifically for other producers, including each other, shows that controlling your own label in Jamaica is not the easiest way to riches.

Having initially established his reputation as a teenager at Studio One, **Dennis Brown** confirmed that he had the talent to last with a series of brilliant 45s on a wide range of Jamaican and UK labels. Winston 'Niney' Holness was the producer for whom he enjoyed the most consistent run of successes, cementing a relationship that went back to Joe Gibbs days, when Niney produced the huge hit "Money In My Pocket" for Gibbs. When Brown and Niney began working together in earnest, they made a series of classical roots statements that was never surpassed by either. Whereas producers like Coxsone and Derrick Harriott tended to cast the young vocalist in a lovers mode – tracks for them like "Concentration" and his cover of the Van Dykes' "No Man Is An Island" were exceptions – the stark productions favoured by Niney threw the strength of Brown's newly matured voice into sharp relief, beginning in mid-1973 with cuts like the soulful love song "Westbound Train". This featured a brash, insistent rhythm from the Soul Syndicate and a guitar sound borrowed from Al Green's hits for Memphis pro-

DAVID CORIO

The Crown Prince: Dennis Brown at Sunsplash, mid-1980s

ducer Willie Mitchell. The next couple of years saw further Niney-produced records in a similar vein, including "I Am the Conqueror" and "No More Will I Roam", but the young singer's lyrics were increasingly becoming message-oriented with tracks such as "Africa" and "So Long" updating proto-roots classics from, respectively, the Gaylads and Count Ossie. Then came one of the most memorable 'cultural' records with 1975's anthemic "Tribulation":

"Rough as the road might seem to be
I'll be toiling on
I'll be myself and no one else
I'll be strutting on
A man must go through tribulation
No matter who or where he's from
If he's man of understanding
He'll know that time alone will tell
Fools know not understanding
And that's why they stumble
They'll never find their way
Cos wisdom is too hard for them."

In the mid-1970s, after the usual Jamaican label-hopping, saw Dennis's profile raised even higher (particularly in the UK) when he returned to Niney, cutting two of his most committed songs for the producer. "Wolf & Leopard" was recorded entirely at Lee Perry's Black Ark; "Here I Come" was voiced in Kingston, but the rhythm, a slow and tortured skank, was laid by Niney and UK band the Cimarons at London's Chalk Farm studio, before being taken to Jamaica for the full 'Yard' mix. Both tunes became staples of Brown's repertoire – he still opens his live shows with the latter. Further hits, as well as remarkably consistent albums with Joe Gibbs, completed the process by which he earned the title of the Crown Prince of Reggae. Marley, of course, remained the King.

DENNIS BROWN

⦿ **Some Like It Hot (Greatest Hits Volume 1)** (Heartbeat, US).

⦿ **Open the Gate (Greatest Hits Volume 2)** (Heartbeat, US).

E The most convenient way of acquiring nearly all of the singer's work for Niney is to pick up these two Heartbeat CDs, which include several tracks not previously available on album.

● **Just Dennis** (Observer, JA; Trojan, UK).
Having established his reputation as a remarkably mature teenager at Studio One, Dennis Brown confirmed that he had the talent to last with a series of brilliant 45s for a wide range of producers. Niney was the one with whom he enjoyed the most consistent run of successes, perhaps because he was only two years the singer's senior. Their first album together, *Just Dennis* (1975) was essentially a collection of hits – "Cassandra", "Westbound Train", "No More Will I Roam", "Conqueror", etc – alongside a few previously unreleased tracks of the same calibre.

◑ **Wolf & Leopard** (Weed Beat, JA; DEB, UK).
This 1977 set – which brought together further Niney productions and those of the partnership of the singer and Castro Brown – was totally made up of singles, and made clear his commitment to Rastafari. Including gems such as the title track, "Here I Come" and "Children Of Israel", this was something of a benchmark album for the roots era.

◑ **Love Has Found Its Way** (A&M, UK/US).
In a somewhat different style from all the above, 1988's *Love Has Found Its Way* is a co-production between guitarist Willie Lindo, Joe Gibbs and Brown himself. The sophisticated mood of the title track, which climbed the US soul charts, is maintained throughout, and the result is the nearest a reggae album can get to the international pop mainstream without losing something very vital in the process.

Gregory Isaacs

Judged by the number of records sold within the reggae market, the only singer to rival Dennis Brown in the last half of the 1970s was **Gregory Isaacs** (b. 1951, Kingston), on whose African Museum imprint appeared possibly Dennis's greatest ever cultural record, "In Their Own Way". Gregory did not have as rich a voice as Dennis, but relied on a cool projection of a masculine vulnerability. For this reason, he was always suited to love songs on which he took the part of the "Lonely Lover", the man always hurt by love, but only because he believes in it so. His first self-produced hit, "My Only Lover", was the template of all the 'lovers' tunes that were to follow; an easy-skanking rhythm supported Gregory's intimate vocal tones as, even before the relationship flounders, he voices the disapproval of others (she is too young; he is not the type for her), and anticipates her leaving him. The chorus, of course, has him expressing his total dedication. Variations of this formula were to keep him a favourite among reggae fans for the next couple of decades.

His vocal approach – before passing years, loss of teeth and reputed substance abuse took their toll – was equally suited to expressions of the sufferer's lot. Early examples of 'reality' commentaries delivered in just as effective a way included "One One Cocoa" (Dwyer), "Way Of Life" (Wambesi), "Village Of the Under Privileged" (Soul Sound) and "The Philistines" (GG. Ranglin). On all of these, Gregory sounded just as wounded by his people's social deprivations as he was so often by women. His most consistently 'conscious' period, however, was in the mid-1970s, when, besides cultural classics for Lloyd Campbell, Joe Gibbs and Ossie Hibbert, he was also responsible for a string of devastating self-produced 'reality' laments, such as "Set the Captive Free", "Thief A Man", "Black A Kill Black", "My Religion" and "Rasta Business". To many of his followers these remain the man's greatest moments, though his return to concerns of the heart in the next decade was to take him to a new pinnacle of popularity.

GREGORY ISAACS

Soon Forward (African Museum, JA; Virgin, UK).

E *Soon Forward*, titled after the monster Sly & Robbie-produced hit, is the first-choice Isaacs album. The programme comprises then-recent hit singles and new material, including the momentous "Universal Tribulation", surely the greatest Isaacs song never to gain release as a single. This set proves he was the number one singer in the reggae world in the period 1977–79.

The Best Of (Volumes 1 & 2) (Heartbeat, US).

Neither the compilations of hits that might be expected from the titles nor the sort of rural reggae usually associated with producer Alvin Ranglin. Instead, the CD comprises two LPs of fresh material, recorded at Channel One, and featuring the then-fashionable 'rockers' style of the Revolutionaries. There are a couple of hit singles – "My Number One" and "The Border" – but plenty else that is just as strong, such as "Cool You" and "No Speech".

Mr Isaacs (Cash & Carry, JA).

According to the label, *Mr Isaacs* was a self-production, though at least one track – the sublime "Slavemaster" – had previously appeared on Lloyd Campbell's Thing imprint. Included are half a dozen of the strongest cultural tracks that the future Cool Ruler was ever to record, including the much-versioned "Storm", plus convincing interpretations of three soul/rocksteady standards.

Cool Ruler (African Museum, JA; Virgin, UK).

Gregory Isaacs' two albums for Virgin failed to bring the crossover success that was deserved, but through no fault of the music. *Cool Ruler* added new tracks of the highest order – most notably "Party In the Slum" – to the already proven 45s "John Public" and "Let's Dance". Its successor, *Soon Forward*, was even better (see above).

Over the Years Volumes 1, 2 & 3 (African Museum, UK).

These compilations draw together hit singles otherwise unavailable on album, and from a welcome variety of sources. Well worth picking up for scarce and wonderful items such as the first volume's powerful "Thief A Man" and his version of the soul hit "Lonely Soldier". On the second set the highlights include the Bob Andy-written "Sunshine For Me" and the Joe Gibbs-produced "Babylon Too Rough", and the third has one of his strongest roots tunes for Alvin Ranglin, "The Philistines", and his sublime version of "Sunday Morning", produced by the man who wrote it, Bunny Wailer.

Freddie McGregor

Once a pre-adolescent singing partner of Ernest Wilson on a couple of 45s (as Freddie & Fitzy), **Freddie McGregor** (b. 1955, Clarendon) has always sounded equally at home with material informed by his membership of the Twelve Tribes of Israel organization as with more romantic types of offering. Several of his Studio One hits of the mid-1970s – "Rastaman Camp", "I Man A Rasta" and "Children Listen To Wise Words" – are convincing examples of the former side of his talent, as are several 45s cut with Earl 'Chinna' Smith's Soul Syndicate band (with whom he performed live) – notably "Revolutionist", a 1977 reworking of "I Man A Rasta", and the apocalyptic "Mark Of the Beast", from the following year. His smooth lovers side was probably best represented in the 1970s by a Chinna-produced version of George Benson's "Love Ballad", which has remained a blues-party favourite since it was released in 1976. Generally, his music of the 1970s was a remarkable display of the singer's ability to combine a rootsman's vision with a sophisticated sense of melody that could approach pure pop. It is perhaps a tribute to his vocal talent and professionalism that, in common with Dennis Brown and Gregory Isaacs, he was to achieve even more in the two decades following the one in which he first came to attention.

FREDDIE McGREGOR

Mr McGregor (Observer, JA; Jackal, US).

This talented singer's debut album from 1980, produced by Winston 'Niney' Holness, and perhaps the most best album-length display of how strong the Soul Syndicate's rhythms could be. "Rasta Have Faith" stands among the strongest versions of the "Satta Massa Gana" rhythm ever, and the same serious feel is maintained on "Zion Camp" and "Walls Of Jericho", as well as reworkings of Little Roy's "Jah Can Count On I" and his own "Rastaman Camp" (originally recorded for Studio One). Amazingly, his interpretations of Maxine Brown's soul number "Oh No Not My Baby" and Neil Diamond's "Brandy" impress almost as much.

Showcase (Observer, JA).

A second Niney-produced set, from the following year, is slightly frustrating in not having the four dubs included directly following their vocals. Followers of the singer will want the album for the superb cultural tracks "The Overseer" and "Chant It", as well as the hit, "Lovers Rock Ja Style", which is much as the title announces.

Other cultural singers

Brown, Isaacs and McGregor were the masters at merging cultural issues with the mainstream tradition of Jamaican vocalizing as established in the previous decade by singers like Alton Ellis, John Holt, Delroy Wilson, Ken Boothe and Slim Smith. Several other established vocalists also adapted to the new mood of the music and its audience with a minimum of difficulty. The often underrated **Max Romeo**, for example, had consistently recorded gospel-influenced tunes about social and cultural topics before they became fashionable. After the usual freelancing between different producers in the first half of the decade, he settled down in the second to making records primarily for Lee Perry, receiving a degree of international interest as a result of the producer's links with Island. Unfortunately, the mutually rewarding relationship between Max and Jamaica's most eccentric and distinctive producer did not long survive this taste of international success, and Max's subsequent work was largely disappointing.

Horace Andy (b. Horace Hinds, 1951, Kingston) was another singer who virtually from the beginning of his career in the early 1970s had cut a fair share of tunes on social conditions. His Studio One oeuvre had included, alongside strong love songs like "Fever" and Al Wilson's soul hit "Show & Tell", self-penned titles 'reality' titles such as "Illiteracy", "Every Tongue Shall Tell", "Help the Children", "Conscious Dreadlocks" and "Skylarking", about the unemployed youth who waste their time idling on the street. After Brentford Road, Andy's unique falsetto voice only ever needed placing in the right setting, and this was provided by numerous producers, most notably Bunny Lee, Leonard 'Santic' Chin, Keith Hudson, Derrick Harriott and Winston 'Niney' Holness in Jamaica, and the Bullwackie and Hungry Town setups based in New York.

Other veterans who adapted to the new era and maintained their popularity included **Cornell Campbell**. While he entered his most commercially successful period by placing his tenderest of falsettos over Bunny Lee's conquering 'flying cymbals' rhythms, he sometimes took time off from Striker's sessions to make equally outstanding records such as "I Heart Is Clean" for Winston 'Niney' Holness, "No Man's Land" for Joe Gibbs and the extraordinary Skin, Flesh & Bones-backed "Them A Bad" for Winston

Riley. Even the ultimate romantic crooner of Jamaican music, **John Holt**, shone on both new love songs (including a popular cover of Lou Rawls' "You'll Never Find Another Love Like Mine" for Bunny Lee) and roots material for Channel One. Both **Leonard Dillon**, who had led the **Ethiopians** but by 1975 was performing solo as the Ethiopian, and the formidable **Joe Higgs** had from the dawn of post-mento music addressed themselves to socially conscious topics, and must have found it fairly straightforward to continue in much the same way as before, but over modern rhythms.

DAVID CORIO

Cool as Candy: the brother Horace Andy

There were several newer singers, as well, whose voices would have ensured them of success in any era, but seemed particularly suited to expressions of the 'dreader' times. One of the most notable was the very consistent **Junior Delgado**, a one-time member of the Time Unlimited group recorded by both Rupie Edwards and Lee Perry. His full-throated and always very anguished-sounding vocal attack is ideally suited for warnings to the less than righteous – and, on occasion, it could seem just as heartfelt tackling love songs.

At the time, however, few could match the popularity of the **Inner Circle** band's rotund **Jacob Miller** (b. 1955; d. 1980) – for a while second in Jamaican popularity only to Marley. As the exception to the rule that Jamaican reputations are made in the recording studio and dancehall, he possessed an extremely exciting stage act. Besides the records produced by Augustus Pablo, he was at his best on the popular 1974 tune "Forward Jah Jah Children" (Sweet City), which was versioned by Augustus Pablo/King Tubby as "Shakedown" (Starapple), and his two largest hits from a year later, "Tenement Yard" (Penetrate) and "Tired To Lick Weed In A Bush" (Arab). Before dying in a car crash, he was also to star in the second most successful movie about reggae, *Rockers*: had he lived longer he might well have achieved the international success that was so often predicted for him.

The self-contained **In Crowd**, led by the very gifted Fil Callender, released records on their own Evolution label, such as "His Majesty Is Coming", expressing rootical enough concerns in most of their lyrics, but usually placed over steady rhythms made for late-night 'rubbing up'. Though favourites at 'blues parties' in the UK, they never came to the attention of the crossover audience for roots reggae, either at the time or since.

Female singers were considerably less well represented on record in the roots era. Nevertheless, with her two Sonia Pottinger-produced albums (*Naturally* and *Steppin'*), **Marcia Griffiths** established herself as the pre-eminent woman singer of the period, a position that would only begin to be challenged from the mid-1990s. She scored big reggae hits with her version of Bunny Wailer's "Dreamland" and "Peaceful Woman" in 1977, followed by a beautiful cover of the Wailers' "Hurting Inside" and her own "Steppin' Out Of Babylon". The latter, her biggest hit, she successfully revived for Donovan Germain in 1995.

At the same time she was a member of the **I-Threes** with **Rita Marley** and **Judy Mowatt**, both of whom also enjoyed solo hits. Mowatt scored with "Black Woman" in 1977, released on the Tuff Gong-distributed Ashandan label, following this up with the well-received album of the same name in 1978. Rita Marley had to wait until her 1981 herb anthem "One Draw" for her hit; until then she had shown a preference for covering early Wailers songs like "Who Feels It Knows It", "Man To Man" and "Thank You Lord". Nothing she cut in the 1970s, however, matched the quality of her sublime "Play Play", recorded for Wail 'N' Soul 'M in the late 1960s.

ADRIAN BOOT

The indomitable Marcia Griffiths

HORACE ANDY

◑ **In the Light/In the Light Dub** (Blood & Fire, UK).

E Complementary vocal and dub sets originally released on Everton DaSilva's Hungry Town label, and much-sought-after by collectors before being brought together for this handy double LP/single CD. Even a recut of "Fever" stands comparison with the original, while the title track, "Problems" (not the lyric he recorded for Santic) and "Government Land" are simply awesome. Prince Jammy's deconstruction of the vocal set confirms the heavyweight nature of the original rhythm tracks, as well as bringing out some even 'dreader' textures.

◑ **Pure Ranking** (Clocktower, US).

The title track of this set is one of several records from the late 1970s concerned with a particularly notorious posse of West Kingston badmen. The rest of the tracks almost match it, their sparseness anticipating dancehall.

JUNIOR DELGADO

● **Taste Of the Youngheart** (Incredible Music, JA; DEB, UK).

The always impassioned-sounding Junior Delgado's debut album of 1978 drew together several of his most successful 45s for the DEB label, including "Devil's Throne", "Love Won't Come Easy", "Famine", and "Storm Is Coming", as well as the great "Armed Robbery" from Joe Gibbs and "Blackman's Heart Cries Out" from Augustus Pablo.

◑ **Treasure Found** (Incredible Music, UK).

Almost two decades after the debut album, an admirer in London compiled the aptly titled *Treasure Found*, repeating a couple of tracks from *Youngheart*, alongside ultra scarce gems such as "Poverty" and the Lee Perry-produced (and momentous) "Sons Of Slaves". Quintessential sufferer's music.

THE ETHIOPIAN

◑ **Slave Call** (Observer, JA; Third World, UK; Heartbeat, US).

By the late 1970s the Ethiopians had become reduced to their frontman and songwriter, Leonard Dillon, though the characteristic style remained intact. This is a Niney-produced album that first appeared in 1978 and was essentially a nyahbingi-based set given a greater individuality through Dillon's unmistakable vocals.

● **Everything Crash** (Studio One, JA).

Leonard Dillon's return to Studio One on the eve of the next decade resulted in an album that was nothing short of masterful, though it met with only limited interest at the time. The versions of "Everything Crash" and "No Baptism" easily stood comparison with the originals, while the Studio One rhythms employed on the other tracks sound as if especially built for the uniformly excellent new lyrics.

◉ **Owner Fe De Yard** (Heartbeat, US).

Useful compilation spanning some eighteen years of Dillon's heartfelt music. What is truly remarkable is the consistency of the vision – the songs sound as though they could have all come from the same session. Interesting notes feature Dillon's own recollections about the music herein.

MARCIA GRIFFITHS

● **Naturally** (High Note, JA; Sky Note, UK).

Jamaica's premier female singer paying tribute to her favourite songwriters, as she reinterprets her Studio One hits, "Feel Like Jumping", "Truly", "Tell Me Now", "Melody Life" and "Mark My Word", all of which were written by Bob Andy – and adds the same singer's "Stay" and "I've Got To Go Back Home", Bunny Wailer's "Dreamland", Bunny and Bob's "Lonesome Feeling", and the Melodians' "Sweet Sensation". Glorious songs, wonderfully sung, and updated for 1978 by the top studio band of the time, the Revolutionaries. This and *Steppin'* are quite possibly the best female vocal albums ever recorded in Jamaica.

● **Steppin'** (High Note, JA; Sky Note, UK).

No reggae diva has been able to touch Marcia Griffiths, even though she remains best known to the general public as a member of Bob Marley's I-Threes. This is the second of the two albums she cut for Sonia Pottinger in the late 1970s, with rhythms again in the prevalent style of the period from the Revolutionaries. Includes three hit singles: "Peaceful Woman", Marley's "Hurtin' Inside" and, most memorable of all, "Steppin' Out Of Babylon" (which she successfully recut twenty years later for Donovan Germain).

JOE HIGGS

◑ **Life Of Contradiction** (Micron, JA; Esoldun, France).

E When this was released at the height of the 'flying cymbals' phase, in 1975, its jazz-influenced rhythms were far from fashionable. Not that the musicianship from Earl 'Wire' Lindo (piano), Val Douglas (drums), Mikey Chung (lead guitar) and US guest Eric Gayle (rhythm guitar) was not impeccable, or failed the purposes of the very distinctive Joe Higgs. The new versions of "There's A Reward", "I Am the Song" (retitled "Song My Enemy Sings") and "Change of Plan" ("Come On Home") were significantly restyled, and possibly improved on the originals. More than anything, this album was a showcase for the most expressive voices in Jamaican music.

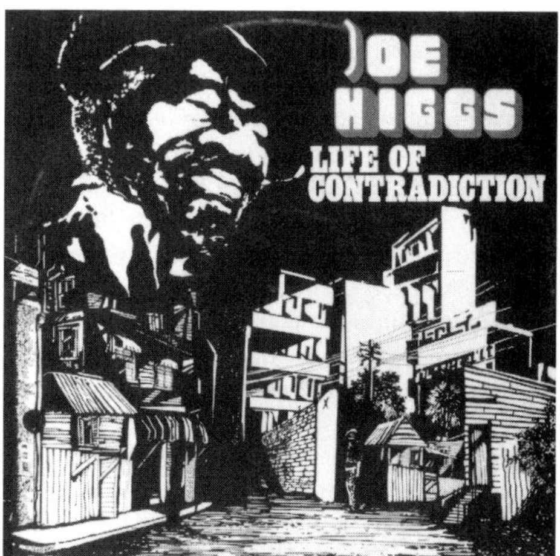

● **Unity Is Power** (Elevation, JA; One Stop, UK).

This appeared four years after the above album, and suffered from comparison with it. Listening to the set now, the second cut of "Sons Of Garvey" still sounds inferior, but the best tracks – "Neither Gold Or Silver" and "One Man Coche (Pipe)" – show a talent hardly diminished.

IN CROWD

● **His Majesty Is Coming** (Creole, UK).

Brings together their four major self-produced hits – "His Majesty Is Coming", "Back A Yard", "We Play Reggae" and "Born In Ethiopia" – and adds another seven tracks of the same easy-rocking-but-tough quality. Fil Callender, the band's lead singer, songwriter and producer, must be the unsung genius of Jamaican music. A definitive CD compilation would need add only "Milk & Honey" (and Fil Callender's popular 'lovers' hit "Baby My Love".

JACOB MILLER

● **Wanted** (Top Ranking, US).

● **Jacob 'Killer' Miller** (Top Ranking, UK; RAS, US).

As Jacob Miller's work with Pablo has received its belated recognition, it would be ironic if the records that were more popular at the time were to be overshadowed. *Killer* and *Wanted* were his best-selling albums in the reggae world, and understandably so. The former includes the hits "Standing Firm", "Peace Treaty Style" and "Healing Of the Nation", and the latter "Forward Ever" and his most popular track not to be released as a 45, "Mrs Brown". There is plenty else on both sets to explain why he was Jamaica's favourite singer of the mid–late 1970s.

◉ **Collector's Classics** (RAS, US).

For a more economical way of exploring almost the full story of the singer's work with Inner Circle, grab this splendid twenty-track CD, which adds both "Forward Jah Jah Children" and his 1976 Song Festival entry "All Night Daylight" to the best of the above sets.

JUDY MOWATT

● **Black Woman** (Ashandan, JA; Grove Music, UK; Shanachie, US).

Like Marcia Griffiths, Judy Mowatt performed in front of hundreds of thousands as one of Marley's I-

Threes, but in the same period made great records under her own name – even if not as many as might have been wished. "Black Woman" was the strongest of these, and a contender for the consummate cultural statement from any Jamaican woman singer. Everything else on her greatest album is in a similar rootsy and gospel-tinged mood – check her self-written "Strength To Go Through" and "Sisters' Chant", or the beautiful treatment given Freddie McGregor's "Zion Chant".

MAX ROMEO

● **Revelation Time** (Tropical Sound Tracs, UK).
A collection of tracks recorded between Max Romeo's 'rebel music' 45s and "Wet Dream" hit of the early 1970s and the *War Ina Babylon* album of 1976. Though not making the same impression on rock critics as the Upsetter-produced album, minor classics like the marvellous title track, "Warning Warning" and "Tackro", make an even stronger set.

DELROY WILSON

◑ **Sarge** (LTD, JA; Charmers, UK).
E Anyone who harbours doubts about reggae's reliance on the version (as opposed to the constant pursuit of 'originality'), should listen to Delroy Wilson's most accomplished post-Studio One set. There might not be one original song here, but with enough of the singer's incomparable vocal style, as well as Lloyd Charmer's undervalued production skills, to make even the much versioned "My Conversation" seem fresh. Some of the original sources might seem unlikely – Jerry Lee Lewis's "Green Green Grass Of Home", Paul Simon's "My Cecilia", Tom Paxton's "Too Late For the Learning" – but the approach works beautifully (someone knew good songs when they heard them).

Roots harmonies

Just as the 'mainstream' solo singers maintained vocal styles established in the late 1960s, so the Jamaican scene in the roots era saw the continuing formation and recording of vocal groups. Some of these could easily have fitted into the rocksteady era, with their sweet (usually tri-part) harmonies updated with fashionable Garveyite lyrics, heavier rhythms and vocal influences from a new generation of US soft soul groups – notably those from Philadelphia. Others, following the lead of the **Abyssinians** (see p.174), arguably the greatest roots harmony trio, represented a more basic shift within this tradition, often employing minor chords in their melodies and 'dreader' vocal tones that owed little to US soul music, for themes of repatriation and black culture. A third grouping, which included the Meditations, incorporated elements from both approaches, as well as a great deal from the original trio form of the Wailers.

Sweet soul influences

The most obvious example of a trio with the smooth approach were the **Mighty Diamonds**, who had clearly spent a lot of time listening to Chicago's Chi-Lites and Philadelphia's Delfonics. Their ground-breaking series of records for Channel One constituted their most important work in the roots era (see p.148), though they had preceded this with fine 45s for Stranger Cole, Rupie Edwards and Pat Francis, and subsequently went on to cut a series of equally strong tunes for Joe Gibbs – in particular "Identity" and "Ghetto Living". The ultra-smooth Philly group the Stylistics also exercised an important influence, particularly on the underrated **Chantells** (Samuel Bramwell, Tommy Thomas, Lloyd Forrester), who for a while seemed the only act that made Roy Francis's Phase One label a going concern. Even the cover photograph of the trio's only album has them clothed in pastel-blue suits in what could have been a publicity picture from Philadelphia International Records. Their major local hits included the cultural "True Born African" and "Children of Jah", while the more romantic concerns of the sublime "Waiting In the Park" could have been voiced by any number of velvety Philly vocal groups (albeit not over such a tough rhythm). Samuel Bramwell also made a couple of worthwhile singles as a solo performer, but had ceased recording when he was shot dead by the Kingston police during an armed robbery on a bauxite company in 1983.

THE CHANTELLS

◉ Waiting In the Park (Phase One, JA).

Like the Mighty Diamonds, the Chantells' harmonies owed more to contemporary soft soul than rocksteady ("Waiting In the Park" itself would have suited the Stylistics). The last four tracks, however, form a sort of 'culture suite', demonstrating just how adaptable their approach was.

Minor chords and dreader harmonies

Most harmony vocal groups of the roots period sounded Jamaican in every way – even if they partly achieved this through melodies and/or rhythms that sounded more 'African'. Mournful minor chord melodies – similar to those employed in the 'Far East' sound of Augustus Pablo – were central to the music of the Abyssinians, the **Royals**, the **Wailing Souls**, the **Congos**, **Culture** and Vivian Jackson's **Prophets**. Just as serious in their musical approach was a trio called **Israel Vibration** – indeed, few groups were so gloriously the product of the late 1970s. Cecil 'Skeleton' Spence, Albert 'Apple' Craig and Lascelles 'Wiss' Bulgrin originally met when housed in a home for polio sufferers, and went on to create a unique style of guileless, off-key harmonizing that is one of the most effective in the entire story of Jamaican music. They perfectly expressed the 'dread' mood of the time in which they first came to notice – initially with the very original 45 "Why Worry" (Orthodox) at the tail end of 1976, and then "The Same Song" (Top Ranking) the following year.

Other gifted and distinctive roots vocal groups, including the **Black Aces**, the **Black Brothers**, the **Jewels**, the **Skulls**, the **Mighty Albijans** and the **African Brothers**, were never given an opportunity to record an entire album's worth of material, instead making their mark with a handful of singles (or less). To these lists of 'dread'-sounding groups can be added the **Viceroys** (Wesley Tinglin, Lineal Williams, Daniel Bernard – the last two eventually replaced by Neville Infram and Norris Reid) and the **Morwells** (Eric 'Bingy Bunny' Lamont, Morris 'Blacka' Wellington, Louis Davis). The former group were formed in the late 1960s, recording for Studio One and then Lloyd Daley, but really came into their own when they returned to Dodd's foundation label in the next decade, recording the roots gems "Slogan On the Wall" and "Struggle". The Morwells mainly recorded for their own label, Morwells Esq., which was launched in 1974 and notched up minor classics such as "Mafia Boss" (an instrumental – they played instruments as well as singing), "Got To Be Holy" and the anthemic "Kingston 12 Tuffy" from 1979. The bassist Errol 'Flabba' Holt joined the group in the late 1970s, and after a couple of years he and Bingy Bunny left to form what was to be the foundation session band of the dancehall era, the Roots Radics.

Not surprisingly, the influence of the three-man Wailers could be heard to varying degrees in the approaches of several trios singing 'cultural' lyrics. Prominent among these were the

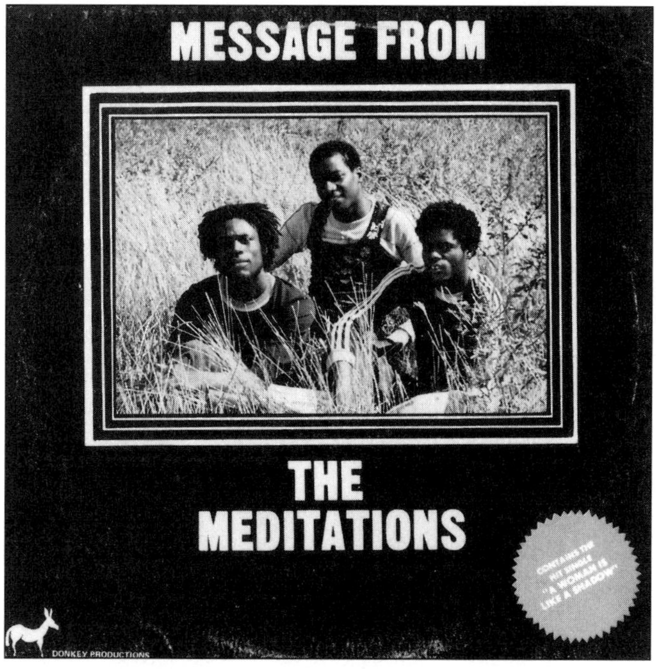

Meditations (Ansel Cridland, Winston Watson, Danny Clarke), who could also sound like a less-sophisticated version of the Mighty Diamonds, and successfully recorded for Dobby Dobson, Channel One, Tuff Gong, Lee Perry and themselves. The most memorable

tunes by the **Itals** (featuring Ronnie Davis, a singer with a following of his own, alongside Keith Porter and Lloyd Ricketts) appeared on Lloyd Campbell's Spiderman label, and included one undisputed classic – "Ina Dis Time". Later, when classic harmonies were no longer fashionable in Jamaica, they were to end up recording regularly for the US Nighthawk imprint, with a far stronger following in that country than anywhere else.

Cultural Roots, one of the few vocal quartets of the time, impressed with thunderous bass-heavy roots tunes for Donovan Germain, when the producer was based in New York (but recording in Kingston). Their 12" 45s, such as the declamatory "Mr Boss Man", were ideal stomach-churning fodder for sound systems of the late 1970s/early 1980s with strict roots and culture policies.

Finally, the Norman Grant-led **Twinkle Brothers**, whose career began as a necessarily versatile North Coast hotel circuit band, transmuted in the late 1970s into one of the heaviest of the self-contained vocal/instrumental groups. Their early work, however, featured some strong harmonies, and "Beat Them Jah Jah", "Jehoviah" and "Never Get Burn" stand as roots classics. The Twinkle Brothers' career is still in full flight (with a changed line-up), largely recording in the UK, performing in Europe and seemingly oblivious of the last two decades of change in Jamaican music (much to the delight of their loyal followers).

CULTURAL ROOTS

● **Drift Away From Evil** (Germain Revolutionary Sounds, JA).

● **Revolutionary Sounds** (Germain Revolutionary Sounds, JA).

Archetypal roots of the later 1970s/early 1980s, covering all the expected ground – ghetto people's suffering, hypocrites and oppressors, Babylon's shaky foundations and the wicked having nowhere to run. *Drift Away* includes their ultimate expression in "Mr Bossman", but *Revolutionary Sounds* is the more consistent set.

CULTURE

⊙ **Trod On** (Heartbeat, US).

A selection of their work for Sonia Pottinger that stands comparison with their best for Joe Gibbs. All the classics that appeared on High Note – "Natty Never Get Weary", "Stop the Fighting", "Down In Jamaica", etc – are here, with one (very welcome) surprise in a previously unreleased track recorded with Count Ossie's Mystic Revelation of Rastafari.

ISRAEL VIBRATION

◑ **The Same Song** (Top Ranking, JA; Pressure Sounds, UK).

E The trio's stunning debut album, titled after their second hit, more than fulfilled the promise already shown, and stands as one of the most completely convincing 'cultural' artefacts of all time. The CD version has disappointing packaging, but compensates with the addition of "Crisis", previously only available as a much sought-after 12" single.

◑ **Unconquered People** (Israel Vibes, JA; Greensleeves, UK).

The rougher edges were smoothed out for the second album, but the rhythms were only slightly less heavy than before – and there is even an exception to the last statement in "Mr Taxman", easily the equal of anything they had recorded before (or have since).

◑ **Why You So Craven** (Volcano, JA; RAS, US).

The meeting of the most cultural of groups and the producer usually associated with hard-core dancehall, Junjo Lawes, might have seemed an unlikely one, but the resulting album, if anything, benefited from the tension between their approaches. Only a less than crisp mix and a couple of weak tracks prevent it from being totally successful.

◑ **On the Rock** (RAS, US).

This much later set (from 1996) has the trio no longer at the cutting edge of the music, but with little decline in the quality of their material or their distinctive vocals.

THE ITALS

◑ **Early Recordings** (Nighthawk, US).

"Ina Dis Time" remains the Itals' one top-flight single, but "Time Will Tell" does not fall far short, and the rest of the generic late-1970s roots material collected here makes pleasant enough listening.

ERIC 'BINGY BUNNY' LAMONT

⦿ **Kingston 12 Tuffie** (RAS, US).

Career-spanning tribute to the gifted singer/guitarist includes work as a soloist and with the Morwells. Duplicates "In God We Trust" and "We Wan' Go A Yard" from the Nighthawk set, but the stirring title track, the militant "Cut Them Down" and the joyous "Reggae Party" more than compensate. The album kicks off with a heartfelt tribute poem recited by his friend from the Radics, Dwight Pinkney.

THE MEDITATIONS

● **Message From the Meditations** (Wild Flower, JA).

The debut album from the Meditations, and more or less a package of their greatest hits up to the point of its release in 1977. Included are "Babylon Trap Them" and "(Rome) Longest Liver" from the pen of the trio's founder, Danny Clarke, alongside "Tricked", "Running From Jamaica" and a new mix of "Woman A Shadow" from Ansel Cridland.

⦿ **Deeper Roots: The Best Of** (Heartbeat, US).

A career-spanning survey of the group's output that just fails to live up to its title. Far too many tracks from the *Message* set are missing, whilst the tracks featuring Cridland with the Linkers sound out of place. The original mix of "Woman A Shadow" is present, as is the Black Ark-recorded "Think So". The sleeve notes feature a fascinating interview with Ansel Cridland.

THE MORWELLS

● **The Best Of the Morwells** (Nighthawk, US).

Certainly not all the Morwells' best by a long way, but a worthwhile selection that includes "In God We Trust", "We Wan' Go A Yard" and "They Hold Us Down".

THE TWINKLE BROTHERS

● **Rasta Pon Top** (Grounation, UK).

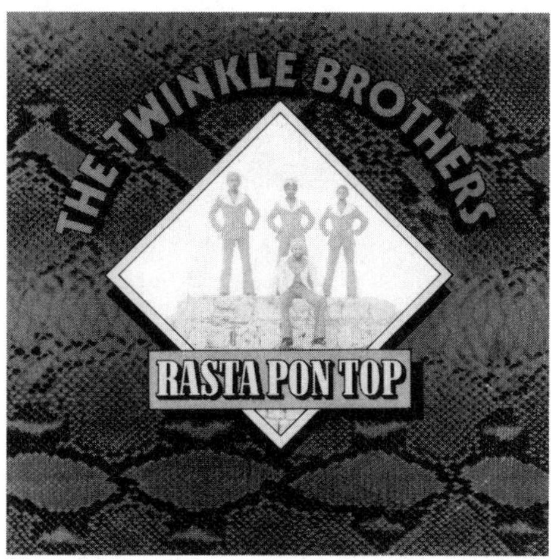

The cover for their debut set has the Twinkles still wearing the sort of matching costumes that they must have worn on the hotel circuit, and a couple of the tracks have echoes of this stage of their trajectory. The rest, however, are full-blooded rockers excursions, recorded at Channel One and in the strictly 'cultural' mode that was then the fashion, with "Beat Them Jah Jah", "Give Rasta Praise" and "Barabas" the most effective.

● **Love** (Virgin Front Line, UK).

● **Countrymen** (Virgin Front Line, UK).

The two Virgin sets that followed the above were even more consistent, particularly the second one, with the group's playing-for-tourists past completely exorcized. Heavyweight steppers tracks – including "Never Get Burned" and "Jah Kingdom Come" – were meant for play on sound systems and make no concessions to crossover tastes.

THE VICEROYS

⦿ **Ya Ho** (Heartbeat, US).

A vocal trio that began, in the usual Jamaican way, at Studio One, but, rather less predictably, went on to greater things. "Slogan On the Wall" is an undisputed classic, and the title track runs it close; everything else is proficient rather than inspired.

Some reflective Rastamen

In contrast to those performers who could handle a cultural or lovers lyric with equal facility, there were more reflective singers who rarely recorded tunes not in a strictly 'conscious' vein, if at all. Several were members of the leading Rastafarian organization of the 1970s, the Twelve Tribes of Israel, and far removed from any 'fashion dreads' hustling the tourists at the North Coast resorts. **Little Roy**, **Pablo Moses** and **Fred Locks** were three of the most distinctive Rasta singers who made a substantial contribution on record, while many others were recorded on a more occasional basis.

Little Roy

Little Roy (b. Earl Lowe, 1950) had recorded for Clement Dodd and Prince Buster without any success before making a series of very fine, mostly Rasta-inspired, records for Lloyd 'Matador' Daley at the beginning of the decade, along with "Cross the Nation" for Scratch and "Father's Call" for Glen Brown. But it was after he had left Daley and teamed up with Munchie Jackson and Lloyd Barnes to launch the Tafari and Earth labels that his most consistent body of work appeared. His best-known single on Tafari, "Tribal War", was a plea for "love and a little harmony" that proved popular enough for Channel One to record a John Holt version, for Joe Gibbs to turn out cuts by George Nooks and Dillinger, and for Vivian Jackson to produce variations from both Wayne Wade and Trinity. "Prophecy" (also Tafari) was at least as powerful a record, and employed a rhythm (based on the old "Peanut Vendor" jazz melody) which was really to take off during the 1980s, when the drum and bass partnerships of Sly & Robbie and Steely & Clevie were to update it for dancehall play.

LITTLE ROY (WITH IAN ROCK & THE HEPTONES)

◑ **Tafari Earth Uprising** (Pressure Sounds, UK).

E This collects everything of consequence that Little Roy recorded for the wonderful Tafari/Earth/Uprising setup, plus superb tracks produced by Gregory Isaacs and Scratch. Even those who have never investigated this less-than-high-profile roots singer are bound to be familiar with at least a couple of the rhythms – including the anthemic "Tribal War" and "Prophecy".

Fred Locks

Fred Locks (b. Stafford Elliot, 1955, Kingston) took on that name in the mid-1970s, by which time he had already recorded with a vocal group, the Lyrics, for Studio One, Randy's and the group's own Lyric label. However, it was as a solo artist that he made a serious impact with the anthemic "Black Star Liners" for the Twelve Tribes-affiliated Jahmikmusik label. His bleating voice could never have suited seductive love songs, but seemed made for expressive cries of the sufferah's pain or affirmations of faith in Rastafari. Fred Locks' music has always seemed totally lacking in guile and as far removed as it is possible to imagine from the more materialistic concerns of the boastful dons who were to dominate the music a few years after his first album appeared.

FRED LOCKS

◑ **Black Star Liner** (Vulcan, UK; Jahmikmusik, JA).

E The handful of singles Stafford Elliot made with the Lyrics in the late 1960s/early 1970s (including the original of "Sing-A-Long", recut here) hardly prepared anyone for the impact of the title track when it appeared as a single in 1975, under

his new name. It became an enduring roots anthem, and was soon followed by an album that helped define the period. His voice was totally apposite to the deep roots rhythms that supported it, as well as to the serious themes of iniquity, faith and repatriation.

FRED LOCKS & THE CREATION STEPPERS

CD Love & Only Love (Greensleeves, UK).

Produced by leading UK sound-system man Lloyd Coxsone at Channel One and Harry J's in Kingston, this features an all-star session band – on drums, for instance, are three legends in Sly Dunbar, Albert Malawi and Leroy 'Horsemouth' Wallace. The title track, "Voice Of the Poor" and "Homeward Bound" were the popular 12" singles, but the entire set stands as superior sound-system music in a serious 'cultural' mode.

Pablo Moses

If both Little Roy and Fred Locks seemed to present their takes on reality in a relatively artless way, **Pablo Moses** (b. Pablo Henry, 1953) was a far more sophisticated artist, though just as committed to a Rasta-inspired view of the world. Rather than sounding like an unworldly Rastaman who suddenly finds that he has the opportunity to express his beliefs in the recording studio, Moses always appeared as a conscious commentator, slightly removed from the feelings he articulated (significantly, the cover of his *Revolutionary Dream* album showed street scenes reflected in his shades). Among the singles that brought his name to attention in 1975/76 were the herb-smoker's anthem, "I Man A Grasshopper" (Jigsaw), which was recorded at Perry's Black Ark studio by Geoffrey Chung; his denouncement of those who would kill for "Blood Money" (also Jigsaw); the topical "We Should Be In Angola" (Penetrate); and yet another call for unity in "One People" (Ja-Man).

PABLO MOSES

Revolutionary Dream (Jigsaw, JA; Tropical Sound Tracs, UK).

E Pablo Moses is another highly original vocalist who has stuck to his chosen path of social commentary infused with spiritual values. His first album, produced by Geoffrey Chung, followed the 45s "I Man A Grasshopper", "Give I Fe I Name" and "Blood Money" (all included), and was marked by thoughtful lyrics and Moses' cool style of delivery. In addition there were suitably imaginative horn arrangements by Tommy McCook.

A Song (Island, UK).

Pave the Way (Island, UK; Mango, US).

Two sets that are well worth investigating. Nothing else he recorded possessed quite the sustained power of *Revolutionary Dream*, but these Geoffrey Chung productions came nearest.

Bim Sherman

Several more dreadlocked singers expressed the Rasta vision of Babylon's fall and corresponding redemption for the righteous in a seemingly artless – but nevertheless effective – way. These included the frail-voiced **Bim Sherman** (b. Jarrett Tomlinson, 1952, Kingston), who scraped enough money together to record almost his entire oeuvre on self-financed labels like Scorpio, Red Sea and Sun Dew, impressing most with the late-1970s titles, "Tribulation", "World Go Round" and "Danger", as well as "Mighty Ruler", which appeared on Dudley Swabey's Ja-Man imprint.

BIM SHERMAN

Danger (Century, UK).

Bim Sherman has always favoured an understated approach when producing himself. *Danger*, based on the earlier *Love Forever* set, brings together the best 45s that appeared on his own Scorpio and Sun Dew labels (as well, in the case of "Danger" and "Mighty Ruler", as the Santic and Ja-Man imprints). Not a weak moment, and unmissable late-1970s roots.

Crucial Cuts Volume 2 (Century, UK).

This CD collects most of the above and all of the subsequent *Lovers Leap* set, and its eighteen tracks represent the best value-for-money package (the sound is pristine, as well). Yes, there is a first volume, perversely comprising later and less essential tracks.

Pablove Black and I. Kong

Several singers already mentioned in this chapter, such as Freddie McGregor, Judy Mowatt and Bob Marley, were aligned with the Twelve Tribes of Israel, and often recorded with fellow members such as the drummer (and sometime singer) Albert Malawi and the melodica/keyboards player, **Pablove Black**

(b. Paul Dixon). Pablove recorded several superb instrumentals for Studio One, employing a variety of keyboard instruments, that more that stand comparison with the best of Augustus Pablo's. Unfortunately for record buyers, he preferred playing over the Twelve Tribes' Jah Love sound system to playing in the studio, though after Brentford Road he did record superb instrumental versions of the Fred Locks hits "Black Star Liners" and "The Last Days". An even more occasional visitor to the recording studio was the mysterious singer known as **I. Kong** (b. Ricky Storme), who was responsible for the haunting "The Way It Is" (Top Cat), which became a favourite of Lloydie Coxsone's sound in London, and "Trod Along (Zion Pathway)".

PABLOVE BLACK

● **Mr Musik** (Studio One, JA).

Pablove Black, a committed member of the Twelve Tribes, was Studio One's resident melodica player, and – as this album displays – no slouch when it came to other keyboard instruments. The treatments given the familiar rhythms of Alton Ellis's "Hurting Me", the Royals' "Pick Up the Pieces", Carlton & his Shoes' "I've Got Soul" and Burning Spear's "Swell Headed" have the most immediate appeal, though the five originals gradually reveal their own qualities, with the title track particularly arresting.

I. KONG

● **The Way It Is** (Top Ranking, JA).

The title track is not the great original that appeared on Top Cat, but an acceptable enough second cut. It remains I. Kong's most memorable composition, though the other seven tracks are effective roots material in the meditative vein associated with Twelve Tribes performers.

Mutabaruka

When the shift to 'dancehall' beckoned, the guitarist Earl 'Chinna' Smith's High Times label carried on the serious roots tradition with excellent 45s by Dennis Brown (in the company of top UK reggae band Aswad), Devon Russell and Freddie McGregor, and the one 'dub poetry' album that can be recommended unreservedly, Mutabaruka's *Check It*. Dub poetry too often seemed bogus – a weak and inept relation to deejaying aimed at those who would not think of coming near a dancehall. But **Mutabaruka** redeemed the form by making records which managed to be both intelligent and impassioned, as well as featuring some extremely strong rhythms. He has also managed still to sound convincing in the 1990s, even to dancehall audiences who bought "Psalm 24", which he recorded with the singer Luciano, and the scathingly witty updating of Prince Buster's "Judge Dread" – "The People's Court".

MUTABARUKA

◑ **Check It** (High Times, JA; Alligator, US).

Mutabaruka's debut set more or less justified dub poetry, a genre that always had more appeal to earnest social-worker types than to the followers of sound systems. He could actually write (having had several volumes of his poetry published), and the guitarist Earl 'Chinna' Smith produced genuinely rootsy backdrops for the invectives.

◑ **The Ultimate Collection** (Greensleeves, UK).

This collection takes up his story after *Check It* to show that Mutabaruka has continued in just as imaginative and serious a manner. Newcomers should check his 'combination' track with Luciano, "Psalm 24", or his updating of the Judge Dread saga, "People's Court" (the latter a major UK reggae hit).

Dub

ADRIAN BOOT

5

5

previous page

Tubby at Tubby's, late 1970s

Dub

The word 'dub' is now used throughout the world of dance music to describe a remix. It's not so widely recognized, however, that the technique of the remix was pioneered in Jamaica as far back as 1967, initially in the quest for sound-system exclusivity, but soon exploited as an economic and imaginative way of reusing already recorded rhythm tracks. Broadly speaking, the history of dub in Jamaica has passed through three phases. First there were the so-called 'instrumentals', not originally conceived as such, but becoming so by the removal of the vocal track. Initially these instrumentals were strictly for sound-system play, but before too long they were being issued commercially. Versions on which the contribution of the studio engineer was more obvious then emerged around the end of 1968, and by 1970 these remixes – called 'versions' – were appearing on the B-sides of most Jamaican singles. The producer would have the engineer remove all, (or most), of the original vocal, leaving the raw rhythm track, which could be spiced up with a deejay adding shouted exclamations and/or extra instrumentation. Besides offering further entertainment to dancers and record buyers, these 'versions' provided sound systems with tracks for their own deejays to talk, or 'toast', over.

Dub, in the now familiar sense of radically remixed versions, arrived in 1972, and was largely the contribution of one man: Osbourne Ruddock, aka **King Tubby**, boss of the leading sound system in Kingston and a superb engineer. Soon many of the leading producers were leaving their tracks at his studio to be given the Tubby treatment. During the remainder of the decade the remixes made by Tubby and his apprentices (**Prince Jammy**, **Prince Philip Smart** and **Scientist**), and by other pioneers such as **Errol Thompson** (aka ET), added a further dimension to Jamaican music, eventually influencing dance culture worldwide.

During 1973–74 record buyers in Jamaica became accustomed to checking labels not just for the producer or artist, but also for the engineer. Records bearing a B-side credit like "King Tubby's Version" or "Drum & Bass by King Tubby's" were often selling on the strength of these, rather than their official top sides. This was also the year in which the first handful of dub albums appeared. They were usually pressed in very small quantities and disappeared quickly, but their followers were the most committed of the reggae public, and over the next few years hundreds of dub albums were issued, as every producer maximized the financial return on his vintage rhythms.

A Jammy dubplate

As every craze must, this eventually ran its course, and by the early 1980s few dub sets were being issued. Still, every single being pressed in Jamaica maintained what by then had become a tradition – the 'version' side. As digital technology became better integrated into Jamaican studios, a new generation of engineers came to prominence. As their experience grew, they in their turn sought to express themselves in dub. Dub has continued to exert a powerful influence on hip-hop and such dance forms as jungle, and the convention of the version continues today in Jamaica itself, even if some modern singles feature variants such as the 'acappella' version, or 'vocal remix'. With increasing frequency in recent years, 'version' sides of new Jamaican 45s have harked back to the form's golden age, particularly those mixed by the young engineers **Colin 'Bulby' York** and **Lynford 'Fatta' Marshall**. However, the revival of interest from the outside world in vintage 1970s dub has yet to prompt any return to a regular supply of new dub albums from Kingston.

VARIOUS PRODUCERS

◑ **Rodigan's Dub Classics – Serious Selections Volume One – Mixed By King Tubby, Prince Jammy & Scientist** (Grapevine, UK).

E A perfect selection, covering the most important seven years (1974–81) in the history of dub. Includes one of the first of Tubby's mixes to make an impression on a significant number of record buyers, "Watergate Rock", and two examples of the form at its most developed – Jammy's "Pablo In Moonlight City" (Earl Zero's second cut of "Please Officer") and Scientist's "Fall Dub" (Johnny Osbourne's "Nightfall").

Instrumental, chapter and version

By 1967 rocksteady had replaced ska in the dancehall, and many newer sound systems had come to rival the established ones. In the former Jamaican capital, Spanish Town, about fifteen kilometres from Kingston, sets such as Seymour Williams's Stereo, Son's Junior and the longer-established Ruddy's the Supreme Ruler of Sound played venues like Prison Oval and Ackee-Wackee Lawn, and were proving tough competitors. **Rudolph 'Ruddy' Redwood** had started a record shop in Spanish Town around 1957; he built a little sound system with just four speaker boxes to entertain friends at private parties. Ruddy continues the story: "Then I started improve on the sound, and start playing at dances and competitions. I get involve with Duke Reid, Coxsone, and then I started gettin' [exclusive] records from Duke Reid mostly – they call it dubs that time, yunno, special records." These 'dubs' were in fact one-off acetates which he was previewing at his sound long before their commercial release, rather than what would later be understood as dub remixes. The next step in the development of dub was the instrumental version of songs that had already been released to the public.

Ruddy Redwood and the first version

With **Duke Reid**'s rocksteady dominating the Jamaican scene in 1967, Ruddy Redwood's became the dominant set in Spanish Town. His long relationship with Duke enabled Ruddy to feature an unrivalled selection of music recorded at Duke Reid's Treasure Isle studio on Bond Street by singers such as Alton Ellis and Phyllis Dillon, as well as legendary vocal-harmony groups the Techniques, the Melodians and, most significantly for the history of dub, the **Paragons**. Late that year, as Ruddy remembers: "I was playin' at a dance one night and I was playin' this record [the Paragons' "On the Beach"] – it was released as a 45 before, but in those times they don't put the version on one side, they only put another record on the other side. So I was playin' it and it was nice for the people, so I went back to Smith [Duke Reid's engineer], Smithy's was his name, he was cuttin' some dubs for me." As he ran through the tapes of "On the Beach", Byron Smith inadvertently left the vocal track off – and Ruddy realized he'd hit on something new.

RICK ELGOOD

Ruddy outside his Spanish Town emporium, 1994

When Ruddy left the studio that evening, he was carrying an acetate with just the backing track on it. Armed with this Paragons 'dubplate', exclusively remixed by Byron Smith, Ruddy went off to his next dance. "They used to call me Mister Midnight in Spanish Town. I used to come in at midnight an' play fifteen, sixteen new music that nobody know about. So, the dance was very nice – I tell you, I love to entertain people. I come at 12 o'clock, and the deejay's name was Wicked, an' he introduce me – 'Mister Midnight, otherwise from S-R-S [Supreme Ruler of Sound].' I start playin' – that time you have two players. I put on "On the Beach" and I said, 'I'm gonna turn this place into a studio,' and I switch over from the singing part to the version part, cut down the sound and, man, you could hear the dance floor rail, man – everybody was singing. It was very happy, an' I get a vibe. So I went into Duke Reid – Duke was my good friend, yunno – an' I says to him, 'Man this ting – you can put the riddim on the other side.' He says, 'What!?' I say, 'Yes man, I play it las' night.' Duke use to depend on me to tell 'im which records goin' good. I tell 'im: 'Well, try it' – yunno? An' 'im try it, an' it work."

Ruddy lost no time in cutting versions of other well-known Duke Reid tracks to play at dances – with the guitarist **Lynn Taitt**, for instance, making instrumental cuts for the sound system of many Treasure Isle classics. Most of these 'instrumentals' appeared only as dubplates for Ruddy's sound, but, as Ruddy says, Duke Reid soon picked up on the idea himself. By 1968, Reid was releasing tunes like "Black Power", which used the rhythm track of the Silvertones' rocksteady cover of "In the Midnight Hour", with Winston Wright's keyboard replacing the group. Reid soon issued other instrumentals using backing tracks from vocal hits – saxman Tommy McCook's "My Best Dress" and organist Neville Hinds' "Sunday Gravy" (treatments, respectively, of the Paragons' "My Best Girl" and Alton Ellis's "Sunday Coming") being good examples of the sort of material that was given a general release (see p.63).

Version to version

Before long practically every producer on the island was following in Ruddy's footsteps. Engineer/producer **Lynford Anderson** (aka Andy Capp) made an undervalued contribution to the development of early remixing techniques. His further 'versions' of Derrick

TWO KINGS: JAMMY ON TUBBY

Before developing into Jamaica's most successful record producer of the 1980s, Lloyd James, aka Prince/King Jammy, was another of King Tubby's apprentices. Here he looks back to the heyday of dub.

"The great King Tubby's – yunno, they don't call people 'great' or 'King' for no reason – the reason why they call 'im great King Tubby's was he was such a nice person. If 'im ever get vex with you for five minutes, the nex' minute he is okay. A lotta good 'im do fe the community. Well, that's like a never-endin' friendship. It's like family, yunno – I grew up with King Tubby's. I used to live on Dromilly Avenue. His loss was of the greatest loss to me – I don't know about the music fraternity, but to me personally, because he was my teacher, yunno. It was so unfortunate that he had to go that way – that was terrible.

In the Seventies at King Tubby's studio, dub records used to sound fantastic to what we hearin' nowadays as dub. The main reason for this is because King Tubby used to have a four-track studio. We way how we used to create the dub, the feelin' of the music, we only had four controls to deal with, four slides to deal with. It was easier to mix with your slides instead of buttons. Nowadays you mix with buttons, because you're mixin' on a 24-track console. But music has to be a fast mixin' thing – most of the instruments were already mixed on one track. So when you draw down like the riddim track, you draw down horns, guitar, piano an' organ. So it was easier for you to mix it, and faster. That's why you got the dub in those days so brilliant. It can be mixed on these modern consoles, but you have to group the instruments. And the slides are not flexible like the mixin' board console that King Tubby's had. Those slides were flexible.

Dub means raw riddim. Dub jus' mean raw music, nuttin' water-down. Version is like your creativeness off the riddim, without voice."

Morgan's second cut of "Fat Man" – "Pop A Top" and "Pop A Top (Ver. 2)" (both Tiger) – were ground-breaking variations of the hit vocal that displayed the potential of the studio mixing board itself as an 'instrument'.

By 1970 the convention of having a different song on each side of a 45 had been replaced in Jamaica with a new one – the B-side now carried an instrumental which used the same rhythm track as the top side. Organ versions predominated, but most other lead instruments had their say on the rhythm. Sometimes they were titled "Chapter 1" or "Volume 2", as on "Stealing Stealing Volume 2", the flip side of **John Holt**'s "Stealing Stealing" (Treasure Isle). This has the straight rhythm track (drums, bass, organ and guitar) augmented by a deejay's percussive effects emerging in and out of the mix: Holt's original vocal can be heard very faintly in the background, but the recording engineer was on his way to becoming the featured artist.

In the same year, **Clancy Eccles** released "Phantom", an instrumental version (credited to his studio band, the Dynamites), of the rhythm employed on the deejay King Stitt's "Herbsman", itself an updating of the Skatalites' "Beardman Ska". What made the record different from other contemporary instrumental 'versions' of hits was that it had been subjected to remixing that reduced the track to its fundamental element – the lethal bassline.

'Version' soon became the favoured term for these new Jamaican remixes. Again in 1970, **Joe Gibbs** released "News Flash, Versions I & II", an instrumental which not only edited together parts of the rhythm tracks of three hits – Lloyd Willis's "Mad Rooster", the Inspirations' "Ease Up" and the Pioneers' "Mama Look Deh" – but was one of the first records to use 'version' in its title. Even more importantly, these versions were used in the dancehall, as the stripped-down mixes allowed the deejays – previously confined to introductions or interjections which spiced up the tune – to take centre stage. Deejays could now invent new lyrics which answered or commented on the original hit vocal – snatches of which had often been left in the mix.

Version galore – the rise of U-Roy

The man who was to rely on the 'version' more than any other in the 1970s was **Bunny 'Striker' Lee**, who also played a crucial role in these early developments. In 1968 he took his friend **Osbourne 'Tubby' Ruddock** (b. 1941, Kingston; d. 1989, Kingston) to one of Ruddy's dances in Spanish Town. Tubby saw for himself the electrifying effect the alternative versions were having in the dancehall. Tubby was a skilled electronics engineer, who also had a Duke Reid connection – he was often called to the Bond Street studio to carry out repair work. He operated a small sound system called the Home Town Hi-Fi, playing local parties in his home patch, the tough Waterhouse ghetto of Kingston. Ruddy's innovations made a strong impression on Tubby: he resolved to upgrade his own set in order to challenge the big sounds.

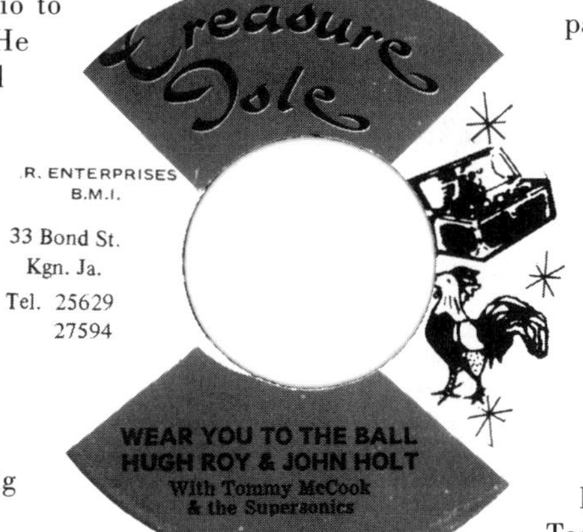

By 1969 he had secured the services of a man who would enable him to achieve this. Ewart Beckford, better known as **U-Roy**, became the deejay for Tubby's sound. An admirer of Jamaica's first selector/deejay/MC, Count Machuki (see p.113), U-Roy had also served his apprenticeship on such legendary 1960s sets as Sir Mike the Musical Thunderstorm and Dickie's Dynamic. MC-ing at Tubby's popular dances during 1969, U-Roy knew exactly how to create exciting and spontaneous lyrics in the new space offered by the 'version', waiting for a track to start and let a line or two of the original vocal be heard before beginning his own 'toasting'. **John Holt**, then lead singer of the Paragons, heard the deejay at a dance and reported back to his producer, Duke Reid, advising him to record this new phenomenon. As Ruddy recalls: "An 'im get U-Roy – that time, firs' time at the dancehall, you only hear – like, a deejay would be talkin' on a record – it's not really a rhythm, the record would be singin' and part of the introduction of the record, the deejay would talk. But U-Roy come in an' mek it a splash, man, an' I couldn't do nothing wrong for Duke Reid."

Treasure Isle
R. ENTERPRISES B.M.I.
33 Bond St. Kgn. Ja.
Tel. 25629 27594
WEAR YOU TO THE BALL
HUGH ROY & JOHN HOLT
With Tommy McCook & the Supersonics

U-Roy had already recorded a handful of titles in 1969 – "Earth's Rightful Ruler" for Lee Perry, "King Of the Road" for Bunny Lee and "Dynamic Fashion Way" for Keith Hudson – before he went in the studio for producer Lloyd Daley in October that year, cutting "Sound Of the Wise" and "Scandal". Early in 1970 U-Roy went down to Bond Street to voice for the Duke. The combination of his new approach – the deejay injecting his high-powered Machuki-inspired jive lyrics with whoops and screams – and some of Reid's sweetest rocksteady rhythms proved unstoppable. The first three U-Roy records on Treasure Isle were massive hits, and nothing would ever be quite the same again. U-Roy's "Wake the Town", a version of Alton Ellis's "Girl I've Got A Date", rapidly rose to the #1 slot on both Jamaican radio station charts. It was soon followed by "Rule the Nation", which rode the Techniques' "You Don't Care" rhythm. By the third release, "Wear You To the Ball", a version of the Paragons' hit of the same name, the deejay is so confident that he lets the group deliver the first two lines of the song:

"I'm gonna wear you to the ball tonight
Put on your best dress tonight"

before making his extraordinary entry:

"Did you heard what the man says baby
Said be your best
'Cos this gonna be your musical test
So come to school
Let I teach you the musical rule
Dig me soul brother, dig me soul sister
Come to I
An' maybe you can make it if you try..."

The deejay's message was to be taken to heart by a whole generation of toasters, boasters and rappers. The modern deejay had arrived, riding the wave on a sea of versions.

Dubwise shower

All of the above variations of the 'version' fed into the later development of dub. But the first vocal record with a full dub version on its flip (ie a dub that dropped parts of the rhythm in and out of the mix, and added other tricks such as equalization effects) is usually recognized as Little Roy's "Hard Fighter" on Lloyd 'Matador' Daley's Syndicate label, recorded in March 1971, with the splendid "Voo-doo" as its strictly drum and bass counterpart from the Hippy Boys. This was probably mixed by the pioneering Lynford Anderson, but the man who really popularized the dub B-side and then entire albums of versions was **King Tubby**. However, Tubby was not the only brilliant mixing engineer. **Errol 'ET' Thompson** was experimenting on the four-track board at Randy's downtown studio, mixing versions for Joe Gibbs – such as 1973's "Echo"/"More Echo" by Johnny Lover and "More Dub"/"Chapter Two" – that clearly indicated his awareness of the new trend. Producers **Prince Buster** and **Herman Chin Loy** also played a part in the spread of the new form, as did **Clement Dodd**, **Augustus Pablo** and the endlessly inventive **Lee Perry**.

Tubby takes the controls

By 1972, Tubby's Hi Fi, deejayed by U-Roy, had become one of the leading sound systems in Kingston, being known especially for its superior sound quality – Tubby's was the first set to employ separate tweeter boxes, and he also introduced a reverb unit to the sound. These technical improvements fed into **King Tubby**'s work in the tiny studio at the back of his home, where he pursued similar goals of aural excellence. There he had a dub-cutting machine on which he would make acetates (known as 'specials') for his set and, increasingly as time went on, for other sound systems. The same year Bunny Lee brokered a deal with Byron Lee's Dynamic Studios that enabled Tubby to buy their old four-track board when they graduated to more sophisticated equipment. Bunny and other producers now began leaving their multi-track tapes with Tubby.

Tubby was not the producer of the rhythms he was mixing at this time; nonetheless, his contribution as remix engineer was to become increasingly crucial over the next few years. Dub really became established with the series of Tubby-mixed dub sides that emerged in 1972–74, principally on Lee Perry's Justice League and Upsetter labels, Glen Brown's Pantomine, Roy Cousins' Wambesi, U-Roy's own Mego Ann, Augustus Pablo's Hot Stuff and Rockers, Winston Riley's Techniques, Prince Tony Robinson's High School, Bunny Lee's Jackpot and Carlton Patterson's Black & White. Tubby's method of mixing on these sides was subtle, with only one or two effects employed on the rhythm tracks; the huge thunderclaps and deeply echoed snatches of vocal would come later. Years later **Lee Perry** said: "Tubby come to meet me, 'cause him was looking for adventure. I am the only adventurer. Because Tubby was there in the beginning, he was looking for that adventure, that make him act from a baby, from nothing, from a sperm to a baby, and he still see the adventure, and recognize the adventure, that this is the adventure, dub's adventure. He was brilliant. I thought he was my student, maybe he thought I was his student, but it makes no matter. I'm not jealous."

Together Tubby and Scratch mixed *Blackboard Jungle*, released in 1973. By the end of the year Scratch would be in his own studio, the Black Ark (see pp.164–169), where he could both build and mix his own rhythms, but his studio never became a centre for dub in the same way that Tubby's did. The sheer number of producers who used Tubby meant that he always had more than enough rhythms to mix, and with which he could experiment endlessly. There is no doubt that the main reason for this experimentation was simply economic, but had the remixes not sounded completely fresh they would not have been so successful, and their freshness was the result of both musical imagination and engineering ingenuity.

Tubby continued to acquire additional studio hardware; he was also very inventive at customizing or indeed making his own equipment. King Jammy, an old friend and fellow sound-system operator who became one of Tubby's apprentice engineers, and later one of Jamaica's most successful producers, gives an insight into this improvisatory aspect of dub: "The reverb unit that we used to use there, it was a Fisher reverb, an' we change it to become a King Tubby and Fisher! The slides that we use to use, we change them from the original slides, because the mixin' console was so old you couldn't get replacement parts. We use other models to incorporate in that console." In every sense, the art of the 'version' was that of taking something old and renewing it. By mid-1973 Tubby had another four-track machine, which enabled him to record vocals, as well as mixing. Roy Shirley was the first to benefit from Tubby's new studio set-up, voicing his song "Stepping Razor" there.

The new style of Tubby's dub versions began to catch on with record buyers, who appreciated the way the song was reconstructed on the B-side. These versions were also a godsend to smaller sound systems; often lacking access to exclusive dubplates, they could use these commercially available dubs for their deejays to 'toast' over.

In 1974 Tubby mixed a dub of former Studio One vocalist **Larry Marshall**'s "I Admire You" for Carlton Patterson. Called "Watergate Rock", it was one of the first dubs to be credited to him on the label – indeed Marshall considers it the dub that really established Tubby's name with the public. The A-side is a beautifully sincere love song; Tubby's dub mix dispenses completely with the vocal and puts the emphasis on the bass and drums, which are subjected to varying amounts of equalization and reverb. Occasionally, the rhythm guitar and melodica slide in; sometimes the bass and drums drop out completely, leaving the the rhythm guitar chipping away on its own. Simple though these techniques may be, Tubby was able nonetheless to make it appear as if the rhythm track was perpetually mutating, and when heard through the massed speakers of a big sound system the effect was even more dynamic. Similar mixes, placing the drum and bass track in the front of the mix, were performed on other Patterson-produced tracks, such as "Locks Of Dub", the version side of another Larry Marshall song, "Can't You Understand".

The first dub albums

The popularity of the 'version' side, particularly when credited to King Tubby, led to the release of entire **albums** of dub versions, but producers were at first tentative. The first few dub albums appeared in 1973 and were pressed in such limited quantities that they cost about three or four times the normal price. There are three contenders for the title of first dub album to hit the street: Lee Perry's epochal *Blackboard Jungle Dub*, mixed by King Tubby; Clive Chin's *Java Java Java Java* (often referred to as *Java Java Dub*), which displayed the distinctive style of Errol Thompson; and Herman Chin Loy's *Aquarius Dub*, probably mixed by the producer himself. Late in 1974, Bunny Lee released his first Tubby-mixed dub album, *Dub From the Roots*, followed by another set, also featuring the producer's 'flying cymbals' sound, early in 1975.

The first dub album to gain a UK release was Keith Hudson's *Pick A Dub*, issued by Atra Records in 1974. Here Hudson had a dozen of his best rhythms deconstructed at Harry J's studio, showcasing the drum and bass artistry of the Barrett brothers from the Wailers band. The results managed to combine an almost scary starkness with just enough melodic touches, and obstinate rhythms aimed squarely at sound-system play. A strong seller in England was Niney's *Dubbing With the Observer* set, released by Trojan just before they went into liquidation in 1975; featuring Tubby mixes of many of Dennis Brown's hits for the producer, it tapped a demand created by the leading UK-based sound system Sir Coxsone, which had been playing similar dubs of many of Niney's rhythms.

HERMAN CHIN LOY PRODUCTIONS AND MIXES

● **Aquarius Dub** (Aquarius, JA).
Another of the initial dub releases and a further link with Pablo as early cuts of both "East Of the River Nile" and "Cassava Piece"/"King Tubby Meets the

Rockers Uptown" are included. Again, the mixing is fairly subdued, but the set makes it on the quality of the Aquarius rhythms – another outstanding one is Alton Ellis's "Alton's Official Daughter", possibly Herman Chin Loy's strongest production.

WINSTON 'NINEY' HOLNESS PRODUCTIONS

● **Dubbing With the Observer** (Observer, JA; Attack, UK).
E The combination of King Tubby's deft touch at the mixing-board and Niney's proven rhythms could hardly have failed. The dub master gets his hands on thirteen of Niney's prime tracks (ranging from Sang Hugh's dread "Rasta No Born Yah", through Dennis Brown's "Cassandra" and "No More Will I Roam", to Ken Boothe's massively popular "Silver Words"), creating a dub set that helped further establish the form when it appeared in 1975.

● **Sledgehammer Dub In the Streets Of Jamaica** (Observer, JA).
A fine set, if not quite in the class of its predecessor. Mostly rhythms from Dennis Brown's *Westbound Train* album – such as "Voice Of My Father", "So Long Rastafari" and "Tribulation" – mixed in particularly raw fashion by an engineer who remains anonymous (in true roots style, the album never received the dignity of a printed sleeve).

KEITH HUDSON PRODUCTIONS

◑ **Pick A Dub** (Blood & Fire, UK).
E One of reggae's greatest innovative spirits, Keith Hudson not only produced distinctive and very strong rhythms, employing the Barrett brothers and the Soul Syndicate, but on *Pick A Dub* mixed what were already fairly sparse tracks down to their bare essentials, without losing any of their musical qualities. Rhythms that are original to Hudson – including Big Youth's "S.90 Skank" and Horace Andy & Earl Flute's "Don't Think About Me" – sit easily alongside his strong interpretations of the Abyssinians' roots anthems, "Satta Massa Gana" and "Declaration Of Rights".

BUNNY LEE PRODUCTIONS

● **Dub Master: Dub From the Roots** (Total Sounds, JA).
The first album under the dub master's own name. The version of Johnny Clarke's "Rock With Me Baby" stands out as the epitome of the producer's and the engineer's approaches at the time.

● **Dub Master: The Roots Of Dub** (Grounation, UK).
A set that was obviously meant to cash in on the success of the above album, and only marginally less effective, with Tubby treatments of the Aggrovators' updatings of Studio One classics like "A Love I Can Feel" demonstrating the seemingly endless possibilities of version-upon-version.

LEE PERRY PRODUCTIONS

● **Blackboard Jungle Dub** (Upsetter, JA).
E The *Blackboard Jungle* set was not only one of the first dub albums but, amazingly, is Scratch's strongest to date. It is helped no end, of course, by the choice selection of early 1970s rhythms, including Junior Byles' "Fever" and "Place Called Africa", the Upsetters' "Bucky Skank", and the Wailers' "Kaya", "Dreamland" and "Keep On Moving". Equally inspired is Tubby's mix – or rather mixes, as the original stereo pressing involved one for each channel, and a third for both. Dillinger celebrates Mr Ruddock's almost alchemical powers on "Dub Organiser", and I-Roy also pops up. One of the half-dozen dub albums that should be in any reggae collection.

PRINCE BUSTER PRODUCTIONS

● **The Message Dub Wise** (Fab, UK).
In contrast to his old rivals Coxsone and Duke Reid, the Prince did not rely on rocksteady rhythms for this, his only dub album. Instead he concentrated on rhythms of more recent vintage. Perhaps even more surprising to those who associate him only with the

1960s, a pronounced 'Far East' feel manifests itself on the opening three tracks: "Swing Low" (a cut of Big Youth's "Revolution Come"), a percussion-heavy version of the Abyssinians' "Satta Massa Gana" and "Java Plus" (another mix of Pablove Black's "Science"/"It's A Fire"/"Java"). Closing with a medley of Big Youth's hits for Buster, this album is as enigmatic and extraordinary in its way as *Blackboard Jungle Dub* or *Aquarius Dub*.

Errol 'ET' Thompson

At about the same time as Tubby's groundbreaking experiments, another engineer, **Errol Thompson**, was developing his own style of 'version' sides at Randy's studio on North Parade. Thompson had worked briefly at Studio One in early 1969 under Sylvan Morris, voicing Max Romeo's enormous hit "Wet Dream" for Bunny Lee there. Unable to get on with Morris, he moved to Randy's, where he completely rebuilt the studio. There he recorded some of the most successful Jamaican music of the next six years, including much of the work of such producers as Lee Perry, Bunny Lee and Winston 'Niney' Holness.

Photographer and reggae journalist Dave Hendley summed up the main difference between Tubby's approach and ET's in terms of the equipment they had at their disposal: "It would be unfair to credit Tubby with the invention of recorded dub, as Errol Thompson was at the same time pioneering bass and drum at Randy's Studio 17 with a great deal of success. But Tubby's was managing to refine the sound using faders, delay echo and a phase shifter to bend the music still further." Thompson was reliant on having to push buttons, rather than sliding tracks smoothly in and out of the mix (as Tubby was able to do to such great effect). Nonetheless, on tracks like the version side to Lloyd Parkes' "Ordinary Man" (Impact), mixed in 1973, Thompson was able to introduce novel sounds – backwards-running and slowed-down vocal tracks – to great effect. This was a precursor of the work he mixed for Joe Gibbs at his new studio on Retirement Road, after the Chin family, Randy's owners, relocated to the USA in mid-decade. In 1974, while still at Randy's, he mixed the *Dub Serial* set for Gibbs; the following year the first of the *African Dub* series appeared. Both sets were characterized by their relative restraint, compared to the dubs which would follow during the next phase.

CLIVE CHIN PRODUCTIONS

⦿ Java Java Java Java (Impact!, JA).

The original Errol Thompson-mixed *Java Java Java Java* set is legendary, not only for being one of the first dub albums ever released, but as one built around a version of Pablo's classic of the same title. Among the

BALPE BRADLEY/KAYA RECORDS

Dubbing at Randy's: from left, Dennis Thompson, Errol Thompson (with phone), Clive Chin and Augustus Pablo

other rhythms given fairly basic but effective dubwise treatments are the Heptones' second cut of "Guiding Star", Junior Byles' "King Of Babylon", and the marvellous Randy's treatment of the Soul Vendors' "Swing Easy". The mixing might seem primitive by later standards, but, like all the best early dub sets, it brings out the essential strength of the rhythms employed. A second variation of the album appeared fifteen years later, on a white-label UK pressing.

● **Randy's Dub** (Impact!, JA).
The second dub excursion from the Chin/Thompson partnership gains from the use of more advanced techniques and studio equipment, and displays just as much of Errol Thompson's imagination on versions of then-recent hits, such as Carl Malcolm's enormous "Miss Wire Waist" and "No Jestering".

Dub from the roots: Augustus Pablo and Yabby You

Singer/producer **Vivian 'Yabby You' Jackson**, who was consistently making heavy-duty roots records (see pp.155–157), had been encouraged by Tubby from the beginning of his career in music. Indeed it was Tubby who gave the singer/producer his *nom de disque* of Yabby You, after the chorus on one of his earliest tunes. Jackson also had Tubby mix the version sides of his self-produced singles, as well as the *Prophecy Of Dub* album, originally released in the UK early in 1976, in a pressing of 500 copies and with a blank sleeve. Yabby You's majestic rhythms were ideal for Tubby's mixing style; over the deep basslines of such as **'Family Man' Barrett** and **Robbie Shakespeare**, Tubby created mixes saturated in delay and reverb effects, which gave the impression of sounds – snatches of vocal, guitar chords, organ stabs, etc – coming across vast distances. In addition, Tubby was responsible for the half-dozen dubs on the vocal/version set variously titled *Chant Down Babylon Kingdom*, *Walls Of Jerusalem* and *King Tubby Meets Vivian Jackson*. The producer used Tubby's studio until 1981, when a crippling arthritic condition forced him to stop recording. In the 1990s, his health improved, he began recording again (he collaborated with UK-based dub master Mad Professor for a couple of sets) as well as repressing his vintage material.

Tubby mixed the earliest releases on the Hot Stuff and Rockers labels run by instrumentalist/producer **Augustus Pablo** (see pp.158–161), who cut many specials for Tubby's sound system, including "Spangler's Clap", a tribute to the well-known bad-man posse that followed the sound before the police destroyed it in early 1975. That year in the UK, Island released "King Tubbys Meets Rockers Uptown", the B-side of **Jacob Miller**'s Pablo-produced "Baby I Love You So". It was a record that introduced many outside of the reggae world to dub, as Island actually issued the dub as the A-side; however, it wasn't until 1976 that the best of the Pablo/Tubby collaborations were compiled on the album that many see as a high point of the entire dub genre: *King Tubbys Meets Rockers Uptown*. The tough rhythms spurred King Tubby on to some of his most imaginative work, with Pablo's plaintive melodica phrases echoed to infinity in the spacey mixes. Other Pablo dub albums almost equalled this, particularly the dub set to Hugh Mundell's "Africa Must Be Free By 1983", with

the majority of the rhythms built at Lee Perry's Black Ark studio and mixed by Prince Jammy at Tubby's. Like Yabby You, Pablo's most artistically successful period coincided with the reign of Tubby's studio as the leader in dub technique – basically, up to the early 1980s.

VIVIAN JACKSON PRODUCTIONS

◑ **King Tubby's Prophecy Of Dub** (Blood & Fire, UK).
E The first dub set on which Tubby took apart and reassembled Yabby You's rhythms, tackling most of the early classics from the singer/producer, several of which were collected on the pioneering *Conquering Lion*. Not unexpectedly, the rhythm for "Conquering Lion" itself crops up, alongside impressive versions of "Run Come Rally" and "Jah

Vengeance", as well as the Jackson-produced Michael Rose gem, "Born Free". The CD adds two equally worthwhile dub sides of much-sought-after instrumentals: "Revenge" and "Death Trap".

Beware (Grove Music, UK).
Three years after the historic *Prophecy Of Dub*, this strikingly packaged set included mixes by Prince Jammy, as well as Tubby himself, that emphasized just how important percussion and horns were to Yabby You's music.

Michael Prophet & Vivian Jackson In Dub (Vivian Jackson [Yabby You], JA).
The track that sold this set, which preceded Prophet's debut vocal album, was "Mash Down Rome". An additional highlight is "Zambia Dub", a cut of "Shank I Shek" that propelled Jammy's first official single release in 1977. Entirely mixed by Prince Jammy, and another rough album that kept interest in dub alive as new styles emerged in the dancehall.

AUGUSTUS PABLO PRODUCTIONS

King Tubbys Meets Rockers Uptown (Yard, JA; Clocktower, US).
Augustus Pablo was among the first producers to employ Tubby-mixed dub sides on his 45s, and their first album together was an instant classic. The title track, the version to Jacob Miller's "Baby I Love You So", became more popular than the vocal side, and remains many people's choice for the definitive Tubby's side. Versions to other Pablo-produced singles – Paul Whiteman's "Say So", the Heptones' "Love Won't Come Easy" and Bongo Pat's "Young Generation" – prove just as impressive.

Rockers Meet King Tubby Ina Firehouse (Yard, JA; Shanachie, US).
Mixes by Tubby, Pablo himself and Prince Jammy of some of the best of the later Rockers/Message material – Hugh Mundell's "Little Short Man" and "Jah Says the Time Has Come", Pablo's melodica treatment of Burt Bacharach's "A House Is Not A Home", Delroy Williams's "Foxhole" and Asher & Trimble's "Humble Yourself". Not ground-breaking, but very satisfying.

Africa Must Be Free By 1983 (Message, JA; Greensleeves, UK).

Eastman Dub (Greensleeves, UK).

One Step Dub (Rockers International, JA; Greensleeves, UK).
These Pablo dub sets are all drum and bass counterparts to well-received vocal albums – respectively, Hugh Mundell's *Africa Must Be Free By 1983*, Tetrack's *Let's Get Started* and Junior Delgado's *One Step More*.

Lee Perry

Interestingly, **Lee Perry** was not as prolific as might have been expected during the boom years for dub albums. However, he pioneered the form with bass-heavy instrumentals like "Clint Eastwood" and "Sipreano", as well as some of King Tubby's earliest mixes on 7", including "French Connection", "Ipa Skank" and "Dub Organiser", as well as sets like *Blackboard Jungle* and *Rhythm Shower* (both 1973). He was also responsible for instrumental sets that can be considered proto-dub, such as *Cloak & Dagger* (1972).

ADRIAN BOOT

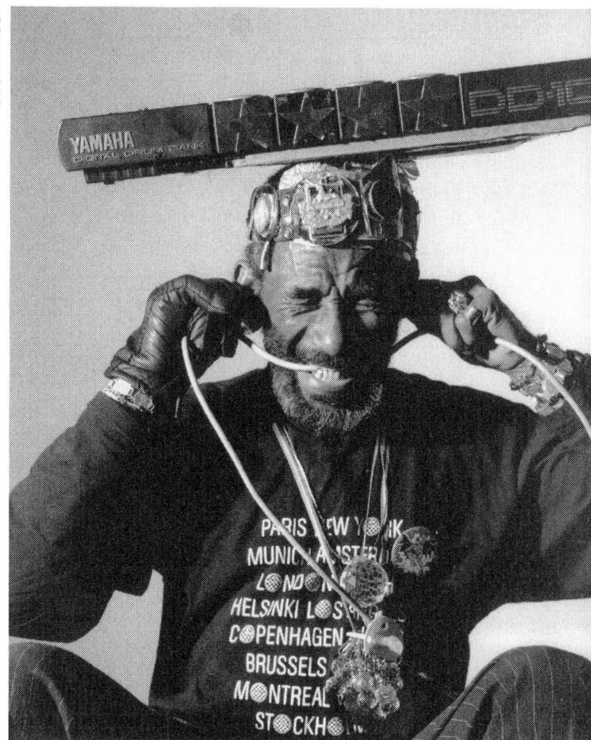

Flossing with Scratch

When he moved into his new studio, he issued further instrumental albums like *Return Of Wax* and *Musical Bones* (1974), but the first pure dub album to come from the Ark was *Revolution Dub*, from 1975. The subsequent *Super Ape* (1976) wasn't a typical dub outing by any means, being an atmospheric solo album from the producer, saturated with dub techniques like reverb and delay; far from stripping the tracks down to their essentials, Perry added layers of sound, including a female chorus, a couple of Heptones, his own vocals and even a Prince Jazzbo toast. Hailed as a *tour de force* by much of the new crossover audience, it disappointed some of his older fans, who were perhaps hoping to hear another raw Tubby-mixed extravaganza in the style of *Blackboard Jungle*. After all, Tubby was still mixing at least some of the 'version' sides to

Perry's singles at the beginning of 1975 – most notably the classic dub to Max Romeo's "Three Blind Mice". Yet, judged on its own terms, *Super Ape* was one of the most progressive and imaginative sets of its time.

Subsequently, Scratch made no more dub albums, although his Black Ark-produced singles continued to carry his trademark dubs – one of his favourite tricks was to take a half-syllable of vocal, throw it into echo and use it to punctuate the mix. The sound that Perry achieved at Black Ark is unmistakable: like Tubby, Scratch was seemingly able to invest his dub mixes with a feeling of wide open space, all the more remarkable taking into account the size of the room, a twelve-foot square box. When he destroyed the studio in 1979, this unique and wonderful sound was lost for ever, although Scratch has had a profound influence on such modern remixers as Adrian Sherwood and the UK 'new roots' producers.

LEE PERRY PRODUCTIONS

◑ **Super Ape** (Upsetter, JA; Island, UK).

E A superb album-length expression of Scratch's vision and technical wizardry. Fortunately the eccentricities with which Perry was to be increasingly associated were kept in check, and the result is a very disciplined, multi-textured exploration of sound. Those who dismissed it for being over-produced missed the point entirely.

◑ **Revolution Dub** (Cactus, UK).

This was released in 1975 and featured some of the first rhythms produced at the Black Ark. British actor James Robertson Justice from the TV sitcom *Doctor In the House* makes appearances every so often (well, Perry was always keen on the odd medical metaphor). Highlights include cuts of Junior Byles' "The Long Way", and a superbly minimal dub of Jimmy Riley's Bobby Womack cover, "Woman's Gotta Have It".

◉ **Upsetter In Dub** (Heartbeat, US)

Strong selection of Black Ark dubs, although the inclusion of a couple of tracks from the early 1970s spoils the overall coherence. With six previously unreleased cuts, this set is a good showcase both for Scratch's Black Ark mixing style (admittedly somewhat limited when compared to King Tubby) and the rugged, moody rhythms he was making there.

Clement Dodd at the dub store

The foundation producer, **Clement Dodd**, of course possessed a far larger stock of classic rhythms than anyone, and from 1974 to 1980 he released a series of twelve Studio One dub albums, all of which are worth at least a listen. As Dodd's talented recording engineer, Sylvan Morris (see p.218), left Brentford Road before the series began, it is likely that Studio One's

DAVID CORIO

Coxsone Dodd outside his Brooklyn store

owner mixed all of these himself. In the final analysis, the mixes on these sets are not really what is most interesting about them. Rather, the albums tend to make it on the strength of the Studio One rhythms, which, however arbitrary their treatment at the mixing-board, always shine through on purely musical grounds. Any developments in the mixing style – on the earlier sets, tracks are dropped in and out in fairly rudimentary fashion – seem largely dependent on what new equipment Dodd had at hand at the time, which at least prevents the albums from sounding too uniform.

CLEMENT DODD PRODUCTIONS

Dub Store Special (Studio One, JA).

E The one essential Studio One dub album. This is partly because of the immaculate selection of rhythms, but also the degree to which the contributions of the musicians – tenorman Cedric 'Im' Brooks and trombonist Vin Gordon, in particular – are allowed space, making this the most musical of the series.

Hi Fashion Dub Top Ten (Studio One, UK).

One of the first Studio One dub albums, and still among the best. The title track is a version of Jackie Mittoo's "One Step Beyond" – indeed "Hi Fashion" has become as well known a title for the much-recorded rhythm.

Better Dub (Studio One, JA).

Rhythms of the calibre of Big Willie's "College Rock", Larry Marshall's "Mean Girl" and the Heptones' "How Can I Leave", mixed down to their essentials. No further recommendation is required.

Sample Dub (Winro, JA).

Rhythms range from the Eternals' "Queen Of the Minstrels" to Horace Andy's more sombre "Love Of A Woman". Includes another rare example of a dub title that became almost as well known as the original hit – "Teasing", a version of the Brentford Road cut of Jo Jo Bennett's "The Lecture".

Bionic Dub (Forward, JA).

The most unforgettable tracks here are probably the versions of the instrumental "Red Blood", "Darker Shade Of Black" and "Exodus", though strong rhythms and intelligent mixing are featured throughout.

Mellow Sounds & Systems [Mellow Dub] (Studio One, JA).

Possibly the most serious in mood of Coxsone's dub albums, with superlative versions of Burning Spear's "Creation Rebel", Horace Andy's "Just Say Who", Slim Smith's "Rougher Yet" and – the surprise of the set – Bob Marley's ska-ballad "Cry To Me".

Roots Dub (Winro/Studio One, JA).

Again, the choice of rhythms is excellent – the Heptones' "Love Me Girl", Alton Ellis's "I'm Just A Guy" and Jackie Mittoo's "Our Thing" to name three – and the mixing is decidedly more adventurous than on previous sets in the series. One for those whose tastes lean more to heavier reggae rhythms rather than rocksteady.

Ital Sounds & System [Ital Dub] (Studio One, JA).

The Eternals' "Stars", Alton Ellis's "Still Trying" and the Heptones' "I Hold the Handle" are among the better-known tracks versioned here. But more surprising rhythms such as Alton Ellis's "Your Heart Is Gonna Pay", Roland Alphonso's "Jazz Rocksteady", the Ethiopians' "What A Fire" and Theophilus Beckford's glorious boogie, "Jack & Jill Shuffle", are just as delightful.

Zodiac Sounds (Forward, JA).

An echo unit was Coxsone's new toy when he worked on these tracks, so the set is noticeably different from its predecessors and more in the dub mainstream. Even the best-known rhythms – such as "Swing Easy", "I'm Still In Love With You" and "Freedom Blues" sound refreshingly different.

Juk's Incorporation (Studio One, JA/US).

Juk's Incorporation Part Two (Studio One, JA).

The first of these two can be heard in digital clarity, and with extra tracks. Both are well worth picking up in any format, with yet more classic Brentford Road rhythms put through their paces The second part, incidentally, also features a fine Lone Ranger toast on the Heptones' "Get In the Groove" rhythm.

African Rub A Dub (Studio One, JA).

A 1979 set, and the last dub album that Coxsone himself released, this has much the same sound as the superb vocal albums he released in this period by the likes of Johnny Osbourne and Freddie McGregor. A strong selection of rhythms, including a dynamite piece of "African Beat". Many of the mixes subsequently turned up on cassettes and live dancehall recordings during the early 1980s.

◉ **Dub Specialist: 17 Dub Shots From Studio One** (Heartbeat, US).

This CD is not a digitally enhanced reissue of a 1970s album, but a well-chosen selection of Studio One dub versions, drawing from both the *Zodiac Sounds* and *Sample Dub* sets, as well as long-unavailable 45s.

Bunny and the dub master

Bunny Lee was the major patron of Tubby's until Channel One and Joe Gibbs wrested dancehall supremacy from him. The huge number of productions that Tubby mixed for Bunny is enough to support this contention, but Bunny also had a qualitative influence on Tubby's style, for he encouraged him to mix in an ever wilder way. As Bunny once said to the dub master: "Yes, Tubbs, madness – the people dem like it!"

Tubby's mixes for Bunny sometimes came complete with sudden and momentous thunder effects (created by striking the spring reverb unit), the sound of the tape being rewound to build up tension, and either the bass or the hi-hat being emphasized for almost intolerable periods. Indeed, the 'flying cymbals' sound that drummer Carlton 'Santa' Davis developed for Bunny Lee seemed made for Tubby's radical deconstructions.

Lee's productions were issued either as the B-sides or, following those already mentioned, as albums like the very popular *Dub From the Roots, Creation Of Dub* (aka *King Tubby Meets the Aggrovators At Dub Station*) and *Roots Of Dub*. Some of the dub albums Bunny and Tubby put out were relatively unexciting, but when the rhythms were above average and Tubby was not just going through the motions, the results were explosive – even psychedelic. Equally strong examples of dubs which created at least as much interest as the vocals they accompanied were the more developed King Tubby's extravaganzas that appeared on Bunny Lee's many labels, primarily Jackpot, Attack and Justice, from 1974 onwards. Johnny Clarke's 45s for Striker always seemed especially well served in this respect – the singer's distinctive tenor seemed particularly suitable for the dub treatment, with the versions to songs like "Blood Dunza", "Declaration Of Rights", "Don't Trouble Trouble", "Crazy Baldhead" and "Poor Marcus" standing out as landmarks of the dub territory. From late 1976 most of Bunny's productions were mixed by Prince Jammy (see p.202); Tubby mixed less and less as the 1970s went on, and newer engineers, like the teenage Scientist (see pp.223–224), emerged at the controls of the mixing desk at 18 Dromilly Avenue.

BUNNY LEE PRODUCTIONS

◑ **Dub Gone Crazy: The Evolution Of Dub At King Tubby's 1975–1979** (Blood & Fire, UK).

◑ **Dub Gone 2 Crazy: In Fine Style (1975–79)** (Blood & Fire, UK).

Ⓔ Two volumes retrospectively compiled of prime Bunny Lee material dubbed almost to oblivion. Both comprise 'version' sides from impossible-to-find 45s (Wayne Jarrett's "Satta Dread" and

Ronnie Davies's "Power Of Love", to mention just one exceptional track from each), as well as previously unreleased tracks drawn from Lee's master tapes. They utilize the mixing talents of not only Tubby himself, but also of his disciples 'Prince' Philip Smart, Lloyd 'Prince Jammy' James and Hopeton 'Scientist' Brown, all working at Tubby's Dromilly Avenue studio. As overviews of the work done there, they are perhaps the best places for the newcomer to either Tubby or Striker to start.

- **Creation Of Dub [King Tubby Meets the Aggrovators At Dub Station]** (Total Sounds, JA; Live & Love, UK).

The strongest of the 'flying cymbals' dub albums, thanks to the generous space allowed Tommy McCook's horn arrangements and an exceptional selection of rhythms, from the opening version of "Creation Rebel" to the end of the set.

- **Rockers Almighty Dub** (Clocktower, US).

Appearing a few years later, this disavowed the gimmicks then prevalent for very musical workouts of some of Bunny's most exceptional hits, including Dennis Brown's "Lately Girl", Horace Andy's "Zion Gate" and Johnny Clarke's heavyweight "Blood Dunza".

Channel One and Joe Gibbs

From late 1975 both the new frontrunners in Jamaican music – **Joe Gibbs** and **Joseph 'Joe Joe' Hookim** – had remarkable success with dub sides and albums of their updated recuts of Studio One and Treasure Isle classics.

The Hookim brothers had moved into recording from jukebox and gambling machine distribution, building Channel One studio on Maxfield Avenue in 1972. By 1973 the studio was operational, with engineer Syd Bucknor in charge of recording, assisted by Ernest Hookim. "Don't Give Up the Fight" by Stranger & Gladdy was the first release on the Channel One label in 1973, and it sold moderately well. Nevertheless, the sound of the studio was not right. Although they had an MCI high-pass filter which let the bass frequencies through, this equipment was not actually being utilized by Bucknor. The deejay **I-Roy** – who was fully tuned in to the sound-system world, having deejayed King Tubby's Hi-Fi when U-Roy was not available – encouraged the Hookims to visit Tubby's to observe for themselves the effect of the same piece of studio outboard in operation there. Subsequently, I-Roy became unofficial house producer at Channel One.

When I-Roy and Joe Joe suggested to drummer **Sly Dunbar** that he make a 'clap' sound on his snare, the result, combined with the improved bass response, was enough to impart just the right amount of freshness to the vintage rhythms updated by I-Roy and the Revolutionaries. These rhythm tracks supported highly successful new vocals, by such outfits as the Mighty Diamonds, but were at least as viable in their stripped-down – and sometimes augmented – forms. Blazing, horns-dominated singles credited to the Revolutionaries, including "MPLA" (also used for Tappa Zukie's popular deejay record with the same title), "IRA", "Angola" and "SNCC" displayed dub techniques on their A-side mixes (the straight instrumentals were relegated to the B-side) which emphasized to maximum effect Sly Dunbar's ground-breaking drumming style and **Robbie Shakespeare**'s equally assured basslines.

Channel One also played a pioneering role in employing dubbed-up rhythm tracks on their vocal records, like the heavy reverb used on the backing for the Meditations' "Woman Is Like A Shadow" or the distinctive klaxon sound effect on John Holt's "Up Park Camp". Joseph's brother Ernest is usually credited with the slightly more drastic remixes of these and many other Channel One rhythms issued on the popular series of dub albums that appeared on the Well Charge label. I-Roy, however, confirmed years later that he had also been heavily involved in these sessions.

When the fashion for dub LPs began to subside towards the end of the decade, the Hookim brothers economized and placed just four different dub tracks – usually titled as variants of a theme – on EP-style 12" singles,. The studio's no-nonsense approach was perhaps best expressed by the titles they used on one disc in the series of dub 12" they issued during 1977–78: "Headache"/"Bellyache"/ "Toothache"/"Heartache".

Former Randy's engineer **Errol Thompson** livened things up yet further (or, some would say, vulgarized the form) with generous use of sound effects such as car horns, barking dogs, ringing telephones and running water, on his dub sides for Joe Gibbs. Even if these effects are not to your taste there's no denying the assured nature of their studio band – essentally the Channel One **Revolutionaries**, usually substituting Lloyd Parkes for Robbie Shakespeare on bass – and their reinterpretations of much of Jamaica's foundation music. Keyboards player **Ossie Hibbert** effectively produced the musicians, while Thompson, if not as innovative as Tubby or Jammy, showed little signs of losing his deft touch at the mixing-board – the music always remained much more than the gimmicks that were tagged on (and helped sell it to a wider audience). The second and third volumes of Gibbs' *African Dub* series sold by the cartload, and remain amongst the best-remembered dub albums of the period.

JOSEPH 'JOE JOE' HOOKIM PRODUCTIONS

● **Vital Dub Strictly Rockers** (Well Charge, JA & US; Virgin, UK).

Ⓔ When the Revolutionaries became the premier studio band in Kingston, the Hookim brothers maximized the return from their popular rhythms by releasing a series of fine dub albums. The most successful was *Vital Dub*, which took nine out of the ten tracks from the Mighty Diamonds' *Right Time/Need A Roof* LP, and showed why no one else at the time was touching the Channel One 'rockers' sound. The dub album that more than any other established Sly & Robbie's names.

● **Revival Dub Roots Now** (Well Charge, JA).

Another excellent selection of rhythms, including the recut of "College Rock" employed for Leroy Smart's massive "Ballistic Affair", alongside versions of the Heptones' "Fight It To the Top" and the Wailing Souls' "Back Out"/"Things & Time". The mixes throughout highlight Sly's furious drumming to particularly good effect, with horns blazing their militant way to the forefront to keep things interesting.

● **Satta Dub Strictly Roots** (Well Charge, JA).

Beginning with a version of Earth & Stone's powerful "In Time To Come", *Satta Dub* is the one for those who prefer the even heavier style developed in 1977 by the Revolutionaries at what had become the island's leading studio.

● **Revolutionaries Sounds** (Well Charge, JA).

With its striking cover picture of Che Guevara, this is a wonderful example of instru-dub, featuring slightly different mixes of the Revolutionaries' hit instrumental 45s, including "MPLA", "Leftist" and "Angola".

JOE GIBBS & ERROL THOMPSON PRODUCTIONS

● **African Dub All Mighty Chapters 1, 2 & 3** (Joe Gibbs Record Globe/Rocky One, JA).

Ⓔ Three albums that decisively helped to popularize dub; the first two within the existing reggae market, and the third beyond it to disparate groups like punks and experimental rock fans. The formula was the same on all three: mainly Studio One and Treasure Isle rhythms updated by the Professionals in the 'rockers' style, and given imaginative mixes by Errol Thompson. The more obvious gimmicks – telephones ringing, toilets being flushed, the odd siren, dogs barking, etc – became more prominent as the series progressed and reached a wider audience. The perspective of time has treated all three albums well.

OSSIE HIBBERT PRODUCTIONS

⊙ Earthquake Dub (Joe Gibbs Record Globe, JA).
Ossie Hibbert is credited as co-producer, which probably means that Joe Gibbs really had very little to do with it, even if the sound is remarkably similar to the second and third in the *African Dub* series. Using the same musicians – Sly and bassist Lloyd Parkes prominent among them – and Gibbs' studio, this is best seen as a more militant extension of those sets. Solid, stepping dub in the style favoured by the dread youth of the last half of the 1970s.

Dub explosion

By the end of 1976 the initial trickle of dub albums had become a flood, and in the summer of the next year it was possible for the UK music weekly *Black Echoes* to publish a three-part article on the genre that included a chart of 125 recommended albums. Some of the sets copied Tubby's style of reverb and echo, while others often consisted of little more than the rhythm tracks with bass and drum 'drop-out' featured. While the earliest dub sides had featured effective but fairly minimal reorderings of the original instrumental mixes, by mid-decade improved studio equipment and the enthusiasm of dancehall crowds for the form led to far wilder remixes. By 1977, virtually every producer had his or her own dub album(s) on sale or were about to release them, and a variety of styles were on offer – based on the divergent kinds of rhythms employed, from rocksteady originals to Pablovian rockers, and the different approaches of the engineers reworking them.

Vintage rhythms, new dub

Errol Brown, a nephew of Duke Reid, had been a junior engineer at his studio and became the senior man after the Duke's death, when Sonia Pottinger took over. He remixed the old rocksteady and early reggae masterpieces, most of which, of course, had already enjoyed a second lease of life through the U-Roy, Dennis Alcapone and Lizzy deejay versions at the dawn of the 1970s. As with those successful deejay cuts, almost all the stripped-down dub versions of Treasure Isle hits retained snatches of the original vocals – pointing to the nostalgia element that was part of dub's initial appeal. Not only were vintage basslines eminently suited to being dubbed up, but voices such as those of Pat Kelly, John Holt or Alton Ellis sounded even more astonishing – even haunting – as echo effects made them disappear into themselves. Brown, who went on to become resident engineer at Tuff Gong studios in the 1980s, also showed himself to be a dab hand at dubbing up Mrs Pottinger's mid–late 1970s productions.

When former Technique **Winston Riley** issued his first dub set in 1976, this too comprised mostly rhythms from the turn of the decade, and mixed in a very similar style. **Derrick Harriott** was another producer who dug out his rocksteady and early reggae rhythm tracks for a couple of excellent dub albums which characteristically retained the very musical qualities of the original hits; indeed the second of the albums was among those that inspired the naming of a further sub-genre, 'instru-dub' (records that bordered on being traditional instrumental albums), and highlighted the talents of the rest of the musicians involved at least as much as the bass player's.

Harry Mudie similarly took time and care over his records, and his classy productions always seemed to have the potential for international appeal. The three dub albums he made with King Tubby are outstanding for highlighting both the strength of his refined rhythms and Tubby's skills at the mixing-board.

DERRICK HARRIOTT PRODUCTIONS

⊙ Scrub-A-Dub (Crystal, JA).
Not the dub set for those who expect the man at the controls to perform an Armageddon job on the original tracks, or to hear outrageous gimmicks every few seconds. Dating from 1974, this is a fairly typical early

dub album, consisting of some of the producer's biggest hits (among them "Shaft", "Know Far I", "Penny For Your Song") reduced to their component parts – mostly just drum and bass, with the odd piece of quite nifty keyboard work.

More Scrubbing the Dub (Crystal, JA).
Issued the following year, this stands as a superb example of the 'instru-dub' sub-genre, with its main strengths lying in the manner in which the individual contributions of the musicians are highlighted. The rocksteady and early reggae rhythms shown to good advantage include Harriott's own "The Loser", "Eighteen With A Bullet" and "Solomon", Rudy Mills's "Long Story", and Keith & Tex's two greatest hits, "Stop That Train" and "Tonight". No fire and brimstone, but great music treated with some subtlety.

HARRY MUDIE PRODUCTIONS

Harry Mudie Meets King Tubby's In Dub Conference Volumes 1, 2 & 3 (Moodisc, JA; Moods, US).
E Harry Mudie combined the sweetness and the heaviness that have always been integral to Jamaican music, even on occasion successfully integrating lush string arrangements. Tubby mostly made obvious the sheer weight of Mudie's rhythms, but wisely maintained snatches of strings on some tracks. All three volumes of the series rank among the most thoughtfully mixed and original dub albums ever, with the hits most associated with Mudie – Lloyd Jones's "Rome", the Ebony Sisters' "Let Me Tell You Boy", Dennis Walks' "Drifter" and the Heptones' "Love Without Feeling" – emerging all the more awesome.

SONIA POTTINGER & DUKE REID PRODUCTIONS

Treasure Dub Volumes One & Two (High Note/Treasure Isle, JA).
Both these albums, which get reissued on a fairly regular basis, draw from Reid's most popular hits. Though the original tracks span a period from 1966 (Alton Ellis's "Cry Tough") to 1974 (Pat Kelly's "Sunshine"), the mixes make them sound strangely contemporary.

Medley Dub (High Note, JA).
Mixed in similar fashion by Errol Brown, but consisting mainly of Pottinger's own late 1960s productions, the originals of which featured the voices of either Ken Boothe or the Melodians (including those artists' hit medleys – hence the title).

Culture Dub (High Note, JA).
Typical Errol Brown mixes – that is, less florid than Tubby's, but serving to bring out and emphasize the melodic qualities of Sonia Pottinger's late 1970s roots style. Only eight tracks, but fully deserving to have the same number again added to them for CD release.

Dub Over Dub: 27 Track Dub Extravaganza (Heartbeat, US).
This collection has Errol Brown applying his skills to Mrs Pottinger's 1970s hits with just as much effect as on the above set, and should have those not already familiar with them hunting for the full vocals, including Bob Andy's "Ghetto Stays In the Mind", Brent Dowe's "Forward Up" and a fair portion of Marcia Griffiths' 45s on High Note.

WINSTON RILEY PRODUCTIONS

Meditation Dub (Techniques, JA).
Winston Riley has been a hit producer since the 1960s without ever receiving the acclaim that's his due, partly because his style of production is not obviously distinctive and partly because his rhythms are too musical for those who judge dub by its ability to give them a headache. Among the wonderful rocksteady/early reggae rhythms shown to good advantage here are the Techniques' "Love Is Not A Gamble" and 'I'm In the Mood For Love", Johnny Osbourne's "Purify Your Heart" and Riley's most enduring track, the instrumental "Stalag 17". Should appeal to anyone who likes the Treasure Isle dub albums mixed by Errol Brown.

The bandwagon rolls on

There was soon a deluge of albums crediting engineers and mixers as the artists, including work by **Prince Jammy** (b. Lloyd James, 1947, Montego Bay), who was to graduate to being one of the most successful producers ever, **Sylvan Morris**, **'Prince' Philip Smart**, **Hopeton 'Scientist' Brown**, **Maximilian** and **Anthony 'Crucial Bunny' Graham**. Yet quite a few dub workouts appeared without any credit being given to the engineer. In this category falls the King Tubby-mixed **Morwells** masterpiece, *Dub Me*, featuring versions of the vocal group's debut album, as does the far from prolific but astonishingly consistent producer **Jimmy Radway**'s one dub classic, a creation possessing all the hallmarks of a vintage Tubby mix. When the UK company Fay Music released the very popular *King Tubby Meets the Upsetter At the Grass Roots Of Dub* set, the back cover simply pictured the different mixing-boards allegedly used by the two dub masters; by now, the technological process itself was recognized as being at least as important as the engineers – let alone the producer, in this case Joe Gibbs associate Winston Edwards. Astutely marketed by Edwards, the album sold widely, and like the Augustus Pablo single, "King Tubbys Meets Rockers Uptown", it played a part in introducing dub to an audience other than sound-system followers. Subsequent attempts by Edwards to repeat this success fell far short of the mark, and he soon moved on to become a pioneer in recording UK lovers rock (see pp.337–338).

Former member of the Treasure Isle vocal group, the Jamaicans, **Tommy Cowan** further displayed his credentials as a rootsy producer with a popular dub set based on hits from his Sweet City, Starapple, Arab and Talent Jamaican labels. Another figure associated with sweet harmonies over strong rhythm was the Royals' leader, **Roy Cousins**, who, despite having some excellent dubs on the backs of the 7" releases on his Wambesi and Tamoki labels, showed little interest in releasing dub albums at the time (he was very much a believer in traditional musical values). A couple of decades would go by before a collection that did his version sides justice would appear. The fact that a marvellous selection of rhythms was not all that was needed for a totally successful dub LP, however, was demonstrated by the slightly disappointing drum and bass counterpart to Burning Spear's classic *Marcus Garvey* set. This was curious, as the Burning Spear singles released by **Jack Ruby** had all featured strong version sides mixed by Errol Thompson or King Tubby. Presumably someone at Island thought that a mix at Hammersmith, London, was what was required to sell the album to Spear's new audience.

The singer/deejay **Pat Francis/Jah Lloyd** not only consistently made exceptional versions to the singles that he produced for himself – often featuring either Bongo Herman or the trombonist Vin Gordon – but had his strongest rhythms reconstructed at King Tubby's and Randy's for a generally underrated set. Another deejay whose heavyweight dub album impressed even those who were not enthusiastic for his work at the mike was **Tappa Zukie**. The mix of *Tappa Zukie In Dub* was made by **Philip Smart**, who later became a successful recording studio owner and producer in New York, but early in 1976 was still working at King Tubby's. The fact that *Tappa Zukie In Dub* was not released in Jamaica and the initial UK pressing was limited to a few hundred copies only added to its later status among collectors.

In the UK, where from the mid-1970s onwards quite a few dub albums from Kingston were released in advance of Jamaica, **Lloyd Coxsone**, the premier sound-system man of the mid–late 1970s, brought together an excellent LP of his own productions and those of Jamaica's **Gussie Clarke** in true sound-warp style. Mixed at King Tubby's Dromilly Avenue studio in West Kingston and various London locations, they eventually appeared to great effect on Coxsone's Safari imprint in 1975, and pointed to London's continuing importance in the reggae market – particularly for dub.

ROY COUSINS PRODUCTIONS

⦾ **Nexus Dub** (Tamoki/Wambesi, UK).

Many of Roy Cousins's strongest rhythms – for his group, the Royals, and other artists – dubbed up in fine fashion by King Tubby, Crucial Bunny, Sylvan Morris, Errol Thompson, Scientist and Barnabus. Wonderful to hear so many pioneering and contrasting styles on one set.

TOMMY COWAN PRODUCTIONS

◑ **Rass Claat Dub [Dubwise Shower]** (Grounation, UK; Lagoon, France).

The first Tommy Cowan dub set features the strongest rhythms that appeared on his labels in 1975–76, including Leroy Smart's "The Road Is Rough", Ras Michael's "None A Jah Jah Children No

SYLVAN MORRIS AND THE SOUND OF STUDIO ONE

The finest recording engineer ever to work at 13 Brentford Road, Sylvan Morris played a considerable role in creating Studio One's foundation sound. In the mid-1970s he moved to Harry Johnson's studio, where he not only contributed to the success of albums such as Burning Spear's *Dry & Heavy*, but was responsible for some outstanding dub workouts.

"I was considered to be a genius at a very young age. I used to work in telecommunications at a place called Comtec. I was called at that time the "Reporter Professor". Because there was a two-way radio by the name of the Reporter, and I was considered to be a genius at fixing these radios. So, Byron [Lee] heard about me, and he sent and asked me if I would like to work with him. So I came, and I was given some training, in the actual music sense, engineering from an audio point of view. I was there for a short time, and then I left.

I went first to Duke Reid. I was there for a short period, about seven, eight months, then went to Coxsone. He had a two-track – everything then was two tracks, Ampex machines. Coxsone had a long console with eight inputs. So we actually recorded, say, drum and bass on one track, and the rest of the rhythm on another. Sometimes we would do like horns; sometimes we didn't want horns. Again we mix everything onto one track of the two-track, and then the horns on another. Then we went from there to another two-track to voice. From the time I went by Coxsone's studio he recognised me for being very sufficient for whatever he had to do. So most of the time he wasn't really even in the studio. When it come to recording, I used to have a lot of input. Sometimes I would say what bass line to play. And if he don't see me dancing, he stop play and say 'Wha happen?' And I say: 'Well, I don't like what the drum sound.' Or: 'I don't like the bass.' In terms of the singers, I was very strict on lyrical perfection. So if a singer came and he wasn't perfect in what he was doing, he had to go home and practise. They used to rely on me for that sort of input.

When I went to Studio One, Jackie Mittoo impressed me in what he was doing, arranging and everything. But he left shortly after I went there. And some other musicians came. Robbie Lynn, if the tune needed a keyboards

Cry", and the Cimarons' version of Marley's "Talking Blues". Strong dub in a strictly roots and culture style. The French CD issue links it with the Jimmy Radway set discussed below.

LLOYD COXSONE PRODUCTIONS

⦾ **King Of the Dub Rock Parts One & Two** (Tribesman/Greensleeves, UK).

Both of the dub albums from London sound-system operator/record producer Lloyd Coxsone brought together in a value-for-money package. The first employs rhythms from Gussie Clarke in Kingston and some built by London-based musicians (mostly from Dennis Bovell's Matumbi band). The stylistic gap between them is not as great as might be imagined, with versions of Don Hutchinson's sombre "What You Gonna Do", Delroy Wilson's sublime "Love" and Louisa Marks's "Caught You In A Lie" coexisting happily. The second set, which did not appear until 1982, is in a heavier mode, with some mixes by Scientist, and is slightly spoilt by the rather dated spoken intros. Standing up to repeated plays are raw versions of Creation Steppers and Fred Locks music, as well as the 'steppers' cuts of the ska classic "Confucius" and Burning Spear's "Travelling".

WINSTON EDWARDS PRODUCTIONS

● **King Tubby Meets the Upsetter At the Grassroots Of Dub** (Total Sounds, JA; Fay, UK).

The set that, more than any other, established the dub album in the UK. Curiously enough, neither the producer nor most of the rhythms were particularly well known, although a cut of the Morwells' version of the Melodians standard "Come On Little Girl" is instantly recognizable. However, the UK release did boast an eye-catching cover – albeit in economical black and white.

PAT FRANCIS PRODUCTIONS

● **Herb Dub** (Micron, JA; DIP/Teem, UK).

Pat Francis/Jah Lloyd was a gifted producer, as well as singer/deejay. His first dub album stood out on account of its colourful sleeve, but the music more

TERO KASHI/MORE AXE

Sylvan Morris: "I was considered to be a genius at a very young age"

player, had a lot of qualities that was very good. Then again, Leroy Sibbles – he and myself were the two main factors for a lot of this music that they're even doing over now. Because he's a very great bass player and writer. And he did a lot of co-ordination when it came to harmonies. Eric Frater, the guitarist, was extraordinary in being very steady on the rhythm. It was a guitar sound that he created and it was brought about by a piece of equipment called the Sound Dimension. It was a catalyst that he moved manually to get the chicka-ta-chick, and eventually he created the sound himself, without the piece of equipment.

In Coxsone's studio I actually created a sound, a bass sound. There was an electro-voice mike which had a very unique bass sound. What happen was the ribbon for it got broke one night, and they couldn't find a another one. So I created a ribbon from one of the tapes. On the end of the tape, you have a piece of silver tape, and I took that and made a ribbon out of it, and put it into the mike. And it seemed to know just how to respond to the right bass frequency. I also designed a box. I remember when listening to speakers, I always notice the back of the bass speaker always get a rounder sound. So I create a box with a support whereby I put the mikes on the back, and that's where I got most of the bass sound heard when I was at Coxsone's. ❞

than lived up to its promise. All the rhythms that he used repeatedly for 45s ("Ain't No Sunshine", "Shame & Pride", etc) are rinsed through yet again – and with good reason. The highlight, though, is a stunning version of Yabby You's "Conquering Lion", using the original rhythm track. The only quibble about the repress is that it comes with artwork that's distinctly inferior to the original.

JIMMY RADWAY PRODUCTIONS

◑ **Untitled [Dubwise Shower]** (Micron, JA; Lagoon, France).

Jimmy 'One Foot' Radway's name has never meant anything outside the Kingston studio scene, but in the mid-1970s he was a remarkably consistent, if hardly prolific, producer, who particularly knew how to employ horns effectively. A collection of his hits with the singers Leroy Smart, Errol Dunkley and Desmond Young is still badly needed; in the meantime, these versions of the same roots classics constitute one of the hardest dub albums ever released. The French CD issue links it with the Tommy Cowan set discussed above.

TAPPA ZUKIE PRODUCTIONS

◑ **Tappa Zukie In Dub** (Blood & Fire, UK).
When it was not serving as an outlet for his own deejay efforts, Tappa Zukie's Stars label issued heavyweight roots vocals from the likes of Ras/Prince Alla, Junior Ross & the Spears, Lynford Nugent and Horace Andy. This 1976 dub set confirms just how fine a producer Tappa was – these rhythms were all over the dances in 1976. Philip Smart at the mixing-board in Tubby's studio brings out qualities you might not have known existed in favourites such as Ras Alla's "Bosrah", Tappa's own "MPLA", Junior Ross's "Judgement Time" and a couple of Linval Thompson tunes courtesy of Bunny Lee. Bonus tracks on the CD are excellent dubs to Junior Ross's "So Jah Jah Say" and "Send Me Over There".

Sylvan Morris: "You had to improvise . . ."

Sylvan Morris, the recording engineer who had been largely responsible for the distinctive recorded sound of Studio One, left the employ of Clement Dodd just as the dub craze was about to take off. He then joined Harry Johnson, mixing early 'version' sides on singles and a couple of dub albums under his own name (*Morris In Dub* and *Cultural Dub*), versioning all over again the classic originals he had recorded at Studio One. In a 1989 interview he remembered the period well: "The dub thing was just coming to the fullness at that time... it was brought about to a degree by the sound men. They came and they wanted probably just a rhythm, a particular rhythm, and if you gave it to one man, another would want a different version. So you had to improvise – you had to give some a little bass and drum – every one of them sound different. This is how the drum and bass thing come about."

Morris also played an important engineering role later in the decade, recording three Burning Spear albums, *Man In the Hills*, *Dry & Heavy* and *Marcus' Children*. He was also responsible for Spear's *Living Dub* sets which featured remixed versions of the tracks on *Marcus' Children*, and the *Hail H.I.M.* set which followed it, in addition to mixing the first two Bunny Wailer dubs. Though Morris made only a handful of dub albums (his forte was recording, rather than remixing), he did engineer some subtle and atmospheric 7" version sides. The dubs on late 1970s records like the Light of Saba's "Lambs Bread Collie" (Light Of Saba), Burning Spear's "Bad To Worse" (Burning Spear) and Peter Tosh's melodica instrumental "Anti Apartheid" (Solomonic) were far removed from the more outrageous dubonic antics of the time, but stand up to repeated listening far better. Several of Big Youth's self-produced singles also have strong version sides by Morris, and the *Reggae Gi Dem Dub* album (the dub counterpart to the deejay/vocal set, *Progress*) further displayed the strength of the deejay's later self-produced rhythms. Since the mid-1980s Morris has supervised cassette manufacture for Dynamic Records in Kingston.

HARRY JOHNSON PRODUCTIONS

● **Jah Jah Dub** (Roosevelt, JA).
Sylvan Morris is in typically fine form at the mixing-board, while Joe White blows the melodica in more assured style than usual on this excellent slice of instru-dub, using musicians from the Soul Syndicate and leading sessioneers like Leslie Butler. The title track, which is a medley of recut Johnny Clarke tunes, takes up the entire first side, while the second side comprises a more conventional five tracks, including a version of Junior Byles' "Curly Locks" that is arguably rougher than the Scratch original.

WINSTON RODNEY PRODUCTIONS

Living Dub Volumes One & Two (Burning Spear, JA).

E The Burning Spear vocal albums *Social Living/Marcus Children* and *Hail H.I.M.* are essential to any roots collection, and their dub versions no less so. In keeping with Mr Rodney's taste for country living, Morris allows plenty of space around instruments and voice as they fade in and out of the mix. Quite eerie, at times, particularly when Winston Rodney's disembodied voice floats across the mix. Note that the Heartbeat CD versions of these albums are completely different 1990s remixes, courtesy of Barry O'Hare.

BIG YOUTH PRODUCTIONS

Reggae Gi Dem Dub (Nichola Delita, JA).

Big Youth's self-produced 45s often featured interesting 'version' sides (including the clavinet cut of his "My Time"), but this Sylvan Morris-mixed counterpart to the *Progress* album was the only dub set of his rhythms ever to appear. Very enjoyable, particularly if your taste inclines towards the more subtle end of the dub spectrum, with outstanding contributions from the American harmonica player Jimmy Becker, saxophonists Glen DaCosta and Deadly Headly Bennett, trumpeters David Madden and Arnold Breckenridge, and percussionists Noel 'Skully' Simms and Jah Youth himself.

BUNNY WAILER PRODUCTIONS

Dubd'sco (Solomonic, JA).

Dubd'sco Volume 2 (Solomonic, JA).

Inspired Sylvan Morris and Carl Patterson dubwise treatments to five of the tracks from Bunny Wailer's *Blackheart Man*, plus the "Roots Radics" and "Love Fire" 45s, and on *Volume 2* nine tracks from *Sings the Wailers*, alongside one from *In I Father's House*. Let's hope that when Bunny puts them on CD he includes versions of the missing tracks.

Dubbing into the 1980s

The advent of the 12" single, with either a dub section or a deejay's commentary added to the vocal, and of the 'showcase' album, which collected half a dozen vocal/dub mixes on one album, kept dub alive as the 1980s dawned. However, dub was becoming less surprising, even formulaic, and Jamaican music was undergoing another major change. A new generation of singers and deejays became known for their ability to improvise lyrics live in the dance over well-loved Studio One rhythms. This became the new dancehall style (see Chapter 6), which would dominate until Jammy led the digital revolution in 1985 with the first totally digital reggae record – Wayne Smith's "Under Me Sleng Teng".

Nonetheless, **King Tubby**'s small mixing and voicing studio continued as a major focal point for dub, though its owner tended to delegate work more and more to apprentices like **Scientist**. While **Prince Jammy** and Scientist were forging their own distinctive mixing sounds using the same equipment as Tubby, there were also newer producers coming to employ the studio's facilities, several of whom were able to make dub albums that equal the triumphs of the earlier years. Among them was the innovative radio deejay **Michael 'Mikey Dread' Campbell**, and two men based in the Greenwich Farm area of West Kingston, both of whom were making particularly hard music in a cultural mode – **Bertram Brown** and **Don Mais**.

Producer Tommy Cowan, working from various studios, released impressive dub sides on 45s – from such as **Jacob Miller**, **Devon Irons** and **Desi Roots** – and heavyweight albums that were simply credited as the work of the studio band, the Fatman Ridim Section, otherwise known as the musical nucleus of the Inner Circle band. **Gussie Clarke** was another producer who omitted from record labels the names of the engineers responsible for both his outstanding early 1970s version sides and the worthwhile dub set from later in the decade – deserving though such credits would have been.

Jammy at the gates of his studio

A king in waiting: Prince Jammy

Prince Jammy had begun his career in music in the late 1960s when he built amplifiers for sound systems, a prelude to running his own system. When he returned to Jamaica for a holiday in 1976 after living in Canada since the early 1970s, **Bunny Lee** persuaded him to make his return more permanent, particularly as Tubby's main engineer, Philip Smart, was emigrating to New York. Soon Jammy was installed at Tubby's tiny studio, and mixing dubs that were firmly in the style of his boss. Jammy mixed most of Bunny Lee and Yabby You's productions from 1977, but the most important album-length dub encounters for which he was responsible were Horace Andy's *In the Light Dub*, for the New York-based Jamaican producer Everton DaSilva, Gregory Isaacs' *Slum* and his own *Jammy's In Lion Dub Style*, largely a stripped-down variation of the debut vocal set he produced by Black Uhuru (see p.142), which had just appeared on his own recently launched label. In general his dubs were characterized by their brilliantly clear sound and the precision with which he marshalled the considerable array of effects now installed in Tubby's studio. The loss to the dub genre when he became Jamaica's most successful producer was, of course, the gain of practically every singer and deejay with whom he then worked – as well as all the other studio owners who followed his lead into the digital era of the late 1980s.

Dread at the controls – Mikey Dread

In the late 1970s **Michael Campbell** (b. 1948, Port Antonio) deejayed a four-hour radio show on JBC that was the rootsiest Jamaica had ever heard. Whereas foreign – that is, largely American – records had been dominant on the airwaves, the dreadlocked Campbell's *Dread At the Controls* show was hip to the latest developments in local music, and displayed an in-depth knowledge of reggae's history – he regularly dropped in the original Studio One cuts to the rhythms currently running things in the Kingston dancehalls. Having built his reputation on radio, the man who called himself **Mikey Dread** then made the obvious move to deejaying on record, and cut his first couple of 45s for Lee Perry. Both of these presented him in the style he used on his show, with the first appropriately having the same title, "Dread At the Controls".

Imaginative singles followed for **Joe Gibbs**, **Sonia Pottinger** and **Carlton Patterson**, but even more important was the launching of his own label, again called Dread At the Control. He produced some of the freshest-sounding records of 1978–81, recording himself as deejay, as well as hard roots singers like **Rod Taylor**, **Earl Sixteen**, **Junior Murvin** and **Edi Fitzroy**. But what made the greatest impact, in Jamaica and in the UK (where tapes of his radio show had been circulated), were the dub sides, and version sides like "Internal Energy", "Robbers Roost", "Parrot Jungle" and "African Anthem" helped create a new interest in the form. People were again buying the records purely for their dubs – and that kind of thing hadn't happened since Tubby's heyday with Bunny Lee a couple of years previously.

ADRIAN BOOT

Michael Campbell: Dread Out Of Control

The Greenwich Farm connection, and Scientist at the controls

As the 1970s drew to a close, a couple of the Greenwich Farm roots producers, **Bertram Brown** and **Errol 'Don' Mais**, also turned out singles with notable dubs. Brown employed King Tubby for all the version sides on his Freedom Sound label, the rhythms built by the Soul Syndicate band for the young producer inspiring the founder of dub to a return to vintage form. Mais, on the other hand, had Tubby's apprentice engineer, the young **Hopeton 'Scientist' Brown** (b. 1960, Kingston), mixing the ground-breaking reworkings of Studio One classics that appeared on his Roots Tradition imprint. Though no one ever quite matched the impact of Tubby's pioneering efforts, it was Scientist who came nearest; Tubby's apprentice was using the same equipment as the original dub master, but he seemed to find parts of the board his mentor had not reached, creating a style that was far more stripped down than either Tubby or Jammy.

Scientist was only 16 when he was first let loose on Mais's rhythms – he had been assisting at Tubby's studio, winding transformer coils and helping out generally, and had already shown Tubby that he could mix, if the chance came. The chance duly came one day when Jammy was too tired to continue with a mixing session that Mais had booked, and the producer asked Tubby to send for the youthful apprentice. The first hit that Scientist mixed was Barrington Levy's "Collie Weed", and he soon gained a lot more attention with version sides of

SCIENTIST: AN APPRENTICESHIP AT TUBBY'S

Born Hopeton Brown, the mixing engineer who became known as 'Scientist' while mastering his craft at King Tubby's Dromilly Avenue studio made the most innovative strides in the development of dub techniques since his mentor's own initial experiments.

" My father, he was a repair technician, repairin' television, radios. He usually have a lotta parts that he would take from televisions, and having the opportunity to be around electronic test instruments and parts, I got to know the names of the components. The first place I ever did work was at King Tubby's studio, an' how I got to bein' a engineer was that I got to the stage on electronics where I started to build amplifiers. After you build a amplifier you need a record that is properly mixed with all the frequency range to be able to test how the amplifier is gonna perform. Usually, the mixes from around Tubby's, they had a heavy bass and real crisp high end. That was a good way to analyze the performance of the amplifier.

How I got introduced to Tubby's is by a next friend that was doing a welding job; he was telling me that I should try and meet Tubby's, because he build amplifiers and he knew that Tubby's could wind some of the transformers that I needed to build my amplifiers. So he had a welding job to do around Tubby's property, and I went there with him. When he introduced me, I told Tubby's that I like the mixes that he were doin', and that they were a good way to analyze the performance of the amplifier.

Science in the mix

After goin' to Tubby's, buyin' parts from him like transformers, I use to tell 'im: 'Hey Tubby's, I can do that sort of work,' and he used to laugh it off and say: 'You're a little kid – you know a lot of big men come here and take years and they still can't do it.' So he had some extra work that he needed done in the shop, windin' transformers, repairin' televisions, he would ask me to help. Then we develop a friendship and he made me a bet one day, when Jammy's was in Canada: 'I bet if I send you in that studio there you don't know the first thing to do.' So I said: 'Okay, I'll go in there!' He gave me the first opportunity. I don't remember exactly which record was the first I get to actually mix, but from that time I didn't pay much attention to repairin' televisions – I found recordin' a little less boring! I did Barrington Levy's, "On My Way To Maverley" ["Collie Weed"]. I think that was the first hit record I ever mixed. At that time I was so anxious to get behind the controls, if somebody want me to go to studio six o'clock in the morning, I would make it there. I had to make use of the opportunity that I was given.

Each day workin' there was completely different. A lotta great things happen there. At first, it wasn't so much of a big deal, but when you 'ave the opportunity to sit back years later and actually remember, so many great things happen there. At the time we all was takin' all these things for granted. One thing I learned from Tubby's, though, like when I would mix a record, I would tek it to 'im and say 'Tubby's how's that sound?' He used to say it don't really sound too good, but his reason for doin' that is to let you always keep tryin' harder. Years after he confess; he said, 'A lot of that stuff you were doin', it was good but I was scared at the time that if I let you know how good you doin', you probably would have gotten swell headed an' stop tryin'. He was truly a genius. "

45s like the True Persuaders' "Roots Man Skanking" and "African Girl", Phillip Frazer's "Never Let Go" and Tristan Palma's "Bad Boys". The young man whom Mikey Dread called the "apprentice master" in his rundown of the Kingston studio talent on 1980's "Jumping Master" was soon to displace Tubby as the dub master. Both before he left King Tubby's employ and after he was hired by the Hookim brothers at Channel One, Scientist was the preferred engineer of **Henry 'Junjo' Lawes**, the dominant producer of the first half of the 1980s (see pp.249–250). Scientist's radical approach to Tubby's mixing-board could not have better suited Henry 'Junjo' Lawes and the **Roots Radics**, the most in-demand session band of the period. The slower Radics rhythms were perfect for a minimalist mixing style that applied reverb to alternate drumbeats or keyboard chords and then punctuated the mixes with them. Scientist put his finger on the originality of the dubs that were created back then, describing the form in terms of: "engineers using the recording equipment to bring about musical changes, a musical environment where reggae music is the music what brought forward the remix, or most of what we hearin' in hip-hop. There is no other music in the world that has the kinda versatility that you could make dub. Hip-hop is slightly there, but not like reggae. With reggae, when you make a mistake, it finds a place and fits in."

As the new decade unfolded, Scientist became even more popular, mixing for other leading dancehall producers like **Linval Thompson** and **Jah Thomas**. He made a series of albums in which he was featured in clashes with opponents such as the Space Invaders or the Pac-Men, utilizing rhythms from Lawes and Thompson. In 1982 he moved to Tuff Gong as second engineer to **Errol Brown**, before relocating to Washington DC in the mid-1980s, where he still continues studio work.

Tubby's new studio

As one decade closed and another began, **King Tubby** occasionally demonstrated that he was still capable – when sufficiently interested – of mixing outstanding dub, as shown by the version sides of practically all of the Glen Brown-produced singles of the period, continuing a mutually rewarding relationship established in the early 1970s. He also maintained links with **Vivian Jackson**, and mixed a particularly strong – and quite traditional – version side for "Influence In Me" (Vivian Jackson), while displaying just as fine a touch with the dub to Leroy Sibbles' "Love & Happiness" (Rock Jam) or Sugar Minott's *Ghetto-ology Dubwise* set.

As the 1970s ended, Tubby began formulating plans to build a studio where he could record music as well as remix it. The studio eventually opened in late 1985, hitting almost immediately with one of his first productions, Anthony Red Rose's "Tempo". After that his apprentices Peego and Fatman recorded early works by such as Ninjaman, King Kong and Courtney Melody, but this promising beginning to Tubby's career as a bona fide producer soon came to a tragic end: King Tubby was gunned down in the early morning of February 6, 1989, outside his home in Duhaney Park, Kingston. The killer has never been found.

BERTRAM BROWN PRODUCTIONS

◑ **King Tubby & Soul Syndicate – Freedom Sounds In Dub** (Blood & Fire, UK).

Bertram Brown's Freedom Sounds label was one of the most consistent of the last half of the 1970s, specializing in raw roots vocals from the likes of Rod Taylor, Prince Allah and Earl Zero. The 'version' sides of the original rhythms were mixed at King Tubby's by the man himself (not always the case after 1976), and it is interesting to hear how much the originator had learned from the apprentices (Scientist and Prince Jammy). Gives a new dimension to classics like Rod Taylor's "Ethiopian Kings" and "In the Right Way", Phillip Frazer's "Come Ethiopians" and Prince Alla's "Lot's Wife" – and those are just the opening four tracks.

GLEN BROWN PRODUCTIONS

◑ **Glen Brown & King Tubby – Termination Dub (1973–79)** (Blood & Fire, UK).

E A previously unreleased dub of the "Dirty Harry" horns classic represents 1973, while the rest of the set concentrates on the last half of the decade, when Glen Brown's South East Music label was associated with particular heavy roots material such as "Lambs Bread", "Cleanliness Is Godliness" and "Away With the Bad". The Tubby-mixed dubs to the same are even more amazing versions of the deadly rhythms, and go a long way to explaining why both producer and engineer have become legends.

MICHAEL CAMPBELL PRODUCTIONS

◑ **African Anthem Dubwise** (Cruise, UK; Ras, US).

● **Mikey Dread At the Controls Dubwise** (Dread At the Controls, JA).

Two superlative dub albums of Mikey Dread's rhythms. The UK one – with mixes by King Tubby, Prince

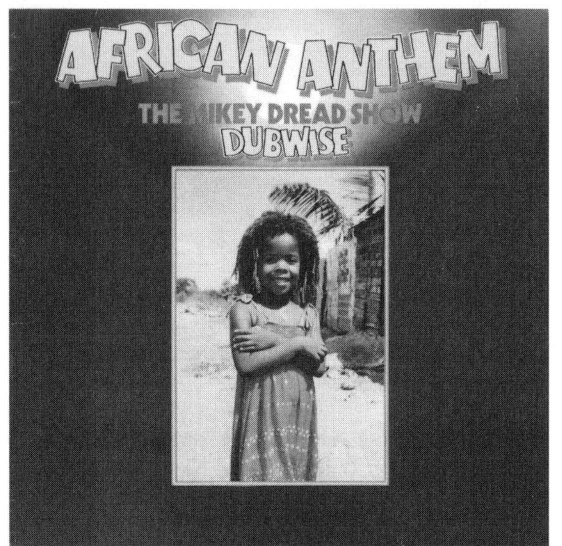

Jammy and Campbell himself – gains from the inclusion of his radio-show jingles which were edited on in London. The Jamaican release brings in the services of Crucial Bunny to mix mostly the same tough but musical rhythms; minus the references to his airwaves persona, it's certainly less dramatic, but still good dub.

AUGUSTUS 'GUSSIE' CLARKE PRODUCTIONS

Black Foundation Dub (Gussie, JA).

Not the Tubby-mixed cuts of the early 1970s' *Simplicity People* tracks, but a set from 1977 that covers some of Clarke's big mid-decade hits in dub fashion. The album still manages to look back to those beginnings, however – there are solid rockers-style recuts of "Skylarking", "Born To Love You" and "No No No". There is also a further cut to Pablo's "No Exit" rhythm ("One Way") and, inspiring the album title, Dennis Brown's "To the Foundation".

TOMMY COWAN PRODUCTIONS

Israel Tafari (Top Ranking, US).

This comprises weighty versions to eight of the ten vocals from Israel Vibration's beautiful and rootsy *Why Worry* album that confirm the majesty and power of the original rhythms from the Fatman Riddim Section. It can only be faulted for omitting dubs to two tracks: everything on the amazing vocal album deserved this sort of treatment.

Rastafari In Dub – Sons Of Negus (Top Ranking, JA).

Mixed in a style like the above set, this is not what the title suggests – ie a straightforward dub companion to the Ras Michael album of a similar name – but instead features versions to the strongest tracks from both that and the subsequent *Kibur Am-Lak*. Plenty of funde and akete drumming, of course, but also some interesting guitar, brass and keyboards brought to the fore.

EVERTON DASILVA PRODUCTIONS

Chanting Dub With the Help Of the Father (Rockers International, JA; Hungry Town, US).

Augustus Pablo is prominent on these rhythms for the New York-based Everton DaSilva, making up one of the heaviest dub albums ever released. Horace Andy's "Problems" particularly stands out, but the entire set has aged very well since its appearance in 1979.

TREVOR 'LEGGO' DOUGLAS PRODUCTIONS

Leggo Dub (Cash & Carry, JA).

Revolutionaries rhythms dubbed up, with plenty of sound effects in the Joe Gibbs style. It is dominated by some half a dozen rhythms from Gregory's *Mr Isaacs* album – including the marvellous "Storm" and "Sacrifice". Other interesting rhythms include Rod Taylor's "Every Little Thing" and, somewhat unexpectedly, a cut to "Don't Think About Me", which Horace Andy recorded for Keith Hudson.

ROY FRANCIS PRODUCTIONS

Phase One Dub-Wise (Phase One, JA).

Mixed by Ernest Hookim, with all the rhythms laid at Channel One, this not surprisingly sounds very much like the series of classic dub encounters that appeared on Well Charge. Hits from both the Chantelles and Lopez Walker appear in slightly variant mixes from the B-side dubs on the original 45s, but are no less entertaining.

KEITH HUDSON PRODUCTIONS

Brand (Joint, UK).

This followed a couple of years after the groundbreaking *Pick A Dub* and introduced the more modern rhythms that were to appear on his *Rasta Communication* vocal set, mixed in a similarly stark and edgy manner.

INNER CIRCLE PRODUCTIONS

Killer Dub (Top Ranking, US).

Heavyweight Dub (Top Ranking, US).

Both these have been long unavailable, but they are thoroughly excellent. Largely featuring dub mixes of Jacob Miller songs, they are strict drum and bass workouts that more than live up to their titles. *Killer Dub* was mixed by Prince Jammy at King Tubby's, with cuts of Miller songs like "10,000 Careless Ethiopians" and Earl Zero's "City Of the Weak Heart". *Heavyweight* has more of the same type of material, but mixed by Maximilian – billed as the new emperor of dub on the sleeve – with a brilliant version of the "Take 5" rhythm ("Down Rhodesia") standing out in particular.

GREGORY ISAACS PRODUCTIONS

Slum: Gregory Isaacs In Dub (Burning Sounds, UK).

The title track of this 1978 set turns out to be a version, not too surprisingly, of "Party In the Slum" from

Isaacs' *Cool Ruler*. Largely the dub counterpart to that classic vocal set, this confirms the importance of Sly Dunbar's drumming to Isaacs' self-productions of the time, but also the keyboard skills of Ansel Collins, which were always as cool as that voice (heard here only sparingly and in fractured form). Prince Jammy never sounded more inspired at Tubby's mixing-board, and after this only the young Scientist would reach new places on it.

JAH THOMAS PRODUCTIONS

⦿ **Jah Thomas Meets Scientist In Dub Conference** (Majestic Reggae, Holland).

⦿ **Jah Thomas Meets King Tubby In the House Of Dub** (Majestic Reggae, Holland).

The deejay Jah Thomas turned out to be a sterling producer of other performers – as well as himself – and the dancehall hits by the likes of Anthony Johnson, Johnny Osbourne and Tristan Palma that appeared on his Midnight Rock and Nura labels were particularly distinguished by their hard Roots Radics rhythms. Tubby's most gifted disciple, Scientist, was by this time teaching the master a trick or two, as both sets confirm.

LLOYD JAMES PRODUCTIONS

● **Jammy's In Lion Dub Style** (Jammy's, JA).

It is the six versions of tracks from Black Uhuru's sensational debut set, *Love Crisis/Black Sounds Of Freedom*, that have made this album's fearsome reputation. *In Lion Dub Style* is a fitting description – the Fisher reverb is in roaring, thunderous effect throughout.

HENRY 'JUNJO' LAWES PRODUCTIONS

◑ **Scientist v Prince Jammy** (Greensleeves, UK).

The first in the series of albums that Lawes's and Tubby's apprentices made for Greensleeves includes intros by gruff-voiced deejay Jah Thomas, with the contrasting vibrant tones of Barrington Levy sometimes emerging out of the mix (all the rhythms are from his *Englishman* album). Several dub albums at this time had spurious credits, but these are genuine, with Scientist and Jammy displaying their very distinct ways at the mixing-board.

◑ **Scientist Heavyweight Dub Champion** (Greensleeves, UK).

The next Scientist/Lawes set again utilized heavyweight boxing imagery for the cover and track titles, as well as featuring Jah Thomas again, and demolishing more of the same singer's tracks – this time, from the equally distinguished *Robin Hood* set.

◑ **Scientist Rids the World Of Vampires** (Greensleeves, UK).

For the third Scientist/Lawes album, the imagery changed to the youthful hero taking on the combined forces of vampires, zombies, werewolves, voodoo practitioners and Frankenstein's monster, over rhythm tracks from, among others, Michael Prophet, Johnny Osbourne and the Wailing Souls.

◑ **Scientist Wins the World Cup** (Greensleeves, UK).

Reverting to athletic metaphors, but switching sport, the *World Cup* set is slightly disappointing, despite the voices of Hugh Mundell, Wayne Jarrett and Johnny Osbourne floating about, and a strong selection of rhythms that includes the latter's "Give A Little Love".

ERROL 'DON' MAIS PRODUCTIONS

◑ **Scientist Dub In the Roots Tradition** (Blood & Fire, UK).

Don Mais's place in reggae history is assured, if only for producing the rhythm tracks that bridged the roots and dancehall phases. Not one of the fifteen rhythms that receive the full Scientific treatment here was an original; at the same time, the versions laid by the musicians from the Soul Syndicate and what would be known as the Roots Radics could not have sounded fresher. Even if you feel that the last thing you need is another version of a dancehall staple like "Never Let Go" or "Pick Up the Pieces", this should be investigated, since these cuts really started the dancehall revolution.

SUGAR MINOTT PRODUCTIONS

● **Ghetto-ology Dubwise** (Black Roots, JA).

The dub counterpart to Sugar Minott's *Ghetto-ology* album. This was one of the last dub albums from Tubby, and well up to vintage standards. An unmissable companion to the vocal set, but one that stands up as good listening in its own right.

PRINCE FAR I PRODUCTIONS

◑ **Cry Tuff Dub Encounter Chapter 3** (Pressure Sounds, UK).

Rockstone toaster Prince Far I's releases on his own Jamaican label, Cry Tuff, were nearly always complemented by interesting version sides, and this is the most interesting of the three album-length excursions into the uncharted regions of his rhythms.

RANKING JOE & JAH SCREW PRODUCTIONS

◑ **Dangerous Dub – King Tubby Meets Roots Radics** (Greensleeves, UK).

Raw and very weighty early 1980s rhythms as played by the Roots Radics, bridging the roots and dancehall phases. This was one of the last dub sets mixed by King Tubby, who – as befits the title – appeared not to have been in the mood to show mercy to anyone; the cut of "Cuss Cuss" is particularly mean and nasty.

LINVAL THOMPSON PRODUCTIONS

◑ **Scientist Meets the Space Invaders** (Greensleeves, UK).

◑ **Scientist Encounters Pac-Man** (Greensleeves, UK).

E Linval Thompson became one of 'Junjo' Lawes's strongest rivals in the early 1980s, specializing in similarly brutal and sparse rhythms from the Roots Radics. Both Scientist-mixed albums contain cuts of his most exciting hits, but the first sounds fresher and includes the teenage engineer beating off the threat from outer space over Wayne Wade's breath-taking "Poor & Humble".

Dancehall

DAVID CORIO

6

6

previous page

Michigan and Smiley: raw-born rub-a-dub in a combination style

Dancehall

All Jamaican popular music, from the r&b of the late 1950s to 1990s ragga, has been directed at the dancehall. As a generic term, however, **'dancehall'** has a more particular sense, which became widely used after the death of Bob Marley in 1981 and the decline in the volume of Rasta-inspired roots records. Some commentators have made a direct link between Marley's death and the rise of what was soon tagged 'dancehall', but even a cursory listen to what was being produced in the Kingston studios of the late 1970s shows this to be false. For some time before his death, Jamaica's only true international superstar had been outside the mainstream of the music being played in the dancehalls, which emphasized pure rhythm to a much greater degree than was apparent on reggae aimed at the international crossover audience. And the dancehalls were now producing a new generation of deejays and singers who learned their craft performing over their sound system's rhythm tracks, either on exclusive dubplates or, with the smaller outfits, the 'version' sides of singles (often from Studio One).

In a sense there was nothing new about this – there's a tape of King Tubby's Hi-Fi sound from 1975 that has U-Roy jive talking his way over recent Horace Andy hits and older Studio One rhythms. But what became different in the dancehall period – roughly 1979–85 – was the degree of influence live dancehall styles exerted on what was apppearing on vinyl. And this was demonstrated not just on deejay records, which became even more popular than they had been before, but on a new generation of singers. There was also a new dominant session band who forged a fresh style of playing mostly vintage rhyhms that perfectly suited both the mood of the time and the recently developed peforming styles. The **Roots Radics**, formed largely from former members of the Morwells vocal group, were to the period what the Revolutionaries had been to the preceding half-decade.

Jamaican music tends to change direction every few years, but to explain why developments followed the particular path they did in the first half of the 1980s it's necessary to place them in the broader context of the decade of Reaganomics and Thatcherism. In 1980, following a period of destabilization (orchestrated by the CIA) and increasing economic problems for Jamaica, Michael Manley's nominally socialist PNP lost the general election to the right-wing JLP, lead by Edward Seaga (or CIAga, according to the wit of West Kingston graffiti). What followed was a respite from the extreme levels of violence that the island had endured prior to, and especially during, the election (more than 800 people died violently that year), but the IMF-prompted deregulation and free market policies of the new government – including significant cutbacks in health provision and other social services, as well as the end of price controls on food – brought hardships that disproportionately affected the poor. A significant rise in unemployment, accompanied by falling wages for many still in employment, made things still worse.

In reaction, the island's music became conservative and inward-looking. The reliance on tried and tested rhythms became more pronounced, while lyrics tended to turn away from social, political or historical themes. Now the emphasis shifted to traditional dancehall concerns – new dance moves, slackness (sexually explicit lyrics) and sound clashes. Furthermore, in the harsher economic climate record producers played safe by using rhythms and lyrics that had already proved successful in the dancehalls. There, a new wave of sound systems had come to the fore, including Gemini Disco, Virgo Hi-Fi, Aces International, Metro Media, the singer **Sugar Minott**'s Youth Promotion, Killimanjaro, Lee's Unlimited, Black Scorpio, Arrows, Emperor Faith Hi-Fi, Black Star and Stereophonic, alongside comparative veterans like the deejay U-Roy's Stur-Gav Hi-Fi and the reborn Ray Symbolic. The former chief engineer at King Tubby's studio, **Prince Jammy**, also expanded his sound-system activities to join the premier league, while the most popular producer of the decade's first half, **Henry 'Junjo'**

ADRIAN BOOT

Lawes, enjoyed similar success with his own Volcano Hi-Power sound from 1983.

The changes in the Jamaican public's mood and taste were clearly reflected by the popularity of young chatters, who mostly seemed to go back to the originator himself, **U-Roy**, as their model. The strongest of the U-Roy-influenced deejays of the late 1970s, **Ranking Joe** and **Brigadier Jerry**, along with two very original stylists, **General Echo** and **Lone Ranger**, in turn served as models for younger men at the mike. These included **Charlie Chaplin**, **Josey Wales**, **Peter Metro** and, most of all, **Yellowman**, who for a while was as popular as Marley had ever been in Jamaica. Some deejays had big dancehall reputations but needed the interaction with an audience, and so impressed less on vinyl (one of Volcano's top men at the mike, Burro Banton, was a prime example), but the most significant shift was that the deejay record became primary to Jamaican music. Deejay records were now being made in unprecedented quantities – in fact, they now outnumbered new 45s by singers, most of the more-established of whom were beginning to seem old-fashioned in comparison to the younger deejays, whose spontaneous and interactive art was the most democratic and populist form of musical expression imaginable. There were still plenty of vocal records being issued, but the only singers who could compete with the deejays were those – such as **Barrington Levy**, **Little John**, **Frankie Paul**, **Michael Palmer**, **Half Pint**, **Cocoa Tea** and **Junior Reid** – who had come up through the same sound-system circuit, and employed similar improvisatory techniques at the mike.

VARIOUS ARTISTS

⦿ **Forward (A Selection Of Greensleeves Top Singles 1977–82)** (Greensleeves, UK).

E Covering the years when roots reggae became dancehall, and Greensleeves went from being a minor player in the UK reggae marketplace to the undisputed major. It should come as no surprise that production credits for over half of the tracks are to Henry 'Junjo' Lawes, while Winston Riley and Channel One receive one apiece, and the deejays Ranking Dread and Doctor Alimantado are represented by self-productions. With not a single weak track, this is an excellent introduction to the period and the label.

Roots Tradition, the Roots Radics and Barrington Levy

A crucial reason for Jamaican producers' increasing reliance on established rhythms – with Studio One as the overwhelmingly popular source – was simply economic. Musicians could record a new version of a rhythm with which they were already familiar far faster than they were able to build a totally original one, thus saving on expensive studio time. In turn, cost-conscious consumers were more likely to spend any spare cash on what was already familiar, as long as it was combined with sufficient elements of the new, whether in the performer's style or a topical lyric.

Most of the ingredients for the dancehall phase were in place before the end of the 1970s: for example, horns on many sessions, an important cost-cutting exercise, and the rise of the **Roots Radics** – built around **Errol 'Flabba' Holt** (bass), **Lincoln Valentine 'Style' Scott** (drums) and **Eric 'Bingy Bunny' Lamont** (rhythm guitar) – as the leading session band (as well as touring musicians with established stars like Gregory Isaacs). Other players associated with the band at various points of their career included Noel 'Sowell' Bailey, Dwight Pickney and Roy Hamilton (all on lead guitar), Eric 'Fish' Clarke and Carlton 'Santa' Davis (both drums) and Wycliffe 'Steely' Johnson (keyboards). All had been active in the Kingston recording scene before coming together as the Radics in 1978, and formed a unique and soon to be dominant sound when they combined – a sparser, slower and at times more threatening sound than what had gone before.

Errol 'Don' Mais: the roots of dancehall

Flabba and Bingy Bunny had been playing together since 1974 as part of the vocal group the **Morwells**, while what was in effect the Roots Radics band supplied some tough updated

BETH LESSER

Roots Radics

versions of vintage Studio One rhythms for **Don Mais**'s Roots Tradition label in the latter half of the 1970s. The down-to-earth style of Mais, a Greenwich Town resident who sang under the name Jah Bible, was perhaps the strongest bridge between roots and dancehall. Commencing his career in 1976 with the occasionally brilliant cultural singer Earl Zero, Mais always concentrated on rougher music and almost exclusively recorded performers from the Greenwich Town area. But his central place in the history of dancehall is not simply defined by the kind of singers and deejays he recorded, nor even by his use of the musicians who became the Roots Radics. Rather, it's most of all based on the fact that he was the man who rediscovered the Studio One rhythms destined to dominate the era. The most successful of these was probably the one initially used for Slim Smith's 1968 hit "Never Let Go", which, rebuilt by Mais's session players, supported hit versions by **Phillip Frazer**, **Little John**, **Peter Ranking & General Lucky** and, most memorable of all, **Brigadier Jerry**. In fact, not one of the rhythm tracks that Mais had the Soul Syndicate or the proto-Roots Radics record at Dynamic and Channel One in the period 1976–79 was an original, yet each cut was as fresh-sounding as anything then emerging from the Kingston studios.

Among the singers to make fine records for Mais were **Rod Taylor**, Philip Frazer and **Michael Prophet**. But the two figures who best exemplified 'dancehall' vocals were the man who called himself **Sammy Dread** and the child star **Little John**, both of whom had the seemingly inexhaustible knack of placing new lyrics (albeit not profound ones) over vintage rhythms, delivering them in an enthusiastic roughhouse manner.

Sammy Dread's vocal style had about as much finesse as his choice of name, but when put on the right rhythms he could create genuine excitement – particularly if heard over several thousand watts of a bass-heavy dancehall sound system. Little John has, however, enjoyed the more enduring career, even if he often sounded as if suffering from a bad cold. Before reaching his teens he could ride a rough rhythm with aplomb, and he injected whatever he was singing with an unstoppable energy, transposing onto vinyl the excitement he created with the Romantic Hi-Fi sound system. He became one of reggae's most prolific stars, and a couple of hundred 45s chart his progress from the precocious child who sings the traditional cultural lyric of "Robe" (Roots Tradition) to the assured dancehall master delivering his boast of how the girls are "All Over Me" (Hitbound).

There were also outstanding deejay records on Roots Tradition that presaged future developments, including Ranking Toyan & Little John's "Gun Fever", which was an energetic take on an old but still relevant topic, and Peter Ranking & General Lucky's "Black I Am", employing a singularly rough cut of the cultural anthem, "Satta Massa Gana". Mais's real stars, though, were his hard and dynamic rhythms, which provided a template for the producer who was to totally dominate the next few years – Henry 'Junjo' Lawes.

LITTLE JOHN

● Early Days (Roots Tradition, JA).

John McMorris was yet to enter adolescence when he cut these eight tracks for Don Mais, and was already something of a sound-system sensation. Though such extreme youth can sometimes be irritating on record, the best tracks here have a genuine dancehall energy. Check his two biggest hits from this period – "Robe" and his precocious take on U-Roy's "Big Boy & Teacher", retitled "What Is Catty".

RANKING TOYAN

● Early Days (Roots Tradition, JA).

Probably owing too much to the Big Youth/Dillinger school to be considered a particularly original talent, the late Toyan successfully adapted the approach of his influences to pioneering Don Mais dancehall rhythms. Little John and Sammy Dread, two of the definitive dancehall singers of the time, also contribute to the excitement, and deserve credits on the sleeve. An unexpected version of the original "Conquering Lion" rhythm has enough verve to appeal far beyond Vivian Jackson completists.

VARIOUS ARTISTS – DON MAIS PRODUCTIONS

◉ Roots Tradition From the Vineyard (Majestic, Holland).

Rod Taylor, Phillip Frazer, Sammy Dread and Mais himself (as Jah Bible) get to grips with some superior Soul Syndicate rhythms. But the vocal standout is the 9-year-old Little John, possessed by the spirit on "Robe", his second-ever record. Tough deejay shots by Toyan and the innovative duo of Peter & Lucky, plus two rough dubs, complete a useful programme.

Enter Barrington Levy

For all the ground-breaking use of the Roots Radics by Don Mais, the first time most reggae followers became aware of the band was with the release in 1979 of the debut album from a new youthman singing sensation called **Barrington Levy** (b. 1964, Kingston). Levy had been part of a group called the Mighty Multitudes and made a couple of singles that did not sell particularly well before the records that thrust him into the public gaze. Recorded at Channel One and produced jointly by Henry 'Junjo' Lawes and New York-based Hyman 'Jah Life', "Ah Yah We Deh", "Callie Weed", "Shine Eye Gal", "Looking My Love" and "Ah Yah We Deh" were all strong sellers in 1979 that signalled the arrival of a major new talent. His subsequent debut album for Lawes/Wright, with its raw rhythms by the Roots Radics, was the template for the whole genre of dancehall vocalizing. The bringing-together of ten tracks by the combination of Levy and the Radics made people aware that yet another fundamental shift was taking place in the island's music – one comparable with that signalled by the Mighty Diamonds debut album with the Revolutionaries for Channel One four years previously. Barrington Levy was soon more popular with the youth audience than any of the new generation of deejays then emerging on record, and in the next few years only the all-conquering Yellowman was more popular.

Unfortunately, a few substandard records were then rushed out to cash in on his phenomenal popularity, and Levy could have very quickly become yet another sensation who burns himself out with far too many releases and too little quality control. But he turned out to be made of more substantial stuff and went on to make a formidable body of work right up to the 1990s – the exuberance of his vocal style was matched in the 1980s only by that of fellow dancehall oriented vocalizers Little John and the even more prolific Frankie Paul. The records that Levy continued to cut with Lawes kept up – or even improved upon – the standard of the ones that established his name, and of particular note were "Hammer", "Robber Man" and, employing the Wailing Souls' "Firehouse Rock" rhythm, "Prison Oval Rock". He also cut equally strong hits for Channel One, George Phang and Joe Gibbs, and occasionally produced himself with excellent results – notably on "Love Of Jah" and "In the Dark". In addition, there were one-off deals that yielded further worthwhile 45s, including "Revelation" for Lloyd Dennis and "M16" for the obscure Peter Callender.

But the producer who enabled Barrington Levy to reach his widest audience was **Jah Screw** (b. Paul Love), formerly the selector for U-Roy's Stur-Gav sound system. "Under Mi Sensi" became a herb smoker's anthem in 1984, and was popular again in the 1990s, when a commentary from the fast-rising deejay Beenie Man was added to a rebuilt cut. A degree of crossover success in the UK came with the follow-up to the original release of "Under Mi Sensi", the more rock-influenced "Here I Come". Yet Levy was unable to follow this with similar pop hits, and cooled off until Jah Screw produced him on a couple of songs written by a singer who had always been a major influence, the great **Bob Andy**. Both "My Time" and "Too Experienced" were successful, commercially and artistically, and demonstrated that the singer who first became a sensation in the early 1980s was still a force to be reckoned with over a decade later. In 1995, Barrington Levy joined forces with the hottest deejay on the island, Bounty Killer, and the next year was once again high in the Jamaican charts (and the UK reggae one) with another Jah Screw production, the infectious "Living Dangerously".

BARRINGTON LEVY

◑ **Collection** (Greensleeves/Time One, UK).

Ⓔ Far from the definitive overview of his prolific career, but an excellent selection of many of his most popular singles, largely for Henry 'Junjo' Lawes and Jah Screw. The selection ranges from the tunes that established him in the late 1970s, through the hits that confirmed his talent in the 1980s, on to his great triumph of the 1990s, "Too Experienced". Not a weak moment, though there are many more Lawes-produced classics that still need to appear on album, including the mighty "Robber Man".

● **Bounty Hunter** (Jah Life, US).

Three of Barrington Levy's early hits are included on his 1979 debut album (two of them retitled) – "Shine Eye

ENTER BARRINGTON LEVY

Girl", "Looking My Love" ("It's Not Easy"), "Reggae Music" ("Don't Fuss Or Fight") – while the title track and "Shaolin Temple" also stand out. Nothing else comes up to quite the same standard, but the set remains well worth picking up for these gems.

Shine Eye Girl (Burning Sounds, UK).
With production credits to Henry 'Junjo' Lawes, this was released in the UK shortly after the debut album appeared in New York. Only eight tracks in all (with "Shaolin Temple" repeated), but the hits "Ah Ya We Deh" and "Collie Weed" were included, and all the material is strong.

Englishman/Robin Hood (Greensleeves, UK).
Two even more impressive Lawes-produced albums that were reggae best sellers in 1980, and now on one CD. Boasts some of the heaviest rhythms from either the singer's or the producer's entire career – the former set's tracks provided the basis for the *Scientist v Prince Jammy* drum and bass extravaganza.

Prison Oval Rock (Volcano, JA).
A 1985 set from Levy and Lawes that fully maintained their past standards. The other hit besides the phenomenal title track is "Hammer", which inspired Johnny Osbourne's popular "Lend Me the Sixteen".

Money Move (Powerhouse, JA).
"Money Move", over George Phang's cut of the "One Step Beyond" rhythm, was one of the biggest hits of Barrington Levy's career, but even stronger is the rootsy "Suffer the Little Children" (aka "Praise his Name"). Perhaps Phang was running short of rhythms from Sly & Robbie, though, as their version of "Mr Bassie" is employed twice.

Here I Come (Greensleeves, UK).
Jah Screw is the producer for this mid-1980s set, which marks a distinctly more cosmopolitan approach. The massive hit "Under Mi Sensi" is pure dancehall, but "Here I Come" shows a rock influence, and there is even a move to more sophisticated territory with "Vibes Is Right" and his second cut of "Moonlight Lover".

Barrington Levy's DJ Counteraction (Greensleeves, UK).
Given the popularity of 'combination' singles since the late 1980s, it is surprising that there have not been more sets like this: several of a popular singer's greatest hits collected together, and various first-league deejays brought in to add their commentaries. This is first-class Barrington Levy, to which ragga chatters of the calibre of Bounty Killer, Lady Saw, Beenie Man and Cutty Ranks add another dimension. The album from which the massive hit "Living Dangerously" was taken.

Cool runnings: celebrations of the dancehall

After Barrington Levy's first hits helped establish the musical sound of the first half of the next decade, the new mood was lyrically best expressed not by some hungry youthman deejay, but two well-established singers. **Gregory Isaacs**' "Tune In" (African Museum) and **Bunny Wailer**'s "Cool Runnings" (Solomonic) were important hits in 1981, and both signalled a move away from militant confrontations and dreams of a paradise in Africa, and towards having the best time possible in the here and now – that is, in the dancehall. The emphasis was on sweetness, and gently rocking the night away, "while", in Bunny's words, "the deejay play your favourite song". The rhythms from the Roots Radics for both records were unhurried and melodic, but at the same time stark and tough.

In the same mood, both **Don (Mc)Carlos** (one of the original members of Black Uhuru) and **Al Campbell** celebrated the delights of the dancehall with strong cuts of the latter's "Late Night Blues". The biggest hit in the career of the young **Triston Palma** (sometimes spelt

GRIMM BEN
ENTERTAINMENT
(TRISTON PALMER)
Triston Palmer
Produced by Jah Thomas
Mfg. & Dist. by G.G.'s Records
MADE IN JAMAICA

Triston Palmer), which employed a Jah Thomas-produced reworking of Vin Gordon's "Heavenless" rhythm, made clear the prime concern of the new generation of dancehall performers – "Entertainment". It is no coincidence that all these records (all of which featured the Roots Radics) were released in the aftermath of the violent 1980 Jamaican general election, which had brought the island to the verge of civil war. In such a context, invitations to enjoy the "Cool Runnings" were far from trivial sentiments.

AL CAMPBELL

Late Night Blues (JB Music, UK).

Self-produced at Harry J's studio with several all-star session musician line-ups, and voiced at King Tubby's, this is almost the perfect showcase for Al Campbell's distinctive voice. The title track remains perennially popular in the reggae world, and deserves to be known to a far wider audience

GREGORY ISAACS

Lonely Lover (African Museum, JA; Pre, UK).

E The first of three albums with the Roots Radics that appeared on Gregory Isaacs' own label, two at least of which can be considered classics. The major hits included are "Tune In", "Poor & Clean" and "Happy Anniversary", and though the title suggests an entire set in a lovers' vein, half of the tracks have cultural/reality themes.

More Gregory (African Museum, JA; Pre, UK).

"Front Door" is the only hit on this set, but there's no drop in quality. Even his reworkings of older triumphs – "My Only Lover" and "Fugitive" – are worthwhile, and fit the mood. The Roots Radics are in an easy-skanking mood, while Gregory is at his most vulnerable and seductive.

Night Nurse (African Museum, JA; Island, UK).

For the final album in Gregory Isaacs' series with the Radics, Island brought in Wally Badarou, whose synthesizer helped sell it to some of the rock audience. The title track might verge on a parody of his seduction technique, but "Hot Stepper", "Cool Down the Pace" and "Material Man" are vintage Gregory.

BUNNY WAILER

Rock & Groove (Solomonic, JA).

Bunny Wailer turns away from the cultural concerns that had dominated his previous albums for a celebration of the dancehall. Those who thought Jamaican singers should only be concerned with the travails of their people thought it lightweight, and missed how completely successful it was on its own terms. The Roots Radics sounded incredibly fresh, and Mr Livingstone fully captured the new mood of the moment.

Sings the Wailers (Solomonic, JA; Island, UK; Mango, US).

A decline in Bunny Wailer's songwriting ability might well have been the main reason for an album of songs associated with the group he founded, but the result was far from a set of sterile reworkings. The original Wailers' recording of "Dreamland" from a decade earlier is included, and sounds quite at home amid the 1980 interpretations.

ADRIAN BOOT

Gregory Isaacs in his three-piece suit and ting

Deejay dominance

Yet, for all the impact of Barrington Levy's work with the Roots Radics, and the manner in which this established Henry 'Junjo' Lawes as the producer with a fresh sound, the new decade was first and foremost about deejays. This plethora of chatters was presaged at the close of the preceding decade, when a handful of deejay versions were released before the corresponding vocals. These included the **Captain Sinbad** and **Ranking Joe** cuts of **Sugar Minott**'s "Hard Time Pressure" and "Too Much Oppression", as well as **Clint Eastwood**'s commentary on Vivian Jackson/Wayne Wade's "Ballistic Dreadlocks". But still the chatters tended to have hits after a singer had made a rhythm popular. This was to change completely in the 1980s. Men like **Yellowman**, **Josey Wales**, **Charlie Chaplin** and **Brigadier Jerry** nearly always recorded over updated cuts of vintage rhythms, but their talk brought them back into favour. Even the best singers, like **Dennis Brown** or **Gregory Isaacs**, would then follow with their own interpretations, either on the same rhythm track or over another producer's hastily recorded version.

Slackness and General Echo

The trend for sexually explicit – or 'slack' – lyrics, which was to reach a peak in the late 1980s, was already popular in the dancehall long before surfacing on vinyl in 1979, when Winston Riley released the deejay **General Echo**'s *The Slackest LP* (the title of which said it all). This was followed by the 45, "Sister Sue" from Madoo, a young singer sounding a lot like a more risqué Horace Andy, and Clint Eastwood's *Sex Education* album. Whatever his choice of topic, General Echo (b. Earl Anthony Robinson) was a first-class chatter, who had built his reputation with work on top sound systems such as Gemini, Stereophonic and Ray Symbolic, and possessed his own very influential voice and way of riding a rhythm. He did record some non-slack material – most notably the Kung Fu-influenced "Drunken Master" for George Phang, and, over the enduring "Stalag 17" rhythm, his Jamaican #1, "Arleen" for Winston Riley – but not enough for an entire set. Perhaps Echo would eventually have tackled a wider range of topics, but we will never know, as in 1980 the car in which he was riding was stopped by the police, and Echo, Leon 'Big John' Johns (the Stereophonic Sound

Master of slack chat, General Echo

owner) and the selector Flux were all shot dead. No satisfactory explanation for the incident has ever been put forward.

GENERAL ECHO

The Slackest LP (Techniques, JA).

The album that began the contentious trend for sexually explicit lyrics. The paradox is that, while many such records can seem degrading to women, men have not been the principal customers for them. Make of that what you will; there is no denying that the Winston Riley rhythms used here were classics, and General Echo's delivery was the most original and influential since Big Youth's.

12 Inches Of Pleasure (Greensleeves, UK).

A title that says it all about the lyrics; Henry 'Junjo' Lawes producing (except for one track from Riley), and brilliant deejaying – just be warned about the subject matter.

Who was that masked man?

Before Yellowman rose to dominate the early 1980s, the way was paved by the arguably more talented **Lone Ranger** (b. Anthony Waldron), who – along with Welton Irie, Ranking Joe, Nigger Kojak, Mikey Dread, Clint Eastwood and Ranking Toyan – negotiated the shift from the 'cultural' chants of the mid-1970s, as exemplified by Big Youth, to pure 1980s dancehall chat. Yet it was one of the most talented of Big Youth's disciples, the man known as **Trinity**, who can be credited with anticipating the shift to more material/carnal concerns of the next decade, with two enormous hits in 1977. On one of these, "Three Piece Suit" for Joe Gibbs, the deejay interacted with Marcia Aitken's "Still In Love With You Boy", itself an updating of an Alton Ellis rocksteady hit, to deliver lines such as:

"Yu should have seem me and the big fat t'ing
Tell yu, when I scrub her in Constant Spring
Tell yu, when I dub her in Constant Spring
Tell yu, when I dub her on the big bed spring
In my three-piece suit and t'ing
In my diamond socks and t'ing
In my Earthman shoes and t'ing."

There were other lines of continuity linking the new breed of deejays with the music's immediate past. Lone Ranger's first records, for instance, appeared on historically the most important of all Jamaican labels, Studio One. His version of Slim Smith's rocksteady classic "Never Let Go" was "The Answer", which subsequently became the much-recorded rhythm's favoured title (as confirmed by a popular Channel One cut from U-Roy apostle, Ranking Trevor, called "Answer Me Question"). Other moderate successes came in the form of "Screw Gone A North Coast" (over Horace Andy's "Skylarking"), "Three Mile Skank" (the Sound Dimension's "Full Up") and, in the company of **Welton Irie**, "Chase Them Crazy" (Horace Andy's "Mr Bassie"). These Studio One 45s established him as a deejay of interest, but the real breakthrough came in 1980. Not only did **Virgo Hi Fi**, with which he was associated, win an award as the best sound system of the year in Jamaica, but he moved on to another producer, Alvin Ranglin, who gave the masked stranger his biggest hit to date, "Barnabus Collins" (GG). The lyrics were inspired by a vampire character from an American TV series called *The Dark Shadows*, but no character in the show ever had lines like:

"Gal, out the candle, lock your door tight
Turn ya neck pon your right angle
He dem the best in the business
Chew ya neck like a Wrigley's".

The disc reached #1 in both the Jamaican chart and the UK reggae one. This was soon followed by a return to Studio One, and hits which involved more humour, and were built around the various abstract "oinks", "bims" and "ribbits" that were to be associated with the men – and women – at the mike for the next couple of years.

The success of the new hits from Brentford Road – "Love Bump" (over Slim Smith's "Rougher Yet"), "Natty Chalwa" (the Gladiators' "Roots Natty Roots"), and "Tribute To Marley" (the Studio One cut of Derrick Harriott's "Solomon") – owed something to the new style of mixing that gave a brighter feel to the studio's seminal music, whether in the form of new 'versions' or re-releases of the originals that practically every other label was 'doing-over'. The Lone Ranger's other important hits included "Fort X" (also for Ranglin), with its appropriate Western theme, and "Rose Marie" (for Winston Riley's Techniques label), "M16" and "Fist To Fist Days Done" (for Channel

One), "Trod On" (for Ossie Thomas's Black Solidarity), and "Tribute To All Mothers" (for the US Absissa label, though over the Sly & Robbie rhythm used on Dennis Brown's "Hold On To What You've Got" hit). No performer was more responsible for ushering in the new era than the Lone Ranger, and his influence on a whole generation of deejays (particularly in the UK) was incalculable.

LONE RANGER

M16 (J&L, US).

E This is Lone Ranger at the height of his powers, and "ribbiting" and "bimming" all over the Niney-produced rhythms that heralded Channel One's renaissance in the early 1980s. The title track was responsible for reviving the popular

LIVE DANCEHALL

Jamaican deejays have traditionally made their reputations the hard way, in front of Kingston dancehall audiences, and there are several whose talents can only be appreciated on recordings of their live performances. The format that best served the underground audience for dancehall music were the cassettes of Kingston dances that began to be played on Kingston minibuses from the late 1970s. The cassettes were also sold overseas, in Brooklyn and Brixton, giving deejays reputations well in advance of their debut on record. In 1982 this live dance phenomenon also arrived on vinyl.

The first official recording of a West Kingston dancehall session to appear on disc was of the **Aces Disco**, featuring the name of the moment, **Yellowman**, and his sparring partner, **Fat Head**. The sound quality was not all it could have been, but what made the album sell in serious quantities and prompt an important if short-lived trend was the chance of hearing the era's top rapper in full flight, complete with mistakes and the noise of an enthusiastic West Kingston crowd. In the wake of *Yellowman & A Fat Head Live At Aces*, other producers and sound systems were soon jumping on the bandwagon. Subsequent live dancehall albums gave a wide audience a chance to hear deejays (or, less often, singers like Little John) performing favourite lyrics over different rhythms, or inserting extra verses prompted by the interaction between performer and audience. But a lack of quality control on many of the albums hurriedly released in 1982–83, along with an over-dependence on many of the same rhythms (especially "Never Let Go" and "Full Up"), contributed to the form's rapid decline – spontaneity and a sense of the moment was often not enough.

The death blow was dealt by improvements in the distribution and sound quality of the cheaper and more immediate cassette tapes of the latest sessions from Kingston – a cassette could arrive in London just days after the session took place in West Kingston. Not surprisingly the popularity of cassettes has continued to the present, remaining the best way of keeping up with what's new in the rapidly changing reggae world.

YELLOWMAN & FATHEAD

Live At Aces (Jah Guidance, JA).

The first ever live dancehall album. Several of the subsequent albums improved on the sound quality found here, but this is worth seeking out for its atmosphere, as well as being one of the best proofs that Yellowman is now unjustly neglected.

"Scandal"/"Secretly" rhythm, and cuts of classics like "Shank I Shek", "I Hold the Handle" and "Cuss Cuss" explain why deejays in general – and this one in particular – were carrying the swing (as they said then).

On the Other Side Of Dub (Studio One, JA; Heartbeat, US).

The Lone Ranger's debut Studio One album was so titled because the second side featured dub cuts of the 'toasts' on the first. Presumably, Dodd had this in the can for quite a while before releasing it in 1981, as it misses the big dancehall hits, but it stands as a good set of next cuts to Studio One rhythms that go beyond the obvious ones.

Badda Den Dem (Studio One, JA).

His second album for Dodd was more obviously in the fully developed dancehall mode. Besides mixes that contrast strongly with the previous set's, there are most of the rhythms that were calling the shots, including "Real Rock", "Shank I Shek", "Throw Me Corn", "Full Up" and a second cut of "Never Let Go". Curiously, his really big Studio One hits are still absent.

Rose Marie (Techniques, JA).

Winston Riley pulled out his most enduring rhythms for this set – including "Stalag 17", naturally – and Ranger had the delivery and enough fresh lyrics to do them justice.

Collection (Grapevine, UK).

Twenty of the masked man's biggest hits, ranging from "Barnabus Collins", through "Fist To Fist Days Done", to "Labour Ward". There is sufficient verbal imagination – as well as variation in rhythms – to maintain interest throughout.

VARIOUS ARTISTS

A Dee-Jay Explosion Inna Dance Hall Style (Heartbeat, US).

E A live dancehall session recorded in Clinton 'Jingles' Davey's renowned Skateland, featuring Gemini Disco as the sound, and the cream of 1982's chatting talent – Michigan & Smiley, Welton Irie, Sister Nancy, Eek-A-Mouse and others. Kicking off with four cuts of Gussie's "Pass the Kouchie" rhythm, before some serious Studio One dubplates, the recording captures the feel of the period where it mattered the most.

The Bibow Posse Live (white label, JA).

This Ossie Thomas release has been reissued at least twice but has never appeared with a proper cover or label. What can be said with certainty is that the session must have taken place sometime in the early 1980s, and serves mainly to provide a showcase for Peter Metro. Among the dancehall favourites he is caught seriously attacking are a scorching dubplate of "Never Let Go", Sugar Minott's "No Vacancy" and Sammy Dread's "Roadblock". Other members of the Bibow Posse present include Metro's sparring partner Zu Zu and journeyman singer Robert French. Essential for anyone wanting to sample the excitement of 1980s dancehall.

Junjo Presents A Live Session With Aces International (Volcano, JA; Greensleeves, UK).

Better sound quality than the first Aces album, and some more of Yellowman at his best, along with a selection of the most serious contenders to his throne.

George Phang & Friends Live At Skateland (Powerhouse, JA).

Producer George Phang's turn at the live dancehall album, with deejays including the likes of Johnny Ringo, Nigger Kojak, Mother Liza, John Wayne and Peter Metro's younger brother, Squidley Ranking. Sound quality is good for this sort of recording.

Live At Negril (Kris Disk, JA).

Recorded at the beginning of 1983 at the Fish Whirl Club, this album captures U-Roy's (King) Stur-Gav sound system at the height of its powers, with Sugar Minott, Don Carlos and Josey Wales running the place hot. Particularly interesting is Josey Wales's delivery of "Cowboy Style", which he was to update in the studio for King Jammy over a decade later.

Josey Wales, Charlie Chaplin & U-Roy's Stur-Gav Hi-Fi

The continuity between dancehall and the past achievements of Jamaican producers and performers is exemplified by the role of veterans like King Tubby's former engineer Prince Jammy and Winston Riley, who had been running his own Techniques label since 1968, and in the way in which established singers like Leroy Smart and John Holt were able to adapt to the demands of the new phase. Another important figure from the music's past who contributed to the dancehall explosion was the Originator himself, **U-Roy**, and he did this mainly through the sound system he was running. His original Stur-Gav Hi-Fi set was out of action for a year after the violent 1980 election and the departure of its main deejay (Ranking Joe) and selector (Jah Screw), but was relaunched to become one of the most popular sounds of the time, boasting the two deejays most seriously to rival Yellowman – **Josey Wales** (b. Winston Sterling) and **Charlie Chaplin** (b. Richard Bennett). Further proof of the music's continuity lay in the way in which the unmistakable influence of U-Roy's tone and phrasing could be detected, to varying degrees, in the styles of both.

Josey Wales was part of the rockstone-voiced deejay tradition that stretches back to Prince Jazzbo and continues today with Buju Banton and Bounty Killer. But the Colonel, as he was called, was always more than just a gruff voice that gave the impression that he had seen it all – which he probably had. His first Jamaican hit – a brilliant slice of dancehall commentary, "Let Go Mi Hand" – was for **Henry 'Junjo' Lawes**, and several more followed for the same producer, including the ultimate expression of his self-assurance at the mike, "What Dem Ago Do" (the rest of the question is "...if Josey shut his mouth"). He then went on to record memorable sides for Bunny Roots, Ossie Thomas, George Phang and, as the music reinvented itself yet again in the decade's second half, King Jammy, Jimmy Cliff and Gussie Clarke. In the 1990s he has continued to impress with recordings for Jammy, Robert Livingstone, Philip 'Fatis' Burrell and Bobby Digital; and with the 'combination' style increasing in popularity, he finally came around to recording with his equally talented Stur-Gav partner Charlie Chaplin, as Courtney Cole released "Do Good" (featuring the two deejays with the singers Yami Bolo and Jack Radics) and 'Fatis' Burrell issued "Rebel Without A Cause" (both deejays with Luciano).

More obviously showing U-Roy's influence in his phrasing, Charlie Chaplin has a less gruff but equally serious tone. Sticking to a strictly cultural approach, even when this was not at all fashionable, he was first recorded by the Royals' leader, Roy Cousins, and then went on to follow almost the same trail of producers as Wales, cutting first-rate sides for, among others, Bunny Roots and Junjo Lawes. His most successful period, though, was with George Phang, for whom he recorded what were probably his most popular tunes, "Que Dem" and "Diet Rock". Incredibly, his obvious talent has never been rewarded with major Jamaican hits, though more recent records for 'Fatis' Burrell suggest this might yet happen – particularly as the 'conscious' lyrics with which he's most comfortable have come back into fashion.

CHARLIE CHAPLIN

◉ **Red Pond/Chaplin Chant** (Tamoki Wambesi, UK).

The two Roy Cousins-produced albums that kick-started the Stur-Gav star's recording career. The more consistent is the debut set – which also features the Killimanjaro deejay, Jim Kelly (who was murdered in the Red Pond district of the title) and includes the two minor hits, "Mother In Law" and "Naw Leave Me Chalwa". But the highlights from its successor match that standard, and "Chaplin Chant" itself might even be his single greatest track.

Que Dem (Powerhouse, JA).

Richard Bennett might not have chosen as hard a movie name as fellow Stur-Gav Hi-Fi chatter Josey Wales, or boasted of his ghetto scars, but he had fully absorbed U-Roy's salutary influence, and had more than enough lyrics of consequence. Updatings of "Shank I Shek", "Won't You Come Home", "Heavenless", "Real Rock", "Never Let Go", "Full Up" and "Johnny Dollar" are quintessential dancehall, and Chaplin's cuts are a great deal better than most.

JOSEY WALES

The Outlaw Josey Wales (Greensleeves, UK).

No Way Better Than Yard (Greensleeves, UK).

His first two albums established Josey Wales's reputation beyond Kingston's dancehalls. The *Outlaw* tracks, from Lawes, use some of the Roots Radics' strongest rhythms, and include his first hit, "Let Go Mi Hand", as well as the updating of Delroy Wilson's "Won't You Come" that helped renew the popularity of the rhythm. For the second set he dispensed with the services of a name producer, employed the High Times Band, and again triumphed. Every track uses a dancehall staple – including "Never Let Go", "Real Rock" and "Throw Me Corn" – and it says something about the deejay's commanding presence that they could not have sounded fresher.

Undercover Lover (Powerhouse, JA).

As with the Charlie Chaplin album on the same label, this has one of the best dancehall deejays over the rhythms that were calling the shots, such as "The Lecture", "Psychedelic Rock", "Keep On Moving", "Throw Me Corn" and, of course, "Real Rock". Pity about the cover.

Dem a mad over Yellowman

The popularity of Lone Ranger only hinted at the impact of the man who was to follow him to the top of the deejay pile. **Yellowman** (b. Winston Foster, 1959, Kingston) was a previously unknown sort of reggae phenomenon, an albino deejay, orphaned from an early age, who came through the familiar route of institutes like Maxfield Park and Eventide Home, as well as the more famous Alpha Boys School (see p.9) before dominating Kingston's dancehalls. Consistently outselling vocalists and fellow deejays alike, during the period 1981–84 he was reggae's figurehead, even though he never had much chance of appealing to as wide and varied an audience as Marley. Listen to the records he made at his peak and you'll hear plenty of style, originality and humour, as well as the necessary ability to ride what were some of the strongest rhythms of the time – practically all the leading dancehall producers lined up to record him once he broke big. His ability to improvise lyrics in the dancehall and in the studio always stood him in good stead: "If you good, you know, you have lyrics come straight to you in the dance. Most of the lyrics I do on record, is in the studio I mek them up. Like "I'm Getting Married" – Junjo just call me an' say I must do an album, and I just listen to the rhythms and the lyrics come to me." Turning the daily events of ghetto life into lyrics came effortlessly to Yellowman.

ADRIAN BOOT

King Yellow at the mike

Initially building his reputation with the highly rated Aces Disco sound (source of the first live dancehall album – see p.240) before moving onto Gemini for a time in the early part of 1981, the albino deejay defied all the odds and won himself a large dancehall following. Perhaps the whole idea of an albino performer aroused people's curiosity, but he would hardly have been tolerated behind the mike if he had not possessed at least as much talent as most of his rivals in West Kingston's dancehall circuit. Like many a deejay, Yellowman seemed obsessed with informing the world that every member of the opposite sex was crazy over him, but there was a very important difference with Yellowman (or 'King Yellow', as he became known) which rested precisely on his status as an albino – just about the lowest rung in Jamaican social stratification – and the wit with which he turned this to his advantage. He was willing to stand up and brag about how sexy he was, and Jamaicans appreciated the courage this took, as well as the good humour with which he was able to deal with his unenviable status.

Furthermore, when not chatting "mad over me" lyrics, he was as capable as any of his peers of perceptive social comment, the best examples being a couple of 45s he made with sometime partner, the late Fat Head, "Operation Eradication" (Spider Man) and "Soldier Take Over" (recorded twice, first appearing on the Tanka label, and then for Sly & Robbie's Taxi). Almost as his reign in the dancehall was coming to an end, he was signed by the US major CBS, the first Jamaican deejay to be thus honoured. His releases for Junjo Lawes have been among the biggest sellers in the entire catalogue of the UK independent Greensleeves, and he continues his career on a lower level to the present. If he had been less prolific, his current standing would perhaps be far higher.

YELLOWMAN

◑ **Them A Mad Over Me** (Channel One, US).

And they really were in 1981, when this first appeared, and Yellowman was the best-selling deejay of all time. Further proof, after the *Live At Aces* set (see p.240), that his early work by no means deserves to be dismissed.

◑ **Mr Yellowman** (Greensleeves, UK).

Yellowman was not slow when it came to displaying his talent over the length of albums, and the sheer number can be offputting – particularly as they are not all from the top drawer. His work with Henry 'Junjo' Lawes was pretty consistent, however, and their first album together has stood the test of time particularly well.

◑ **Bad Boy Skanking** (Greensleeves, UK).

Yellowman's second set for Lawes in the same year – 1982 – kept up the standard, not least thanks to the excellent High Times Band rhythms and his total confidence. The CD has three additional tracks, all of which are worthwhile.

YELLOWMAN & JOSEY WALES

◑ **Two Giants Clash** (Arrival, JA; Greensleeves, UK).

A fitting title, as no one was bigger than Yellowman when this appeared in 1984, and Josey Wales was his most serious rival. As things have turned out, the popularity of the Outlaw has outlasted that of the then bigger star. Tackling the same tough Roots Radics rhythms, and produced by Lawes, they seem quite equally matched here. The Jamaican and UK presses have slightly different tracks, but either is worth picking up.

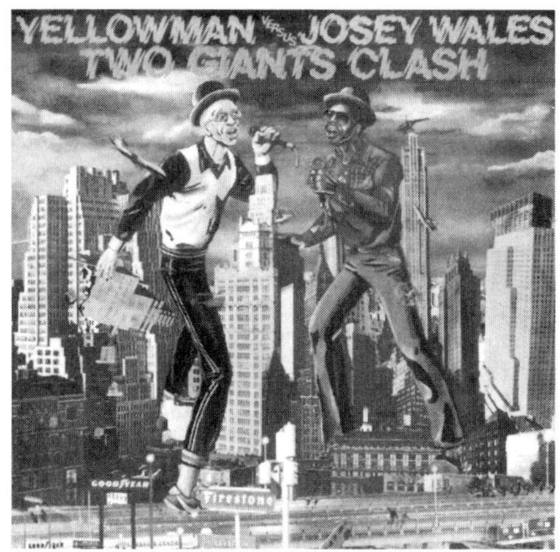

Dance pon the riddim

'Versions' were nothing new. Throughout the 1970s, producers had often followed their big vocal hits with deejays or musicians giving their variations on a theme, employing the same rhythm track. They also sometimes looked further back to the music's past, particularly the rocksteady era, issuing their own cuts of earlier producers' rhythms. Beginning in 1972, **Augustus Pablo** – one of the most original figures in the history of reggae – had begun self-production with updated versions of old Jackie Mittoo hits from Studio One. Singer/producer **Rupie Edwards** had taken the original cut of "My Conversation" from **Bunny Lee** in 1974, and treated it to an entire album's worth of deejay and instrumental versions, in what had then seemed an eccentric experiment. Bunny Lee's own very successful 'flying cymbals' sound, launched in the same year, had involved disco-influenced updatings of vintage Brentford Road and Bond Street material. The **Channel One** and **Joe Gibbs** operations were then simply the most commercially successful of those who followed Striker's lead in what soon became the financially sound modus operandi for record production, and these labels dominated the later 1970s with versions of classic rocksteady rhythms from the same foundation studios.

What was different now was that the rhythms were becoming all-important, with virtually all the producers rushing to cut their own versions of the most popular ones. By 1983, indeed, it was unusual for anyone to have a Jamaican hit employing a completely original rhythm track. Those who didn't experience the excitement of the dancehalls might view the arrival of twenty new versions of, say, "Real Rock" as indicating a lack of creativity, and some people have for this reason dismissed the dancehall phase of reggae as more shoddy than the music that had preceded it. But the real imagination came in making the familiar sound fresh, with each producer struggling to make his own cut the freshest of all.

The Lone Ranger's "Barnabus Collins" was of crucial importance, for besides giving younger deejays a new tone of delivery and several fresh catchphrases, it also revitalized the rhythm for Slim Smith's late 1960s hit, "My Conversation". Soon almost every producer on the island had his own cut on the street. Deejay Jah Thomas stepped in with his self-produced celebration of "Cricket Lovely Cricket" (Midnight Rock), while Barrington Levy praised the qualities of "Collie Weed" (Roots From the Yard) to score his best-selling single to date, and Al Campbell revisited the original lyric for London's Soferno B. Yet "Barnabus Collins" only reflected what was already happening in the dancehalls. There a popular rhythm track would be played repeatedly, with a succession of performers lining up to take their turn in performing over the 'dubplate', each attempting to make it his – or sometimes her – own.

Real rocking in the dancehall

Having already enjoyed a massive local hit with "Rub A Dub Style" (Studio One), a version of Alton Ellis's "I'm Just A Guy", the deejay duo of **Papa Michigan & General Smiley** (b. Anthony Fairclough and Errol Bennett) then released "Nice Up the Dance", which employed a sprightly remix of the Soul Vendors' 1967 rocksteady instrumental, "Real Rock". Needless to say, the title of the new cut neatly summed up the mood of the moment: hedonism rather than a return to Africa was the order of the day. It was not the first time the "Real Rock" rhythm had been versioned. Augustus Pablo recorded four classic cuts in 1973, and Joe Gibbs had released several more five years later. But it had never previously enjoyed quite the popularity it did in 1979–80, when Michigan & Smiley's hit was rapidly followed by vocals such as **Willie Williams**'s "Armageddon Time", which employed the same Studio One rhythm track and mysteriously struck a chord with punk rockers in the UK. Cuts like **Barrington Levy**'s "Looking My Love" (Busy) and **Baddoo**'s "Kinarky" (Scorcher), on the other hand, were little heard outside the reggae specialist market. Further deejay cuts that were almost as successful as the Michigan & Smiley hit included **Nigger Kojak**'s "Nice

Up Jamaica" (Nigger Kojak) and **Jah Thomas**'s "Dance Pon Me Corner" (Jah Guidance), both of which stuck pretty close to the duo's original theme, while more amusing and outrageous variations were offered in the form of **Errol Scorcher**'s biggest hit "Roach In the Corner" (Sir Collins) and, perhaps the most off-the-wall of all the versions, **Archie & Lynn**'s only known record, "Rat In the Centre" (High Note). The Archie & Lynn tune related the tale of rodents infesting a community hall, with only producer Sonia Pottinger's cat able – eventually – to provide the answer to the problem. Three years later, Channel One reworked "Real Rock" again for **Johnny Osbourne**'s very successful "Lend Me Your Chopper" (Hitbound), which in turn prompted yet more versions, and the rhythms seem to have been revived on more or less an annual basis ever since.

Never let go of a hot riddim

The story of dancehall was largely about a succession of (mostly revived) basslines. Vintage instrumentals like **Roland Alphonso**'s "Jah Shakey", **Vin Gordon**'s "Heavenless", **Baba Brooks/Bobby Ellis**'s "Shank I Shek", **Jackie Mittoo**'s "Drum Song", the **Soul Vendors**' "Full Up" and **Jo Jo Bennett**'s "The Lecture" were particularly popular as a source. Classic vocals were also plundered for their rhythms, with the **Maytals**' "54-46 That's My Number", **Alton Ellis**'s "Mad Mad" and the **Heptones**' "Party Time" typical of the rhythms from the 1960s/early 1970s that were given a sometimes excessive number of new treatments. None was quite as popular, though, as the one that had been employed originally for another Slim Smith hit, this time from Studio One – "Never Let Go".

"Never Let Go" has one of the most striking horn riffs in the history of Jamaican music, along with a juggernaut bassline that sounds as if nothing will ever stop it. Clement Dodd himself successfully revived the rhythm with the **Lone Ranger**'s "The Answer" in the mid-1970s, but the flood of versions arrived at the beginning of the dancehall era. The first and one of the best of the new cuts employed a devastating updating by the Greenwich Town producer, **Don Mais**. A vocal from **Phillip Frazer** appeared in 1982, and was soon followed by perhaps the ultimate version, "Pain", from one of the few under-recorded deejays, the very influential **Brigadier Jerry** (b. Robert Russell, 1957, Kingston). A member of the Twelve Tribes of Israel Rastafarian organization, the Brigadier initially honed his strictly 'cultural' approach to mike work on U-Roy's King Stur-Gav Hi-Fi sound, before further building his reputation as the most serious 'reality' deejay of the new decade with appearances on several sound systems, most notably the Twelve Tribes' own Jahlovemuzik. "Pain", released in 1982 on Delroy Stansbury's Jwyanza imprint, was a *tour de force* that demonstrated that the dancehall style was not necessarily at odds with a serious 'cultural' message.

To list all the versions of "Never Let Go" that appeared over the next couple of years would require a chapter in itself. Outstanding deejay cuts included **Josey Wales**'s best ever tune, "Kingston Hot" (for Bunny Roots' Kris Disc label), **Peter Metro & Zu Zu**'s humorous "In the Army" (for Dynamite) and **General Tree**'s "Heart, Mind & Soul" (for Maurice Johnson's Black Scorpio), all of which were enormous Jamaican hits. There was even a second, equally distinguished, cut from Brigadier Jerry – the celebratory "Jamaica Jamaica", for Jahlovemuzik. Among the singers' versions, **Dennis Brown**'s "I Can't Stand It", (Jammy's), **Barrington Levy**'s "Like A Soldier" (Hitbound), **Patrick Andy**'s "Cowhorn Chalice" (Ujama) and **Sugar Minott**'s "Rydim" (Powerhouse) were significantly different to attract attention. But the most different of all – thanks to an advanced semi-digital rhythm track – was the seriously progressive "Rub A Dub Soldier" (Studio Worx) from **Paul Blake & the Blood Fire Posse**, a vocal/instrumental group that failed to maintain their initial impact. "Never Let Go" has proven its classic status by refusing to disappear – and there are likely to be more new cuts in the future.

The foundation studio answers back

Studio One, which had supplied the original cuts for nearly all the rhythms now being recorded in the Kingston studios, responded to the wholesale 'versioning' of its rocksteady/early reggae hits by releasing remixes of the originals along with new cuts of its own. In fact, *Live Loving*, the 1978 debut Studio One album from **Sugar Minott** (b. Lincoln Minott, 1956, Kingston) preceded fully fledged dancehall and played an important part in its development by showing how new lyrics could be seamlessly grafted onto old rhythms. Two similar Studio One LPs – *Truths and Rights* from **Johnny Osbourne** (b. 1948) and *Bobby Babylon* from **Freddie McGregor** (b. 1955, Clarendon) – followed in the next year with comparable success. Though Osbourne had cut the beautiful "All I Have Is Love" for Clement Dodd back in 1969, and Winston Riley had released the "Warrior " and "See & Blind" 45s, as well as the *Come Back Darling* album the same year, his career had lost its impetus during an extended stay in Canada. Upon his return to the island in 1979 he went back to Studio One, and turned out three very strong singles – "Forgive Them", "Love Is Here To Stay" and "Jealousy, Heartache & Pain". These were followed by the album, and soon he was one of the most prolific and popular singers around, even if not all his lyrics matched those of the Studio One set.

Freddie McGregor also has claims to veteran status, having made a couple of records with Ernest Wilson of the Clarendonians in the mid-1960s, when the pre-teen had to stand on a box to reach the mike. He had also been responsible for a string of quality singles under his own name at Studio One in the 1970s, but it was only after he had left Brentwood Road to record with the Soul Syndicate that Dodd released the exceptional LP he had been holding back. Modern mixes made material that was at least a couple of years old seem totally modern, and vintage rhythms sounded as if they'd been specifically built for the songs.

Three years later, the vintage keyboard maestro **Jackie Mittoo** – working with fellow keyboards player Pablove Black, the jazz-oriented guitarist Ernest Ranglin, the bassist Bagga Walker and the drummer Horsemouth Wallace – came up with *Showcase*, his best set for several years, featuring refreshing new interpretations of classic Brentford Road rhythms. Those busy versioning Studio One rhythms were being answered in their own terms: with completely fresh reinterpretations of classic rhythms, recorded at the studio where they were originally put together. Dodd then pressed a superb series of 10" 45s in New York that presented some of his finest direct responses to the dancehall revolution, including Freddie McGregor's "Africa Here I Come", a marvellous cut of the Soul Vendors' instrumental "Full Up" that equalled the Mighty Diamonds' very well-received "Pass the Kouchie" version for Gussie Clarke, and the former Paragon **Tyrone Evans**'s sublime vocal, "How Sweet It Is", which employed Jackie Mittoo's vintage "Jericho Skank".

BRIGADIER JERRY

◑ **Jamaica Jamaica** (RAS, US).

The most respected – and imitated – deejay of the dancehall era, though far from the most prolific. Committed to the Twelve Tribes of Israel organization, he has always considered performing for their Jah Love sound system far more important than the treadmill of Kingston studio work, and has not

DAVID CORIO

Serious reasoning from deejay Brigadier Jerry

appeared on disc a great deal, by Jamaican standards. This, however, does him almost full justice, with the title track and "Kushunpeng" particularly standing out.

FREDDIE McGREGOR

◑ **Bobby Babylon** (Studio One, JA; Heartbeat, US).

E Dodd didn't exactly rush Freddie McGregor's first set for Studio One. This most gifted of singers had recorded for the label since the mid-1960s (if his work with the Clarendonians is included), yet this exceptional album was not released until 1980. Five of his 45s were reworked to even greater effect, and there was even a successful version of the Ethiopians' first hit, "I'm Gonna Take Over Now", while the other tracks follow the example of Sugar Minott's debut LP, with well-crafted new songs placed over classic Studio One rhythms.

SUGAR MINOTT

◑ **Live Loving** (Studio One, JA; Heartbeat, US).

E Few debut albums have made such an impact as Sugar Minott's. Besides the sweetly expressive voice, which inspired the name change from the more prosaic Lincoln Minott, there was also the ability to write quality new songs over vintage rhythms. This fusion of the new and old was to become the norm of the dancehall era, but few were to accomplish it in quite such an accomplished manner. Arguably the first dancehall album, released in 1978, and certainly one of the best from any era of Jamaican music.

◑ **Showcase** (Studio One, JA).

His second album for Studio One employed the same formula of new lyrics over established rhythms, but with dub versions following the vocals, and the then-fashionable syndrums making its presence felt throughout. Maybe not quite the equal of the ground-breaking debut, but near enough, and including the ultimate herb dealer's anthem, "Oh Mr DC".

JACKIE MITTOO

◉ **Showcase** (Studio One, US).

What makes this album really interesting is that it made no attempt to imitate the Roots Radics' approach, but to answer it on the foundation studio's own terms. Classic rhythms associated with Carlton & his Shoes, the Abyssinians and Alexander Henry never sounded quite like this before, and – alongside a second cut to Mittoo's own "After Christmas" and a version of Marley's "No Woman No Cry" – confirmed that veteran musicians could still take the music another step forward.

JOHNNY OSBOURNE

◑ **Truths And Rights** (Studio One, JA; Heartbeat, US).

E Released a couple of years after Sugar Minott's *Live Loving*, Johnny Osbourne's only Studio One album follows much the same formula with comparable success. He was never to leave vintage Studio One rhythms completely behind, but he obviously spent a little longer on the lyrics when he was recording this, and that makes the difference.

PAPA MICHIGAN & GENERAL SMILEY

◑ **Rub A Dub Style** (Studio One, JA; Heartbeat, US).

The two deejays who popularized the 'combination' style at the close of the 1970s, particularly with "Rub A Dub Style" and "Nice Up the Dance". The album presents the two hits, adds their versions of the Soul Vendors' "Full Up", the Heptones' "Pretty Looks Isn't All" and "Heptones Gonna Fight", and the Paragons' "Danger In Your Eyes", and completes the package with their dubs. Clement Dodd's answer to those who were making money with 'versions' of his rhythms.

Henry 'Junjo' Lawes rules the dancehall

The dancehall era saw the rise of a new generation of sound-system operators and record producers, and the most consistently successful for the first half of the 1980s was a former singer from the ghetto around Olympic Way, West Kingston. In a reversal of the usual CV, **Henry 'Junjo' Lawes** first earned his reputation in the studio rather than behind a sound system's massed speakers. Altough he had first ventured into production with Linval Thompson the previous year, in 1979 Lawes more or less launched dancehall as a fully developed musical style. He held a series of sessions at Channel One that resulted in, first, the important series of hit 45s from the 15-year-old **Barrington Levy**, and then the young singer's ground-breaking debut LP, *Bounty Hunter* (see p.235). Levy's powerful vocal attack would have made an impact in any era, but it was the combination of his distinctive voice and the raw, uncompromising rhythm tracks from the Roots Radics that particularly grabbed the attention of reggae lovers. Lawes's employment of the innovative young engineer, Hopeton 'Overton' Brown – better known as **Scientist** – at the mixing desk was the final ingredient that guaranteed the album's success, and that of most of the producer's subsequent work.

VARIOUS ARTISTS – HENRY 'JUNJO' LAWES PRODUCTIONS

◑ **Volcano I (Total Recall)** (VP, US).

◑ **Volcano II (Total Recall)** (VP, US).

The dancehall era's leading producer had too many hits in the reggae marketplace for two albums to cover them all, but these at least draw together the most important. Each album has fourteen tracks – vocals on the first, deejays the second – and the faultless selection ranges from the most rootsy (Barrington Levy's "Prison Oval Rock"), through singers with lighter concerns (Michael Prophet's quite incredible "Here Comes the Bride"), to many of the most memorable deejay records (Michigan & Smiley's "Diseases"). Better compilations of early 1980s dancehall are hard to find.

Junjo calls the tune

Never owning his own studio, but usually using Channel One, Junjo operated from Myrie Avenue, just off Spanish Town Road in Kingston 11 – an area that had been celebrated by the Royal Rasses. More hits on his Volcano label quickly followed his triumphs with Barrington Levy, all employing driving rhythms from, first, the Roots Radics and then the guitarist Earl 'Chinna' Smith's High Times Band. Among the most striking was one by a performer calling himself **Eek-A-Mouse**, whose very original "Wa Do Dem" set another trend. The younger singers performing in the dancehalls had been rapidly learning a thing or two from the deejays, but no one brought the two approaches closer than the man previously known as Ripton Hilton (b. 1957, Kingston). He

DAVID CORIO

Eek-A-Mouse – originator of singjay style

had begun his recording career in the late 1970s, as a conventional roots singer in the reflective Pablo Moses mould, cutting a couple of minor masterpieces under his real name. The real break came when he changed his name – reputedly after a racehorse he had followed and lost money on – and began adding abstract and oriental-sounding utterances to his vocals, in the style originated by **Ranking Joe** (see p.232) on Stur-Gav at the end of the previous decade. Joe Gibbs held back on releasing the original cut of "Wa Do Dem", and allowed Junjo to have a hit with Eek-A-Mouse's second recording of the lyric, supported by a deadly metal-tipped Roots Radics rhythm. Thus was born 'singjay' – a style that was not quite straight singing or deejaying.

Among Lawes's other important hits was **(Papa) Michigan & (General) Smiley**'s "Diseases", which proved that the deejay partnership was not entirely reliant on original Studio One rhythm tracks – this utilized a stinging Roots Radics updating of Alton Ellis's rocksteady hit, "Mad Mad". Both **Barry Brown**'s "Give Israel Another Try" and **Michael Prophet**'s "Gunman" demonstrated, in turn, how the young producer could handle more orthodox roots singers with equally convincing results, and the latter record boasted Lawes's most enduring original rhythm. Barry Brown was always one of the most impassioned of the youthman singers who recorded mostly 'cultural' lyrics at the turn of the decade, and after establishing himself with uncompromisingly heavy 45s for Bunny Lee, impressed equally with work for such as Sugar Minott and Tony Robinson, along with his own Jabba Roots label. At the beginning of the 1980s, Michael Prophet was primarily associated with Vivian Jackson, for whom he had recorded the album that established his name outside of Jamaica, *Serious Reasoning* (see p.158). But it was his far more prolific work for Junjo that ensured the emotive singer of a wider and younger audience.

For the most part, however, Lawes tended to concentrate on those vocalists with closer links to Kingston's dancehall circuit, including two relative veterans who had reinvented themselves – **Tony Tuff** and **Johnny Osbourne**, both of whom had made excellent 'cultural' records in the previous decade, but adapted to the new one with apparent enthusiasm. The latter in particular could fill out what were often fairly thin lyrical ideas with more than enough style, and both were rewarded with instant dancehall popularity. Osbourne's main rival as the dancehall singer *par excellence* was the younger **Frankie Paul** (b. Paul Blake, 1965, Kingston), who was obviously influenced by both Stevie Wonder and Dennis Brown, but applied his talent in true dancehall fashion in seemingly endless runs of hits for every producer on the island. His tunes for Junjo – especially "Pass the Tu-Sheng-Peng" and "Dem A Talk 'Bout" – were among the best of his early years, and at the very least hinted at the arrival of an enduring star.

EEK-A-MOUSE

◑ Wa Do Dem (Volcano, JA; Greensleeves, UK; RAS, US).

Under his real name, Ripton Hilton, Eek-A-Mouse made a handful of straight roots records, rather in the style of Pablo Moses. Major success, however, came with the change of name and the 'singjay' style that went with it. At first listen, the combination of singing and deejay styles, with its generous use of oriental-sounding abstract utterances, can sound gimmicky; closer attention reveals a more serious level to the rodent's art. The title track is a dancehall masterpiece, and nothing disappoints.

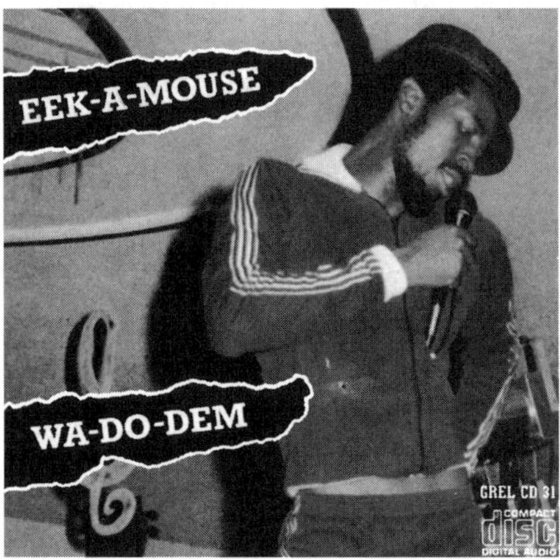

◑ Mouseketeer (Greensleeves, UK).

His final set for Lawes confirmed he could handle a 'reality' lyric as well as anyone, with titles like "Queen Elizabeth" and "Star, Daily News Or Gleaner". "How I Got My Name" explains precisely that in a tune that is just as much about reality – albeit of a less serious kind.

JOHNNY OSBOURNE

◑ Fally Lover/Never Stop Fighting (Greensleeves, UK).

If Johnny Osbourne was a little too prolific in the 1980s, quality control was seldom forgotten in his output for Lawes, as demonstrated in the two albums brought together here. "Too Bad Daughter" employs the same rhythm as the Wailing Souls' "Kingdom Rise Kingdom Fall" tour de force, while our hero's further complaints about women – "Fally Lover", "Too Sexy" and "Ice Cream Love" – are over Roots Radics workouts of the same high order. The lyrics are sometimes lightweight, but, with the rhythm tracks taking no prisoners, that is hardly the main concern.

PAPA MICHIGAN & GENERAL SMILEY

◑ **Downpression** (Greensleeves, UK).

The album on which the ground-breaking deejay duo showed they were not dependent on original Studio One rhythms, but could sound equally at home on Roots Radics versions of the same – or an exceptional cut of Harry J's "Cuss Cuss". The sound could not be purer dancehall, but, the lyrics – as befits the album title – are strictly 'cultural'. "Diseases" was one of Lawes's biggest hits, and probably Michigan & Smiley's greatest record.

FRANKIE PAUL

⦿ **Pass the Tu-Sheng-Peng/Tidal Wave** (Greensleeves, UK).

Both the albums brought together here – one from 'Junjo' Lawes, the other from George Phang – helped confirm Frankie Paul's growing reputation in the mid-1980s. The Lawes-produced tracks include at least four classics – "Tu-Sheng-Peng" itself, "Jump No Fence", "Them A Talk About" and "War Is In the Dance" – along with tracks that fall only a little short. The George Phang part is almost as strong, with the singer's energy amazingly infectious throughout, and Sly & Robbie showing they were not keeping all their best rhythms for their own label.

MICHAEL PROPHET

⦿ **Gunman/Righteous Are the Conqueror** (Greensleeves, UK).

The singer sounded just as much at home on these Roots Radics rhythms produced by Lawes as those of Vivian Jackson that brought him to most people's attention, though the quality of the material gathered here does vary. "Gunman" remains the singer's greatest single track.

Junjo's vintage singers

Even the veteran **John Holt**, whose hits with producers like Duke Reid, Clement Dodd and Bunny Lee were already considered classics, was served well with rugged Lawes-produced Roots Radics rhythms for the hits "Ghetto Queen", "Police In Helicopter" and a superb updating of his own Brentford Road chestnut, "A Love I Can Feel". Among the other established vocalists to benefit from the Lawes touch, and to reach a new audience with modern dancehall rhythms, were **Alton Ellis**, **Leroy Smart**, **Ken Boothe** and **Junior Murvin**, but none of the vintage acts expanding their audiences with Roots Radics rhythms flourished more under his guidance than the **Wailing Souls** (see pp.174–175), always one of the most consistent of Jamaican vocal-harmony groups. They simply maintained standards set with Studio One, Channel One and their own Massive label on a series of 12" singles that combined their customary cultural concerns with some of the most brutal and inspired of the Junjo's rhythms.

Singers performing in the increasingly more popular declamatory style associated with the Waterhouse area were also represented on Junjo's labels, with former Black Uhuru member **Don Carlos** and Augustus Pablo protégé **Hugh Mundell** (see p.161) both cutting strong records, often with fairly traditional cultural themes.

DON CARLOS

◑ **Day To Day Living** (Greensleeves, UK).

Don Carlos suffered from the sort of overexposure that stifles the long-term careers of all but the most exceptional Jamaican performers. This third album exposed his reliance on a limited number of melodic and lyrical ideas, though benefiting from Lawes's handling of the Roots Radics, as well as Scientist and Soldgie at the mixing board.

JOHN HOLT

◑ **Police In Helicopter** (Greensleeves, UK).

A mostly 'reality' set that might surprise anyone who thinks of the former Paragon simply as

Jamaica's finest interpreter of love ballads. Curiously, the two straight love songs are the least inspired on the album – while the title track, "Chanting" and "I Got Caught" show him as much a roots man at heart as anyone.

HUGH MUNDELL

Mundell (Greensleeves, UK).

A good example of the indivisibility of early 1980s roots and dancehall, with Augustus Pablo's prodigy wailing over hardcore Roots Radics rhythms. Most of the time his thematic concerns are unaltered, and lyrics like those of "Red, Gold & Green" and "Tell I A Lie" could have been recorded with Pablo. "Jacqueline", however, shows him equally at ease with more typical dancehall fare.

THE WAILING SOULS

Fire House Rock (Volcano, JA; Greensleeves, UK).

E The veteran vocal-harmony group adapted easily to the new era and recording with the Roots Radics – or perhaps the Lawes approach did not represent such a sharp break with the past as it seemed at the time. Whichever view you take, there can be no argument that the first album made by the Wailing Souls with Junjo is as flawless as either their Studio One debut or the self-produced *Wild Suspense*. The apocalyptic "Kingdom Rise Kingdom Fall" might make the greatest initial impact, but everything eventually reveals classic qualities.

Inchpinchers (Greensleeves, UK).

The Souls' second album for Lawes is very worthwhile, without quite reaching the heights of its predecessor.

Volcano's deejays

Junjo's Volcano label also had hits with practically every deejay who meant anything in the dancehalls of the day. The first rank of these included the Stur-Gav stars **Josey Wales** and **Charlie Chaplin** (see pp.242–243), both of whom had obviously learned much of their craft from U-Roy, but skilfully applied the older man's tuition to Junjo's modern rhythms. The man known as **Nicodemus** (b. Cecil Wellington, 1957), who had come to notice playing sound systems such as Socialist Roots, Taurus and Tapetone, could also be placed in a particular deejay tradition – his abrasive, lived-in voice made him sound totally authoritative, in the manner of Prince Jazzbo. **Early B** (b. Earlando Neil), who had played with the Sound Imperial and King Majesty sounds, belonged to a line of deejays stretching back to I-Roy, who always excelled when relating a story; Early's tone and delivery were very much his own, and he managed better than many of his contemporaries to adapt his skills at the dancehall mike to the recording studio.

It helped for a deejay to have some unique characteristic, and **Peter Metro** (b. Peter Clarke) made a speciality of chatting some of his lyrics in Spanish. Taking his name from the Metro Media sound with which he worked at the Gemini Club on Halfway Tree Road, he had the kind of looks more suited to a romantic balladeer than a rough-and-tough mike man, and was arguably best heard on live session recordings, where there is no mistaking either his energy or hold on dancehall patrons. **Ranking Toyan** (see p.234), a slightly asthmatic-sounding deejay from the Socialist Roots and Romantic Hi-Fi sound systems, was another highly rated live performer who only sometimes lived up to his dancehall reputation on record; Junjo, along with Don Mais (his first producer), caught him at very near his best – most notably on the *How the West Was Won* album, which made a considerable impact in London, partly thanks to the attractive packaging given it by Greensleeves. The same UK company served future producer **Captain Sinbad** just as well with a similarly eye-catching cover, and Junjo's pairing of Trinity's younger brother **Clint Eastwood** (b. Robert Brammer) with the UK deejay **General Saint** (Winston Hislop) even reached the lower regions of the British pop charts. But when it came to sales, nothing could quite match the alchemy between the fastest-rising producer and the most popular chatter of the era – Yellowman (see p.243).

CAPTAIN SINBAD

Seven Voyages Of Captain Sinbad (Greensleeves, UK).

Now concentrating on his own label and producing other performers, Sinbad was formerly a very accomplished deejay in his own right, as shown over these rough Roots Radics rhythms for Junjo.

CLINT EASTWOOD & GENERAL SAINT

Two Bad DJ (Greensleeves, UK).

To dismiss the music of this successful deejay combination as 'pop-reggae' is to overlook the toughness of the Roots Radics rhythms used on their debut album together. "Tribute To General Echo", their first 45, was obviously aimed directly at a dancehall audience already familiar with the late slackness master, and even their minor pop hit, "Another One Bites the Dust", employed Michael Prophet's hard "Gunman" rhythm. One of Greensleeves' best-selling albums, and deservedly so.

RANKING TOYAN

How the West Was Won (Volcano, JA; Greensleeves, UK).

The title track employed the "Gunman" rhythm before the Michael Prophet tune had reached the streets, while other 'Junjo' Lawes hits used include Johnny Osbourne's "Backra" and "Ice Cream Love", as well as the Wailing Souls' magnificent "Bandits Taking Over". With no gaps between the tracks, the feel is very much that of a sound-system session of the time, and Toyan – for all his obvious talent – never quite repeated the feat.

Junjo's last dancehall days

Before moving to New York in 1985, and then temporarily bowing out of the music business, he also launched a singer who was to be one of the most successful of the subsequent digital age, the very gifted **Cocoa Tea** (b. Calvin Scott, 1960, Clarendon), whose honeyed voice would have brought him a healthy following in any era of Jamaican music. His records for Junjo, including his initial hits "Rocking Dolly" and "Lost My Sonia", displayed a marvellous vitality as well as purity of vocal tone, and were only let down by weak lyrics. We can only speculate on what might have happened had dancehall's most prominent producer stayed in Kingston for the early days of computerized rhythms in the second half of the decade, but after a spell in an American prison Junjo did successfully relaunch himself in the 1990s, when he again worked with Josey Wales, Yellowman and Cocoa Tea, as well as a new generation of performers.

DAVID CORIO

Singing sweet: Cocoa Tea

COCOA TEA

Rocking Dolly (RAS, US).

The sweet-voiced one from 1985, just before digital rhythms took over, and featuring the Roots Radics at their finest. "Lost Me Sonia" and "Rocking Dolly" were the enormous hits that established the appropriately named Cocoa Tea, and the rest of the tracks all employ the popular Junjo Lawes dancehall rhythms of the day. Only the sometimes-less-than-inspired lyrics prevent this from being an essential choice.

Prince Jammy

Henry 'Junjo' Lawes's main rival, and the man who would eventually take his crown, was Lloyd James, aka **Prince Jammy** (later promoted to King Jammy). Jammy had been active in the music business since the 1960s, running a small sound system in West Kingston, as well as building and repairing amplifiers for others. The first few years of the next decade he had spent in Canada, and upon his return to Jamaica in 1976 he worked with the dub master himself, King Tubby, before throwing himself wholeheartedly into the sound-system business and record production (see p.217).

The first hits – Half Pint and Junior Reid

Jammy had released music even before he had set up his own studio in his house at 38 St Lucia Road (just around the corner from where he was born). Taking advantage of the contacts he made in the music business after returning to Kingston, in 1976 he released a couple of Vivian Jackson productions (one a killer Jah Stitch version of "Judgement On the Land"), but did not enter into production until a year later, selling the debut **Black Uhuru** album to the UK Third World label in the winter of 1977. But it was at the beginning of the next decade that both his sound system and new label – with the 's' on **Jammy's** printed as a dollar sign – really made an impact.

From the same notorious Waterhouse area in West Kingston where Jammy had his headquarters came a new dancehall singer, **Half Pint** (b. Lyndon Roberts, 1962, Kingston), who – along with Johnny Osbourne – made the greatest impact of the performers Jammy recorded in 1983. Half Pint had already gained experience and something of a reputation playing on sound systems like Mellow Vibes Hi-Fi and Black Scorpio when he was taken into the recording studio by the up-and-coming production partnership of Myrie Lewis & Errol Marshall. Then Jammy provided him with his first hits ("Pouchie Lou", "One In A Million" and "Money Man Skank"), employing confident, infectious rhythms from the High Times Band that possessed many of the qualities of vintage rocksteady, with a totally modern dancehall brashness. Over these rhythms, the young singer added his own vibrant vocal styling – his excitement at being let loose in a recording studio was only too obvious, and an important part of his appeal. Such was the positive response of record buyers to these singles that an exceptional debut album, *Money Man Skank*, was rushed out for the local market (as well as export), and another, *One In A Million*, appeared in the UK the next year. Half Pint was always limited in the melodies he used, but his best records – and this certainly included those for Jammy – possessed all the energy, style and ebullience that exemplified early 1980s dancehall at its most positive.

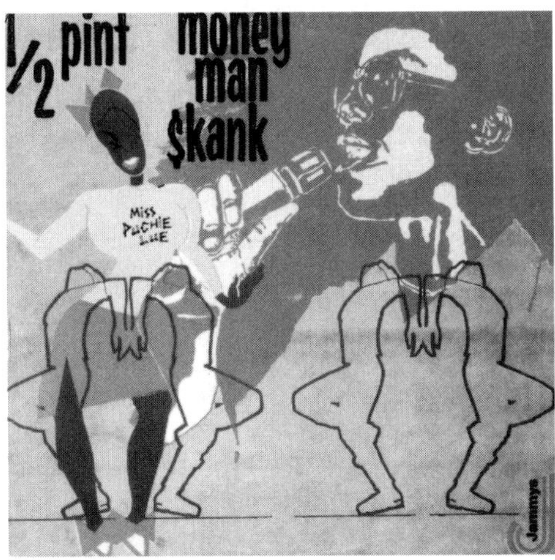

Alongside his triumphs with Half Pint, Jammy scored best sellers in both the Jamaican and the UK reggae markets by another distinctive youthman singer, **Junior Reid**. Since his debut single for Hugh Mundell, recorded when he was only 13, Reid's vocal technique had improved considerably. Besides sounding a great deal more assured and on key, he had also incorporated the techniques of the fast-talk deejays – one of the best examples of the positive influence of deejays on the new generation of singers. His career has outlasted those of the majority of his dancehall contemporaries, but he has only occasionally recaptured the degree of excitement of hits such as "Higgler Move" and "Boom Shack A Lack" for Jammy. Perhaps he has always needed the fresh ideas of another producer – in the dancehall period he gained from the varied approaches of not only Jammy, but also Sugar Minott, Robert Palmer, Errol Thompson, Delroy Wright and Lewis & Marshall.

HALF PINT

Money Man Skank (Jammy's, JA).

E Half Pint might have always relied on very similar melodies, but Prince Jammy's no-prisoners-taken approach to building rhythms ensured that interest was maintained throughout his debut set. "Mr Landlord" is perhaps the finest version of "Hypocrites" after the Wailers' original.

One In A Million (Greensleeves, UK).

Repeats two tracks from the above LP, and adds another eight prime Prince Jammy productions. The hit singles not on the previous set are the title track and "One Big Ghetto".

JUNIOR REID

Boom Shack A Lack (Greensleeves, UK).

Another album that argues for Prince Jammy having brought out the best in the High Times Band. The future Black Uhuru singer's vocal approach is not quite as predictable as it was to become when he produced himself, and he only puts a foot wrong when attempting Billy Stewart's soul classic, "Sitting In the Park". A pity that "Higgler Move", his best single for Jammy, was not added for the CD release.

The hits continue

The most consistent hitmaker among all of Jammy's vocalists was **Johnny Osbourne**, an older performer who, after spells with Winston Riley and Studio One, had reoriented his style towards the dancehall audiences of the day, and was particularly successful with the biggest reggae hit of 1983, "Water Pumping" (a reworking of Hopeton Lewis's rocksteady classic, "Take It Easy", that celebrated the dance of the record's title). This was followed by a series of sound-system anthems, such as "Rewind" and "In Your Area", and he regularly returned to Jammy during the digital age with similarly successful results.

Sugar Minott's "Give the People" was another good example of Jammy's confident approach to hard-hitting dancehall tunes, and continued the run of outstanding numbers the singer had been notching up for a variety of producers. Sounding just as comfortable on his rhythms was the well-established **Dennis Brown**, who was on vintage form with "They Fight I" – as spirited a record as anything he ever made.

Jammy was not to change his title until a couple of years after the digital revolution he initiated, but by the close of 1984 he was king in all but name – ruling on both sound system and record.

DENNIS BROWN

Slow Down (Greensleeves, UK; RAS, US).

The usual mixture of love and cultural lyrics from reggae's most consistent singer, distinguished by Jammy's tough rhythms. The versions of the Gaylads' "Joy In the Morning" and John Holt's "Let's Build Our Dreams" might seem superfluous, but the other ten tracks – including "They Fight I" – show singer and producer in top form.

JOHNNY OSBOURNE

Folly Ranking (Positive Sounds, JA; Jammy's, UK).

The title track, a warning to a particular bad boy posse, was the one to signal that Johnny Osbourne was about to be a major force. "Mr Walker" and "Bet You A Fret" are the other exceptional tracks, and the entire set showcases both producer and singer on the brink of real success.

VARIOUS ARTISTS – KING JAMMY PRODUCTIONS

King Jammy: A Man & His Music Volume 3 – Hits Style (RAS, US).

E The fifteen hits collected here cover roots (Black Uhuru's "I Love Selassie" and Hugh Mundell's "Jah Fire") and computerized ragga (Cocoa Tea's "Come Again" and Frankie Paul's "Sarah"), as well as early 1980s dancehall (Johnny Osbourne's "Water Pumping", Junior Reid's "Higgler Move" and Half Pint's "Mr Landlord"). The spirit of dancehall is dominant (just about), and there is not yet a better selection on CD of Mr James's early 1980s dancehall hits.

Sugar Minott

If Henry 'Junjo' Lawes remains the producer most associated with dancehall, several of his less prolific rivals deserve credit for developing styles of their own and releasing music that was occasionally just as good. Among the most obviously gifted of these was **Sugar Minott** (b. Lincoln Minott, 1956, Kingston), whose major contribution to the period was threefold: as an extremely individual and popular singer; as an accomplished producer; and as a very successful sound-system operator. He was also a tireless promoter of fresh singers and deejays – invariably youthful strugglers from the same tough ghetto background as himself.

ADRIAN BOOT

Youth promoter Sugar Minott

The singer at Studio One

Sugar Minott's singing career began in 1974 with the **African Brothers**, an impressive vocal-harmony group that teamed him with another future dancehall star **Tony Tuff** (b. Winston Morris) and **Derrick Howard**. A handful of their singles from this period have remained 'revive' session favourites in the UK – "Party Night" for an obscure producer called Duke Thelwell, "Mysterious Nature" for Rupie Edwards, and the self-produced "Torturing". On their own Ital imprint they also adapted the Abyssinians' style of close harmonizing on minor-chord melodies for three roots classics – "Lead Us Father', "Youths Of Today" and "Righteous Kingdom" – and even approached the standard of their most obvious influence.

Minott then went solo at Studio One, where he foreshadowed much of what was to happen in the dancehall era. The difference between the material collected on his debut album for Dodd and the many youthman singers who were to follow in his wake was simply that he had the chance to record over the original cuts of some of the rhythms that were already beginning to provide the basis of the dancehall style. Besides the honeyed quality of his tone, which gave him the first name by which he became best known, Minott's music was also characterized by the sheer quality of his songwriting, particularly in the way in which he made new lyrics perfectly fit the old Brentford Road rhythm tracks. It was this ability, more than any other, that was to make him eminently suitable for the dancehall era just around the corner.

Black Roots and Youth Promotion

In 1978, Sugar Minott left Brentwood Road to set up his own labels, **Black Roots** and **Youth Promotion**. The first self-produced he released was "Man Hungry", a well-structured sweetly sung sufferer's lament that was easily the equal of his Studio One gems. This was soon followed by "Hard Time Pressure", his initial UK release and another excellently performed, written and produced record that confirmed he had made the right move. A string of high-calibre tunes, including "River Jordan", "Rome" and "I Wanna Be With Jah", further demonstrated that he had spent his time at Clement Dodd's studio learning all he could about producing quality records.

The title Youth Promotion was thoroughly apposite, as Minott showed a very real commitment to helping develop new talent from the West Kingston ghettos he knew so well. He offered assistance not only as a forward-looking producer but also through his sound system, also named Youth Promotion, on which the young, often raw, performers sometimes received their first exposure to the dancehall public. (The selector for the sound was **Jah Stitch**, the former Tippertone deejay who had enjoyed hits with Bunny Lee in the late 1970s.) Commercially, few of the records released on Sugar's labels were as successful as his own efforts, but **Barry Brown**'s "Not So Lucky", **Junior Reid**'s "Original Foreign Mind" (credited as a co-production between Reid and Minott) and **Tenor Saw**'s "Lots Of Sign" sold well and stand among the most enduring of the period. Another accomplished singer he recorded was **Michael Palmer** (sometimes known as Palmer Dog), who had sung with the Stereophonic sound, and showed traces of Leroy Smart's gritty vocal attack in his approach. "No Run Long Ketch" was a dancehall classic, as was his first Jamaican hit "Smoke the Weed" for Channel One and "My Region" for Black Scorpio; unfortunately, he fell into the familiar trap of simply recording too much in his few months of glory, and his career never developed in quite the way it should have. The UK-based **Trevor Hartley** had one consummate 45 released on Black Roots, "Africa", which was one of the more positive results of Sugar's increasingly spending time in London, where he had gained a large following.

As might be expected from anyone so involved with the sound-system scene in both countries, Minott also produced several interesting deejay singles, the most interesting being **Ranking Joe**'s excellent "Youthman Promotion", **Captain Sinbad**'s "51 Storm" (featuring an uncredited 9-year-old Little John) and **Ranking Dread**'s "Super Star". Nevertheless, Youth Promotion's main contribution to the dancehall phase of reggae was as a popular and influential sound system that enjoyed enough stature to play opposite such as Prince Jammy's and Black Scorpio. Sugar Minott himself would perhaps have been a more dominant force in Jamaican music but for his popularity in the UK and subsequent absences from the Kingston studios and dancehalls.

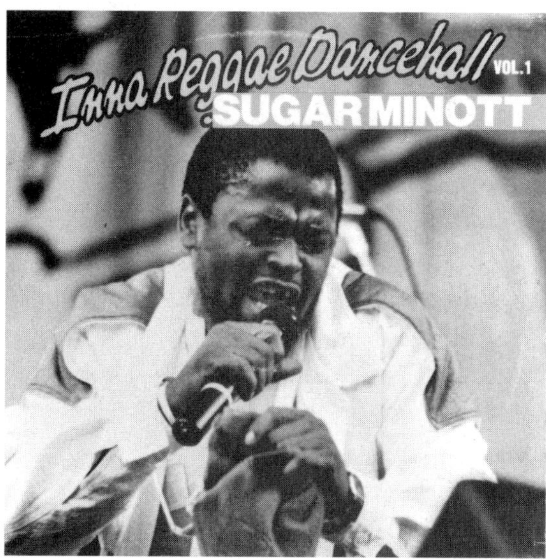

Minott also financed his producing activities and sound system by freelancing in typical Jamaican fashion for numerous other producers, including King Miguel, Carlton Patterson, Barry Brown, Mikey Dread and Martin 'Mandingo' Williams. Even after his own labels were well established, one of the busiest men in Jamaican music also cut equally strong records for Tristan Palma, Prince Jammy's, Sly & Robbie, George Phang, Niney and Maurice Johnson. Practically any Sugar Minott record from the first half of the 1980s is worth investigating, though his output in the last half of the decade was less consistent.

JUNIOR REID SPEAKS THE TRUTH

Junior Reid was one of the singers who bridged roots and dancehall, beginning with a single released by Augustus Pablo in the late 1970s, and then making records for top dancehall producers of the next decade, such as Sugar Minott, Prince Jammy and Delroy Wright. A spell with Black Uhuru took away from his dancehall credibility for a while, but this returned with a rough series of self-productions that included the anthemic "One Blood".

"As I start to understand myself, as a youth at the age of about 12 to 13, so I used to sing around my yard. That was in Waterhouse, on Balmagie Avenue, Kingston 11, near King Tubby's – that's the same road Jammy's grew up on. Then when we start sing-sing, me sing 'pon mi corner, fe mi friends dem. In the evening, when my grandmother go into her bed, she always sing, sometimes me an' her singing "Meet Me By the River" and "Old Rugged Cross", and all dem tune deh. And me just keep on singing till I meet this youth name Locksley Castell. Locksley involved in the music, so it kinda make me want to involve in the music. Hugh Mundell like my style as Junior Reid and give me a lot of encouragement. So Mundell start to visit where me and Locksley live, an' we start to hold a vibes, an' is like the three a we start to sound the same way. After Mundell missing for a while, he wants to see me, beca' 'im want to take me unto the studio fe work pon some a de songs 'im hear me with. At the time when I check Mundell, me a deejay. But Mundell say, 'No, not deejay, me like the singing one yu did', so me sing "Speak the Truth", an' 'im say 'Yeah, that one deh!'

After I sing about two song for Hugh Mundell, he were looking to do an album with me, 'cause at the time I never want to sing for no other producer. But Mundell pass away in '83, and when 'im pass away now it's like me nah have no musical director. So me did have to start and go out there to search. So we start to work for Negus Roots – "Mini Bus Driver", "If I" and "Sister Dawn". But at the time, it's like dem wasn't coming up fast enough with the right sound behind my voice, so I just branch off now. Me start link up with Sugar Minott, doing "A-1 Lover", and produce this song name "Foreign Mind". We still need foreign, but you can't forget where you coming from, and we start to build up the Junior Reid name. Then Black Uhuru have a problem and is me was the only solution at the time. So me go in a Black Uhuru and give them x-amount of support.

While I was in Black Uhuru I jus' keep learning the business and start my own JR label. Barrington Levy the first artist to come out on the label with "'Nah Go Settle Down". Then [Black Uhuru's] "Pain On the Poorman's Brain", "Nah Get Rich And Switch", "Dreadlocks In the Mountain". When we leave Black Uhuru, we seh how married life is a serious ting! That was the first track to come out on the JR label for Junior Reid. Then after "Married Life" came "One Blood" an' the album named after that tune."

NSOMBI JAJA/JR MUSIC

Junior Reid with his One Blood Band, 1988

BARRY BROWN

● Not So Lucky (Black Roots, UK).

The title track was the only hit that Sugar Minott had with Barry Brown, but the entire album caught the singer at his youthman best. The six heartfelt vocals are accompanied with their dubs, which leave little doubt as to the strength of the rhythms.

SUGAR MINOTT

◑ Black Roots (Black Roots, JA; Mango, US).

E The first set from the granulated one to appear on his own label, and something of a masterpiece. Perhaps it says something about his status at the end of the 1970s that Don Carlos, Locksley Castell and Ashanti Waugh contribute harmonies, while the roster of musicians includes Horsemouth Wallace and Albert Malawi on drums, Bingy Bunny on guitar, Junior Dan on bass, Ansel Collins and Steely on organ, Gladstone Anderson on piano and Zoot 'Scully' Simms on percussion. "Hard Time Pressure" and "River Jordan" were the hit singles, but the quality is consistent throughout.

● Roots Lovers (Black Roots, US).

By the time this showcase album was cut the following year, Sugar Minott was even more popular in the UK than Jamaica, and had adapted – very easily it would seem – to the 'lovers rock' form that was ruling there. As the title suggests, *Roots Lovers* brings the two facets together, with each given its own side, though any thematic division is overridden by the rocksteady/lovers feel of the music throughout. Studios in New York, London and Kingston were used, which makes it seem way ahead of its time.

◑ With Lots Of Extra (Channel One, US).

Sugar Minott's sojourn at Channel One here coincides with producer Niney's, making this well worth checking. The album brings together singles that sold well at the time – "Babylon" (over the popular "Secretly" rhythm), "No Vacancy" and "Give Thanks & Praise" – and supplements them with at least three tracks that are their match for quality: "People Of the World" (over the Channel One cut of "Java"), "Only Jah Jah" (over "Party Time"), and "Why You Acting Like That" (over "Pretty Looks Isn't All").

● Buy Off the Bar (Powerhouse, JA).

The title track was one of George Phang's biggest hits, though it is not necessarily the strongest here. As on all the albums to appear on the label, Sly & Robbie are very much in the driver's seat, and several already-familiar rhythms reappear.

● Showcase (Uptempo, UK).

A 10" album that features original Studio One rhythms throughout, and was always open to legal doubt, so unlikely to be re-released as a CD. Well worth seeking out, though, to hear the Brentford Road alumnus tackling the rhythms he did not have a chance to use when recording there. The opening cut of the Wailing Souls' "Mr Fire Coal Man", complete with dub, is just one of the highlights.

● Dancehall Style (Black Roots, UK).

Another 10" set, but with Youth Promotion cuts of classic dancehall rhythms, and each of the four tracks followed by its dub. "Easy Squeeze (Make No Riot)" is one of four vocal cuts he recorded over the "Scandal"/"Secretly" rhythm, and just as strong as "Babylon" (for Channel One) or "Living A Rough Ole Life" and "Rough Ole Life (Babylon)", produced by himself.

◑ Sugar & Spice (Taxi, JA; RAS, US).

Sly & Robbie took long enough to release this set, which rather took away from its impact at the time. In retrospect, though, it stands as one of Minott's most consistent, and a handy way of obtaining the hits "Rub A Dub Style", "Devil Pickney" and "Herbman Hustling".

JUNIOR REID

● Original Foreign Mind (Black Roots/Harry J, JA).

The title track was Junior Reid's most successful 45 before the anthemic "One Blood", and the record to establish that it was not only Jamaican deejays who could learn from the 'fast style' of UK chatting. Despite appearing on a Sugar Minott label, this was an early self-production that anticipated Reid's own JR All Stars label at the close of the decade.

VARIOUS ARTISTS – SUGAR MINOTT PRODUCTIONS

● Presenting the Posse (Uptempo, UK).

The posse in question is Youth Promotion's, and besides Sugar himself it includes Trevor Junior (Locksley Castell's brother), Don Carlos, Anthony Johnson, Michael Palmer, Junior Reid and Ashanti Waugh. A couple of the tracks come complete with dubs mixed by Peter Chemist, just to give a flavour of developments in that particular facet of the music.

Sly & Robbie

For all the commercial dominance of Junjo Lawes and Jammy, you could argue that the most innovative dancehall was to be found on **Sly Dunbar** and **Robbie Shakespeare**'s Taxi label. In addition to running their own business, the dynamic duo or rhythm twins, [as they were variously called] contributed to countless sessions for other producers, offering the one commercially viable alternative to the studio hegemony of the Roots Radics and the High Times band. They particularly shaped the sounds found on imprints such as **George Phang**'s Powerhouse, **Clive Jarrett and Beswick 'Bebo' Philip**'s Dynamite, **Myrie Lewis and Errol Marshall**'s Sun Set and **Philip 'Fatis' Burrell**'s Vena – all of which were heavily dependent on their progressive sound.

ADRIAN BOOT

Robbie Shakespeare (left) and Sly Dubar, mid-1980s

Call a Taxi

After **Gregory Isaacs**' "Soon Forward", the initial hit on Taxi in 1979, startlingly different and popular records from **Junior Delgado**, the **Wailing Souls**, the **Viceroys**, **Dennis Brown** and the Michael Rose-led **Black Uhuru** provided a glorious last phase to the Rasta-inspired roots music of the 1970s, while looking towards the next two decades. The difference between these tunes and those from practically anyone else lay, not surprisingly, in the rhythms, a metallic, almost non-human sound tagged 'robotic' by some – and which anticipated the digital revolution. Sly made far more imaginative use of the newly imported syndrums than anyone in Jamaica.

With "Trouble You A Trouble Me", Sly & Robbie also successfully launched **Ini Kamoze** (b. Cecil Campbell), possibly the most progressive singer to emerge in the dancehall era. He never took the mike in West Kingston's dancehalls to perform over Studio One dubplates, but came to Sly & Robbie's attention through Jimmy Cliff, who he had made a tape of the six songs that would make up the astounding 1984 debut album. Island Records got it a little wrong when they tried to present him to a broader audience as a poetic singer-songwriter; rather, Kamoze was as concerned as anyone with the usual dancehall topics, but addressed them with lyrics that were a little more distanced than those of his contemporaries.

Working with musicians of the calibre of guitarists Radcliffe 'Duggie' Bryan, Ranchie McClean and Willie Lindo, and keyboards players Robbie Lynn and Keith Sterling, Jamaica's most talented drum and bass partnership forged an independent path that avoided what was tried in the styles they bridged, managing to sell their records to both roots traditionalists and the new generation of sound-system followers. Among the other established artists to benefit from their consistently inventive approach were the **Tamlins**, a sweet-harmony vocal trio who triumphed with a masterful interpretation of Randy Newman's "Baltimore". As always, a quality song from outside of reggae lost nothing in being welded onto a tough Jamaican rhythm of the first order. Former Unique **Jimmy Riley** proved just as adaptable to the new era when he cut a couple of songs associated with his old group, but transformed by Sly's imaginative drum beats and Robbie's penetrating basslines. Sly & Robbie could also be proud of their recordings with **Bobby Floyd**, a soulful vocalist who has never quite achieved the success he deserves, and the prolific **Sugar Minott**, who maintained his usual standards with "Devil's Pickney" and "Rub A Dub Sound Style". The latter hit featured a particularly blistering rhythm that was nothing if not original; nevertheless, the duo's progressive spirit was most consistently shown in a benchmark series of instrumentals credited to Sly & Robbie or the **Taxi Gang** – notably "Maxi Taxi", "Unmetered Taxi", "Soldier Man Rock", "Rent A Car"– that could not have sounded more modern, while steeped in the musical values of classic rocksteady.

ADRIAN BOOT

The Hot Stepper: Ini Kamoze

Taxi for hire: Sly & Robbie's sessions for other producers

Nobody could accuse Sly & Robbie of taking things easy. Rather than being content simply to build advanced rhythms for their own label, they worked for a wide range of international stars. These included the few reggae performers to achieve a degree of crossover success, namely Peter Tosh and Black Uhuru, but also include genuine pop stars – from Jamaican-born Grace Jones to the most unlikely of matches, Bob Dylan. In the same period, they generously ensured major local hits for other Jamaican producers, the notable of which were **George Phang**, the partnerships of both **Clive Jarrett & Beswick 'Bebo' Phillips** and **Myrie Lewis & Errol Marshall**, and the first hits for one of the most successful producers of the forthcoming digital era, **Philip 'Fatis' Burrell**.

Sly & Robbie's work for others during this period was not their most innovative, but they applied techniques and ideas already tried and tested on Taxi with results that were well received in the dancehalls. Jarrett and Phillips' Dynamite label was particularly successful with **Carlton Livingstone**'s "Rumours", which employed a typical Sly & Robbie updating of Derrick Harriott's "Solomon" rhythm, and was the best-selling disc of the singer's entire career. Further Jamaican hits that also created a stir in the world's other reggae capitals included "Bad Boy" from **Al Campbell** (b. 1954, Kingston), on which a familiar topic of the bad boy and his likely fate was refreshed by the singer's understated approach and the menacing rhythm track.

From the deejay camp came a couple of significantly different hit singles from Peter Metro that paired him with first his usual partner, Zu Zu, and then Yellowman – respectively, the tale life of "In the Army" and an interpretation of Michael Jackson and Paul McCartney's 'The Girl Is Mine".

Myrie Lewis and Errol Marshall's were another producing partnership that for a while enjoyed consistent success with Sly & Robbie rhythms. Their now somewhat over looked Sun Set label (not to be confused with Harry J's Sunset) gave **Half Pint** one of his first hits with the appealing "Winsome" (later covered by the Rolling Stones in rather inept fashion), and was responsible for **Patrick Andy**'s most popular record, "Get Up, Stand Up", and **Junior Reid**'s very fine "Youthman". As with most of the producers who relied on Sly & Robbie during this period, it is hard to determine whether either man spent much time in the studio or simply handed the keys to Sly & Robbie and let them get on with the sessions – though from the audio evidence the latter is more than likely.

Inexplicably, the hits from Dynamite and Sun Set tailed off with the digital revolution inaugurated by Prince Jammy. Similarly, George Phang's real success was limited to the supply of Sly & Robbie rhythms built for him in 1984, reputedly in return for a favour involving the producer's political connections. These rhythm tracks were used on a string of classic dancehall 45s that included **Barrington Levy**'s "Money Move", **Sugar Minott**'s "Buy Off the Bar" and "Rydim", **Michael Palmer**'s "Lick Shot", **Little John**'s inspired revival of the Silvertones' "True Confession", **Frankie Paul**'s "Alesha" and "Tidal Wave", **Half Pint**'s "Greetings" and **Tristan Palma**'s "Folly Rankin'". All were sprightly performances, with lyrics fully in tune with the time, over rhythms that were brash versions of dancehall staples given new life by the premier rhythm team. Phang's Powerhouse label is also fondly remembered for a couple of discs on which more traditional vocal performances were allied to similar up-to-date rhythmic excursions – the **Tamlins**' version of "Smiling Faces" (a Motown hit by the Undisputed Truth), and **Freddie McGregor**'s superb and soulful "Don't Hurt My Feelings". In accordance with the vibe of the time, Phang successfully recorded top deejays as well, with particularly strong discs from **Charlie Chaplin** ("Que Dem"), **Josey Wales** ("Undercover Lover"), **Ranking Toyan** ("Hot Bubblegum"), **Yellowman** ("Walking Jewellery Store") and **General Echo** ("Drunken Master").

DAVID CORIO

Half Pint (right) with Powerhouse producer George Phang

In contrast, Philip 'Fatis' Burrell's Vena label was not launched until 1987, but relied upon Taxi rhythms that sounded contemporary with the earlier ones to support exciting performances like **Frankie Paul**'s "Hungry Belly" and "Warning", **Sanchez**'s "Zim Bam Zim" (featuring perhaps the strongest rhythm of the lot) and **Pinchers**' "Grammy" and "Mass Out". Sly & Robbie were also, of course, to play a major role in the even greater success of Burrell's subsequent Exterminator/Xterminator label, but that story belongs to the ragga era.

DENNIS BROWN

Brown Sugar (Taxi, JA).

Essentially a collection of his hit 45s on the Taxi and Powerhouse labels, as well as the singer's own Yvonne's Special (named after his wife). Dennis Brown was at the peak of his popularity, emanating total confidence, and the rhythms were the brightest and most dynamic around. Seven tracks might not appear particularly good-value, but three of these have extended mixes that confirm the juggernaut power of the Taxi Gang. Includes "Revolution", "Sitting & Watching" and "Hold On To What You've Got".

AL CAMPBELL

Bad Boy (CSA, UK).

Something of a journeyman singer, Al Campbell has worked in a number of styles, and occasionally come up with something a little special. His roots records for Phil Pratt – as well as the lovers favourites "Gee Baby" and "Late Night Blues" – are well worth searching for, as is this dancehall/roots set from Clive Jarrett and 'Bebo' Phillips. The title track employs a dangerously mixed cut of "Take Five"/"The Russians Are Coming", while the horns team – Dean Fraser, David Madden, 'Nambo' Robinson and Chico Chin – help even the most familiar dancehall rhythms sound fresh.

HALF PINT

Greetings (Powerhouse, JA).

The basic similarity of all of Half Pint's records does not stop some of them from standing out, and the anthemic title track has only been equalled by "Winsome" (for Lewis & Marshall) and "Money Man Skank" (for Jammy).

In Fine Style (Sun Set, JA).

Only eight tracks, but they do include his best record, "Winsome", and the powerful "Political Fiction". Another dancehall set produced by Lewis & Marshall on which Sly & Robbie are well in evidence.

INI KAMOZE

Ini Kamoze (Island, JA).

The singer's debut album, and one he has yet to better. Each of the six vocals comes complete with its dub version, and the hit 45 that established him, "Trouble You A Trouble Me", is (amazingly) matched by tracks such as "World A Music", "General" and "Hail Mi Idrin". Sly & Robbie's best shot in reply to the dominant Radics sound.

LITTLE JOHN

True Confession (Powerhouse, JA).

Little John might always have possessed an excessively nasal tone, but there is no denying the excitement of his best discs, among which must be numbered the title track – an upfront Sly & Robbie-powered reworking of the Silvertones' rocksteady classic. Pure dancehall fever all the way.

MICHAEL PALMER

Lick Shot (Powerhouse, JA).

Michael Palmer was a dancehall star for a couple of years, but recorded too much mediocre material in his brief moment of glory. As with most of the Powerhouse albums, there are only eight tracks, but "Mr Booster" (over the "Mr Bassie" rhythm) bears comparison with the hit singles "Lick Shot" and the lyrically similar "Gunshot A Burst".

FRANKIE PAUL

Warning (RAS, US).

One of producer Philip 'Fatis' Burrell's earliest albums, featuring two of the hits that established his Vena label (the predecessor to Xterminator): the amusing "Hungry Belly" (about a girlfriend with a taste for hamburgers) and the more serious "Warning" (railing against the trend for slack lyrics). Frankie Paul in typically fine form throughout, over excellent Sly & Robbie rhythms. It's also available as half of a value-for-money CD with the Pinchers album below (on RAS).

PINCHERS

● **Mass Out** (Exterminator, JA; RAS, US).

The singer's best work prior to his sojourn with Jammy's, featuring the hits "Mass Out" and "Grammy". The gospel wail was already in evidence, as well as echoes of the fast style picked up from UK MCs – or maybe Junior Reid. What he lacked in vocal finesse was more than made up for in panache and enthusiasm.

VARIOUS ARTISTS – MYRIE LEWIS & ERROL MARSHALL PRODUCTIONS

⊙ **Waterhouse Revisited** (High Tone, US).

⊙ **Waterhouse Revisited (Chapter 2)** (High Tone, US).

All of Lewis & Marshall's dancehall classics, alongside more standard generic items. Contributions from Half Pint, Junior Reid and Patrick Andy are particularly memorable.

VARIOUS ARTISTS – SLY & ROBBIE PRODUCTIONS

● **Crucial Reggae** (Mango, US).

This compilation contains a couple of the label's less essential moments, but more than makes up for them with classics like Dennis Brown's "Hold On To What You Got" and Carlton Livingstone's "Chalice In Hand".

● **Taxi Fare** (Heartbeat, US).

Far from the complete collection of the major Taxi hits from the early 1980s, but a worthwhile selection. Standouts include Junior Delgado's "Fort Augustus", Sugar Minott's underrated "Devil Pickney", Dennis Brown's "Sitting & Watching", the Tamlins' definitive version of "Baltimore", and Sly & Robbie's own "Unmetered Taxi" (an excellent cut of the "Peanut Vendor"/"Prophecy" rhythm). But why Jimmy Riley's "Bang Bang", rather than his far superior "My Woman's Love"?

Channel One and Joe Gibbs

Both **Joseph 'Joe Joe' Hookim**'s Channel One and **Joe Gibbs**' setup at 20 North Parade put out good stuff during the early dancehall period. Channel One enjoyed a minor renaissance both as a studio used by producers who didn't have facilities of their own, and with the Hitbound label, the flagship for its own rootsy productions. Channel One's refreshed new sound was contemporaneous with the appointment of Joe Joe Hookim's nephew, Wayne, as the studio manager, though the two men who can perhaps take the greater share of credit for the label's success through 1983–84 might be a former rival, **Winston 'Niney' Holness**, and the hottest mixing engineer then working, **Hopeton 'Scientist' Brown**. At least a couple of first-rate 45s appeared on Niney's own Observer label in this period – Sugar Minott's boastful "Lovers' Race" and Third World's aptly named "Roots With Quality" – but most of his energies were concentrated on production for Hitbound. Joe Gibbs (see pp.152–155) also continued to release popular and strong records, updating the sound that had been so successful for him in the late 1970s, finding particular success with **Dennis Brown**, with whom he had first worked in 1973.

The 'new' Channel One

As of 1979 the Channel One studio had new sixteen-track equipment, and besides having Scientist at hand, Niney was no doubt further helped by the mixing skills of **Soljie** (a former member of the Jamaican Defence Force: *Soljie* = "soldier") and a youth known as **Chemist**. The Roots Radics took care of the rhythms most of the time, though Sly & Robbie or the High Times Band sometimes stepped in. The result was a more militant version of the sound pioneered by 'Junjo' Lawes – the tempo was generally slower, the sweeter element was banished, and the effect was more threatening. Among those to benefit from the revitalized Channel One touch were established performers such as **Barry Brown**, the **Gladiators**, **Horace Andy**, **Johnny Osbourne**, **Sugar Minott**, **Barrington Levy** and **Al Campbell**, and newer names that included **Michael Palmer**, **Little John**, **Sammy Dread**, **Don Carlos** and the man destined to be the most prolific singer of the era, **Frankie Paul**. Paul had cut his first record at the studio, the cultural "African Princess" for Chinna Smith and Bertram Brown's High Times, and the hit that first aroused real excitement about him was "Worries In the Dance", originally taken from a best-selling Channel One album shared with Sugar Minott. In addition, there were deejays like **Lone Ranger**, **Wayne & Johnny**, **Ranking Toyan** and **Welton Irie**. Fortunately, most of the Channel One albums that appeared then have been re-released in the 1990s, though a compilation of the most worthwhile 45s missing from those – particularly the couple credited to the enigmatic 'cultural' singer, Mac Warner/McWoner – is still needed.

Joe Gibbs – the final days

Channel One's main rival in the late 1970s, **Joe Gibbs**, went out of the business in the mid-1980s, but only after being responsible for several excellent singles that – like those from Maxfield Avenue – bridged the roots and dancehall styles. The always extremely expressive **Dennis Brown** continued as his major star, with hits like "Let Me Love You", "A Little Bit More" and "I Can't Stand It", which boasted exceptional rhythms, and on which his singing was still of vintage standard (even if some of the lyrics were not). The most successful producer of the previous decade also produced one of the new stars who was to make a very big name for himself elsewhere. One of the strongest records by the extraordinary **Eek-A-Mouse**, "Once A Virgin", appeared in 1980 on the familiar Record Globe label. Curiously though, Gibbs held back the original cut to "Wa Do Dem", which the singjay performer then re-recorded (with considerable success) for Henry 'Junjo' Lawes (see p.249).

Further important Jamaican hits of the time from Joe Gibbs and his right-hand man **Errol Thompson** included **Barrington Levy**'s "My Woman", **Cornell Campbell**'s "Boxing" (one of the few durable original rhythms of the era), **Freddie McGregor**'s "No Competition", **Lady Ann**'s "Informer", **Barry Brown**'s "Dem A Fight", and the instrumental/vocal band **Chalice**'s best record, "Good To Be There". There was also **J.C. Lodge**'s beautiful version of the country singer Charley Pride's US hit, "Someone Loves You Honey" – a song which, because of a question of unpaid royalties, brought an end to recordings from Gibbs. Unfortunately, a collection concentrating solely on his work in the dancehall era has yet to be compiled, and it remains undervalued.

BARRY BROWN & LITTLE JOHN

Showdown Volume 1 (Channel One, US).

Hard-core dancehall music from two masters of the genre. Each has a side apiece, and is helped no end by the extra-tough Channel One rhythms.

DON CARLOS & GOLD

Them Never Know Natty Have Him Credential (Hitbound, US).

Don Carlos never developed the potential shown by tracks like "Dice Cup" and "Hog & Goat" over the length of an entire album, but this is as close as he got, and features typically rugged Maxfield Avenue production values.

SAMMY DREAD

Road Block (Hitbound, US).

Sammy Dread's approach was about as subtle as his name, though he pretty much summed up a new generation of singers' response to the roughhouse deejays. The title track, over the Channel One cut of "Full Up", was his best 45, and it is joined here by versions of nearly all the popular dancehall rhythms employed on the label.

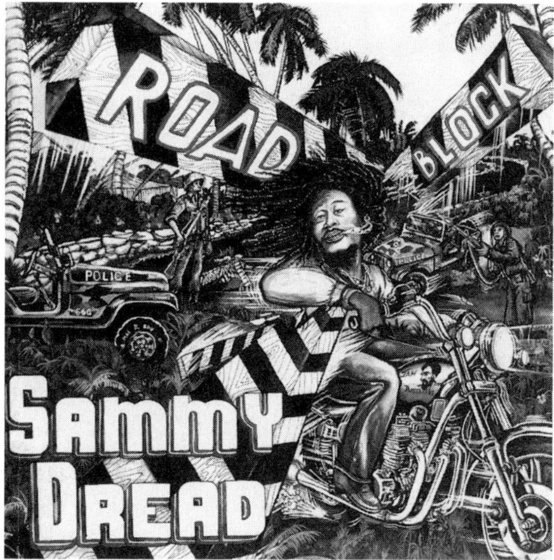

BARRINGTON LEVY

Reggae Vibes (Rocky One, US).

All of Barrington Levy's best work for Joe Gibbs – including the marvellous "My Woman" and "Wife & Sweetheart" – plus some Sammy Dread tunes from the same period that employ similar hard-hitting dancehall rhythms.

SUGAR MINOTT & FRANKIE PAUL

Showdown Volume 2 (Channel One, US).

Sugar Minott in the role of the established star, and Frankie Paul as the hot new contender. The inclusion of the latter's first hit, the searing "Worries In the Dance", along with mixes by the innovative Scientist, just about tips the *Showdown* in the direction of his side.

FRANKIE PAUL

⊙ Give the Youth A Chance (High Times, JA).
Recorded at Channel One, Paul's debut in the studio is a remarkably assured affair, the 16-year-old singer giving measured and mature performances on the reality-themed songs.

FRANKIE PAUL & LITTLE JOHN

⊙ Showdown Volume 6 (Empire, US).
Four volumes later in the *Showdown* series and Frankie Paul now stands as the dancehall champion, with Robin Hood's sidekick his worthy challenger. Dancehall was always the rawest of reggae styles, and both men are in their element here. Paul's "Slave Driver", over the Channel One cut of "Darker Shade Of Black", is exceptional.

Worries in the dance: more producers join the crowd

The producers discussed above were the most prolific and influential during the first half of the 1980s. Yet there was no shortage of records appearing on other labels which, if not as original, were still massive hits in the reggae world. Generally, these producers simply followed the lead set by the majors, but an exception to this was **Gussie Clarke**, who attempted to create a glossier form of dancehall that would have international crossover potential. Fellow veteran **Winston Riley** remained abreast of new trends, and on more than one occasion caught performers before they broke big. There continued to be a sizeable number of worthwhile smaller labels, nearly all relying for their rhythms on the incredibly busy **Roots Radics**, **Sly & Robbie**'s Taxi Gang or **Chinna Smith's High Times Band**. Among these was the Midnight Rock label owned by the popular deejay **Jah Thomas**, while the singers **Linval Thompson** and **Tristan Palma** (with associate **Ossie Thomas**) became dependable producers of generic fare that worked in the right place – the dancehall.

Continuing the even older tradition of sound-system-man-turned-producer was **Maurice Johnson**, owner of the **Black Scorpio** sound, which went on to become a major force with deejay **Sassafrass** then with **General Trees**. Johnson opened his own studio in his home area of Maverley, below Washington Boulevard, in the mid-1980s. It has since become one of the leading studios in Kingston. Originating from the Chisholm Avenue area was the Thrillseekers label, controlled by Leon Synmoie and his brother. The outfit scored quite a few hits during 1979–80: Barry Brown's "Two House Department" and Welton Irie's "Bill Fold Wa You Fa", and several more from Lone Ranger. In 1981 they struck with the early Yellowman tune "Eventide Fire", and they had further dancehall success during 1982–84 with such as Robert French, Danny Dread and Michael Palmer, but Synmoie had ceased production by mid-decade. The much less prolific Trevor Elliott's Musical Ambassador imprint is best remembered for local hits from the immediately recognizable **Edi Fitzroy**. Fitzroy's father, Vasco Edwards, had been a sound-system operator in the 1950s, but Fitzroy, who started with local hits for Mikey Dread, was not a typical dancehall singer. He scored with "Check For You Once Girl" and "Youthman Penitentiary", and his album titled after the former hit was largely cultural, as was **General Plough**'s "This Society", on the same label.

Winston Riley

The former Technique **Winston Riley** continued with his well-established Techniques imprint, not only releasing the debut album that introduced **General Echo** (see p.238) to a wider world, but similarly launching both **Sister Nancy**, the first really popular female deejay, and the singer who was to be the most recorded of the decade, **Frankie Paul**. The records that Frankie Paul cut for Riley were, along with those for High Times and Channel One, the material that initially established his name, and made clear that a major new talent had arrived. Sister Nancy, who performed with Stereophonic when only 15, sometimes seemed under the shadow of her brother, the highly esteemed **Brigadier Jerry**, but her approach was sufficiently different, and she had local hits with both "Papa Dean" and "Transport Connection" for Riley. If nothing else, she was important for giving other would-be women deejays a style and the confidence to hold their own in the very male world of the sound system. Among those for whom she paved the way were Lady Ann, Mama Liza and Sisters Charmaine and Verna, who in turn would be followed by such powerful performers of the 1990s as the Ladies G, Patra and Saw. **Maddoo**, **Tristan Palma**, **Lone Ranger** and **Errol Scorcher** were among the other dancehall favourites to benefit from the producer's assured touch, and if practically everyone Riley produced on more than a couple of sides was given the potent "Stalag 17" to version, he had enough top-calibre rhythms to ensure at least one killer album from each.

Gussie Clarke

Augustus 'Gussie' Clarke, who had been producing since he was 18, had ambitions to run the Jamaican answer to Motown, envisaging a totally professional operation with its own studio, in-house songwriters and business practices in line with international copyright law. By 1987, when he opened his Music Works studio, these ambitions were largely realized, but in the early 1980s he was still using the Channel One studio for his label's releases. In an ideal world, he would have gained a crossover hit with the **Mighty Diamonds**' "Pass the Kouchie", the record that brought the "Full Up" rhythm back into favour in 1981. In the event, a version by the UK pop-reggae group Musical Youth cleaned up on the global market with a weaker cut of the rhythm and a bowdlerlized take on the lyric (a cooking pot rather than a pipe of herb was passed on their record). Needless to say, it was the Gussie dub cut, alongside the Studio One original, that ruled the Kingston dancehalls, providing a platform for practically every deejay or singer of thc day. Gussie went on to release extremely well-crafted discs from **Tetrack**, **Freddie McGregor**, **Hopeton Lindo**, **Gregory Isaacs** and the deejay daddy, **U-Roy**, though few of these connected with the dancehall audience, and the label would not really fulfil its potential until the computerized sound of the decade's closing years.

Jah Thomas

Among the successful performer-owned labels was Midnight Rock, belonging to the popular deejay **Jah Thomas** (b. Nkrumah Thomas, 1955, Kingston). The imprint was named after his initial Jamaican hit for GG Ranglin, which topped the Jamaican charts in 1976; the man who would be the Roots Radics bass player **Errol 'Flabba' Holt** had supervised that session, and would play a part in Thomas's subsequent success with his own label. More local hits followed over the next two years, leading to his first album *Stop Yu Loafin'*, produced in 1978 at Channel One by Joseph 'Joe Joe' Hookim. In 1979, the gruff-voiced chatter made his next important career move and went into self-production, working with Errol Holt's band, the Roots Radics, at about the same time they took on the name that was to be synonymous with dancehall. Midnight Rock label very soon notched up its first major hit, "Cricket Lovely Cricket", one of the most popular of the numerous "My Conversation" versions then making waves in the dancehalls.

More of his own efforts then regularly surfaced on the label, and Thomas proved as adept at producing dancehall hits for other performers as for himself. Of his fellow deejays, the most successful for him were **Early B**, from the Soul Imperial Hi-Fi and King Majesty sound systems, and **Ranking Toyan**. Alongside these were offerings from singers who had recently come to the forefront on the recording scene, including **Michael Palmer**, **Barrington Levy**, **Barry Brown** and **Little John**, plus veterans like **Johnny Osbourne** and **Sugar Minott.** None of Thomas's productions were better received, though, than **Tristan Palma**'s 1981 hit "Entertainment", and the same youthman singer's more caustic "Joker Smoker". The latter tune was another that boasted a brutal Roots Radics rhythm, but was also distinguished by an original lyric about the familiar dancehall figure who wants to build a spliff by hustling all the ingredients from those around him – including the lighter. Just as strong was **Anthony Johnson**'s "Gun Shot" of 1982, one of the many warnings of the time to the gun-happy youth, delivered over an aggressive Roots Radics rhythm.

Ossie Thomas

Tristan Palma also recorded for Black Solidarity, a label he owned in partnership with **Ossie Thomas**. The imprint is still active today but will always be most associated with the raw dancehall hits it scored in the first half of the 1980s. Practically every name that appeared on it was a dancehall stalwart – **Frankie Paul, Little John, Sugar Minott** and **Robert French** among the singers, and **Josey Wales, Peter Metro, Early B, Lone Ranger** and **Captain Sinbad** from the ranks of the deejays. Thomas's rhythms also proved just as suited to the enduring chat of **U-Roy** ("Get Ready") and the sweet tri-part harmonies of the **Mighty Diamonds** ("Putting On the Ritz").

Linval Thompson

A veteran from the Bunny Lee camp of the mid-1970s, **Linval Thompson** arguably proved a more interesting producer than singer, and matched tough Roots Radics rhythms with mostly established performers to good effect. Not surprisingly, his production style was close to that of 'Junjo' Lawes (the first time Lawes's name appeared on a record was as co-producer with Linval) and both men employed the same session musicians. Among those who appeared with distinction on his Thompson Sound label were the **Wailing Souls, Freddie McGregor,** the **Viceroys** and the **Meditations**, their 1970s roots sensibilities enhanced by the tough dancehall rhythms they sang over. More stylistically radical, and just as suited to the Thompson touch, was Lawes's singjay stylist **Eek-A-Mouse**.

DENNIS BROWN & GREGORY ISAACS

◑ **Judge Not** (Greensleeves, UK).

One of the CD's two bonus tracks – the hit 45, "Let Of Supm" – has both singers together, but the other tracks are divided evenly between them. The Gussie Clarke rhythms are crisp, the material – mostly written by Carlton Hines – worthy of the talents involved, and Dennis and Gregory show why they were the reggae audience's favourite singing stars of the 1980s.

EARLY B

● **Four Wheel No Real** (Midnight Rock, JA).

Early B had more to say on a three-minute track than most, and did so over hard-core dancehall rhythms. Fellow spiel merchant Jah Thomas caught him at his best, when he seemed ready to challenge both Josey Wales and Charlie Chaplin.

● **Ghostbusters** (Black Solidarity, JA).

The reliable Ossie Thomas released this about the same time as the above set, and there is little to choose between them. Check both albums' cuts of "College Rock" for a comparison between their production styles.

EEK-A-MOUSE

◑ **The Mouse & the Man** (Greensleeves, UK; RAS, US).

The Roots Radics rhythms that Linval Thompson produced for Eek-A-Mouse were the equal of the Lawes classics, and the rodent more than kept up standards with his inventive vocal approach. Thankfully, the lyrical inspiration that seemed missing for most of *Skidup* returns for the following year's album, which includes the phenomenal "Terrorist In the City".

GENERAL TREES

● **Heart, Mind & Soul** (Black Scorpio, JA).

● **Ghost Rider** (Black Scorpio, JA).

Two albums released in the same year for producer Maurice Johnson. The choice is between the 'showcase' format of *Heart, Mind & Soul*, where each of the General's tracks is followed by a worthwhile dub, and the pure deejay music of *Ghost Rider*. Both sets include the popular "Heart, Mind & Soul" and "Ghost Rider", but only the latter has the record that launched Trees, "Monkey & the Ape", an enormous hit in Jamaica.

GREGORY ISAACS

◑ **Private Beach Party** (Greensleeves, UK).

This came three years before Gussie Clarke took himself and Gregory Isaacs to a new digitally enhanced plane with the epochal "Rumours". But it was already obvious that the reunion of producer and singer was mutually advantageous (particularly with Carlton Hines providing lyrics that the singer could get his teeth into). The duet with Carlene Davis is outstanding.

FREDDIE McGREGOR

◑ **Big Ship** (Thompson Sound, JA; Greensleeves, UK).

E The dancehall era showed that Linval Thompson was a producer of consequence, and his work with the Roots Radics is comparable with that of Henry 'Junjo' Lawes. The title track was later to be the name of McGregor's own label, which reflects how popular it was at the time. No weak tracks at all, and a good mixture of quality love songs and 'cultural' material. A pity that "Sinking Sand", his most impressive 45 for Thompson, is missing.

THE MEDITATIONS

◑ **No More Friend** (Greensleeves, UK).

The Ansel Cridland-led Meditations, one of the few 1970s roots vocal groups to keep up previous standards in the following decade, did so by placing their thoughtful material over Roots Radics rhythms. "Carpenter Rebuild" is the massive Linval Thompson-produced hit included here, though the entire set demonstrates the durability and adaptability of the trio's approach.

THE MIGHTY DIAMONDS

Changes (Music Works, JA).

E "Pass the Kouchie" was the most exciting record from the Mighty Diamonds since their mid-1970s heyday at Channel One – an inspired combination of the right rhythm (a new cut of the Studio One instrumental "Full Up"), the group's peerless harmonies and a good lyrical idea. The album opened by the hit showed that it was more than a lucky one-off, and how the trio could glitter away from Maxfield Avenue, with both original material and reworkings of rocksteady classics.

Struggling (Live & Learn, US).

The sublime heights of the Mighty Diamonds' Channel One output has tended to cast a shadow over most their subsequent work somewhat unfairly, as this Delroy Wright-produced album demonstrates. Both the title track and "Heathen Children" are minor masterpieces.

FRANKIE PAUL

Strange Feeling (Techniques, JA).

The Winston Riley-produced debut set that announced the arrival of a major vocal stylist – though few could have predicted then that he was to become the most prolific Jamaican singer of all time. At this stage of his phenomenal career, there were strong traces of Dennis Brown in his tone and phrasing, but an exuberance all his own.

SISTER NANCY

One Two (Techniques, JA).

The 1982 album that introduced Brigadier Jerry's sister to the world beyond Kingston's dancehalls, and an important influence on all the female deejays to follow. Includes her biggest hit for Winston Riley, "Transport Connection".

THE VICEROYS

We Must Unite (Trojan, UK).

Brethren & Sistren (CSA, UK).

The Viceroys also established their reputation in the dread 1970s, though their career stretches back to the rocksteady era. Their most consistent body of work, however, was facilitated by Linval Thompson and the Roots Radics, in the dancehall years. These albums are far superior to most of the work collected on their Studio One collection.

VARIOUS ARTISTS – JAH THOMAS PRODUCTIONS

Midnight Rock Presents Reggae Veterans Volume One (Midnight Rock, JA).

A good collection of early dancehall hits from Jah Thomas's Midnight Rock label, featuring Anthony Johnson, Barry Brown, Sugar Minott, Tristan Palma and other youthman talents of the time, along with the deejay-producer's own gruff tones.

VARIOUS ARTISTS – LINVAL THOMPSON PRODUCTIONS

Jah Jah Dreader Than Dread (Majestic, Holland).

Seventeen tracks, mostly new to album, that demonstrate what a good producer Thompson is – he gets superb performances from Freddie McKay, Wayne Wade and Freddie McGregor in particular. Sammy Dread, Tristan Palma and Thompson himself also contribute songs that match these in dancehall vibes, if not intensity. A song apiece from vocal groups the Viceroys and Wailing Souls, plus three dubs and two deejay versions, complete an exemplary dancehall package.

Ragga

EVERTON SHARP

7

7

previous page

All the ladies in the house say "Forward!": Buju Banton, 1992

Ragga

Ragga – essentially reggae played entirely (or mostly) with digital instrumentation – has been the most commercially successful Jamaican music since the heyday of Bob Marley, with ragga stars like Shabba Ranks, Chaka Demus & Pliers, Red Dragon, Cobra, Super Cat and Terror Fabulous selling in such quantities that a new style of pop-ragga – as represented by Snow, C.J. Lewis and Louchie Lou and Michie One – has emerged. Ragga is also the most populist of all forms of Jamaican music. Drawing freely from practically every aspect of Jamaican popular culture, including spirituals and hymns, it ranges from rougher-than-rough deejay music, through romantic crooning, on to a new generation of cultural wailers.

A minimum of completely new rhythms were built during the first half of the 1980s, but the lower production costs of digital tracks meant that producers could again afford to take chances on untried rhythms. **King Jammy** (formerly Prince Jammy) initiated the use of digital rhyhms in 1985 and was the undisputed ruler as both sound-system operator and producer for the second half of the decade, prompting an unprecedented proliferation of producers and labels. Each year of the 1990s has seen, on average, a staggering five thousand new titles released, testifying to the irrepressible vitality of dancehall culture.

Of course, producers never gave up 'versioning' what was old and trusted. Jammy, for instance, was hugely adept at reinterpreting the best-known hits from Studio One – the rhythm under **Admiral Bailey**'s massive hit "Politician", for instance, was a digital update of Larry Marshall's "Throw Me Corn" from 1969. Similarly, reworkings of hits of the late 1960s and early 1970s supported the voices of a new generation of performers. Inventive as always, in 1991 **Sly Dunbar** built a rhythm modelled on the Maytals' 1966 "Bam Bam", but incorporated an Indian water-drum sample – and vocalist **Pliers** duly scored a big Jamaican hit singing

7

DAVID CORIO

Dancehall goes international: Chaka Demus (left) and Pliers

the original lyric over it. And when deejay **Chaka Demus** and Pliers did "Murder She Wrote" on the same rhythm it went international, charting in the UK and the US pop charts.

Samples lifted from the originals further enlivened the Jamaican 'version', extending its possibilities yet further, but the fact remains that a significant number of ragga rhythms have been originals. The totally new rhythms that underpinned **Anthony 'Red' Rose**'s "Tempo" for **King Tubby**, Admiral Bailey's "Punaany" for Jammy's, Chaka Demus's "Young Gal Business" for **Skengdon** and **Gregory Peck**'s "Pocoman Jam" for **Steely & Clevie** were to become the new dancehall standards, and are now well on their way to being themselves 'versioned' as often as the rocksteady staples.

The next development for Jamaican music is anyone's guess, for it's never been more open to fresh influences. In 1996, for example, the **Taxi Gang** incorporated a country and western element for the instrumental "Western Farm", while the deejay **Buccaneer** had a go at grand opera with the totally outrageous "Sketel Concerto". No single trend is all-encompassing, but two strands continue to run strongly: the sampling of old hits and the emphasis on new drum beats, sometimes both being found in the same record – particularly if **Sly Dunbar** is involved. **Dave Kelly**'s "Pepper Seed" from 1995 has proved to be the single most influential rhythm of recent years – at least as far as new rhythm styles are concerned. The same producer's "Arab Attack" and "Joy Ride", **Stone Love**'s "Corduroy" and **Malvo & Redrose**'s "Quarter To Twelve" are further originals that have been much-versioned favourites in the dancehall. A contrasting return to 'conscious' lyrical themes, as well as musical

ONE-RHYTHM ALBUMS

The 'one-rhythm' – or 'version' – album, consisting entirely of different cuts of the same rhythm track, is a uniquely Jamaican phenomenon, and a very important part of a market that is largely singles-oriented. Though the concept became particularly popular in the late 1980s, its history stretches back further. Deejay versions began seriously in the early 1970s, to be followed by stripped-down dub cuts. The instrumental version was also very popular throughout the 1970s, with, say, a saxophonist, an organist or bongo player let loose over a currently popular track. The one-rhythm album was a logical progression from this, but it did not become an institution overnight.

The first LP in this mode was Rupie Edwards's *Yamaha Skank*, released in 1974, and made up of twelve cuts of Slim Smith's "My Conversation" hit (a rhythm given to Edwards by Bunny Lee). The next such album was not to follow until the beginning of the 1980s, when Mikey Dread unleashed an eight-track set utilizing the rhythm track from his last great hit, "Jumping Master". Things picked up a little after that, with Channel One releasing four albums in 1984 based on big dancehall rhythms, the most exciting of which was *General For All General*, featuring a Maxfield Avenue recut of the Heptones' "Love Me Girl". The flood came when the music became computerized, and to the uninitiated such albums can seem merely proof of the old adage that "all reggae sounds the same". It has to be admitted that without a strong rhythm and sufficiently varied mixes and performances the results can be pretty yawn-inducing. But when some imagination has been applied, and the right ingredients are all there, one-rhythm albums are among the most exciting in reggae.

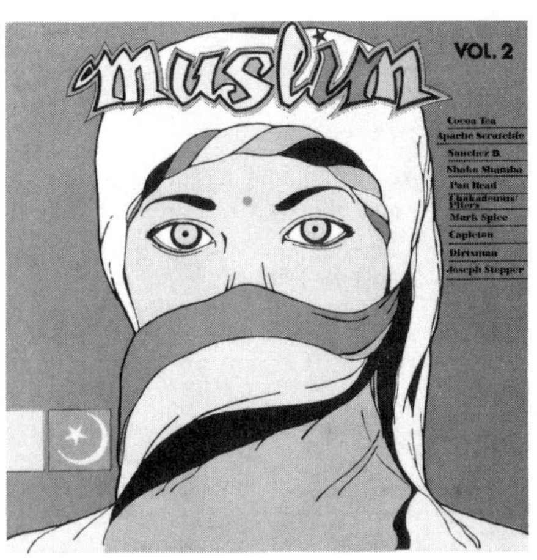

motifs, has also been widespread, with three leading ragga deejays, **Shabba Ranks**, **Capleton** and **Buju Banton** turning their backs on slackness and gun lyrics, in favour of uncompromising 'cultural' statements. Popular rhythms in this sphere have included fresh cuts of Bob Marley's "Heathen" and a new nyahbingi-flavoured track from Penthouse – "Kette Drum".

The number of new Jamaican labels – often owned by artists wanting a greater control over their output – continues to increase. The most obvious examples of this trend include Bounty Killer's Priceless, Buju Banton's CB 321 and Junior Reid's longer-established JR Productions. At the same time, major international record companies are more than likely to continue their interest in this Third World music as an untapped source of talent (and profit), without ever really coming to terms with its sheer fecundity, or mode of production. In their turn, producers and performers in Jamaica will remain tantalized by prospects of crossover success, while still concentrating on meeting the demands of the critical audience of the Kingston dancehalls. A wild card in any attempts to predict the future must be the large-scale defection of young black Britons from music made in Jamaica to the UK's indigenous form, techno-derived **jungle**. The sampling of ragga hits by the junglists momentarily fed back into renewed interest in Jamaican music, as did participation by ragga/reggae singers in dance music projects, but at the moment jungle and its successor **drum and bass** are the preferred youth musics in Britain's urban centres, along with rap and modern US r&b. The success of the deejay Bounty Killer in the UK market is linked to his use of such rap stars as Jeru Da

Examples of the genre are scattered throughout this chapter, but as an introduction to the one-rhythm album you can't do better than listen to the following.

PHILIP 'FATIS' BURRELL PRODUCTIONS

Muslim Volumes 1 & 2 (Xterminator, JA).
For these two sets Fatis employs one of Sly Dunbar's best rhythms, made popular initially with Capleton's "Almshouse". He also draws a good balance between top singers (including Pinchers, Thriller U, Cocoa Tea, Sanchez) and deejays (notably Dirtsman, Shaka Shamba, Pan Head, Papa San, Cutty Ranks).

DAVE 'RUDE BOY' KELLY PRODUCTIONS

Pepper Seed Jam! (Mad House, UK).
E The 'jam' concept, initiated on record by Dave 'Rude Roy' Kelly, takes the version album to its logical conclusion. Rather than ten or twelve separate cuts placed alongside each other, the jam presents them segued together in a seamless piece of extended music – or 'megamix'. The cuts are edited down so that 26 versions of the most infectious rhythm of 1994, "Pepper Seed", appear here.

Arabian Jam (Mad House, JA/UK).
E The second, equally impressive, megamix album released on Mad House brings together the label's next couple of dancehall throbbers, "Heartbeat" and "Arab Attack", with more than thirty tracks. The cast is much the same as before – Terror Fabulous, Beenie Man, Spragga Benz, Louie Culture, etc – though with Buju Banton's "The Only Man" inexplicably missing.

ROOF INTERNATIONAL PRODUCTIONS

Bam On the Roof (Roof International, JA).
This features the Courtney Cole and Barry O'Hare cut of "Bam Bam", over which Cutty Ranks declared that he was not done yet, proving it with one of the biggest hits of his career. Just as notable is Max Romeo's reworking of "Jordan River", with cuts from Tyrone Taylor, Garnett Silk and Jack Radics not far behind.

ANTHONY 'RED' ROSE AND ANTHONY MALVO PRODUCTIONS

Quarter To Twelve (How yu fi sey dat?, JA; VP, US).
Simpleton's title track and Cobra's "Don Wife" are the megahits here, but as always it is the roughneck rhythm that is the true star, with names like Future Troubles, Fabby Dolly, Snagga Puss and Beenie Man in fine supporting roles.

SLY & ROBBIE PRODUCTIONS

Reggae Bangara (Taxi, JA).
Sly & Robbie give their "Murder She Wrote" rhythm the full version treatment. The Chaka Demus & Pliers hit, Pliers' solo "Bam Bam" and the Taxi Gang's hypnotic instrumental, "Santa Barbara", are the popular 45s, while other highlights include former Melodian Brent Dowe revisiting his own "Rivers of Babylon".

Damaja, Raekwon, Busta Rhymes and the Fugees. In order to develop, Jamaican producers, artists and musicians might have to make more of an effort to reach their audiences outside the island.

RAGGA COMPILATIONS

◑ **Just Ragga Volumes 1–11** (Charm, UK).
This series is an easy and economical way of keeping up with the continually changing face of ragga. Be warned, though, this is the genre at its most hard-core – which means deejays predominate, and there are plenty of triple-X lyrics.

◑ **Reggae Hits Volumes 1–20** (Jet Star, UK).
A similar series to the above, but offering a greater balance of singers and deejays, not to mention themes. Every track on each volume has been a hit in the reggae marketplace, and the selection is far more consistent than on the overrated Tighten Up series from the 1970s.

◑ **Ragga Ragga Ragga Volumes 1–8** (Greensleeves, UK).
Equally reliable series that lives up to its name – hard-core dancehall music from the biggest names of the moment. Invaluable compilations for anyone not regularly buying new reggae singles, or unable to keep up with the flood of material.

◑ **Greensleeves Sampler Volumes 1–14** (Greensleeves, UK).
A series that began as a promotional set for the label's other albums, but has since become a regularly released, mid-price selection of current reggae hits. Over the years, the albums have drawn from an ever-increasing range of producers, which has been all to the good. Newcomers are advised to begin with any of the last half-dozen sets.

◑ **Strictly the Best Volumes 1–18** (VP, US).
This is the New York label's equivalent to the Jet Star or Greensleeves series, and perhaps the most consistent of all the compilations aimed at this market.

The birth of ragga

Jamaican music never stands still for very long, as the hothouse atmosphere of the Kingston studios and the competing sound systems continually produce new variants of established formulas. But even when developments establish an unmistakable shift from the preceding period, the break is never total. Reggae's most recent manifestation, **ragga**, is no exception to this law. Though the first fully digital rhythm was not built until the beginning of 1985, the so-called 'robotic' sound of many **Sly & Robbie** dancehall productions of the first half of the decade was a precursor of the computerized style. The most obvious examples include the **Viceroy**'s "Heart Of Stone", and two popular records by **Sugar Minott** from 1984, "Rub A Dub Sound" and "Herbman Hustling". In retrospect it seems obvious that Sly was embracing the new technology of the electronic drum kit (or syndrums) with ever-increasing enthusiasm, and could hardly wait for the developments that were to come. Although they did not go as far in the direction of robotic rhythms, the **Roots Radics** were also pushing the music forward by pioneering a sparseness that would only find its full expression with computerization. Yet it was **Paul Blake and the Blood Fire Posse** who most closely anticipated the sound of digital ragga, with their pioneering semi-computerized hits of 1984, "Rub A Dub Soldier" and "Every Posse Get Flat" (both on the band's own Studio Worx label).

Everything gone digital – Under Me Sleng Teng

The cheapness of rhythms built with computerized keyboards meant that their acceptance by cost-conscious Jamaican producers was inevitable. But credit still has to be given to King Jammy for kick-starting the digital phase of reggae with one crucial record, **Wayne Smith**'s "Under Me Sleng Teng" (Jammy's). According to Beth Lesser's book, *King Jammy's*, the young Smith and another struggling singer, Noel Bailey, discovered the rhythm – a close relative to that heard on Eddie Cochran's "Something Else" – on Bailey's Casio. An alternative account has Smith and **Tony Asher** finding the rhythm on the singer's computerized keyboard, but whatever the source, it was then slowed down and re-recorded by Asher at Jammy's studio, and completely turned Jamaican music around. Jammy had already established himself as one of the most successful producers and sound-system operators of the decade, though it is doubtful if his dancehall hits with Johnny Osbourne and Half Pint had quite prepared him for the phenomenon of "Sleng Teng". When played at the historic sound clash between Prince Jammy and Black Scorpio at Waltham Park Road on February 23, 1985, its impact was immediate. Versions, whether on Jammy's original rhythm track or variants hurriedly built by rival producers, followed by the trailerload, while close relations of "Sleng Teng" – such as the **King Tubby**-produced "Tempo" from another new singer **Anthony 'Red' Rose**, and the Jammy-produced "Agony" from Pinchers – were also massive hits. Many producers – including Jammy – then jettisoned most of the non-digital rhythms they had stockpiled, in favour of computerized novelties. Many traditional reggae fans were appalled at the new development, often refusing to admit that the latest stage of Jamaican music was anything but a temporary aberration.

Two dancehall anthems

For all the success of "Under Me Sleng Teng", a couple of non-Casio numbers kept the old techniques alive in the dancehalls. The rhythm for **Tenor Saw**'s contemporary dancehall vocal "Ring the Alarm" (for Winston Riley) was an overdubbed cut of "Stalag 17", Ansel Collins's 1973 organ instrumental. Tenor Saw (b. Clive Bright, 1966, Kingston) had come to prominence on Sugar Minott's Youth Promotion system (see p.256), where he had been first recorded on dubplate by the selector for the set, Jah Stitch. The lyric of "Ring the Alarm" was to set the standard for all the sound-boy burial tunes to follow, neatly epitomizing the competitive spirit that has been one of Jamaican music's main driving forces:

"Hey, woah, ring the alarm
Another sound is dying
Woah, another sound is dying
Come, listen to this sound – a champion
Ram the dance in any session
Rock up the man, rock up the woman
Another sound go down like a tin pan
Tee-ta-toe, see them all in a row
Four big sounds in one big lawn
One sound play, and the others go down."

Buju Banton's scorching deejay version of a few years later used Tenor Saw's vocal in a posthumous 'combination' style (Tenor Saw was killed in 1988), and the rhythm is now as well known by the singer's title as by the original – another example of how Jamaican music continually feeds on its own past, turning out new bench-mark records in the process.

The second significant post-"Sleng Teng" hit that didn't employ a fully computerized rhythm was **Half Pint**'s anthemic "Greetings" (Powerhouse), which used a furious Sly & Robbie-propelled version of Vin Gordon's

"Heavenless". Along with Junior Delgado's "Ragamuffin Year", this George Phang production helped to re-establish the term 'raggamuffin' as an identity for the ghetto youth. Shortened to 'ragga', this went on to become the most widely accepted generic term for their music.

TENOR SAW

◑ **Fever** (Blue Mountain, UK; RAS, US).

A Sugar Minott-produced debut set for Tenor Saw that includes the hits "Lots Of Sign", "Roll Is Called" and "Pumpkin Belly", as well as "Fever" (his own varia-

tion of the "Tempo" theme). It would only need "Ring the Alarm" for the full picture.

VARIOUS ARTISTS – GEORGE PHANG PRODUCTIONS

● **Final Mission** (Powerhouse, JA).

An album's worth of the "Greetings" rhythm track. A pity that George Phang didn't include Frankie Paul's brilliant "Alesha", the second major hit on the rhythm, but he almost makes up for it with sterling efforts from the likes of Super Cat, Conroy Smith and Little John.

VARIOUS ARTISTS – WINSTON RILEY PRODUCTIONS

● **Stalag 17, 18 and 19** (Techniques, JA/UK).

Built around Winston Riley's "Stalag 17" rhythm, this remains the most popular one-rhythm album ever. Several premier division names are present – including Michael Prophet, Sugar Minott and Little John – though the true highlights are Ansel Collins's original instrumental, the Tenor Saw smash, and Brigadier Jerry's "What Kind Of World", one of the under-recorded deejay's best.

● **Original Stalag 20** (Techniques, UK).

The second set of "Stalag" versions from Riley is even more consistent, collecting vintage shots from such as Big Youth, Horace Andy, Augustus Pablo, General Echo and Frankie Paul. The best of the new cuts was saxman Dean Frazer's magnificent "Burial".

King Jammy

For several years after "Sleng Teng", **King Jammy** was the undisputed ruler of the dancehall. By the end of the 1980s there were at least 150 albums in his catalogue, with countless other songs appearing on singles. Like Clement Dodd in the 1960s, Jammy was catching the best of the new performers and recording them over the most progressive rhythms then being built; additionally. And like Dodd, he had the intelligence to surround themselves with very gifted associates. Musicians and arrangers like Jackie Mittoo, Roland Alphonso, Larry Marshall and Leroy Sibbles, as well as the engineer Sylvan Morris, all contributed to the success of the Brentford Road studio. Similarly, Jammy employed the mixing talents of **Bobby 'Digital' Dixon** and Squingy Francis, combining them with the arranging and songwriting skills of **Mikey Bennett**, and the musicianship of bass player **Wycliffe 'Steely' Johnson**, drummer **Cleveland 'Clevie' Browne** and the brilliant saxophonist **Dean Frazer** (one of the very few to continue the tradition of the reggae instrumental after the digital revolution). A final, refining, touch to Jammy's productions – at least from 1987 onwards – were the polished harmonies of the unrelated **Brian and Tony Gold** (b. Brian Thompson and Winston Hislop), who chose a professional name that fitted the luxurious feel of their voices.

Not surprisingly, when Bobby Digital and Steely & Clevie moved on to form their own labels – both in 1988 – they almost immediately began to present the first serious challenge to Jammy's position. As things turned out, Jammy survived remarkably well.

DAVID CORIO

Jammy: the T-shirt says it all

DEAN FRAZER

● **Big Bad Sax** (Jammy's, JA; Super Power, UK).

E Dean Frazer is heard here at his most exciting over Jammy's rhythms. This is the 1980s equivalent of the classic Brentford Road albums by Roland Alphonso and Cedric Brooks: a first-class sax player let loose over a selection of proven rhythms – including "Agony", "Punaany" and "Tune In".

KING JAMMY PRODUCTIONS – COMPILATIONS

◑ **King Jammy: A Man And his Music Volume 2 – Computer Style** (RAS, US).

E Several boxed sets would be necessary to give anything like a full picture of Lloyd James's role in ragga, but this – part of a three-volume series – at least gives some idea. Seminal hits such as Wayne Smith's "Under Me Sleng Teng", Chuck Turner's "Tears", Lieutenant Stitchie's "Wear Yuh Size" and Leroy Gibbons' "This Magic Moment" make this an invaluable introduction to the work of a master.

● **Electrocutioner Phase I Sound Wars** (Jammy's, JA).

A strong selection of sound-boy boasts, with Cocoa Tea's "Ballin' For Sound Clash", Thriller U's "My Sound Is the Ruling Sound" and Johnny Osbourne's "For A Few Dollars More" representing the genre at its most exciting.

KING JAMMY PRODUCTIONS – ONE-RHYTHM ALBUMS

Sleng Teng Extravaganza (Jammy's, JA; Tads, UK).

The one extra track on the UK press makes it the one to pick up – unless you already have Johnny Osbourne's superb "Buddy Bye Bye" as a 45. Using the "Sleng Teng" rhythm throughout, this album sold hugely at the time; countless versions later, these remain some of the best, with Tenor Saw 's "Pumpkin Belly" particularly outstanding.

Ten To One (Jammy's, JA).

Ten Jammy's cuts to King Tubby's "Tempo", a near relation to his own "Sleng Teng". His initial hit on the rhythm – Nitty Gritty's "Hog Ina Me Minty" – is replaced with another cut by the singer, while Johnny Osbourne, Little John, Tonto Irie and Junior Delgado are among those helping to make up for Tubby never releasing a version album of his most successful digital rhythm.

DJ Confrontation (Jammy's, JA).

"Agony", another rhythm with more than a passing resemblance to the initial digital hit, is given a serious seeing-to by ten deejays, two of whom enjoyed massive hits with their cuts: Admiral Bailey, with "Big Belly Man", and Major Worries, with "Me No Response".

Further East Volume 1 (Jammy's, JA).

The rhythm given the treatment here began life as "Jah Shakey", a Studio One instrumental by Roland Alphonso. Later, it was recut at Channel One for Barry Brown's "Far East", to resurface yet again in the digital era as Cocoa Tea's anthemic "Tune In". This version excursion is built around "Tune In", with Barry Brown (yes, another cut of "Far East"), Gregory Isaacs, Home T (with Brian and Tony Gold) and Horace Andy standing out.

Superstar Hit Parade Volume 3 (Live & Love, UK).

Steely & Clevie's reworking of Larry Marshall's "Throw Me Corn" for Jammy is put through the paces here. Cocoa Tea's hit "Come Again" is missing, as is Admiral Bailey's popular "Politician", but notable inclusions are Johnny Osbourne's "On the Right Track", Chuck Turner's "I Need You" and Lieutenant Stitchie's "Wear Yuh Size".

TREVOR JAMES PRODUCTIONS

The Score Of Love (Uncle T, JA; Hawkeye, UK).

When Jammy handed the rhythm for Frankie Paul's "I Know the Score" to his brother, Trevor James, another monster hit was forthcoming – Cocoa Tea's "Uptight Saturday Night". Top vocal stylists like Brian and Tony Gold, Sanchez, Horace Andy and Thriller U were then pulled in for the obligatory rhythm album. Wisely, Uncle T included the two hits, and the result is a very romantic, computerized-rocksteady type of ragga album.

WAYNE SMITH & PRINCE JAMMY

Sleng Teng/Prince Jammy's Computerised Dub (Greensleeves, UK).

Two of Jammy's earliest digital LPs brought together in CD clarity. Wayne Smith's "Under Me Sleng Teng" is one of the dozen or so seminal reggae singles, though other tracks on the first set remain more rooted in their period. Several of the rhythm tracks also appear on part two, which is certainly computerized, but only arguably dub.

Singing for the King

Among Jammy's vocalists were three who shared a broadly similar style that seemed made for the early digital rhythms. **Nitty Gritty** (b. Glen Augustus Holness, 1957, Kingston), **King Kong** (b. Dennis Anthony Thomas, c. 1964, Kingston) and **Tenor Saw** all sang in the same oddly expressive flat wail that was a digital counterpart to the 'Waterhouse' style established by such as Michael Rose and Junior Reid during the early 1980s. This expressiveness was particularly apparent in the case of Tenor Saw, who incorporated gospel influences picked up as a child in church, and was the most gifted of the three as a songwriter, although Nitty Gritty was the most vocally accomplished. (Both Tenor Saw and Nitty Gritty were to die young in the USA, the former found dead on a Texas roadside in 1988, the latter perishing in a New York shooting three years later.) Nitty Gritty recorded for a variety of producers, but his greatest impact was with King Jammy. Beginning with "Hog Ina Me Minty" (a cut of the "Tempo" rhythm), he went on to record a string of hits that captured the feel of the era's dancehall fever: "Run Down the World", "So Them Come, So Them Go" and "Gimme Some A Your Something" among them. King Kong did not add a great deal to the style established by Tenor Saw and Nitty Gritty, but made strong dancehall records when given the right rhythms – namely "Legal We Legal" and "Trouble Again" for Jammy, and "AIDS" for King Tubby. Also at Jammy's at this time was the more eccentric stylist **Pinchers**, with his tongue-twisting lyrics, who after "Agony" scored his biggest hit with the cowboy-styled "Bandelero".

These were soon followed by the sweeter voiced **Sanchez** (b. Kevin Jackson, 1967, Kingston) and **Thriller U** (b. Eustace Hamilton, 1969, Kingston), who were to develop into two of the most popular performers of the digital era. They remain virtually onknown outside the dancehall, but on his home patch the good-looking Sanchez continues to occupy a position analogous to that of Bobby Brown in the swingbeat world, and has a comparable vocal approach. He has continued to cover the best US r&b hits by the likes of Anita Baker and Babyface, but his strong, flexible and expressive tenor has recently been heard on more cultural material. Thriller U has an altogether more self-effacing and vulnerable personality – and there is a large audience who prefer such singers to the hard-core, unromantic deejays.

To these have to be added talents as diverse as **Pad Anthony**, **Chuck Turner**, **Anthony Malvo** and the under-valued **Leroy Gibbons**. The last, in particular, seemed set for real stardom at the close of the 1980s. Having previously lived in Canada, he had developed a powerful vocal style that put him in a classic soul-influenced tradition. Upon his return to Jamaica, he soon notched up major hits for Jammy – most notably "Four Season Lover", "This Magic Moment" and a strictly dancehall version of Sam Cooke's "Cupid". The mystery is why so little has been heard of him since.

Jammy's production skills proved just as useful in helping more established names return to their best form in years, including **Alton Ellis**, **Cornell Campbell** and the late **Delroy Wilson**, all of whom cut excellent 45s at his studio. Alongside these names from the 1960s, he produced entire albums demonstrating that his digital approach was also suited to roots heroes like **Dennis Brown** and **Gregory Isaacs** – the compatibility of the **Wailing Souls**' time-honed harmonies and hard digital instrumentation was particularly surprising to some. More predictable perhaps were his successes with two vocalists who had emerged in the dancehall explosion of the first half of the 1980s – **Cocoa Tea** and **Frankie Paul**.

DENNIS BROWN

● **The Exit [History]** (Jammy's, JA; Trojan, UK; Live & Love, US).

Dennis Brown's best years were incontrovertibly in the 1970s, but he has been responsible for more than a few gems since then. His second set for King Jammy, released in 1987, showed the degree to which the producer's digital approach fitted into a much older tradition, and how the singer had lost none of his powers.

LEROY GIBBONS

◑ **Four Season Lover** (Jammy's, JA; Super Power, UK).

All his major hits for Jammy are here, along with tracks that could have been just as successful as 45s – including a wonderful interpretation of Clyde McPhatter's "Lover's Question" and the infectious "Build Up the Vibes". His one album for Jammy is a *tour de force*, employing some of the producer's strongest rhythms of the late 1980s, and with the new tracks bearing out the promise of the hits.

GREGORY ISAACS

● **Let's Go Dancing** (Jammy's, JA).

The best of the Isaacs albums produced by the King, with some stunning rhythms. "Dancing Time" and "My Heart Is Aching" were both popular as 45s, though a greatest hits CD is badly still needed from this quarter.

KING KONG

● **Trouble Again** (Jammy's, JA; Greensleeves, UK; Live & Love, US).

The title track and "Legal We Legal" were King Kong's best-selling 45s, and they are joined here by another eight examples of prime Jammy's music from the mid-1980s. Most notable are "Mix Up", another hit 45, and "Bruk Rock Stone" (aka "Emmanuel Road" on the UK press), his adaptation of a Jamaican folk song.

NITTY GRITTY

◉ **Trials & Crosses – Tribute To Nitty Gritty** (VP, US).

E An excellent retrospective set that gives the best overview of the late Nitty Gritty's sojourn at Jammy's, with nearly all his hit 45s, from "Hog Ina Me Minty", through "Agony" and "Good Morning Teacher", to "So Them Come, So Them Go". Curiously, his final hit with Jammy, "Letting Off Steam", is omitted, but there is no better introduction to dancehall fever, circa 1985.

◑ **Turbo Charged** (Jammy's, JA; Greensleeves, UK).

His remarkably consistent debut album on Jammy's, which made clear that he was not just dancehall flavour of the month. It misses some of the hits, but has impressive tracks not included in the VP collection.

PINCHERS

◑ **Bandelero** (Jammy's, JA).

A talented dancehall singer who deserves a greatest hits package. In the meantime, this is Pinchers' most consistent album, and the only alternative to taping 45s from a friend's record collection. The title track was arguably the reggae hit of 1991, and certainly his most popular since "Agony".

THE WAILING SOULS

◑ **Stormy Night** (Rohit, US).

Perhaps the greatest relief on hearing this 1989 set lies in finding Winston Matthews's songwriting ability unimpaired. Don't be put off by the lack of hits (no doubt the reason this was never released in Jamaica): one to be heard by followers of the Wailing Souls (of any period) or the King.

Super Power deejays

From the ranks of Jammy's **Super Power** sound came several deejays who were to be among major names in the digital age. The most immediately successful (particularly as a live performer) was **Admiral Bailey** (b. Glendon Bailey, Kingston), who made up for limitations in his lyrics by bringing a likeable avuncular presence and a sly sense of humour to Jammy's most popular rhythms. Another high-ranking deejay, **Major Worries** (b. Wayne Jones, 1966; d. 1987), initially built his reputation with Jammy's sound system, GT Hi-Fi and King Mellow, then impressed with highly original and amusing tunes like "Babylon Boops" and "Topa", before his life was cut short in a shooting incident. Pliers' future partner, **Chaka Demus** (b. John Taylor, 1965, Kingston) also made his mark with his first few tunes, and at one point seemed on the brink of stardom on his own, particularly when he appropiated elements of the revival church style. Former Stur-Gav deejay **Josey Wales** – by this time a relative veteran – appeared to have no difficulties adapting to digital rhythms, and the eccentric **Tiger** (b. Norman Jackson, 1960, Kingston) made the first of what would be several returns to favour with dancehall audiences.

ADRIAN BOOT

Dancehall poster, 1995

Closely following Admiral Bailey on Jammy's label (and in popularity) was another chatter who gave himself a military title – **Lieutenant Stitchie** (b. Cleveland Laing, Spanish Town), whose debut album, like the Admiral's, was released by Jammy in 1987. One of deejay music's great originals, the Lieutenant possesses a gift for amusing and sharp storytelling – he had been a schoolteacher – and is capable of adopting several different voices on the course of a single. His talent was sufficient for him to make a successful comeback almost a decade later, with few alterations in his very distinctive style.

ADMIRAL BAILEY

Undisputed [Kill Them With It] (Jammy's, JA; Live & Love, UK).

In the absence of a greatest hits collection, this at least includes at least two of the high points of Admiral Bailey's work with King Jammy: "Big Belly Man" and the exuberant "Kill Them With It".

LIEUTENANT STITCHIE

Wear Yu Size [Great Ambition] (Jammy's, JA; Super Power, UK).

E Surprisingly, no-one has ever titled a Lieutenant Stitchie album after his early 45, "Story Time", for it sums up what his records are all about. He is nothing if not a storyteller, usually a very funny one, with some perceptive insights into ghetto life. The humorous "Wear Yu Size" and "Broad Hips" were the major hits, but tracks like "The Wedding", "Great Ambition" and "The Visit" are accomplished pieces of reportage.

MAJOR WORRIES

Babylon Boops (Jammy's, UK).

Before falling victim to West Kingston's gun culture, Major Worries was another deejay seemingly set for the premier league. Possessor of a unique and easily recognizable style, with no shortage of original lyrics, he made his best work for King Jammy, and it's all here. The title track remains his best-known hit, though there is plenty else to confirm how important a talent was lost.

JOSEY WALES

Ha Fi Say So (Jammy's, JA).

Yellowman's main rival from the early 1980s survived the transition to new technology better than most, sounding particularly at home on Jammy's rhythms. "It's Raining" and "Must Say Something" were the hits

on his first set for Mr James, a selection of the producer's most popular rhythms ensuring that interest was maintained throughout.

⊙ **Nah Left Jamaica** (Mango, UK).
The second Jammy's album is at least the equal of its predecessor. Particularly outstanding are the title track, a major local hit, and "Solomon Style", his version of a rhythm that had supported successful 45s for Hugo Barrington and Admiral Bailey.

⊙ **Cowboy Style** (Greensleeves, UK).
After a couple of quiet years, Josey made a strong comeback in the mid-1990s with the title track of this set, which revisited an old lyric over a remixed "Sleng Teng" rhythm; a similarly rejuvenated Frankie Paul joins him for "Curfew" to provide another highlight. But it is "Bible Never Fail Mi Yet" that best sums up the conscious ragga attitude: "Mi love mi gun, mi woman and mi bag of gold, but mi Bible never fail me yet".

Jammy's first rivals

Even before the setting up of the Steely & Clevie and Digital B labels, King Jammy occasionally had to look over his shoulder at the competition. Jammy's rival in the sound wars of the early 1980s, Jack Scorpio, might have been temporarily sidelined by the success of "Sleng Teng", but the low cost of digital rhythms allowed a dramatic proliferation of new producers. Even so, the first serious pretenders to Jammy's throne were both veterans: **Winston Riley** a founder member of the Techniques singing group and a successful producer since the early 1970s, and **King Tubby**, Jammy's former employer – even if the latter took on more of an executive producer role, usually leaving it to others to take care of the sessions in his Dromilly Avenue studio. The first new producer to challenge Jammy was a sound-system operator called **Hugh 'Redman' James**, who brought his own take on the King's approach.

Winston Riley

The most important of **Winston Riley**'s digital tunes of the time was the first hit from the man who had been top deejay for the Stur Mars and Killimanjaro sound systems, **Super Cat** (b. William Maragh, 1963, Kingston). His "Boops", on which he showed traces of Lone Ranger's way of attacking a rhythm, used a stinging Steely & Clevie updating of Marcia Griffiths' "Feel Like Jumping" rocksteady rhythm, and began a craze for records about sugar daddies. As the Cat said:

"She nah tek 'im 'pon a Monday, neither a Tuesday
She 'ave fe find her boops on a Friday
And when ya check it out, Friday a pay day
He come round the lane and give her dollars on the way."

Soon contributing their own views on the topic, on the same Techniques rhythm track, were both Michael Prophet, who had begun by singing cultural material, and the deejay **Junie Ranks**. (Naturally other producers cashed in with their own cuts, with vocalists such as Sugar Minott, King Kong, Anthony 'Red' Rose and even reggae's elder statesman Bunny Wailer adding their views, along with the deejays Lone Ranger, Papa San, Pompidoo and Lyrical.)

Further enormous deejay hits from Riley included some original advice on cleanliness from **Red Dragon** (b. Leroy May). The deejay, originally known as Redman, had built a reputation with his appearances on the Stone

Love, Small Axe and People's Choice sounds, but neither his debut disc for fellow deejay Charlie Chaplin nor a couple of 45s for Harry J matched the impact of his commentary on personal hygiene, "Hol A Fresh". His brother, **Flourgon**, followed it with the "Hol A Spliff" variation to give Riley yet another dancehall favourite. The combination of **Papa San & Lady G** gave Riley a further winner with "Legal Rights", a three-minute saga of domestic tensions.

Besides top deejay outings, Riley was also among the first producers to record **Admiral Tibet** (b. Kenneth Allen), one of the few 'conscious' singers of the first years of digital reggae, and **Courtney Melody**, a quintessential (and sometimes off-key) dancehall performer then having his first fifteen minutes of fame. The strong reality messages of "Leave People Business" and "Badminded People" were Tibet's most successful records for Riley. Melody scored with two hits delivered in his urgent roughhouse style, "Bad Boy" and "Exploiter".

WINSTON RILEY PRODUCTIONS

◑ **Techniques Vaults** (VP, US).

A very consistent compilation from the Techniques label, including Tenor Saw's "Ring the Alarm" and, on the same rhythm, General Echo's "Arleen", as well as Red Dragon's first hit, "Hol A Fresh", Sanchez's "Loneliness" and practically every Winston Riley production that meant anything in the dancehall from 1980 onwards.

King Tubby

Jammy's other main rival of this period, **King Tubby**, had made fitful attempts at producing his own music before (as opposed to mixing other people's), but it was only with the opening of his new studio, and the setting up in 1985 of his Firehouse, Waterhouse and Taurus labels, that he seriously launched himself in this capacity. His first hit on Firehouse, "Tempo" (a misspelling of "Temper"), from the young singer **Anthony 'Red' Rose** (b. Anthony Cameron), was calculated to make the same sort of showing as "Sleng Teng". The rhythm lacked quite the originality of Jammy's bench-mark tune, and the almost expressionless vocal owed much to the style pioneered by Nitty Gritty (who soon had his own version of the rhythm on Jammy's, with "Hog Ina Me Minty"), King Kong and Tenor Saw. Where "Tempo" gained, though, was in the aggressive mix, the work not of the Dubmaster himself, but his two apprentice engineers Peego and Fatman.

Tubby then released records – of varying quality – from youth performers and veterans alike. Among the latter were **Johnnie Clarke** and **Cornell Campbell**, whose hits for Bunny Lee had been accompanied by dubs mixed by Tubby and his apprentices at Dromilly Avenue. Neither was as successful on Tubby's digital rhythms, however, as the resurgent **Gregory Isaacs** – though the former Cool Ruler's one brilliant album for Tubby only surfaced after the producer's murder. One of the most memorable of all the tunes from the younger singers was "Rude Boy" from **Lloyd Hemmings**, also a veteran of sorts, as he had originally recorded a tune called "Africa" ten years previously, aged only 12. Nothing much had been heard from him in the interim, but he again moved centre stage with a fresh-sounding 45 that brought together two different elements from the past: an updating of the Wailers' 1960s hit of the same title, plus a chorus that drew upon Amos Milburn's r&b chestnut, "One Scotch, One Bourbon, One Beer". King Kong's warning about "AIDS" was in the same class, as was young Courtney Melody's boastful "Ninja Mi Ninja".

DAVID CORIO

The voice in the tweeter box: Anthony 'Red' Rose

AN INTERVIEW WITH PHANTOM

Phantom (b. Noel Gray) was King Tubby's right-hand man during the first years of ragga, when the former dub master was concentrating on running his own labels and, for the most part, passing mixing duties to younger engineers. When photographer Paul Coote met him at Sonic Sounds in August 1996, he gave the following account of the last years of Tubby's studio.

"I started at King Tubby's studio in 1985. Professor, who was the engineer, and me used to go to school together at Norman Manley Secondary School, but we know music first amongst Henry 'Junjo' Lawes, and spar with Captain Sinbad and Sugar Minott at Youth Promotion. Tubby's used to make music and the majority just dub, but he did one and two song. The guy me used to go to school with, Professor, was the engineer at King Tubby's, and him come for me one day in 1985, and say 'King Tubby's want a man who know music beside him.' Through Junjo had so much man 'round him, me say: 'All right. I will go to Tubby's.' So we went to Tubby's, and through him buy some sixteen-track tapes. We build about thirty rhythms.

Me took three days at Channel One and build rhythm, and back to Tubby's, where we transfer the rhythm to two-track and four-track, as Tubby's never have no sixteen-track machine, and start voice. The first sing we put out was "Hard Time Rock" with Sugar Minott, "Tickle Me" with Little John and a tune with Patrick Andy name "Love Me Forever". "Hard Time Rock" was the first hit tune we make in '85. We find out we can't just make tune 'round a Tubby's and them hit, and a couple nah hit. Jammy's now make a tune name "Slim Ting", so we get Anthony 'Red' Rose sing "Under Me Fat Ting", and we hit again. Out next big hit was when we make Anthony 'Red' Rose sing "Tempo". That was a big hit, then – a #1 tune! And from we make, that a 1985, we start gwan, and we get a singer name King Kong, and we get Singing Melody, Super Black, Lily Melody, Banana Man, Derrick Irie.

So, in '86, Professor come to me and say: 'Phantom, I going away now. Me mother send for me a foreign. You haffe take care of this business, now. You must control the business, now, cut stamper, labels to look 'bout.' Me say: 'Bwoy, I don't know 'bout that.' Anyway, we put it to Tubby's, say Professor a go away and Tubby's get frighten, and say: 'Professor, why you going away? Who going' look after 'bout the business?' Professor say: 'Phantom will take care of business." So from there, we take care of Tubby's business and look after the labels, audition. Like a singer come, we have to audition and pass them. Me pass Thriller U, me pass Admiral Tibet, Junior Demus, Pliers, Wayne Wonder. We get Wayne Palmer – him do a song name "Hell Ina Town', and it hit up the place.

When Professor left, we get a youth name Peego. Him used to live near and him did a work for Jammy's. Peego love how we gwan, and him start engineer fe Tubby's. Then we get Banton, and we get Fatman who deh a Jammy's now. We get together and put out 'nuff song, and we mek the label call Firehouse, and Waterhouse, Kingston 11 and Taurus. Tubby's, him happy fe all of us to carry the business. When money fe pay, him say 'Carry this money' and 'Cut this stamper', and we pay Tuff Gong and pay Dynamic fe cut it. Me used to look 'bout them thing deh.

King Tubby's was still repairing electronics and if a dub cut bad, he show them how fe cut it back. But him mostly in the office those times deh. Some time when a song a mix, him just come help mix the song, or show how to mix it. Him sit down inna office until some song never mix too right, so him get a new youths call Fire House Crew. We bring them now and start work, and cut a lot of hit tune. Hit by hit, right up until '89 we do good in a music business, and put an album name *Dubplate Clash*. It was a sound-boy killing album, and sell forty odd thousand over the world. It just sell like a 45. Me run the business side for Tubby's, but just wake up one morning and hear say 'im get shot. Him daughter take over the business. We put out about another seven tune when I was there, and they never sell. So the daughter was vex and say: 'The tune no sell.' And me just say: 'I have to go to England.' Things then run down and so Sonic Sounds a buy up the whole things."

But Tubby didn't fully repeat the commercial success of his initial hit until the album that emerged shortly before his untimely death in 1989, the innovative *King Tubby Presents Soundclash Dubplate Style*, which presented the sort of sound-clash boasts and taunting introductions normally only heard in the dancehall itself. From this set came **Little John**'s "Fade Away", an exemplary sound-boy interpretation of Junior Byles' roots classic, with lyrics aimed not at those lacking consciousness but at rivals at the clash.

GREGORY ISAACS

◑ **Warning** (Serious Business, UK).

The one incontestably great Isaacs album of the digital era, with sharp Firehouse Crew rhythms that include "Lonesome Side"/"Fade Away". The opening track, "Long Sentence", sums up the mood of the entire set: one for paranoid rude-boys everywhere.

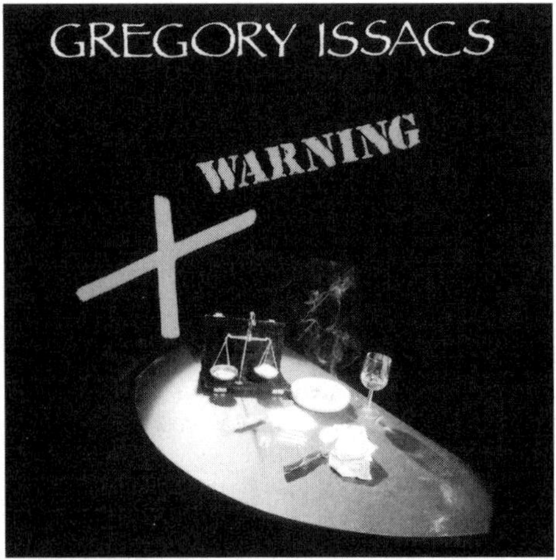

KING TUBBY PRODUCTIONS

● **King Tubby Presents Soundclash Dubplate Style** (Taurus, JA/UK).

Ⓔ King Tubby was responsible for hundreds of dubplates, and it this ammunition for 'sound clashes' that is celebrated here. The tracks feature amusing intros by Alty 'Fuzzy Jones' Salmon (who found fame doing just this), followed by the singers extolling Tubby's sound.

Hugh 'Redman' James

A couple of years after "Sleng Teng", another sound man-turned-producer joined the fray, and for a brief period **Hugh 'Redman' James** was considered a contender for Jammy's throne. The sound of his productions was a rootsier version of the King's, which is not so surprising as he used the same musicians, notably the almost omnipresent Steely & Clevie. Admiral Tibet's "New Tactics", Carl Meek's "Wey Dem Fa" and Conroy Smith's one great tune "Dangerous" were the strongest of the first flurry of hits in 1988. The momentum was kept running over the next year with excellent tunes from Johnny Osbourne, Courtney Melody, Frankie Paul and the veteran John Holt, while the deejay Clement Irie was responsible for Redman's most popular tune outside of Jamaica – the powerful anti-coke warning "Kola Ko". After that Redman seemed to lose interest. Though from time to time there have been rumours about his plans for a serious return to the sound-system arena and record production, only the former has been fulfilled so far.

HUGH 'REDMAN' JAMES PRODUCTIONS

◑ **Total Recall Volume 8** (VP, US).

This might not give the complete Redman story – missing are classic records from Admiral Tibet, Courtney Melody and Carl Meeks – but it does include the producer's greatest single, Conroy Smith's "Dangerous", as well as Frankie Paul's fine "Slow Down" and much else that explains the esteem in which he was held in the late 1980s.

● **Rough, Mean & Irie Volume 1** (Redman International, JA/UK).

One of the best rhythms built for Redman was a digital variation of Delroy Wilson's "Run Run", employed for Clement Irie's "Kola Ko". This version album then placed the deejay's hit alongside further strong offerings from such as Johnny P, the duo of Rappa Robert & Tipper Lee, and Daddy Lilly, Carl Meeks and Thriller U. A wild dub completes the package.

Gussie Clarke

The next step forward for dancehall music occurred three years after the first digital hit, and again with just one ground-breaking 45: **Gregory Isaacs**' "Rumours" (the rhythm of which was used for an even bigger club hit in the United States: J.C. Lodge's "Telephone Love"). Producer **Augustus 'Gussie' Clarke** had first established his reputation in his late teens, progressing from owner/operator of his own small sound, through the record export business, before venturing into production in 1972 (see pp.119–120). A hard-working businessman, he was also a great organizer with a gift for assembling superior performers, writers and engineers into hitmaking teams.

By 1987 he was in control of his own studio, **Music Works**, which was to become the studio of choice for many developing producers, offering state-of-the-art equipment. Gussie's innovation, like so many in the history of reggae, was really a timely synthesis, for with "Rumours" he broadened the scope of computerized ragga by showing that the dread feel of the previous decade could be incorporated into a hi-tech sound for the modern dancehall. After the success of "Rumours", Gussie continued with the same approach, building original rhythms and employing professional songwriters – **Mikey Bennett**, **Hopeton Lindo**, **Dennis Croary** – for quality material with a distinctly dread ambience. This paid off with several more hits from Gregory Isaacs, as well as Dennis Brown and the Mighty Diamonds. Even the top UK lovers-rock singers **Peter Hunningale** and the late **Deborahe Glasgow** benefited from the Gussie touch. Gussie had originally made his mark with U-Roy, I-Roy and Big Youth but avoided recording deejays in the prolific way most of his rivals were, concentrating on the occasional quality record with Cutty Ranks, Shabba Ranks, Papa San, Lady G or Ninjaman.

Another inspired move on Gussie's part was the popular pairing of Shabba – then on the brink of global stardom – with women singers like **Krystal** and **J. C. Lodge**, as well as the sweet tones of the male trio **Home T** and Cocoa Tea. The results were some of the most refined examples of the 'combination' genre. Gussie must have been disappointed when **Freddie McGregor & Snagga Puss**'s "This Carry Go Bring Come" (1993), which employed a sample from the Justin Hinds ska original, failed to repeat the crossover success of Shaggy's similarly styled "Oh Carolina". In 1997, however, Freddie McGregor topped the UK reggae chart with a Gussie-produced lovers song called "Rumours" (a relation to Gregory's hit).

Mikey Bennett, who provided most of the vocal arrangements for the records that appeared on Gussie's labels in the late 1980s, joined forces with **Patrick Lindsay** in 1990 to form another forward-looking label, Two Friends, which also used the Music Works studio (as well as Maurice Johnson's Black Scorpio). The glossy sound created for **Two Friends** was similar to that on Gussie's own productions, and several of the same performers were featured (eg Gregory Isaacs, Dennis Brown, Cocoa Tea, Shabba Ranks, Brian & Tony Gold).

DEBORAHE GLASGOW

◑ **Deborahe Glasgow** (Greensleeves, UK).
One of the finest of the UK 'lovers rock' singers placed in the hi-tech setting of Gussie Clarke's

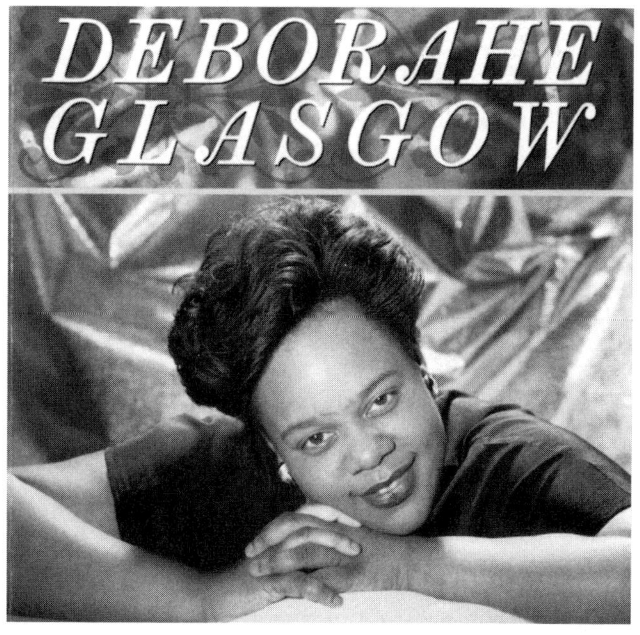

Music Works. The satin sheet of the sleeve photograph pretty much sums up the smooth and sexy approach, with the singles "Don't Test Me" and "Champion Lover" showing a more assertive side to the singer. Obviously a labour of love on Gussie's part, and a set intended to outlive any trend.

HOME T, COCOA TEA & CUTTY RANKS

◑ **Another One For the Road** (Greensleeves, UK).

After Shabba signed with Epic, Cutty Ranks was brought in to take his place. The Two Friends team produced the new permutation; and the resulting album was just as successful as the above – with Cocoa Tea's powerful "No Blood For Oil", the title track and "The Going Is Rough" standing out.

HOME T, COCOA TEA & SHABBA RANKS

◑ **Holding On** (Music Works, JA; Greensleeves, UK).

The 'combination' style was taken a step further when the rockstone tones of Shabba Ranks were placed alongside the sweeter voices of Cocoa Tea and Home T. Jammy was responsible for "Who She Love", their initial hit together; Gussie stepped in to record them on the popular "Stop Spreading Rumours" and "Pirate's Anthem". The album features two more combination tracks, plus another two from each act.

GREGORY ISAACS

◑ **Red Rose For Gregory** (Music Works, JA; Greensleeves, UK; RAS, US).

The fact that Gussie made a return to the cutting edge of the music at the same time as Isaacs decided to revitalize his career by recording for almost every producer in Jamaica must be one of reggae's happiest coincidences. This presents the groundbreaking "Rumours", plus the hits "Rough Neck" (with the Mighty Diamonds) and "Mind Yu Dis", along with the equally strong "Intimate Potential" and "Teacher's Plight".

GREGORY ISAACS & DENNIS BROWN

◑ **No Contest** (Greensleeves, UK).

Five years separated this set from the first Gussie album that brought the two stars together (see p.268), and this is similarly divided into duo and solo tracks, complete with dubs. The difference this time lay in the strictly hi-tech digital rhythms featured. The pair's popular single "Big All Round" is included, with two more combination efforts. Dennis Brown's "No Camouflage" is the best of the solo tracks.

HOPETON LINDO

◑ **The Word** (Greensleeves, UK).

Not unexpectedly Hopeton Lindo's first album, produced by Two Friends, features his own compositions exclusively, with his unassuming vocal style shown to good effect over the sharp rhythms.

FREDDIE McGREGOR

◑ **Carry Go Bring Come** (Greensleeves, UK).

Two cuts of the title track – one a straight vocal, the other with Snagga Puss – stand out as decidedly different for both Freddie and Gussie. There is also an interesting version of Gregory Isaacs' "Night Nurse". Everything else is more predictable – though given the standards of both singer and producer that is not such a bad thing.

THE MIGHTY DIAMONDS

◑ **The Real Enemy** (Greensleeves, UK).

◑ **Get Ready** (Greensleeves, UK).

The Mighty Diamonds albums released by Gussie before and after the breakthrough of "Rumours". The difference between them, however, is minimal, both employing essentially the same musicians and a semi-computerized sound. The group continue as if nothing had changed from their Channel One days, with the familiar harmonies delivering the usual mixture of love and 'reality' lyrics. A pity that the second set omits "Heavy Load", their version of Gregory's hit.

VARIOUS ARTISTS – GUSSIE CLARKE PRODUCTIONS

◑ **Hardcore Ragga** (Greensleeves, UK).

E This compilation could not be better – Gregory's "Rumours", the J.C. Lodge and Lady G cuts, Home T, Cocoa Tea & Shabba Ranks' "Pirate's Anthem", Papa San & Lady G's "Twice My Age" and practically every important Gussie hit of the late 1980s, in digital clarity. This is some of the most adventurous music ever to emerge from Jamaica.

◉ **Music Works Showcase '88 & '89** (Greensleeves, UK).

Two strong 'version' albums bought together. While many producers use the one-rhythm format to expose new names, these sets feature only bona fide stars. Thus "Rumours" is treated to cuts by, among others, Ken Boothe, Dean Frazer, the Mighty Diamonds and Josey Wales. J.C. Lodge's US hit, "Telephone Love", is here as well, though not "Rumours" itself. The following year's set is built around the same singer's "Mind Yu Dis Rudeboy", and includes Shabba Ranks, Jackie Mittoo and Johnny Osbourne. Again, it is assumed that you have the original hit.

VARIOUS ARTISTS – TWO FRIENDS PRODUCTIONS

◑ **Hardcore Ragga 2** (Greensleeves, UK).
A similar collection to the above, but displaying the production skills of Mikey Bennett and Patrick Lindsay. Their Two Friends label might have always seemed in the shadow of Music Works, but hits like Cocoa Tea's "No Blood For Oil", Dennis Brown's "Poison" and Hopeton Lindo's "Slaughter" come very near to matching Hardcore Ragga.

Jammy's employees go it alone

The most serious contenders for King Jammy's throne were former employees who set up their own outfits after making crucial contributions to his initial success with digital instrumentation. Foremost among these was engineer **Bobby Digital** who, following in Jammy's footsteps, soon proved just as accomplished in every area of production – a point acknowledged by the King himself. **Steely & Clevie**, who for a while occupied Sly & Robbie's place as the premier bass and drum team in Jamaica, launched their own eponymous label, which was a successful showcase for both singers and deejays.

HORSEMAN/VINE YARD RECORDS

Pre-eminent dancehall engineer, Bobby Digital

Bobby Digital

Robert Dixon – aka **Bobby Digital** – earned his now familiar moniker when he helped shape the computerized phase of Jamaican music at Jammy's headquarters. He rose to the position of Jammy's chief engineer and right-hand man, and it was at the St Lucia Road studio that he formed relationships that were to be important to his later career –with Steely & Clevie, who were building the ground-breaking rhythms, and then with a relatively unknown deejay called **Shabba Ranks** and a more established singer whose voice was as sweet as his name, **Cocoa Tea**.

When, in 1988, Bobby Digital formed his Digital B label, its first releases included Cocoa Tea's moody "Lonesome Side", and the even more popular cut from Shabba, "Peanie Peanie", both riding a variation of Junior Byles' "Fade Away" rhythm. (Bobby Digital had a talent for spotting a past rhythm that had not been versioned to death, and then giving it a fresh lick of paint.) Shabba's impact at Jammy's had been relatively muted, but he is reputed to have played a key role in encouraging Bobby Digital to strike out on his own, and quite a few of the earliest hits on Digital B featured the gravel-voiced deejay. "Hot Like Fire", "Wicked In Bed", "Roots & Culture" and "Just Reality" were among the 45s that helped to establish both the future crossover star and Bobby's label. The strength of the relationship between the two men was later shown by the series of Shabba 45s that appeared on Digital B in the mid-1990s, long after the deejay's fame had gone far beyond the reggae marketplace. But then it was Bobby Digital who had played the major production role in the success of Shabba's best-selling albums for Epic-Sony, at the same time helping ensure that the world's best-known ragga did not lose his original dancehall audience.

Cocoa Tea, too, has regularly returned to the producer with whom he first worked at Jammy's, and their hits together have taken in the full range of contemporary reggae, including sound-clash anthems, 'reality' tunes and tender lovers outings – as well as some great 'combination' discs with Shabba.

After his initial successes, Bobby Digital played a key part in the establishment of the late **Garnett Silk**'s career, with the singer's initial hit 45s and well-received debut album. Records of the first order from **Sanchez**, **Frankie Paul**, **Pinchers**, **Johnny Osbourne**, **Admiral Tibet** and **Wayne Wonder** further confirmed his reputation as a premier league producer, and even veterans like **Gregory Isaacs**, **Leroy Smart** and **Leroy Sibbles** have benefited from his studio skills. As might be expected from his success with Shabba, Bobby Dixon has shown himself equally at ease with deejays. He has produced strong-selling tunes by most of the 'name-brand' deejays of the last few years, including **Ninjaman**, **Admiral Bailey** and **Red Dragon**; additionally, he has produced interesting but less prolific contenders like **Junior Demus**. Most importantly, his hits with **Terror Fabulous**, **Tony Rebel**, **Cobra**, **Lieutenant Stitchie** and **Beenie Man** contributed to bringing them to the attention of major labels overseas.

BOBBY DIGITAL PRODUCTIONS

● **Ripe Cherry** (Blue Mountain, UK).
Eric Donaldson's best-selling "Cherry Oh Baby", a Festival Song Competition winner from 1971, had already been covered by both the Rolling Stones and UB40 when Bobby Digital showed how it could be updated for the digital age. This album brings Digital's successful singles together – including Cobra's remarkable "Tek Him".

● **Hotter This Tear** (Blue Mountain, UK).
After the late Dirtsman declared he was "Hot This Year" over the rhythm, Philip Smart gave his successful cut of "Drum Song" to Bobby Digital, who allowed a selection of hot performers the chance to stamp their identities upon it. Pick of a fine bunch: Papa San's "Run the Route", where Dirtsman's brother successfully makes the same sort of claim for himself.

◑ **Things A Gwan** (Digital B, UK).
The Bobby Digital approach has mostly involved reviving vintage rhythms, but here he successfully tackles one from the digital era itself: Cocoa Tea's "Ruling Cowboy". Several of the cuts were successful as 45s – including the title track from Ninjaman.

Steely & Clevie

Given the nature of Kingston's studio system, it is hardly surprising that most of Jammy's competitors employed his rhythm section of Steely & Clevie to build their own digital tracks. Much the same principle had operated in previous eras, when rival producers used nominally different studio bands, drawn from the same nucleus of musicians. The difference made by computerization was that just two musicians could make a session band, and in the immediate post-"Sleng Teng" period two seasoned professionals were the dominant band: **Wycliffe 'Steely' Johnson** and **Cleveland 'Clevie' Browne**, graduates respectively of the Generation Gap and the Browne Bunch. Like Sly & Robbie before them, they found time to build superb rhythms for practically every producer in Kingston, while keeping their most progressive efforts were kept for their own label. There they proved equally suited to hard-core deejays like Ninjaman, Tiger, Johnny P and Cutty Ranks, and to singers of the calibre of Gregory Isaacs, Frankie Paul and Freddie McGregor.

The first release on the duo's eponymous label was in the newly fashionable 'combination' style, bringing together one of the most talented emerging singers and a vintage deejay whose biggest hits had come a decade before. **Leroy Gibbons & Dillinger**'s "Bruk Camera" – an updating of Freddy McKay's "Picture On the Wall" – confirmed Steely & Clevie's status as the master builders of hard computerized rhythms that still retained very musical qualities. Subsequent discs demonstrated that Steely & Clevie were establishing their own finely crafted sound, with inspired touches in the pared-down mixes and advanced use of sampling.

Important local hits like **Ninjaman**'s "Murder Dem", and **Cutty Ranks**' "Retreat" showed their knack of bringing out the best in the new generation of deejays then coming out of the dancehalls. The vocal tunes they released alongside them were no less inspired, further showing the duo's respect for tradition. **Freddie McGregor**'s version of Little Roy's "Prophecy" rode the same fresh-sounding cut of the "Peanut Vendor" rhythm that supported **Foxy Brown**'s interpretation of Tracy Chapman's "Fast Car". But there was no better example of Steely & Clevie's knack of picking and matching different elements from musical history than **Frankie Paul**'s reading of Dennis Brown's "Cassandra". This included a quote from the same singer's "Westbound Train", and was placed over a new version of the "Sleng Teng" rhythm, in a juxtaposition of styles that worked exquisitely. Freddie McGregor's best-received records of the 1990s have mostly been his treatments of old Jamaican favourites, all treated in much the same way as the several he versioned for Steely & Clevie.

Furthermore, Steely & Clevie also utilized rhythms derived from the music associated with the religious cult of Pocomania (see p.5). Donovan Germain (see p.292) had already had a hit with Chaka Demus's exuberantly joyous "Chaka On the Move", and records with the same back-to-church feel then appeared in quantity, though few rode as interesting a rhythm as **Gregory Peck**'s furiously paced "Pocoman Jam" for Steely & Clevie. Employing an overdubbed cut of the same rhythm track, Cutty Ranks then scored another massive hit with "(Ugly Girl) Retreat". The Pocomania trend was short-lived, though the style has remained another cultural resource – like mento or ska – upon which Jamaican musicians have periodically drawn.

FREDDIE McGREGOR

Now (Steely & Clevie, JA).

This 1991 set features excellent reworkings of Little Roy's "Prophecy", Dobby Dobson's "Loving Pauper", the Heptones' "I Hold the Handle" and his own "Africa Here I Come". Best of the new material is the bittersweet "Bad Boys". An indispensable Steely & Clevie album, and the singer's best for almost a decade.

Freddie McGregor Sings Jamaican Classics: Volumes 1, 2 & 3 (Big Ship, JA/UK).

All three sets demonstrate what a superb interpreter of proven material Freddie McGregor can be. An unsurpassable choice of songs, including the Gaylads' "Joy In the Morning", Derrick Harriott's "The Loser" (retitled "I Was Born A Winner") and the Paragons' "Danger In Your Eyes" – to give but one from each volume.

STEELY & CLEVIE COMPILATION

Steely & Clevie Play Studio One Vintage (Steely & Clevie, JA; Heartbeat, US).

Rather than have performers voice new lyrics over modern reworkings of Studio One rhythms, Steely & Clevie bought in the original artists to again sing the original songs. The result is exemplary, mainly because of the enthusiasm that the process obviously involved. Dawn Penn's "You Don't Love Me" was the crossover hit, but everyone – including Alton Ellis, Leroy Sibbles and the Cables – deserved similar success.

STEELY & CLEVIE ONE-RHYTHM ALBUMS

Real Rock Style (Steely & Clevie, JA).

Classy digital update of the Sound Dimension instrumental classic, jointly produced by Steely & Clevie and Bobby Digital. Featuring big hits like Cocoa Tea's "Love Me" and Shabba & Flourgon's "Shock Out" as well as cuts by such dancehall favourites as Little John, Pad Anthony and Clement Irie.

Poco In the East (Steely & Clevie, JA).

More Poco (Steely & Clevie, JA).

The first of these presents only half a 'version' album for the "Pocoman Jam" rhythm, as the other side is devoted to slightly disappointing cuts of "Far East". Worth picking up, however, for the "Pocoman Jam" side, which includes the Gregory Peck hit that began the excitement. The remixed rhythm was then employed for an entire album's worth of cuts, built around the popular Cutty Ranks version. The title track samples all the versions, creating something quite different in the process.

● Lion Attack (Steely & Clevie, JA).
Here Steely & Clevie freshen up to the "Punaany" rhythm which they originally recorded for Jammy, and have singers and deejays stamp their mark on it. The "Fever Medley" hit from Freddie McGregor is given some serious competition from Cocoa Tea's "Sonia" and Shabba Ranks' "Ca'an Dun", as well as strong cuts from the likes of Cutty Ranks, Carl Meeks and Tony Tuff.

● Godfather (Steely & Clevie, JA).
Steely & Clevie revive the digital rhythm that began it all. Ninjaman's "Murder Dem", Johnny Osbourne's "Salute the Don" and Frankie Paul's "Cassandra" were all popular singles on the reworked "Sleng Teng", to which are added cuts by such as Cocoa Tea, Carl Meeks, Little Twitch, Anthony 'Red' Rose and Reggie Stepper.

Donovan Germain

After the efforts of the various pretenders to the throne, the man who finally took Jammy's place as Jamaica's leading record producer was **Donovan Germain**. Like the producer who initiated digital reggae, his involvement in music dates back to the 1970s, when he ran a record shop in New York and began producing. By the beginning of the 1980s he had a label called Revolutionary Sounds, which was run from New York though all the recording sessions took place in Kingston. Outstanding among the productions on his own label were **Sugar Minott**'s UK hit, "Got A Good Thing Going", and the heavyweight steppers' anthem, "Mr Boss Man", from the appropriately named **Cultural Roots**. More success came to Germain half a decade later: first, with a second British pop hit, **Audrey Hall**'s "One Dance Won't Do" (answering Beres Hammond's "What One Dance Can Do"), and then in more sustained fashion with the setting up in Kingston of his own **Penthouse** studio in 1987.

Digital reggae in the mid-1980s was very much a youth music – it was all about excitement, immediacy and newness. But the Penthouse studio at 56 Slipe Pen Road – like its neighbour, Gussie Clarke's Music Works (see p.267) – was a source of a more considered ragga. Clarke and Germain were Kingston's two most sophisticated contemporary producers, with long careers in the business and a very similar professionalism. But while Gussie gives the impression of wanting to leave the dancehall behind, Germain has been more interested in consolidating this base and building outwards from there. He sought to improve the quality of the music being played in the dancehall, and succeeded in re-establishing superb vocalists like **Marcia Griffiths** and **Beres Hammond** in that context, while working just as successfully with most of the major new deejays, including **Buju Banton**, **Tony Rebel**, **Cobra** and **Cutty Ranks**.

The only area where Germain's achievements fail to match Jammy's is in his lack of first-rate and completely original rhythms. He has yet to produce his own "Sleng Teng" or "Punaany". Rather, his talent lies in his selection of the right vintage rhythms for the time, and in what he has **Steely & Clevie**, **Mafia & Fluxy** or the **Firehouse Crew** do with them. He was also one of the first Jamaican producers to build rhythm tracks around samples, beginning with one taken from the Channel One cut of Leroy Sibbles' "Love Me Girl", the first of several occasions on which he has chosen the streamlined late-1970s Maxfield Avenue version over the Brentford Road original.

VARIOUS ARTISTS – DONOVAN GERMAIN PRODUCTIONS

● Dancehall Hits Volumes 1–6 (Penthouse, JA).
Almost anyone who has meant anything in the ragga era is represented on these six hit-packed compilation albums, which means singers of the calibre of Beres Hammond, Tenor Saw and Wayne Wonder, alongside deejays such as Buju Banton, General Degree, and the still underrated Terry Ganzie.

● Fire Burning (Penthouse, JA).
Having Marcia Griffiths sing Bob Andy's "Fire Burning" over the same singer's "Feeling Soul" rhythm was an inspired move. This version album adds Cutty Ranks' superb combination with Marcia Griffiths, "Half Idiot", another combination featuring Beres Hammond and UK-based deejay Cinderella, plus seven cuts of comparable quality.

◑ **Frontliners** (Penthouse, UK/US).
Versions of Marcia Griffiths & Cutty Ranks' "Really Together" on one side, and Cobra's "Gundolero" on the other. The other reliable names to make an appearance: Sanchez, Carlene Davis, Beres Hammond and Johnny P for the former excursion; Tony Rebel, Sugar Black and Wayne Wonder for the latter.

● **Good Fellas** (Penthouse, JA).
The first side has cuts of Beres Hammond's "Tempted To Touch", including the Cutty Ranks and Tony Rebel hits. These are backed with the Penthouse version of Jammy's "Run Down the World" rhythm, with Sanchez's "Soon As I Get Home" and Tony Rebel's "The Herb" of particular note.

● **Penthouse Celebration Part 2** (Penthouse, JA).
An attempt to recreate the dancehall vibe in the studio, with the 'juggling' style, is brought off with elan, utilizing the full range of sound effects, introductions and dedications. It benefits from the presence of stars like Cutty Ranks, Beres Hammond, Tony Rebel, Cobra and Sanchez, all of whom ride the successful recut of "Love I Can Feel". Part I had more participating stars, but lacked the focus given by the killer rhythm.

● **Penthouse Dancehall Hits Volume 7** (Penthouse, JA).
Ten cuts of the updated "Swing Easy" rhythm, all of which were strong enough to be released as 45s. Buju Banton's cutting "Sensimellia Persecution" and Beres Hammond's "Kid's Play" were particular favourites at the time, but tracks from Terror Fabulous, Cobra and Buccaneer are hardly put in the shade, and there is a healthy balance between top deejays and singers.

Deejays at Penthouse

The Penthouse records of the late 1980s were distinguished by their clean and bright sound, even if the early hits only hinted at the sophisticated approach of the next decade. The future became clearer in 1990. To begin with, Germain began producing one of the deejays about to seriously challenge Shabba, the rock-stone-voiced **Cutty Ranks** (b. Philip Thomas, 1965, Kingston), a deejay who had been a mainstay on sound systems since the early 1980s. There was no denying the authority of the ex-butcher's attack on 45s like "Dominate" and "Russia & America", the latter a fine illustration of Germain's approach to rhythm-building, which has tended to favour new cuts of rhythms that have yet to be overexposed. In this case, the rhythm went back only to 1987, when it had supported two major Jamaican hits on the Miami-based Skengdon label, Chaka Demus's "Young Gal Business" and Super Cat's "Mud Up".

The deejay with whom Cutty shared his first Penthouse album, *Die Hard*, was **Tony Rebel** (b. Patrick Barrett, Manchester, Jamaica), who had already established his style with the Germain-produced 45s, "Mandela Story", "The Armour" and "Instant Death". More than any other deejay in this period, Rebel consistently tackled cultural themes on record, providing a focus for similarly inclined younger artists, like

his friend the singer **Garnett Silk**. Both the Cutter and the Rebel were to continue as part of the regular Penthouse stable (Germain commands an uncommon loyalty from his artists), sometimes joining forces with singers such as **Beres Hammond**, **Marcia Griffiths**, **Wayne Wonder** and **Twiggy**.

A third very gifted deejay who was to make his mark at Penthouse was **(Mad) Cobra** (b. Ewart Everton Brown, 1968, Kingston), who rose to the top very quickly in 1991, with uncompromising rude-boy hits like "Yush", "Bad Boy" and "Gundolero", as well as the appropriately titled debut album, *Bad Boy Talk*.

As Penthouse became more established, there were further top-drawer deejay records from new and established names, including **Capleton**, **Lieutenant Stitchie**, **Terry Ganzie**, **Beenie Man**, **Lady Saw**, **Spragga Benz**, **Terror Fabulous** and **Buccaneer**. None, though, were quite to equal the success of **Buju Banton**. In common with most popular Jamaican performers, Buju has worked for several producers, while most often recording – and having the best brought out of him – at

Penthouse. His ascent to the status of Jamaica's most acclaimed mike man was obviously helped by Germain's hottest rhythms – his cuts were often released alongside as many as nine other versions, and inevitably came out on top.

COBRA

◑ **Badboy Talk** (Penthouse, JA).

This Donovan Germain-produced set, from 1992, includes the major hits "Bad Boy" and "Gundolero" (both titles meaning much the same, with the latter adding some Wild West glamour), as well as the extraordinarily popular "Yush", whose title celebrates the slang form of greeting then prevalent among the rude boys.

● **Merciless Bad Boy** (Sinbad Production, JA/UK).

Not a Germain production, but a fine complement to the debut album. The first side warns West Kingston's gun-crazy youth while celebrating their culture. Even his response to the Gulf War takes the form of addressing Bush and Hussein as a couple of ghetto

GUN TALK AND SLACKNESS

If ragga's digital rhythms were contentious in certain circles, so too were some of the lyrics that accompanied them. Cultural sentiments had become thin on the ground during the dancehall onslaught of the early 1980s, when they were replaced by lyrics about the dancehall itself, guns and sex (slackness). Now those themes became even more dominant and the increasingly explicit descriptions of female anatomy and automatic weaponry proved unacceptable to many who had come into reggae through Bob Marley albums. Some critics found this material grossly materialistic and lewd, especially in comparison to the uplifting values of 1970s reggae, but such charges ignored much older traditions within Jamaican music and, even more importantly, the harsh facts of ghetto life, which the gun and 'punaany' lyrics mirrored. In addition, the critics failed to recognize the role of irony in some of the lyrics, and to hear that the new voices were not entirely homogeneous.

Violence had increased in Kingston's ghetto areas during the political wars around the 1980 election, and after the JLP government took power many members of the 'posses' who had enforced their agenda found new criminal activities. When crack came on the scene the situation worsened, with gangs locked into deadly fighting for control of the trade. The most sophisticated weaponry soon appeared on the streets of Kingston's ghettos, and the government responded by introducing special squads drawn from the army, whose attitudes and hardware matched those of the gangs. (The first of these units, the '(E)Radication' squad, was celebrated on an early Yellowman record.) Under one name or another, they continued to operate throughout the decade, and their brief was simple: to remove the gunmen, by force when necessary. This situation – akin to a civil war – found its reflection in the dancehall, where many records directly addressed it, while others merely utilized the image of the gun figuratively, as an expression of power otherwise denied to most ghetto dwellers.

Cobra, one of the most talented of the ragga deejays, namechecks two of the most feared 'posses' on his 1991 tune called "T'ink A Little Gun" (Wild Ninja):

"You t'ink a little gun
bad boy sit down pon
respect bad boy from all direction
Me want hear
the rude boy gun a clean
Me want hear
when dem change the magazine
Me want hear
Junglist gun dem a clean
Me want hear
Shower man gun dem a clean
Bad boys, yes we run the scene
Nah run when we hear police sireen."

Cobra similarly comments on the reality of the bad-boy life on "Price Gone Up" (Penthouse), where his lyrics deal in matter-of-fact fashion with the price rises of guns and ammunition, while his "Shot A Talk" (Steely & Clevie) makes it clear that "Gunshot don't talk, gunshot a kill".

rude boys. The second side deals just as successfully with the other ragga preoccupation, girl business.

CUTTY RANKS

◑ **The Stopper** (Fashion, UK).

This 1991 offering is one of the deejay's two most consistent albums. The title track uses a hip-hop-influenced treatment of the "Punaany" rhythm – it was the first Jamaican record to use the US form in this way – and epitomizes what a classic Cutty record is all about: rapid-fire delivery, fresh lyrics delivered in a voice of pure rockstone, and a gritty rhythm. He was never hotter than when he was recording these tracks, using facilities in Kingston and at London's Fashion studio.

◑ **Lethal Weapon** (Penthouse, JA; VP, US).

The other unreservedly recommended Cutty Ranks set features all Penthouse rhythms, and includes the hits "Lambada" (with Wayne Wonder), "Half Idiot" and "Really Together" (both with Marcia Griffiths) and "Love Mi Hafi Get" (with Beres Hammond). As good a place as any to discover either the deejay or producer Donovan Germain.

But in the tradition of the rude-boy records from the 1960s, some of the deejays' gun talk was ambivalent. Thus **Cutty Ranks** on both his early hits, "The Bomber" and "The Stopper", proclaimed that Jah gave him "strength and power" to bring "roots and culture" wherever he goes, while boasting how his state-of-the-art gun can shoot down both policeman and soldier. The 'conscious' ragga deejay Tony Rebel entered the same arena early in his recording career with "The Armour", a shot aimed directly at Cutty Ranks' head, while Cobra has recorded 'conscious' tracks alongside those that both glamorize or condemn West Kingston's gunplay.

Given that they are often degrading to women, it is hardly surprising that sexually explicit ragga lyrics have come in for almost as much condemnation as the guntalk. There have been plenty of crude tunes like Grindsman's "Benz Punaany" (Dragon) and Major Bones' "Sticky" (Steely & Clevie), unredeemed by any wit or imagination. But the interesting thing about tunes such as these is that they have been bought largely by Jamaican women – sex is one area where women in Jamaica can assert some sort of power, and these lyrics perhaps show men's uneasy response to this. Furthermore, not all slack lyrics are one-dimensional. A record like "Lone Cocksman" from **Little Lenny** (b. Nigel Grandison) might be judged obscene by politically correct Western standards, yet it is not merely sexual posturing. It functions simultaneously as a parody of macho attitudes, delivered in imagery – the "lone cocksman riding west" – derived from the Hollywood Western. Another example of a slackness expressing more than appears on the surface is **Shabba Ranks**' "Ca'an Dun" (Steely & Clevie). This celebrated the inexhaustible sexuality of women, but the hardcore lyric of the original 12" single also conveyed a strong sense of personal resolution in the face of harsh ghetto conditions.

Showing that a new generation of female deejays could be just as slack as the men, **Lady Saw** (b. Marion Hall, c. 1971) gained a reputation for her outrageous sexual boasting – on one record she claims that one man is not enough, but two or three might satisfy her. Accordingly, she recommended that women should only have sex with the "hardest workers" in bed, not giving their favours away lightly – in short, that sex should be satisfying for the woman as well as the man. What is more, for Lady Saw true obscenity exists more in the world outside the bedroom. As she puts it on "What Is Slackness":

"Me seh: society a blame Lady Saw fi de system dem create
When culture did a clap dem never let me through the gate
Now as me seh 'sex'
Dem want fi jump on a mi case
But pick the beam out of your eye
Before you chat in a mi face.
Slackness – is when the road wan' fi fix
Slackness – when government break dem promise
Slackness – when politicians issue out guns
So the two party a shoot one another down."

Less talented female deejays than Lady Saw have also, just like the men, used slackness merely for publicity, in contrast to the generally more demure work of singers such as Twiggy, Chevelle Franklin and Nana McLean.

CUTTY RANKS & TONY REBEL

◑ **Die Hard** (Penthouse, JA/UK).

A side apiece for two of the most regular visitors to Penthouse, and an interesting contrast of styles. While Cutty attacks the stinging rhythms with his usual intensity, Tony Rebel 'singjays' along with them in fairly melodic fashion. Both were heading for the top of the ragga pile when they cut these tracks, and this set helped them on their way.

TONY REBEL

● **Rebel With A Cause** (Penthouse. JA).

The first album that the conscious ragga had to himself, and one he still has to surpass – not least because of the ratchet-sharp Penthouse rhythms. Guest appearances from Marcia Griffiths, Wayne Wonder, and the UK's Macka B. Early hits like "War & Crime" and "Fresh Vegetable" are included.

The singers

Proving that he was equally at ease working with quality singers, Germain's best seller in 1990 was **Beres Hammond**'s "Tempted To Touch". The reworking of John Holt's "A Love I Can Feel" rhythm that supported Hammond's soulful vocal provided further hits the following year, with Cutty Ranks' assertive commentary, "Love Mi Hafi Get", and Tony Rebel's lyrically original "Fresh Vegetable". The major importance of the Hammond hit, however, was that it began a string of wonderful Germain-produced Hammond records that have represented the high ground for Jamaican vocal music in the 1990s – titles like "Falling In Love", "My Wish" and "Is It A Sign" sold heavily in the reggae market, albeit without coming to the attention of the outside world. (For more on Hammond, see p.297.)

Wayne Wonder's "Hold On" was another impressive vocal favourite of 1990, part of another ongoing series of 45s by a singer who can do no wrong as far as the dancehall audience is concerned, while remaining totally unknown to most of the world beyond it. Other superb vocals on Penthouse have come from **Garnett Silk**, **Sanchez**, **Richie Stephens**, **Jack Radics**, **Thriller U** and **Junior Tucker**, all on their very best form.

Ragga sing a hit song

The mainstream media have consistently identified ragga with the men at the mike. While it is undoubtedly true that deejays have retained the popularity they achieved during the early 1980s, by the beginning of the 1990s the most interesting of the younger singers had re-established the place of the vocalist alongside the roughneck talkers. What follows is a look at just some of the singers who have consistently made interesting records since "Sleng Teng", beginning with five relative veterans, before moving on to the new breed of lovelorn crooners, as well as the under-recorded women singers who have made their mark.

DAVID CORIO

Pure Worries in the Dance: Frankie Paul

Frankie Paul

As the jump from dancehall to ragga was more a matter of technology than aesthetics, it is not surprising that the outstanding vocal stylist produced by early 1980s dancehall,

Frankie Paul, continued to cut records of the first order. He has been an extraordinarily prolific singer, making more than one hundred albums in fifteen years on a bewildering number of labels, including Jammy's, Techniques, Supreme, Steely & Clevie, Redman International, Skengdon, Sinbad Production and Fashion – to name just a few. After a dip in popularity at the first half of the 1990s, he made a triumphant return in 1995, with a well-received performance at Sunsplash and a series of sterling 45s on Digital B, Xterminator and Stone Love. At one time, Motown were said to be interested in signing the almost blind singer (he has been tagged "Jamaica's Stevie Wonder"), though it is hard to imagine how a contract with any major US recording company could have been reconciled with his tireless enthusiasm for studio/label hopping – an album a year has never been the man's style.

FRANKIE PAUL

◑ **Sara** (Jammy's, JA; Live & Love, UK).

Ⓔ It was impossible to walk around certain areas of London in the summer of 1987 without repeatedly hearing Frankie Paul's "Sara". In the reggae world a great single does not always mean an album of anything like the same calibre, but Paul and Jammy – with the help of Steely & Clevie – managed precisely that. The other hit, "I Know the Score", is at least as memorable, and the emotive love songs, sound-boy boasts and cultural commentaries more than hold their own.

◉ **Live & Love** (Jammy's, JA).

This set from three years later was almost a greatest hits collection in everything but name, including as it did "(Posse) Run Come", "Be Mine Tonight", "Kibba Your Mouth Shut" and "I Wanna Love You All Over", plus tracks of the same rank – like the magnificent "Long Run Short Ketch".

◑ **Money Talk** (Jammy's, UK).

Paul's popularity had slipped by the time this appeared in the UK in the early 1990s, and as a result it has never been released in Jamaica. Proceedings are dominated by a cut of Nitty Gritty's "Run Down the World", where one of Jammy's top rhythms combines with Frankie P's exquisite vocalizing.

Beres Hammond

Another singer with even more potential for crossing over to larger markets is the soulful **Beres Hammond** (b. Beresford Hammond, 1955, Kingston), who has only risen to real prominence in the digital age, despite a career stretching back to the mid-1970s. The former Zap Pow vocalist has shown himself equally at home with the most anguished romantic ballads and the deepest roots, which places him in the

DAVID CORIO

The awesome talent of Beres Hammond

company of talents such as Gregory Isaacs, Dennis Brown and Freddie McGregor. Although making excellent records for a variety of labels (while never stretching his talent as thin as many of his compatriots), Jamaica's greatest contemporary has perhaps been captured most consistently at his finest by Penthouse, Tappa, Xterminator and Star Trail, as well as his own Harmony House. The fact that Elektra released one superb album by him and then failed to renew his contract says more about the perspectives of an international record company than it does Hammond's awesome talent.

BERES HAMMOND

◑ **A Love Affair** (Penthouse, JA/US).

Ⓔ The set that established Beres Hammond as the major vocalist of the digital age. Singles such as the sublime "Tempted To Touch" had validated Donovan Germain's move in placing Jamaica's top soul stylist over dancehall rhythms. Rather than hurriedly adding a few fillers to the hits, each track obviously had time and care taken over it, with talented musicians like Mafia & Fluxy, Steely & Clevie and the Firehouse Crew providing the rhythms, while the cream of the island's singers made guest appearances. The CD's bonus tracks let top deejays Cobra, Cutty Ranks and Tony Rebel have their say.

◑ **In Control** (Harmony House, JA; Elektra, US).

Some fans were initially disappointed by Hammond's debut on a US major. Rather than repeating the formula of *A Love Affair*, a contemporary r&b-influenced approach was employed. There were still some out-and-out dancehall killers – "I Could Beat Myself", for example, and a track with Buju Banton – but they are joined by soulful ballads more reliant on well-structured songs than on already familiar rhythms. A set that deserved far more of a push from Elektra than it received.

◑ **Full Attention** (Charm, UK).

A Philip 'Fatis' Burrell-produced set that places the wonderful title track alongside the searing "Emptiness" and "All In the Game", former singles that demonstrated his ability to handle rootsier rhythms.

◑ **Putting Up Resistance** (Tappa, JA).

Tappa Zukie proved himself an excellent producer when he made a welcome return in the 1980s. The album titled after his most successful 45 with Beres Hammond includes further hits in the form of "Strange", "Look Fi Mi Girl" and "Love On the Wire", plus several previously unavailable tracks of the first order.

◑ **Sweetness** (VP, US).

This collects together most of the hit singles that did not appear on Penthouse or Xterminator. Dancehall followers will possess all these as singles, but for anyone else it is a wonderful opportunity to catch up on his best from Steely & Clevie, Star Trail, Sting International and Mister Tipsy.

◑ **Love From A Distance** (VP, US).

A mixture of self-produced gems and equally impressive tracks from Richard Bell, Mikey Bennett and Bulby & Fatta. Nothing very different from his past sets in this 1996 collection, but with music of this soulfulness only the gimmick-hungry would complain.

◑ **Life Time Guarantee** (Greensleeves, UK).

A full set from producer Richard Bell, and confirmation of the singer and producer's compatibility. This is another from 1996, and it seems as if the title has it about right: he does not look likely ever to make a wrong move.

⦿ **Reggae Max** (Jet Star, UK).

A mid-price set with undistinguished packaging but a more than worthwhile collection of hits from a range of producers, including Philip 'Fatis' Burrell, Donovan Germain, Tappa Zukie and Richard Bell. With twenty tracks, this value-for-money package serves as a wonderful introduction to the major Jamaican vocal talent of the 1990s.

Ini Kamoze

A very original stylist who was associated with Sly & Robbie in the early 1980s then made a triumphant return in the digital age, **Ini Kamoze** has never been prolific – at least, not by reggae standards. However, his crossover success in the mid-1990s (his reworked "Hot Stepper" reached #1 in the US charts in 1995) has to some extent obscured the body of work that immediately preceded it – particularly the self-productions that appeared on his Selekta imprint. He is nothing if not his own man, and his recent work for Philip 'Fatis' Burrell has been just as individual. The *Lyrical Gangsta* album, which followed his hit, was targeted squarely at the hip-hop crowd, but Kamoze's next singles, on Burrell's Sounds Klik label, were firmly back in the dancehall style. The brooding "Jah Never Fail I Yet", "Hill And Gully Ride" (both 1995) and "No Watch No Face" (1996) were impressive records, the pair riding heavy-duty updates of Horace Andy's "Mr Bassie" and Marley's "Heathen", respectively.

INI KAMOZE

◑ **Shocking Out** (Greensleeves, UK; RAS, US).

The title track introduced his Selekta label to the world in 1987, and dominates the self-produced set that appeared the following year. Original lyrics, wicked rhythms (from Steely & Clevie, with Danny Browne, Danny Thompson and Tyrone Downie) and a delivery that is totally his own.

Romantic raggas

Sweet-voiced and romantic singers such as **Sanchez**, **Thriller U**, **Wayne Wonder**, **Cocoa Tea** and **Junior Tucker** are just as representative of the modern dancehall as the more publicized deejays, even if their stardom is more localized. Pliers' brother, **Spanner Banner**, also fits into this grouping stylistically, and is equally at home with 'lovers' or 'cultural' lyrics – like Cocoa Tea, who wears Rasta locks and in recent years has cut plenty of records informed by his faith. To understand how the seemingly divergent styles of sweet-voiced ladies' men and abrasive deejays can complement each other, you just listen to any of the popular 'combination' records from such as Shabba Ranks, Home T and Cocoa Tea, Red Dragon and Brian & Tony Gold, Johnny P and Thriller U, or Buju Banton and Wayne Wonder.

In comparison with the sweet-as-molasses approaches of the above singers, there are more traditional artists who are more influenced by either classic Jamaican vocalists – such as Delroy Wilson and Ken Boothe – or mature-sounding American r&b stylists of the Brook Benton mould, while concentrating just as much on 'lovers' material, and commanding an equally large female following. These include a big-voiced veteran of the North Coast tourist circuit, Mikey Spice (b. Michael Johnson), who became the sensation of 1995 with his incredibly popular version of Barry White's "Practise What You Preach", though subsequent hits have shown him equally confident with just as heartfelt 'cultural' offerings. Then there is **Richie Stephens**, who began as a Dennis Brown clone, but has since developed his own style, while still waiting for the really massive hit to lift him into the first division. Already with several best sellers to his credit is the vocally eccentric **Jack Radics**, who sometimes allows his exaggerated vowel sounds to approach self-parody.

Perhaps the most underrated balladeer of all is **Glen Ricks**. Born in Jamaica but raised in Canada, he began his career when he joined the Fabulous Flames while they were on tour. Ricks then returned to Jamaica for a couple of years, gaining a hit for producer Clancy Eccles in 1969 with Neil Diamond's "Holy Holy". After this, he lived in Canada again, where he earned a solid critical reputation with two deep-soul albums. Back in Jamaica by 1990, Ricks was soon in demand with producers like Bobby Digital, Sly & Robbie, Captain Sinbad and Fatis Burrell. A gifted singer, he grafts soul vocal techniques onto dancehall rhythms for under-rated gems such as "Baby I'm For Real" (Taxi) and "Give Love" (Sinbad). Third World's **Bunny Rugs**, who has not made nearly enough solo records, also works this approach to particularly good effect.

COCOA TEA

◑ **Come Love Me** (VP, US).

E The improvement in Cocoa Tea's lyrics was witnessed by the hits for Bobby Digital collected here: "We Do the Killing", the much-versioned "Lonesome Side", "Too Much Gun Lyrics" and "Love Me Truly". There is also strong material that did not appear on singles, while things are roughed up by two generations of rockstone deejay voices in the shape of Josey Wales and Shabba Ranks.

◑ **Authorised** (Music Works, JA; Greensleeves, UK).

The titles "Chilling Out" and "Cooling Out" give an idea of the general mood of this Gussie Clarke-produced set from 1991. The neo-steppers side of Clarke's music is represented by "Hunted Wanted" and "Get Rotten", but for the most part the rhythms are sweet and easy.

◑ **Kingston Hot** (Greensleeves, UK; RAS, US).

The album that marked the resurgence of the man who successfully recorded Cocoa Tea in the early 1980s, Henry 'Junjo' Lawes – an event celebrated in one of the most immediately appealing tracks, "Return". "Bust Outta Hell" was a Jamaican #1, and the entire set is a triumph for both singer and producer.

◉ **Israel's King** (VP, US).

The best of Cocoa Tea's collaborations with Fatis Burrell. Several rhythms are perhaps more familiar supporting songs by Luciano, but they are just as suited to the sweet-voiced one's approach. The duet with Luciano, "Rough Inna Town", is a real stormer, while the love song "Don't Want To Live Without Your Love" stands out from the remaining cultural material.

JACK RADICS

◑ **I'll Be Sweeter** (Penthouse, JA).

Jack Radics' highly mannered vocalizing can be hard to take. But here he is relatively restrained, and heard over some of Donovan Germain and Dave Kelly's strongest rhythm tracks.

◉ **Open Rebuke** (Heartbeat, US).

Produced by Richard Bell, and employing a variety of studios and musicians, this album nonetheless maintains coherence throughout, drawing committed vocals from the singer which fully match the overall seriousness of the lyrics. Two combinations – one with deejay Kulture Knox, the other with Yami Bolo

– are both outstanding. An album of modern roots that is Jack Radics' best effort to date.

GLEN RICKS

◉ **Ready For Love** (RAS, US).
A highly accomplished set that shows love songs needn't be equated with softness. Strong Xterminator rhythms throughout – including the label's interpretation of Aswad's "Love Fire" – and Glen Ricks's soul pedigree is well in evidence in the emotive vocals.

BUNNY RUGS

◉ **Talking To You** (Greensleeves, UK).
Produced by Jack Scorpio (with some help from Clive Hunt and fellow Third World member Cat Coore), this has a smoother sound than usual from Black Scorpio's owner, and one that is nearer to the Jamaican mainstream – partly thanks to appearances from deejays Papa San, Cobra and General Trees. The material is chosen with care, ranging from two new cuts of "Now That We Found Love", through a successful reworking of Desmond Dekker's "Shanty Town", to some strong new songs.

SANCHEZ

◉ **Sweetest Girl** (Dennis Star, JA).
This album for producer Dennis 'Star' Hayles in 1988 created the template from which Sanchez would rarely deviate – largely covers of US r&b hits, with the odd reality tune and sound-boy boast thrown in for variety. This has the hits which sent girls wild in 1988 – "Old Friends" and his first cut of "Let Me Love You Down" – plus rhythms by Firehouse Crew and Dave Kelly.

◉ **Loneliness** (Techniques, US).
Another set from 1988, this time with veteran producer Winston Riley. Riding an understated Steely & Clevie cut of Pat Kelly's "In the Mood", the single "Loneliness Leave Me Alone" sold by the cartload and gave the set its title. Seven of the ten tracks are covers, including Aaron Neville's "Tell It Like It Is" and an assured medley of the r&b standards "Since I Fell For You" and "Never Let Me Go", which transforms them into a hot dancehall blend.

◉ **Number One** (RAS, US).

◑ **Boom Boom Bye Bye** (Greensleeves, UK).
Phillip Burrell is the producer who has drawn the best from the sweet-voiced singer in recent years, as demonstrated on both of these sets. Along with the expected r&b covers, Sanchez exercises his songwriting skills to good effect, and there are typically strong Xterminator rhythms. The RAS album has the earliest tracks – including his popular version of Tracy Chapman's "Baby Can I Hold You Tonight"; the Greensleeves set spices things up with guest spots from Marcia Griffiths, Flourgon and Shaka Shamba (with the CD adding the UK deejays, Macka B and Sweetie Irie).

MIKEY SPICE

◑ **Happiness** (RAS, US; Runnetherlands, Holland).
Included in the Barry O'Hare-produced debut set is his version of Barry White's "Practise What You Preach", a strong contender for the reggae vocal of 1995. Plenty of pure rub-up-a-girl music here, though tracks like "Signs & Wonders" and "Chant Down Babylon" have him handling 'consciousness' lyrics with aplomb.

◑ **So Much Things To Say** (Big Ship, UK).
A similar and equally strong mixture of lovers and roots tracks appear on this set, which was produced by Freddie McGregor. The title track stands as one of the best ever cuts of a Marley song, and was a major hit in the reggae world.

RICHIE STEPHENS

◑ **Forever** (VP, US).
The title track remains one of the best cuts of the "Tempo" rhythm released by Donovan Germain (there were at least seven), while a variety of producers display the degree to which a former Frankie Paul clone has developed his own very impressive style.

THRILLER U

● **Waiting For You** (Live & Love, UK).
The crossover market tends to have an antipathy towards Jamaican versions of soft-soul songs, however tough the rhythms used. Thus the appeal of Thriller U, a singer with a penchant for just that, has been limited to the reggae marketplace, where his records never fail to sell. The rhythms here are Jammy's, which means the best, and the songs include "I've Been Sitting", "My Love" and "Greatest Love Affair": beautiful stuff, and part of a Jamaican tradition dating back to rocksteady.

JUNIOR TUCKER

◑ **Secret Lover** (Charm, UK).
Once heard, Junior Tucker's records refuse to be ejected from the memory bank, so it's hard to explain why a massive reggae hit like "Move Along" wasn't a wider success. Here his most successful 45 is joined by tracks from producers of the calibre of Donovan Germain, Danny Browne and Bobby Digital. A near-perfect summer soundtrack.

WAYNE WONDER

◑ **Don't Have To** (Penthouse, JA).
By the time he cut this second album for Germain, Wayne Wonder had developed into one of Jamaica's leading ladies' men. A fair portion of hits is included – "I'd Die Without You" and "Bonafide Love", to name two – plus much else that's guaranteed to melt the hearts of his dancehall fans. And for those wary of too much sweetness, there are tough contributions from deejays Buju Banton, Terry Ganzie and Tony Rebel.

Dancehall divas

Jamaican women have played a major role in setting trends as consumers, but their role in front of the mike has tended to be restricted to the traditional role of backup singers – or heavy breathers on slacker offerings. Happily, this situation has shown signs of changing over the last decade, with the veteran **Marcia Griffiths** initiating this development. With a CV stretching back to hits in the late 1960s, Jamaica's most accomplished woman singer re-emerged in the ragga age, employing her warm, soulful voice over state-of-the-art rhythms for Penthouse, Taxi, Xterminator and Fat Eyes.

Since the 1980s no other Jamaican woman singer has been recorded as often as the former I-Three, but several have made interesting records on a more sporadic basis. **Dawn Penn** and **J.C. Lodge** have even received international attention with Yard-style hits, even if they have been consigned to the status of one-offs – a particularly unfair situation in the case of Lodge, who possesses a hugely expressive voice. One of the most promising discoveries of 1989, **Foxy Brown**, has yet to have a crossover hit, and while she made a serious impact in the reggae world with covers of Tracy Chapman's "Fast Car" and "Baby Can I Hold You Tonight" (both Steely & Clevie), her subsequent releases have demonstrated how badly she needs the guiding hands of Messrs Johnson and Browne – and, perhaps even more important, songs of the calibre of Tracy Chapman's.

The relatively few records by women singers that have surfaced suggests a vast potential still to be fully realized. Well-put-together and-promoted albums are still urgently needed from **Twiggy**, **Nadine Sutherland**, **Carol Gonzalez**, Toots Hibberts' daughter **Leba**, **Chevelle Franklin**, **Juliet Nelson** and **Krystal**, all of whom have made excellent singles for a variety of producers. The superb **Nana McLean** has an album currently available, but she still lacks the regularly released 45s that her male counterparts take for granted. Presumably, many more Jamaican women are underselling their vocal talents in church choirs or the occasional talent show.

MARCIA GRIFFITHS

◑ **Indomitable** (Penthouse, JA/US).

Ⓔ A 1993 album that displays a talent that can accommodate the best of the old and new with assurance. The set begins and ends with her biggest Penthouse hits – wonderful readings of Bob Andy's "Fire Burning" and Miriam Makeba's "I Shall Sing" – and the tracks in between feature several versions of Jamaican classics. Cutty Ranks joins her on the LP, while the CD adds Buju Banton, Tony Rebel and Bunny Rugs.

J.C. LODGE

◑ **Selfish Lover** (Greensleeves, UK).

Gussie Clarke lavishes time and care on the considerable vocal talents of J.C. Lodge. It says something about the quality of the material and the production that her most successful single, "Telephone Love", by no means dominates.

NANA McLEAN

⊙ **Collector's Series** (Penthouse, JA).

Donovan Germain's production skills were always particularly suited to romantic material and women singers, as shown on this polished set. Ms McLean remains another seriously underrated and under-recorded talent.

Deejay confrontation

Shabba Ranks has been ragga's most widely known figurehead for several years, and though his contract with Epic has slowed the flow of 45s his music has remained essentially the same – give or take the odd guest appearance by US guest stars like KRS-1, Queen Latifah and Johnny Gill. In the early 1990s he had to fend off a challenge to his supremacy from **Ninjaman**, and there's been no shortage of more durable rivals. At least as acclaimed in the Jamaican dancehalls of the past few years have been two deejays working in the same rockstone voice tradition, **Buju Banton** and **Bounty Killer**, who in turn have inspired another generation of younger deejays. Approaching them in popularity are **Beenie Man**, **Cobra** and **Capleton**, while many more young hopefuls continue to flood the market – almost every shipment of 45s that arrives in London or New York from Kingston contains at least a couple of new and attention-grabbing deejays. On the international stage the combination of the singer **Pliers** and the gruff-voiced **Chaka Demus** have mattered the most, consistently reaching a broad-based audience who might never think of going to a ragga dance, while at the same time appealing in the dancehalls as well.

ADRIAN BOOT

Two-Grammy Shabba Ranks

Shabba Ranks

Ragga's international icon, **Shabba Ranks** (b. Rexton Gordon, 1965, St Ann's), occupies a position not dissimilar to that of Bob Marley in a previous decade, but his reception outside Jamaican has been rather different. His contribution to the row stirred by the homophobia of Buju Banton's "Boom Bye Bye" (Shang Muzik) was ill-considered, and was immediately seized upon by the international media, who are not usually concerned with what Jamaican performers have to say. The outcry added to the notoriety earned by the 'slackness' of his work, creating a distorted image of his success in the reggae world. This is not to deny the popularity of his risqué stuff, but this is just one facet of his work – alongside records such as "Hard & Stiff" (Digital B) and "Love Punaany Bad" (Jammy's) have been pertinent commentaries on 'reality' themes, and some boasts about his sexual prowess that have an irony that seems lost on some people.

In common with a fair percentage of the top deejays to emerge in the mid-1980s, Shabba first started to build his reputation with records for King Jammy. More unusually, he went on to surpass the quality of this early material with work for other producers – even if Jammy has to be given the credit for first linking him with the singers **Cocoa Tea** and **Home T**, a team that was to have more sustained successes together for Gussie Clarke. Shabba's first album for Jammy, in 1989, was shared with **Chaka Demus** (his colleague at Jammy's unassailable sound system), and though it was an acceptable enough generic set, neither deejay more than hinted at his future potential (if anything, Chaka Demus seemed the stronger talent).

Shabba's leap into the premier league came with a series of 45s for the label recently set up by Jammy's main engineer, **Bobby Digital**. "Peanie Peanie", over the rhythm used for Cocoa Tea's "Lonesome Side", raised his profile in the reggae world, and further titles confirmed the arrival of an exceptional new force. The next move for a deejay who has worked with relatively few producers (by Jamaican standards, at least), was to Gussie Clarke's Music Works studio. There his international potential became more obvious, largely thanks to Gussie's glossy, more melodic rhythms and some inspired couplings with singers of the quality of **J.C. Lodge**, the UK's **Deborahe Glasgow** and, again, Cocoa Tea & Home T.

Real crossover success came with his signing to the US major, Epic, who had enough nous to call on the services of Jamaican producers and studios, and not to make any obvious attempts to water down his roughneck style. In other words, he was allowed to continue doing what he did best – which sounds like an obvious approach, but contrasts sharply with how the international majors had dealt with reggae in the 1970s. This has allowed Shabba to reach a far wider audience than any previous Jamaican deejay. The general high profile of chatters in the reggae marketplace cannot have done him any harm, but to this must be added the important role of hip-hop in preparing the wider world for the once exotic concept of someone talking over rhythm tracks.

Wisely, Clifton 'Specialist' Dillon's Shang Muzik have continued to release Shabba 45s in Jamaica – such as "Ting A Ling", "Respect" and "Shine & Criss" – that are aimed squarely at the local market, and as raggamuffin-rough as anything he has ever voiced. A series of vintage cultural statements – "Flag Flown High", "God Bless", "Satan", "Who Calm the Lion", "Think You're Having It All", "Heart Of A Lion" – also appeared in 1995 and 1996, all on Digital B.

SHABBA RANKS

◑ **Golden Touch** (Two Friends, JA; Greensleeves, UK).

Ⓔ Released immediately prior to his move to Epic, this remains Shabba's most consistent set. Producers Mikey Bennett and Patrick Lindsay ensured variety by using top studios in London and New York, as well as Kingston, and the world's most successful ragga dropped the easy option of slackness, to show just how inventive – and good-humoured – he could be. He made plenty of great records both before and after this, but something very special was captured here.

◉ **King Jammy's Presents Shabba Ranks** (Melodie, France).

Jammy was Shabba's first producer, and this is more or less a reissue of his ground-breaking *Star Of the Nineties* set (released in 1990!). The album to let you know where he began, while Jammy's rhythms of the period are always a joy.

◑ **Best Baby Father/Just Reality** (Vine Yard, UK).

The two Bobby Digital albums that really established Shabba's name, brought together on one CD. Upon its release in 1989, *Best Baby Father* caused the kind of excitement that is usually the preserve of hit 45s in the reggae world, and the following year's *Just Reality* confirmed its promise. Jamaican hits like "Wicked Ina Bed", "Are You Sure" and "Peanie Peanie" are the equal of anything that was to follow.

◑ **Rappin' With the Ladies** (Greensleeves, UK).

◑ **Mr Maximum** (Greensleeves, UK).

The first of these is a collection of his 'combination' hits with female vocalists. All the Gussie-produced hits are here, including those with Krystal, Rebel Princess & Cocoa Tea, J.C. Lodge and Deborahe Glasgow. The gravel-voiced one also rejoins J.C. Lodge for another cut of her "Telephone Love". A second collection of such cuts has four remixed solo pieces to complete the package, alongside combinations with Maxi Priest, Dennis Brown, Home T, Cocoa Tea, Lady G and Fabiana. Obviously scraped together after Shabba had found crossover success, but made worthwhile by the inclusion of five full-length 12" mixes.

◑ **As Raw As Ever** (Shang Muzik, JA; Epic, US).

◑ **X-Tra Naked** (Shang Muzik, JA; Epic, US).

◑ **A Mi Shabba** (Sony, US).

Three albums into his contract with the international major, Sony-Epic, and our rude boy is still as rough as ever. Indeed, the first two titles make a virtue of just this. There are US guest stars, but from a world of dance music that is as hard-core as Shabba's own (the only combination that does not quite work is the one with Chuck Berry). All that is missing, really, is any example of his cultural side, which he has consistently displayed on Jamaican 45s for Bobby Digital.

Ninjaman

Ninjaman (b. Desmond Ballentine, Kingston) was once seen as Shabba's main rival, and for a couple of years his output showed at least as much verve. Set to become one of the most original of deejays, he first established his reputation beyond Kingston's dancehalls on a series of 'combination'-style 45s – alongside first, Courtney Melody, and then the veteran Tinga Stewart. Successful records without a singer in tow soon followed, including "Lick Out" (Selekta), "Peddle & Wheel" (Music Master) and the particularly strong "Hortical Don" (Steely & Clevie).

But, popular as these were, his reputation really took off in 1990, with far more original hits like "Murder Dem" (Steely & Clevie), "My Weapon" (Mr. Doo) and "Border Clash" (Jammy's). The shift in approach that put him in the first league involved chatting against the rhythm in what might be called a 'conversational' style (complete with a very distinctive stutter), rather than riding it in the conventional sense. This might sound artless, but it was anything but – as shown on a stunning series of 45s for a wide variety of producers, including Bobby Digital, John John, Trevor James, Junior Reid, Fatis Burrell, Lloyd Dennis and Gussie Clarke. The overall effect of these records was like listening to authentic arguments from Kingston streets that had somehow been grafted onto rhythm tracks, with Ninja expounding on every topic under the Kingston sun.

As soon as any performer becomes hot in Jamaica, he is bound to have producers offering him their best rhythms, so ensuring the roll continues – at least, until the next hot name appears. For this reason alone, almost any record from 1990 to 1992 bearing Ninjaman's name is worth hearing. In addition to recording over some of the toughest rhythms of the time, the Original Gun Tooth, Front Tooth, Gun Pon Tooth, Don Gorgon – as he was then calling himself – was then at his peak of verbal inventiveness. Confidently projecting a bad-boy image – one LP cover has him posing as if for a police photograph – he boasted of his misdeeds on "My Weapon". As he has been arrested twice since 1992 for firearm possession, his 'outlaw' image would appear to have some substance. He dissed his rivals – especially Flourgon and Shabba Ranks – with some of the most lethal 'burial' tunes ever, but the Don Ninja displayed another side of his persona with a particularly outstanding series of 45s for Bobby Digital that included warnings to the rude boys ("Cowboy Town"), apocalyptic social comment ("Serious

DAVID CORIO

Ninjaman: the Original Gun Tooth, Front Tooth, Gun Pon Tooth, Don Gorgon

Time") and even the occasional expression of his spiritual faith ("Fulfilment").

Though his creativity – and popularity – declined after a couple of years of prolific activity, Ninjaman gained a new audience through the sampling of his hits on jungle records – a development that inspired Steely & Clevie to record him on one of the few junglist pieces to come out of Jamaica itself, "Donette". Then he fully regained his old form in 1996 with two consummate singles – "Old Picture Frame" and "Many More Miles" – for the producer who has always brought out the best in him, Bobby Digital. Deejays seldom make successful comebacks, but the 48 Gun Bad Bwoy Talker – to use another of his titles – always stood more chance than most. By early 1997 the deejay had rediscovered the Christian religion and sound tapes featuring him in this mode have been selling like there's no tomorrow.

NINJAMAN

◑ **Bounty Hunter** (Digital B, JA; Blue Mountain, UK).

E Ninjaman's freelancing activities mean that his best work is dispersed over several albums, as well as many obscure 45s. This set, though, brings together most of his essential work for Bobby Digital, and has no weak moments. Variety is ensured by the appearance of Gregory Isaacs on three tracks ("Last Of the Warning", "Cowboy Town", "Set Me Free"), and Admiral Tibet and Shabba Ranks on another ("Serious Time"). An LP that captures both producer and DJ at their peak.

◑ **Out Pon Bail** (Xterminator, JA; Gold Disc, UK; Exterminator, US).

Philip 'Fatis' Burrell provides the rhythms for a tough album that almost reaches the standards of the above. Check "A So We Stay" for a spiritual statement that contradicts both album title and cover picture.

◑ **Reggae Sunsplash** (Pickout, JA/US).

The title track – an account of his renowned Sunsplash clash with Shabba – remains one of the deadliest 'burial' tunes ever. The rest of these Lloyd Dennis-produced tracks are not that far behind.

Buju Banton

After Shabba signed to Epic and his output in Jamaica slowed down, the deejay who initially took his place as the prolific voice of the ghetto youth was **Buju Banton** (b. Mark Myrie, 1973, Kingston). He too was signed to a US major – Mercury – but his music, like Shabba's, remained unchanged. He started out in his early teens on small sound systems; by the time he was 15 he had recorded for fellow deejay Red Dragon, as well as vintage producers Bunny Lee and Winston Riley. These early efforts showed him to be competent but no more so than much of the competition.

DAVID CORIO

Hand on heart: Buju Banton pre-Rasta conversion

Like many aspiring deejays he gravitated towards Penthouse studio, where by late 1990 he had met the innovative engineer/musician **Dave Kelly**. The dancehall hits started in the summer of 1991 with "Love Mi Browning", celebrating his love for his light-skinned girl. When darker-skinned women took offence, Buju responded quickly with the placatory "Love Black Woman". In the interim, his voice had become noticeably rougher and deeper. Throughout 1992 it was heard on more Penthouse hits, both solo and in combination with top singers such as Wayne Wonder and Beres Hammond. When Kelly started his own imprint that year, the deejay scored an immediate hit with the first release, "Big It Up", riding a powerful new drum-based rhythm loaded with catchy vocal samples. "Batty Rider" was the next smash for the outfit, commenting on the lat-

PAN HEAD: A TALENT GUNNED DOWN

The deejay known as Pan Head (b. Anthony Johnson, 1966, St Mary; d. 1993, Spanish Town), had already scored a massive reggae hit with "Punny Printer" and was on the brink of real success when he was shot dead in his own home. The crime, which remains unsolved, inspired Buju Banton's outspoken "Murderer". Conducted six months before his death, the following interview offers insights into the processes by which a young deejay establishes himself.

"The firs' set that I deejay on is by the name of Love Vibration. Firs' night I hold a big mike was with Professor Nuts, Tenor Saw, Yami Bolo, an' Lecturer. That was in late '85; an' den from there I move on to Scorpio. But all dose time, I never deejay Scorpio full time, not till me come live a Maverley now, which is Kingston 20. So all dem time me live near Scorpio me use to go over dere, tho' most a the time man nah want to give me the mike still, but me know seh one day me would affi hold it, beca' everybody know hard work yield success in a

DAVID CORIO

Pan Head and friends at Arrow's Studio, 1993

est dancehall fashion – ultra-brief shorts then being worn by flamboyant dancehall 'donettes'.

Buju had become the voice of the moment, but was already extending his range beyond the dancehall staples of guns, girls and his own prowess at the mike. "How Massa God World A Run", employing a wicked Channel One sample, was the first in a series of powerful critiques of the sociopolitical system as viewed from a ghetto perspective. Incorporating striking images, like the rich man feeding the ghetto food of 'chicken back' to his dogs, the lyrics focused on the evils of hard drugs, corrupting materialism and the denial of real opportunity:

"Though the poor can't afford the knowledge, dem no get none
The rich man 'ave the dollars an' no want give we some
Bragadocious and boasty talk him a fling down
Pure 190-E Benz 'im bring down
Sell the mos' crack, cocaine, heroin an' opium
Dem no want see ghetto youth elevate out a the slum
So dem give we all type a things, try turn we down."

In late 1992 he recorded the anti-gay "Boom Bye Bye", sparking a controversy that set his career back – an appearance by the Penthouse Revue at the Womad Festival, in which he would have featured, was cancelled. For a while he kept a lower profile. Then his anger at the death of his friend and fellow deejay Pan Head was brilliantly conveyed on 1993's "Murderer", a tune instrumental in changing the focus of deejay lyrics away from celebrations of the gun. Buju began to grow dreadlocks, although he could still rock the dancehall with hits like "Champion". An early release in 1994 was "Operation Willy", a "safe sex" number from which all proceeds were donated to a charity running a home for children with AIDS. He was able to launch his own CB 321 label in late 1994 with the singularly uncompromising "Rampage" 45. But then 1995's "Untold Stories" pointed to a resolution of his anger in a more pronounced spirituality. Delivered as a semi-acoustic song rather than as a straight deejay rap, this remains his most mature statement on record and it became the high point of his album *'Til Shiloh*.

business. So Exodus was the right sound now, when time people start know who Pan Head lickle-lickle, ca' dem start put mi name pon posters, was 1987, a dance with dem an' Stereo One – Pan Head special guest, Professor Nuts, Papa San so. Dat day was a Saturday night. Thursday night, go back to Scorpio, and 'im say 'Yu mash up the place', and from deh so dem gi' me the mike, an' me jus' start go on, Do some wickeder lyrics – ca' I nah talk 'bout no gun ting, was a deejay weh people could a lissen – everything we talk – culture, jus' name it, girl pickney ting – me nah do slack deejay talk.

Scorpio release the firs' tune with me, in 1988; was a tune by the name of "Gimme Lickle Lovin', Gimme Lickle Lovin' Before It Done". Play pon 'im program, and' den me find me do a nex' tune with Thriller U jus' a burst a tune name "Some Girl A Run Down the Man An' the Man No Match Dem". Dem was my type a girl pickney tune. An' den after, me find me all lef' outa music ting, that was about '89 or so. I end up in a church name of Pentecost somewhere on Molynes Road – was a tent, but is a nice church; start go a church an' me start flex – but the music ting stay in deh – beca' inborn ting, cyaan come out. After dat, now, me get me lyrics book an' burn it up, ca' me seh me done with deejay ting. But it still in me, so me jus' come back inna it. After me leave the church and ting, first Thursday night me a go hold back the mike a Scorpio again, everyting 'appen – me draw lyrics and me me a go hold back the mike a Scorpio again, ever'ting 'appen, me draw lyrics and me seh:

"Heaven was created by God inspire me
Laws an' order that's a Bible statement
Unni can't get a place in 'eaven to rent
Unu better follow the father fi live permanent
Follow the word an' – seen?"

'Nuff lickle lyrics down the line now! From dere on – as me seh, hard work yield success an' the mercy a God, beca' me is a youth weh – me know psalms that me live to the 'eart, and when me in a trouble, a psalm one 'undred an' twenty one. Nah true a man hear Pan Head talk 'bout gun. A jus' a ting fi get the break, fi mek the people dem know a deejay name Pan Head, ca' the 'ardest part a the business is to mek yu name. ❞

BUJU BANTON

◑ **'Til Shiloh** (Penthouse, JA; Loose Cannon, UK).

E This brilliantly conceived set would rank as essential just for two of the tracks in a reflective cultural mood: "Till I'm Laid To Rest" and the wondrous "Untold Stories" (the latter bringing to mind Marley's "Redemption Song"). As it is, nothing else falls very far short of their standard. The former single "Murderer" and a version of Garnett Silk's "Complaint" continue the 'conscious' feel of an album that was clearly the product of much time and thought.

◑ **Mr Mention** (Penthouse, JA/UK).

"Mr Mention" is simply a term for someone who is being mentioned a lot, which young Buju Banton certainly was, even before making public his views about other people's sexual proclivities. His first album for Germain fully explains why he was such a talking point in the reggae world: this is the sharpest, most confident deejaying since Shabba's. Largely a collection of his first hits – including "Love Me Browning", "Batty Rider", "Woman No Fret" – this set alone would have ensured a lasting reputation.

◑ **Voice Of Jamaica** (Penthouse, JA; Mercury, US).

For Buju's major label, debut producer Germain employs his usual stable of singers (Wayne Wonder, Beres Hammond, Brian & Tony Gold) with fellow deejays Cutty Ranks, Tony Rebel and Terry Ganzie also making guest appearances. Buju mixes his concerns to take in political violence, deportees from the States, personal relationships and, yes, his woman's good body. The voice of Jamaica, indeed.

Bounty Killer

If any deejay can lay claim to be the raw voice of Jamaican ghetto youth over the last three years, it has to be **Bounty Killer** (b. Rodney Pryce, Kingston). Not simply a gruff-toned chatter, he has deployed several different voices, employing them in intricate and striking vocal patterns which further emphasize his distinctive lyrics. Born in Trench Town, he entered

PAUL COOTE

Lord 'Ave Mercy: Bounty Killer

music as a youth after moving to the equally tough Seaview Gardens and Riverton City areas. His early influences were **Brigadier Jerry** (see p.246) and **Ranking Joe** (see p.178); they stood him in good stead when, encouraged by his cousin the deejay John Wayne, he voiced his debut "Gun Must Done" in 1990 under the name Bounty Hunter for King Jammy's brother, Trevor 'Uncle T' James. A change of name quickly followed, as did the tune "Dub Fi Dub" for the same producer. This gained him more attention, but it was not until he voiced "Spy Fi Die" for Jammy's son John John that he gained his first bona fide hit.

Since then he has not looked back. Jammy released three albums that contain most of his hits for the label, plus another in which he was opposed by his rival, Beenie Man. Although some of his lyrics celebrate gun culture, others condemn violence; furthermore he is chillingly convincing on reality themes, and has recorded a moving tribute to his mother, "Miss Ivy Last Son". By 1995, chafing under his tenure with Jammy and family, he founded his own Priceless label, since then going on to international success – the first album recorded under his own control, *My Experience*, has reportedly sold more than 300,000 units worldwide, registering strongly with hip-hop fans.

BOUNTY KILLER

◑ **My Xperience** (VP, US).

E A double album by a hard-core ragga deejay might seem a daunting prospect, but Bounty Killer's imagination, self-assurance and ability to stay in touch with his dancehall followers (while reaching out to a wider world) ensures the set's success. The guest appearance from compatible hip-hoppers – including Erick Sermon, Blahzay Blahzay and the Fugees – work well, as do those with more predictable sparring partners like Junior Reid snd Barrington Levy. A generous portion of major reggae hits is placed alongside fresh material of the same scintillating standard.

◑ **Jamaica's Most Wanted** (Greensleeves, UK).
While frantic studio-hopping is the usual course for Jamaican performers eager to make the most of their moment of fame, Bounty Killer chose to keep it largely a family affair, before striking out on his own: his first three albums brought together tracks for King Jammy, his son John John and brother Trevor James. On this debut set, "Roots, Reality And Culture" has to be one of the strongest of the many cuts of the "Real Rock" rhythm released by Jammy over the years, and the entire album is full of similarly incisive commentaries on ghetto life.

◑ **Down In the Ghetto** (Jammy's, JA; Greensleeves, UK).
The second album for ragga's royal family more than kept up the standard of its predecessor. The title track, employing the "Shank I Shek" rhythm, might be his most electrifying to date, but listen to anything here and be convinced of the man's serious talent.

◑ **No Argument** (Greensleeves, UK).
Eight of the tracks on *No Argument* were successful 45s, and there is no drop in quality for the remaining four. "Seek God" is one of the many versions of a nyahbingi drum rhythm that was unexpectedly popular at the close of 1995, and is perhaps the most "different" track here; other tracks are more typical – but brilliant – rude-boy talk.

BOUNTY KILLER & BEENIE MAN

◑ **Guns Out** (Greensleeves, UK).
Concerns on this set are those most commonly associated with raggas at the mike: guns and self-promotion. Suitable hard-core rhythms all the way, as well, and the talents proving evenly matched.

Beenie Man

The deejay who has been cast as Buju's main rival is **Beenie Man** (b. Moses Davis, 1972, Kingston), who is something of a veteran in the business. A product of the rougher-than-rough Waterhouse area, he voiced his first record for 'Junjo' Lawes when he was only 8 years old, with a tune called "Too Fancy". He then featured on Lee's Unlimited sound system, often in company with **Papa San**. Three years later he cut an album's worth of material for Bunny Lee, titled fittingly *The Invincible Beenie Man The Ten Year Old Deejay Wonder*. The next few years were spent refining his verbal skills, recording occasionally, but principally appearing on sounds – he was a mainstay of the celebrated Black Star, alongside the deejay Tiger and vocalist Anthony Malvo.

DAVID CORIO

Brand new veteran, Beenie Man

In 1989, Beenie Man linked up with producer Patrick Roberts, who was already recording Beenie's brother, the singer Little Kirk, on his Shocking Vibes label, and gained dancehall success with titles like "Kip Wey" and "Cu-Cum Looks". The real breakthrough then came in 1994, with the incisive anti-gun lyric of "No Mama No Cry" (Taxi), yet another tribute to Pan Head. The record was a Jamaican #1, making Beenie Man the hottest deejay in Kingston and initiating a stunning series of 45s which continues to the present. Included among these are titles for virtually every top producer working in Kingston: Bobby Digital, King Jammy, Jack Scorpio, Colin 'Bulby' York & Lynford 'Fatta' Marshall, and Danny Browne. Beenie Man has proved to be a wittily inventive deejay, capable of coining a telling phrase derived from dancehall slang; when in 1992 he began interjecting the phrase "People Dead" into his lyrics it was soon copied by Bounty Killer, prompting a feud that has continued, in spite of several public reconciliations. Following Bounty's appropriation of the phrase, Beenie returned the compliment by plundering Bounty's style of delivery.

Outside of the Shocking Vibes setup, Beenie Man's biggest successes have come when collaborating with dancehall supremo Dave Kelly, the pair enjoying huge hits with "Slam" and "Wicked Ride" in 1995.

BEENIE MAN

◑ **Gold** (Charm, UK).
After a decade in the business, Beenie Man rose to the premier league with an exceptional series of 45s in 1994. Those on Taxi, which made the initial impression, are not included here, but that still leaves hits of the calibre of "Mobster", "Never Dis A Mobster" and "Veteran".

◑ **Blessed** (Island Jamaica, UK).
This album features the hit that became the dancehall anthem of 1995, "Slam" from Dave 'Rude Boy' Kelly's Mad House setup, plus other almost-as-popular 45s.

◑ **Maestro** (Greensleeves, UK).
This Patrick Roberts-produced set stands best as a complete album, with far greater variety of mood than most people expect from a single deejay set. "Nuff Gal" might not boast his strongest lyrics (the title gives

you the idea), but is delivered with more than enough panache over the most imaginative rhythm he has been given to date, while "Black Board" and an alternate cut to his dancehall anthem of 1996, "Old Dog", impress just as much.

Capleton

Besides possessing one of the most arresting deliveries in the business, **Capleton** (b. Clifton Bailey, 1974, Kingston) is interesting for the way in which his career has taken in two seemingly disparate facets of modern reggae. He first came to public attention in 1990/91 as one of the slackest of deejays, with titles like "The Red" (Jammy's), "Rough Rider" (Uncle T) and "Bumbo Red" (Exterminator) leaving little to the imagination, while demonstrating he knew how to ride a rhythm. Interspersed with these slack tunes were some incisive 'reality' lyrics – most notably "Too Warsome" (Fresh Breed), "God Mi Love, We Nuh Love Satan" (Bravo the Best Baby Father) and "Ghetto Youth" (Black Scorpio). Even "Gun Talk" (Jammy's) was as much a warning to the gun-crazy ghetto youth as the usual bad-boy braggadocio. The major shift in attitude, however, came about in 1992, when he enjoyed two massive hits with 'cultural' themes – "Almshouse" (Xterminator) and "Prophet" (Penthouse), followed by the almost as successful "Mankind" (Colin Fat). These seemed to point the way forward for Capleton: he openly declared his Rastafarian beliefs, and has since concentrated on lyrics informed by his faith.

PAUL COOTE

The prophet Capleton

The sound system and record label with which he has been most regularly associated in the last few years has been Stuart Brown's African Star, which specializes in culture lyrics over progressive dancehall rhythms. His "Tour" for African Star – a vintage sufferer's tune – was among the best sellers of 1994 within the reggae market, and a hip-hop version did the business in the US market. Capleton's next cut of the same rhythm, "Chalice", actually featured nyahbingi drumming mixed to the fore – preceding both Buju Banton's employment of the sound on *'Til Shiloh* and the success of the "Kette Drum" rhythm. Philip 'Fatis' Burrell's Xterminator, another label that tends towards the rootsier side of ragga, has followed with more first-order Capleton, either solo or in tandem with a singer like Cocoa Tea or Beres Hammond. In 1995, the hip-hop imprint Defjam signed Capleton, and released the uncompromisingly conscious *Prophecy* album. Sales didn't meet their expectations and he was dropped two year later. His Jamaican 45s, however, continue to meet the same very high standards.

CAPLETON

◑ **Prophecy** (Defjam/Ral/African Star, US).

Ⓔ Comparable with Buju Banton's *'Til Shiloh*, all fifteen tracks on this album demonstrate just how serious ragga deejays can be. Included are "Obstacle", "No Competition", "Don't Diss the Trinity" and two mixes each of "Wings Of the Morning", "Heathen Reign" and the phenomenal "Tour". The nyahbingi drumming on several tracks preceded its serious return with the various "Kette Drum" versions – Mr Bailey is no mere fashion follower.

◑ **Almshouse** (Greensleeves, UK; Ras, US).
Over tough Philip 'Fatis' Burrell-produced rhythm tracks, Capleton tackles a variety of topics, all of them reflecting his West Kingston audience's preoccupations.

◑ **Good So** (VP, US).
Capleton's rejection of 'slackness' in favour of culture and reality is nowhere better captured than on his work for the 'conscious' sound system/label, African Star. This excellent set brings together several of his hits for the label, all from 1993, while Black Scorpio and Colin Fat are represented with a track apiece.

Chaka Demus & Pliers

While several Jamaican deejays have made inroads into charts around the world via the hip-hop market, no ragga act has struck a greater chord with mainstream pop fans than **Chaka Demus & Pliers**. What makes the story of this deejay and singer's joint success interesting is that it has far exceeded anything they had achieved in their solo careers – even within the confines of the reggae market. Chaka Demus (b. John Taylor, 1965, Kingston) had enjoyed the greater popularity, particularly with his Jamaican hits for Jammy, Black Scorpio and Penthouse, but by the close of the 1980s had been eclipsed by, most obviously, Shabba Ranks (with whom he once shared an album), along with more recently established deejays such as Cobra, Capleton and Cutty Ranks. His best days seemed behind him when he joined forces with Pliers (b. Everton Banner, 1965, Kingston), a singer who also seemed stuck in the second division, unable quite to challenge dancehall favourites like Sanchez, Wayne Wonder and Thriller U – or, for that matter, the similarly named Pinchers.

The 'combination' style of deejay and singer performing together in the studio (as opposed to the former talking over the latter's already completed record) had been popular for about four years when in 1991 Chaka Demus's gruff but good-humoured deejay voice was paired with Pliers' more delicate tones, initially for veteran producer **Ossie Hibbert**. They almost immediately clicked with the reggae public, with tunes like "Wining Machine", "Gal Wine" and "Worl' A Girls". The next move was to record for **Sly & Robbie**'s Taxi outfit; a fortunate move, as Sly Dunbar was entering a new phase of experiment with drumbeats – his incorporation of rhythms from the UK Asian form of popular music known as bhangra.

The first result of their team-up with Sly & Robbie was "Murder She Wrote", a re-recording of a tune that Pliers had previously cut on his own. The union of deejay and singer, along with Sly's new drumbeats, gave the song a resonance that it had previously lacked, and made it a dancehall smash in the world's reggae capitals. "The Boom" and "Mr Mention" were further hits on the reggae charts, but it was with "Tease Me", released by Island, that they entered the UK pop charts, a feat repeated with "She Don't Let Nobody" and their interpretation of the Isley Brothers' "Twist And Shout", on which they were joined by singer Jack Radics. They are now considered a little too commercial by many of their old fans, though the occasional tune like "War A Gwan Down the Lane" or "Murder Story" demonstrates that they have not entirely forgotten their roots.

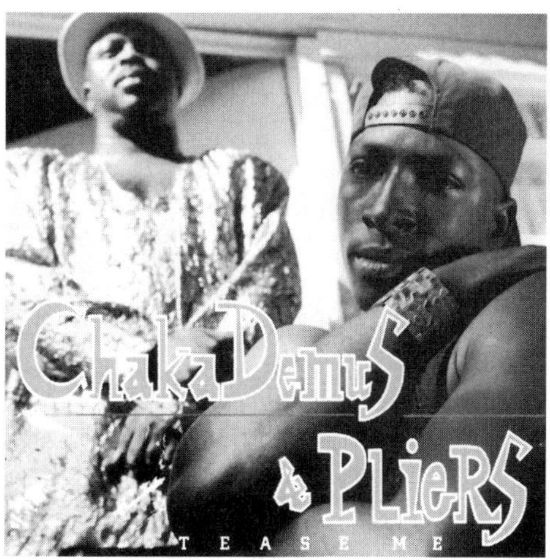

CHAKA DEMUS & PLIERS

◑ **Tease Me** (Mango, UK/US).
Ⓔ Sly & Robbie (plus guitarist Lloyd 'Gitsy' Willis) lay down the innovative rhythms that took ragga another step forward, providing the deejay and singer team with several international hits. "Murder She Wrote", "Tease Me" and the UK chart-topper "Twist and Shout" are all included, as is Pliers' solo "Bam Bam".

◑ **Gold** (Charm, UK).
Chaka Demus & Pliers' greatest moments have been with Sly & Robbie, but this varied collection of 45s shows they were never entirely dependent on Taxi-driven rhythms. Tracks like "Wining Machine", and "Worl' A Girls" were only hits within the reggae market, but incredibly popular with their target audience, and deserve to be heard by a wider one.

Other voices, other mikes

These dominant deejays have carved out their careers in a crowded arena. In addition to a continuous flow of new talent, there are longer-established chatters who are not to be discounted as yesterday's men. Prominent among these are **Cobra** (see p.293) and **Cutty Ranks** (see p.293), both with recent releases on US majors, the ever-inventive **Lieutenant Stitchie**, who made a sensational return to form in 1994/95, and **Red Dragon**. The last of these, whose releases always make up in quality what they lack in quantity, had one of the strongest tunes of his career with 1996's "Explode Gal" (Techniques), having broken into the UK pop charts two years previously – in the company of Brian & Tony Gold – with the very different "Compliments On Your Kiss" (Taxi). The salacious **General Degree** will probably never appeal far beyond the dancehall, but can be relied to come up with something a little different – as with his most outrageous record to date, "Granny" (Main Street), which he delivered in the voice of the old woman of the title.

The deejay who broke big at the same time as Red Dragon and on the same label, **Super Cat**, has been among those seriously attempting to broaden his audience. He has released two albums with US major Sony, the second a mix of hip-hop and reggae that failed to sell in either market. Illustrating the compromises that are made by majors, the Cat's brilliant 12" mix of "Too Greedy" was not on the album, which substituted a later version of the lyric. Needless to say, the album version has none of the urgency or power of the single, a lyrical diatribe against the perils of crack which was released on Super Cat's own Wild Apache imprint.

The remarkably consistent **Papa San** (b. Tyrone Thompson) had a big hit in 1991 with the self-produced "Strange" (Survival), and since then has cut inventive 45s for producers like Sly & Robbie, Jack Scorpio, Bobby Digital, Steely & Clevie and Fatis Burrell. His brother **Dirtsman** (b. Patrick Thompson) looked set for a serious career but was shot dead soon after making his presence felt with "Hot This Year" for the NY-based producer Phillip Smart. **Tiger**, an innovator of deejay styles since the mid-1980s, suffered a serious motorbike accident in 1993, following a less than successful stint with Sony. His humour – well to the fore in 1992's "When" for Steely & Clevie – is much missed. **Little Lenny**, too, has proved a far more enduring deejay than many expected when he broke through with the lewd "Gun In A Baggy" in the late 1980s.

As always, though, there are there are plenty of ambitious youthmen aspiring to the premier league of deejays. Those nearest to Buju, Bounty and Capleton appear to be **Terror Fabulous**, **Merciless**, **Buccaneer** and **Spragga Benz**. After them, there's a legion of talented young deejays who are likely to continue making interesting records and enjoy some measure of success, including **Daddy Screw**, **Poison Chang**, **Frisco Kid**, **Gospel Fish** and **Simpleton**. Predictably, Buju and Bounty are the most influential deejays at the moment, and the best of the former's disciples is **Mega Banton**, who brings a youthful energy to his sound-boy boasts and commentaries on the topics of the moment. Several talented female deejays have also emerged, the most consistent

PAUL COOTE

Lady Saw contemplates Life Without Dick

being **Lady Saw**, who has as much presence at the mike as Shabba or Buju, tackles 'slack' material from a woman's perspective, and can even sing an effective country ballad. Perhaps the most unexpected recent deejay success has been that of the early 1980s chatter Dickie Ranking, who changed his name to **Snagga Puss** and his style to one that's a good deal more original than before.

Lastly, there has developed in the 1990s a school of culture-oriented deejays, following on from the success of Tony Rebel. The U-Brown-influenced **Prezident Brown** (b. Fitz Albert Cotterell) first gained a reputation on the Roof International label before making a striking series of traditional cultural records for another Ocho Rios-based imprint, Barry O'Hare's X-Rated. The relative veteran **Louie Culture** – he first recorded as half of duo Wayne & Louie in the mid-1980s – is another who has consistently made strong reality tunes, such as his biggest hit to date "Ganga Lee" for the Stone Love sound system's Father Pow imprint. He has continued with superior releases for Mad House, John John, Star Trail, Sampalue, and Buju's CB 321 label. Another who mixes chanting and deejaying is **Anthony B**, whose incisive lyrics and considerable stage presence suggest real stardom might lie ahead. Fatis Burrell's Xterminator labelmates **Jesse Jender** and **Sizzla** have made similarly militant cultural music over the last three years, as has **Lady G**, who first came to prominence with Gussie Clarke in the late 1980s, and consistently voices pertinent social commentary over Fatis's best rhythms.

MEGA BANTON

◑ **First Position** (VP, US).

Several hits from one of the rawest youth talents about – the title track, "Sound Boy Killing" and "No Ninja, No Buju" – plus more of a similar quality. The material is drawn from Black Scorpio, Stone Love and Wizzard, the most hard-core of the Jamaican ragga labels.

SPRAGGA BENZ

◑ **Jack It Up** (VP, US).

Deejays' debuts are often their best albums– especially if packed with the hits that established them. This could easily be the case with young Spragga's *Jack It Up*, which brings together the Stone Love 45 that brought him to wide attention ("Jump Up & Swear"), Dave Kelly's "Things A Gwaan", Arrows' "Jack It Up" and Winston Riley's "You Could A Deal", as well as hits from John John, Bobby Digital and Steely & Clevie.

BUCCANEER

◑ **Classic** (Greensleeves, UK).

The title is no exaggeration for a set that has the "Bad Man Sonata", the "Sketell Concerto" and the "Man Tief Sonata", complete with snatches of the Moonlight Sonata and the Blue Danube waltz. In between he sticks mainly to mainstream dancehall topics yet holds attention easily with humorous lyrics and in-your-face delivery.

DIRTSMAN

◑ **Acid** (Blue Mountain/Vine Yard, UK; VP, US).

The main body of Dirtsman's tragically limited output was for Bobby Digital, as represented in this package – with the addition of his biggest hit, "Hot This Year", from New York's Philip Smart. His topics were the usual ones for a ragga chatter – guns, girls and his prowess at the mike – to which he brought good humour and a very likeable personality (even when cleaning his gun).

GENERAL DEGREE

● **Fi Real** (Pretty Boy, UK).

Essentially a collection of General Degree's hits from the mid-1990s, drawn from various sources. "When I Hold You Tonight" was particularly popular as a 45, and employs one of the most memorable rhythms of the period.

LADY G

◑ **God Daughter** (VP, US).

Lady G might not sound very different from all the other women deejays, but her records are more consistent. Thoughtful cultural and ghetto reality lyrics are underpinned by strong rhythms from Philip 'Fatis' Burrell; there is a guest appearance from the underrated Chevelle Franklyn.

LADY SAW

● **Bare As You Dare** (Diamond Rush, JA).

◑ **Give Me the Reason** (VP, US).

The debut includes the hit "Find A Good Man" which really established her on the dancehall scene, along with the explicit "Stab Out the Meat". The second set has its fair share of slackness – "Good Wuk" and "Life Without Dick" – but there are also more reflective lyrics like "What Is Slackness" and "Glory Be To God". Lady Saw further confounded critics with "Condom", which recommends safe sex, and the title track, a remarkable country-style ballad.

LITTLE LENNY

◑ **Gun In A Baggy** (Greensleeves, UK; RAS, US).

The diminutive Lenny is a talented deejay who came from nowhere with the title track, still his best-known record, and followed it with a surprisingly strong album. His youthful enthusiasm over minimalist rhythms from the Firehouse Crew was the template for subsequent successes on Patrick Roberts' Shocking Vibes label.

PAPA SAN

◑ **No Place Like Home** (VP, US).

Papa San continues making some of the best deejay records around, working several styles with clever arguments and witty lyrics. This 1995 set is produced by Fatis, so the rhythms are first-class. The obligatory combination is with Cocoa Tea and rides a fast cut of the "Solomon" rhythm. San is particularly scorching on "It Bun Them", a classic rap that invokes memories of Ranking Joe & Charlie Chaplin on Stur-Gav.

PREZIDENT BROWN

⦿ **Prezident Selections** (Runnetherlands, Holland).

Mostly produced by Barry O'Hare, who contributes a fair bit of the musicianship as well, with solid rhythms ranging from modern roots to jump-up ragga. Prezident Brown has been one of the most consistently interesting deejays to emerge in the 1990s, as shown by his cut of the "Heathen" rhythm, which stands comparison with those by Shabba, Tony Rebel and Ninjaman.

CUTTY RANKS

⦿ **Six Million Ways To Die** (Priority, US).

This 1996 set from the Cutter shows no diminution of the power that has made him one of the greatest modern deejays. This is underlined by the inclusion of "Who Say Me Dun", his riposte to those who thought that Buju and Capleton had overtaken him.

SIZZLA

⦿ **Burning Up** (RAS, US).

1990s-style deejaying over state-of-the-art Xterminator rhythms, but with traditional enough cultural concerns. A surprise that the 45s that brought Sizzla to attention – "True God", "Ins & Outs", "Bruk Down" and "Ready Ghetto Youths" – are omitted, but everything is of a similar standard, and points to how much material this talented youth must have.

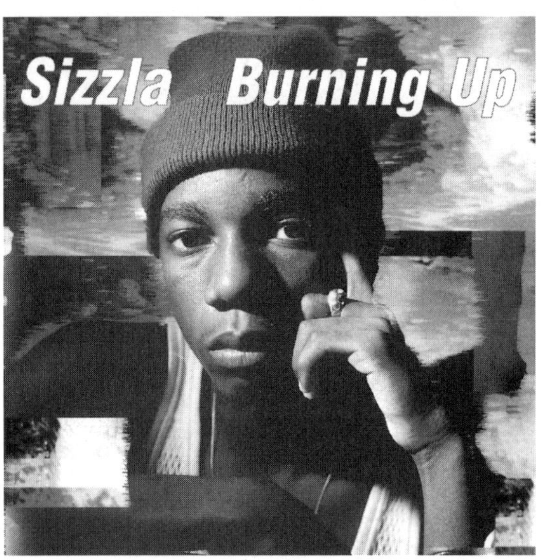

SUPER CAT

◑ **Don Dada** (Columbia, US).

Super Cat was one of several ragga deejays signed to American majors in the wake of Shabba, and the resulting album is among the most successful. This is partly because of his own inclination to think in international terms anyway – his hip-hop-influenced "Mud Up", with its scratch-mix version, was recorded six years earlier – and Columbia wisely included several of his best Jamaican hits: "Nuff Dead A Ready", the title track and the ferocious "Ghetto Red Hot".

TERROR FABULOUS

◑ **Gwaney Gwaney** (Shocking Vibes, JA).

Sparse, hard-core ragga rhythms from Patrick Roberts' Shocking Vibes setup were balanced by fuller Penthouse ones for the deejay's impressive debut album. The title track has the 'slogle' feel of Cobra's "Flex", and there is sufficient variation to maintain interest throughout.

◑ **Terror** (VP, US).

Bobby Digital received the production credits for this second album, and if anything this displayed Terror Fabulous's talent to even greater advantage. The hard-hitting "You Would Ah Bawl" is just one of the reggae hits included in a well-put-together set.

◑ **Yaga Yaga** (East West, US).

A total hard-core album on a label that reached beyond the committed ragga constituency. Not that it made any difference to the music, which was produced by Dave Kelly in his usual fashion, and included quite a few of the backlog of popular 45s on his Mad House label: the hugely popular "Action" with Nadine Sutherland, "Gangster Anthem" and both his versions of the notorious "Pepper Seed" rhythm.

TIGER

● **Shocking Colour** (Jammy's, JA).

Even by ragga deejay standards, Tiger's style is far from harmonious, usually provoking wild animal metaphors appropriate to his name. But while he doesn't say a great deal other than the expected self-aggrandizement, you should listen to how one of the most inventive and original deejays says it. "Boom Bastic" (his cut of "Who She Love") is the only big hit included, but the same standard is kept up for all the tracks.

◑ **Deadly** (Penthouse, JA).

Deejays are, of course, even more dependent than singers on the right rhythms, which is why the pick of the Tiger albums are those on Jammy's and Penthouse, the most important labels of the 1980s and 1990s respectively. Germain packs his album with more hits than Jammy, as well as including a deadly combination track with Cutty Ranks.

ZIGGY MARLEY & THE MELODY MAKERS

Bob and Rita's second child, **David 'Ziggy' Marley** (b. 1968, Kingston) has had to overcome two major obstacles. The first was that comparisons with his illustrious father were inevitable; the second was his distance from the West Kingston dancehall vibe that has informed practically all of the best Jamaican music. Unlike most young performers on the island, he didn't have to tirelessly freelance on the Kingston studio circuit, but whether that helped or hindered his music remains debatable. Beyond question is that by the 1980s he had reached a far larger audience in America than his dad ever did while still alive.

ADRIAN BOOT

Marley Jnr

Ziggy's career began at the close of the previous decade, when he and his siblings – Cedella, Sharon and Stephen – formed the **Melody Makers** and cut a single for the Tuff Gong label, "Children Playing In the Streets", one of the few instances when they have recorded a song written by their father. This was followed by "Sugar Pie" and "Trodding" in 1980, and their appearance at Bob Marley's funeral the following year. The next 45, "What A Plot" (Rita Marley Music), appeared in 1982, and remains one of their most convincing performances to date – with Ziggy sounding just like a 14-year-old version of his father. The record might have lacked originality but had one of the toughest rhythms ever to support his voice, and it deservedly sold well in Jamaica. A promising debut LP, *Play the Game Right*, then appeared in 1985, again on Tuff Gong.

The potential shown on the album was fully borne out on *Joy & Blues*, which appeared on their own Ghetto Youth United imprint in 1993. The majority of all their records, however, have been aimed too obviously at the American market (which tends to lag well behind Jamaica), and sound as if neither the dancehall phase nor ragga's digital revolution ever took place. Yet it would be unfair to dismiss him as an anachronism, for he has voiced dubplate specials for several leading Kingston sound systems (admittedly adapting his dad's songs), and he has made at least one superb single – the reflective "Black My Story (Not his Story)", released in 1989 by Rita Marley Music.

ZIGGY MARLEY & THE MELODY MAKERS

● **Play the Game Right** (Tuff Gong, JA).
Recorded with an all-star line-up of session players, including the Barrett brothers on drums and bass, at its best this set could almost be taken for a late album by Bob Marley. It includes a remix of their best early 45, "What A Plot".

◑ **Joy & Blues** (Ghetto Youth United, JA).
The one completely successful album from the Bob Marley progeny. Ziggy's composition, "Garden", particularly stands out among the originals, though the real surprise is the aplomb with which they handle two songs recorded by the Wailers (when with Lee Perry) – "African Herbsman" and "There She Goes" (formerly titled "Stand Alone" on the *African Herbsman* album).

New roots: Rasta in the dancehall

Gussie Clarke's success with "Rumours" left no doubt that digital instrumentation was compatible with more traditional values in Jamaican music – including those of the roots era. Gussie produced modern, hi-tech counterparts to 'steppers' rhythms, and others soon worked along similar lines, creating suitable platforms for those who would rather sing about 'cultural' concerns rather than love, rude boys or the dancehall. This extended the careers of some performers from the previous decade, but more importantly allowed a few younger 'cultural' singers to emerge. **Admiral Tibet** and **Yami Bolo** seemed the only fresh 'conscious' vocalists being recorded regularly in the late 1980s; by the next decade, however, a significant shift had taken place, and a new generation of singers with cultural perspectives had emerged. Most prominent among these were the late **Garnett Silk**, **Luciano** and **Everton Blender**, but in these rootsmen's footsteps followed such as Jamali, Uton Green, Ras Shiloh, Ebun Abeo, Daweh Congo, the vocal group Morgan Heritage and a host of others.

VARIOUS ARTISTS – SKY HIGH PRODUCTIONS

◑ **Sky High & Mau Mau Present Marcus Garvey Chant** (Sky High, JA).

E The cover was obviously a rush job, but the music is far more interesting: modern cultural singers Yami Bolo, Half Pint and Garnett Silk, along with the conscious deejays Tony Rebel and Ricky Chaplin. What makes the set essential is the first side, taken up by three versions of Jackie Mittoo's "Drum Song" classic, and including the voice of Marcus Garvey from half a century before: one of the most atmospheric sides in reggae.

VARIOUS ARTISTS – TONY REBEL PRODUCTIONS

◑ **Flames Presents Lalabella** (Flames, JA).

Tony Rebel features on three tracks of this coherent various-artists compilation on his own label. Highlight is Everton Blender's stirring "Ghetto People Song", but the set – fourteen cuts of an original rhythm – also showcases new names like Aaron Silk, Honey Comb and Lebanculah (and Shanty Plus on the CD), alongside relative veterans like Sugar Black, Little Kirk, Uton Green and Mutabaruka. Committed modern roots music.

VARIOUS ARTISTS – BOBBY DIGITAL PRODUCTIONS

◑ **Digital B Presents Kette Drum** (Digital B, JA).

E One of the pleasant surprises of 1995 was the return of nyahbingi drumming, a trend helped by the success of the ten or so cuts Bobby Digital put out on the "Kette Drum" rhythm. This album collects together the 45s – which include Garnett Silk's "Silk Chant" and Bounty Killer's "Seek God" – and adds fresh cuts from Prezident Brown, the dub poet Mutabaruka and Morgan Heritage (the first on the LP, the other two on CD only). Every track works in its own right, and few rhythms of the year were more suited to the one-rhythm album treatment.

VARIOUS ARTISTS – BOBBY DIGITAL AND X-RATED PRODUCTIONS

⊙ **Heathen Chant** (Runnetherlands, Holland).

A total of 24 cuts of the popular "Heathen" rhythm from the Digital B and X-rated labels, presented in a 'mega-mix' style, and complete with interjections from Irie FM deejay Mighty Mike. Shabba's "Heart Of A Lion" stands as one of best of his career, while variations from Morgan Heritage, E.T.

Webster, Yami Bolo, Carlton Coffie, Prezident Brown and Cocoa Tea run it very close. Curious that the excellent Ninjaman version, "Old Picture Frame", is missing.

VARIOUS ARTISTS – BOBBY DIGITAL, X-RATED AND HOW YU FI SAY DAT PRODUCTIONS

⦿ **Drum Song** (Runnetherlands, Holland).

Following the above album, this set comprises nineteen cuts of the Studio One "Drum Song" chestnut played by Sly & Robbie, Dean Frazer and Bongo Herman, presented again in 'mega-mix' style. The range of styles is as varied as before, with the measured, meditative rhythm motivating Bounty Killer, Capleton, Louie Culture and Prezident Brown to give brilliant deejay performances, and Morgan Heritage, Cocoa Tea and Frankie Wilmott standing out among the singers.

VARIOUS ARTISTS – ASSORTED PRODUCTIONS

◑ **Conscious Ragga Volumes 1 & 2** (Greensleeves, UK).

Hit tracks, from a variety of producers, demonstrating the return of 'conscious' themes to Jamaican music in the 1990s. The excellent selection ranges from the relatively traditional approaches of Luciano & Louie Culture's "Real Rastaman" and Frankie Paul's "Praise Him", to the completely modern, hard-core rhythms of Simpleton's "1/4 To 12" (all on the first volume). Just the thing to introduce roots fans to ragga, or vice versa.

Modern Jamaican roots: the foundation

Usually recognized as the first 'cultural' singer of the deejay-dominated period that followed "Under Me Sleng Teng", **Admiral Tibet** has built on his initial hits with Winston Riley and Redman, making particularly strong records for King Jammy, Bobby Digital and the African Star setup, while never achieving a lasting breakthrough. His voice can occasionally seem in danger of descending into a whine – a real problem over the length of an album – but at its best has a convincing, vulnerable quality entirely suited to sufferers' laments.

Yami Bolo (b. Rolando Ephraim McClean 1970, Kingston) had established himself on Youth Promotion sound by 1983, and recorded dubplates for the sound before scoring with "When A Man Is In Love" for Winston Riley in 1985, at the beginning of the digital era. He then recorded a handful of 45s with Sugar Minott, Skeng Don and Riley before joining the group of artists associated with roots master Augustus Pablo. But he only found his mature style when he began cutting music for Trevor Leggo Douglas's label in 1991. Further discs for King Jammy, Bobby Digital, Fatis Burrell and Taxi have brought him more into the dancehall mainstream; his rootsier material appears on his own Yam Euphony imprint, Leggo or Tappa Zukie's Tappa label. In 1994, "Love Is Dangerous", his collaboration with Japanese star Kazafumi Miyazawa (aka Miya) sold in excess of 500,000 albums in Japan. He has been recording most recently with Sly & Robbie's Taxi label; an album, apparently called *Worldwide Corruption*, is expected in 1997.

An even more obvious bridge between the music's past and the computerized era was built by **Junior Reid**. He also had a connection with Pablo (his debut recording for the producer appeared in 1979), but only came to prominence after incorporating the fast-style influence of the 1980s deejays, scoring important hits for the leading dancehall producers Prince Jammy and Sugar Minott. In retrospect the time spent with the Grammy-winning roots/crossover act Black Uhuru seemed a diversion en route to hard-edged digital hits like the anthemic "One Blood", "Sound" and "All Fruits Ripe", which combined cultural themes with a dancehall delivery. He gained a UK chart entry in 1988 with leading UK remixers Coldcut, following this with another shot in 1990 when he collaborated with the indie band Soupdragons on a cover of the Rolling Stones song "I'm Free" which reached #5 in the UK chart. A steady stream of music flows from his new studio, with a healthy portion of newer talents featured alongside Junior himself, veterans like **Dennis Brown** and **Gregory Isaacs**, and deejays **Ninjaman** and **Junior Demus**.

Michael Rose (who sometimes gives his first name the more African spelling of Mykal) is also an important talent of the digital era, especially since his resurgence in 1991 with "Bad Boys" for Sly & Robbie. Further ragga-roots classics by Rose have appeared on Taxi, as well as cutting-edge labels like Penthouse, Tappa, Star Trail, High Power and Record Factory, along with the revived Observer and Volcano. The erstwhile voice of Black Uhuru shares with Junior Reid and Yami Bolo the "Waterhouse" style of wailing vocal, an approach eminently suited to the sort of serious 'reality' lyrics that he writes. The last couple of years have seen four new albums by the singer; interestingly, though, his best-selling record to date in the UK has been "Last Chance", an untypical lovers outing cut with London's fine Ruff Cutt Band.

ADMIRAL TIBET

● **Come Into the Light** (Live & Love, UK).
Before the widespread return to 'cultural' lyrics in the 1990s, Admiral Tibet was the most consistently 'conscious' singer of the ragga age. His greatest hits with Jammy are still to be collected for one essential package, but this set contains enough highlights to be worthwhile – including "Serious Time", which would have been as appropriate a title.

◑ **Reality Time** (Digital B, JA; Vine Yard, UK).
Much the same can be said about the album produced by Jammy's former right-hand man, Bobby Digital. The title track, on which he rejects 'slackness' in favour of 'reality' lyrics, pretty much sums up his appeal, though he convinces just as much on the sound-boy burial tunes, "Execute A Sound" and "My Sound Is Champion".

YAMI BOLO

◑ **Up Life Street** (Leggo, JA; Heartbeat, US).
This eloquent cry from the heart of the ghetto is one of the most impressive modern roots statements to date. The dense rhythms – there are six keyboard players and five percussionists amongst the session musicians – provide the perfect modern steppers backdrop for songs like "Iniquity Worker", "Blood A Go Run" and "Greedium".

⊙ **Born Again** (Ras, US).
Tappa Zukie has always got good performances from the singer; this 1996 set features singles like "Trample the Dragon", and "Dominion" alongside tracks recorded at Leggo studio – including a cover of the Jackson 5's "Happy Sings the Blues".

JUNIOR REID

● **One Blood** (JR All Stars, JA).
One of the biggest hits of Junior Reid's career was "One Blood", which has become something of a Jamaican anthem. The other single from this self-produced set named after it, "Sound", attempts a similar effect, while most of the tracks stand as worthwhile examples of the Waterhouse style of wailing.

◑ **Visa** (Greensleeves, UK).
"All Fruits Ripe" was deservedly Reid's biggest Jamaican hit since "One Blood", and boasts the most interesting rhythm his JR Productions team has built to date. Other Jamaican 45s around which *Visa* is built are "Gun Court", "Friend Enemy", "No Loating" (a cut of Horace Andy's "Skylarking") and "Youthman".

MICHAEL ROSE

● **Sly & Robbie Present the Taxi Sessions** (Taxi, UK).
 The combination of Michael Rose's gloomy warnings to the less than righteous and Sly &

Robbie's rhythms and imaginative sampling has created some of the most adventurous and serious music of the digital age. Their album collects the innovative hits "Bad Boys", "One A We, Two A We", "Visit Them" and "Monkey Business", and adds six new tracks in the same ragga-dread vein. Music that simultaneously looks back and forward, and does so with consummate grace.

◑ **Michael Rose** (Heartbeat, US).
This Niney-produced set looks back more directly to Rose's work with Black Uhuru (as well as the earlier solo singles), though it still has a modern edge and is just as convincing as the above. Includes the singles "Don't Play With Fire" and "You Too Short Temper", the latter a genuinely different-sounding cut of "Tempo".

Garnett Silk

The late **Garnett Silk** (b. Garnett Smith, 1970, Manchester, Jamaica; d. 1994) seemed the most talented of the new 'reality' singers who emerged in the early 1990s. He had begun as a 12-year-old deejay called Little Bimbo, before linking up with the cultural deejay Tony Rebel in his mid-teens, working with him on Destiny Outernational sound system along with Uton Green, Everton Blender and Culture Knox. The direct influence of the dancehall would linger in his phrasing when he concentrated on his singing and signed with Steely & Clevie. Although he recorded an album with them, it never saw release until after the singer's untimely death in a gas canister explosion.

Tony Rebel had introduced him to songwriter Anthony 'Fire' Rochester, and the pair began working together, first for Courtney Cole's Roof International label, then for Bobby Digital, who released his debut album in 1992. The release of this set, together with a swing back to cultural lyrics by deejays like Buju and Capleton, marked a turning point in dancehall: he sang of both 'culture' and romance in a smooth tone that befitted his name change, but in a style that bore the mark of the previous ten years of Jamaican music. In his brief recording career he cut sides for most of the main production outfits, including Jammy's, Black Scorpio, Star Trail and Sly & Robbie, but was under contract with Atlantic at the time of his death, probably poised on the threshold of an international breakthrough. In the aftermath of his death, the cultural current that he played a major role in re-establishing has, if anything, grown stronger.

PAUL COOTE

Zion in a Vision: the very dapper Garnett Silk

GARNETT SILK

◑ **Gold** (Charm, UK).
E A collection of Garnett Silk's initial hits that goes a long way to explaining what all the excitement was about: Jammy's "Fill Us With Your Mercy", Star Trail's "Hello Africa" (his biggest UK hit), Germain's "Lion Heart", Bobby Digital's "The Rod", Jack Scorpio's Jamaican chart-topper, "Zion In A Vision", and another five of the same calibre.

◑ **Nothing Can Divide Us** (Roof International, JA; VP, US).
Courtney Cole's Roof International studio, situated in Ocho Rios, provides a refreshing alternative to the Kingston mainstream – as witnessed by the Garnett Silk material here. "Mama", "I Can See Clearly Now" and "Seven Spanish Angels" were the popular early 45s, but the entire set displays an artistry already fully developed. Jammy's beautiful "Lord Watch Over Our

Shoulders" is the one track not to emanate from the north coast resort.

◑ **It's Growing** (Digital B, JA; Vine Yard, UK; VP, US).

The album that established Garnett Silk as one of the prime vocal stylists of the 1990s. At the time of his death he was widely seen as the leading light in the return to cultural lyrics, but here he divides his attention between 'reality' and romantic themes, on a set that features several of Anthony 'Fire' Rochester's strong compositions. The result is one of the most successful celebrations of love, physical and spiritual, since Marley's *Exodus*.

◑ **Lord Watch Over Our Shoulders** (Greensleeves, UK).

A posthumous compilation that draws together seven tracks from King Jammy (including both the title track and "Fill Us With Your Mercy"), a couple each from Jack Scorpio and E.J. Robinson and one from Phillip Smart. One of the Robinson tracks is below par; the rest are the sort of heartfelt numbers for which Silk will be remembered.

Everton Blender

Everton Blender (b. Everton Dennis Williams, Clarendon) similarly concentrates on 'conscious' themes in a sweetly expressive vocal style wrought in the modern dancehall. He started in the early 1980s, singing on small sounds like Master Voice and Santex, then recorded "Ba Ba Black Sheep" for producer Danny Barclay in 1985, but returned to his trade of house painter when the record flopped. For the next few years he worked on the Destiny Outernational sound with Garnett Silk, who introduced him to Richard 'Bobo' Bell in 1993. Bell issued a stunning series of singles beginning with "Wi Nuh Jus A Come" that year, and has produced both the singer's albums to date. He has been helped no end by the tough but melodic rhythms built for producer Bell by the Firehouse Crew and Steely & Clevie. Blender has also

XTERMINATOR – A NEW ROOTS LABEL

Luciano's producer **Phillip 'Fatis' Burrell** (see p.000) operates one of the most progressive production outfits currently working in the Jamaican studios, utilizing the master drummer **Sly Dunbar** and the Firehouse Crew to build its rhythms. Fatis started in 1984, releasing a couple of Sugar Minott tunes on his Kings & Lions label. In 1986 he started his Vena imprint, kicking off with 12" singles by Leroy Mafia; the following year he was recording dancehall singers like Pinchers, Sanchez and Thriller U. Since then he has produced most of the established singers, and has been responsible for launching the careers of such as Lukie D and fast-talking deejay Daddy Freddy. By the 1990s he was in full swing with his Xterminator label (at first Exterminator), recording modern gems by such as Marcia Griffiths, Freddie McGregor, Sugar Minott, Cocoa Tea, Beres Hammond, Luciano and Nadine Sutherland. His productions are among the best crafted, whether on refreshed vintage rhythms or innovative drum-dominated tracks. He continues to record new talent, notably the cultural deejays **Sizzla** and **Jesse Jenda**, as well as a couple of very talented singers – the Garnett Silk-influenced **Ras Shiloh** and a former London resident who cut strong tunes for Fashion Records, **Mikey General** (b. Michael Taylor), who now lives in Jamaica, waiting for the right rhythm to bring him to mass attention. His Burrell-produced *Sinners* was perhaps a little too understated to do the job in 1994, but could one day be very collectable. He remains with the Burrell crew to the present, and is a strong presence on the live shows of the Xterminator Revue that has been supporting Luciano on tour.

MIKEY GENERAL

◑ **Sinners** (Charm, UK).

A former UK-based singer, Mikey General built a solid reputation recording for Fashion Records. This is his first set for Philip 'Fatis' Burrell in Jamaica, and fully confirms the faith that many in London expressed in him. Anyone who has enjoyed Luciano's records for Mr Burrell will ignore this at their peril – though, strangely, it has yet to be released on Xterminator in Jamaica.

recorded for Black Scorpio and Malvo & Redrose's *How yu fi say that* label, including the hit "Blend Dem" for the former. The self-conscious references to his own name on this and several other records is perhaps his most obvious legacy from the dancehall.

EVERTON BLENDER

◑ **Lift Up Your Head** (Star Trail, JA; Heartbeat, US).

◑ **World Corruption** (Greensleeves, UK).

Everton Blender's most successful record in Jamaica to date has been "Blend Dem" for Black Scorpio, which topped the charts. But there is even stronger material on these two sets from Richard Bell's Star Trail setup. An interesting meeting of a strictly dancehall vocal style and 'conscious' themes, with *Lift Up* – which features the hits "Create A Sound", "Family Man" and "Man Is Unjust" – the slightly stronger.

Luciano

The very talented **Luciano** (b. Jepther McClymont, 1974, Davey Town) can be included as a major figure in the development of modern roots. When he started out in 1992, with releases on Hartnol 'Sky High' Henry's Mau Mau label and then with Castro Brown's New Name outfit, he had not yet shaken off his major influences – Dennis Brown, Frankie Paul and Stevie Wonder. In 1993 he recorded with Freddie McGregor's Big Ship label; more importantly, he began an association with Phillip 'Fatis' Burrell that ultimately led to his signing with Island. Burrell chose to develop the roots side of the singer, beginning with sides like "Chant Out" and "Poor & Simple", and has produced a body of work – some thirty singles and three albums – that supplies convincing evidence of a major talent. Most of this material has been modern cultural music with a pronounced spirituality, although he is clearly at home with a traditional 'lovers' offering, like one of his most successful records to date in the UK, "Shake It Up Tonight" (Big Ship). Many of his righteous cuts have a gentle, reflective feel about them – as witnessed by "It's Me Again Jah" and "How Can You" (both Xterminator), although both tunes come supplied with insinuating hooks. His audiences habitually sing along on these anthems during his live performances, a sure sign of classics in the making.

LUCIANO

◑ **Where There Is Life** (Xterminator, JA; Island Jamaica, UK).

E This Fatis Burrell-produced album was obviously designed to set Luciano apart from the other

DAVID CORIO

Roots Messenger, Luciano

new Jamaican singers similarly concentrating on real songs (as opposed to stringing together dancehall catchphrases). "It's Me Again Jah" topped the Jamaican charts, and its relaxed, dignified feel carries over to the rest of this exceptionally well-crafted set. A landmark in modern roots music.

◑ **One Way Ticket** (VP, US).
The first Philip 'Fatis' Burrell-produced set gives a chance to catch up with the 45s that signalled the arrival of a major talent. The title cut, "Black Survivors", "Chant Down Babylon", "Give Thanks To Jah", "Turn Your Life Around" and "Raggamuffin" are all among his finest, and extra tracks on the CD include an exceptional version of the "Sleng Teng" rhythm, "Mr Governor", on which he is joined by Cocoa Tea.

◑ **The Messenger** (Island Jamaica, UK).
The best tracks from the follow-up to *Where There Is Life* had already appeared, or were shortly to appear, as singles, and as a complete album it lacked its predecessor's cohesion.

◑ **Shake It Up Tonight** (Big Ship, UK).
The title track from this Freddie McGregor-produced set has been one of Luciano's most popular singles in the UK, exemplifying the 'lovers' side of his approach. The more urgent "It's A Jungle Out There" is the other single included, and the entire set strikes a healthy balance between 'blues-dance' rocking and Mr McClymont's social conscience.

Morgan Heritage

Surprisingly, the tradition of roots harmonizing has also made something of a return, with **Morgan Heritage**, a vocal group comprising the three sons and two daughters of US-based singer Denroy Morgan. They visited Jamaica in the summer of 1995 for that year's Reggae Sunfest, and there linked up with Bobby Digital, for the first time going into a Kingston studio. The resulting three tracks were strong enough for the group to return at the close of the year to complete the fifteen songs that would make up their CD for the producer. It more than confirmed the promise of tough 45s like "Protect Us Jah" (one of the best of the "Heathen" versions for Bobby's Digital B label), "Give Wi A License" and "Praise To Jah" (both for King Jammy's) and "One Rasta Man" (for Trevor James). An album from King Jammy is eagerly awaited.

MORGAN HERITAGE

◑ **Protect Us Jah** (VP/Brickwall, US).
E On the evidence of this album (their second, but the first to be recorded in Jamaica), Morgan Heritage have the talent for major success. A clear Garnett Silk influence on some of the lead vocals – most notably "What Man Can Say" and "Set Yourself Free" – doesn't detract from the freshness and power of five voices interacting. A return to roots and culture, but the two lovers tracks impress just as much.

Reggae in Britain

8

ADRIAN BOOT

8

previous page

Any vacancies for reggae musicians? Matumbi line up outside the Job Centre, late 1970s

Reggae in Britain

Long before 1972, when Chris Blackwell handed the Wailers a cheque to record the first reggae album for an international rock audience, Jamaican migration had ensured that the island's music reached far beyond its shores, with the UK as a major market. The musical tastes of communities of Jamaican émigrés in Britain, affluent by standards back in the Caribbean, provided an important impetus for the development of Jamaica's recording industry and by the 1950s records were being produced with export principally in mind. The producer **Stanley Motta**, for example, thought that discs of rural **mento** music had an international potential to rival the then-fashionable Trinidadian calypso.

Mento, as it turned out, was something of a false start for the Jamaican recording industry, for while it was popular with the island's rural population, younger Jamaicans living in Spanish Town or fast-growing Kingston opted for American r&b. But it was a sign of things to come, as Jamaican variants of r&b developed into ska.

Sales of Jamaican-produced ska thrived in Britain's inner-city areas where Jamaicans had settled and, not surprisingly, British Jamaicans soon turned to recording music themselves. London in particular became an important centre for first ska and rocksteady, and in the 1960s reggae.

London's ska and rocksteady pioneers included **Sonny Roberts**, who started the **Planetone** label in 1962, working out of the same premises as **Chris Blackwell**'s fledgling **Island** label. He began by recording tunes by Jamaicans who had arrived in the UK, among them trombonist **Rico Rodriguez** and vocalists **Dandy Livingstone** and **Mike Elliott**. He later founded the Orbitone and Tackle labels, recording sentimental r&b ballads with **Roy Alton** and the incredibly successful Tim Chandell.

Much of the 1960s UK output was less accomplished than the Jamaican originals, but by the mid-1970s talented musicians and singers had emerged from the expatriate communities to form strong self-contained bands. Outfits such as the **Cimarons**, **Aswad**, **Matumbi** and **Steel Pulse** cut records in the late 1970s/early 1980s that were quite different from those being recorded in Kingston. Aswad, in particular, have enjoyed years of success, both on the roots circuit and, sporadically, in the UK and international pop charts.

An even more distinctive contribution to reggae of the 1970s and 1980s was the merging of soft-soul styles and reggae basslines known as **lovers rock**, a style that Britain made its own. It remains hugely popular in the UK's inner cities – and, twenty years on, still pretty much ignored by the music media.

The **dancehall** phase of the early 1980s saw the emergence of UK-based artists as original, fresh and varied as deejays **Smiley Culture**, **Tippa Irie** and **Macka B**, or singers like **Andrew Paul** and **Mikey General**. The digital revolution of the late 1980s meant an even greater explosion of talent and, as techniques became more refined by the 1990s, distinctive chatters such as **Top Cat**, **General Levy**, **Starkey Banton** and **Glamma Kid** proved themselves the match of the roughest from Kingston. Meantime, a Birmingham-born Asian, **Apache Indian**, took a combination of ragga and UK Asian bhangra into the UK pop charts.

The top figure in contemporary UK reggae, however, and a man leading the field by multiple lengths, is undoubtedly **Maxi Priest**. He developed his craft in the 1980s singing on the Saxon sound system, had his career handled in the right way, and has subsequently become the most popular international reggae singer since Bob Marley.

Early sounds 1954–74

With the establishment of expatriate Jamaican communities in Britain's major cities in the early 1960s came the maintenance of musical links with home through the sound system. As early as 1954, **Duke Vin**, the former selector for Tom The Great Sebastian, arrived in England, and set up the country's first genuine Jamaican-style sound.

Meantime, many Jamaican musicians who had settled in Britain were forging careers in London, with the ranks led by virtuoso guitarist **Ernest Ranglin**, an original member of the Skatalites, and trombonist **Rico Rodriguez**. Both played around the jazz and r&b scene, Rico gigging with, among others, Georgie Fame's Blue Flames. There were Jamaican singers, too, who had already made their names on the Kingston studio circuit and became important figures in London; they included, notably, **Jackie Edwards**, **Dandy Livingstone** and **Laurel Aitken**. Unsurprisingly, most of these performers concentrated their efforts on styles popular in Jamaica – ska, rocksteady and then reggae – though the music often emerged filtered through its exposure to a new culture.

UK ska & rocksteady

The guitarist **Ernest Ranglin** was one of the most distinguished Jamaican expatriates to make an impact in the UK. In London, in 1964, he produced and played on **Millie Small**'s (b. Millicent Small, 1942, Clarendon, Jamaica) international pop hit, "My Boy Lollipop", a record which went on to sell over seven million copies. Millie herself was a somewhat limited vocalist and had little success with her follow-ups. "Sweet William" contrived to sound like Lollipop-2 but made only a brief appearance at #30 in the UK pop charts, while her revival of Wynonie Harris's "Bloodshot Eyes" barely scraped in for a week in the Top 50. Nothing she recorded after that made much of an impression

ADRIAN BOOT ARCHIVE

Lollipop girl Millie Small

at all, though her international smash did allow her to tour Africa twice in the mid-1960s, and secured a place in the history of how the wider world became familiar with Jamaican music.

The sweet-voiced balladeer **Jackie Edwards**, who recorded an album with Millie, was another early arrival in London from Jamaica, accompanying Chris Blackwell to London in 1962 to help him establish Island Records in the UK. Edwards subsequently found a degree of pop success: not as a singer, but through the Spencer Davis Group's renditions of two of his compositions – "Keep On Running" and "Somebody Help Me" (both sung by a teenage Stevie Winwood and topping the British pop charts in 1966). White youth, especially in the same run-down inner city areas as the migrants, were already into black American r&b and proto-soul from Chicago, Detroit and Memphis, and they turned easily to ska. Derrick Morgan, Prince Buster and the Skatalites played to multiracial audiences in clubs like Wardour Street's **Flamingo**, Forest Gate's **Upper Cut** and Brixton's **Ram Jam**, and slotted in easily with the offerings of such American heroes as Phil Upchurch, Inez & Charlie Foxx and Jimmy McGriff.

Another 1960s UK resident was the Cuban-born vocalist **Laurel Aitken**, whose approximations of New Orleans r&b styles had helped establish the fledgling Jamaican record industry in the late 1950s. He was to make an incalculable contribution to the British reggae scene over the decade, and the records he made in Jamaica for Chris Blackwell, Duke Reid, Ken Khouri, Prince Buster and Leslie Kong had a big impression on the expatriate community in the UK. After moving to London, he returned sporadically to Kingston for recording sessions for **Emil Shallit**'s Blue Beat label, **Graeme Goodall**'s Rio and **Rita & Benny King**'s R&B (R&B after their names). These popular discs, however, hardly prepared anyone for Aitken's distinctive self-productions that emerged in the next phase of the music – reggae.

The arrival of reggae: the singers . . .

Ska and rocksteady played second to black American music on the British club scene of the early 1960s. However, the next shift in Jamaican music coincided with changes in white British youth culture – the emergence of hippies and skinheads. It was the **skinheads** who embraced what was by then being called 'reggae' and though few followed subsequent developments – ganja smoking, dreadlocks and calls for "peace and love" were a little too reminiscent of the despised hippies – for four years from 1968, those who signified their tribal allegiance through Dr. Martens footwear and shorn hair made up a committed audience for the faster, more jerky, sounds then emerging from the Kingston studios, as well as records produced nearer at hand and (partly) aimed at them.

It was when rocksteady was changing into 'reggae' at the end of the 1960s that **Laurel Aitken** began producing himself and others for the **Palmer Brothers**-owned Crab and NuBeat/New Beat concerns (the 1970 name change coinciding with a new policy of releasing

ADRIAN BOOT

Boogie in his bones: Laurel Aitken

mostly UK productions). His audience then widened to take in the white skinheads. Records like "Woppi King", "Jesse James", "Haile Selassie" (one of the very few Rasta-slanted records to find favour with the skins) and "Pussy Price Gone Up" stand among the more enduring UK productions of the period – in part because they employed the slower rhythms emerging from Jamaica itself. Aitken also made a couple of credible deejay records as **Tiger** (not to be confused with the ragga star) and produced other performers over similar rhythms, including **Winston Groovy** ("Island In the Sun") and the **Classics** ("History Of Africa").

The movie that brought Jamaica to Britain

The veteran **Derrick Morgan** similarly enjoyed a following among skinheads. His self-produced "Moon Hop" released on the Crab label in 1969 was his first (and hugely successful) atttempt to reach this wider market; Derrick's UK-based backing group the Pyramids went on to recut Morgan's composition as the far less subtle "Skinhead Moonstomp".

Another singer who had enjoyed youthful success in Jamaica before moving to the UK, at the ripe old age of 15, was **Dandy Livingstone** (b. Robert Livingstone Thompson, 1944, Kingston). He made his name with Sugar Simone, recording as **Sugar & Dandy**, but these releases were put into the shade by his solo work in the UK, which included 1967's popular "A Message To You Rudy" (Ska Beat), featuring the trombonist **Rico Rodriguez**. "Reggae In Your Jeggae" (Down Beat), a skinhead favourite, followed in 1969, and the catchy "Suzanne Beware Of the Devil" (Horse) made the UK pop charts in 1972.

Dandy was also a fairly successful record producer, being given Giant, his own subsidiary label to the R&B imprint, and then Down Town and J-Dan by Trojan. **Brother Dan's All Stars**' "Donkey Returns" and Dandy's own "Move Your Mule" were popular singles on the former label in 1969, and the Music Doctors instrumental "Bush Doctor" on the latter the following year; all three were notable examples of the type of UK reggae designed to appeal beyond transplanted Jamaicans to white youth resistant to 'hippy' rock. Dandy's most successful production of the period was **Tony Tribe**'s interpretation of Neil Diamond's "Red Red Wine" which twice scraped into the pop charts in 1969, and was revived over a decade later by pop-reggae band **UB40.** (The Specials had paid a similar tribute with their version of "A Message To You Rudy".)

For British audiences, though, the best-known Jamaican figure of this period was undoubtedly **Jimmy Cliff**. He had come to London in the mid-1960s and Island initially attempted to sell him to the rock audience. That failed, but his career in Britain took off with a trio of unashamedly commercial pop hits in 1969 – "Wonderful World, Beautiful People", "Vietnam" and the Cat Stevens song "Wide World" – and, with his lead appearance in the 1972 Perry Henzell film, *The Harder They Come*, the first glimpse of Jamaica for many white audiences.

Although Cliff lived in London for several years, his strongest records were all cut in Jamaica, so he remains fairly marginal to the story of UK reggae. Much the same can be said for talented men like **Alton Ellis**, **Owen Gray** and **Desmond Dekker**, none of whom repeated the artistic success of their Jamaican discs when recording in the UK (though both Ellis and Gray would sometimes return to Kingston with fruitful results). The undervalued **Errol Dunkley** was in a similar position, though he made a few records in London worthy of his talent, including a Dennis Bovell reworking of his early 1970s hit "A Little Way Different" (1978) and the lovers-rock favourites, "Happiness Forgets" and "Betcha By Golly Wow ". He even entered the UK pop charts of 1979 with a catchy version of John Holt's "OK Fred".

... and the producers

Besides Laurel Aitken and Dandy Livingstone, a number of other London-based producers produced records aimed, at least in part, at the skinhead audience. They included three Jamaicans from Brixton, in Southwest London – Lambert Briscoe, Nat Cole and Joe Mansano. **Lambert Briscoe** ran Brixton's popular Hot Rod sound system and in 1970 Trojan gave him a record label of the same name; among its titles were "Skinhead Speaks his Mind" and "Skinheads Don't Fear", credited to the **Hot Rod All Stars**. **Nat Cole**, a seller of Afro wigs on the Atlantic, expended only a relatively small part of his energies on music, but produced two records that have become collectable among those nostalgic for UK productions of the period: his own "Sugar Sugar" (Jackpot) and **Rina Alston**'s "Popcorn Funky Reggae" (Trojan). Meantime, **Joe Mansano** was selling reggae discs in Brixton before producing skinhead anthems like "Dracula Prince Of Darkness", "Brixton Cat" (both in 1969) and "Skinhead Revolt" (in 1970).

Two other London-Jamaican producers of note, again for skinhead discs, were **Clancy 'Sir' Collins**, with his Down Beat label, and **Sydney Crooks**, an original member of the Jamaican vocal group the Pioneers, who produced skinhead favourites with a science fiction/comic book flavour like the **Sidney All Stars**' "Outer Space" and "Return Of Batman", as well as a number of discs by the talented singer, **Junior English**, who made fine 'lovers rock' before the term was coined.

LAUREL AITKEN

High Priest Of Reggae (Pama, UK).

The acceptable side of UK-produced reggae of the skinhead era with the likes of "Jesse James", "Landlords & Tenants", "Mr. Popcorn", "Haile Selassie" and "Woppi King". The addition of "Pussy Price Gone Up" would make this a wonderful *Best Of Laurel Aitken In the UK* CD.

DANDY LIVINGSTONE

Your Musical Doctor (Downtown, UK).

A late 1960s self-production that catches his voice at its best, and places it over rhythms that rise above the general standard for the time and place. The advice on the sleeve to "take as often as possible" might be overstating the case a little, but worthwhile early UK reggae.

Roots, rock, reggae, UK style

If most early UK reggae records now seem excessively crude, production standards soared from 1974 as self-contained reggae bands found a new maturity and confidence. They had a different generation of black youth for their audience – one largely born in Britain – and an ideology, Rastafarianism, that helped give themselves and their followers a new self-affirming identity. The strongest influence on the music of these instrumental/vocal groups was, of course, Bob Marley and the Wailers.

The fact that the mid–late 1970s were dominated by bands – as opposed to singers recording with session musicians – had a couple of obvious advantages. Most important was that they found it much easier to earn money playing live, boosted by the crossover success of Marley, who was selling out major rock venues around Europe and the US for nights on end in the mid-1970s. For UK reggae bands, in turn, this meant a move from community halls and clubs in migrant areas to student union venues and support slots for rock bands at large-capacity halls.

Working as self-contained bands also led to different skills – and sounds – being developed than those of the largely studio-oriented Jamaican performers. In retrospect this can be seen as one of the strengths of outfits such as London's **Cimarons**, **Aswad**, **Reggae Regular**, **Matumbi**, **Black Slate** and **Misty In Roots**. Similarly, Birmingham's **Steel Pulse**, Bristol's **Black Roots** and Wolverhampton's **Capital Letters** forged styles that were rooted in what was heard from 'Yard', but informed by the musicians' own immediate environments.

Dread youth ina Babylon

Another reason why reggae produced in the UK in the mid–late 1970s seemed removed from that of the Jamaican model was the different social background: the lives of even the poorest and most discriminated against in Britain in the 1970s was not comparable with the sufferers' lot in West Kingston. Arguably, the imagery of Rastafarianism also meant something different to second-generation black Britons: the sense of identity being given by 'cultural' lyrics often seemed to be as part of a Jamaican diaspora as much as an African and, while some of the British-born youth shared the ideal of Africa as their spiritual homeland, many others dreamed of a 'return' to a Jamaica known only through their parents' memories – or reggae records.

Equally important was the fact that these UK reggae outfits were bands and equipped for the most part with their own instruments – a luxury denied to most of their Jamaican counterparts. Independent of the sound systems, the home-grown bands' musical styles were developed over much longer periods and shaped by the need to play lengthy sets before a variety of audiences – from dreads to (predominantly white) university students.

Most of the bands came together after the initial impact of Island's signing of the Wailers in 1972 (two earlier exceptions were the Cimarons and Dennis Bovell's Matumbi), and unsurprisingly they tended to look to the world's most successful reggae group for their model. Around this time increasing numbers of UK black youth were beginning to wear their hair in dreadlocks, and after Bob Marley's historic Lyceum concert in 1975, before a rapturous multiracial audience, the image of the dreadlocked Rastaman entered decisively into popular iconography.

The Cimarons

The **Cimarons** – **Sonny Binns** (keyboards), **Franklyn Dunn** (bass), **Locksley Gichie** (guitar), and singer **Winston Reid**, later to find solo success as Winston Reedy – were the first self-contained reggae band in Britain. Formed in northwest London as early as 1967, they developed their craft backing visiting Jamaican singers on the club circuit. An early tour of Africa helped them hone their skills as a live band, though their first efforts in the recording studio – including a version of Neil Diamond's "Mammy Blue" and an album of soul covers – lacked focus.

Nevertheless, they continued building their reputation as a strong performing band and eventually visited Jamaica to record. The experience of working in a Kingston studio was obviously what the band needed and resulted in the acclaimed *On the Rock* album, one of the great british reggae albums of the 1970s. The band failed to keep pace, however, and by 1982's pop-oriented *Reggaebility*, their last album release, seemed well out of time with the new decade. Nonetheless, with roots rock in revival, a version of the band, including original bassist Franklyn Dunn and vocalist Winston Reedy, still performs and retains a following.

VULCAN

Northwest London's finest: the Cimarons with Winston Reedy (bottom centre)

CIMARONS

● **On the Rock** (Vulcan, UK).
The band's second and best album, recorded in Jamaica and including their deserved #1 on the island – a cut of Marley's "Talking Blues".

Matumbi

Formed in 1971 to back the singer **Tex Dixon**, **Matumbi** comprised **Dennis Bovell** and **Errol Pottinger** (guitars), **Uton Jones** (drums), and vocalists **Bevin Fagan**, **Glaister Pottinger** and **Nicholas Bailey**. Over the decade, they were to prove a major force, both live and on record, and in their own right and as session musicians. Bovell was also to forge an important career in production.

The band's first few singles, for Trojan, were inconsequential, but in 1976 they had UK reggae chart hits with the lovers rock songs "After Tonight" and an exemplary version of Bob Dylan's "Man In Me". Much to Trojan's chagrin, the band members also pursued various outside projects, released under a variety of names and imprints. These included a couple of interesting dub-based albums (Bovell was a dub pioneer in Britain), and a bunch of fine singles: "Daughter Of Zion" (Matumbi), "Sunshine" (Tempus), "Run Rasta Run" (K&B) and "Raindrops" (More Cut).

There was never any doubt that Matumbi could roots-rock with the best of them – witness the Dennis Bovell-written "Guide Us" (Matumbi Music Corp), one of the strongest UK productions of 1977. Nevertheless, they are best remembered for helping define British 'lovers rock', drawing from soft soul in contrast to the harder, male-oriented roots records. In addition to their own releases, Matumbi were in demand as a backing group for lovers rock singers such as **Louisa Marks**.

After three of the original members – Bailey, Dixon and Jones – had left, and the drummer **Lloyd 'Jah Bunny' Donaldson** had joined, Dennis Bovell and the band signed with EMI, for whom they cut a couple of worthwhile albums. The second of these was titled after an experimental 12" single, "Point Of View" (1979), which had come complete with a vintage-style I-Roy toast and echoes of Glenn Miller in the arrangement. An aesthetic and commercial success, it was one of the few 'lovers rock' songs to enter the UK pop charts.

Few figures have been as important to the UK reggae scene as **Dennis Bovell** (b. 1953, St Peter, Barbados), who, coming from a Caribbean island other than Jamaica, possessed a wider perspective about the sort of reggae he wanted to make than many of his contemporaries. Before launching Matumbi, he was involved with the esteemed **Jah Sufferer** sound system in North London, which gave him the necessary feel for making music suited for the one medium then giving exposure to reggae in Britain. With fellow Matumbi members, he also contributed consid-

UK producer-dubmaster Dennis Bovell

erably to the acceptance of the dub poet **Linton Kwesi Johnson** (b. 1952, Chapelton, Jamaica), who was adopted by rock/punk audiences (and anti-racist campaigns) in the late 1970s. Bovell provided the 'dub' treatment and a roots credibility to Johnson's work.

After Matumbi went their separate ways at the beginning of the 1980s, Bovell worked for a while with punk rock group the Slits. He has gone on to do considerable TV work, and has produced albums for Linton Kwesi Johnson's LKJ label – including excellent instrumental outings from saxophonist Steve Gregory, guitarist John Kpiaye, and trumpeter Shake Keane, blending reggae with jazz and other influences. Bovell continues to produce Johnson's own occasional records, as well as those of poet Jean Binta Breeze, along with dub releases and live work with his **Dennis Bovell Dub Band**.

MATUMBI

Ah Fe Wi Dis (Rama, UK).

Ah Who Seh? Go Deh (Rama, UK).

These self-produced sets from the late 1970s, dominated by dub techniques, stand as the best showcases for Matumbi's talents. Reeking of dread atmosphere, there is enough classic musicianship and variety in the different tracks to maintain interest when heard away from a ganja-filled sound clash.

LINTON KWESI JOHNSON

Forces Of Victory (Island, UK).

Politically conscious dub poetry, with every patois term enunciated clearly enough for Johnson's white audience. Flawless musical contributions are from the likes of Dennis Bovell, Jah Bunny and Rico.

STEVE GREGORY

Bushfire (LKJ Records, UK).

Formerly with UK jazz-funk band Gonzalez, and veteran of a long session career, Steve Gregory finally gets a whole album to himself. Playing with guitarist John Kpiaye, trumpeter Eddie 'Tan Tan' Thornton, and with guest spots from Georgie Fame's Hammond organ, the saxophonist/flautist delivers a cleverly crafted and gutsy programme of originals that blend jazz-funk and reggae in a satisfying new hybrid.

JOHN KPIAYE

Red Gold & Blues (LKJ Records, UK).

Guitarist Kpiaye, long associated with producer/bassist Bovell, features on a set of originals and covers – a hypnotic version of Ben Tucker's "Comin' Home Baby" stands out – in company with Steve Gregory and Eddie 'Tan Tan' Thornton. The result is a well-judged synthesis of reggae, ska, jazz and funk, in the manner of Ernest Ranglin's work with Monty Alexander.

VARIOUS ARTISTS – DENNIS BOVELL PRODUCTIONS

Force To Deal (Pressure, UK).

A compilation of releases by Arawak, one of the 1970s labels that demanded UK reggae be taken seriously. Gaining immeasurably from the production skills of Bovell, both lovers-rock records like Janet Kay's 1979 pop hit "Silly Games" and rootsier offerings such as Errol Dunkley's 1978 updating of his own "Little Way Different" stand up well twenty years on.

Black Slate

Black Slate came together in 1974 from a variety of backgrounds: **George Brightly** (keyboards) and **Elroy Bailey** (aka Ras Elroy, bass) were London-born; **Keith Drummond** (lead vocals), **Chris Hanson** (lead guitar) and **Desmond Mahoney** (drums) from Jamaica; **Cledwyn Rogers** (rhythm guitar) from Anguilla. Their shared experiences of being black in London united them, as it did much of a new, enlarged audience for reggae in the UK, and in many ways they typified the generation of British reggae bands that emerged in all the cities with sizeable migrant communities after the release of the Wailers' *Catch A Fire* album. Marley had presented a fresh model for reggae, both live and on record, and one much more in sync with the established conventions of youth music in Britain.

Nonetheless, Black Slate received their first exposure playing behind touring Jamaican stars, such as Delroy Wilson and Ken Boothe, before, in 1976, entering the UK reggae charts with their own excellent "Sticks Man" (Slate). Over a rumbling skank bassline made for sound-system play burst lyrics forthrightly condemning mugging. UK pop hits would follow in 1980 with "Amigo" and to a lesser extent with "Boom Boom", though neither had quite the uncompromising power of "Sticks Man", one of the high-water marks in British reggae of the 1970s.

Black Slate's magic was never captured over the full length of any of their albums, and nothing new from this gifted band has appeared since the mid-1980s.

Steel Pulse

Steel Pulse was the most successful of all the UK reggae bands of the 1970s, gaining recognition at home, in the US, and with the ultra-critical Jamaican audience. The band was formed in 1975 by three school friends in the Handsworth area of Birmingham, which they were to celebrate with the title of their first album. **David Hinds** was their dominant force, both as songwriter and lead vocalist, as well as rhythm guitarist; **Basil Gabbidon** played lead guitar and contributed to the vocals; and **Ronnie McQueen** was on bass.

This original trio recorded a couple of singles, "Kibudu, Mansetta and Abuka" (Dip) and "Nyah Love" (Anchor), before expanding to a seven-piece, adding **Alphonso Martin** and **Michael Riley** (both on vocals and percussion), **Selwyn Brown** (keyboards, vocals and percussion) and **Steve Nisbet** (drums). This line-up attracted a big multiracial live following, which led to their being signed to Island Records. Their first release on the label was the popular anti-racist single, "Klu Klux Klan", the centrepiece of their always arresting stage act. Then came their brilliant debut album, *Handsworth Revolution* (1978), a record that put to rest any remaining doubts concerning the quality – or 'authenticity' – of reggae made in the UK. It was a set clearly the equal of the best that arrived from Jamaica that year, and superior to a great many.

Steel Pulse made two further (and lesser) LPs for Island before moving to Elektra in 1982, and then MCA four years later. After their initial impact with *Handsworth Revolution*, however, they tended to be taken for granted in Britain and gradually spent more time touring abroad. They remain one of the few roots-rocking UK groups from the 1970s to continue to record and perform regularly – though their main following is now in the US.

STEEL PULSE

◑ **Handsworth Revolution** (Island, UK).

Ⓔ This devastating debut album presented both a forceful social and musical vision, expressed with thoughtful writing, heartfelt vocals and stunning musicianship. It surely said something about the band's confidence that three of their most exceptional tracks

ADRIAN BOOT

Steel Pulse displaying heavy-duty dreadlocks, led by David Hinds (centre)

– "Prodigal Son", "Klu Klux Klan" and "Prediction" – were placed on the second side.

◑ **Sound System** (Island Jamaica, US).

This double CD neatly collects the three Island albums, substituting 12" mixes for certain tracks and adding a couple of live takes for good measure, including a fine version of "Nyah Love".

◑ **True Democracy** (Elektra, JA/US).

This 1982 set stands as the band's most consistent release since their debut, with songs like "Chant A Psalm", "Blues Dance Raid" and "Worth his Weight In Gold (Rally Round)" showcasing their musicianship.

Aswad

While never breaking through to either US or Jamaican audiences in quite the same way as Steel Pulse, **Aswad** were a fixture on the British music scene of the 1970s and 1980s, and eventually had that rarity for reggae bands – pop chart success, with "Chasing the Breeze" in 1984 and the chart-topping "Don't Turn Around" in 1988.

The band formed in the same year as Steel Pulse, (1975), this time in the Westbourne Grove area of West London. Their nucleus was **Brinsley 'Dan' Forde** (vocals, guitar), **George Oban** (bass), **Tony 'Gad' Robinson** (vocals/keyboards) and **Angus 'Drummie Zeb' Gaye** (drums). After Oban left in 1980, Robinson took over bass duties.

The 1980s saw Aswad's sound enhanced in the studio and on stage by a great horns section built around variations of **Michael 'Bammi' Rose** (alto saxophone), **Eddie 'Tan Tan' Thornton** (trumpet) and the veteran Jamaican trombone player **Vin 'Don D Junior' Gordon.** The contributions of Gordon and Rose particularly added to the effectiveness of their 1980 12" single "Warrior Charge", which was featured in the film *Babylon* – a vehicle for the acting talents of Brinsley Forde – and remains their most powerful track to date.

They were at this time – and for the best part of a decade – the foremost roots band in Britain, and repeatedly demonstrated they could also successfully take on the role of a top session band, enhancing their reputation with rhythms of the very hardest quality for the Jamaican singers **Johnny Osbourne**, **Michael Palmer** and **Dennis Brown.**

Aswad's forays into pop territory – "Don't Turn Around" in 1988 was the first, followed by "On And" the next year – lost them part of their original following, though recording 1990's *Too Wicked* album at Gussie Clarke's Music Works studio in Kingston (and including a guest

DAVID CORIO

Aswad founders Brinsley Forde and Tony Gad Robinson lay down a bass overdub

appearance from Shabba Ranks) demonstrated they could return to their roots whenever they felt like it. They went on to gain more crossover success with glossy lovers tunes like "Next To You" and "Best Of My Love", building a huge following in Japan, where they currently enjoy gold and platinum album sales.

ASWAD

● **New Chapter** (CBS, UK).

Ⓔ Aswad's first album for CBS, in 1982, confirmed their solid roots credentials and displayed the ease with which they could tackle virtually any facet of reggae, with the rhythms ranging from steppers-style roots to lovers rock, and touching most points in between. It is a consistent set, featuring memorable melodies, inspired horn arrangements and melliferous vocals, while "Love Fire" had a rhythm Jamaican producers were to seize upon a few years later.

● **Showcase** (Grove Music, UK; Mango, US).

The first part of the Aswad story is conveniently summarized on *Showcase*, which presents all their early reggae hits, complete with dub versions, from 1976's "Back To Africa" to 1980's "Warrior Charge" and "Babylon".

● **Hulet** (Grove Music, UK).

If the tracks on *Showcase* appeal, and you want to hear more of their work from the late 1970s, it is also worth picking up this 1978 set that defined their approach for the next few years.

● **A New Chapter Of Dub** (Island, UK).

The dub companion to *New Chapter* takes some of best rhythms, and gives them a new dimension with Michael 'Reuben' Campbell and Angus 'Drummie Zeb' Gaye's inspired mixing.

● **Not Satisfied** (CBS, UK).

The second CBS album continued in the same vein as *New Chapter*, balancing raw roots tracks with lighter material like "Pass the Cup" and the exquisite "I Need Your Love".

◑ **Live & Direct** (Island, UK).

The recording of Aswad's crowd-pleasing performance at the 1983 Notting Hill Carnival meant a triumphant return to Island, and one of the very few live reggae albums of real interest – in part because of their versions of recent dancehall favourites, such as the "Heavenless" rhythm, Dennis Brown's "Revolution" and Johnny Osbourne's "Water Pumping".

◑ **To the Top** (Simba, UK; RAS, US).

Appearing on their own label, this saw Aswad moving even further from their previous militant roots style into easy summer-skanking territory, but performed with just as much grace and aplomb. Includes their major hits, "Bubbling" and "Kool Yah".

Misty In Roots

Formed in Southall, one of London's largest migrant areas, **Misty In Roots** were a major roots-era band. They had a big following both among West Indian and white rock audiences, the latter achieved through tours alongside punk rock bands in the late 1970s, "Rock Against Racism" festivals (which they often co-headlined with punk bands), and appearances on John Peel's radio 1 show in the UK. Membership fluctuated, but the core of the band was **Walford Tyson** (lead vocals), his brother **Delvin Tyson** (vocals, rhythm), **Chesley Samson** (lead guitar), **Delbert McKay** (guitar, vocals), **Tony 'Thungy' Henry** (bass) and **Dennis Augustine** (rhythm guitar).

Always keen to pursue an independent path and stay true to their Rastafarian principles, Misty turned down major label offers and formed their own, People Unite. The singles and albums that appeared on their imprint were melodic enough to appeal to a broad cross-section of the public, and it was possibly only their refusal to make the compromises involved with signing to a mainstream record company that stood in the way of the national chart hits enjoyed by the likes of Black Slate, Aswad and Matumbi.

Though no longer at the forefront of British reggae, Misty continue to record, and in 1997 celebrated their twentieth anniversary with a well-attended concert in London. In addition, their entire back catalogue of albums has been re-released in recent years.

MISTY IN ROOTS

● **Live At the Counter-Eurovision** (People Unite/Kaz, UK).

Another of those rare beasts – an essential live roots album. Check the impassioned "Judas Iscariot" for an outstanding example of Misty's energy, musicianship and panache.

◑ **Wise & Foolish** (People Unite/Kaz, UK).
Their debut studio album, appearing a couple of years after *Eurovision*, gained from having Godson Bedau on saxophone, and remains unsuperseded by the band. By this time, it was obvious that among the UK reggae outfits, only Aswad and Steel Pulse stood comparison with this very committed collective.

Reggae Regular

The highly successful London-based Greensleeves label was launched in 1977 with two singles – and there could be no greater words of praise for **Reggae Regular**'s "Where Is Jah" than it was not put in the shade by its co-release, Doctor Alimantado's "Born For A Purpose".

Reggae Regular – a seven-piece London- based band – clearly owed much to contemporary Jamaican roots music but they were also a distinctly UK reggae product. Their second, equally enduring 45 for Greensleeves, 1978's "The Black Star Liner", again drew from orthodox Rastafarian imagery and presented it over a rhythm unmistakably built in the UK.

Comprising **Allan 'Kingpin' King** and **Tony 'Benjamin' Rookwood** (lead vocals), **Norman 'Junior' Ebanks** (lead guitar), **Trevor 'Seal' Salmon** (bass), **Patrick 'Chiki' Donegan** (rhythm guitar, vocals), **George 'Flea' Clarke** (keyboards) and **Errol 'Sly Jnr.' Francis** (drums), the Regulars (as they became known) always impressed in live performance. On record, they were less impressive, attempting to match Aswad's pop, and never repeated the impact of their first two singles. These, however, were significant achievements and did much to set the standards by which reggae made outside of Jamaica was judged for the rest of the decade.

Capital Letters

Wolverhampton's roots champions, **Capital Letters** played in the easy skanking style of the Wailers' international reggae, though with a distinctly British flavour. As they themselves put it, "Jamaican people have a special way to rock and sway in a Jamaican way/My UK brethren just got no way to shake a leg and play in that Jamaican way". They were a big, eight-piece outfit, comprising **Roderick 'the Dude' Harvey** (drums), **Junior 'JB' Brown** (bass), **George 'Bulk' Scarlet** (guitar), **Earl 'Wizard' Lynch** (keyboards, vocals), **Danny 'Teacher' McKen** (guitar, vocals), and backing singers **Wenty 'Country Boy' Stewart, Pauline 'Dell' Spence** and **Paulette 'Lee' Hatden.**

The band made just one album, *Headline News* in 1979, though they had some strong 12" releases (coming to the fore at the time in the UK reggae market), including tough dub mixes of "Smoking My Ganja" and "Natty Walk". Like most 1970s UK reggae groups, they did not long survive that decade, and never followed their impressive debut album.

CAPITAL LETTERS

◑ **Headline News** (Greensleeves, UK).
Archetypal UK roots rocking of the late 1970s that still sounds good. To the original ten-track LP, which was always an impressive debut, the CD adds the full 12" single mixes of "UK Skanking", "Natty Walk" and "Smoking My Ganja".

Solo singers

As well as the roots reggae bands of the 1970s, a number of British-based singers represented the older and more Jamaican tradition of recording over rhythms built by session musicians (often from the bands mentioned above). These included **Ijahman Levi** (b. 1946, Manchester, Jamaica), a London resident for most of his life, who recorded a trio of singles – including the sublime "Jah Heavy Load" – for UK label Dip Records before returning to Jamaica to make his unique debut album at Joe Gibbs' studio in Kingston.

Other 45s of comparable merit included the blues party favourite "Rebel Woman" (Queen Bee) from **Gene Rondo**; "Give All the Praise To Jah" (Virgin) from **Delroy Washington**, an underrated singer at the time who is now all but forgotten; "We Nah Go Suffer" (Daddy Kool) from the **Black Stones**, rare UK representatives of the Jamaican harmony-trio tradition; "Long Time" (Lightning) from **Winston Fergus**; and "Jah Find Babylon Guilty" (Terminus) from **Junior Brown**. Even one of the more gifted of the London producers from the skinhead era, **Sir Collins**, surfaced again in 1976 to release a completely convincing record in the Burning Spear mould – the **Unity Stars**' "Africa" (Nice 1).

Moving into the 1980s, **Pablo Gad**'s self-produced "Hard Times" (Burning Vibrations), on which this underrated performer both sang and deejayed, was a 'steppers' anthem for a time of deteriorating social conditions in the UK. The resilient deejay part delivered lines that were favourites with sound-system followers: "When I was a youth, I used to burn collie weed in a Rizla/Now I'm a man I just burn collie weed in a chalwa".

PABLO GAD

◑ **The Best Of Pablo Gad** (Pablo Gad, UK).

Roots anthems like "Hard Times" and "Blood Suckers" manage to sound heartfelt as well as simply heavy. A set that should be compulsory listening for all the would-be roots revivalists of the 1990s.

Lovers rock

The early years of '**lovers rock**' have two main resonances: London 'blues parties' and discs by girl singers who sounded as if they were still worrying about their school reports. The record that kick-started the phenomenon was the 14-year-old **Louisa Marks**'s plaintive reading of Robert Parker's soul hit, "Caught You In A Lie". With Matumbi as backing group and production by sound-system man **Lloyd Coxsone** (b. Lloyd Blackwood, Jamaica), this appeared on Coxsone's Safari imprint in 1975 and was impressive enough to see release in Jamaica by Gussie Clarke. Several of Louisa Marks's subsequent titles, including "All My Loving" (Safari) and "Six Sixth Street" (Bushays), repeated the success and have remained favourites at revive sessions ever since.

Louisa Marks's hit was followed by **Ginger Williams**'s "Tenderness" (Third World), and a genre was born – essentially Philly/Chicago soul ballads played over fat reggae basslines. The style was consolidated by the husband and wife team of **Dennis and Eve Harris** who had a big hit with the white singer **T.T. Ross**'s massively popular "Last Date" (Lucky), another key record, and set up a new imprint, Lover's Rock, giving the genre its name.

Later labels like **Fashion Records** and **Ariwa** would go on to take lovers rock to more sophisticated plains and beyond the music's original market of working-class teenagers. And while the music media largely ignored their performers – singers like **Peter Hunningale**, **Sylvia Tella**, **Michael Gordon** and **Keith Douglas** – they have deservedly scored hit after hit with audiences who trust what they hear rather than read.

VARIOUS ARTISTS

◑ **Lovers Rock – Serious Selections Volumes 1, 2 & 3** (Rewind Selecta, UK).

Ⓔ Not just UK lovers rock in these thoughtfully compiled selections, but many of the most popular romantic offerings from both Kingston and London, in the mood principally set by the latter city. All three volumes are chock-a-block with the most enduring examples of the genre, mostly in their 12" mixes, ranging from Louisa Marks's "Caught You In A Lie" to Barry Biggs's "Wide Awake In A Dream" (Volume 1); from the Heptics' "Natural Woman", through to Sugar Minott's "Lovers Rock" (Volume 2); and from the African Brothers' "Torturing", to Winston Reedy's "African Daughter" (Volume 3).

◑ **Pure Lovers Volumes 1–9** (Jet Star, UK).
Again, not just the UK variety but quality lovers from all the reggae capitals of the world, and featuring both long-established names (such as Freddie McGregor, Janet Kay, Delroy Wilson and Dennis Brown), and younger lovers (including Carol Gonzales, China Black and Wendy Walker). A wonderful opportunity to catch up on the best in the field for minimum outlay.

◑ **Lovers For Lovers Volumes 1–10** (The Business Records, UK).
A similar series to the above, and another that can be trusted. UK talent of the calibre of Louisa Marks and the still under-recorded Trevor Walters sits easily alongside vintage Jamaican greats like Freddie McGregor, Larry Marshall and Alton Ellis, with several tracks transcending common definitions of 'lovers' or 'roots'. Collections to be heard by anyone who equates 'lovers rock' with sickly sentiment and off-key schoolgirl voices.

First flowering

Among the groups that helped establish both the Lovers Rock label and genre were **Brown Sugar**, a south London trio discovered at a Sunday talent show at a Brockley Rise record store. They had a hit with a version of Barbara Lewis's "Hello Stranger", and followed it with a pair of singles, "I'm In Love With A Dreadlocks" and "Black Pride", that signalled a sub-genre – 'conscious lovers'. The records' easy-rocking rhythms were clearly aimed at the same audience as the Louisa Marks hits, but added a layer of black consciousness. The group also provided a first outing for **Caron Wheeler**, later to find fame with Soul II Soul, before embarking on her current solo career.

After Brown Sugar's hits, the sweet-voiced **Cassandra**'s "I'll Never Let You Out Of My Life" was probably the most popular record on the Lovers Rock imprint. Major records from other labels in the late 1970s/early 1980s included the appropriately named **15, 16 & 17**'s "Black Skin Boy" (Morpheus), **Portia Morgan**'s "Let Be Me Your Angel" (Hawkeye), **Revelation**'s "With You Boy" (Rite Sound) and **Donna Rhoden**'s "It's True" (Santic). All of these titles – and there were many more – have stood the test of time pretty well. Far better, certainly, than any critic might have predicted when they were being bought by teenage girls in pleated skirts, clumpy shoes and dark berets (or boys who wanted to attract them to their parties).

Further developments came from female singers who sounded less like schoolgirls. One of the first to surface was **Carroll Thompson**, a singer with assured phrasing and pitch, whose

"I'm So Sorry" (Santic) was one of a run of hits produced by the Jamaican producer (and by now London-resident) **Leonard Chin**. The most adult-sounding of the female lovers rock singers of the era, however, was **Joy Mack**. She possessed a strong voice that would not have sounded out of place in a Memphis or Muscle Shoals recording session of a decade before; indeed, her records, including the enormous hit, "You Had Your Chance" (Rite Sound), were indebted to southern soul in their arrangements.

A string of hits from **Janet Kay** (b. Janet Kay Bogle, 1958, London) took lovers rock to an ever more sophisticated level. A highly gifted singer, and an accomplished actress, Kay was first recorded by the veteran Jamaican singer Alton Ellis in 1977, resulting in best-selling "Loving You" (Stonehouse). This was followed by several more reggae chart singles including "I Do Love You" (D-Roy) and the Dennis Bovell-produced "Silly Games" (Arawak), which soared up the UK pop charts, too, peaking at #2 in 1979.

ADRIAN BOOT

Janet Kay: Silly Games, serious sales

JANET KAY

◑ **The Ultimate Collection** (Arawak, UK).

An album that deserves its name, bringing together the queen of lovers' most memorable hits for Arawak, D-Roy, Lloyd Charmers, Black Roots, Fergus Jones and Clem Bushay. The crossover hit, "Silly Games", sublime as it is, remains only part of the story.

CARROLL THOMPSON

◑ **The Other Side Of Love** (Ariwa, UK).

A 1993 album that confirmed the enduring nature of Thompson's talent. Her seductive vocals are so well complemented by the Mad Professor's production techniques it seems amazing that they have not met in the studio more often.

Lover boys

Male balladeers, who fitted into an older tradition of Jamaican singers, also appealed to the lovers rock market. **Tex Johnson**'s gloriously romantic "Pillow Talk" (Discotex) was an example of the genre at its best, and similar accolades could be given to gems such as **Tradition**'s "Breezing" (RCA), **Trevor Hartley**'s "Hanging Around" (PC) and **Vivian Jones**'s "Good Morning" (Third World).

The overwhelming majority of these 'lovers' hits involved singers recording over rhythms laid by session musicians, but there were a few self-contained bands (besides the pioneering Matumbi) on the scene. **One Blood** introduced the multi-talented **Paul Robinson** (aka **Barry Boom**) to the record-buying public, but were hit by tragedy – in the death of group and family member Errol Robinson – and folded before fulfilling their full potential. **Motion** were formed by Aswad's original bass player, George Oban, and were particularly successful with their interpretation of Dionne Warwick's "Walk On By" (Mojo Blank). From south London came the **Investigators**, who notched up hit after hit in the UK reggae charts, including marvellous treatments of Barbara Lewis's sultry "Baby I'm Yours" (Inner City), and – as the **Private I's** – the Spinners' "I'll Be Around" and Curtis Mayfield's "Romancing To the Folk Song" (both Cruise). The polished vocal and songwriting talents of member **Michael Gordon** ensured later solo success with 1980s hits such as "Magic Feeling" and "Love Is What You Make It". Another equally impressive outfit was North London's **Instigators**. They included the brothers **Leroy 'Mafia ' & David 'Fluxy' Heywood**, who were to become one of the most in-demand rhythm sections of the ragga age (and not just on the London studio scene, but in Kingston as well). Instigators singles like "We Ain't Been

Getting Along" (Mafia & Fluxy) remain among the most enduring of the genre.

BARRY BOOM

The Living Boom (Fine Style, UK).

Three massively popular singles in the reggae market – "Number One Girl", "Making Love" and "Hurry Over" – demonstrated that Barry Boom belonged to the same class of effortless serenador as the man he helped to international stardom, Maxi Priest. His debut album is built around this trio of 45s, but with other tracks of the same immaculate, soulful standard.

THE INVESTIGATORS

Investigators Greatest Hits: Rare Grooves (Sweet Freedom, UK).

This best-selling album brings together most of the band's finest moments. The fact that they were little heard beyond their target audience at the time says a great deal about British radio. Every track is a genuine classic of its genre.

MAFIA & FLUXY PRODUCTIONS

Mafia & Fluxy Lovers Connection Volume I (Mafia & Fluxy, UK).

Mrs Heywood's boys have always imparted classic rocksteady qualities to their lovers rock productions, as displayed on this collection from the likes of the Instigators (naturally), Winston Reedy, Leroy Mafia himself, and the seriously underrated Black Stones.

The 1980s

Critics wrote off lovers rock as a passing phase but it remained popular through the **1980s**, both in its original form, with many of the early hits remaining 'revive' session favourites, and in more sophisticated shape. For teenage black girls, whose dreams of escape were more likely to involve marriage to a caring man than repatriation to Africa, lovers rock 45s presented a welcome alternative to the diet of militant roots being presented by many UK sound systems.

Many of the artists mentioned above kept the hits coming, while among the most notable records from a newcomer was **Dee Sharp**'s pivotal version of Leo Hall's 1975 Jamaican hit, "Let's Dub It Up", which in the first year of the new decade launched what was to become the leading UK label producing its own music – Chris Lane and John MacGillivray's **Fashion Records**.

The same imprint also recorded **Keith Douglas**, another very accomplished singer who had already cut a couple of roots titles, as well as singing harmonies on Pablo Gad's "Hard Times". His own tastes included Marvin Gaye, as well as Jamaican favourites like Alton Ellis, Dennis Brown and Bob Marley, and as the 1980s unfolded he demonstrated that his rich voice was even more suited to the emotive lovers tunes that Fashion excelled in. "Specialise In God Girls" was the first in this vein to make an impact on dance floors, and more reggae chart hits followed, including the exquisite "Try Love Again" and "Cool Down Amina".

Equally distinguished hits from Fashion over the next few years included **Peter Spence**'s "Yesterday's Magic", **Winsome**'s "Born Free" and **Nerious Joseph**'s "No One Night Stand".

Not that Fashion had become the only label in the game. Enduring blues-party favourites came from a variety of sources. The Greensleeves subsidiary UK Bubblers gave the late **Deborahe Glasgow** her first hit with "You're My Sugar"; the **Administrators**' own label, Groove & A Quarter, scored with **Vivian Jones**'s "Sugar Love", as well as several successful discs by the band itself; the Inner Light label had the tune that remains the biggest hit from **Winston Reedy**, "Dim the Lights"; **Leonard Chin**, who had moved from Kingston to London in 1975, helped further define the genre with **Jean Ademambo**'s consummate "Paradise" (Santic).

Although lovers rock was very much a UK phenomenon, one Jamaican singer who had no problems adapting to its demands was **Sugar Minott**. In 1981, the Studio One graduate celebrated the form with a track called

"Lovers Rock", recorded at the Easy Street studio in London, and duetted with its then reigning queen, Carroll Thompson, on one of the more inspired versions of David Gates's "Make It With You".

Alongside Fashion, the most consistent of all the labels regularly releasing lovers rock was **Ariwa Sounds**, run by **Neil Fraser**. Fraser, like Dennis Bovell, was not a Jamaican – he was from Guyana – and like Matumbi's leader he applied himself equally to satisfying the markets for both sweet lovers rock and raw dub (earning himself the sobriquet of the **Mad Professor** for his mixing skills).

Beginning with basic four-track equipment at his home in Thornton Heath, South London, Fraser showed a mastery of lovers rock with the first disc by **Deborahe Glasgow** (b. 1965; d. 1994), releasing "Falling In Love" when the singer was only 12 and calling herself Debbie G. In the early 1980s he relocated to another South London area, Peckham, where he set up a more professionally equipped studio.

Among major 80s hits for Ariwa were **John McLean**'s "If I Gave My Heart To You" and **Paulette Tajah**'s "Let's Make A Baby". However, the label's two great discoveries of the decade were Sandra Cross and Kofi. **Sandra Cross**, a clear, tuneful singer, emerged from the ranks of the **Wild Bunch**, one of the earliest Ariwa acts. Her string of hits in the UK reggae charts included an inspired cut of the Stylistics' "Country Living" and the exquisite "Best Friend's Man". She has remained loyal to the label. **Kofi**, another pretty-voiced singer who benefitted from Fraser's accomplished produc tion techniques, was best known for her beautiful updatings of "I'm In Love With A Dreadlocks" and "Black Pride".

ARIWA

Kofi: reflective lovers rock at its best

SANDRA CROSS

◑ **This Is Sandra Cross** (Ariwa, UK).

The Mad Professor hardly puts a foot wrong when it comes to classy lovers rock outings, and Sandra Cross is the perfect honey-toned singer for his well-crafted settings. This collects practically everything of interest she recorded at Ariwa Sounds, including her version of the Stylistics' "Country Living" soul hit, now considered as much a reggae classic as the Mighty Diamonds' one.

JUNIOR DELGADO

● **It Takes Two To Tango** (Fashion, UK).

Recorded at Fashion's A-Class Studio when it was still under the record shop, and an album designed to show Junior Delgado's versatility. The popular title track combines lovers lyrics with a roots feel (partly courtesy of longtime associate Augustus Pablo), and a healthy balance of concerns is provided with fine outpourings of the heart ("Magic Of Love" and "It's True"), out-and-out dancehall offering ("Labba Labba") and powerful 'cultural' diatribes ("Rebel Sold In Captive").

KEITH DOUGLAS

● **Love With Style** (Hot Pepper, UK).

A easy-going self-produced set that is mostly concerned with affairs of the heart, as suggested by the title, but also touching on 'reality' for the equally assured "Frontline" and "Fit For the Fire".

KOFI

◑ **Black... With Sugar** (Ariwa, UK).

◑ **Friday's Child** (Ariwa, UK).

Kofi has the kind of enticing voice and crisp arrangements associated with lovers rock, but a lot more thoughtful lyrics than usual for the genre. This debut album includes her best-selling 45s, "Black Pride", "Looking Over Love" and "Didn't I", while the equally impressive *Friday's Child* revisits lovers classic, "I'm In Love With A Dreadlocks".

WINSTON REEDY

● **Dim the Lights** (Inner Light, UK).
The title track, a 1983 blues-party favourite, was Winston Reedy's fourth in that vein to reach the UK reggae charts, and remains his most enduring hit. The album demonstrated another side to his talent, as he showed himself just as capable of handling 'reality' themes (albeit still with something of a lovers vibe about them).

WINSOME

◑ **Story Of A Black Woman** (Sir George, UK).
The ten tracks presented here are best described as 'conscious lovers'. Music with serious intent, written as well as superbly sung by Battersea's own Winsome, but with a glorious 'lovers' feel throughout.

VARIOUS ARTISTS: FASHION PRODUCTIONS

◑ **Lovers Fashion Volumes 1 & 2** (Fashion, UK).
E The first of these two exemplary sets begins with the first Fashion hit, Dee Sharp's "Let's Dub It Up", the bench mark by which future releases were judged. Then there are equally impressive best sellers – like Winsome's "Am I the Same Girl", Carlton Lewis's "Sweet Soul Rocking", Michael Gordon's "Magic Feeling" and Keith Douglas's "Try Love Again". The second volume keeps up the standard with such as Barry Boom's sublime "Making Love" and Winsome's "Homebreaker". Hear these, and ponder on why lovers rock remains the least acknowledged of reggae forms.

● **Rock With Me Baby – The Fine Style Collection** (Fashion, UK).
Nerious Joseph and Winsome's amazingly infectious remake of the Delano Stewart classic is joined by other Fashion hits from the likes of Peter Spence, Michael Gordon, Winsome on her own and Aston Eson. A couple of previously unreleased gems keep up the standard of the already-proven tracks.

VARIOUS ARTISTS: NEIL FRASER (ARIWA) PRODUCTIONS

◑ **Lovers Delight** (Ariwa, UK).
The romantic side of the Mad Professor. Some might get excited by his experiments in the dub laboratory, but it has been the lovers offerings from the likes of Trevor Hartley, Kofi, Sandra Cross and John McLean that have long rocked blues dances in Brixton, Chapeltown and Handsworth.

The 1990s

If anything, lovers rock has enjoyed even greater success in the UK reggae charts in the **1990s**, with romantic male crooners often outselling the more high-profile deejays. The perfectly controlled voice of **Mike Anthony**, for instance, has graced several major hits, including "How Long", "Don't Play Games" and, the most perfectly realized of them all, "Spread Love". Another new star, **Don Campbell**, has upheld traditional vocal values with records that would probably sell in their millions if he was an American singer, and much the same could be said of **Neville Morrison** and former member of the Investigators, **Michael Gordon**. Even **Vivian Jones**, an expressive singer who made his reputation with roots material for the likes of Jah Shaka, has shown he can convincingly slip into a lovers mood.

Over the decade, however, the sweet-voiced and exquisitely soulful **Peter Hunningale** has been the most consistently popular of all lovers stars – and he had rightful recognition in Jamaica as part of a triumphant UK contingent at the 1996 Sunsplash festival.

The genre's women singers have continued in the forefront, too, with significant discs including **Donna Marie**'s "Think Twice" (Londisc), **Janet-Lee Davis**'s "Do You Remember" (Fashion) and **Sylvia Tella**'s most sublime single to date, "Happy Home" (Mafia & Fluxy). On the latter, Tella's lyrical celebration of family values showed how far lovers rock had developed from when there was no more apposite a name for a group than 15, 16 & 17.

MIKE ANTHONY

◑ **Back 4 More** (Gussie P, UK).
Anthony's greatest hits, along with hitherto-unreleased tracks of a similar calibre, make you wonder why he remains an unknown quantity to most British record buyers. Check the exquisite "Spread Love" for some of the most soulful music of modern times.

DON CAMPBELL

◑ **The Album** (Juggling Records, UK).
An exceptional debut set. The hits "See It In Your Eyes", "Lovers Do" and "Sun Shines For Me" are among a dozen gems collected here, and there are no weak moments.

JANET-LEE DAVIS

◑ **Missing You** (Fashion, UK).
E One of those debut albums that just radiate freshness, marvellous vocal technique and feeling, ensuring the singer's reputation in the unlikely event of her never making another record. Standouts among a beautifully crafted set include the sublime title track and "Do You Remember".

MICHAEL GORDON

Feeling For Love (Fashion, UK).

The first solo outing from this incredibly gifted singer after he had left the Investigators is something of a milestone in lovers rock's development. Easy skanking material given bite by immaculate musicianship and Gordon's ever soulful intonation.

PETER HUNNINGALE

Reggae Max (Jet Star, UK).

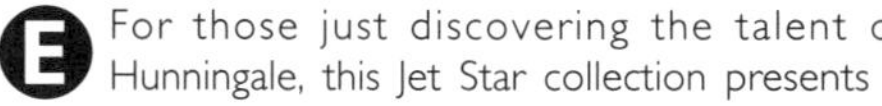

For those just discovering the talent of Hunningale, this Jet Star collection presents a way to catch up with no less than twenty of his most successful singles, all of which sold incredibly well in the UK reggae market.

VIVIAN JONES

Reggae Max (Jet Star, UK).

Another singer who has yet to receive the recognition he deserves. A twenty-track, almost entirely self-produced set that can be bought with confidence, brimming as it does with hits of the quality of "Strong Love", "The Hurt" and "Love Is For Lovers".

LEROY MAFIA

Finders Keepers (Mafia & Fluxy, UK).

The bass-playing half of the UK's top rhythm section steps forward to show he can handle the vocal department with equal assurance. In accordance with his background in the Instigators, the approach is UK lovers rock of the type (and standard) with which the north London band were synonymous. The title track, "You Are the One For Me", "Can't Get Enough" and "There She Goes Again" were enormous hits in the reggae market, and the rest easily come up to their polished standard.

SYLVIA TELLA

Spell (Charmers, UK).

One of the best-selling lovers rock albums of all time, and one that has worn very well. Immaculate arrangements, and just the right amount of soulful rasp in the voice. A CD re-release is long overdue.

From deejays to ragga

For all the popularity of lovers rock in Britain in the early 1980s, nothing could take the limelight away from the relentless rise of the **deejays** – not just from the Jamaican dancehalls, but UK ones as well. The sound system at the heart of this coming-of-age for home-grown MCs (as UK deejays of the time preferred to be known) was **Saxon Sound International**, which supplanted **Sir Coxsone** as London's ruling sound in the first half of the decade.

Coxsone's main rival from the close of the previous decade, **Jah Shaka**, was doggedly sticking to 'cultural' material, over the most militant steppers rhythms, and with the emphasis on stomach-churning dub mixes; the only deejay business on Shaka's set was its owner's own righteous chanting. In contrast, the Saxon posse were keeping abreast of the latest developments in Jamaica and allowing the most talented of the local MCs to dominate proceedings at their dances. The fact that sometimes there might be more heard from the likes of **Peter King**, **Asher Senator**, **Daddy Colonel** and **Smiley Culture** than the records was the cause of complaint from some quarters; yet a new generation of dancehall patrons thought the chat the main focus of interest.

Part of the excitement that the MCs created lay in their being local lads, commenting very directly on their audience's experiences. At first, the major stimulus for young chatters living in the UK came in the form of cassettes that captured live sound-system sessions from Kingston. These often poorly recorded tapes were the reggae phenomenon of the early 1980s, allowing those who had never visited Jamaica to hear deejays like Nicodemus, Ranking Joe, Brigadier Jerry and General Echo interacting with their dancehall followers, and without the compromises or refinements involved in transposing their performances to the different environment of the recording studio.

Fast chat

Stylistically the major innovation for which the Saxon MCs were responsible was the

DAVID CORIO

The ever-faithful Jah Shaka plays sounds for His Imperial Majesty

The fastest talkers: Smiley Culture (left) and Asher Senator

'fast chat' style – originally heard from Yard deejays like Ranking Joe but taken to new levels by men like the much-copied **Peter King** (a talent little known beyond his peers on the sound-system scene). In turn the UK chatters then influenced Yard deejays and singers (most notably Junior Reid, who still employs it).

It was **Smiley Culture** (b. David Emmanuel, c. 1960, London) who propelled fast chat into the mainstream. His Fashion single "Cockney Translation" was a UK reggae chart-topper in 1984 and its follow-up, "Police Officer", employing the "Never Let Go" rhythm, made its way into the national pop charts the next year. Meantime, plaudits for first UK deejay record to top the Jamaican charts went the same year to **Philip 'Papa' Levi** (b. Philip Williams), with "Mi God Mi King" (Bad Breed).

In their wake, **Asher Senator**'s "Abbreviation Qualification" (Fashion) successfully competed with all the Jamaican versions of "Feel Like Jumping" that were popular in 1984, and **Tippa Irie** (b. Anthony Henry, 1965, London) scored a UK Top 30 pop hit with "Hello Darling (UK Bubblers) in 1986.

ASHER SENATOR

◉ Born To Chat (Fashion, UK).

One of the liveliest, most inventive MCs from the Saxon Studio sound, fast chatting over both digital and (slightly) older-style dancehall rhythms, and living up to the promise of his performances on the inspired "Abbreviation Qualification"/"Fast Style Origination" 45.

PHILIP 'PAPA' LEVI

◑ Code Of Practice (Arrow, UK).

Papa Levi was one MC who did not desert the sound on which he made his name, Saxon, after he started recording. This set is a good deal nearer the dancehall mainstream than most on Ariwa, with all the rhythms courtesy of Mafia & Fluxy, and one of the UK's finest deejays showing – six years after his Jamaican #1 – that he still had lyrics and style.

SMILEY CULTURE

◉ The Original (Top Notch, UK).

Smiley Culture's popular "Cockney Translation" and "Police Officer" always possessed just the right balance of light-hearted pop values and genuine musical muscle designed to rock the dancehalls. Here they

are along with tracks that are just as distinctive, amusing and infectious.

TIPPA IRIE

Original Raggamuffin (Mango, UK).

Released almost a decade after Tippa Irie made his initial impact with Saxon Sound, this is the most satisfying album-length example of the talented deejay's work. It benefits from the Tippa's own production ideas and from variation in the material – ranging through fun lyrics, to 'reality' reflections, to the expected dancehall celebrations.

VARIOUS ARTISTS FASHION PRODUCTIONS

Great British MCs (Fashion, UK).

The album that confirmed in no uncertain terms the abundant talent and energy of UK MCs. The music of the 'mic' men does not always date well, but Philip Levi's "Mi God Mi King" stands as a true classic of the genre, while contributions from the likes of Smiley Culture, Peter King and Asher Senator show why UK MCs were – for a while – causing more excitement than their Jamaican counterparts.

VARIOUS ARTISTS – SAXON PRODUCTIONS

Coughing Up Fire: Saxon Studio International Live (UK Bubblers, UK).

Recorded in November 1984, this shows some of the best of the UK MCs of the immediate pre-digital period – 'Papa' Philip Levi, Daddy Colonel, Sandy, Tippa Irie, Daddy Rusty, et al. – caught in their natural dancehall habitat. Not quite the same as being there – but the best you can hope for a decade later – and in your own home.

ARIWA

Ever fertile wit: Macka B

Birmingham chatters

Away from the London dancehall circuit, Birmingham's **Wassifa** sound system was building a reputation for itself, along with their leading deejay, **Macka B** (b. Christopher MacFarlane, Wolverhampton). The possessor of a gruff voice in the Prince Jazzbo tradition, but with more humour to his approach, Macka had an initial hit for Fashion with the irresistibly catchy "Bible Reader". He then moved on to Neil Fraser's Ariwa set up, whose rootsier rhythms were better suited to his style, debuting with the *Sign Of the Times* album, a triumph in its serious yet never po-faced approach.

Macka B's subsequent sets for Ariwa – one a year to date – have proved almost as successful, while visits to Jamaica have shown him to be just as at home in studios catering more directly to dancehall demands – as witnessed by the Donovan Germain-produced "DJ Unity", on which he sparred with Tony Rebel, and "Tongue And Nuh Gun" for Fatis Burrell.

Another talent to emerge from Birmingham was **Pato Banton** (b. Patrick Murray, Birmingham). He first came to national attention at the end of the 1970s with pop-ska, two-tone band, **The Beat**, before distinguishing himself with releases for Fashion, the Mad Professor and Greensleeves. These records were aimed squarely at the reggae market, though his lightness of vocal tone and humour always made a shift back to more pop-oriented material (and success) inevitable. Reggae is now just one of the elements in his eclectic approach.

MACKA B

Sign Of the Times (Ariwa, UK).

E Released in 1986, this was Macka B's impressive debut, and several tracks – including "Invasion" – remain among the strongest of his always interesting career. His lyrics (as well as delivery) alerted the world to a talent who stood out in any company. The Mad Professor's rootsy rhythms and mixing provide the perfect complement to his intelligent, pertinent chat.

PATO BANTON

Never Give In (Greensleeves, UK).

Released in 1987, Pato Banton's second album ignored the digital revolution for earlier-sounding roots rhythms from two Birmingham bands, the Studio Two Crew and (for one track) Steel Pulse. The seeds of crossover success were already apparent.

The next generation at the mike

Inevitably, many of the UK MCs of the 1980s failed to keep momentum in the next decade. But Macka B, Philip Levi and Tippa Irie continued to develop and remain relevant, while newer figures have demonstrated a vitality and invention on a par with their ragga counterparts in Kingston. **General Levy** (b. Paul Levy), **Top Cat**, **Ricky Tuffy** and **Sweetie Irie** (b. Dean Bent), for instance, have been totally in tune with post-Shabba developments from Yard, while having the confidence to draw from their immediate environment for lyrical inspiration.

Levy, in particular, has proved himself a roughhouse deejay with as much originality and flair as any in Kingston. His "Heat" was a dancehall anthem, and he soon became a junglist hero as well as a ragga one. Top Cat is in a similar position and probably the most vital and good-humoured of all the current crop; he has a delivery owing something to the similarly named Super Cat, but an original London take on topics – and accent. Both the General and the Cat cut impressive versions of an updated cut of Scratch's "Lock Jaw" rhythm – "Mad Them" and "Request the Style", respectively – and the two records provide an interesting comparison of their talents.

Another rising star, discovered by the UK's premier bass and drums partnership, **Mafia & Fluxy**, in their Tottenham, North London, base, is teenage boy-wonder deejay **Glamma Kid**. His juggernaut approach is extraordinary, making him sound the graduate of years on the Kingston dancehall circuit. His debut single, the exuberant "Fashion Magazine", not only reached the upper region of the UK reggae chart in 1996, but was a Jamaican #1. A year later he repeated the success with the brutally infectious "Moschino" (Clarkey & Blakey), leading to a deal with major label BMG.

Any of these deejays has the potential to enjoy one of those occasional summertime reggae hits in the UK pop chart, though to date none has approached the crossover popularity of the Asian ragga deejay **Apache Indian** (b. Steve Kapur, 1967, Birmingham). Yet another product of Birmingham's lively multiracial culture, this son of Indian immigrants established himself in the reggae marketplace with singles like "Chok There" and "Don Raja", which drew from bhangra, the dance music of young British Asians, as well as ragga. The success of these records brought Apache Indian to the attention of Island, who sent him to Jamaica in 1993 to record with the likes of Sly Dunbar (who had already been experimenting with bhangra-style drums beats). A real crossover artist, he had both reggae and pop hits with original and appealing 45s like "Moving On" and "Arranged Marriage". The hits then dried up, however, and he was subsequently dropped by Island.

APACHE INDIAN

◑ **No Reservations** (Island, UK).

Apache's debut album, produced in Jamaica by Sly Dunbar, Bobby Digital and Robert Livingstone, convincingly demonstrated that the Indian/Birmingham ragga star was no novelty act and deserved to be taken seriously as a force in reggae music.

GENERAL LEVY

◑ **Wickedness Increase** (Ffrr, UK).

E General Levy's 1993 debut set for Fashion, *The Wickeder General*, was a landmark in the development of post-Shabba/Buju deejaying in the UK. The ground-breaking hits, "Heat", "Breeze" and "The Wig" were all included, alongside previously unreleased tracks that confirmed the arrival of a major talent. *Wickedness Increase* was essentially the same set, but with a new sleeve, and the addition of further gems.

FASHION RECORDS: THE A-CLASS STORY

Since its launch in 1980, Chris Lane and John MacGillivray's **Fashion** label has been a dominant player among UK reggae studio-cum-record companies. The business began as a small four-track studio under MacGillivray's Dub Vendor record store in Clapham Junction, South London, and from the outset it encompassed all facets of reggae, taking inispiration from Studio One (whose *Hi Fashion Dub* album inspired the label's name), and, in Kingston tradition, building its own in-house production style at its revamped **A-Class** studio (in nearby Forest Hill). There, the label creates its own rhythms with people like Mafia & Fluxy, Jazwad, and members of Aswad and the Massive Horns, as well as employing tracks from Donovan Germain's Penthouse setup in Kingston.

In addition to success with practically every sort of deejay, from **Smiley Culture** to **General Levy**, Fashion has established itself as the premier UK outfit for quality singers. Its first release was **Dee Sharp**'s brilliant vocal "Let's Dub It Up" but this was soon followed by dancehall hits from **Andrew Paul** and **Mikey General**, and immaculate lovers rock 45s from soulful vocalists such as **Keith Douglas**, **Michael Gordon**, **John McLean**, **Nerious Joseph**, **Peter Hunningale**, **Carlton Lewis** and **Vivian Jones**, the superb **Janet-Lee Davis** and **Winsome**. The label has also been graced by **Barry Boom** (aka Maxi Priest's producer Paul Robinson), who has had a series of 1990s solo hits, notably "Making Love" and "Number One Girl".

Besides the strongest local talent, almost every Jamaican visitor of note has also visited A-Class. These have included long-established stars like roots heroes **Johnny Clarke**, **Junior Delgado** and **Glen Brown**, as well as Studio One alumni **Horace Andy**, **Alton Ellis** (a long-term resident in London) and **Carlton Manning**. In most cases these singers have been caught in their finest form in years. Alongside the veteran names have been equally distinguished recordings from some of the most talented performers to emerge in the 1980s/1990s – including **Frankie Paul**, **Leroy Gibbon**, **King Kong** and **Wayne Wonder** among vocalists, and deejays such as **Papa San** and **Cutty Ranks**.

Rhythms and lyrics employed by Fashion's performers have covered a similarly wide area, taking in dancehall anthems, sweet-skanking lovers and hard roots, as well as cultural tunes with a sweet lovers vibe. Fashion have always been sharp to trends from Kingston and responded to the popular 'combination' format of the late 1980s with **Philip Leo & C.J. Lewis**'s "Why Do Fools Fall In Love", a spirited and original interpretation of Frankie Lymon & the Teenagers' doo-wop hit. Likewise, when Sly & Robbie were a little slow in releasing Thriller's "Tickle Me" in 1984 (the most popular dubplate on the London sound-system scene), Fashion beat them to it with two equally compelling cuts of their own – Nerious Joseph's "Sensi Crisis" and Horace Andy's "Gateman".

The label was also quick to accept the biggest upset reggae music had ever known, competing with all the Jamaican versions of the initial digital hit, "Under Me Sleng Teng", with **Peter King**'s "Step On the Gas" and **Andrew Paul**'s "Who's Gonna Make the Dance Ram", cuts that brought something fresh to 1985's most-versioned rhythm.

In the 1990s, Fashion responded to the rise of **jungle**, initially a British offshoot of techno that often incorporated samples from reggae classics, recording junglist figures like DJ Rap and DJ SS. They also made the case for the opposition, issuing deejay **Starkey Banton**'s amusingly dismissive "Jungle Bungle" ("One bag a noise and a whole heap a sample/That's something my ear holes can't handle!").

VARIOUS ARTISTS – FASHION PRODUCTIONS

⦾ **A Fashion Statement: The Fashion Records Story** (RAS, US).

A well-presented selection of Fashion's reggae (and on a couple of occasions pop) hits. It's pointless to talk of highlights: the set draws together the best from what is anyway an exemplary catalogue. If fault has to be found it surely lies in neither Papa San or Glen Brown being represented.

◑ **Not Just Ragga** (Fashion, UK).

A tongue-in-cheek but apt title for a collection of hits (plus a couple of fresh tracks) that demonstrates the true breadth of 1990s reggae: from the immaculate lovers rock of Janet-Lee Davis's "Do You Remember 2", through Starkey Banton's no-nonsense "Jungle Bungle", to Vivian Jones & Nico Junior's 'cultural' "Dedicated To His Majesty".

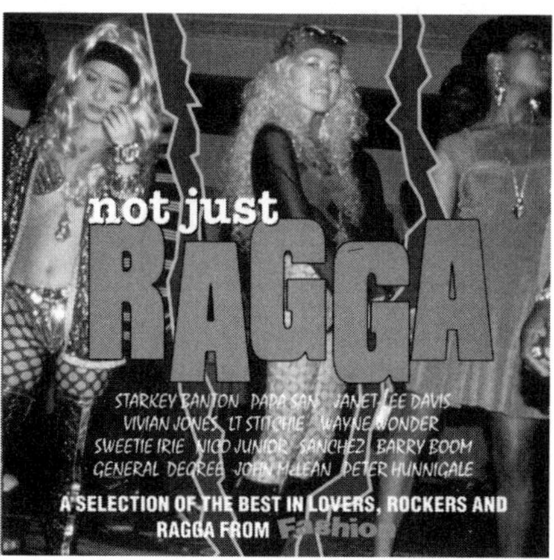

◑ **Heat** (Fashion, UK).

This one-rhythm album is based on "Heat" – one of the 45s that established London deejay General Levy – with Sly Dunbar and the UK's Leroy Mafia supplying drum and bass. Here, Mike Anthony, Singing Melody, Winsome and Top Cat step forward to sing or deejay.

GLEN BROWN

● **Play Music From the East** (Fashion, UK).

Not one of Fashion's best-selling albums, though Brown's distinctive melodica over superb A-Class roots rhythms was pretty compelling. Includes great versions of Junior Delgado's "Bus I Skull", Shako Lee's "None A Jah Jah Children" and Frankie Paul's "A No Nutten".

NERIOUS JOSEPH

● **Love's Gotta Take Its Time** (Fashion, UK).

Nerious Joseph is another consistent UK-based singer awaiting due recognition. His initial reggae hit, "Sensi Crisis", voiced typical dancehall/roots concerns, but this 1987 debut album has him in predominatly lovers mood, with a full, rather traditional, vocal approach proving the equal of any in the field. Includes "No One Night Stand", the best known of his romantic offerings.

◑ **Guidance** (Fashion, UK).

This more culturally oriented album arrived five years later, and benefited from excellent originals and sensitive interpretations of the Meditations' "Babylon Trap Them", Bob Marley's "Sun Is Shining" and the Light of Saba's "Words Of Wisdom". All the classical qualities of the best Jamaican vocal music, but produced and mixed by Chris Lane and Gussie P in south London.

FRANKIE PAUL

● **FP the Greatest** (Fashion, UK).

Recorded at both Fashion's own A-Class studio in South London and Donovan Germain's Penthouse in Kingston, this has Frankie Paul in his usual vocally exuberant mood and touching all his favourite topics – love, the dancehall, rude boys and a little self-promotion. Not a weak moment, and among his strongest albums after those for King Jammy.

SWEETIE IRIE

◑ **DJ For the Future** (Mango, UK).

Of the generation of UK deejays to emerge after the initial MC boom of the early 1980s, Sweetie Irie has most successfully merged the rockstone tradition of Jamaican chatters with a recognizably British style. This album is built around the hits that brought him to public notice, "On And On", "Magga Man", "New Talk" and "She Want It", and the only possible reservation is that a voice of his power could be dealing with weightier topics.

ADRIAN BOOT

Maxi Priest takes off

TOP CAT

◑ **9 Lives Of the Cat** (9 Lives, UK).

◑ **Cat O'Nine Tales** (9 Lives, UK).

E Top Cat's debut set drew together his initial hits from several labels, including Fashion, Gussie P, his own Nine Lives and Saxon – and it's hard to find deejay records from anywhere that match tracks like "Over Yu Body" or "Request the Style" for sheer panache and sense of style. *Cat O'Nine Tales*, the follow-up, had hits every bit as accomplished, including "Wine Up Your Body" and the anthemic "Smoke the Sensi".

Saxon singers: Maxi Priest and Roger Robin

In the same period as the Saxon deejays were redefining what it meant to be a UK MC, a couple of singers were performing alongside them on the sound. The first to develop fully his own style and take it beyond the dancehall was **Maxi Priest** (b. Max Elliot, London). He was trained as a carpenter and first worked for Saxon in that capacity, after which he joined the sound as a singer, performing over the same rhythms as the MCs. Again, the model had been provided by what was heard of Jamaican sounds and their employment of dancehall vocalists like Sugar Minott, Sammy Dread and Little John, who sang over exclusive rhythm tracks in a similar manner as the deejays chatted. Blessed with a voice more than a cut above the dancehall average, and rooted in the rich soil of both vintage Jamaican reggae and US soul, Priest had by the mid-1980s linked up with producer and writer **Paul Robinson** (aka the singer Barry Boom – see the box on Fashion Records).

Maxi Priest's accomplished debut album *You're Safe* resulted from this partnership, and after that it was only a matter of time before crossing over on an international scale. Crisp 45s like "Let Me Know", "Good-bye To Love" and "Close To You" (all Ten) have been among the most impressive recorded offerings from any UK reggae artist. Few people might have expected it when he was singing with Saxon in South London community centres, but his blend of dancehall, lovers rock, roots and soul not only struck a chord with the mainstream pop audience in the UK but has found acceptance in the far larger market of the US.

The Jamaican dancehall tradition of performers beginning their careers at remarkably young ages also manifested itself on Saxon sound. For the second important singing talent to emerge from Saxon, **Roger Robin** (b. Roger Williams, 1967, Bristol), was only 11 when he first took the mike on the sound. By the time he was in his early twenties, he had developed a bitter-sweet singing style that placed him in a tradition of reflective Jamaican roots singers like Little Roy. By then he was also writing well-crafted songs that perfectly suited his vocal approach. "More Love", for Saxon's own record label, topped the UK reggae charts in 1990, and two years later he was being produced by Rowen 'Spider Ranks' Johnson, who contributed strong songs of his own to the Robin repertoire. "Show Me the Way" and "It's Your Choice", along with the 'combination' effort with Dennis Brown, "Keep It Burning", were among further Robin successes for Saxon, while the Spider Ranks imprint was responsible for a string of hits, including his most haunting record to date, "Fist Full Of Dollars".

MAXI PRIEST

Bonafide (Ten, UK; RAS, US).

E This appeared in 1990 at about the same time as Maxi Priest's first entry into the UK pop charts, and with worldwide acceptance just around the corner (the soul track, "How Can We Ease the Pain", was his initial US hit). He covers all aspects of contemporary reggae, from roots to the most romantic of ballads, and recording sessions took place in London and Kingston, using both reggae capitals' most distinguished musicians. Includes the popular "Close To You".

You're Safe (Ten, UK; RAS, US).

Maxi Priest's assured debut set from 1985 had the blend of roots, dancehall and soulful lovers rock already perfected. Listening to tracks like "Should I" and "In the Springtime" now, it is only too easy to hear why luminaries as diverse as Shabba Ranks, Sly & Robbie, Soul II Soul and Shaggy would eventually want to work alongside him.

Intentions (Ten, UK; RAS, US).

The all-important second album from the following year, *Intentions* paired Priest with Aswad and more than confirmed his promise. Rather than being built around already successful singles, this was obviously conceived as an album and as such represented another step forward.

ROGER ROBIN

Undiluted (Spider Ranks, UK).

"Fist Full Of Dollars" is the highlight on this debut set recorded at the Mixing Lab studio in Kingston, though "Matter Of Time", "Working" and another hit, "Wisdom Grows", are not far behind. Deservedly the winner of the British Reggae Industry's "Best British Reggae Album" award for 1993.

VARIOUS ARTISTS – SAXON PRODUCTIONS

The Best Of Saxon Volumes One, Two & Three (Saxon, UK).

These three sets are the perfect introduction to Saxon's bright, clean but still weighty sound, and rank among the most important reggae hits of the 1990s (from anywhere). Among the gems on the first volume are Peter Hunningale's "Baby Please" and Roger Robin's "I'll Give You More", while the second and third volumes have equally strong selections. All music that needed no hype to sell to its target audience.

Saxon Studio Presents Dance Hall Specials Volume One (Saxon, UK).

E Released not long after Saxon Studio International had won the World Cup Sound Clash against rivals from both Jamaica and New York, and featuring the kind of 'specials' necessary for flopping the competition at such events. Top names suitably adapt their most popular records in praise of the sound in question, including Michael Rose with "Stalk Of Sensemilla", Dawn Penn with "No No No" and The Abyssinians with "Declaration Of Rights" (worth the price of the set by itself).

The roots revival

While the musicians employed by Fashion provide a UK mirror to mainstream reggae developments, the UK also has an insular **roots revival** scene, playing a new wave roots and dub that has little following in Jamaica. This emerged in a low-key way during the second half of the 1980s, through the efforts of both black and white followers of roots reggae from over a decade before. They had grown disillusioned with new Jamaican music during the dancehall era (slackness, celebrations of the dancehall, and reworkings of Studio One rhythms), and alienated even more (at least at its onset) by "Under Me Sleng Teng" and the switch to digital instrumentation.

Jah Shaka keeps the faith

The roots scene's main point of focus over the past two decades has been **Jah Shaka**'s sound system, the only significant system that kept faith with 1970s ideals. A self-styled Zulu warrior, Shaka defied fashion (and falling audiences) with his commitment to Rastafarian beliefs – and relentless steppers rhythms as the most fitting vehicle for their expression throughout the 1980s. He played old roots recordings, a few fresh ones from Yard that met his criteria, and his own productions, and by the close of the decade audiences had returned, among them a strong showing of whites and Asians, who felt far more at ease at his dances than ragga ones.

Shaka collaborated with many UK-based musicians, including the Twinkle Brothers and, perhaps most satisfying, Aswad, with whom he produced a dub set in 1984. The Shaka dubs, with their pronounced emphasis on foot-drum, can become wearing, but his work with the Disciples generally manages to avoid the clichés of the UK new dub style. By the early 1990s Shaka, a frequent visitor to Jamaica, was using the Jamaican session band the **Firehouse Crew** for his rhythms. This combination produced albums by Studio One veteran Willie Williams, Icho Candy, and two worthwhile Max Romeo sets. Shaka has also worked with Horace Andy and Prince Alla.

Norman Grant's **Twinkle Brothers** were among those who became associated with the Jah Shaka crowd. The original band had established itself as an accomplished vocal/instrumental group on Jamaica's North Coast hotel circuit in the early 1970s, cutting records for Bunny Lee among others, before relocating to the UK, where their records and gigs provided another alternative to those who would not set foot in a modern dancehall.

JAH SHAKA PRODUCTIONS

● **Commandments Of Dub Volumes 1–10** (Shaka Music, UK).

This is where the UK roots revival started, and to a large extent remains centred: relentless 'steppers' rhythms reduced to their bas(s)ics. Followers will already have the entire series; newcomers should try the third chapter, subtitled *Lion's Share Of Dub*, which gains from a touch more imagination in both the rhythm tracks and the man's mixing.

◉ **Jah Shaka Meets Aswad In Addis Ababa Studio** (Shaka Music, UK).

Tough dub set from 1984 that avoids the routine dub-by-numbers approach. Aswad's rhythms are uniformly propulsive, whether their own originals or the fine versions of Pablo's "Cassava Piece" ("Aswad Special") and the Soul Vendors' "Drum Song" ("Drum Dub").

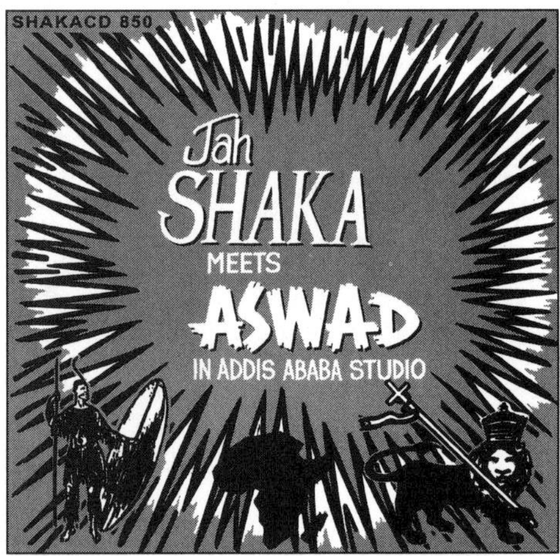

TWINKLE BROTHERS

◑ **Don't Forget Africa** (Twinkle, UK).

◑ **Dub With Strings** (Twinkle, UK).

◑ **Higher Heights (Twinkle Inna Polish Stylee)** (Twinkle, UK).

Anyone interested in true international reggae should sample these three sets. The Twinkle Brothers have a strong following in Eastern Europe and this led to their recording in Warsaw with the Tribunia-Tutee Family, a Polish wedding band featuring violins and cello. The results are at least intriguing, with the *Higher Heights* set taking the experiment the furthest, and featuring the Polish family singing their folk songs over the Twinkles' rhythms. Those not quite ready for that might like to ease themselves in gently with the dub counterpart to the first collaboration: a typically heavy Norman Grant dub set, but with the Polish musicians' contributions in curiously supportive sync.

On-U-Sound

Equally important have been the dub excursions to emerge from the **On-U-Sound** label, owned by **Adrian Sherwood** (b. 1958), and Neil Fraser/Mad Professor's more traditional **Ariwa Sounds**. These too have been out of kilter with the directions of Jamaican reggae – though not backward-looking as both producers employed 1970s dub techniques and steppers rhythms as a base for aural experiment.

On-U man Adrian Sherwood mixing it up

Sherwood in particular is a true eclectic, moving effortlessly between reggae, post-punk, blues and indie rock fields. He worked for UK distributor Carl Palmer in the mid-1970s and by 1978 was running the Hitrun label and releasing Jamaican-recorded music by such as Bobby Melody and the deejay Prince Far-I. When Far-I toured the UK in 1979 he was backed by **Creation Rebel**, a band featuring longtime Sherwood associate **Clifton 'Bigga' Morrison** (currently a member of the excellent **Jazz Jamaica** ska-jazz band), and drummer **Valentine 'Style' Scott**, shortly to join Roots Radics. Sherwood formed his label On-U-Sound in 1980 and began releasing music by Far-I, Creation Rebel, Bim Sherman, London Underground and the Mothmen. Over the next few years he fused elements of reggae with rock, dance and funk influences, achieving a coherent and individual production style, and gained chart success with **Gary Clail**.

The music created by On-U has been released under a confusing array of group identities – among them **New Age Steppers**, **African Head Charge**, **Singers and Players** and **Dub Syndicate** – but what is clear is that it laid the foundation for much of the modern UK dub scene, with its emphasis on layered percussion and sound effects. Sherwood's projects often feature Jamaican vocalist **Bim Sherman** and Carlton 'Bubbler' Ogilvie, along with former Sugarhill sessionmen **Keith Leblanc**, **Doug Wimbish** and **Skip McDonald**. Recent and innovative outings have included an album by Bim Sherman fusing acoustic reggae with strings from an Indian movie playback orchestra; Skip McDonald's wonderful **Little Axe** discs, with their seamless blend of blues and dub; **Two Bad Card** – Morrison and Sherwood with guests like deejays Dennis Alcapone and U-Brown; and **Akabu**, an accomplished, seriously underrated all-women band.

Sherwood has also continued to do production work with visiting Jamaican artists, including Lee Perry, Congo Ashanti Roy and 'Deadly' Headley Bennett, as well as remixing for dance and rock artists. Since 1994 he has operated out of his own studio in Walthamstow, East London.

VARIOUS ARTISTS

⦿ **Reggae Archive Volumes I & 2** (On-U, UK).
These two compilations cover the years 1977–82 and measure Sherwood's transition from Jamaican-recorded music to a more eclectic UK sound. The first set has Hitrun releases by Carol Kalphat (the excellent "African Land") and Prince Far-I, Jamaican productions by Bim Sherman, including his "Golden Locks", and early Creation Steppers material. The second collects most of the tracks from Jamaican saxophonist Headley Bennett's "35 Years From Alpha", along with Creation Steppers with mad soprano jazz saxophonist Lol Coxhill and more Sherman vocal tracks.

CREATION REBEL

● **Starship Africa** (4D, UK).
One of the earliest Sherwood productions which attempted, pretty successfully, to blend reggae rhythms with a range of studio textures and industrial/sci-fi effects. On-U family members like drummer 'Style' Scott and keyboard player 'Bigga' Morrison are in the line-up; the programme features just two compositions, the title cut and "Space Movement", each extended over a side of vinyl.

DOCTOR PABLO & THE DUB SYNDICATE

● **North Of the River Thames** (On-U, UK).
Predominantly atmospheric melodica instrumentals – the album includes a dedication to Augustus Pablo – this is exemplary UK roots made during 1982–84, and the presence of Roydel Johnson (congos), Style Scott and former Matumbi bassist George Oban ensures high authenticity factor.

DUB SYNDICATE

⦿ **Research & Development** (On-U, UK).
An appropriate title for a selection of tracks from the most exciting UK new wave roots outfits, all given the Adrian Sherwood treatment at the controls. The Disciples, Zion Train, Dougie Wardrop, Iration Steppas and practically everyone who matters on the scene are represented.

BIM SHERMAN

⦿ **Miracle** (Mantra/Beggars Banquet, UK).
Disparate elements – 'playback' strings orchestrated by Suraj Sathe, Talvin Singh's tablas, former Sugarhill sessioneers (guitarist Skip McDonald and bassist Doug Wimbish) and Sherman's meditative lovers and cultural songs – are brought together beautifully on *Miracle*. The lack of a conventional drum kit is barely noticed and yet this is still recognizably reggae, albeit of a uniquely mutated kind.

LITTLE ROY

⦿ **Longtime** (On-U, UK).
Apt title for this first album in eight years from the veteran Jamaican vocalist. Sherwood's production is conventional by his standards, with no trace of the dub excesses, and the On-U studio has rarely sounded better. Little Roy delivers nine new songs and a recut of his Rasta-affirming "Righteous Man".

Ariwa

Working out of his studios in Peckham and Thornton Heath in South London, **Neil Fraser** (aka **Mad Professor**) has created an equally recognizable mixing style. His studio musicians – often featuring **Black Steel** on bass – were able to forge their own strong sound over a series of dub albums which did much to maintain market interest in the form when Jamaican producers stopped releasing their own dub sets. As well as scoring notable successes with reggae styles from lovers through roots and dub, Mad Professor has produced veteran Jamaican deejays – U-Roy, Ranking Joe and Dennis Alcapone – with considerable empathy. His many collaborations with **Lee Perry** are both funny and brilliant, even if they don't get near the heights attained by Scratch at the Black Ark. Mad Professor has toured ceaselessly and very successfully with Ariwa artists for many years, most notably with UK-based deejay **Macka B**.

Dub Me Crazy: Neil Fraser, the Mad Professor

THE MAD PROFESSOR

◑ **Dub Me Crazy Parts 1–10** (Ariwa, UK).

Alongside – and sometimes in collaboration with – Jah Shaka, Neil Fraser/Mad Professor pursued a course of dubonic experiment throughout the 1980s, and still likes to dabble at the controls in between turning out accomplished lovers rock hits. All of his *Dub Gone Crazy* series of albums have been well received, and none more so than parts 3, 5 and 10. Music that possesses a strong appeal to indie rockers while being equally suited to a spot of warrior stepping.

VARIOUS ARTISTS

◑ **Roots Daughters** (Ariwa, UK).

Lovers rock might be the area of UK reggae in which women have been best represented, but Neil Fraser has employed the female voice in a more roots context. The best-known track here is Audrey's "English Girl", originally available as a Jah Shaka 12" single, but equally worthy of note are Aisha's "Guide & Protect", Rasheda's "Mr. Roots Man" and Fabian Miranda's "Fire". The first and best of three such collections from the Mad Professor.

The new wave of sound systems

As the 1980s progressed, a number of Shaka's followers decided to take a more active role, forming their own sound systems (invariably based on the Shaka approach). These new roots sounds – including **Mannasseh**, **Boom-Shacka-Lacka** (linked to the roots fanzine of the same name), **Channel One**, **Iration**, **Jah Trinity** and **Aba Shanti-I** (run by a former deejay from the esteemed Jah Tubby's East London sound) – helped to spread the gospel. Dub played an ever-growing role, following the examples of Shaka, Adrian Sherwood and Neil Fraser, and late-1980s records such as "Seventh Seal" from **Sound Iration** (associated with the Mannasseh sound system) and "Warrior Stance" from **Dread & Fred** (released on Jah Shaka's imprint). Both discs were instrumental/dub workouts, in the tradition of Aswad's 1980 'steppers' classic, "Warrior Charge", and have acted as templates for much that has followed.

Even before the brothers **Russ** and **Lol Bell-Brown**, who came from a Surrey suburb, began the Boom-Shakka-Lacka sound system, they had been experimenting with rhythm tracks of their own. It was inevitable that others on the same underground circuit would eventually begin to create their own music and rhythms – if for no other reason than the shortage of fresh material from Jamaica that fulfilled their demands. The models for such committed figures as the **Disciples** (Russ and Lol, again), **Jonah Dan**, **Alpha & Omega**, Dougie Wardrop's **Bush Chemists** and **Centry**, **Aba Shanti-I** and **Dub Judah** were Jamaican 'steppers' records from the late 1970s/early 1980s, and above all Lee Perry and Augustus Pablo. Yabby You is another much-cited inspiration, though any direct influence of his reflective music remains harder to detect.

Not least because of the understandable reluctance of these musicians, far removed from the Kingston ghettos, to sing about slavery days, the new wave roots outfits have concentrated on instrumental/dub excursions. But a handful of promising vocalists have emerged, including **Tenna Stelin**, **Donette Forte**, **Willy Stepper** (formerly of respected Jamaican vocal trio, Creation Steppers), **Kendrick Andy** and **Empress Rasheda**.

Perhaps the most promising and individual of the bunch is **Danny Red**, who was signed by Columbia in 1993 on the strength of *I Don't Care*, an album recorded in Nick Mannasseh's Brixton studio. It showcased his singjay and chant-based style – derived from such as Junior Reid – to great effect. Red followed the album with a series of 12" singles, working brilliantly with UK dance outfits like Leftfield, and ragga deejays like Top Cat, Gospel Fish, Danger B and Starkey Banton, and his major label album debut, *Riddimwize*. Chart success didn't come, however, and the first roots artist to be signed to a UK major label in twenty years was dropped. He remains an artist with great potential.

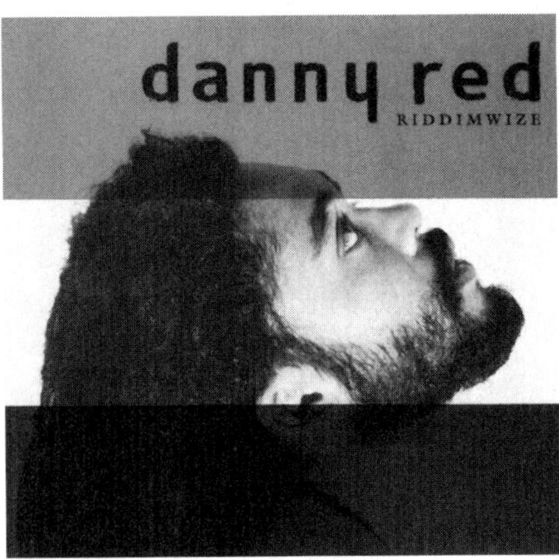

KENDRICK ANDY

◑ **Another Night In the Ghetto** (Fence Beater, UK).

A promising debut album from the West Country-based roots singer. Sufferahs' music that does not rely on heavy basslines at the expense of everything else and which looks to classic-period Studio One for inspiration.

THE BUSH CHEMISTS MEET THE DUB ORGANISER

◑ **Fashion Records & Conscious Sound Present A Dub Convention** (Fashion/Conscious Sounds, UK).

Cover imagery of a mixing-board and dope leaves (along with track titles like "Four Wise Men") might be yawn-inducing, but the music manages to maintain interest. One side is mixed by Dougie Wardrop at his Conscious Sounds studio, the other by Chris Lane at A-Class, and both men clearly knew what they wanted to achieve.

THE DISCIPLES

◑ **Hail H.I.M. In Dub** (Roots Records, UK).

The Disciples have consistently been among the more imaginative new wave roots outfits in the UK. *Hail H.I.M In Dub* consists, not too surprisingly, of versions to tracks from the Empress Rasheda album (see below), with said voice drifting effectively in and out of the intelligent mixes. A worthy companion piece that stands just as well on its own.

◑ **For Those Who Understand** (Roots Records, UK).

This comes with a photograph of the Boom-Shaka-Lacka sound system on the cover to help the listener slip into the required mood, and represents raw dubplate material familiar to the sound's followers. Concern with texture and thoughtful use of samples lift it some way above the generic norm.

DREAD & FRED

◑ **Ironworks** (Jah Shaka, UK).

A seminal work in the development of the modern UK roots movement, with instrumentals in the accustomed Shaka steppers mould played by two Bedford-based dreads employing digital instrumentation. "Warrior Stance", which as a 1988 12" 45 was something of a milestone for the genre, is included, with other weighty tracks such as "African Dawn" and "Mission Dub" brimming with the same confidence.

EMPRESS RASHEDA

◑ **Hail H.I.M.** (Roots Records, UK).

Committed vocals in the Fabian Miranda/Dhaima/Sister Frika mould, over sturdy Disciples rhythms. The audience for this particular facet of reggae knows exactly what it likes, and so – quite obviously – do all the people involved in this project. Includes "Give Jah Praise", which gained some attention as a 12" single on Rasheda's own label.

DANNY RED

◑ **I Don't Care** (Roots Records, UK).

Red's debut is a wonderful album, revisiting in an entirely independent spirit. He tackles Burning Spear's "Old Jill" with worthwhile results, as well as a cut of Horace Andy/Keith Hudson's "I'm Alright" rhythm.

⊙ **Riddimwize** (Columbia, UK).

It's a mystery why this major label debut didn't have a bigger impact. Perhaps the problem lay in covering too many bases: the set moves from the distinctly Burning Spear-influenced "Be Grateful" to "Rolling Stone", a slightly uneasy attempt to follow Chaka Demus and Pliers into the charts. However, excellent roots songs like "Rise Up" ensure this album will last longer than the major label interest.

Reggae in the USA

DAVID CORIO

9

previous page

Mr Boombastic: Shaggy

Reggae in the USA

Reggae took root in the **USA** in much the same way as in Britain – through the Jamaican community established in New York and other major cities. In contrast with London, though, it was not until the 1980s that the **Brooklyn** and **Bronx** areas of the Big Apple became important as more than distribution centres for reggae from the Kingston studios. Other American black music forms – soul, funk, jazz – were immediately accessible to the Jamaican émigré musicians and offered a more lucrative range of outlets for their own talents.

Nevertheless, by the mid-1970s, **Lloyd 'Bullwackie' Barnes** had set up the first reggae recording studio in New York, and successfully bid for attention with a roots sound that was its own. Barnes, originally a singer who had recorded for Prince Buster in the early 1960s, initially started producing in partnership with 'Munchie' Jackson in the early 1970s. By the end of the decade, he was recording on his own account locally based Jamaican singers and musicians like **Wayne Jarrett**, and illustrious visitors from Jamaica, including **Sugar Minott** and **Horace Andy**. Barnes also recorded a series of sometimes stunningly good dub albums during the same period.

As the 1980s progressed several other reggae-oriented studios became established in the US, among them the **HC & F Studio** on Long Island, owned and operated by **Phillip Smart**, an engineer who had worked closely with King Tubby in Jamaica up to 1976. By 1991 Smart was hitting in the Jamaican dancehalls with US-recorded music like Dirtsman's "Hot This Year"; today it is the leading reggae studio in the US. Other pioneering studios in the 1980s included Hyman Wright and Percy Chin's **Jah Life** in New York and **Delroy Wright**'s studio in Washington DC, and from the mid-1980s **Don One** and **Living Room** in **Brooklyn**, and Kenneth Black's **Skengdon** and Willie Lindo's **Heavy Beat** in **Miami**. Both Miami studios notably succeeded in scoring with the ultra-partisan Jamaican dancehall crowd. Deejay Chaka Demus's massive "Young Gal Business" was recorded at Skengdon in 1987, while Lindo's version of the Studio One/Slim Smith rhythm "Rougher Yet" propelled hits for Kashief Lindo and Wayne Wade in 1992, as well as a big-selling one-rhythm album, *Nice & Ruff*.

The **dancehall** phase of the early 1980s – driven in the US by a strong sound-system scene in the Bronx and Brooklyn – did not see any major American reggae stars emerge; the focus still rested largely on visiting Jamaican 'supas'. Nonetheless, performers like vocalist **Scion Sachay Success** and deejay **Mikey Jarrett**, indicated that NY-recorded reggae was maturing fast. Then, mid-decade, the highly original and eclectic deejay/singer/rapper **Shinehead** came up through the Brooklyn sound-system circuit – he worked on the African Love set – to conquer both the Jamaican and UK reggae worlds.

Shinehead was followed in the next decade by the even more popular **Shaggy**, one of the great crossover successes of the ragga era. Shaggy's rise was due in no small part to the exceptional NY-based producer **Robert Livingston**, and as the 1990s progressed his ragga/hip-hop fusion developed as the dominant American reggae sound, with labels such as Bobby Konder's **Massive B** and **Profile**, and artists like **Red Fox**, **Louie Ranking**, the deejay/vocal duo **Born Jamericans** (Horace 'Headley Shine' Payne and 'Notch' Howell), and ragga rappers **Jamal-ski** and **Mad Lion** joining the crowd of Jamaican-based deejays in chatting over hip-hop beats.

US reggae takes root

Despite a long-established Jamaican community in New York, there was just one US studio – Lloyd Barnes's **Bullwackies** – producing significant reggae before the 1980s. The US was an important market for reggae from the early 1970s on, but labels such as Brooklyn-based **Clocktower** were receiving more than enough material from Jamaican producers like Bunny Lee and Lee Perry to need to worry about financing sessions of their own. About the only significant US-based reggae performer pre-international-period Wailers was **Johnny Nash**, a Texan soul singer who visited Kingston to record.

Johnny Nash: Texan reggae star

America's reggae roots could hardly have found a more bizarre soil than Houston, Texas. Yet this was the home of soul singer/actor **Johnny Nash**, a man responsible for some of the first US-produced reggae tracks and for promoting American interest in the (then) little-known Bob Marley.

In the late 1960s Nash had enjoyed a major hit in the US soul charts with "Let's Move & Groove Together" and was also running the JODA and JAD labels with his manager Danny Simms. He visited Jamaica in 1968 with a view to recording there and found the island pulsating to the confident strains of rocksteady, the coolness of which could not have been better suited to the American singer's own refined vocal style.

Nash embarked on a series of recordings with some of Kingston's finest session musicians, cutting "Hold Me Tight" and a version of Sam Cooke's "Cupid", both of which became international pop chart hits. The Texan also met Bob Marley and immediately recognized the strength of Marley's songwriting. Danny Simms produced several albums' worth of tracks with Marley that were aimed at the US market but failed to take off. Better received at the time were Nash's own interpretations of Marley material, recorded in 1971 with the **Wailers** providing the rhythms, and including the sensuous "Stir It Up" and "Guava Jelly".

JOHNNY NASH

⦿ **The Best Of Johnny Nash** (Sony Music, US).
Nash's forays into rocksteady/early reggae are easy to dismiss as lightweight but they were successful in their own terms and milestones in the international acceptance of Jamaican music. The Texan soul singer adapted seemingly effortlessly to recording in Kingston, and his hits – "I Can See Clearly Now", "Hold Me Tight", "Cupid", "Guava Jelly" and "Stir It Up" – have dated well. Pop-reggae, certainly, but entirely delightful.

Lloyd Barnes and Bullwackies

Lloyd Barnes (b. c. 1948, Jamaica), aka **Wackie**, did some recording in Jamaica, as a singer for Prince Buster, before migrating to New York in the early 1970s. There, he set up a studio at 4731 White Plains Road, in the Bronx, recording both visiting and resident Jamaicans with consistently interesting results. Employing his own session band, the **Reckless Breed**, he developed a hard roots style that was highly distinctive (for all its debt to Perry's Black Ark sound), and can be heard on records that appeared on his **Bullwackies** label, and its many subsidiaries, including Wackie's, City Line, Aries, Wisdom Track, Senrab, Footprints, Dougies, Hamma and Rawse.

Among the established Jamaican luminaries with whom Wackie worked to striking effect were **Horace Andy**, **Sugar Minott**, former Heptone **Leroy Sibbles**, **Tyrone Evans** and the veteran tenor saxman **Roland Alphonso**. Among the less celebrated but gifted were **Wayne Jarrett** (one of the better singers who modelled his approach on Horace Andy), **K.C. White**, **Lloyd Hemmings**, **Annette Brissett** and one of Lloyd Daley's star performers from the early 1970s, **Audley Rollins**.

Sessions with new US-based artists were as remarkable. Outstanding 45s that appeared in the late 1970s/early 1980s included **Happy Love**'s "Down In the Valley", **Ras Ifton & the Zionites**' "Look Over Yonder", **Joe Auxmite**'s "No Equal Rights In Babylon", **Noel Delahaye**'s "Working For the Rentman" and **Joe Morgan**'s "Basement Session". These and many more still wait for the CD compilation that Wackie's productions deserve.

Dubbing up 241st Street

In common with Jamaican producers, Bullwackie issued plenty of dub on album, as well as the customary B-side versions. The **African Roots dub series** began in 1977 when **Clive Hunt** – then living in New York and a key member of Wackie's session crew – kicked off with the initial volume, released on the Five Arts label, again based in the Bronx. The album carried a distinct Black Ark influence, audible in its use of drum machines and sound effects.

The series was then continued on the main Wackie's label. Working with Jamaican musicians of the calibre of Jackie Mittoo, Clive Hunt and Leroy Sibbles, Wackie and co-engineer Douglas Levy created a recognizable studio sound and deployed it to startling and original effect. They continued to maintain an interest in mixing dub long after most Jamaican producers had abandoned the form, and in 1985 produced one of the earliest digital dub sets – *African Roots Chapter V* – with longtime Wackie's musician **Fabian Cooke** handling the drum, keyboard and DX programs.

Around this time Wackie began a partnership with Sonny Ochai of Tachyon Records in Japan, producing ragga and dancehall discs primarily for the Japanese market, a partnership that lasted until 1994 when Wackie returned to Jamaica in order to begin the construction of a new studio with Sugar Minott. In 1996 the Wackie back catalogue started to be reissued on CD through Wackie's London associate, Rae Cheddie.

ROLAND ALPHONSO

Roll On (Wackie's, US).

The sort of understated instrumental album that easily gets overlooked at the time of its release, while possessing just the sort of subtle qualities that ensures enduring appeal. The title track is yet another inspired version of "Declaration Of Rights" to add those to those you already treasure.

HORACE ANDY

Dance Hall Style (Wackie's, US).

E The Wackie's approach proved particularly suited to Horace Andy's individual vocal style. Given that he played a major role in the building of the rhythms – playing bass, and both rhythm and lead guitar – it is perhaps not too surprising that his fragile but moving voice has few better contexts in which to express itself. Even the re-recordings of old favourites – his own "Money Money" and "Lonely Woman", as well as Lloyd Robinson's "Cuss Cuss" – manage to sound inspired, and the fresh material is their equal.

LLOYD BARNES PRODUCTIONS

African Roots Act V (Wackie's, US).

This pioneering digital dub sounds contemporary ten years on. Featuring saxophonist Jerry Johnson, guitarist Jerry Harris and Fabian Cooke on programming, these are the Wackie's versions of staples like "Far East" ("Cudjo"), "The Whip" ("Accompong Dub") and "Cyrus" ("Zulu Dub"). But the standout must be the dubbed-up sax cut of the "A Get A Lick" (aka "Billie Jean"), called here "Tor-Osaze Dub", which gets a furious workout from engineers Barnes and Levy.

● **The Dub Generals** (Wackie's, US).
An excellent 1997 compilation which brings together long-unavailable 12" mixes – "Rockfort Rock" – with similar versions of legendary Studio One rhythms. Hence the cuts of "Drum Song" and "Fatty Fatty" (here retitled "Song Maker" after the Cedric 'Im' Brooks & David Madden version called "Money Maker"). The hugely accomplished Clive Hunt both arranged the material and features strongly throughout this refreshing set.

CLIVE HUNT PRODUCTIONS

● **African Roots Act I (Five Arts Records, US).**
Highlights of this set include the mysterious "Addis Ababa Dubba", which sounds a lot like Lee Perry from his Super Ape period, as do several other tracks.

WAYNE JARRETT

◑ **Bubble Up** (Wackie's, UK/US).
Horace Andy imitator Wayne Jarrett can on occasion rise to the heights of his model. This remains his most scintillating album-length work, with six examples of impressive falsetto complemented by their dub workouts. Even his version of Andy's "Every Tongue Shall Tell" is effective, not least because of the superb Wackie's rhythm track behind it, while original material like "Brimstone & Fire", "Holy Mount Zion" (over a particularly lethal cut of "Drum Song") and the title track represent Bronx-style roots at very near its best.

SUGAR MINOTT

● **Wicked Ago Feel It** (Wackie's, US).
At the pinnacle of his popularity in the early 1980s. Sugar Minott's talent shone anywhere he decided to apply it, and Mr Barnes's Brooklyn studio was no exception. As with most of his albums after *Black Roots*, both lovers and 'cultural' topics are covered with equal feeling and flare. Includes a very different cut of his UK pop hit, "A Good Thing Going".

NY dancehall and ragga

US reggae reached new heights during the dancehall and ragga phases of the music, with forward-looking labels such as **Hyman Wright**'s Jah Life Time in the 1980s, and veteran studio engineer **Philip Smart**'s Tan Yah in the following decade. The former introduced **Barrington Levy** to the reggae world with his classic debut album recording Jamaican singers such as **Carlton Livingstone**, **Michael Prophet**, **Sammy Dread** and **King Kong**, and the New York-based **Scion Sachay Success**; while the latter has been responsible for excellent records from important Jamaican talents such as the late **Garnett Silk** and **Dirtsman**, and under-recorded New York ones like **Alton Black**, **Bajja Jed**, **Nike Fungus** and **Shelene & Andrew Bell**.

In these last two decades a trio of New York-based artists have emerged to make an impression in Jamaica itself, too. The first of these was **Shinehead** (b. Edmund Carl Aitken, Kent, England), who was born in the UK, then lived with his parents in Jamaica, before moving to New York in the mid-1970s. There, in the 1980s, he began his musical career with the local Downbeat International sound system, before joining Claude Evans's African Love, where he made his reputation as an extraordinarily talented deejay-rapper-singer-whistler. His first major hit,

DAVID CORIO

The brilliant Shinehead: a man ahead of his time

a take on Michael Jackson's "Billie Jean" (African Love Music), might have been based on one of the more obscure old Studio One rhythms – Bumps Oakley's "A Get A Lick" – but subsequent versions, of which there have been many, have owed everything to the track that propelled this unique figure to the fore.

Shinehead followed up with an equally brilliant album, *Rough & Rugged*, showcasing his incredible versatility of vocal styles, and his work since has been of similar high standard, whether rapping, singing or deejaying in Jamaican fashion. He is clearly the most influential US reggae artist to date, his fusion of dancehall with modern r&b and hip-hop beats anticipating the crossover success of such as Maxi Priest and Shabba Ranks a few years later. However, he has never had the success he deserves, maybe due to an unfocused image. Although his albums for US major Elektra have always contained brilliant tracks – and none better than "Strive" from 1990's *The Real Rock* – he has managed only one minor chart success, with a version of Sting's "Englishman In New York" in 1993. His most recent album, 1994's *Troddin'*, showed a more coherent approach but, whatever happens, his reputation is assured.

At about the same time as Shinehead was making international waves, a dancehall singer with the name **Scion Sachay Success** was also notching up hits in both the UK reggae charts and Jamaica. He faded pretty quickly – nothing has been heard of him for quite a while now – but there is no denying the dancehall excitement of the records he made for Jah Life Time (another label that grew out of a leading New York sound system) in the mid-1980s.

The next New York reggae performer to make an international impact turned out to have the widest appeal of all, and possibly the most enduring talent. The first international hit from **Shaggy** (b. Orville Richard Burrell, 1968, Kingston, Jamaica) was thought by many to be an inspired one-off, and few imagined New York ragga would repeat its phenomenal success. But Shaggy's updating of the Folks Brothers' 1958 Jamaican hit, "Oh Carolina" – exploiting the full potential of the original song in a totally modern setting – was to prove only the first of such flashes of inspiration. In 1995 Shaggy and producer **Robert Livingstone** superseded the success of the initial hit with the equally amazing "Boombastic" (Big Yard), which simultaneously topped the national charts in both the UK and US (aided in the UK by an attention-grabbing Levi's jeans commercial).

Shaggy's brilliant combination disc with **Mikey Spice**, "Shake Your Body" (Big Yard), bore further witness to a serious talent at work, and one capable of holding his own with the brightest of new Jamaican singing stars. Livingstone is also closely associated with another gifted Brooklyn deejay, **Red Fox** (b. Gareth Shelton), whose approach might be just a little too hard-core for the mass acceptance enjoyed by the always likeable Shaggy.

BORN JAMERICANS

⊙ Kids From Foreign (Delicious Vinyl, US).

Born in the USA to Jamaican families (hence the name) the duo of Horace Payne and Notch Howell

deliver their 1994 US hits like "Boom Shak-A-Tak" and "Cease & Seckle", fusing classic dancehall rhythms – "Stalag", "Hi-Fashion", "Prophesy" and "Shank I Shek" – with rugged hip-hop drums. The pair mix roughneck Jamaican style deejaying with yearning vocals, and sustain it with considerable style.

RED FOX

◑ **As A Matter Of Fox** (Elektra, JA; Elektra, US).

An uncompromising fourteen-track assault that, like most of the best reggae to emanate from New York in the late 1980s/early 1990s, is strongly informed by the city's hip-hop culture. Big Apple productions from Sting International, Bobby Kondors, Brand Nubian, DJ Premier and Sir Raphael sit easily alongside those from Kingston's Dave Kelly, Bobby Digital and Mikey Bennett to demonstrate the parallels between the two cities' musical cultures. Raw and not a little brutal, but the most consistent New York reggae album since Shinehead's debut.

SCION SACHAY SUCCESS

● **Success** (Jah Life Time, US).

Scion Sachay Success was one of the first New York-based reggae singers to mean anything in Kingston or London, and most of the records that put him on the map are gathered here, including "Pain A Back", "Put It On" and "Can't Leave Jah Alone". A blend of roots and dancehall hard as Brooklyn concrete.

SHAGGY

◑ **Pure Pleasure** (Greensleeves, UK; Virgin, US).

◑ **Boombastic Full Length Album** (Greensleeves, UK; Virgin, US).

Inevitably perhaps, given the 100 percent classic qualities of the 45s "Oh Carolina" (included on *Pure Pleasure*) and "Boombastic", neither of these albums quite keeps up the same standards of imagination and verve, and much of the time Shaggy comes across as just another solidly good deejay. The highlights on both sets, however, justify purchase, with *Boombastic* having the slight edge. And Shaggy is bound to come up with a classic album in time.

SHELENE

● **Shelene** (Tan-Yah, US).

Impressively soulful US lovers (plus the conscious, self-composed "Black Woman") from former backing singer Shelene Thomas, recorded at Phillip Smart's HC & F studio. Rhythms – original and recut – feature NY's finest reggae sessioneers including Rafael 'Sir Raf' Allen, Nass-T Hackett and Andy Bashford, as well as such as Jamaican-based Danny Browne. Among the highlights: "Can You", a duet with Andrew Bell over a tough piece of Alton Ellis's "Breaking Up" rhythm, and "Just Give Me Love", which rides a superb loop-driven cut of Marley's original "Stir It Up".

SHINEHEAD

● **Rough & Rugged** (African Love, US).

◑ **Troddin'** (Elektra, US).

Ⓔ Shinehead's inspired debut album, *Rough & Rugged* marks the point where Brooklyn reggae came of age. It had been preceded by a remarkable 12" 45, "Billie Jean"/"Mama Used To Say", which welded the Michael Jackson/Junior Giscombe songs onto an update of an obscure Studio One rhythm. The other rhythms on the album came from a variety of sources, and were incredibly well selected (from "The Lecture" to "Under Me Sleng Teng"); even more attention grabbing were Shinehead's own (very varied) performances, ranging from the latest deejay styles to tender soul balladeering. His output afterwards was variable, but *Troddin'* came near to recapturing the first set's excitement, even if having to revisit the "Billy Jean" rhythm (twice) to do so. A cracking version of Dave Kelly's then hot "Pepper Seed" showed that he was still in touch with dancehall developments.

African reggae

PIERRE TERRASSON/EMI FRANCE

10

10

previous page

Côte d'Ivoire superstar Alpha Blondy

African reggae

Africa, as an original homeland/pastoral paradise, has been the topic of some of the most moving music to emerge from Jamaica, so it's fitting – and maybe not surprising – that the music of the Kingston ghetto 'sufferers' has taken root in the continent. Without the communities of Jamaican migrants that have supported and developed the music in the UK and US, however, the various strands of **African reggae** have drawn inspiration from divergent sources, and developed along very different lines. There is a kind of 'pure' African reggae – modelled predominantly on Bob Marley and the Wailers and other roots rock artists – but African bands and musicians often use reggae rhythms as just one component in a mix of local and international styles.

Reggae artists began making their way to Africa back in the 1960s. One-hit wonder ("My Boy Lollipop") **Millie Small** toured Nigeria and Ghana a couple of times, performing with local musicians. During the early 1970s, UK reggae band the Cimarons also successfully toured Africa, while in the last half of the decade the deejay **U-Roy** sold more of his albums in Africa than in the rest of the world put together. **Jimmy Cliff**, too, was a superstar in several African countries, especially Nigeria where he performed to huge audiences in the Lagos football stadium. Local musicians, meantime, had picked up on reggae rhythms. **Sonny Okosun** – whose first band had played the music of Elvis Presley, Cliff Richard and the Beatles – was by 1977 playing an Africanized reggae on albums that sold 150,000 copies each in Nigeria alone.

It was **Bob Marley**'s now legendary Zimbabwe independence concert of 1980, though, that proved inspirational to many African musicians seeking new directions after the trends for rock, soul, funk and disco had run their course. The appeal lay in both his music and lyrics – Marley's songs of freedom finding a receptive market. The result was reggae taking hold right across the continent, played on cassette and echoed by local bands from Morocco to South Africa, by Africans who possessed no links with Jamaica beyond a love of the island's music.

As the 1980s progressed, two genuine African reggae superstars emerged: Ivory Coast's **Alpha Blondy** and South Africa's **Lucky Dube**. Both have recorded in Jamaica, though their records have yet to register there – and, indeed, are unlikely to do so given their out-of-time Marley/roots reggae influences. A significant difference with African reggae is that its overwhelming influences have been not the hot 45s ruling Kingston's dancehalls, but albums (circulated in Africa on cassette) aimed at an international crossover audience in the first place – namely those of Bob Marley, Peter Tosh, Third World, Jimmy Cliff and Steel Pulse.

Tellingly, when Blondy visited Jamaica in 1986, he was uninterested in having Kingston's hottest session musicians of the time, Steely & Clevie, lay down the rhythms, or going to Prince Jammy's studio; he wanted the (post-Bob Marley) Wailers emblazoned on his new album. The result was immaculate musicianship and production values but about as far as it was possible to get from the music's cutting edge.

Nonetheless, both Alpha Blondy and Lucky Dube have huge followings in Africa and established places on the European and American 'world music' circuits. And the superstars are only the tip of the African reggae pyramid, laying down roots reggae rhythms in alliance with everything from Nigerian fuji to räi (Algeria's räi superstar **Cheb Khaled** recorded much of his last album, *Sahra*, in Jamaica, employing the I-Threes for vocal support). And of course the lyrics, often overtly political, are sung in every language going.

The music of an island crosses a continent

Nigeria's **Sonny Okusuns** paved the way for an explosion of African reggae with his series of best-selling records of the late 1970s that blended the Jamaican form with West African highlife and juju. It was during the next decade, however, that African variations of reggae really took off, with not only **Lucky Dube** and **Alpha Blondy** coming to the fore, but many other performers emerging with their own takes on the music.

Alpha Blondy

The Ivory Coast-born **Alpha Blondy** (b. Seydou Kone, 1953, Dimbokoro) first became interested in the music of Bob Marley and in Rastafarianism when studying at New York's Columbia University, and it was from there that he made his first visit to Jamaica in the late 1970s. When he returned to the Ivory Coast in 1980 and announced to his parents his new beliefs, as well as his ambition to become a musician rather than a teacher, they placed him under psychiatric supervision. Determined, Blondy kept on course and, two years later, cut the successful single "Brigadier Sabari", and followed it with a series of albums that sold massive quantities of cassettes in West Africa and eventually brought international attention.

To help ensure the widest possible audience for his music, Blondy employs English, French and the Dioula language in his lyrics, which are informed by both Rastafarianism and local conditions. His signing by the US reggae label Shanachie in 1987 further ensured a broadening of his audience, especially after his extensive touring of American cities.

Lucky Dube

In South Africa, **Lucky Dube** (b. 1967, Ermelo, Eastern Transvaal) was also taking

TA'BU

Reggae from the Townships: South Africa's Lucky Dube

on board Rastafarian imagery, alongside a taste for the reggae of Peter Tosh, Bob Marley and Joe Higgs. As with other African reggae performers, the Rasta influence in his lyrics was modified – none of the Africa land of "milk and honey" often found in Jamaican reggae – while the influence of Tosh extended beyond Dube's vocal style to the anger of many of his lyrics (albeit rarely supported by an equal bite to the music). Not surprisingly, this language of black rights ensured the banning of Dube's first reggae album, 1985's *Rasta Never Die*, by the South African government.

Further sets got through the censors, among them 1986's *Slave* (also the name of a new band Dube formed that year) and 1989's *Together As One*, the latter promoted with acclaimed tours of France and the USA. Neither success, however, probably meant as much to him as an invitation in 1991 to take part in Jamaica's Reggae Sunsplash festival – the first South African artist to grace the stage.

Other contenders

While not in the same league as far as record sales were concerned, performers from a range of African countries in the 1980s made an impact with reggae stylings, including Nigeria's **Mandators**, **Ras Kimono** and **Evi Edna Ogholi-Ogosi**, Zimbabwe's **John Chibadura** and Senegal's **Adioa**.

This was also the period when Zimbabwe's dreadlocked **Thomas Mapfumo**, who had been jailed for ninety days during the war for that country's independence, fused elements of reggae with local musical traditions.

In Ghana, a similar synthesis took place when the well-established **African Brothers** incorporated reggae strands into the highlife with which they originally made their name.

Other fusionists included South Africa's **Senzo Mthetwa**, who grafted reggae with both gospel and the local mbaganga style, and the Ivory Coast's **Tangara Speed Ghoda**, who combined Jamaican rhythms with a mixture of local styles.

Askia Modibo, from Mali, is also interesting in this context. A former associate of Alpha Blondy when living in the Ivory Coast, he calls his music Wass-reggae, though it is informed by the musical traditions of several peoples besides the Wassoulou – namely the Songhai, Bambara and Tamachek. The reggae influences, rather more predictably, have echoes of Bob Marley, Peter Tosh and Bunny Wailer.

There is little doubt about the care with which these leading African reggae bands put their music together, or their genuine creativity – particularly in merging reggae with local musical traditions. Some of the brass sections, in particular, are stunning. Just don't expect to hear the bassline drop as it does on a rhythm like "Real Rock" – or indeed to hear anything that sounds remotely contemporary in a Jamaican context.

ALPHA BLONDY

⊙ **The Best Of Alpha Blondy** (EMI, France).
Tracks taken from nine of the Ivory Coast star's albums, including the best-selling *Apartheid Is Nazism* from 1985, and *Jerusalem* recorded the following year with the Wailers. Tracks from later albums are not quite as powerful, though the musicianship is always beyond reproach. "Rendez-Vous (Cool Summer Mix)" is particularly charming.

LUCKY DUBE

⊙ **Serious Reggae Business** (Lucky/Gallo RSA)
⊙ **Taxman** (Lucky/Gallo RSA).
The first of these is a career-spanning CD-ROM compilation, with most of his best-known songs – "Slave", "Prisoner", "House Of Exile" – present in digital clarity. Although his style is heavily derivative of Tosh/Higgs/Cliff, he manages to steer clear of outright imitation; the interactive portion of the disc contains many images and song lyrics, although an interview in which Dube claims "I am reggae" strains your creduli-

ty. Taxman shows him mining the same vein, apparently oblivious to developments on the Jamaican scene; nonetheless, this set sold 40,000 units in Ghana alone soon after release in early 1997.

THE MANDATORS

⊙ **Power Of the People: Nigerian Reggae** (Heartbeat, US).

A collection of the popular Nigerian band's best-known tracks, all with a strong Marley influence. The later work of band members Victor Essiet and Peggy Umanah, along with their former lead guitarist, Majek Fashek, could do with a similar compilation.

THOMAS MAPFUMO

⊙ **Corruption** (Mango, US).

The classic 1989 set that most successfully combined reggae influences with musical styles from both South Africa and Mapfumo's own Zimbabwe. Many of his albums are currently available, but this is the one of greatest interest from a reggae perspective.

ASKIA MODIBO

⊙ **Wass Reggae** (Stern's Africa, UK).

For all the red, yellow and green on the cover, and his dreadlocks, Askia Modibo's lyrics do not simply replicate Jamaican rastaspeak, but are in French and address local concerns. Like several African reggae albums, this was recorded in Paris.

VARIOUS ARTISTS

⊙ **Reggae Africa** (EMI UK).

This set illustrates the penetration of reggae throughout Africa. Performers from South Africa, Mali, Cote d'Ivoire, and Cameroon are all featured, with Alpha Blondy and Ismael Isaac the best-known outside the continent. As expected, Marley and Tosh are the dominant models, although P.J.Ray from Cote d'Ivoire breaks the mould convincingly on his anti-imperialist "Politic Warrior".

Glossary

Agony
The sexual act, or a style of dancing that involves moving the waist around in simulation of it.

Almshouse
Anything that is negative.

Babylon
Oppressive Western society in general, or the police in particular.

Baby mother
A young woman with child.

Baggy
A woman's knickers. When she is described as having a "a gun in her baggy", wise rude boys will avoid her as she carries a sexually transmitted disease.

Bakra
A white man.

Baldhead
Someone who is not a Rastafarian.

Balm
A system of folk healing, employing Jamaican herbs.

Bandulu
A swindle, as in "bandulu business".

Bangarang
Noise or disruptive commotion, often used by rival sound systems.

Bashment
Originally from a "a big bash", the works, the ultimate, whether applied to a sound-system session or a woman passing on the street.

Batty boy
A homosexual.

Batty-rider
A skimpy pair of shorts.

Beanie or **beenie**
Small.

Big people music
Sentimental ballads, often covers of 1950s/1960s soul records, as released on labels like Orbitone in the UK, and bought in serious quantities by older Jamaicans.

Big up
To praise someone.

Blood claat
See 'Rass claat'.

Bobo dread
A Rastafarian follower of Prince Emanuel Edwards, who wears his locks in a turban and carries a broom to signify his own cleanliness.

Bongo
A small drum played with the fingers, as it is elsewhere, but also a term used to describe someone with African cultural traits. Thus the Linkers' equation of the "Bongo Man" with the Rastafarian returning to Africa.

Boops
A man who keeps a woman, a sugar daddy.

Boopsie
A woman kept by the above.

Bow
Oral sex.

Brawta
A little more, a little extra.

Bredda
A brother or friend.

Browning
A light-complexioned Jamaican woman, as loved by Buju Banton – though he then attempted to soothe any hurt feelings (and sell even more records) by recording "Love Black Woman".

Cabin stabbin
Fucking.

Carry go bring come
To spread rumours, tell tales about someone.

Chalice
A pipe for smoking the 'herb', with deliberate connotations of 'chalice' in the sense of a communion cup.

Cho
An expression suggesting that the speaker's patience is wearing thin.

Chronic
A particularly potent strain of the 'herb'. Is to the 1990s what 'sensi' was to the 1970s, and strongly recommended by both Michael Rose and Beenie Man (among others).

Combination
When a singer and deejay work together in the studio, as opposed to the latter chatting over a performance from the former that might have been recorded months or even years before. Chaka Demus & Pliers are the most successful practitioners of this style to date.

Coolie
Someone of East Indian descent.

Copasetic
Everything is fine. An expression taken from US jive talk.

Craven
Greedy.

Culture/cultural
Used in the reggae world, these terms refer specifically to a pan-African culture that places the injustices suffered by that continent's diaspora in the context of an eventual dispensation. Used to describe records or lyrics, the term is usually interchangeable with Rastafarian.

Cuss-cuss
An argument, a dispute.

Dancehall
[1]
Where the music is primarily heard. In Jamaica this is usually not a hall in the sense of part of a building, but an enclosed open space into which gigantic speakers and record-playing equipment have been placed.

[2]
Virtually all recorded Jamaican music has been designed for the dancehall in the above sense, but the term is also used to label a particular stage of reggae that began in the late 1970s. This was when, after tasting international attention with Marley, the music became more insular, and styles were developed primarily in the dancehalls themselves. There both singers and DJs would perform over pre-recorded rhythms, often with lyrics commenting on the dance and the prowess of the singer or sound system. There is no great aesthetic difference between the dancehall and early ragga – simply a technological one, as the latter employed computerized instrumentation.

Dibby dibby
Inferior, weak, as used to describe the sound system that is competing against yours, or tunes that don't deserve a place in your selection.

Diss
To show disrespect.

Don
The big man in the area, or gang chief, taken from American Mafia films like *The Godfather*. It is also possible to be a fairly harmless sort who is simply the 'don' on record.

Don Gorgon
Combines two terms meaning much the same, suggesting an even greater degree of awesome power.

Do-over
A new version of a lyric from an old – or foreign – record.

Downpresser
Someone who oppresses you.

Dread
Abbreviated form of 'natty dread', but also used to describe anything that is serious – we're living in a "dread time", say.

Dub
The remixed version of a record, with the vocal either entirely or partly removed, and usually with the foregrounding of bass and drums. The great majority of reggae singles from 1973 onwards have had dub versions on their flips. Outside of the reggae world, 'dub' is now a buzz word used in a much looser way to indicate practically any record where the mixing engineer's skill is apparent, so making it virtually meaningless.

Dubplate
An acetate, produced in very limited numbers for the play on particular sound systems. This helps attract patrons to a particular sound (because of the exclusivity of their plates), but also tests public response to a new tune, and builds up demand prior to its release on vinyl.

Dunny or **Dunza**
Money.

Duppy
A ghost.

Flex
To behave, how one relates to someone.

Ganga Lee
A gangster (usually used with some respect).

Ginnal
A con man, or anyone that cannot be trusted.

Gorgon
A gorgon is someone to be afraid of (or at least respected). Cornell Campbell's 1975 record of this title used an updated version of the rhythm from Derrick Morgan's "Conquering Ruler", and expressed similar sentiments.

Gow
An empty boast.

Gravalicious
Greedy.

Grounation
A large gathering of Rastafarians that involves Bible readings, drumming, chanting and much reasoning.

Heartical
Used to describe someone with the necessary qualifications for the job – often used before the noun 'don', for instance, to describe someone well prepared to handle what happens in the area he controls. Connotes authenticity, integrity,

Herb
Cannabis leaves, and to many Rastas a sacrament.

Higgler
A sidewalk vendor.

ICI
Informal commercial importer, or the modern version of the 'Higgler', who travels to buy the goods which she sells.

Irie
Fine or good; often used as a greeting.

Ital
Natural, as with the organic food preferred by Rastafarians.

Joe Grind
The other man who visits a woman when her husband/regular boyfriend is away.

John Crow
A scavenger bird similar to the turkey buzzard. The "John Crow Skank" was so named because of the sudden changes in direction and wheeling motions of the dancers.

Juggling
The sound-system practice of employing twin decks to play several versions of a rhythm, without interruption. What is known in the wider world of deejay/dance culture as segueing.

Kiss me neck
An exclamation meaning "I'm somewhat surprised".

Labba labba
Talk. Often preceded with the phrase "too much".

Labrish
Gossip. Lee Perry and Bunny Lee's record of this title is the last word on the topic.

Lick shot
Either the firing of a gun, or the imitation of such, to express approval.

Lovers rock
A type of reggae concerned almost solely with romance, developed in the UK as an alternative to the militant roots records dominant in the late 1970s. Often employs US soft-soul songs over crisp reggae rhythms. The one area of reggae where women have been given considerable opportunities and enjoyed enduring popularity.

Macca fat
A fruit that is not quite as tasty as the Jackie Mittoo album so named.

Mampy
A fat woman.

Massive
Large or important. Becomes a noun when the talk is of a sound system's 'massive' – meaning its group of followers.

Matie
A man's mistress, and a popular topic with ragga deejays such as Cobra.

Mega-mix
The 'one-rhythm' album taken to its logical conclusion, with all the tracks segued into each other to form one continuous piece of music. Saves you having to develop the necessary skills for a spot of your own 'juggling'.

Mento
The first indigenous musical form to be recorded in Jamaica. The island's answer to the calypso craze from Trinidad and an enduring influence on subsequent developments (including ragga deejays like Captain Bailey).

Name brand
In fashion, as applied to performers appearing in a dancehall or on an album.

Natty
An abbreviated form of 'natty dread'.

Natty dread
A Rastafarian with dreadlocks.

Nyahbingi drumming
A style of drumming favoured by Rastafarian communities, and including the use of a large bass drum, which is beaten with a padded stick, and smaller "funde" and "repeater" hand drums. Nyahbingi drumming forms the basis of the music of Rasta musical aggregations such as Count Ossie's Mystic Revelation of Ratafari, the Light of Saba and Ras Michael & the Sons of Megus, but every now and then surfaces on more commercial reggae records.

Obeah
A Jamaican form of magic, originating in West Africa.

One-rhythm album
Otherwise known as the 'version' album. Ten or twelve 'versions' of a rhythm track presented on one album, with different mixes, and various singers or deejays competing to make it their own. The sort of set that confirms the outsider's view that "all reggae sounds the same", but consistently selling within the reggae marketplace itself.

Peenie wallie
A species of firefly, and the title of an excellent Jackie Mittoo instrumental.

Pickney
A young child.

Pre-release
Originally the first limited press of a 45 with a blank label to test public response, before official release. Later the term applied to all Jamaican pressed singles meant for export to the UK (and thus pre the record's release in that country).

Punaany
A woman's genitalia. The deejay Admiral Bailey said "Give me punaany, want punaany... any punanny is the same." Even in the digital/ragga age, singers have tended to employ a slightly more subtle approach.

Ragga
Abbreviation of the above and the generic name given the type of digital reggae enjoyed by such. The music of the Jamaican dancehall since 1985.

Raggamuffin
A young streetwise ghetto dweller.

Ras
Ethiopian for "prince" or "head".

Rass
A swear word, meaning menstrual blood, and so not to be confused with the above.

Rass claat
"Claat" means cloth, so add it to the above for a curse, literally meaning a used tampon.

Reality
Specifically, the ghetto sufferer's reality. Usually employed as an epithet: "reality lyrics". As Robert Nesta Marley said: "Who feels it knows it."

Reason
A lengthy discussion, particularly about matters of social and spiritual import among the Rastafarian brethren.

Revive
An old record. What would be a "golden oldie", but for having originally sold in the hundreds – or maybe thousands – rather than millions.

Rhythm
The rhythm, or backing, track of a reggae record, particularly the drum and bass part. The rhythm of a successful record will often (nowadays, always) be 'versioned' by competing producers. There are literally hundreds of versions of certain rhythms, with several entire 'one-rhythm albums', devoted to them.

Risto
Derived from "aristocrat", someone of the upper echelons of society, or who puts on airs.

Rockers
A militant style of rhythm developed in the 1970s, mostly based on the updating of old rocksteady classics, and associated with, first, Augustus Pablo and then the drummer Sly Dunbar and the crack Channel One session band, the Revolutionaries.

Rude boy
A young ghetto criminal or hooligan, as immortalized in the mid–late 1960s by, among others, the Wailers, Desmond Dekker and the Clarendonians. Predecessor to various bad boys, bandulos and 'yush' (the term 'rude boy' itself reappears every so often, as well).

Samfi-man
A swindler.

Satta
To rejoice.

Screwface
To scowl, or someone who habitually wears such an expression.

Seen
Understood.

Sensi
Short for "sensimilla", or seedless (and very strong) 'herb'.

Showcase album
An album on which vocals are followed directly by their dub versions. A particularly useful format when a producer is short of material by the performer in question.

Sipple
Slippery – when Max Romeo sang that it was "Sipple Out Deh" he meant it was dangerous.

Skank
[1]
Early 1970s dance movement, as in "John Crow Skank".

[2]
To con (UK).

Sketel
A dance.

Skylark
To loiter or idle. Something that Horace Andy advised the youth not to do.

Slack
Sexually explicit.

Slam
A fuck. The deejay Beenie Man proclaimed that the "wickedest slam" was with a real ghetto girl.

Slogle
An amalgamation of the adjective "slow" and the noun "bogle" (a dance popular in the reggae world of the early 1990s), and used to describe a relaxed, more soul-influenced type of rhythm. The record credited with beginning the trend was Cobra's US hit "Flex", which employed the bassline from the Temptations' "Just My Imagination".

Sound system
The Jamaican version of a mobile disco, with massed gigantic speakers (or "boxes") for play in the dancehall (in Jamaica, usually an open space that has been fenced off). International dance culture has now appropriated what was once a uniquely Jamaican form of entertainment.

Spar
Partner or friend.

Specials
Custom-made dubplates on which currently popular performers will sing/chat the praises of

the particular sound system for which they have been cut. 'Specials' now entirely dominate sessions from Jamaica's top sound systems.

Steppers
An even more militant development of the 'rockers' style of rhythm, and dominant in Jamaica during the late 1970s/early 1980s. What hard bop was to bebop, 'steppers' was to 'rockers'. A facet of roots reggae that has never gone out of fashion with groups of fans in the UK, and some sound systems there – such as the redoubtable Jah Shaka – are still expected to play nothing but 'steppers' records.

Sufferer or **sufferah**
A Jamaican ghetto dweller. Mid–late 1970s roots reggae was "suffarah's music".

Toasting
The deejay's performance over records in the dancehall. In the 1970s, Jamaican deejays were often called 'toasters', though by the end of the decade 'MCs' was the preferred term. They are now deejays again, and the term 'toasting' has largely fallen into disuse.

Trailer-load
A large amount. Shabba Ranks boasted of having a "Trailer Load Of Girls".

Version
Another cut of a popular rhythm. This can be a vocal, deejay, instrumental or dub version, employing the same rhythm track as the original, or another producer's recording of the rhythm (as in Channel One or Joe Gibbs versions of Studio One rhythms).

Version album
See 'One-rhythm album'.

Wagonist
Derived from "bandwagonist" – that familiar figure who jumps on a bandwagon or popular trend.

Work
Sex.

X-amount
Countless, as in "x-amount of versions".

Yard
A Jamaican's home, after the government built housing projects built around open spaces (which served as the focus for communal and commercial interaction). Also Jamaica as "home" for expatriates.

Yardie
Derived from the above, this originally applied to anyone from Jamaica. Appropriated by the UK media in one of their periodic moral panics, it is now usually understood to mean a Jamaican gangster, with connotations of excessive violence and ruthlessness.

Yush
Term of greeting among rude boys.

A Jamaican chronology

1494
Christopher Columbus lands at what will be known as 'Discovery Bay', "discovering" Jamaica for Europeans and claiming it for the Spanish Crown. In the next decade, Spanish violence and disease will wipe out the peaceful Arawak inhabitants of the island that the Spanish name Xaymaca.

1518
Gold is discovered in Jamaica.

1523
Three hundred slaves are sent to the island.

1655
The British take Jamaica from the Spanish.

The maroons (slaves that the Spanish left behind) rebel. Runaway slaves of the British will later join them.

1663
The undefeated maroons, under the leader ship of Juan de Bolas, are acknowledged as a free people.

1670
The Treaty of Madrid is signed, under which Spain recognizes British sovereignty of Jamaica.

1675
Charles II appoints Sir Henry Morgan, a former buccaneer, as Governor of Jamaica.

1692
Port Royal, the pirate capital of the world, is destroyed by an earthquake.

1700–86
In this period an average of seven thousand slaves are imported each year into Jamaica. Some will work the sugar plantations there; a quarter will be re-exported to other countries.

1738
Nanny, one of Jamaica's national heroes, leads a successful slave revolt against the British settlers.

1739
The British give the maroons rights over the land they have settled in the Central Mountains.

1831
The largest of the slave uprisings is led by Sam Sharpe, a Baptist deacon. He declares when waiting execution: "I would rather die on yon gallows than live a slave."

1833
Jamaica's most influential newspaper, the *Cleaner* (later the *Daily Gleaner*), is founded.

1838
Slavery is abolished in Jamaica.

1865
The Morant Bay Uprising takes place, and its leaders, Paul Bogle (the son of a freed slave) and George William Gordon (a Jamaican legislator of mixed race), are executed.

1884
William Alexander Bustamante, the future founder of the Jamaican Labour Party (JLP), is born.

1887
On August 17, Marcus Mosiah Garvey, proponent of Black self-determination, is born in St Ann's Bay on the north coast of Jamaica.

1893
Norman Washington Manley, the founder of the People's National Party (PNP), is born.

1916
Marcus Garvey organizes the Universal Negro Improvement Association in the United States.

1924
On December 10, Norman Washington Manley's son, Michael Norman Manley, future leader of the PNP and Jamaican Prime Minister during its most turbulent times, is born in Kingston.

1930
On November 2, Ras Tafari Makonnen, the supposed 225th descendant of King Solomon and the Queen of Sheba, is crowned Emperor of Ethiopia, receiving the title of Haile Selassie, King of Kings, Lord of Lords, Conquering Lion of the Tribe of Judah. To many Rastafarians this fulfils the prophecies of both Marcus Garvey and the Book of Revelation.

1935
Marcus Garvey establishes the Black Star Line shipping company (the name in parody of Cunard's famed White Star Line). The company is intended to transport all black people in the New World who wish to return to their ancestral home in Africa.

1938
Jamaica's two main political parties, the PNP and JLP, are founded by the cousins Norman Washington Manley and William Alexander Bustamante.

1944
The first Jamaican general election based on universal suffrage is held.

1945
On February 6, Robert Nesta Marley is born, of an English father and Jamaican mother, in St Ann's Bay – also the birthplace of Marcus Garvey and Winston Rodney (aka Burning Spear).

1948
Large-scale emigration of Jamaicans to Britain begins with the arrival of almost five hundred on board the Empire Windrush. The establishment of Jamaican communities in the country's major urban centres will provide an important market for the Jamaican record industry, which is just beginning.

1951
Wynonie 'Mr Blues' Harris's "Bloodshot Eyes" is released on Cincinnati's King label, and becomes one of the best-selling r&b discs ever in Jamaica, and an inspiration to the island's aspiring performers.

1954
Ken Khouri starts Federal Records on Bell Road, Kingston, initially to release US recordings as 78s.

1956
For the first of three consecutive years, Duke Reid is crowned the 'King of Sound & Blues' at the Success Club on Wildman Street.

Duke Vin, the selector for Tom the Great Sebastian, moves to the UK, where he establishes the first Jamaican-style sound system to play there – The Tickler.

1958
Edward Seaga starts WIRL (West Indies Record Label) to record local musicians and singers, mostly performing the Jamaican variant of American r&b.

Chris Blackwell produces his first Jamaican hit, Laurel Aitken's "Boogie In My Bones", which reaches #1 in the local charts.

1959
Clement Dodd and Duke Reid, who will dominate the 1960s, hold their first recording sessions. Theophilus Beckford's "Easy Snapping", one of the most enduring Jamaican r&b discs ever released, appears on the former's Worldisc label.

1960
Prince Buster leaves Clement Dodd to establish his own sound system, The Voice of the People.

The Folks Brothers' original version of "Oh Carolina", with nyahbingi drumming from the legendary Count Ossie, is recorded at radio station RJR, and appears on Buster's Wild Bells label.

In June an encampment of militant Rastas and black American radicals in the hills above Kingston is attacked by the West India Regiment. Two soldiers are killed and three others wounded by escaping followers of the Jamaican-born Claudius Henry.

1961

All Star Top Hits, a collection of tracks recorded at the Federal recording studio, is released on Clement Dodd's All Stars label.

1962

In May, Chris Blackwell moves his Island operation to London, where he is soon releasing most of his former rivals' best recordings.

Jamaica is granted its formal independence from British rule on August 6, an event celebrated by Lord Creator's "Independent Jamaica", as well as Derrick Morgan's "Forward March" and Jimmy Cliff's "Miss Jamaica".

1963

In June, the island's most important musicians – including Don Drummond, Roland Alphonso, Tommy McCook, Lester Sterling, Ernest Ranglin, Johnny 'Dizzy' Moore, Lloyd Nibbs, Jah Jerry and Lloyd Brevitt – begin to call themselves the Skatalites, and become the ska period's most successful group.

At the close of the year the Wailers record their first Jamaican #1, "Simmer Down", a hit that helps initiate the trend for records about Kingston's rude boys.

1964

Michael Manley first acquires the nickname 'Joshua', while leading a march of striking communications workers to the JBC (Jamaican Broadcasting Company) building, outside of which he declares: "These are the walls of Jericho!"

In February Millie Small's "My Boy Lollipop" becomes the first international hit by a Jamaican performer, reaching the Top 5 in both the UK and the US.

1966

The transition to the cooler rocksteady phase is signalled by Hopeton Lewis's "Take It Easy", produced by Winston Blake, and appearing on his Merritone label.

On April 21, the Emperor of Ethiopia, Haile Selassie, makes a state visit to Jamaica, to be greeted by hundreds of enthusiastic Rastafarians at Kingston airport.

1968

Several records appear with claims to being the one to initiate the shift from rocksteady to reggae, among them Larry Marshall's "Nanny Goat", the Beltones' "No More Heartaches" and the Race Track Fans' "Time Marches On".

Walter Rodney, Guyanese academic and advocate of Black Power, is refused readmission into Jamaica after a lecture tour of Canada. Serious rioting breaks out in Kingston; Prince Buster releases "Dr Rodney" in tribute.

1969

Don Drummond, the trombone virtuoso and founder member of the Skatalites, dies in the Belle Vue mental hospital, where he had been incarcerated five years earlier for the murder of his common-law wife.

1970

The deejay craze begins when U-Roy, toasting vintage Treasure Isle rocksteady tunes, holds the top three places in the Jamaican charts for twelve weeks.

1971

Jimmy Cliff stars in *The Harder They Come*, the film (and soundtrack album) that will bring reggae to new international audiences.

1972

On February 29 the left-leaning PNP, led by Michael Manley, wins the general election, and ends ten years of JLP rule.

1973

The practice of 'version' sides on the flips of reggae 45s is extended to the first dub albums: Herman Chin Loy's *Aquarius Dub*, Clive Chin's *Java, Java, Java, Java Dub* and Lee Perry's *Blackboard Jungle Dub*.

International reggae is born with the release by Island – then a successful progressive rock label – of the Wailers' *Catch A Fire* album. Packaged and promoted in the manner of their rock LPs, it is bought by students and hippies who had previously dismissed the music. The Wailers also cease to be simply the best vocal-harmony group in Jamaica to become a self-contained band, a move calculated to give them greater appeal to global audiences.

1974

Singer and producer Rudie Edwards releases the first one-rhythm or 'version' LP, *Yamaha Skank*, made up of twelve cuts of Slim Smith's "My Conversation" hit. The trend for such albums, however, will not take off until the next decade, when they will become at least as significant a trend as dub albums were in the mid-1970s.

Faced with growing violence, Prime Minister Michael Manley puts the island "Under Heavy Manners", passing the Gun Court Act, which imposes indefinite detention on anyone caught in illegal possession of a firearm.

1975

Through their work with the Channel One house band, the Revolutionaries, Sly Dunbar and Robbie Shakespeare become the most-sought-after drum and bass partnership in Kingston.

The release in the UK by Island of Burning Spear's *Marcus Garvey* album ensures an even higher profile for Rastafarian-influenced 'cultural' music.

On November 14, Cuban troops save the MPLA government in Angola by defeating an invading South African army. Several Jamaican 45s – including the Revolutionaries' "MPLA" and "Angola" – express solidarity with liberation struggles in southern Africa.

1976

Another wave of violence makes Michael Manley declare a State of Emergency, which authorizes the security forces to "detain all persons whose activities are likely to endanger the public safety". Leroy Smart's "Ballistic Affair" and Max Romeo's "Sipple Out Deh" are just two of the many local hits about the "tribal war" that grips the island.

Virgin's release of the Mighty Diamonds' *The Right Time/I Need A Roof* album confirms the dominance of Jo Jo Hookim's Channel One studio, as well as showing how fashionable roots reggae has become in the rock/pop world.

Early in December gunmen break into Bob Marley's house, shooting and wounding both the singer and his manager, Don Taylor. Michael Manley includes this incident in his diary of actions that he considers are intended to destabilize the country.

On December 15, Michael Manley is re-elected, but sees the PNP's support among the upper working class and lower middle class dramatically reduced.

1977

Rock journalists manage to convince bondage-gear-wearing punks that living on an art college grant in Notting Hill is analogous with the Kingston sufferer's lot. Enough believe they would be happier living in Ethiopia to help make Culture's *Two Sevens Clash* one of the best-selling reggae albums of all time.

1978

On January 4, an incident known as the Green Bay Massacre takes place. Five suspected gang members associated with the JLP are murdered, apparently by an army firing squad, at a bay west of Kingston, and another five escape to tell the story. Big Youth, Jah Lloyd and Lord Sassafrass are among the deejays to pass comment on disc.

On April 22, the One Love peace concert initiated by rival gang leaders Bucky Marshall and Claudie Massop brings both of the political parties' gunmen together. Bob Marley – himself the survivor of an assassination attempt – forces Manley and Seaga, who hitherto has been mentioned solely as a record producer, to hold hands.

1979

In February, Claudie Massop is shot dead by police. During the same year Bucky Marshall is assassinated by a gunman at the Starlite Ballroom in Brooklyn.

1980

The general election is the most violent to date. The Jamaican electorate elects Edward Seaga's conservative JLP.

1981

On May 21, the Hon Robert Nesta Marley, OM, is given a state funeral, at which Jamaica's Governor General, Florizel Glasspole, Prime Minister Edward Seaga and the leader of the opposition Michael Manley are among those who make speeches in his honour.

1982

The first live dancehall album – *Live At Aces* from Yellowman – is released.

1984

With the Taxi release of his "Mi God Mi King", Saxon Sound's Philip 'Papa' Levi becomes the first UK MC (deejay) to have a Jamaican #1. The record also helps establish the influential "fast style" of delivery that is taken into the upper regions of the UK pop charts by fellow Saxon Sound MCs Smiley Culture and Tippa Irie.

1985

On December 5, the first fully digital reggae recording, "Under Me Sleng Teng", is cut at Prince Jammy's studio at 38 St Lucia Road, so launching the ragga stage of reggae.

1988

The high-tech rhythm that Gussie Clarke builds for Gregory Isaacs' "Rumours" hit demonstrates the compatibility of digital instrumentation and late 1970s 'steppers'-style rhythms.

Hurricane Gilbert strikes Jamaica, causing havoc and – not unexpectedly – inspiring several records.

1989

On February, Osbourne Ruddock, aka King Tubby, the single most important figure in the development of dub in the 1970s, and a successful producer since the mid-1980s, is shot dead outside his home in Waterhouse. His killer was never caught, though robbery was the assumed motive.

1992

Chaka Demus & Pliers' "Murder She Wrote" becomes an international pop hit, paving the way for other ragga records to cross over.

Cobra's "Flex" is a massive US hit, while the mainstream media pay more attention to the anti-gay sentiments of Buju Banton's cut of the same rhythm, "Boom Bye Bye".

1995

Shaggy's "Boombastic", aided by a Levi's commercial, becomes the first reggae record to enter the UK pop charts at #1, simultaneously reaching the same position in the US, there helped only by massive play in clubs and on urban radio.

Producer Bobby Digital's success with numerous versions of the "Kette Drum" rhythm brings back traditional nyahbingi drumming in a serious way. Buju Banton's "Untold Stories" and everything from Capleton confirms that raggas are becoming 'conscious'.

Books and Web sites

General reggae and Jamaican music

John Collins *West African Pop Roots* (Temple University Press, US, 1992). Includes informed essays on the popularity of reggae in West Africa, and local practitioners such as Sunny Okosum.

Grant Goddard *Reggae On The Internet* (privately printed, 1993).

A collection of Internet newsgroup items that contain lots of information; also a great way to see what concerns reggae fans – at least those who have access to the Net.

Ray Hurford, Geoff Sullivan, Colin Moore and Dave Hendley *More Axe* and **Ray Hurford, Dave Katz, Ian McCann, Ardella Jones and Tero Kaski** *More Axe 7* (Muzik Tree, UK/Black Star, Finland, 1987 and 1989). Interesting interviews and articles from the *Small Axe* fanzine, including a pioneering article on King Tubby and the evolution of dub in the former volume.

Brian Jahn and Tom Weber *Reggae Island – Jamaican Music In The Digital Age* (Kingston Publishers, Jamaica, 1992). One of the few books concerned with developments of the last decade in Jamaican music. Producers and performers are allowed space to express their views, and the interview material is complemented by Jahn's superb photographs.

Howard Johnson and Jim Pines *Deep Roots Music* (Proteus/Channel 4, UK, 1982). The book that accompanied the TV series, with great photos. Difficult to find now, but well worth seeking out.

Tero Kaski and Pekka Vuorinen *Reggae Inna Dancehall Style* (Black Star, Finland, 1984). Illuminating interviews with practically everyone associated with Junjo Lawes, the most important producer and sound-system operator of the early 1980s.

Colin Larkin (ed.) *The Guinness Who's Who Of Reggae* (Guinness Publishing, UK, 1994). The only A–Z encyclopedia of reggae that has been published to date, this volume in the Guinness series was overseen by Noel Hawkes with contributions from almost all the cognoscenti.

Beth Lesser *King Jammy's* (Muzik Tree, UK/Black Star, Finland, 1989). Beth Lesser and Dave Kingston's account of how Jammy became King in 1985 is an essential book; it captures a crucial shift in the music – the arrival of the *Sleng Teng* digital rhythm – as it happened, and from the inside. Lesser's photos of everyone involved complement perfectly the affectionate narrative.

Dennis Morris *Reggae Rebels,* (Epoch, UK, 1984). As a photographer for *Black Music* magazine, Morris took some of the best photos of the mid-1970s Kingston music scene. *Reggae Rebels* collects 32 poster-size images, including famous pictures of Tosh, Marley and Bunny Wailer, as well as Dennis Brown and Doctor Alimantado.

Paul Oliver (ed.) *Black Music In Britain – Essays On The Afro-Asian Contribution To Popular Music* (Open University Press, UK, 1990). Academic in tone but invaluable for information about the first recordings of Jamaican musicians in the UK; it also covers the calypso scene as well.

Bob Marley

Adrian Boot and Chris Salewicz *Bob Marley – Songs Of Freedom* (Bloomsbury, UK, 1995). The best book published on Marley, full of anecdotal material, background and insight. Extensively illustrated, with wonderful shots from Boot, as well as archive sources.

Dennis Morris *Bob Marley: Rebel With A Cause* (Epoch, UK, 1986). The pick of Morris's Marley archive.

Don Taylor (as told to Mike Henry) *Marley And Me – The Real Story* (Kingston Publishers, Jamaica, 1994). Bob's manager tells the story from his perspective. The original Yard edition is the unexpurgated one.

Timothy White *Catch A Fire: The Life Of Bob Marley* (Corgi, UK, 1984). White's self-proclaimed "vivid and dramatic" style – utilizing invented conversations and thoughts combined with actual interview material – ultimately mitigates against the authenticity of his biography. A pity, because this *Billboard* editor includes much material from family and musicians that is useful and illuminating.

Discographies

Rob Chapman *DownBeat Special – Studio One Album Discography* and *Never Grow Old – Studio One Singles Listing & Rhythm Directory* (privately printed, UK, 1985 and 1989). The definitive Studio One listings – a wealth of information. Available by mail order from Rob Chapman, PO Box 98, Paignton, TQ3 2YJ.

Ray Hurford, *Rhythm Wise* (Muzik Tree, UK/Black Star, Finland, 1989). Can't quite place that familiar rhythm? Here's an invaluable guide to versions of some of the best-known rhythms (or backing tracks) of Jamaican music. This useful work continues in two further volumes compiled by Jean Scrivener – *Rhythm Wise Two* and *Rhythm Wise Three* (Black Star, UK/Finland, 1990 and 1991).

Charlie Morgan *Coxsone's Music* (Outernational Records, US, 1997). The first attempt at a complete Studio One discography, complete with matrix numbers and a cross-referencing system for thousands of 45s. A lot of work has gone into this book; invaluable for the serious/fanatic collector, although the high price will put off casual readers.

Jamaican culture

Leonard Barrett *The Sun And the Drum – African Roots In Jamaican Folk Tradition* (Sangster's Book Stores/Heinemann Educational Books, Jamaica, 1976). Covers the influence of African traditions in Jamaican folk culture. Valuable background reading.

Louise Bennett *Anancy And Miss Lou* (Sangster's Book Stores, Jamaica, 1979). Jamaica's leading folklorist interprets the traditional Anancy stories.

Miguel F. Brooks (ed. & trans.) *Kebra Nagast* (Kingston Publishers, Jamaica, 1995). A modern translation of the *Kebra Nagast, the Glory Of Kings*, an Ethiopian text excised from the Authorized Version of the King James Bible of 1611. It provides insight into the fascinating background material underpinning Rasta theology.

Horace Campbell *Rasta & Resistance From Marcus Garvey To Walter Rodney* (Hansib, UK, 1985). Thoroughgoing study of the Rastafarian movement includes sections on Bob Marley and reggae, and much more of political interest.

Joseph Owens *Dread – The Rastafarians Of Jamaica* (Heinemann, UK, 1976). An important historical overview of the development of the Rastafarian faith.

Kim Robinson, Walcott Harclyde and Trevor Feaaron *The How To Be Jamaican Handbook* (Jamrite Publications, Jamaica, 1987). Highly amusing guide to Jamaican styles and manners.

Olive Senior *A–Z Of Jamaican Heritage* (Heinemann Educational Books [Caribbean]/The Gleaner Company, Jamaica, 1983). A useful guide to Jamaica that includes entries on Rastafariansm and reggae, as well as much of historical and social relevance.

Laura Tanna *Jamaican Folk Tales And Oral Histories* (Institute Of Jamaica Publications, Jamaica, 1984). A superb collection of songs, riddles, proverbs and narratives, including Anansi, Trickster, Duppy and Big Boy stories and other "old-time" tales, collected by Dr Tanna in 1973–74, that show the incredible richness of this vanishing artform.

Joan Williams *Back A Yard* (Yard Publications, Jamaica, 1990). One of Jamaica's foremost columnists casts a humorous eye on crucial aspects of Jamaican life that range from Gambling to Grammar, Places of Interest to Potholes, and not forgetting Urination.

Politics

Laurie Gunst, *Born Fi Dead* (Payback Press, UK, 1995). No better account exists of the Kingston street gangs, covering both the political wars of the Manley–Seaga years and the violent drug trade that followed these. Essential background reading.

Darrell E. Levi *Michael Manley – The Making Of A Leader* (Andre Deutsch, UK, 1989). Biography of the late Jamaican political leader for those who want further background reading.

Anita M. Waters *Race Class and Political Symbols* (Transaction Books/Rutgers, US, 1985). Subtitled "Rastafari and Reggae in Jamaican politics", this important sociological study concentrates on the use of reggae music in Jamaican elections from 1967 to 1983.

Fiction

Roger Mais *Brother Man* (Cape, UK, 1954). The first novel to feature a Rastaman as a central character – and it's a great read as well!

Orlando Patterson *The Children Of Sisyphus* (Houghton Mifflin, US, 1965). A fine novel that offers further insight into the music's social background.

Michael Thelwell *The Harder They Come* (Pluto, UK, 1980). The novelization of the film, and far better than might be expected. Essential background reading, in fact.

Proverbs/language

Desmond D. Green *Vintage Jamaica: Yard Style Philosophy* (Oasis Publishing Co, Jamaica, publication date unknown). An entertaining collection of traditional Jamaican phrases and proverbs. Make up your own reggae lyrics from these.

Barbara Lalla and Jean D'Costa *Language In Exile – Three Hundred Years Of Jamaican Creole* (University Of Alabama Press, US, 1990). A scholarly look at Jamaican language by analysing eighteenth- and nineteenth-century documents. Specialist but fascinating reading for anyone who wants to understand the development of the island's language and speech patterns.

Vivien Morris-Brown *The Jamaican Handbook Of Proverbs* (Island Heart Publishers, Jamaica, 1993). Gives the Jamaican proverbs as spoken on the island with standard English translations and explanations. Many will be familiar through reggae lyrics.

Dictionaries

Joan Williams *Original Dancehall Dictionary* (Word Publications, Jamaica, date unknown).

Ray Chen *The Jamaican Dictionary* (Periwinkle, Jamaica, 1994).

Chester Francis-Jackson, *The Official Dancehall Dictionary*, (Kingston Publishers, Jamaica, 1995).

We found these invaluable when compiling our own glossary, which includes only a fraction of their terms and meanings.

Magazines

We have been inspired by the work of writers in various magazines worldwide. Respect is due to: Chris Lane in *Blues and Soul* and *Melody Maker;* Carl Gayle in *Black Music*; Dave Hendley in *Blues & Soul*; Beth Lesser and Dave Kingston in *Reggae Quarterly*; Penny Reel and Nick Kimberley in *Pressure Drop*; David Katz in *The Upsetter;* John Williams in *Black Echoes* and *Top*; Richard Williams in *Melody Maker;* Ray Hurford and Colin Moore in *Small Axe*; Lol Bell-Brown in *Boom Shacka Lacka*; David Rodigan, Simon Buckland, Ian McCann and John Masouri in *Echoes*; Roger Steffens and Michael Turner in *The Beat*; and Lascelles 'Trainer' Adams in *Dub Missive*.

Credit also to Jamaica for the first all-reggae publication in the world, Johnnie Golding's *Swing* magazine, Dermot Hussey's many writings in journals and magazines, and Balford Henry's articles and reviews in the *Jamaica Gleaner* and elsewhere. And a final tip of the tam to *Reggae Magazine* (Japan), *Riddim* (Japan), *Dubcatcher* (NY), Bruno Blum at *Best* in France, Rene Wyands in Germany, and Tero Kaski in Finland.

Web sites

Reggae is finding its way onto the Internet. The main newsgroup, for email discussion, is *rec.music.reggae*, while among the growing roster of web sites worth checking are:

Jammin Reggae Archives

http://www.arrowweb.com/jammin/
Possibly the top reggae web site, including full text of Dub Missive, details of (mainly US) festivals and gigs, plus masses of links to labels, artists and other Internet sites.

400 Years

http://incolor.inetnebr.com/cvanpelt/Years.html
Carter Van Pelt's wide-ranging site includes fanzine features and photos plus links to hundreds of sites of reggae interest.

Russian Reggae Rasta Roots Review

http://www.zhurnal.ru:8083/music/rasta/links.html
Kaeta Maeda's very informative pages are especially useful for fans of current dancehall.

Index of artists

C

D

E

F

G

H

I

J

K

L

M

N

O

P

R

S

T

U

V

W

Y

Z

PRESSURE SOUNDS CATALOGUE

LPPS 1/CDPS1	Santic And Friends - An Even Harder Shade Of Black
LPPS 2/CDPS2	Prince Far I and the Arabs - Dub to Africa
LPPS 3/CDPS3	Israel Vibration - The Same Song
PSCD4 /PSLP4	Keith Hudson - Brand
PSCD5 (CD only)	* Sounds And Pressure Volume 1
PSCD6 /PSLP6	Little Roy With Ian Rock And The Heptones - Tafari Earth Uprising
PSCD7/PSLP7	Prince Far I - Cry Tuff Encounter Chapter 3
PSCD8 /PSLP8	Enos McLeod Freaturing Mighty Diamonds - Genius Of Enos
PSCD9 /PSLP9	Lee Perry - Voodooism
PSCD10 (CD only)	* Sounds And Pressure Volume 2
PSCD11/PSLP11	Earth And Stone - Kool Roots (Double Vinyl)
PSCD12/PSLP12	Psalms Of Drums - Carlton Patterson And King Tubby
PSCD13/PSLP13	Prince Far I And The Arabs - Cry Tuff Encounter Chapter 1
PSCD14/PSLP14	Channel 1 Compilation - Well Charged
PSCD15/PSLP15	The Techniques - Techniques In Dub

Pressure Sounds. Fax: 0171 288 1339.
E-Mail on-u@obsolete.com. http://www.obsolete.com/on-u

For mail order send payment to Beatback Ltd:-
P.O. Box 12757 London E8 1P2 England.
VINYL £8.00 DOUBLE VINYL £9, CD £11.00 & * £5
Postage cost per item: UK £0.90. Europe £2.00.
USA/Canada £5.90. Elsewhere £6.60.

ON-U-SOUND CATALOGUE

*African Headcharge	My Life In A Hole On-U CD 0013
African Headcharge	Environmental Studies On-U CD 0019
*African Headcharge	Drastic Season On-U CD 0027
*African Headcharge	Off The Beaten Track On-U CD 0040
African Headcharge	Songs Of Praise On-U CD 0050
African Headcharge	Songs Of Praise On-U LP 0050
African Headcharge	Pride And Joy Live On-U CD 0058
African Headcharge	In Pursuit Of Shashamane Land On-U CD 0065
African Headcharge	In Pursuit Of Shashamane Land On-U LP 0065
*African Headcharge & Professor Stretch	Drums Of Defiance On-U CD 0093
*African Headcharge & Professor Stretch	Drums Of Defiance On-U LP 0093
Audio Active	We Are Tokyo Space Cowboys On-U CD 0073
Audio Active	Happy Happer On-U CD 0077
*Audio Active	Apollo Choco On-U CD 0094
*Audio Active	Apollo Choco On-U LP 0094
Audio Active	Weed Specialist On-U DP/DPCD 0041
*Bim Sherman	Across The Red Sea On-U CD 0017
*Barmy Army	The English Disease On-U CD 0048
Compilation	Disco Plates Vol. 1 On-U CD 0012
*Compilation	Disco Plates Vol. 2 On-U CD 0052
Compilation	On-U-Sound 15 Years + More On-U CD 0092
Compilation	Pay It All Back 6 On-U CD 0096
*Creation Rebel	Psychotic Jonkanoo On-U CD 0004
*Creation Rebel	Starship Africa On-U CD 0008
*Deadly Headly	35 Years From Alpha On-U CD 0014
*Dub Syndicate	Pounding System On-U CD 0018
Dub Syndicate	Tunes From The Missing Channel On-U CD 0038
*Dub Syndicate	Strike The Balance On-U CD 0047
Dub Syndicate	Stoned Immaculate On-U CD 0056
Dub Syndicate	Stoned Immaculate On-U LP 0056
Dub Syndicate	Echomania On-U CD 0064
Dub Syndicate	Echomania On-U LP 0064
Dub Syndicate	Ital Breakfast On-U CD 0084
Dub Syndicate	Research And Development On-U CD 0085
Dub Syndicate	Ital Breakfast On-U LP 0084
*Dub Syndicate And Dr. Pablo	North Of The River Thames On-U CD 0030
Dub Syndicate Featuring	Bim Sherman, Akabu Live @ T&C On-U CD 0059
Gary Clail's On-U-Sound System	End Of The Century Party On-U CD 0049
Lee Perry And Dub Syndicate	Time Boom De Devil Dead On-U CD 0043
Lee Perry And Dub Syndicate	Time Boom De Devil Dead On-U LP 0043
Little Roy	Longtime On-U CD 0087
*Levi Judah	T.B.C. On-U CD 0089
*Levi Judah	T.B.C. On-U LP 0089
Levi Judah	T.B.C. On-U DP/DPCD 0042
*New Age Steppers	Foundation Steppers On-U CD 0021
Missing Brazilians	Warzone On-U CD 0034
Mark Stewart And The Maffia	Learning To Cope With Cowardice On-U CD 0024
Revolutionary Dub Warriors	Deliverance Part 1 On-U CD 0068
Revolutionary Dub Warriors	State Of Evolution On-U CD 0083
Revolutionary Dub Warriors	State Of Evolution On-U LP 0083
*Singers And Players	War Of Words On-U CD 0005
Singers And Players	Revenge Of The Underdog On-U CD 0011
*Singers And Players	Staggering Heights On-U CD 0023
*Singers And Players	Vacuum Pumping On-U CD 0039
Tribal Drift	A Priority Shift On-U CD 0088
Tribal Drift	A Priority Shift On-U LP 0088
2 Badcard	Hustling Ability On-U CD 0078

* Scheduled For Release 1998-1999
* All "On-U-Sound Master Recordings" will be released on compact Disc and mastered from the original 1/4" master tapes, they will also feature comprehensive sleeve notes and will retail in the mid-price range.

Distributed in :

UK & UK EXPORT
SRD Tel: 00 44 (0) 181 802 2000
Fax: 00 44 (0) 181 802 2222

G.A.S / ITALY / SPAIN / USA / CANADA
EFA Tel: 00 49 (0) 40 78 91 700
Fax: 00 49 (0) 40 78 27 83

FRANCE / BENELUX
MUSIDISC Tel: 00 33 1 41 49 42 08
FAX: 00 33 1 41 49 42 00